The Tuttle Story: "Books to Span the East and West"

Many people are surprised to learn that the world's leading publisher of books on Asia had humble beginnings in the tiny American state of Vermont. The company's founder, Charles E. Tuttle, belonged to a New England family steeped in publishing. Immediately after WWII, Tuttle served in Tokyo under General Douglas MacArthur and was tasked with reviving the Japanese publishing industry. He later founded the Charles E. Tuttle Publishing Company, which thrives today as one of the world's leading independent publishers.

Though a westerner, Tuttle was hugely instrumental in bringing a knowledge of Japan and Asia to a world hungry for information about the East. By the time of his death in 1993, Tuttle had published over 6,000 books on Asian culture, history and art—a legacy honored by the Japanese emperor with the "Order of the Sacred Treasure," the highest tribute Japan can bestow upon a non-Japanese.

With a backlist of 1,500 titles, Tuttle Publishing is more active today than at any time in its past—inspired by Charles Tuttle's core mission to publish fine books to span the East and West and provide a greater understanding of each.

Published by Tuttle Publishing, an imprint of Periplus Editions (HK) Ltd

www.tuttlepublishing.com

Copyright © 2012 by Periplus Editions (HK) Ltd
Cover photo © Dreamstime

ISBN 978-0-8048-4206-8

Distributed by

North America, Latin America & Europe
Tuttle Publishing, 364 Innovation Drive
North Clarendon, VT 05759-9436 U.S.A.
Tel: 1 (802) 773-8930;Fax: 1 (802) 773-6993
info@tuttlepublishing.com
www.tuttlepublishing.com

Japan
Tuttle Publishing
Yaekari Building, 3rd Floor
5-4-12 Osaki, Shinagawa-ku, Tokyo 141 0032
Tel: (81) 3 5437-0171; Fax: (81) 3 5437-0755
sales@ tuttle.co.jp
www.tuttle.co.jp

Asia Pacific
Berkeley Books Pte. Ltd.
61 Tai Seng Avenue #02-12
Singapore 534167
Tel: (65) 6280-1330; Fax: (65) 6280-6290
inquiries@periplus.com.sg
www.periplus.com

Indonesia
PT Java Books Indonesia
Kawasan Industri Pulogadung, Jl. Rawa
Gelam IV No. 9, Jakarta 13930
Tel: (62) 21 4682-1088; Fax: (62) 21 461-0206
crm@periplus.co.id
www.periplus.com

17 16 15 14   8 7 6 5 4 3   1411CP
Printed in Singapore

The Ultimate Guide
to the World's Most Spectacular
Tropical Island

revised by LINDA HOFFMAN

TUTTLE Publishing

Tokyo | Rutland, Vermont | Singapore

CONTENTS

Part 1:

INTRODUCING BALI

Welcome to Paradise!

It is said that the world knows about the cultural delights of Bali, but many people don't know where Indonesia is. It is true that Bali is only one of the sprawling archipelago's over 17,500 islands, and it is also a fact that Bali is its most famous. Relatively small, Bali is only 144 km (89 miles) from east to west and 90 km (56 miles) from north to south and is densely populated in some regions, housing over 4 million souls in a space that can environmentally support only 1.5 million.

There is a certain magic about Bali. The longer the stay on the island, the more impressive the many exquisite sights and the scores of talented and charming people encountered become. All the tourist hype aside, Bali truly is exceptional.

Bali presents a modern paradox, an ancient, traditional society that is still incredibly alive and vital. While the basic conservatism of the Balinese has enabled them to preserve many of their past achievements, it has never hindered the acceptance of new and innovative elements, whether home-grown or foreign. A fortuitous congruence of circumstances—accidents, really—of geography and history seem responsible for the island's fabled cultural wealth.

First and foremost, Bali is extraordinarily blessed by nature. Lying within a narrow band of the tropics where wet and dry seasons fall roughly into balance—providing both adequate rainfall and long periods of sunshine—the island's soils, topography and water resources are all remarkably well suited to human habitation. As a result, the island has supported a civilization since early times.

This is also the only island in "inner Indonesia" that has enjoyed centuries of more or less uninterrupted cultural continuity.

The island's natural beauty is one of the many reasons that lure visitors to often return to Bali.

While other traditional states in the region suffered major disruptions due to Islamization and Dutch colonization, Bali was — for the most part — isolated, left to go her own way.

As a result, this is the only area of Indonesia that remains primarily "Hindu" today, retaining elements of the great fusion of indigenous and Indian cultures that developed here over 1,000 years ago. When Bali was finally colonized by the Dutch at the beginning of the 20th century, the European invaders were so fascinated by what they found that a concerted effort was made to preserve and foster the island's traditional culture.

In addition, Balinese society remains strong and vital because it promotes family and communal values. This is the key: a self-strengthening system in which religion, custom and art combine with age-old child-rearing techniques and deeply-entrenched village institutions to produce an exceptionally well-integrated society. Feelings of alienation from parents and peers, so common in the West, are rare in Bali.

Children are carried everywhere until they are at least three months old, held at all times in the warm, protective embrace of family, friends and neighbors. Elaborate rituals are performed at frequent intervals to ensure their wellbeing. Every aspect of village life is organized to the nth degree, the individual's rights and responsibilities within the community being carefully defined by tradition.

Despite all this, it should be noted that traditional Bali was far from perfect. For the majority of Balinese peasants, it was in fact a world wracked by warfare, disease, pestilence, and famine. In the 20th century, Bali was continuously plagued by political violence, over-population, and poverty. The 21st century has introduced new challenges: tremendous development and new communication tools resulting in nearly every teen being able to Facebook during rituals. Traffic gridlocks all the main thoroughfares.

Bali's unique culture can be viewed as a response to difficult, uncertain conditions. Its strong village institutions serve as bulwarks against the ever-present threat of natural disaster; their inherent flexibility a guarantee of survival in the face of a changing world.

The rapid changes now occurring on the island must be seen from this historical perspective. Certainly there are problems, some perhaps as serious as those faced in earlier times. But the Balinese are eternal optimists, fervently believing that their "Paradise Island" enjoys a very special place in the grander scheme of things.

GEOGRAPHY AND ECOLOGY

An Island Built by Volcanoes

Every aspect of Bali's geography and ecology is influenced by the towering range of volcanic peaks that dominate the island. They have created its landforms, periodically regenerated its soils, and helped to produce the dramatic downpours that provide the island with life-giving water. The Balinese recognize these geophysical facts of life, and the island's many volcanoes, lakes, and springs are considered by them to be sacred.

Bali is continually being re-formed by volcanic action. The island lies over a major subduction zone, where the Indo-Australian plate collides with the rigid Sunda plate. A violent eruption of Mt. Agung (3,142 m/ 10,308 ft pre-eruption; 3,031 m/9,944 ft now) in 1963 showered the mountain's upper slopes with ash that slid off as mudflows, killing thousands of people and laying waste to irrigation networks and rice fields that had been built up over many years. Mt. Batur (1,717 m/5,633 ft) to the west is also active, with greater frequency but less violence.

A mild, equatorial climate

Lying between 8 and 9 degrees south of the equator, Bali has a short, hot wet season and a longer, cooler dry season. The mountains are wet year round, averaging 2,500 to 3,000 mm of rain annually, with warm days and cool nights. The lowlands are hotter and drier, but fresh and persistent winds make the climate less oppressive here than elsewhere in the equatorial zone.

The wet season lasts from November to March, and is also the hottest time of year (30–31° C by day, 24–25° C at night). The dry season is from April to October, when south-easterly winds blow up from the cool Australian interior (28–29° C by day, and a pleasant 23° C at night), with nearly 12 hours of sunshine daily.

By itself, the rainfall in the lowlands is not enough for wet rice cultivation. In other parts of Indonesia, particularly Java, flood waters following heavy rains can be collected behind dams, but the steep, narrow valleys of Bali

Volcanoes, such as the magnificient Mt. Agung, are considered holy and dominate the landscape.

offer no good dam sites. Over the centuries, the Balinese have instead devised many sophisticated irrigation systems that optimize the water available from rain and rivers. Bali's volcanic soils are, in fact, not naturally well suited to wet rice cultivation. They are deep, finely textured and well-drained, so water soaks through them rapidly. While this reduces the risk of floods, it wastes precious water. Paradoxically, the solution is vigorous and repeated plowing, which actually renders the soils less permeable. Irrigated areas also receive a supply of nutrients from river water enriched by domestic effluents.

Man has extensively modified the natural vegetation of Bali. The entire forest area now covers only 121,271 ha, or 23 percent of Bali's total area, mainly in the western mountains and along the arc of volcanic peaks from Mt. Agung to Mt. Batukaru. About a quarter of the forest is protected in four nature reserves, the largest of which is Bali Barat National Park (19,000 ha). Further reserves are planned to protect another quarter of the island's forests.

In the 21st century, attention is also being paid to coastlines. Recent studies show that Bali's shores are receding at an alarming rate, accounting for a loss of 181.7 km (113 miles) of land in the last decade, amounting to 41.5 percent of the island's total shoreline. Primarily resulting from environmental neglect, it is obvious that solutions must be found before more damage occurs.

An island of great contrasts

Bali may be small, but its physical geography is complex, creating an island of great variety. In simple outline, three major areas emerge: the mountains, the coastal lowlands and the limestone fringes. The mountains are lofty and spectacular, dominated by Mt. Agung and its neighbors, Abang and Batur. Dramatic lava flows on the northeastern flanks of Agung are Bali's newest land-forms, demonstrating what the entire island probably looked like a million years ago.

The western mountains provide the last major wildlife sanctuary. Cultivation here is limited to coastal areas that are very dry in the north, but more prosperous and fertile in the south. Coconut groves, cattle pastures and rain-fed fields line the foothills, while rice fields are found along the coast. Unique canals vanish into foothill tunnels excavated as protection from landslides. In the extreme southwest, the Palasari Dam forms the island's

Large lakes inside of Bali's volcanic craters serve as reservoirs to store water, which emerges from springs further down the slopes.

only manmade lake. On Bali's western tip, the coral reefs and clear waters around Menjangan Island provide fantastic scuba diving.

The southern lowlands formed the cradle of Balinese civilization. Here it is possible to grow two or more irrigated rice crops per year. Based on this agricultural surplus, eight small but powerful kingdoms arose, symmetrically lining the parallel north-south river valleys that shaped their early growth.

In contrast to the south, the north coast hosted only a single kingdom, centered on the less extensive but equally productive rice lands around Singaraja. Terracing here continues well into the hills, on slopes that elsewhere would be regarded as a severe erosion hazard. On Bali, these terraces stand as firm as masonry because of peculiar clay minerals within the soil. Further east, the dry coast is relieved by several major springs that emerge from fissures in the lava flows. The spring water is used for irrigating table grapes, a crop that thrives here.

The southern limestone fringes stand in complete contrast to the rest of Bali. These are dry and difficult to cultivate. The Bukit Peninsula south of the airport has impressive southern cliffs and many large caves. Across the sea to the east, Nusa Ceningan, Nusa Lembongan and Nusa Penida are dry limestone islands with scrubby vegetation and shallow soils. Villagers on Penida have built ingenious catchments to collect rainwater. Springs also emerge from the base of its high southern cliffs, and locals have built precarious scaffolds to collect water. Just as water is the measure of richness in the interior, so is it the measure of survival around the periphery. In Bali, water is truly sacred.

—*Stephen Walker*

BALINESE AGRICULTURE

Nourishing Body and Soul

Wet rice cultivation is the key to the agricultural bounty in many areas of Bali. The greatest concentration of irrigated rice fields is found in southern-central Bali, where water is readily available from spring-fed streams. Here, and in other well-watered areas where wet rice culture predominates, rice is planted in rotation with *palawija* cash crops, such as soybeans, peanuts, onions, chili peppers and other vegetables. In the drier regions corn, taro, tapioca and beets are cultivated.

Rice is, and has always been, the essence of life for the Balinese. As in other Southeast Asian countries, rice is synonymous with food and eating. Personified as the "divine

nutrition" in the form of the goddess Bhatari Sri, rice is seen by the Balinese to be part of an all-compassing life force of which humans partake.

Rice is also an important social force. The phases of rice cultivation determine the seasonal rhythm of work as well as the division of labor between men and women within the community. Balinese respect for their native rice varieties is expressed in countless myths and in colorful rituals in which the life cycle of the female rice divinity is portrayed, from the planting of the seed to the harvesting of the grain. Rice thus represents "culture" to the Balinese in the dual sense of *cultura* and *cultus*: cultivation and worship.

Bali's subak *irrigation system is unique.*

Irrigation cooperatives (*subak*)

Historical evidence indicates that since the 11th century, all peasants whose fields were fed by the same water course have belonged to a single *subak,* or irrigation, cooperative. This is a traditional institution that regulates the construction and maintenance of waterworks, and the distribution of life-giving water that they supply. Such regulation is essential to efficient wet rice cultivation on Bali, where water travels through very deep ravines and across countless terraces in its journey from the mountains to the sea.

The *subak* is responsible for coordinating the planting of seeds and the transplanting of seedlings so as to achieve optimal growing conditions, as well as for organizing ritual offerings and festivals at the *subak* temple. All members are called upon to participate in these activities, especially at feasts honoring the rice goddess Sri.

Subak cooperatives exist entirely apart from normal Balinese village institutions, and a single village's rice fields may fall under the jurisdiction of more than one *subak,* depending on local drainage patterns. The most important technical duties undertaken by the *subak* are the construction and maintenance of canals, tunnels, aqueducts, dams, and waterlocks.

Other crops

Visitors often get the impression that nothing but wet rice is grown in Bali, because of the vast, unobstructed vistas of extensive irrigated rice fields between villages in southern and central Bali, but this is not so. Out of a total of 563,286 hectares of arable land on Bali, just 81,482 ha (about 14.47 percent) are irrigated rice fields (*sawah*). Another 136,796 ha (24.29 percent) is non-irrigated dry fields (*tegalan*), producing one rain-fed crop per year. A further 127,271 ha (23 percent) is forested lands primarily belonging to the central government, and 121,797 ha (21.62 percent) are estate crops such as coffee (both arabica and robusta), cloves, coconut, and cacao; 99,151 hectares are devoted to cash crop gardens (*kebun*) with tree and bush culture. From the mid-1980s through the late 1990s, vanilla experienced a boom period, with over 50 percent of Indonesia's production coming from Bali. A downward trend occurred from 1998–2003 during the global vanilla crisis, spurred by the advent of plant disease. Currently, Bali produces about 2 percent of the world's vanilla. Balinese tobacco production declined to about 1,800 tons in 2008 (according to the Statistics Bureau) from previous levels of over 5,000 tons. The production of cloves, vanilla and tobacco has also increased, and in mountainous regions, such as Bedugul, new vegetable varieties have been intensely cultivated to supply the tourist trade.

Compared with 1980, there has been a decrease in the total area under cultivation, resulting mainly from population pressures and tourism development. The real estate and building boom that is now happening over much of the island has led to a new tongue-in-cheek nickname for Bali: "Villa Island".

Other export commodities include copra and related products of the coconut palm. For subsistence cultivators, the coconut palm remains, as before, a "tree of life" that can be utilized from the root up to the tip. It provides building materials (the wood, leaves, and leaf ribs), fuel (the leaves and dried husks), kitchen and household items (shells and fibers for utensils), as well as food and ritual objects (vessels, offerings, plaited objects, food, and drink).

The "green revolution"

Changes in Balinese agricultural practices have brought about fundamental alterations

Coffee is an important estate crop in Bali.

in the relationship of the Balinese to their staple crop. Rice production can no longer be expanded by bringing new lands under cultivation. Nor is mechanization a desirable alternative, given the current surplus of labor on the island. For these reasons, the official agricultural policy since the mid-1970s has been to improve crop yields on existing fields through biological and chemical means.

The cultivation of new, fast-growing, high-yielding rice varieties, in concert with the application of chemical fertilizers, herbicides and pesticides, lies at the core of the government's agricultural development program (BIMAS). Further aims have been to improve methods of soil utilization and irrigation and to set up new forms of cooperatives to provide credit and market surplus harvests. Over 80 percent of Bali's wet rice fields have been subjected to these intensification processes.

Under the Suharto regime, Indonesia was able to meet most of its own rice needs, thus relieving some of the pressures that created the original "Green Revolution" of the 1960s. But as more land was gobbled up with the development of resorts and golf courses, the effort failed in the late 1990s.

In the 21st century, however, self-sufficiency has once again returned. As a result, an ecologically more meaningful "green evolution" is now possible, and rice varieties better suited to local conditions are being introduced. The 21st century has brought on an explosion of new agricultural techniques (such as Sustainable Rice Intensification, a kind of all-inclusive permaculture) and organic farming. Bali's governor, I Made Mangku Pastika, initiated a "clean and green" campaign in 2010 that will hopefully address some of these agricultural issues.

— Urs Ramseyer

BIRDWATCHING

Bali's Amazing Avifauna

W ell, did you see the birds in Bali
When you were staying there last year,
Or was your time assigned entirely
To seeing sights and swilling beer,
Sifting sand or shifting gear?

Birdwatching is above all a delightful recreation and no longer merely the province of collectors and academics. And what better place than Bali to indulge the urge? What pleasanter island, what wilder domain, and what fresher air in which to nurture it?

Indonesia's zoogeographic range embraces not only both hemispheres but also the Asian and Australian regions, which are divided by the "Wallace Line" running between Bali and Lombok islands. Extending from Sumatra's mountain forests to those of Papua, there rests an unrivalled diversity of avian life.

Bali alone boasts some 300 different bird species, including of course migrants, from massive hornbills and storks to diminutive

sunbirds and spiderhunters, to say nothing of one of the world's rarest and most beautiful birds, the Rothschild's Myna (also known as the Bali Starling), which occurs only on Bali.

Our view of such marvels need not be confined to the aviary. In the wild, readily accessible to all, even to those who inhabit the crowded tourist beach resorts or Denpasar city — an hour's drive at most to Ubud or Bedugul — there is more than enough on which to feast the eyes.

In a garden situated in the central foothills of Bali, there can be as many as 80 different bird species. In a dense curtain of greenery, mainly of flowering shrubs, coconut palms and fruit trees, arboreal birds thrive, the most remarkable being the Black-naped Oriole and Ashy Drongo — the former a glorious golden-yellow with a broad black band through the eye to the nape, and the latter an acrobatic wonder of unrelieved dark gray with deeply forked tails.

Various species of herons and egrets are ubiquitous on Bali.

Australian pelicans are found in coastal areas.

Many of the birds found on Bali are migratory and can only be seen seasonally.

Highly endangered, Bali Starlings are now being bred and released on Nusa Penida.

Beneath the canopy, the Magpie Robins endlessly disport and vent a rich vocabulary of imprecations and sweet fluting calls, while the restless Pied Fantail dashes to and fro, pirouettes and trips the light fantastic, characteristically flirting its tail all the while. Always in evidence are the ubiquitous Yellow-vented Bulbuls, chattering and chortling as they race each other from palm to palm.

Of the smaller birds, the most commonly occurring are the lively, darting Bar-winged Prinias and Ashy Tailorbirds; the vivid scarlet-headed flowerpeckers and metallic blue-throated Olive-backed Sunbirds, busily rifling the hibiscus blossoms to sate their appetite for minute insects and nectar; and the cheerful greeny-yellow Common Iora, which hops about in the thick crown of a rambutan tree, now and again betraying its presence with a long drawn-out mellow whistle, slowly increasing in pitch and ending abruptly on a lower note: *tweeeeeeeeeeeeeeeeeee-tyou.*

Birds of the field

An open expanse of terraced rice fields is the seasonal haunt of watercock and Cinnamon Bittern, of Ruddy-breasted Crake and flocks of stately snowy-white Plumed and Little Egrets. Consorting with the latter, and usually distinguishable by the buffy-rufous patches of their nuptial plumage, are the Cattle Egrets, while scattered about in frozen attitudes, some Javan Pond Herons stare warily at passers-by, the breeding birds richly adorned in buff, cinnamon, and black, which is curiously transformed to white when they erupt into flight.

Overflying the fields are swiftlets and swallows, and tiny tumbling Fantail-Warblers, while swarms of marauding munias wheel this way and that to escape the clappers defending their crops, before descending *en masse* to ravage another patch of unguarded grain. There patiently sits the little Pied Bushchat, rather resembling a miniature Magpie Robin, likewise perched and keenly espying its prey, and the spectacularly caparisoned Javan Kingfisher, whose radiant presence makes an indelible impression on all who behold it. Like others of its tribe, it may be found along the riverbeds of verdant ravines, but it also frequents the paddy fields, where it may more readily be observed perched atop a slender pole or the thatched roof of a small shrine to Dewi Sri, goddess of agriculture and fertility.

Other regular visitors include the Magpie Robins, those conspicuously pied and vocal denizens of all the gardens of the East. In pops the Ashy Tailorbird, insignificant mousy gray thing with a rufous face, and elegant little olive-grey-brown Bar-winged Prinias (wren-warblers) clambering down in the variegated copper-leaf and croton bushes while emitting a plaintive *twee-wee-wee*, succeeded by utterances of quite explosive force. They sport long, white-tipped tail feathers, white throats and upper breasts, twin white wing bars, amber eyes and lemon-yellow bellies, and seem to thrive in any habitat from montane forest to coastal mangrove, and especially in ornamental gardens. Their geographic range is confined to Sumatra, Java and Bali: nowhere else are they found.

— Victor Mason

EARLY BALINESE HISTORY

Artifacts and Early Foreign Influences

The early history of Bali can be divided into a prehistoric and an early historic period. The former is marked by the arrival of Austronesian (Malayo-Polynesian) migrants, beginning perhaps 3,000–4,000 years ago. The Austronesians were hardy seafarers who spread from Taiwan through the Southeast Asian islands to the Pacific in a series of extensive migrations that spanned several millennia. The Balinese are thus closely related, culturally and linguistically, to the peoples of the Philippines and Oceania, as well as other neighboring Indonesian islands.

Stone sarcophagi, seats and altars

Though precious little is known about the long, formative stages of Bali's prehistory, artifacts discovered around the island provide intriguing clues about its early inhabitants. Prehistoric gravesites have been found in western Bali, the oldest probably dating from

Bali's contact with Javanese Hinduism and Buddhism dates back to the 8th century A.D.

the first few centuries B.C. The people buried here were herders and farmers who used bronze, and in some cases iron, to make implements and jewelry. Prehistoric stone sarcophagi have also been discovered, mainly in the mountains. They often have the shape of huge turtles carved at either end with human and animal heads with bulging eyes, big teeth, and protruding tongues.

Stone seats, altars and other large rocks dating from early times are housed in several Balinese temples. Here, as elsewhere in Indonesia, they seem to be connected with the veneration of ancestral spirits who formed (and in many ways still form) the core of Balinese religious practices.

Also apparently connected with ancestor worship is one of Southeast Asia's greatest prehistoric artifacts, the huge bronze kettledrum known as the "Moon of Pejeng". Still considered to have significant power, it is now enshrined in a temple in Pejeng, central Bali, in the Gianyar Regency. More than 1.5 meters in diameter and 1.86 meters high, it is decorated with frogs and geometric motifs in a style that probably originated from near Dong Son in what is now northern Vietnam. This is the largest of many such drums discovered in Southeast Asia.

Hindu-Javanese influences

It is assumed (but without proof so far) that the Balinese were in contact with Hindu and Buddhist populations of Java from the early part of the 8th century A.D. onwards, and that Bali was even conquered by a Javanese king in A.D. 732. This contact is responsible for the advent of writing and other important Indian cultural elements that had come to Java along the major trading routes several centuries earlier. Indian writing, dance, religion and architecture were to have a decisive impact, blending with existing Balinese traditions to form a new and highly distinctive culture.

Stone and copperplate inscriptions in Old Balinese dating from around A.D. 882 onwards, coincide with finds of Hindu- and

The "Moon of Pejeng"—the largest prehistoric kettledrum in Asia

Buddhist-inspired statues, bronzes, ornamented caves, rock-cut temples, and bathing places. These are often found in areas near rivers, ravines, springs, and volcanic peaks. At the end of the 10th and the beginning of the 11th centuries there were close, peaceful bonds with the Indianized kingdoms in east Java, in particular with the Kadiri realm (10th century A.D. to 1222). Old Javanese was thereafter the language of prestige, used in all Balinese inscriptions, and evidence of a strong Javanese cultural influence. In 1284, Bali is said to have been conquered by King Kertanegara of the east Javanese Singhasari dynasty (1222–1292). It is not certain whether the island was actually colonized at this time, but many new Javanese elements appear in the Balinese art of this period.

According to a Javanese court chronicle known as the *Nagarakertagama* (dated 1365), Bali was conquered and colonized in 1334 by Javanese forces under Gajah Mada, the legendary general or *patih* of the powerful Majapahit kingdom, which established hegemony over east Java and all seaports bordering the Java Sea during the mid-14th century. It is said that Gajah Mada, accompanied by contingents of Javanese nobles, came to Bali to subdue a rapacious Balinese king. A Javanese vassal ruler was installed at a new capital at Samprangan, near present-day Klungkung in east Bali, and the nobles were granted appanages in the surrounding areas. A Javanese court and courtly culture were thus introduced to the island. The separation of Balinese society into four caste groups is ascribed to this period, with the *satriya* warrior caste ruling from Samprangan. Those who did not wish to participate in the new system fled to remote mountain areas, where they lived apart from the mainstream. These are the so-called "original Balinese", the *Bali Aga* or *Bali Mula*.

Around 1460, the capital moved to nearby Gelgel, and the powerful "Grand Lord", Dewa Agung, presided over a flowering of Balinese arts and culture. Over time, however, the descendants of the *aryas* became increasingly independent, and from around 1700 began to form realms in other areas.

Reconstructing the past

Because ancestor veneration plays such an important role in Balinese religion, many groups possess family genealogies known as *babad*. In such texts, the *brahmana, satriya,* and *wesya* clans trace their ancestry to the Majapahit kings, while the *Bali Aga* assert descent from even earlier Javanese rulers. There are also groups that claim as their ancestors Javanese Hindus and Buddhists who are said to have taken refuge in Bali from invading Muslim forces. This probably gave rise to the story that entire Hindu-Buddhist populations of Java, with their valuables, books, and other cultural baggage, fled to Bali after the fall of Majapahit. It is not known if this is true, as even up to the present day it is common for families to rewrite and improve their *babad,* depending on their current circumstances.

—Hedi Hinzler

THE TRADITIONAL BALINESE KINGDOMS

History in a Balinese Looking Glass

Most of what is known about Bali's traditional kingdoms comes from the Balinese themselves. Scores of masked dance dramas, family chronicles and temple rituals focus on great figures and events of the Balinese past. In such accounts, the broad outline of Bali's history from the 12th to the 18th centuries is an epic tale of the coming of great men to power. These were the royal and priestly founders of glorious dynasties—some mad, some fearsome, some lazy and some proud—who together with their retainers and family members determined the fate of Bali's kingdoms, as well as shaping the situation and status of the island's present-day inhabitants.

It is possible to see the Balinese as both indifferent to history and yet utterly obsessed by it. Indifferent because they are not very interested in the "what happened and why" that make up what we know as history, while at the same time they are obsessed by stories concerning their own illustrious ancestors.

Balinese "history" is in fact a set of stories that explain how their extended families came to be where they are. Such stories may explain, for example, how certain ancestors moved from an ancient court center to a remote village, or how they were originally of aristocratic stock although their descendants no longer possess princely titles. In short, they provide evidence of a continuing connection between the world of the ancestors and present-day Bali.

Major events are thus invariably seen in terms of the actions of great men (and occasionally women), yet to view them as mere individuals is deceptive. They are divine ancestors, and as such their actions embody the fate of entire groups. Above all, they are responsible for having created the society found on Bali today.

Each family possesses its own genealogy that somehow fits into the overall picture. Some focus on kings, their followers or priests as key ancestors. Others see the family history in terms of village leaders,

blacksmiths (powerful, as makers of weapons and tools) or villagers who resisted and escaped the advance of new rulers.

The fact that such stories sometimes agree with one another should not necessarily be taken as proof that this is what really happened. There are many gaps, loose ends and incon-sistencies, often pointing to the fact that gen-erations of priests, princes and scribes have recast these tales about the past to serve their own ends. The sagas must be retold, neverthe-less, in order to know what is open to dispute.

Ancestors and origins

Bali's history begins in ancient Java, in the legendary Kadiri and Majapahit kingdoms, where Javanese culture is regarded (by Javanese, Balinese and Western scholars alike) as having reached its apex. From these rich sources flowed the great literature, art, and court rituals of Hindu Java that were later transplanted to Bali.

One of the prime reasons for holding such rituals was to elevate Hindu-Javanese leaders to the status of god-like kings who were in contact with the divine forces of the cosmos. As these Javanese kingdoms expanded to take over Bali, they brought with them their art, literature, and cosmology. At the same time, the Javanese also absorbed vital elements of Balinese culture, eventually spreading some of these throughout the archipelago and elsewhere in Southeast Asia.

The great Airlangga, descendant of Bali's illustrious King Udayana, is said to have ascended the east Javanese throne and to have founded the powerful Kadiri kingdom in the 11th century. Thus it was proper that his descendants would later install priests and warriors from Java to rule over Bali. Foremost among these was the son of a priest, Kresna Kapakisan, who became the first king of Gelgel (now in Klungkung Regency) in the mid-15th century.

The transition to Gelgel from a previous court center at Samprangan (now in Gianyar Regency) was made by a cockfighting member

Ancestors are considered sacred and are revered.

of the Kapakisan dynasty who became embroiled in a struggle for the throne and attempts to save the kingdom from the mismanagement of his elder brother, or so the account goes. There is little reason to doubt this version of events, yet there are huge gaps in the story of how power moved from Java to Gelgel in previous centuries and the relationship of the Kapakisan line to earlier kings appointed by the Javanese conquerors.

Bali's "Golden Age"

Most Balinese trace their ancestry back to a group of courtiers clustering about the great King Baturenggong, a descendant of Kapakisan, who is seen to have presided over a Balinese "Golden Age" in the 16th century. Balinese accounts describe him as "a king of great authority, a true lion of a man who was wise in protecting his subjects and attending to their needs, and an outstanding warrior of great mystical power, always victorious in war". European records do not mention him by name, but attest to the wealth and influence of a Balinese kingdom which at this time had a more centralized and unified system of government than was the case in subsequent centuries.

Of equal if not greater importance in the collective Balinese memory of this era is the super-priest Nirartha. He is remembered for his great spiritual powers: a man who could stop floods, control the energies of sexuality through meditation, and write beautiful poetry to move men's souls. In the genealogies it was he who founded the main line of Balinese high priests, those whose worship is directed to Siva, Lord of the Gods. His name is associated with many of Bali's greatest temples and a corpus of literature produced by himself and his followers.

In Balinese eyes, the descendants of King Baturenggong and Nirartha presided over a period of decline, even though Baturenggong's son, Seganing, upheld some of his father's greatness and, after the texts, fathered the ancestors of Bali's key royal lines. Balinese sources tell of the destruction of Gelgel by a rebellious chief minister, Gusti Agung Maruti, who was distinguished by possessing a tail and an overwhelming thirst for power. After his defeat by princes who established themselves in the north and south of the island, new independent kingdoms arose from the ashes of Gelgel. The Gelgel dynasty itself survived—albeit in a much reduced state—as the kingdom of Klungkung, maintaining some of its moral and symbolic authority over the rest of the island, but having direct control of only its immediate area.

Slave trading and king-making

To the outside world, as to later Balinese writers, the period following Gelgel's "Golden Age" was one of chaos in which fractious kings ruled from courts scattered about the island. This was not necessarily so in contemporary Balinese terms, where the new states

This vintage 1930s portrait shows all eight Balinese kings gathered in the Gianyar palace grounds.

must have represented a more dynamic way of conducting the affairs of state and external trade. Bali became known on the international scene at this time as a source of slaves, savage fighters, beautiful women, and skilled craftsmen.

According to traditional accounts, the fate and status of present-day Balinese families was also largely determined at this time. Kingdoms rose and fell with alarming rapidity, clans split and were demoted or even enslaved, and aspiring princes waged war and organized lavish ceremonies. Such human dramas were punctuated by a series of natural disasters such as earthquakes, epidemics, and volcanic eruptions.

Bali's principal export throughout the 17th and 18th centuries was slaves. Warfare and a revision of Bali's Hindu law codes helped provide a steady supply of slaves to meet an ever-increasing overseas demand. War captives, criminals and debtors were sold abroad indiscriminately by Balinese rulers, who maintained a monopoly on the export trade. In northern Bali, Europeans were even invited in to oversee the trade, and the Dutch in particular purchased large numbers of Balinese to serve as laborers, artisans, and concubines in their extensive network of trading ports, especially their capital at Batavia (now Jakarta), where Balinese slaves made up a sizeable portion of the population. Balinese were even sent to South Africa, where in the early 18th century they constituted up to a quarter of the total number of slaves in that country.

Likewise, Balinese wives and concubines were very much favored by wealthy Chinese traders for their industriousness and beauty and the fact that they had no aversion to pork, unlike the Muslim Javanese. An early 19th-century trader noted that Balinese women were among the most expensive slaves, costing "30, 50 and even 70 Spanish dollars, according to her physical qualities". The same observer later commented that the Balinese "regard deportation from their island as the worst possible punishment. This attitude results from their strongly-held conviction that their gods have no influence outside Bali and that no salvation is to be expected for those who die elsewhere".

The principal kingdoms which emerged during this period were Buleleng in the north, Karangasem in the east and Mengwi in the southwest. At various times, these realms expanded to conquer parts of Bali's neighboring islands. Mengwi and Buleleng moved westward into Java, where they became embroiled in conflicts with and between rival Muslim kingdoms. The Dutch came to play an ever larger role in these conflicts, until eventually the Javanese rulers discovered that they had mortgaged their empires to the gin-drinking Europeans. The Balinese were finally pushed out of eastern Java by combined Dutch and Javanese forces.

In the east, Karangasem conquered neighboring Lombok Island, and at one point even moved into the western part of the next island, Sumbawa. It also annexed Buleleng, and knocked at the gates of Bali's august, but largely impotent central kingdom, Klungkung.

By the beginning of the 19th century, the island's changeable political landscape had stabilized to an extent, as nine separate kingdoms consolidated their positions. A massive eruption of Mt. Tambora on Sumbawa in 1815 —the largest eruption ever recorded—proved to be a catalyst. A tide of famine and disease swept Bali in the wake of the eruption, shredding the traditional fabric of Balinese society and with it many of the fragile political structures of the two previous centuries.

Paradoxically, Tambora's devastating eruption brought in its aftermath a period of unprecedented renewal and prosperity. Deep layers of nutrient-rich ash from the volcano made Bali's soils fertile beyond the wildest imaginings of earlier rulers. Rice and other agricultural products began to be exported in large quantities at a time when vociferous anti-slavery campaigns throughout Europe were bringing an end to Bali's lucrative slave trade.

Two other factors served to transform the island's political and economic landscape. The first was a dramatic decrease in warfare as ruling families focused more and more on internecine struggles and competing claims for dynastic control, and the monopolies on duties, tolls and corvee labor that came with it. The second was the changing nature of foreign trade, particularly with the founding of Singapore as a British free trade port in 1819. To Singapore went Bali's pigs, vegetable oils, and rice. Back came opium, Indian textiles, and guns. Bali was now integrated with world markets to a degree unknown in the past, a fact that did not escape the ever watchful eyes of colonial Dutch administrators in Batavia.

— *Adrian Vickers*

Conquests and Dutch Colonial Rule

In the 19th century, Europe took up the fashion of empire building with a vengeance. Tiny Holland, once Europe's most prosperous trading nation, was not to be left behind and spent much of the century subduing native rulers throughout the archipelago, a vast region that was to become the Netherlands East Indies, later Indonesia.

A steady stream of European traders, scholars and mercenaries visited Bali in this period. The most successful of the traders was a Dane by the name of Mads Lange, one of the last of the great "country traders" whose local knowledge and contacts permitted them to operate on the interstices of the European colonial powers and the traditional kingdoms of the region.

A literary character
Lange was perhaps the prototype for Joseph Conrad's *Lord Jim*, a man who failed to pick the winning side in an internecine dynastic struggle that wracked Lombok in the first half of the 19th century, but who then settled in southern Bali and found a powerful patron in Kesiman, one of the lords of the expanding Badung kingdom. He soon combined this patronage with knowledge of overseas markets and familiarity with the largely female-run internal trading networks of Bali to become extremely rich for a brief period in the 1840s.

The Dutch, determined to establish economic and political control over Bali, became embroiled during this period in a series of wars in the north of the island. They came, as they saw it, to "teach the Balinese a lesson", whereas the words of Buleleng's chief minister best expressed the prevailing Balinese view: "Let the *keris* decide." The first two Dutch attacks, in 1846 and 1848, were repulsed by north Balinese forces aided by allies from the Karangasem and Klungkung kingdoms, as well as by rampant dysentery among the invading forces. A third Dutch attempt in 1849 succeeded mainly because the Balinese rulers of Lombok, cousins of the Karangasem rulers, used this as an

opportunity to take over east Bali. Not wishing to push their luck, the Dutch contented themselves with control of Bali's northern coast for the next 40 years. As this was the island's main export region, they did succeed in isolating the powerful southern kingdoms and in controlling much of the export trade. Lange's fortunes soon declined as a result, and he died several years later, probably poisoned out of economic jealousy.

The end of traditional rule
Not long after the cataclysmic eruption of Krakatau in 1883, on the other side of Java, a series of momentous struggles began amongst the kingdoms of south Bali, struggles that were to result in a loss of independence for all of them over the next 25 years. These conflicts began with the collapse of Gianyar following a rebellion by a vassal lord in Negara. The rebellion ultimately failed, as Gianyar was revived by a hitherto obscure but upwardly-mobile prince in Ubud, but it in turn touched off a series of conflicts that produced a domino effect across the island.

The first kingdom to go was once mighty Mengwi, former ruler of east Java, which was destroyed by its neighbors in 1891. The Islamic Sasak inhabitants of Lombok then rebelled against their Balinese overlords, which gave the Dutch an excuse to intervene and conquer Lombok in 1896.

Greatly weakened by these events, Karangasem and Gianyar both ceded some of their rights to the Dutch, leaving only the independent Badung kingdoms, Tabanan, Bangli and prestigious Klungkung, by the turn of this century.

Shipwrecks, opium, and death
The Dutch found excuses to take on these kingdoms in a series of diplomatic incidents involving shipwrecks and the opium trade. These culminated in the infamous *puputans*, or massacres, of 1906 and 1908 that resulted in not only many deaths, but completed Dutch mastery of the island.

This contemporary illustration from the French newspaper Le Petit Journal *depicts the death of the Raja of Buleleng in 1849.*

In the 1906 *puputan*, the Dutch landed at Sanur and marched on Denpasar, where they were greeted by over 1,000 members of the royal family and their followers, dressed in white and carrying the state regalia in a march to certain death before the superior Dutch weaponry. As later expressed by the neighboring king of Tabanan, the attitude of the unrelenting Balinese ruler of Badung, when asked to sign a treaty with the Dutch, was that "it is better that we die with the earth as our pillow than to live like corpses in shame and disgrace".

A macabre massacre
In 1908 the bloody *puputan* (meaning "end-ing" in Balinese) was repeated on a smaller scale in Klungkung. The ghastly scene was one in which, according to one Dutch observer, the corpse of the king, his head smashed open and brains oozing out, was surrounded by those of his wives and family in a bloody tangle of half-severed limbs, corpses of mothers with babies still at their breasts and wounded children given merciful release by the daggers of their own compatriots.

Ostensibly because they felt guilty about the bloody nature of their conquest, which was widely reported and condemned in Europe, the Dutch authorities quickly established a policy designed to uphold "traditional" Bali. In fact this policy supported only what was seen to be traditional in their eyes, and only if those bits of tradition did not contradict the central aim of running a quiet and lucrative colony.

Marketing ploys
Preserving Bali largely meant three things to the Dutch: creating a colonial society that included a select group of the aristocracy, labeling and categorizing every aspect of Balinese culture with a view to keeping it pure, and idealizing this culture so as to market it for the purposes of tourism. Although these may sound contradictory, they meshed well together. There were slight hic-cups: those Balinese who refused to cooper-ate and did their best to avoid the demands of the Dutch-run state. Some were killed, while others were forced to work on road construc-tion projects or to pay harsh new taxes on everything from pigs to the rice harvest.

Indirect rule through royalty
Another aspect of "preserving" Bali was that the traditional rulers were maintained. As on Java, the Dutch adopted a policy of ruling the villages indirectly through them, while running their own parallel civil service to administer the towns. At least this was the general idea, although here, too, there were some hitches. It took decades before a cooperative branch of the old Buleleng royal family was in place, and many members of the other royal families had to be exiled. In the case of the Klungkung royalty, the exile lasted for some 19 years after the *puputan*.

The Gianyar and Karangasem royal families adapted best to the new conditions. Gusti Bagus Jelantik, the ruler of Karangasem, embarked on an active campaign to strengthen and redefine traditional Balinese religion. In large part, he did this to head off the sort of split that had earlier occurred in the north between modernist commoners or *sudras*, who argued for a social status based on achievement, and members of the three higher castes, or *triwangsa*, who were given hereditary privileges. Ironically this split came about because of a new emphasis on rigidly-defined caste groups under Dutch rule.

The Dutch had to intervene and exile some *sudra* leaders, but modernizing moderates such as the Karangasem ruler realized the need to shape and control the changes taking place in Balinese religion and society. In this, they found ready allies among intellectuals in the Dutch civil service with a passion for Balinese culture and an international influx of artists, travelers, and dilettantes who poured into Bali during the 1920s and 1930s.

Hints of sex and magic

Some, like Barbara Hutton and Charlie Chaplin, were rich and famous and stayed only for a short time. Others, like painter Walter Spies, cartoonist Miguel Covarrubias and composer Colin McPhee, are now famous principally because of their long association with Bali.

The attraction for these well-heeled, well-connected, or simply talented Westerners was the developing image of Bali as a tropical paradise where art exists in overabundance and people live in perfect harmony with nature, an image tinged with hints of sex and magic that was officially sponsored by Dutch tourism officials. And it was certainly promoted by genuinely enthusiastic reports from those who visited and witnessed the island's intricate life, art, and rituals.

The positive contributions of these foreign scholars and artists, working in conjunction with enlightened Balinese and Dutch civil servants, included such institutions as the Bali Museum and the Kirtya Liefrinck-van der Tuuk (now the Bali Documentation Center).

But there was a negative side as well. Although the Bali lovers claimed to be the complete opposite of colonial authorities, they in fact represented the other side of the coin of Western rule. With the fan dance performances for tourists came forced labor, and in their writings Bali-struck foreigners always conveniently ignored the poverty, disease, and injustice that made the colonial era a time of continuous hardship and fear for many Balinese.

— Adrian Vickers

The streets of Denpasar, as depicted in an oil canvas by Balinese artist Mangu Putra in 2005

MODERN BALI

From Chaos to Tourism Development

The Dutch, complacent in their cocoon of colonial supremacy, were shocked when the Japanese invaded the Indies in 1941, so shocked that they gave up with hardly a fight. More shocking still to the colonialists was the fact that after the war, the majority of Indonesians failed to welcome their former rulers back with open arms. *Revolution!* and *Freedom!* had instead become rallying cries around the archipelago, and these were taken up with fierce determination by the Balinese.

Those who had come to believe in colonial "peace and order" and in "Bali the Paradise" were appalled by the intensity of violence and social divisions that wracked the island in subsequent decades, from the beginning of World War II until the middle of the 1960s. In many ways the violence was worse here than in any other part of Indonesia, a situation which had its roots in the way that the Dutch had ruled Bali and the fierce pride and independence of the Balinese people themselves.

Japanese rule, brief as it was, was a period of increasing hardship, punctuated by torture and killings and the conscription of men for forced labor and women as sex slaves of the Japanese military. Although the Japanese had initially been welcomed as liberators, members of the Balinese upper class soon found themselves bearing the brunt of a campaign of terror designed to beat them into submission. Military requirements for rice and other products also dictated that the niceties of wooing the Balinese masses into devotion to the Japanese cause eventually gave way to harsher measures.

As the war dragged on and Japan's position became precarious, most Balinese suffered from serious shortages of all basic necessities. At the same time, Balinese youths were radicalized by being made to join paramilitary organizations with strong nationalistic overtones. When the Japanese surrendered, a few Balinese did welcome the Dutch back, but many others acted swiftly to seize the Japanese weapons and take up the struggle for independence. As the Dutch readied themselves to return with the triumphant Allied forces, preparations were made on Bali for a violent "welcome for the uninvited guests".

Bali's foremost revolutionary was Gusti Ngurah Rai, who led a brave but badly outnumbered and outgunned guerilla group. Some 1,400 Balinese freedom fighters died in the struggle, but with few resources Ngurah Rai was defeated and killed. Bali then became the headquarters of the new State of Eastern Indonesia, which the Dutch hoped to later merge into a pro-Dutch federation. Even this state, under the leadership of the Gianyar ruler, Anak Agung Gede Agung (later Foreign Minister of the Republic), turned against the Dutch when they broke their treaty with the fledgling Republic, and so contributed to the achievement of independence, which the Indonesians declared in 1945 but was not recognized by the Netherlands until 1949.

Mayhem and mass murder

Throughout the 1950s and early 1960s, social divisions that had crystallized during the

Sukarno reads the declaration of independence (Proklamasi Kemerdekaan) *on 17 August 1945.*

The 2002 terrorist bombings in Kuta killed over 200 people, most of them foreigners.

Revolution continued to widen. Political conflicts and assassinations were rife, the key split being between those who favored the old caste system and traditional values and those who rejected the caste system as a form of aristocratic "feudalism" designed to oppress the majority. By the mid-1960s the conflict had taken political form as a contest between the Indonesian Nationalist Party (PNI) and the Indonesian Communist Party (PKI). Attempts by the latter to organize a program of land reform exacerbated the already high level of rhetoric and bad feelings, and both sides organized rallies and pressed the Balinese to choose one side or the other.

On September 30, 1965, an unsuccessful leftist military coup in Jakarta resulted in a takeover of the government by pro-Western military leaders under General Suharto. In the wake of the coup, a tidal wave of killings swept Java and Bali, as the military sought first to dismantle the extensive structure of the PKI and rightist supporters then turned this campaign into one of wholesale slaughter. As many as 500,000 Indonesians died, and up to a fifth of them—5% of the island's population at the time—may have been Balinese. Most Balinese have family or friends who were involved in the conflict in one way or another, but even now few will talk about it, so extensive and brutal were the killings.

Bitter memories

Suharto emerged from the political storm as President of Indonesia. His "New Order" government first stabilized the country then ushered in a long period of relative peace and development, in sharp contrast to the chaotic Sukarno years that preceded it, providing basic health care, food, housing, and education to a rapidly growing population.

Over the past four decades Bali has played a key role in Indonesia's development. The tourist "paradise" begun by the Dutch has been updated and given modern form, providing a lucrative income for tens of thousands of Balinese and foreigner investors and significant amounts of foreign exchange for the nation. By the beginning of the 1990s, deregulation of the economy created uncontrollable growth in luxury hotels and other types of tourist developments. Local politicians continued to struggle with the national government, even after the fall of Suharto brought about greater local autonomy.

The downfall of the Suharto regime in 1998 inaugurated Indonesia's return to democracy. The Balinese had great hopes when Megawati Sukarnoputri, daughter of the first president and of Balinese heritage, became president in 2001.

The first few years of this period of "Reformation" brought upheaval and un- leashed a national struggle for power that opened the way for violent confrontation. On a late Saturday night, October 12, 2002, two bombs exploded in the heart of Kuta's night- club district, Bali's most popular tourist area. The effects of the blasts were devastating, resulting in an appalling loss of life, terrible injuries, and a disastrous downturn in the economy. Three years later in 2005, when Bali was on the road to recovery, further terrorist attacks were staged in the Jimbaran and Kuta areas, again bringing death and tragedy. It took another five years for the tourist industry to rebuild, but by 2010 visitor numbers were higher than ever.

Even for the Balinese, Megawati proved to be a disappointing president, and in a 2004 election a Javanese ex-military officer, Susilo Bambang Yudhoyono (familiarly called SBY), succeeded her as president, to be reelected by a landslide majority vote in 2009. SBY's leadership weathered the economic storm of the Global Financial Crisis of 2007–2012, and has faced challenges both from extremist groups and from an unruly and inefficient parliament. Nevertheless, Bali continues to prosper as part of the world's third largest democracy, in a nation of 240 million, home to the largest Muslim population in the world. The importance of this mainly-Hindu island in such a complex state demonstrates Indonesia's ability to survive as a nation while successfully managing plurality.

—*Adrian Vickers*

"Bali-style" resort hotels are famous the world over and widely imitated elsewhere.

THE BALINESE VILLAGE

A Place of Communal Order

The Balinese village is a closely knit network of social, religious, and economic institutions to which every Balinese belongs. Most Balinese live in villages, yet even those who now reside and work in cities like Denpasar still identify with, and actively participate in, organizations and rituals in the village of their birth.

Spatial layout of the village

Spatial orientation plays an eminent role in all things Balinese. The most important points of reference are *kaja* ("upstream" or "toward the mountain") and *kelod* ("downstream" or "seawards"), although *kangin* (east), *kauh* (west) and the intermediary compass points are of almost equal importance. Note that *kaja* in south Bali lies to the north, whereas in north Bali, on the other side of the mountains, it refers to a southerly direction.

At the heart of every traditional Balinese village (*desa adat*) is the *kahyangan tiga*, the three core village temples that are physically located in close accordance with this system of orientation. Thus the *pura puseh* ("temple of origin") lies nearest the mountains, the *pura bale agung* ("temple of the great meeting hall") lies in the center of the village, and the *pura dalem* (temple of the not-yet-purified deceased and of magically charged and potentially dangerous forces) lies to the seaward side of the village.

Clustered around the *pura desa* ("village temple")—generally between the *pura puseh* and the *pura dalem*—lie the residential quarters of the village, known as *banjar*, sometimes translated as "hamlets" but actually comprising distinctive neighborhoods within the village. These are usually referred to as "eastern", "western", and "central", but are often named according to the dominant profession or caste of their residents. Thus, there are *banjar pande*, where smiths live, and *banjar brahmana*, where members of the *brahmana* caste predominate.

Each *banjar* has its own meeting hall (*bale banjar*), which is the secular counterpart of the *bale agung* temple. These *bale banjar* are the social centers of the community, today often equipped with ping pong tables and televisions and surrounded by small, portable food stalls in the late afternoon.

Each *banjar* is surrounded by rice fields and gardens. The outer boundaries of the village are usually clearly marked by hedges, valleys, streams, forests, and other natural features. There are many local and regional variations in village layout, often determined by topography and population density, but there is a common pattern for all.

The family compound

In stark contrast to the open social and religious spaces of the village, the family living quarters are enclosed and private. House compounds are surrounded by a wall and from the outside nothing much can be seen.

A family compound consists of several buildings whose location and function are strictly defined and spatially determined.

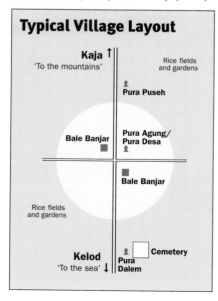

Typical Village Layout

Kaja ↑
'To the mountains'

Rice fields and gardens

Pura Puseh

Bale Banjar

Pura Agung/ Pura Desa

Bale Banjar

Rice fields and gardens

Kelod
'To the sea' ↓

Pura Dalem

Cemetery

Most Balinese still return to their home villages several times each year for ritual ceremonies.

In the mountain-ward eastern corner of the compound lies the family temple. Also toward the mountains is the *bale gunung rata* or *meten bandung,* in which the parents and grandparents usually live.

The *bale dangin* or *bale gede* (the "east" or "great" pavilion) is where family ceremonies such as tooth filings and weddings are held, but the grandparents may also sleep here. Guests are normally received in the eastern pavilion. The western pavilion (*bale dauh*) is where children normally sleep. In the sea-ward or downhill section of the compound are the more mundane and functional structures: the kitchen (*paon*), rice granary (*lumbung*), pigsty, and the bathroom (if there is one).

It is within the house compound that a child is reared and integrated into the ways of village life with the help and care of parents, aunts and uncles, siblings and, most especially, the grandparents. Male children continue to live here; a girl moves to the compound of her in-laws when she marries.

Social and religious organization

The Balinese village may be said to be "semi-autonomous" in the sense that it is largely responsible for its own socio-religious affairs and yet still forms part of wider governmental and religious networks. The *desa adat* is the lowest administrative level of the state. A number of *desa adat* form a "sub-district" (*desa* or *perbekelan),* several of which form a district (*kecamatan*), which in turn make up the regency (*kabupaten*). The boundaries of the latter are for the most part identical with those of the former Balinese kingdoms.

The semi-autonomous status of the village creates the need for a dual village administration, a *kliang adat* or chief responsible for internal village affairs and a *kliang dinas* who is responsible to the regional government. Below these are several *banjar* chiefs.

The village is further characterized by the existence of numerous groupings, membership in which is only partially voluntary. Before marriage, a person is a member of the boys' or girls' club. These have specific duties in the context of village rituals and may be regarded as a "training ground" for the person's later participation in village affairs as a married adult. Upon marriage, a Balinese becomes a member of the neighborhood association (*banjar*), the village association, the irrigation society (*subak*) and several other groups, such as the local music club and the rice harvest association.

Every Balinese thus lives within a complex matrix of interconnecting and overlapping associations. He or she has multiple duties to fulfill as members of these various institutions, as well as in the complex rounds of regional, village, and family-based ceremonies. It is due to the great complexity of these groups and their attendant support of the individual's personal identity that the village has retained its vital role as the focal point of Balinese life, even in the face of rapid modernization and change.

—Danker Schaareman

THE TEMPLE

A Sacred Space for God and Man

Above all, the Balinese temple is a sacred space in which the deities are honored with rituals and offerings. Whether a simple enclosure with only one or two tiny shrines or an elaborate complex with scores of sacred structures, the basic function of each temple is the same: to serve as a site where the Balinese pay reverence to the spiritual powers that play such a large role in their lives.

Temple types

There are literally tens of thousands of temples in Bali, and new ones are being constructed all the time. Throughout much of the year they lie eerily deserted, but on the date of their anniversary festival (*odalan*) they come to life in a brief but glorious burst of activity as the congregation adorns the temple with beautiful ornaments and arrives dressed in their finest apparel bearing elaborate gifts.

The English language has only one word for temple, but the Balinese distinguish two important types. A *sanggah* (*merajan* in the refined language) refers to private or family temples, generally translated as "house temples". Each family compound has one, containing shrines to the family's deified ancestors (*sanggah kamulan*). Thus there are several hundred thousand house temples in Bali. The other word for temple in Balinese is *pura*, originally a Sanskrit term referring to a town or palace.

On Bali, the word *pura* has come to refer to a temple in the public domain, generally located on public land. These cannot always be neatly classified, but there are generally three types associated with the three most important foci of social organization on Bali: locale, irrigation cooperative (*subak*) and descent group.

Within the group based on locality are temples of the local village, as well as temples with greater regional and island-wide significance. Irrigation cooperative temples can belong to a single *subak* or to a whole group of *subaks*. And within the group of temples based on descent are temples supported by "clans" of greater or lesser degrees of ancestral depth, variously known as *pura dadia*, *pura kawitan*, and *pura padharman*. Altogether there are at least 10,000 temples on Bali belonging to these various types.

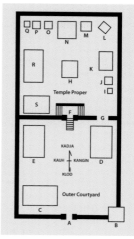

Ground plan of typical Balinese temple

A – Split gate, *candí bentar*
B – *Kulkul* tower
C – Kitchen, *paon*
D – *Balé gong*
E – *Balé* for pilgrims
F – Ceremonial gate, *padú raksa*
G – Side gate
H – *Paruman* or *pepelik*
I – *Ngrurah alit*
J – *Ngrurah gedé*

K – *Gedong pesimpangan*
L – *Padmasana*
M – *Gunung agung*
N – *Meru*
O – *Gunung batur*
P – *Maaspait*
      (*menjangan seluang*)
Q – *Taksú*
R – *Balé piasan*
S – *Balé*

Offerings and prayers are made frequently at many thousands of temples throughout Bali.

Three village temples of special significance are the *kahyangan tiga* ("three sanctuaries"): the *pura puseh* ("temple of origin"), at the upper end of the village, the *pura desa* ("village temple") or *pura bale agung* ("great meeting hall temple") in the village center, and the *pura dalem* (death temple or "temple of the mighty one") lying near the cemetery and cremation grounds at the lower or seaward end of the village. These temples are linked with the gods of the Hindu trinity: the *pura puseh* with Brahma the Creator, the *pura desa* with Wisnu (or Vishnu) the Preserver, and the *pura dalem* with Siva the Destroyer.

The famous temple sites that tourists visit are regional or island-wide temples. These include Besakih, the "Mother Temple" high up on the slopes of Mt. Agung, as well as the major temples Ulun Danu (Mt. Batur), Lempuyang, Goa Lawah, Uluwatu, Batukaru, Pusering Jagat (Pejeng), Andakasa, and Pucak Mangu. These are nearly all mountain or sea temples, marking the primary poles of the sacred landscape in Bali.

Lesser regional temples, numbering in the hundreds, are sometimes called *pura dang kahyangan*, or "temples of the Sacred Ones", because they are associated with legendary priests who brought Hinduism to Bali from Java. Their supporting congregations are drawn from a wide area, and in the past such temples were often supported by local princely houses. Nowadays, regional governments have taken on the same role. Important regional temples include Pura Sakenan, Pura Tanah Lot, Pura Kehen, Pura Taman Ayun and many others.

Shrines and pavilions

A temple may contain just one or two shrines within a small courtyard, or it may contain dozens of shrines and other structures within two, or often three, courtyards. The innermost courtyard is the most sacred. Shrines are usually located here in two rows, one lining the mountain (*kaja*) side and the other lining the eastern (*kangin*) side. Toward the center of the courtyard is a large structure where the gods gather during rituals. A variety of open pavilions complete the arrangement.

Among the shrines lining the mountainward side there is often a pair of small, closed shrines (*gedong*), one with an earthenware dish on its roof, the other with a pointed roof. These honor protective deities of the greatest importance: Dewi Sri, goddess of rice and prosperity, and her consort Rambut Sedana, god of wealth. A small shrine with a deer's head is called *menjangan saluwang* and honors the legendary priest Mpu Kuturan or a deity called Bhatara Maospahit.

A particularly striking structure is the *meru* or Balinese pagoda, which has an odd number of roofs, up to a maximum of 11. A *meru* honors a god or a deified ancestor, depending on what kind of temple it is. It was probably introduced from Java during the 14th century.

In the mountain-ward eastward corner, between the rows of shrines, there is often an open seat-type shrine. In its fully developed form, adorned with cosmic turtle and serpents, this is called a *padmasana* ("lotus throne") and honors the high god Sanghyang Widhi in his manifestation as Siva Raditya, the sun god. Modern Balinese Hinduism stresses its monotheistic aspect, and the *padmasana* has recently become more prominent.

Temple festivals are held according to one of two calendrical systems. When it appears on the 210-day *wuku* (Balinese) calendar, a festival is called an *odalan*; when it follows the lunar calendar, it is often referred to as an *usaba*. Various factors, such as local tradition and the size of the ritual, determine whether a festival is officiated by the temple's own priest (*pemangku*) or by a *brahmana* high priest (*pedanda*).

— David Stuart-Fox

BALINESE RELIGION

A Life of Ritual and Devotion

The majority of Balinese practice a form of the Hindu religion which they call *Agama Hindu Dharma* ("Religion of the Hindu doctrine"). Also called *Agama Tirtha* ("Religion of the Holy Waters"), it represents a unique amalgamation of foreign Hindu and Buddhist elements that were grafted onto a base of preexisting, indigenous religious customs. After Indonesia declared independence in 1945, the Balinese became more self-conscious of their religion and strengthened their religious organization. This resulted in the establishment of the Satya Hindu Dharma in 1956 and the Parisada Hindu Dharma Bali in 1959. The state philosophy, Pancasila, also had an impact on Balinese Hinduism as well.

Hinduism and Buddhism arrived in Bali partly via Java and partly direct from India between the 8th and 16th centuries. Elements

Villagers are blessed with sprinkled holy water during a temple anniversary festival.

of the two religions have developed further and merged here. The Indian division into four castes was adopted, and religious practices are closely connected with social hierarchy. Balinese society is separated into four main groups: *brahmana, satriya, wesya* and *anak jaba* or *sudra*, which are in turn subdivided into many more.

Basic principles

Balinese Hinduism encompasses a vast range of practices and doctrines, dominated by Siva-type characteristics. Siva is the main god, manifesting himself as Surya, the Sun. Buddhistic elements in the Balinese *Hindu Dharma* derive from a Tantric form of Mahayana Buddhism (the main branch of Buddhism, practiced in China, Tibet, Korea, and Japan). Only small groups of Balinese Buddhists exist today, mainly Brahmans living in Budakling village in Karangasem Regency. However in Banjar, in northwest Bali, a Buddhist monastery is strongly influenced by Theravada Buddhism (practiced today in Sri Lanka, Burma and Thailand).

The three basic principles of the Hindu religion are knowledge of the epics (the *Mahabharata, Ramayana* and commentaries), knowledge of philosophy and theology, and ritual worship (*puja*) connected with devotion (*bakti*) and offerings (*banten*). The central questions in Balinese Hindu philosophy are: where from and where to? Where does humanity come from, how can we attain release? In which offspring will he or she reincarnate? What is the origin of the cosmos, and how should one behave to guarantee the continuation of cosmic processes? These questions and their answers can be expressed in visual symbols, such as a mountain with a tree of life, a lotus pond, or a heavenly nymph.

The stability of the cosmos is expressed by emphasizing the quadrants of the compass and their colors, and the gods with their mounts and attributes. Oppositions like creation-annihilation, good-bad, heaven-earth, and fire-water are visualized in the nadir and the zenith. The swastika, wheel of the sun, is the symbol for the Hindu religion in general and shows the perpetual cycle of life.

The five ritual categories

The purpose of every ritual is to cleanse objects and people. Holy water, fire, and ash can all be used. This can also be done by rubbing or touching with objects symbolizing purity—for instance eggs, geese, ducks, and leaves of the *dapdap* tree. It is believed that one's soul may have accumulated impurities through evil deeds during one's life or previous lives, resulting in punishment in hell followed by rebirth as a miserable creature. In order to avoid this, the deceased and his or her soul must be purified by means of fire (the cremation) and holy water. A soul that has been released becomes a god (*bhatara*).

All Balinese rituals—tooth-filings, cock-fights, cremations, and others—can be held only on specific occasions according to the Balinese calendar. In all, there are literally hundreds of rites and festivals that each person participates in during his lifetime, and a great deal of time and expense is devoted to them.

Yadnya is a term of Sanskrit derivation meaning "worship" or "sacrificial rite" that is collectively applied to all Balinese ceremonies. Each rite may have any number of meanings ascribed to it, but all serve to create a sense of wellbeing and of community, both of which are important concepts to the Balinese. They are also a means of maintaining a delicate balance among the various forces in the Balinese cosmos. The Balinese themselves distinguish five ritual categories, the *panca yadnya*.

Ritual exorcisms

The first of these, the *bhuta yadnya*, are rites carried out to appease the spirits of chaos, personified in the form of ogres, witches, and demons, and to cleanse humanity and their surroundings from those influences. Ritual offerings known as *pacaruan* are set out by the women of the household every 15 days to appease and banish these baleful influences from the house compound.

An annual *pacaruan* offering ritual on a much larger scale, the Tawur Agung, is carried out on the day before Nyepi, the Balinese "New Year". Its aim is the purification of an area from the bad influences that have

A high priest performs purification rituals.

accumulated during the previous year. The rite is usually carried out at a crossroads, supervised by a *pedanda* high priest. Five sorts of fluids are used: water, *arak* (palm liquor), palm wine, rice wine, and blood. Blood is thought to be one of the most purifying ingredients and in most cases has been taken from a cock which has been killed during a ritual cockfight. Afterwards, men carry torches through the village and make a huge commotion beating gongs and bamboo tubes to expel the demonic forces. Simultaneously young men carry ornate papier-mâché *ogoh-ogoh* or demon images through the streets, which are consequently burned at the night's end, symbolically extinguishing their negative energies. The same is done in every house compound, without the *ogoh-ogoh*.

More elaborate exorcisms are undertaken once in 5, 10, 25, and 100 years. In 1979 and 1989 elaborate Panca Wali Krama rites took place in Besakih temple, and the greatest ritual exorcism of them all—the Eka Dasa Rudra purification of the universe, which is held only once every century—was also celebrated in Bali's "Mother Temple" in 1979 to mark the transition to the Saka year 1900.

Rites of passage

The *manusa yadnya*, or life cycle rites, are designed to ensure a person's spiritual and material wellbeing. From conception until after death a person is believed to be in the company of the "four companions" (*kanda empat*). After birth these are expressed as personifications of the amniotic fluid, the blood, the *vernix caseosa*, and the afterbirth. The latter is buried by the entrance of the sleeping house and covered with a river stone. The umbilical cord is often kept in a little silver box hung around the baby's neck.

The companions will protect if treated well; if not, they may create problems.

Twelve days after birth the ceremonial cutting of the navel string occurs. At this time the child is given a temporary "baby-sitter", a deity called Dewa Kumara. This deity is instructed by his father, Siva, to protect the baby until its first tooth appears. A small shrine next to the child's bed is hung with flowers and bananas as an offering for the protecting spirit.

Forty-two days after birth, a ceremony is held to cleanse the mother, who is thought to be impure after birth. On this day also the natural force of a "brother/sister", which has accompanied the baby since birth departs, and the child is now considered to be fully human. Another ceremony is held three months after birth to consolidate the baby's body and soul. At this time, the child's official name is announced, and he or she may touch the earth for the first time.

After 210 days, the baby's first "birthday" or *otonan* is celebrated. The hair is cut for the first time and the mother makes an offering in the village temple to announce that her child has arrived in the village.

In some communities, the onset of puberty is celebrated by a ritual held in the house, followed by the young person involved being paraded around the streets to announce their new status. This is held for girls on the occasion of her first menstruation; for boys when his voice changes. The next major ceremony occurs as the child reaches the end of puberty. This is the well known "tooth filing" ceremony whose aim is to symbolically eradicate the animal or "wild" nature in a person symbolized by the six enemies: greed, lust, drunkenness, anger, envy, and confusion. During the ceremony, the six central upper canine teeth are filed down slightly. A person should now behave as an adult, able to control his or her emotions.

Full adulthood begins after marriage, and the person is then treated as a full-fledged member of the community. If the child is the eldest or youngest son, he will replace his father in carrying out certain village duties.

Completing the cycle and returning the soul safely to the other world are the *pitra yadnya* or ceremonies for the dead (see "The Ceremony Cremation"). After death, the soul of the deceased joins the ancestors and is worshipped with the gods in special shrines within the house compound. The hope is to regularly communicate with one's ancestors,

and every Balinese has a sense of wellbeing, knowing he or she is protected by them.

Rites for gods and priests

Dewa yadnya ceremonies are performed to honor the divinities. Such ceremonies are a communal responsibility, taking place during temple anniversaries either once every 210 days of the *wuku* year, or once in a lunar-solar year of 360 days. The gods or divine ancestors are then invited to come down to earth and reside in their temples. For at least three days they are feasted and regaled with offerings, music, dance, and hymns. Priests perform the rituals to summon the gods; those who support the temple pay their homage.

Apart from these anniversaries, major temple festivals are held on Galungan and Kuningan, two holy days according to the Balinese calendar. Another important festival

The entire village regularly participates in elaborate offerings, processions, and performances.

is Tumpek Uduh—held every 210 days—when useful trees and garden plants are honored with offerings. On this day no tree may be cut or fruits taken. In a similar way, rituals are performed for household and agricultural tools and other objects made out of metal on Tumpek Landep, for domesticated animals on Tumpek Kandang, and for puppets and performing arts objects on Tumpek Wayang.

Ritual worship is supervised by specialists: the priests. Their main task is to prepare holy water for the believers. People of higher castes cannot receive holy water from priests belonging to a lower caste. The highest and most distinguished priests are the Brahman *pedanda*, who can offer holy water to any person, because they occupy the highest rung in the social hierarchy. Members of the *satriya dalem* and *wesya* castes may use priests from their own class, the *resi*, but they prefer a *pedanda*. The

Pasek, Sengguhu, Pande and Bali Aga groups all have their own priests as well, but being so low in the hierarchy, they can only offer holy water to members of their own group.

The *resi yadnya* are rituals to ordain priests. To be ordained as a *pedanda*, a Brahman must study with a high priest for many years. A ritual ordination, or *padiksan*, is then organized for him by the family with the help of other villagers. During the ritual, the candidate undergoes a symbolic death and cremation. Thereafter, he is "reborn" as a pure man. After his ordination, his guru continues to act as his advisor, and it is only after another year of study that he is able to perform rituals on his own. Male priests are consecrated along with their wives, meaning the wife may take over the priesthood after the death of her husband.

—*Hedi Hinzler & Ida Ayu Agung Mas*

Pitra Yadnya: Rites for the Ancestors

Life, death, rebirth. This cyclical conception of existence lies at the very heart of Balinese Hinduism. During each life on earth the eternal soul occupies a temporary vessel—the physical body—which at death must be returned to the *pancamahabhuta*, the five elemental substances: solid, liquid, radiance, energy, and ether. Only then can the soul be released and reincarnated. Of all Balinese rituals, the cremation (*pangabenen, palebon*) is the most complex, lasting for many days and culminating with the spectacular burning of not only the corpse, but vast quantities of valuable ritual objects especially created for the occasion.

Calling the soul

Due to the huge amount of time and expense involved, a cremation is usually postponed for months or even years. In the meantime the body of the deceased is temporarily buried. Family members first wash and groom the corpse, then wrap it in cloths and mats. A raw egg is rolled across it and smashed to the ground, removing all impurities. The body is then transported to the cemetery on a simple bier and buried without a casket.

Once a favorable day has been set, an army of ritual specialists, artists, priests, family members, friends, and neighbors of all ages and sexes is mobilized, calling upon an encyclopedia of communal knowledge in the creation of offerings of every imaginable shape, color, and ingredient and the performance of a series of elaborate rites.

Before cremation a "soul calling" ritual must be held at the grave. Offerings are made, and as the corpse cannot be returned to the house once it has been buried, the soul is taken home in a *sangah urip* effigy containing soil from the grave. Outside the house a paper and coconut shell lamp—a *damar kurung*—is hung to guide the soul home.

The washing of the corpse is symbolically repeated on an *adegan*, a small board with a human figure drawn on it. The day before the cremation, a priest prays for favorable treatment of the soul in the afterlife. Various types

Cremations are expensive affairs: bodies may be buried for years until families can afford one.

of holy water are made and offerings are purified. The *angenan*, an eggshell lamp mounted on a decorated coconut, serves as a memorial.

The procession
On the day of the cremation, once the sun has passed the zenith, loud gong music is played and a lively procession starts the journey to the cemetery. Dozens of offerings and ritual objects lead the way, and the body is carried in a colorful tower (*wadah, bade*) fashioned of wood, bamboo, and paper, shouldered by scores of shouting men. Platforms at the base represent the earth, sometimes resting on the cosmic turtle and serpents of the underworld. On the back of the tower may be a winged and fanged face of the son of the earth, and higher up a goose symbolizing purity.

Above these platforms is an open space for the body, and crowning the tower is an odd number of roofs representing the heavens. The caste and clan of the deceased determine the number: 11 for royalty, less for persons of more humble birth. Attached to the front of the tower is a long, white cloth (*lantaran*) held by family members to represent their ties to the deceased. The tower is rotated at each crossroads to disorient and prevent the soul from returning to disturb the living.

Release through fire and water
Arriving at the cemetery, the body is taken down and a pair of birds set free, symbolic of the soul's release. On a bamboo platform under a high roof stands a wooden sarcophagus (called a *patulangan* or *palinggihan*) decorated with cloth and paper, sometimes carried in procession ahead of the tower. The sarcophagus is generally in the shape of a mythical animal such as a bull or winged lion.

The sarcophagus is opened and the body or newly exhumed remains (sometimes simply an effigy) are carried around it and placed inside. The shroud is opened; jars of holy water are poured over the body and shattered. Cloths, letters of introduction to the gods, and effigies are piled inside, and the sarcophagus is closed. Offerings are placed below to start the fire, and the sarcophagus and corpse are consumed by flames. The tower is burned separately.

Death brings with it the opportunity to fulfill all duties toward the deceased, and there is no public display of mourning if the deceased has lived a long and full life. Weeping near a corpse disturbs the soul,

A cremation tower holds the body of the deceased so that its soul may be sent to heaven.

making it unwilling to leave. Grief is expressed in private, however, especially if a young person has died prematurely as the result of serious illness or a tragic accident.

Purification and deification
When the corpse has finally been reduced to ashes, the flames are doused and the family hunts for bone fragments, forming them into a small human shape. The bones are pulverized and placed in an effigy made from a coconut, which is taken on a bier to the sea or river and cast into the waters. Three days later another ceremony removes the ritual pollution brought by death upon the living.

Twelve days after the cremation, the soul of the deceased is purified in a *ngrorasin* rite, often accompanied by rituals (*mukur, nyekah, ngasti, maligia*) designed to deify the ancestor. A *sekah* effigy is made for the soul and placed in a high pavilion. In the evening, family members pray and offer their respects. Early the next morning, the image is broken and burned, and the ashes placed in a decorated coconut. A tower (*bukur, madhya*) then transports them to the sea for disposal.

Finally, in the *nyagara-gunung* ceremony, the family expresses thanks to the gods of the oceans and the mountains. Offerings are brought to important sea and mountain temples, often including Besakih, after which the deified soul is enshrined in a clan or family temple as a protective ancestral spirit.

—*Garrett Kam*

A Cycle of Holy Days and Anniversaries

Except in a number of once-isolated mountain villages and ancient court centers, most of Bali follows both a 12-month lunar calendar and a 210-day ritual cycle. Together these two parallel calendrical systems determine the incredibly complex and busy schedule of holy days and anniversaries observed throughout the island, with many important festivals being determined by the conjunction of particular dates in the two systems. Every day also has associated with it numerous auspicious and malevolent forces that must be considered when selecting dates for everything from construction to cremation.

Two parallel systems

The lunar calendar, similar to that used in parts of India, is based upon phases of the moon. Each 29- to 30-day lunar month (*sasih*) begins on the day after a new moon (*tilem*), with the full moon (*purnama*) occurring in the middle.

Twelve lunar *sasih* months comprise a normal year, with an intercalary 13th month added every two or three years to keep it synchronized with the longer solar year. The years are numbered from the founding of the Indian Saka Dynasty in A.D. 78, so that the year 1900 in Bali began in 1979.

The 210-day *pawukon* cycle, on the other hand, is indigenously Balinese, and its repetitions are not numbered or recorded as years. It may have had its roots in the growing period for rice, but the following Oedipal myth is associated with it as well. A woman discovers that her husband is in fact her own son, who ran away as a child. Vain with power, he challenges the gods but is defeated; 27 children by his mother and aunt are sacrificed. The 30 weeks (*wuku*) of the calendar are named after these characters.

The 210 days of the *pawukon* "year" are divided into many shorter cycles, which run concurrently. The most important of these are the 3- (Pasah, Beteng/Tegeh, Kajeng), 5- (Umanis, Paing, Pon, Wage, Kliwon) and 7-day "weeks", whose conjunctions determine most

holy days. Each day has its own deity, constellation and omen that indicate good or bad times for a variety of activities.

The *pawukon* year is also subdivided into 35-day "months" (*bulan*) determined by a complete cycle of 5- and 7-day weeks. Each date in the *pawukon* calendar is referred to according to the combination of days in the various weeks, for example: Kajeng Kliwon Menail, Anggarkasih Dukut, Buda Cemeng Ukir. The passage of six *bulan*, a full *pawukon* year, marks a birthday (*otonan*) or anniversary (*rahinan, odalan*).

Sasih holy days

Purnama and *tilem* in the *sasih* calendar are for praying and making offerings, a time when rituals and sacred dances are held in many temples. Temple anniversaries (*odalan*) often take place on the full moon. Siwalatri, the "Night of Siva", falls on the eve of the new moon of the seventh *sasih*, in January. On this night many Balinese meditate, sing classical poetry and keep all-night vigils in temples of the dead.

The days immediately before the start of the lunar new year are especially full of activity. Processions of offerings and loud gong music accompany the icons of every temple to the coast for a ritual cleansing (*malasti, makiis, malis*). On the eve of the new year, demon-appeasing sacrifices are held everywhere. That night, a great commotion is made to chase demons away, sometimes accompanied by torch processions of huge bamboo and paper monsters (*ogoh-ogoh*).

The next day is Nyepi, literally "the day of silence", when Bali appears completely deserted. No fires are lit or electricity used, visiting and entertainment are not permitted, and people stay at home to meditate. This continues until the following morning, when normal activity resumes.

Pawukon holy days

Kajeng Kliwon is the only significant conjunction of the 3- and 5-day weeks. Offerings are placed at house entrances to bar demonic forces. Ceremonies and sacred dances are held at temples, many of which celebrate an *odalan* anniversary. On Anggarkasih, when Tuesday coincides with Kliwon, household offerings are made to safeguard its members, and many temple *odalans* take place.

The influence of Buddhism can be seen in the holy days falling on Buda or Wednesday. Buda Umanis is a very auspicious day for ceremonies. Buda Cemeng is a day for praying and meditating. Buda Kliwon is often a particularly holy day, when prayers and offerings are made to ensure the blessings of the gods.

Pagerwesi falls on Wednesday of the week Sinta and means "Iron Fence", a time when humanity must stand firm to protect the world and its creatures. Rituals begin two days before and prayers are said for the continued wellbeing of the universe.

Galungan and Kuningan

The days between Galungan (Wednesday of the week Dunggulan) and Kuningan (Saturday of the week Kuningan) are full of celebrations. Kuningan marks the end of a series of festivals. This 42-day holy period is based on an ancient harvest festival, and it is still forbidden to begin planting at this time.

Each day before Galungan is marked by a special activity: ripening fruits, making offerings and slaughtering animals. Temples are cleaned and decorated for the upcoming visit of the ancestral spirits. On Galungan eve, *penjor* bamboo poles are set up in front of every house and temple, arcing over roads with flowers, fruits and palm leaf ornaments hanging from them, symbols of fertility.

Nearby altars for offerings are decorated with *lamak* scrolls of delicate palm-leaf cutouts as welcome mats for the ancestors. On Galungan day, prayers are intoned, people visit and feasts are held. *Barongs* dance from house to house and receive donations in return for their blessings. On Kuningan day, new offerings and decorations are put out and tools are honored.

— *Garrett Kam*

A pelelintingan, *or traditional astrological chart*

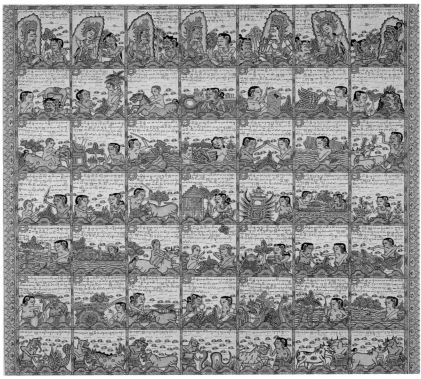

BALINESE LANGUAGE AND LITERATURE

A Rich Literary Heritage

Three languages are spoken on Bali: Balinese and its dialects, Indonesian, and a kind of Old Javanese called Kawi. Contacts with Hindu-Buddhist Java between the 9th and 16th centuries exerted a strong influence on the language and literature of Bali. Later contacts with Muslim Java, Blambangan and Lombok between the 17th and 19th centuries also left their traces. The Indonesian language, which derives from Malay, is used in schools, in the mass media, and as the *lingua franca* of commerce and government, has also had a great impact on the Balinese language.

Standard Balinese uses different levels, each with its own set of parallel vocabulary, to indicate the caste or status of the speaker vis-à-vis the person spoken to. There are three main levels: *alus* (high), *kasar* (low) and *mider* (middle). This means that a low caste person uses formal high Balinese words in speaking to a person of higher status, while the latter will reply using the low vocabulary. Only several hundred words are covered by these parallel vocabularies, but they tend to be the most commonly used ones.

Indonesian is spoken and taught at school, and children from six years onwards are thus brought up bilingually with a stress on Indonesian. Additionally, intellectuals and many Balinese parents in towns like Denpasar and Tabanan consider it more fashionable to speak only Indonesian. As a result, knowledge of formal or "high" Balinese among the younger generation is declining.

Kawi is now mainly a literary language, surviving in spoken form only in the theater. Heroes representing high caste characters from the classical literature express themselves in Kawi, but it is only understood by a few specialists, by *dalangs* (puppet masters) and by some of the older people in the audience.

Courtly literary genres

Much of the diversity displayed by Balinese literature today has historical roots. Written sources can be found in the following languages on Bali: Sanskrit, Old Balinese, Old Javanese, Middle Javanese, Balinese, Sasak (from Lombok), Malay, and Indonesian.

Sanskrit was used in royal edicts dating from the 9th to the 11th centuries and still today in hymns (*stuti, stawa*) recited by priests. There are many Sanskrit loanwords in Old Javanese, Balinese, and Indonesian. Old Balinese was used in edicts issued between A.D. 882 and the early 10th century.

A sample of the traditional Balinese Kawi script, based on a southern Indian script

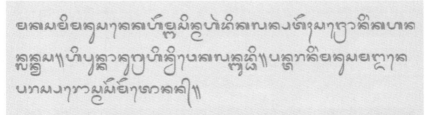

Makasami manusane kaembasin mahardika lan pateh. sajeroning kahanan lan kuasa. ipun kanugrahin wiweka lan budi. pantaraning manusa mangdane paras-paros masemetonan.

By the end of the 10th century, when close links were established with east Java, Old Javanese was used in the inscriptions, and it is likely that Javanese literature came to Bali at this time also. Ironically, while Old Javanese is still known and used in Bali, it has all but disappeared on Java. Poems and prose works on religion, grammar, metrics, magic, medicine, history, and genealogy are still being produced there in Old Javanese.

During the culturally rich Gelgel period (1550–1600), the kings of Bali kept Balinese or Javanese scribes in their service who wrote in Middle Javanese and introduced a whole new genre of laudatory poems on the beauty of women (the queen in particular) or the death of a beloved. They also produced works on politics and ancient history to legitimize the position of the king.

Later east Javanese literature, including stories of Muslim knights such as the Menak and Kidung Juarsa tales, became known in Bali in the 17th century. When Karangasem took control of western Lombok at the end of the 18th century, Sasak literature was brought to eastern Bali as well. Many Sasak words occur in poems in Karangasem.

As Balinese nobles formed their own independent courts and became more powerful around 1700, they began to sponsor works of court literature. Brahman authors were very popular, probably because they knew Old Javanese and were well-versed in religion, politics, and the classical literature. The language of these new *kidung* poems was Old Javanese with many Balinese elements added.

A new genre of poetry (Geguritan or Parikan)—epic histories and love stories about Balinese kings, princes, and heroes written in Balinese—developed at the end of the 18th century. Folktales, riddles and rhymes were also noted in Balinese from the end of the 19th century onwards.

When the Dutch began their conquest of Bali early in the 20th century, at a time when the Balinese themselves were constantly at war, a new genre came into being: poetry about the devastation (*rusak* or *uug*) of a realm.

Most works of Old Javanese and Balinese literature are anonymous. The manuscripts consist of *lontar* palm leaves, prepared and cut to size (usually 3.5–4.5 cm high and 35–50 cm long), and then bound together by means of a string run through perforations in the center or the left hand side of the leaves. An iron stylus is used to inscribe them and

The Balinese language has different vocabularies that are used on more or less formal occasions.

the lines are then blackened with soot. Other illustrated manuscripts also date from the late 19th and beginning of the 20th centuries.

For the most part, Balinese literature is meant to be read silently but should be sung and recited, for example during rituals and in theater performances. Certain passages are sung or adapted for the *wayang* (shadow puppet play) or the stage. There are also special clubs (*seka bebasan*) devoted to the singing and recitation of poems.

New ideas, new language

With the increase of Western influence during the 1920s and 1930s, many Balinese, especially the Brahmans, came to feel that the Balinese were becoming alienated from their religion and culture. To counter this, they composed religious treatises in Balinese. Dissertations on Balinese script, grammar, and language were also produced under the influence of Dutch scholarship.

After the Indonesian Revolution against the Dutch, Balinese authors began to write novels in Indonesian, and later also poetry, and a Balinese literary movement came into being. The Balai Penelitian Bahasa library in Singaraja, now in Denpasar, began a Balinese folktale series in 1978.

In the 21st century, the local newspaper, *The Bali Post*, its electronic counterpart, Bali TV and other competitors such as Dewata TV all have sections and programs made completely in Balinese. Even though Indonesian is spoken by nearly all segments of the population, Balinese is still the main language heard on the streets.

—*Hedi Hinzler*

ARTFUL OFFERINGS

Gifts for Gods, Ancestors, and Demons

The many unseen inhabitants of Bali—gods, ancestors, and demons—are treated by the Balinese as honored guests through the daily presentation of offerings (*banten*) of every imaginable shape, color, and substance. These are first and foremost gifts expressing gratitude to benevolent spirits, and placating mischievous demons to prevent them from disturbing the harmony of life.

Simple offerings are presented daily as a matter of course, while more elaborate ones are specially produced for specific rituals. After the daily food is prepared, for example, tiny packets are presented to the resident gods of the household before the family eats. Every day, too, the spirits are presented with tiny *canang*, palm leaf trays containing flowers and betel as a token of hospitality.

Being gifts to higher beings, these offerings must be attractive, and a great deal of time and effort is expended to make them so. Leaves are laboriously cut, plaited and pinned together into decorative shapes (*jejaitan*). Multi-colored rice flour cookies (*jajan*) are modeled into tiny sculptures and even into entire scenes, which have a deep symbolic significance quite apart from their decorative function. In many ways, therefore, the production of offerings may be regarded as an important traditional art form that still flourishes on Bali.

Materials and preparation

Aside from a few durable elements employed, such as coins, cloth and an occasional wooden mask, offerings are generally fashioned of perishable, organic materials. Not only the materials, but also the function of these objects is transitory. Once presented to the gods, an offering may not be used again and similar ones must be produced again and again each day.

The preparation of offerings is one of the many tasks undertaken by every Balinese woman. Within the household, women of several generations work together, and in this way knowledge and skills are handed down to the young. To a limited extent, men also

cooperate; it is their task to slaughter animals and prepare most meat offerings.

Many women in Bali even make a living by acting as offering specialists (*tukang banten*). Their main task is to direct the armies of people who collectively produce offerings for large rituals at home or in the communal temple. They are able to coordinate this work because they know the types and ingredients of offerings required for each occasion.

As more and more Balinese women work outside the home in offices or tourist hotels, they have less time to undertake elaborate ritual preparations. This results in an increasing demand for ready-made offerings that many *tukang banten* produce in their own homes. In spite of this commercialization, the meaning and ritual use of offerings is not diminishing in Bali.

Ritual uses

For almost any ritual, the enormous number and variety of offerings required is quite astounding. There are literally hundreds of different kinds, the names, forms, sizes, and ingredients of which differ greatly. There is also considerable variation from region to region, and even from village to village. The basic form of most offerings is quite similar, however. Rice, fruits, cookies, meat, and vegetables are arranged on a palm leaf base and crowned with a palm leaf decoration called a *sampian*, which serves also as a container for betel and flowers.

Certain offerings are used in many rituals, whereas others are specific to a particular ceremony. Basic offerings form groups (*soroh*) around a core offering, and since most rituals can be performed with varying degrees of elaboration, depending upon the occasion and the means and social status of the participants, the size and content of these offering groups vary also according to the elaborateness of the ritual.

The size of an offering may be scaled up or down to match the occasion. For example, an ordinary *pula gembal* contains, among other

Offerings are a central feature of everyday life in Bali and a focal point for all religious ceremonies. Holy water is sprinkled over the offerings to consecrate them.

things, dozens of different rice dough figurines in a palm leaf basket. In more elaborate rituals, this becomes a spectacular construction of brightly colored cookies, measuring several meters from top to bottom.

Besides the major communal offerings associated with a particular ritual, each family brings its own large and colorful offering to a temple festival. It is a spectacular sight when women of a neighborhood together carry offerings in procession to a temple.

At the temple, offerings are placed according to their destination and function. Offerings to gods and ancestors are placed on high altars, whereas demons receive theirs on the ground. An important difference is that offerings to demons may contain raw meat, while those for the gods and ancestors may not. Specific offerings required for a ritual are placed in a pavilion or temporary platform.

During the ceremony, a priest purifies the offerings by sprinkling them with holy water and intoning prayers or mantras. The smoke of incense then wafts the essence of the offerings to their intended destination. The daily presentation of offerings at home takes place in a similar way, through the use of holy water and fire. After the ritual is over and their "essence" has been consumed, the offerings may be taken home and eaten by the worshippers.

Symbolism

The elements that make life on earth possible are transformed into offerings and thus returned as gifts to their original Creator. But an offering not only consists of the fruits of the earth, but also mirrors its essential structure; decorative motifs often symbolize the various constituents of the Balinese universe. The colors and numbers of flowers and other ingredients refer to deities who guard the cardinal directions. The requisite betel on top of every offering symbolizes the Hindu Trinity, as do the three basic colors used: red for Brahma, black or green for Wisnu, and white for Siva.

Conical shapes, whether of offerings as a whole or of the rice used in it, are models of the cosmic mountain whose central axis links the underworld, the middle world, and the upper world, symbolic of cosmic totality and the source of life on earth. Rice dough cookies represent the contents of the world: plants, animals, people, buildings, or even little market scenes and gardens. Pairs of such cookies, like the sun and moon, the mountain and sea, the earth and sky, symbolize the dual ordering of the cosmos in which complementary elements cannot exist without one another.

The unity of male and female, necessary for the production of new life, is in many ways represented in the composition of offerings. By recreating the universe through the art and medium of offerings, the Balinese hope that the continuity of life on earth will be assured.

—Francine Brinkgreve

TOURISM IN BALI

Creating a New Vision of Paradise

Bali has long been characterized in the West as the last "paradise" on earth, a traditional society insulated from the modern world, whose inhabitants are endowed with exceptional artistic talents and concentrate a considerable amount of time and wealth staging sumptuous ceremonies for their own pleasure and for that of their gods, now also for the delectation of foreign visitors.

This image is due in large part, of course, to the positive effect Bali's manifold charms have on visitors, but it is also the result of certain romantic Western notions about what constitutes a "tropical island paradise" in the first place. Additionally, it should be understood that Bali's development into a popular tourist destination has been the result of specific actions and decisions on the part of governing authorities for more than a century.

Colonial beginnings

To become a prime tourist destination, Bali had to fulfil two conditions. First, an island which had previously been known mainly for the "plunderous salvage" of shipwrecks and "barbarous sacrifice" of widows on the funeral pyre had to become an object of curiosity for Westerners in search of the exotic. Secondly, the island had to be made accessible. Barely a decade after the Dutch conquest of Bali, both conditions were met.

It was in 1908, just after the fall of Bali's last raja, that tourism in the Indonesian archipelago had its beginnings. In this year, an official tourist bureau was opened in the colonial capital, Batavia (now Jakarta), with the aim of promoting the Netherlands Indies as a tourist destination. Initially focusing on Java, the bureau soon extended its scope to

Titled "President Reagan Visits Bali", this painting by I Made Budi shows a Balinese view of foreigners.

include Bali, then described in its brochures as the "Gem of the Lesser Sunda Isles".

In 1924, the Royal Packet Navigation Company (KPM) inaugurated a weekly steamship service connecting Bali's north coast Buleleng (Singaraja) port with Batavia and Surabaya on Java and Makassar on Sulawesi. Shortly thereafter, the KPM agent in Buleleng was appointed as the tourist bureau's representative on Bali, and the government began allowing visitors to use the rest houses or *pasanggrahan* originally designed to accommodate Dutch functionaries on their periodic rounds of the island.

In 1928, the KPM erected the Bali Hotel in Denpasar—the island's first real tourist hostelry—on the very site of the *puputan* massacre and mass suicide of 1906. Following this, the KPM also upgraded the *pasanggrahan* at Kintamani, which from then on hosted tourists who came to enjoy the spectacular panoramas around Lake Batur.

Early visitors to Bali sometimes arrived aboard a cruiser that berthed at Padangbai for one or two days, but more often aboard the weekly KPM steamship via Buleleng. Passengers on this ship usually disembarked on Friday morning and departed aboard the same boat on Sunday evening, giving them just enough time to make a quick round of the island by motorcar. The number of people visiting Bali in this way each year increased steadily from several hundred in the late 1920s to several thousand during the 1930s.

The Master Plan

With the landing of Japanese troops at Sanur in 1942, tourism on Bali came to an abrupt halt, and recovery after the war was slow. In fact, until the late 1960s, Balinese tourism was severely hampered by the rudimentary state of the island's infrastructure and by unsettling political events in the country. Yet President Sukarno adopted Bali as his favorite retreat (his mother was Balinese) and made it a showplace for state guests. Eager to use the island's fame to attract foreign tourists, he undertook construction of a new international airport in Tuban and the prestigious Bali Beach Hotel in Sanur, the latter financed with Japanese war reparation funds. Opened in 1966, rebuilt in 1994, and now called the Inna Grand Bali Beach Hotel—owned by the Indonesian government—it remains a major landmark and the tallest building on Bali.

When General Suharto became President of the Republic in 1967 his New Order government rapidly moved to reopen Indonesia to the West. This move coincided with a period of high growth in international tourism, and from this time onward tourism expanded rapidly on Bali.

This development was the direct result of a decision made by the government in their first Five-Year Development Plan (1969–74), primarily in order to address a pressing national balance of payment deficits. Bali's prestigious image, formed during the pre-war years, meant that the island naturally became the focus of tourism development in Indonesia.

Accordingly, the government heeded the advice of the World Bank and commissioned a team of French experts to draw up a Master Plan for the Development of Tourism on Bali. Their report, published in 1971 and revised in 1974 by the World Bank, proposed the construction of a new 425-hectare tourist resort at Nusa Dua and a network of roads linking major attractions on the island.

With the Master Plan's official promulgation in 1972, tourism was ranked second only to agriculture in economic priority in the province. The Master Plan was designed to attract tourists in the upper-income range who were expected to stay at luxury hotels. But it turned out that a considerable proportion of visitors were not of the target group but comprised young, low-cost travelers staying in small homestays and budget accommodations. As the Balinese were quick to adapt to this unexpected clientele—for years derogatorily described as "hippies"—new resorts sprang up in places like Kuta, Ubud, Lovina, and Candidasa.

Further developments

In the late 1980s, tourism development on Bali shifted into high gear with a sharp upsurge in visitors arrivals followed by an even more rapid rise in hotel investment and other tourism related facilities. In 1988, alleging the pressure of demand, the governor designated 15 tourist areas around the island, thus in effect lifting the regional restrictions imposed by the Master Plan which had prohibited the building of large hotels outside of Nusa Dua, Sanur, and Kuta. From then on, there has been a frenzy of investment and development by leading international hotel chains, enticed by the deregulation of the banking system and solicited by Asian investors, most of them backed by Jakarta-based conglomerates.

In 1993, the tourist areas were increased to 21, covering roughly one quarter of the total surface of the island. Tourism development continued apace, proving remarkably resilient to world events. But when in October 2002 bomb blasts killed over 200 people—foreign tourists for the most part—visitor arrivals dropped sharply. Tourism had begun to recover in earnest when Bali was hit for the second time by a terrorist bombing in October 2005. The damage was fortunately far less than the first time, with fewer casualties, most of whom were Indonesians. Unlike in 2002, there was no mass exodus of tourists. Nonetheless, arrivals went down markedly, rising anew in 2007 and increasing ever since.

The number of new accommodations built in the last five years is nothing short of amazing, not only in traditional tourist areas but also in regions heretofore almost totally unaffected by tourism in the past, for example in west, east and north Bali, particularly along the coastlines. From fewer than 30,000 in the late 1960s, foreign and domestic arrivals reached 5.75 million in 2009, 1.5 times the island's 3.9 million population (2010 census estimate). During the same period, hotel capacity increased from less than 500 rooms to over 78,000.

Tourism: bane or boon?

One significant result of this development has been spectacular economic growth on Bali, so that the province now has one of the highest average income levels in all of Indonesia, with more automobiles per capita in Denpasar than in the nation's capital, Jakarta. Another highly visible result has been the ever-accelerating physical transformation of the island as more and more hotels, villas, restaurants, and souvenir shops dot the landscape.

While tourism has boosted the economic growth of Bali, the uneven distribution of economic benefits within the population and throughout the island, as well as the growing encroachment of foreign interests, have become matters of serious concern. While the resorts employ local staff, they are mostly low-skilled, and many of the tourist dollars end up with the owners in Jakarta or overseas. Land prices have soared in many areas, and rural Balinese, unable to pay the increasing land taxes, have sold their lands to investors below market values. Agricultural output

is falling, as more and more farm land is given over to tourism developments.

Additionally, as a result of inadequate planning and lack of control, the environment on Bali has been heavily taxed, to the point that the island is now rife with air and water pollution, beach erosion and reef destruction, water and electricity shortages, saturation of solid waste disposal; not to mention traffic congestion, urban sprawl, overpopulation, crime, and social tensions. Worse in the eyes of the Balinese is the transformation of land into a marketable commodity and its massive conversion, which has caused family as well as communal feuds and has uprooted the local population, alienated from land ownership. This shift in the function of rice fields has important implications for food production and the livelihood of farmers, and it poses serious threats to the perpetuation of traditional Balinese culture, which grew out of a communal-agrarian society.

More difficult to assess, however, are the implications of tourism on Balinese society and culture, and opinions on this subject are as contradictory as they are passionate. Many foreign visitors, after only a day or two on the island, are quick to say that Bali is finished —almost. The Balinese, so the story goes, have been thoroughly corrupted by tourist dollars and the entire island is up for sale. Authentic traditions are being packaged to conform to tourist expectations, legendary Balinese artistry is being harnessed to create souvenir trinkets, and age-old religious ceremonies are being turned into hotel floor shows. In short, tourism is engulfing Bali, and the island's culture cannot survive much longer. So hurry up and see what you can; next year may be too late....

Other observers who deem themselves better informed will counter that this kind of apocalyptic attitude is neither very accurate nor even very new. Travel narratives penned during the 1930s tell a similar tale, these authors having already persuaded themselves that they were witnessing the swan-song of Bali's traditional culture, while in fact that culture is as vibrant as ever, with tourism now sparking a cultural renaissance of sorts by providing the Balinese with much-needed economic outlets for their artistic talents.

This view is reinforced, in turn, by deeply-rooted assumptions about the resilience of Balinese culture. Indeed, the Balinese have been universally praised for their ability to borrow foreign influences that suit them while maintaining their own unique identity. Witness, for example, the blend of Hindu-Javanese and indigenous ideas that inspire current Balinese religious practices. Today, so the argument goes, the Balinese are coping with the tourist invasion of their island by taking advantage of their culture's appeal without sacrificing their basic values on the altar of monetary profit.

What the Balinese think

Faced with such contradictory statements by foreigners, it is interesting to examine how the Balinese themselves feel about the tourist "invasion". To tell the truth, the Balinese did not really have a say in the decision of the central government to trade on their island's charms in order to refill the coffers of the state, and they were never consulted about the Master Plan. Presented with a *fait accompli*, they attempted to appropriate tourism in order to reap its economic benefits. In 1971, Balinese authorities proclaimed their own conception of the kind of tourism they deemed suitable to their island, namely a "Cultural Tourism" (*Pariwisata Budaya*) that is respectful of the values and artistic traditions that brought fame to the island in the first place.

From the start, the Balinese have evinced an ambivalent attitude towards tourism, which they perceived as being at once filled with the promise of prosperity and yet fraught with danger. The foreign invasion was seen to contain the threat of "cultural pollution", which might destroy those very traditions that provided Bali's main attraction for tourists.

By official accounts, "Cultural Tourism" has achieved its mission, reviving Balinese interest in their traditions while reinforcing a sense of cultural identity. In actual fact, tourism has neither "polluted" Balinese culture nor entailed its "renaissance", much less simply contributed to "preserving" it, to quote the terms which have tended to monopolize the debate. This is because tourism should not been seen as an external force striking Bali from the outside, as over the years it has instead become an integral part of Balinese society. In addition, tourism is only one of many factors bringing about rapid change on the island, which is enmeshed in both national Indonesian policy and globalization.

Still, it could be said that the interest shown by foreign tourists has made the Balinese aware of the fact that they are the lucky owners of something precious and perishable, their "culture", which they perceive at once as a capital to be exploited and as a heritage to be protected. And so it is that their culture became reified and externalized in the eyes of the Balinese, turning into an object that could be detached from themselves in order to be displayed and marketed for others, but also, consequently, of which they risked becoming dispossessed.

— *Michel Picard*

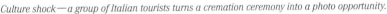

Culture shock — a group of Italian tourists turns a cremation ceremony into a photo opportunity.

BALINESE FOOD

Everyday Fare and Ritual Feasts

Ngajeng! or Makan! (meaning "Eat!" in Balinese and Indonesian respectively) are expressions often heard when passing people in Bali who are enjoying their food. In fact, this is not an invitation to join the meal, but rather an apology for eating when the passerby is not. It is a reflection of a strong sense of community found on Bali and of the great cultural importance attached to food and eating.

Basic ingredients
The staple food of Bali is white, polished rice. Nowadays cooked rice (*nasi*) is of the fast-growing "Green Revolution" variety found everywhere in Asia. The traditional Balinese rice (*beras Bali*) tastes better and is more aromatic, but is restricted to a few areas and is now mainly used as a ritual food. Other, less frequently grown varieties are red rice (*beras barak*), black rice (*ketan injin*), sticky rice (*ketan*) and a variety (*padi gaga*) grown in non-irrigated fields in the mountains. Rice consumption averages 0.5 kg per day.

Many local vegetables grow in a semi-wild state. These include the leaves of several trees and shrubs, varieties of beans (including soybeans), water spinach (*kangkung*), the bulbs and leaves of the cassava plant, sweet potatoes and maize. The flower and trunk of the banana tree, young jackfruits (*nangka*), breadfruits (*sukun* and *timbul*) and papayas may also be cooked as vegetables. Foreign vegetables such as cabbage and tomatoes are now also commonly found.

Though they form a major part of the diet, vegetables are considered low-status; high status foods are rice and meat. Because it is expensive, however, meat is reserved for ritual occasions. Like their Hindu counterparts in India, many Balinese do not eat beef. Surprisingly, fish plays a relatively minor role as a source of protein; though the seas surrounding Bali are rich, the Balinese are not avid fishermen.

The distinctive flavor of Balinese cuisine derives from a *sambal* condiment and spice mixtures. A standard mixture will include shallots, garlic, ginger, turmeric, galangal, and red chilli peppers ground together in varying proportions depending on the recipe.

*Satay (*sate) *is ubiquitous throughout Indonesia, and the Balinese have their own version.*

A distinctive flavor is also imparted by strong-smelling shrimp paste (*terasi*) and chopped *cekuh* root.

The usual drink served with Balinese food is water or tea. Apart from this, there are three traditional alcoholic drinks, drops of which are sprinkled onto the earth during rituals to appease the *bhuta* or negative forces. *Tuak* (or *sajeng*) is a mild beer made from the juice of palm inflorescence. Before the flowers bloom, the inflorescence is tapped in the afternoon, the juice collected overnight in a suspended container, and the next morning it is collected and the fresh juice is ready to drink. To ferment it, it is either left to set a bit longer or other ingredients, such as the bark of certain trees, are added.

Arak or *sajeng rateng* ("straight *sajeng*") is a 60-100 proof liquor distilled from palm or rice wine. It is basically colorless, but may have a slight tint from the addition of ginger, ginseng, turmeric, or cloves. Visitors should be aware that "fire *arak*" or *arak api,* which sold locally is mixed with dubious ingredients (perhaps even gasoline) to make it more potent, has resulted in a number of deaths.

Brem is a sweet, mildly fermented wine made from red or white sticky rice. Yeast is added to the cooked rice, which is wrapped, and after about a week liquid squeezed from it is ready to drink.

Everyday fare

Upon waking around 5:00 or 6:00 each morning, the typical Balinese woman goes to the kitchen to boil water for the morning coffee and cook rice and other dishes for the day. Cooking is done only once and the food is then eaten cold throughout the day. Breakfast in most cases consists only of coffee and fried bananas or rice cookies. Some Balinese eat small portions of rice with vegetables, often bought in a nearby *warung* (kiosk).

When the woman has finished cooking, she will prepare a number of small banana leaf mats on which she places rice and other foods. These are then offered to the gods, placed in the house shrines, on the ground by the entrance gateway and in front of all buildings in the compound. Only after this has been done can the main meal of the day commence, usually at about 11 am. A smaller evening meal is had between 5 and 7 pm, just before or after dark.

It is quite unusual for a family to sit and eat together, in sharp contrast to ritual meals,

Babi guling *(roasted pig) is a Balinese specialty.*

which stress togetherness. Everyday meals are taken in private; one goes into the kitchen, takes what is there and retreats to a quiet place to eat alone, more or less in a hurry, with the right hand. Nothing is drunk with meals; afterward there is lukewarm tea or plain water to rinse the mouth and hand.

Everyday meals consist of rice, one or two vegetable dishes, *sambal*, peanuts, grated coconut with turmeric and spices, and perhaps a small piece of fried fish bought in a nearby *warung*. Usually, the same meal is eaten several times, and in general there is not much variation from day to day.

Vegetables are cooked with coconut milk and spices and served dry or with plenty of broth. Cooked maize with grated coconut and sugar, boiled sweet potatoes, fried bananas, and rice cookies are popular snacks. *Rujak*, a plate of raw fruits mixed with lots of chillies, shrimp paste and/or palm sugar is also popular.

Ritual feasts

Special ritual foods are prepared for each ceremony by the family or community involved. Villagers contribute materials and labor, and the dishes are prepared in the temple's own kitchen. Usually there is a strict division of labor. Men slaughter and butcher the pigs, mix the spices, grate the coconuts, and prepare the *sate* (meat skewers) and other dishes such as blood soup and pork tartar, usually very early in the morning (between 3 and 5 am). Women cook the rice and prepare vegetable offerings, which may be consumed after their consecration.

Each village or area has its own ritual cooking specialists who direct the work. There is a great deal of local variation in dishes, and people from different regions can spend hours discussing differences in traditional foods. For instance, the ritual meat dishes from Gianyar are said to be "sweet" while those from Karangasem are "hard" or "biting."

—*Danker Schaareman*

Cloths of Great Power and Artistry

Indonesia enjoys an enviable reputation as a veritable paradise for textile connoisseurs. On Bali, as elsewhere in the archipelago, traditional textiles are much more than simply decorative pieces of cloth. To the Balinese they represent a mark of cultural identity and religious exclusivity, while the use of certain cloths also convey subtle differences of birth, age, sex, title and caste. Traditional fabrics also serve many sacred and ritual functions, distinguishing the holy from the profane and the good from the evil.

Humans are not the only ones who wear clothes; the Balinese cover with fabric almost everything which possesses a head, a body and feet. Buildings, shrines, altars, ancestor stones, and statues are all wrapped in costly

A Balinese bride is dressed like royalty.

or magically permeated apparel during rituals. The cotton yarns are said to bring strength to both men and objects, protecting them and warding off harmful influences. Red, white and black threads when braided together are called *tridatu* and when these colors are combined, the wearer is protected from the spirits of chaos, particularly those that visit Bali during the sixth month of the Balinese calendar, when disease is more rampant due to the rains.

The ritual wardrobe

The ritual or *adat* wardrobe of the Balinese consists of several lengths of cloth of various sizes. These are not tailored, but are used in the form in which they are woven, and then draped artfully around the body. Boys and men wrap a large skirt (*kamben* or *wastra*) around themselves and tie it in such a way that a long fold hangs down in front between the legs, nearly touching the ground. Girls and women wrap their bodies below the waist clockwise as tightly as possible.

In some rituals, an inner cloth is wound around the body as an undergarment (*tapih* or *sinjang*). A *kamben* or *wastra*, which can extend down to the ankles, is then wrapped over the undergarment. The end is tucked in at the waist near the left hip, and the *kamben* is generally secured by a narrow sash wound around the body several times.

Tube skirts (*sarung*) do not belong to the traditional wardrobe, though imported Javanese cloths with batik patterns are commonly used as *kamben*. During the past few years, Balinese woven *ikat* cloth from Gianyar, Sidemen, Singaraja, and Bayan (East Lombok) have increasingly come into use.

A smaller sash, known as *saput* or *kampuh*, is wound round the hips or the chest by boys and men, falling approximately to the knees. The belt (*umpal*) attached to the end of this cloth is wrapped around the body and knotted below the upper edge of the *saput*. Another type of sash, known as *sabuk*, is generally so long that it is wrapped once around the body and then knotted. Men also wear a graceful head cloth, sometimes in the form of a little boat-shaped hat (*destar udang*).

Women's outer garments consist of a long band similiar to a belt (*sabuk, setagen*) holding the skirt together and a breast-cloth (*anteng*) wrapped tightly around the upper part of the body. Sometimes a part of the *anteng* will be draped over one shoulder. In former times, women also wore loose shoulder sashes (*selendang*).

Until the 1930s, Balinese women were usually naked above the waist in everyday situations, but always covered the upper parts of their bodies when bringing offerings to the temple or taking part in festive court events. Even though traditional bare-shouldered dresses are still seen at temple feasts and family rituals, this has now been replaced in many parts of Bali by long-sleeved, lacey *kebayas* from Java, which are now considered part of the national dress. In the 21st century, most women wear a tube top of similar color to their *kebaya* underneath, providing a modicum of modesty under these often transparent blouses.

Traditional textile forms

The art of Balinese textile decoration is best expressed in men's skirt, chest, and head cloths, and women's chest and skirt cloths. There are three distinguishable categories, the first comprising cloths decorated with gold leaf, called *prada*, traditionally produced for royalty and still used by girls and boys during tooth-filing and marriage ceremonies. The outlines of the design are first drawn on the cloth and coated with glue before applying the gold leaf. Stylized blossoms, plants, and birds are the most common motifs, and the edges of the cloth are often decorated with intertwined swastikas, the symbol of Balinese Hinduism. Other pieces show a distinct Chinese influence.

A second group just as brilliant and expensive as the *prada* cloths are the Balinese *songket* brocades. Supplemental gold- and silver-colored weft threads are added for decoration when these cloths are on the loom. The range of patterns extends from simple crosses and stars to elaborate compositions with trees, vines, flowers, and snakes as well as stories from the *Ramayana* and *Mahabarata* epics.

Gold painted prada *cloth is used for important occasions.*

From a historical point of view, the production of brocaded fabrics with ornamental wefts of gold and silver was for centuries the exclusive preserve of the higher castes. Today, Brahman women, along with wives and daughters in the princely *satriya dalem* and *satriya jaba* families, continue to show considerable skill in this art. Centers of *songket* production are still found in the aristocratic and brahmanical neighborhoods Karangasem (Amlapura and Sidemen), Buleleng (Bubunan and Bratan), Klungkung (Gelgel) and Jembrana (Negara).

In 1980, the then-governor of Bali, Professor Ida Bagus Mantra, appealed to his fellow citizens to employ Balinese textiles in their ceremonial dress. Apart from promoting village crafts and encouraging the development of the Balinese economy, it had the effect of reducing the role of these textiles as aristocratic symbols. Thereafter, anyone of a certain position or wealth was able to flaunt their *songket* publicly at religious and social events. As a result, the demand for *songket* cloth increased dramatically.

The third major type of Balinese textile is weft *ikat* or *endek*, the weft threads of which are dyed prior to weaving. Areas to remain uncolored are bound tightly together to resist the dyes. Different color combinations may be achieved by repeating the binding and dyeing process several times. Dye is also sometimes applied by hand to the unwoven weft.

Endek is by far the most popular Balinese textile form, and its designs are consequently more reliant on fashion and current trends. The demon heads and *wayang* figures of the older cloths have nearly all been replaced by finer geometric motifs. The popularity of *endek* has spread beyond Bali to the rest of Indonesia and abroad as enticing new designs are created.

Since the turn of the century, natural dyes have become much more popular, in part thanks to the efforts of the Ubud based foundation, Yayasan Pecinta Budaya Bebali (www.threadsoflife.com), which encourages the planting of natural dye plants and community weaving cooperatives. Natural dye textiles with intricate designs are unique and appeal to a more elite Balinese market that takes pride in wearing such works of art.

Magical textiles from Tenganan

The famous double *ikat* cloths from Tenganan Pegringsingan, eastern Bali, rank among the masterworks of Southeast Asian textile art. In double *ikat*, the weft and the warp threads are both patterned using the *ikat* tie and dye method. This is an immensely difficult process, requiring great precision not only in dyeing but also in maintaining the proper tension in the threads on the loom so that the patterns will align properly.

Each region of Bali has its own style of handwoven textiles.

The showpieces of Tenganan are called *geringsing*, instantly recognizable by their muted colors—red and reddish brown, eggshell, and blue-black—achieved by dyeing or over-dyeing with red *sunti* root bark and *taum* or indigo dyes. It is often claimed that the traditional production of the fabric required blood from human sacrifices. These wild rumors have been refuted many times over but persist in the tourist literature, despite the protests of scholars and the people of Tenganan.

All *geringsing* are made of cotton yarn decorated with geometrical or floral motifs, lozenges, stars, or small crosses. The *geringsing wayang* is best known: large four-pointed stars (*lubeng*) surrounded by four scorpions divide the main field into semi-circular segments, while inside each section are buildings, animals, and *wayang* figures in the style of ancient east Javanese bas-reliefs ranging across the cloth in groups of twos and threes.

Geringsing cloths are said to possess the power to protect against malevolent earthly and supernatural enemies. Produced only in two other small villages in the world—in Japan and India—the fame of the cloths' power has spread throughout Bali, making it conceivable that the independence and wealth of the Tenganan community might be due in part to a monopoly in the creation of these magically potent fabrics.

Geringsing are of importance to all Balinese, irrespective of whether they are used as protective or destructive agents. It is still the custom in quite a few villages to wind the *geringsing* cloths around the seats and sedan chairs in which the gods are carried to the sea or the river to be bathed. Outside of Tenganan, the *geringsing cemplong* textile is also used in tooth-filing ceremonies, and for cremation purposes the *wayang kebo* is used.

Narrow cloths called *geringsing sanan empeg* ("broken yoke") are worn by men or women when a younger or older sibling has died, leaving them as the remaining middle child. During their ritually impure period of bereavement and its associated rites, the cloths are thought to be instrumental in protecting the wearer. It is noteworthy that the people of Tenganan do not use *geringsing* to heal disease in people and animals as is done on other parts of the island. Instead, they used fragments of Indian double *ikat*, which are reputedly just as magical as *geringsing*.

Black and white poleng *cloths represent the Balinese philosophy of duality.*

These cloths, called *pitola sutra* (also *patola*) are woven of silk and were traded to Indonesia for many centuries during the spice trade era. However, since most of these *patola* cloths have been sold to collectors, the *geringsing* cloth is used for this purpose.

Holy stripes and squares

The red weft *ikat cepuk* cloth has the same structure of the *pitola sutra* or *patola* textiles but has its own specific function in Balinese ceremonial life. *Cepuk* is used for all types of ceremonies: Pitra Yadnya, Manusa Yadnya, and Dewa Yadnya as well as for animal sacrifices (*mepada*) and at cremations. They are also worn by Rangda dancers as a protective cloth. The centers for weaving the *cepuk* cloth were formerly Kerambitan (Singaraja) and Nusa Penida Island. Today, Tanglad village on Nusa Penida is the main production center for these cloths, which can be found in larger markets throughout Bali, sold together with other sacred textiles.

Sacred hip and breast cloths with simple checkered patterns (*poleng*) or small, circular fabrics (*wangsul, gedogan*) are usually worn during rites of passage (especially the three-month birthday, the 210-day birthday, and for tooth-filing ceremonies). The *gedogan* is referred to as *kadang kuda* or "that which can harness what is difficult to control", such as human appetites. This cloth is used for the inauguration ceremonies for high priests or priestesses.

The *poleng*, or black-and-white checked cloth, relates to the philosophy of duality (*Rwa Bhinneda*) and teaches believers to maintain a balance between the polarities of dark and light.

—*Urs Ramseyer; revised by I Made Raiartha*

BALINESE ART

A Fusion of Traditional and Modern

Modern Balinese "export" art has been charming visitors and collectors around the world for many decades and is generally far more popular than the traditional, sacred, and ritual pieces that the Balinese originally produced for themselves. It is notable that while displaying many Western and other influences, modern Balinese art has important traditional roots.

Art of the tradition

In the past, Balinese artists were patronized by kings, princes, and temple councils. The majority of their works served ritual and magical functions, emphasizing the symbolism of a temple ceremony or domestic sanctuary, or supporting claims of divine authority by the ruler. Traditional calendars, with their attendant astrological symbols, also formed an important category of works.

A major center of traditional painting was and still is located at Kamasan, near Gelgel in Klungkung Regency. Village craftsmen here once served rulers who reigned over the whole of Bali. Other centers were located in Gianyar, Bangli, Karangasem, Tabanan, Sanur, and Singaraja, where local rulers resided or were influential. After the Dutch conquered Bali in the 19th and early 20th centuries, the authority of the rulers waned and new patrons had to be found. As a result, modern influences soon manifested themselves.

Traditional drawings for magical purposes (*rerajahan*) were inscribed with a stylus on palm leaves, pot shards, and metal, then blackened with soot. Others on cloth or paper were executed in black ink. The ink formerly made of soot, and paints handmade from natural dyes have been replaced with Chinese ink and imported acrylics. Cloth

A traditional-style painting from the village of Kamasan depicting an episode from the Mahabharata, *"The Temptation of Arjuna" (by an unknown artist)*

paintings were only displayed during religious ceremonies; the subject matter being chosen to harmonize with the intent of the ritual.

Artistic conventions were passed down from father to son, and there are fixed elements of style, ornamentation, and overall composition. Human figures are represented in the *wayang* style, a reference to the leather figures in *wayang kulit* puppet plays. The figures have characteristic clothes, jewelry, coiffures, and headdresses, and their facial features and figures indicate their class, age, and character. Sky, rocks, and ground are indicated by specific shorthand ornaments. There is no perspective.

Stories are often depicted, the scenes being divided by rock ornaments that act as frames. A back-to-back arrangement of the figures is another way of indicating different scenes. Important scenes are placed in the center and those containing gods are at the top, with demons or animals are at the bottom.

The subject matter of traditional paintings derives from religious texts, in particular Old Javanese and Balinese versions of the *Mahabharata* and *Ramayana* epics, the Pancatantra fables, Javanese tales about the wandering Prince Panji, and Balinese folk-tales, such as the story about Pan and Men Brayut, who were blessed with many children.

The oldest extant Balinese paintings are on two wooden planks in the Pura Panataran and Pura Batu Madeg temples in Besakih. They date from 1444 and 1458 and depict a small lotus flower and the elephant-headed deity, Ganesha. The next oldest work is the wooden cover of a *Ramayana* manuscript dating from 1826, containing painted scenes from the epic at the top and sides.

Cloth paintings dating from the 1840s are in museums in Denmark and Germany, depicting among other things scenes from the *Ramayana*.

Traditional Balinese art should not be thought of as static. Important innovations occurred at the end of the 19th century. In drawings from Sanur and Singaraja of this period some perspective was used, and figures and scenery were given naturalistic features. More important innovations date from the end of the 1920s, when a naive, naturalistic style incorporating *wayang* elements developed in the Gianyar area. Apart from traditional subjects, scenes from daily life were also depicted on paper in crayon or gouache.

The influence of Western artists

German artist Walter Spies (1895–1942) settled in Campuan, near Ubud, in 1927 and was the first and most influential of a number of Europeans who made Bali their homes around this time. Dutchman Rudolf Bonnet (1895–1978) visited Bali in 1929 and settled in Ubud in 1931. The paintings of these two exerted a great influence on local artists. Spies' dense landscapes are characterized by trees with bright leaves, stylized animal and human figures, and double or triple horizons. Bonnet painted naturalistic, romantic portraits. The Mexican painter Miguel Covarrubias, who spent the early 1930s in the Sanur area, was another important figure.

Three modern art centers developed in the 1930s, each with its own characteristic style and subject matter. The first of these was in Ubud, where the style was characterized by refined, polychrome *wayang*-type figures surrounded by Spies-like scenery or Bonnet-like men and women, naked to the waist amidst plants and trees. The figures are harvesting, planting, making offerings, and dancing. Witches and scenes from the Old Javanese and Balinese epics were also popular. Illustrious artists from the Ubud

A work by Dutch artist Rudolf Bonnet entitled "Two Balinese Girls" (1955)

area are: Ida Bagus Kembeng (1897–1952), Ida Bagus Made Poleng (1915–1999), Anak Agung Gede Sobrat (1917–1992), his cousin Anak Agung Gede Meregeg (b. 1902), and Wayan Tohjiwa (1916–2001).

A second center developed around Sanur, where the style is characterized by softly-colored or black-and-white ink drawings with half-*wayang*, half-naturalistic animals in human dance poses, huge insects, and birds (for example, by I Sukaria, Gusi Made Rundu, I Regig); or naive village scenes and land-scapes with trees bearing huge leaves (by Ida Bagus Made Pugug, Ida Bagus Rai).

The third center was Batuan, characterized by its stylized half-*wayang*, half-naturalistic figures with pronounced, heavily-shadowed vertebra, leafy Spies-like trees, and a very distinctive use of perspective. Originally only black ink and crayon were used on paper. The idea of coloring with crayon came from the Neuhaus brothers, who began selling Balinese drawings from their art shop in Sanur in 1935. Today, watercolors, gouache and canvas are used as well.

Typical early representatives of this style are Ida Bagus Made Djata (*sura*) (1910–1946) and Ida Bagus Made Togog (1916–1989). Some Balinese painters refused to imitate Spies or Bonnet. I Gusti Nyoman Lempad (b. 1862 or 1875, d. 1978) made naturalistic but highly stylized flat human figures with almost no scenery. I Gusti Made Deblog (1906–1987) placed figures clad in *wayang* gear in romantic landscapes.

In the 1930s, many paintings were already being sold to tourists in art shops in Ubud, Denpasar, and Sanur. At this time, Spies, Bonnet, and the Dutch archeologist W. F. Stutterheim feared that tourism was having a negative impact on the quality of paintings and drawings being produced, and so with the help of Cokorda Gede Raka Sukawati, they formed the Pita Maha artists' association in Ubud on January 19, 1936.

About 150 painters, sculptors and silversmiths became members, with Lempad playing an important role. The main aim was to organize sales exhibitions in Java and abroad, and to make the artists aware of the importance of quality standards. In this way modern Balinese art began to be purchased by collectors and museums abroad. The Pita Maha ceased operation in 1942 following the

"The Bumblebee Dance" by Anak Agung Gede Sobrat of Ubud, one of the original Pita Maha artists

A painting in the intricate Batuan style by I Made Budi, well known for non-traditional subjects such as tourists and surfers

Japanese occupation. Spies died as a prisoner aboard an Allied troops ship; but Bonnet returned to Bali from a Japanese prison camp in 1947 and tried to reorganize the artists. Combining again with Cokorda Gede Raka Sukawati, he formed the Ubud Painters' Club (Ratna Warta), and painters from Batuan and Sanur began to work as well as before.

A new style of painting was introduced by Dutch painter Arie Smit (b. 1916), who came to Bali in 1956 and became an Indonesian citizen. In Penestanan near Ubud he taught groups of young boys. Their naive style, characterized by strong colors and primitive, naturalistic human figures soon became well known; their subjects of daily life, festivals, animals and birds are now widely imitated. The group was dubbed the "Young Artists", from which a third generation has emerged today.

Balinese painting today

As Bali opened up to tourists after 1965, young Balinese painters and sculptors as well as many Javanese, Sumatran, and Western artists settled in the area between Mas and Ubud. Almost every year a new art style (Pop Art, Macro Art, Magic Realism) emerges and new materials and techniques (batik, silk-screen) have become highly fashionable.

Only a small number of Balinese painters receive formal art training either abroad or at the Indonesian art academies in Yogyakarta (operating since 1950) and Denpasar (founded in 1965). Formally trained artists work in styles and with subjects that differ completely from those of other Balinese painters.

The work of the non-academic painters is still heavily influenced by stories from the epics and folktales, to the extent that many cannot be understood without knowledge of Balinese literature. All painters, however, are fond of depicting daily Balinese life, with its rituals and dramatic performances. Most non-academic painters produce primarily for the tourist market. Many less talented ones, often children, engage in mass production of imitations of works by their more talented colleagues for sale in "art markets" and shops.

Balinese art is now displayed in many galleries and several museums in Bali. Through Bonnet's efforts, a museum for modern Balinese art, the Puri Lukisan, was built between 1954 and 1956 in Ubud. In 1979, an Arts Center, also designed for tourists, was opened in Denpasar. Expositions of paintings and sculptures are now held there, especially in conjunction with the yearly Bali Arts Festival from July to August. The galleries that host the most contemporary local artists of today are Komaneka and Gaya in Ubud, Tony Raka in Mas, Griya Santrian in Sanur, and Ganesha at the Four Seasons in Jimbaran.

— *Hedi Hinzler*

BALINESE DANCE AND DRAMA

A Vibrant World of Movement and Sound

Dances and dramatic performances form an important part of nearly every ritual on Bali. They are seen as an integral part of Balinese religion and culture and are employed as an expression of devotion to the gods (*ngayah*) as well as a means of instilling centuries-old values in each new generation of Balinese through the medium of movement, music, and words.

Training and *taksu*

Balinese children are exposed to dance at a very early age. They are taken to performances long before they can walk, and begin to take dance lessons soon after. Most take great pleasure in this, whether or not they perform, as they are just as interested in the learning experience as in the final product.

There are no warm-ups before a lesson begins, and the teacher plunges right into the dance. The movements are not taught individually; the child stands behind the teacher and follows her movements. When the teacher feels that the pupil understands the basic sequence, she will move behind the student, take her wrists or fingers and move them through the desired positions. The student's body must be both full of energy and relaxed, "listening" to the teacher's fingers as much as to her words, which are soft syllables imitating the music.

After many hours of such manipulations, the movements are said to have "entered" the student. He or she then dances alone, with the teacher correcting from behind as needed. Only after completely memorizing a dance will the student practice with a full *gamelan* orchestra.

Balance is essential in Balinese dance, as in everything the Balinese do; rarely do they trip or fall. Control is also important; the dances demand domination of every limb, muscle, and emotion. The dancer must learn how to express the character of his or her role as opposed to expressing one's "true self" (a very un-Balinese concept). It could be said that dance involves a displacement of the ego.

The most important aspect of Balinese dance is that of *taksu* or "divine inspiration", the electrifying presence that mesmerizes audiences and transports performer and viewer to another time and place. *Taksu* can transform a plain-looking dancer into a great beauty and a technically deficient one into a stellar artist. A dancer studying Topeng (masked dance) will often sleep with a mask above his bed so he can absorb its character. Masks have their own special *taksu*. One who lacks *taksu* is likened to a "weak flame", and dancers pray to the god of *taksu* before each performance. It doesn't always come though; even the Balinese have off nights.

Sacred versus secular dances

There are literally hundreds of dance forms on Bali, from the starkly simple Rejang to the highly intricate Legong. Concerns about the impact of tourism caused a team of scholars to convene in 1971 to determine which dances were to be deemed sacred and which secular, to keep the sacred ones from becoming secularized. The result was that all dances were placed into three categories depending on the area of the temple in which they are performed, and this has now become the standard classification system used for Balinese dance forms.

Wali dances are those performed or originating in the *jeroan*, or innermost courtyard of the temple, where the sacred icons are kept and worshipped. These dance forms are often performed in groups with no dramatic elements. They are considered indigenously Balinese, and as with all Balinese dances, are performed to propitiate the ancestral spirits. Rejang, Baris, and Sanghyang trance dances all fall into this category.

Bebali dances are ceremonial, performed in the *jaba tengah* or middle courtyard of the temple, the meeting point of the divine and the worldly. These are primarily dance dramas whose stories derive from the Hindu-Javanese epics, including Gambuh and Wayang Wong.

Balih-balihan dances are secular and are performed in the *jaba* or outer courtyard, usually beyond the prescribed sacred space itself (although often this space will be consecrated by a priest before the performance). Into this category fall a number of classical and modern forms, like Legong, Baris, Arja, Kebyar, Sendratari and others.

As with most things Balinese, these categories are not rigidly adhered to. Dance dramas may be performed in the *jeroan* and magically-charged sacred dances may be held in the *jaba*. As the Balinese are fond of saying, everything has a place, a time, and a circumstance (*desa, kala, patra*), and things vary greatly from district to district, from village to village, and even from time to time. The performing arts are no exception, which is why the *barongs* in different villages are unique. This variety is one of the delights of Bali.

Rejang, Baris, and Mendet

The most truly indigenous dances of Bali are the sacred Rejang, Baris Gede, and Mendet, which are considered temple "offerings" in and of themselves. These are usually performed in stately lines by groups of men or women, with an occasional priest or priestess leading, in the *jeroan* of the temple. The dancers often bear holy water and offerings which they present to the gods.

On the first days of an *odalan* or temple festival, the Rejang and Baris Gede are usually performed in the early morning or late afternoon, sometimes in tandem. The **Rejang** dance consists of a procession of females ranging in age from two up to 80. They move in a slow and stately fashion toward the altar, twirling fans or lifting their hip sashes. Costumes range from simple temple attire (Batuan) to elaborate gold headdresses and richly-woven cloths (Asak and Tenganan).

Baris dances are rooted in courtly rituals of war; the term *baris* refers to a formation of warriors. In the Baris Gede or Baris Upacara, a weapon of some sort is used, while in the Baris Pendet an offering is carried. Various Baris dances are named after the particular weapon involved, and a mock battle between two warriors is often re-enacted. Trance sometimes occurs, and the main function of this dance is devotional; it matters not if the dancers are in unison with one another or with the music. Baris Upacara is performed in mountain villages near Lake Batur, in the Sanur area, in Tabanan, and now in Ubud.

Late at night at the end of a temple festival a **Mendet** dance is performed by the married women of the village, although in some cases young women and girls join in as well. The women carry woven offering baskets, holy water, or libations of distilled liquor to offer up to the gods on their divine journey home. A procession is formed and they weave around the temple grounds, stopping before each shrine to offer up their gifts. Mendet, like Rejang and Baris Upacara, is not taught but learned through performance.

The divine descent

The word *sanghyang* means "deity" and performers of the sacred Sanghyang dances are said to be possessed by specific deities who enable them to perform supernatural feats. Their role is an overtly exorcistic one; they assist in warding off pestilence and ridding the village of black magic.

Trance is induced through incense smoke and chanting by two groups of villagers: women who sing the praises of the gods and ask them to descend, and a chorus of men who imitate the *gamelan*, using the word *cak* and other sounds.

There are many kinds of Sanghyang. In **Sanghyang Dedari**, two pre-pubescent girls (chosen through a "trance test") are gradually put into trance, dressed in costumes very similiar to the Legong. In fact, many scholars feel that the Legong developed from this form. They are then carried on palanquins or shoulders around the village, stopping at magically-charged spots such as crossroads, bridges, and in front of the homes of people who can transform themselves into *leyak* or witches. After this, the *sanghyangs* lead the villagers back to a dancing arena at the temple or *bale banjar*, where, with eyes closed, they dance for up to four hours. Stories from the Legong repertoire or dramatic forms based on the Calonarang and Cupak are re-enacted. In some villages, the *sanghyang dedari* execute the entire dance mounted on the shoulders of men, performing astounding acrobatic feats. This part of the ritual is accompanied by a complete *gamelan* group who have been thoroughly trained and rehearsed.

In **Sanghyang Jaran**, a small number of men are put into trance, but their transition is much more violent: they fall, convulsed, to the ground and rush to grab hobby horses. During the pre-trance chanting, coconut shells are lit, leaving red hot coals. The trancers are said to be attracted by all forms of fire and onlookers are required not to smoke. The entranced dancers leap into the coals, prancing on top of them, picking up the hot pieces and bathing themselves in fire. The *sanghyangs* are accompanied only by a *kecak* chorus of chanting men.

Both types of Sanghyang are performed several times a week in Ubud, where the trance state is better left to the viewer's imagination.

Dramatic courtly forms

In the 14th century, Bali was conquered by East Java's great Majapahit kingdom. As a result, a number of Javanese nobles and courtiers settled in Bali, bringing with them their dances, their caste system, and a variety of ceremonies which quickly became interwoven with the rich tapestry of indigenous beliefs and rituals.

The stories of the **Gambuh** dance drama are principally based on the Malat tales concerning the adventures of a Javanese prince, Panji Inu Kertapati, and his quest for the beautiful princess Candra Kirana. However, the dramatic action centers around the courts and the pomp that infuses royal battles. The ideals and manners of 14th century Java and Bali are thus preserved in this form.

The language of Gambuh is Kawi or Old Javanese, which very few Balinese understand. There is little clowning, as more attention is paid to the choreography than to the story. Perhaps because of this, there are very few active village troupes left on the island, most of them in Batuan.

Gambuh is definitely worth seeing, as all Balinese dance and musical forms may be said to stem from it. Gambuh is accompanied by a small ensemble in which four to eight men play meter-long flutes. These, along with a two-stringed *rebab*, provide hauntingly beautiful melodies.

Topeng mask dramas

Topeng literally means "pressed against the face" or mask. All actors in Topeng dramas are masked. Refined characters wear full masks, and clowns and servants sport a half-mask, which facilitates speaking. Topeng is a tremendously popular form in Bali, as it relates local lore and historical tales concerning the royal lineages in scenes of everyday life. Topeng is also immensely entertaining,

as the use of humor and clowns is extensive. Topeng, along with the *wayang kulit* shadow play, is the primary medium through which Balinese history, values, and even knowledge of current events are transmitted. In the end, the two factions contend, and the "bad guys" admit defeat.

Prembon

The Balinese love to create new genres by melding together different forms. In the 1940s the king of Gianyar, I Dewa Manggis VIII, summoned his royal dancers and asked them to create a new dance called **Prembon**, taking elements from the Gambuh, Arja (a kind of operatta), Topeng, Parwa (a non-masked form based on the Mahabharata), and Baris.

A night of Prembon often begins with a solo Baris and some other *tari lepas* (nondramatic dance). A story of Balinese kings with characters from all these forms is then presented, although it most resembles a Topeng performance. Watching Prembon gives the uninitiated an excellent glimpse of all of these genres in a way that is easier to follow than other forms, Gambuh or Arja, for example. And often it is the best dancers of each tradition that perform these pieces.

Calongarang: battling the dark side

Every 15 days, on Kajeng Kliwon, the dark forces of Bali gather to frolic and inflict illness on unsuspecting souls. These witches or *leyaks* are humans who, through the study of black magic, are able to transform themselves into grotesque animals, demons, even flying cars. They haunt crossroads, graveyards, or bridges, and this particular day, due to its inauspiciousness for *dharma*, or the correct path, is auspicious for Rangda, queen of the *leyaks*. A performance of the **Calonarang** dance is then often held.

There are many variations on the Calonarang dance, but all involve the Barong, a mythological beast with an immense coat of fur and gilded leather vestments. The most common and sacred is the Barong Ket, a cross between a lion and a bear, although the Barong Macan (tiger), Barong Bangkal (wild boar), Barong Celeng (pig) and Barong Gajah (elephant) also exist.

The Barong is considered a protector of the village. Of demonic origin, the people have made a beast in his image and transformed him into a playful, benevolent creature. Upon entering, he prances about the stage, shaking his great girth and clacking his jaws. He is often followed by the *telek* and *jauk*, two masked groups of men depicting deities and demons, respectively. They fight, but no one wins, a common theme in Balinese performances. Their role is simply to help restore and maintain balance.

The exquisite Legong

Perhaps the most famous of Bali's dances, the **Legong** is also by far the most exquisite. Performed by three highly-trained young girls, it is said to have been the created by the king of Sukawati, I Dewa Agung Made Karna (1775–1825), who meditated for 40 days and 40 nights in the Yogan Agung temple in Ketewel and saw two celestial angels, resplendent in glittering gold costumes. When he finished his meditations, he summoned the court musicians and dancers and taught them what he had seen, calling it the Sanghyang Legong. This was first performed in the temple with nine masks, and is still performed there every seven months.

Most scholars agree that the Legong grew out of the Sanghyang Dedari. All Legong pieces are for two young girls. Some are totally abstract with no narrative; others tell a story and the *legongs* act out different roles.

In 1932, Ida Bagus Boda, a celebrated Legong teacher, created the *condong* or female attendant role, which serves as an

In the Legong, *a young female dancer wearing a glittering costume plays the role of a lovely princess.*

introduction to the piece. In shimmering costume, her body wrapped like a gilded cocoon, the *condong* makes her entrance. After a solo of about 10 minutes, she spies two fans on the ground, scoops them up and turns around to face the two *legongs*. Dancing in complete unison, they take the fans from the *condong*, perform a short piece called *bapang*, and the *condong* exits. It is here that the narrative begins.

The most commonly performed tale is that of a princess lost in the woods of the wicked king of Lasem. He kidnaps her and tries to seduce her, but she spurns his advances. Upon hearing of her fate, her brother, the king of Daha, declares war on the king of Lasem. As they go forth into battle, the *condong* reappears wearing gilded wings, a *guak* (crow) or bird of ill omen. The two kings fight, with evil Lasem invariably meeting death at the hands of King Daha.

Other stories portrayed include **Jobog**, where the two monkey kings, Subali and Sugriwa, fight over the love of a woman, Kuntir; **Kuntul**, a dance of white herons; and **Semaradhana**, where the god of love Semara takes leave of his wife Ratih and goes to awaken the god Siva (represented by a Rangda mask) out of meditation. The traditional centers for Legong are Saba, Peliatan, and Kelandis, but today it is also performed in Teges, Ubud, and many other villages.

New forms: the Kecak

In the 1930s when tourism to Bali was just beginning, two Western residents, painter Walter Spies and author Katharine Mershon, felt that the *cak* chorus of the Sanghyang dances, taken out of its ritual context with an added storyline, would be a hit among their friends and other visitors. Working with Limbak and his troupe in Bedulu village, they incorporated Baris movements into the role of the *cak* leader. Eventually the story of the *Ramayana* was added, though it wasn't until the 1960s that elaborate costumes were used.

The **Kecak** dance, as it is now called, involves a chorus of at least 50 men. They sit in concentric circles around an oil lamp and begin to slowly chant: *cak-cak-cak-cak*. Up to seven different rhythms are interwoven, creating a tapestry of sound similar to the *gamelan*. One man is the *kempli*, or time beater, and his "pong" cuts through the chorus. A *juru tandak* sings the tale of the *Ramayana* as the drama progresses.

The exhilarating Kecak *is perhaps Bali's best known dance performance.*

Tourists call this the "Monkey Dance", because at the end of the play the men become the monkey army sent to rescue the heroine, Sita. The *cak* sound also resembles the chattering of monkeys. Kecak is performed solely for tourists; never in temple ceremonies. Even though it has its roots in the Sanghyang trance dances, the Kecak dancers themselves do not go into trance.

Kebyar: lighting strikes

At the turn of the last century, north Bali was the scene of great artistic ferment, as *gamelan* competitions were common and each club vied to outdo the other. In 1914, **Kebyar Legong** was born, a new dance for two young women who portray an adolescent youth, the prototype for the dynamic Taruna Jaya, choreographed by I Gede Manik in the early 1950s. There was no story, the emphasis being instead on interpretation of the music, which was a new phenomenon. This form swept the island like lightning, which is what *kebyar* literally means. The music is equally electrifying, full of sudden stops, starts, and complex rhythms.

Four years later, the king of Tabanan commissioned a *gamelan kebyar* to perform at an important cremation. One member of the audience was so taken with the music that he began to compose and choreograph his own pieces in this style. This was I Ketut Maria (also known as "Mario"), the most illustrious Balinese dancer of the 20th century.

In 1925 Mario debuted his **Kebyar Duduk**, a dance performed entirely while seated on the ground. With no narrative to tell, the Kebyar dancer presents a range of moods, from

coquettishness to bashfulness, and from sweetly imploring to anger. Mario himself performed this while playing the *trompong* (a long instrument with 14 inverted kettle gongs), using theatrics and flashy moves to coax sound from the instrument.

In 1951, Mario was approached by British enterpreneur John Coast and Anak Agung Gede Mantera of Peliatan to create a new piece. They wanted a boy-meets-girl theme for their world tour in 1952. Tambulilingan Ngisap Madu ("a bumblebee sips honey"), now known as **Oleg Tambililingan**, was the result, created for I Gusti Raka, one of the tiny Peliatan *legongs*, and Gusti Ngurah Raka, Mario's prize Kebyar student. It is a story mimed in abstract terms of a female bumblee sipping honey and frolicking in a garden. A male bumblebee sees her, encircles her in a dance of courtship, and they finally mate.

Into the spotlight: Sendratari

During the political upheavals of the 1960s, many new ideas in dance and music were ushered in. A team of Balinese artistes at KOKAR (now SMK, the High School for Performing Arts) in 1962 created a new form called **Sendratari**, from *seni* ("art") and *tari* ("dance"). Instead of having dancers speak their lines, as in Gambuh, Topeng and Arja, a *juru tandak* sits in the *gamelan* and speaks to them in Kawi and Balinese. The dancers pantomime the action on stage. Since then, KOKAR and SMK artistes have created new Sendratari every year for the **Bali Arts Festival**, filling to capacity the open-air theater at the Art Center, which seats 5,000. These are lavish spectacles with casts of hundreds. The stories are usually taken from the *Ramayana* and the *Mahabharata*.

The Arts Festival showcases some of the best dance and music on the island. It begins in mid-June and runs through mid-July. Schedules are available from the Regional Tourism Office in Denpasar.

Birds and other beasts

The 1980s ushered in new forms which added to the classical repertoire of Balinese dance. These Kebyar style forms may be popular for a year, a decade, or a century, and most of them are created by teachers and students at SMK in Batubulan and ISI (Indonesia Institute of Art) in Denpasar. In 1982 these teachers inserted a bird scene into one of the Mahabharata Sendratari episodes. This team effort was then refined into Tari Manuk Rawa ("long-legged bird dance") by I Wayan Dibia, one of Bali's most prolific modern choreographers.

Such was the popularity of Manuk Rawa that other bird forms sprung up, notably Tari Kedis Perit ("sparrow dance") by Ni Ketut Arini Alit, and Tari Belibis (a story of a mother swan and her young) and Tari Cendrawasih ("bird of paradise dance") both by Ni Luh Suasthi Bandem, also a lecturer at STSI.

Two dances that can be seen everywhere are **Kijang Kencana** (by I Gusti Ngurah Supartha), a "golden deer dance" performed by tiny girls with abundant energy, and **Jaran Teji** by I Wayan Dibia, a humorous dance of horseback riders that has become a real hit.

New creations

The *kreasi baru* or "new creations" once referred to the colossal Sendratari productions of the dance schools. Today, however, this term encompasses what in the West would be called "performance art", which means in Bali, anything quite out of the ordinary. Most of these *kreasi* come out of the academies, SMK, and ISI. There are national festivals every year of new music and modern dance that encourage these forms. Some of the young composers and choreographers are fusing elements of East and West into spectacular and original forms; others are wallowing in mediocre attempts at self-expression and self-indulgence.

Many Japanese and Western composers and choreographers are coming to Bali to collaborate with Balinese performance artists and create innovative works. Some of the groups to see are: **Bona Alit** (*gamelan* fusion), **Balawan Ethnic Fusion** (guitar and *gamelan* fusion), **Wayang Listrik** by I Made Sidia of Bona, contemporary dance by **I Nyoman Sura**, and *gamelan* fusion by **I Nyoman Windha**.

The tradition of dance in Bali is a strong and a rich one. Even with the influx of modern, Western culture the classical Balinese forms are still the most popular and will undoubtedly remain so for a very long time to come.

— *Rucina Ballinger*

The famous Mario (I Ketut Maria) from Tabanan performing the electrifying Kebyar Duduk, which he invented and popularized (photo by Walter Spies).

BALINESE MUSIC

The Deep Resonances of the *Gamelan*

Few places in the world have as concentrated a musical tradition as Bali. The sheer quantity of ensembles and musical forms is impressive enough: there are thousands of active *gamelan* ensembles composed of more than 20 distinct types on an island barely 140 km (87 miles) across. Almost all are intertwined with dance, recitation, theater, puppetry, or other artistic traditions. But Bali's musical achievements go far beyond mere quantity. Considering the sophistication and stylistic breadth of its orchestral compositions, the famed ensemble skills of its musicians, and the fact that its performing arts traditions are still evolving, it becomes clear what an unusual living musical tradition this tiny island has nurtured.

Music in Balinese culture

Part of the vitality of Balinese music rests in its cultural resonance. Fundamental aspects

The frames for gamelan *instruments are carved of jackfruit wood by skilled artisans.*

of Bali-Hindu cosmology—the way people perceive the universe and humankind within it—are reflected. Ideas of interdependence, balance, and unity are manifest in the very fabric of the music, the tuning of the instruments and in the ways musicians interact as an ensemble. Dazzling interlocking melodies composed of two complementary parts reflect *rwa bhineda*, the Balinese belief in dualism and interdependence. The same idea is expressed in paired tuning systems, in which partner tones separated by small frequencies "beat" together in a vibrating, co-dependent relationship. The deep resonances of the large suspended gong—the heart of most bronze *gamelan* orchestras, born of the fires of ancient bronzesmithing traditions—bring unity to musical, spiritual and sonic realms.

Music and dance are practiced and performed intensively in Bali. This may arise partly from the sheer love of theatrical display, of which the Balinese are justly famous. Or perhaps it is an outgrowth of the communal nature of Balinese society, since playing *gamelan* is one of the most sublime expressions of shared, coordinated effort. Regardless of the underlying impulse, it is evident that the performing arts are highly valued and integrated into daily social and religious life. This integration has helped to maintain the vitality of the arts in the midst of a century of social change, strife, rapid modernization and mass tourism. Ceremonies in the temple or home are considered incomplete without music and dance. They are essential not only in the creation of the right atmosphere but to the enactment of many core rituals. Performances are felt to entertain gods and humans alike, an attitude that largely helps bypass the divide between "secular" and "sacred" or between "classical" and "popular", familiar in other traditions. An offering dance in the inner temple, a performance for tourists and a *gamelan* competition before thousands of screaming fans have far more in common than is apparent at first glance.

Balinese musicians not only maintain but actively develop their musical traditions. New works are composed and premiered alongside established repertoire, which is also continually developed. In fact, there is often no clear distinction between new and traditional, since Balinese musicians borrow, rework, and rearrange existing material and forms with great freedom. Theirs is still a collectively shared musical language; musical evolution arises more from collaborative endeavor than individual genius.

As a result, music seems ubiquitous even in the modern, bustling Bali of tourist buses and instant messaging. From a quiet vantage point — now rare — the ringing tones of metallophones, gongs, and drums drift across the rice fields from a nearby village temple ceremony as they have for centuries. From a more typical present-day perspective, senses are assailed by the crash of cymbals competing with the din of motorcycles and trucks as a local *baleganjur* (marching *gamelan*) group rehearses in their *bale banjar*. Surroundings may change, but the excitement derived from making music has not faded.

What is a *gamelan*? Who plays it?

Technically the term *gamelan* refers to a set of instruments: bronze, iron, or bamboo percussion instruments that are created and tuned together to form an indivisible whole. But in common usage "*gamelan*" also refers to the group of musicians who play them. They come together in the spirit of a club *(seka)*, with a strong collective identity and organizational structure that often outlives its original membership. Players, *seka gong*, come from all layers of Balinese society, from farmers and laborers to civil servants to well-to-do descendants of the princely castes. In this sense it is a true popular art. The cooperative atmosphere of a *gamelan* club is a reflection of the *banjar*, the fundamental unit of village or neighborhood community that hosts most groups. This is evident not only in the team spirit and de-emphasis of individual virtuosity but in the ensemble interaction itself. Unity and precise synchronization of the various parts are essential to the musical flow. It is no surprise that solo performance is nonexistent in Bali.

Although ISI Denpasar (Indonesia Institute of the Arts Denpasar) has helped elevate *gamelan* performance to a professional level for many of its graduates, most musicians are amateurs. Aside from the rare commissioned performance or international tour, there is little money to be made from playing *gamelan*. The lure to play still comes primarily from the prestige of performance in community and religious contexts: village

A four-piece ensemble consisting of ugal, kempli, *and two* kendang.

Every banjar *has its own* gamelan *troupe that performs at rituals and temple ceremonies.*

celebrations (both religious and secular), festivals and the ever-popular "battle of the bands"-style *gamelan* competitions. Any income generated is typically used for instrument upkeep, costumes, refreshments during rehearsals, and an occasional feast for the players. However, there is a rise of private music and dance centers, *sanggar,* which seek some income to complement the great fun of playing *gamelan* and dancing.

Styles, instruments, and tuning

The diversity of musical ensembles on Bali and styles is striking. More than 20 forms of *gamelan* have been documented, with numerous sub-varieties depending on dramatic function. And the number is increasing as a younger generation experiments with new ideas of instrumental combination. Ensembles range in size from the small *gender wayang,* a quartet of musicians that accompanies the *wayang kulit* (shadow puppet play), to the massive *gamelan gong gede* ensemble of 35–40 musicians who perform a repertoire of ancient and stately ceremonial pieces in the temple.

A variety of materials are used in the production of instruments. The most common types of *gamelan* instruments have bronze keys suspended over bamboo resonators in carved wooden frames. These are combined with a variety of tuned gongs, drums, cymbals, and flutes to make a complete orchestra. With the exception of the largest gongs made on Java, the bronze instruments are all hand-forged by Balinese smiths using techniques essentially unchanged over the last few centuries. Each set of instruments is laboriously tuned by filing and hammering the metal keys and gongs to match a pentatonic (5-tone) or heptatonic (7-tone) scale that is unique to that particular set of instruments. While *gamelans* of a particular type—for example, the *gamelan angklung*— are tuned to approximately the same interval structure, there is no uniform standard of reference for *gamelan* tuning. This is another indication of the unique identity of each orchestra. However, two large families of tunings, in scales known as *pelog* and *slendro,* are known and easily distinguished by their intervals.

The *gamelan gong kebyar,* which appeared about a century ago, remains the most common type of *gamelan* on Bali. As described by anthropologist Miguel Covarrubias as early as the 1930s, it is the "modern orchestra par excellence". Like most *gamelan* (and not dissimilar to a Western orchestra), the *gamelan gong kebyar* is composed of instrumental families that are subdivided according to the instrument's range, function, timbre, and performance technique. The eight or 10 *gangsa* or highest-pitched, 10-keyed metallophones play the main melodic material. The *calung* or *jublag*, five-keyed midrange metallophones, play the *pokok* or core melody lines. The lowest *jegogan*, also five-keyed, reinforce the *pokok* by regularly stressing certain tones (for example, every fourth *jublag* note). The *reong*, a row of tuned gong chimes played by four musicians, plays another layer of figuration or melodic doubling, parallel to the *gangsa*; at other moments it joins the drums in non-pitched rhythmic patterns. Various small gongs are struck to punctuate the phrases in regular fashion. The *kajar*, for example, keeps the beat, a difficult task in this syncopated and rhythmically complex music. The medium-sized gongs, called *kempur*, *kemong*, and *kempli*, punctuate the phrases at important junctures, while the largest gong is reserved to mark the phrase endings: periods at the end of sentences.

Leading the entire group is a pair of drummers (*kendang*), accompanied by the cymbal or *cengceng* player, that cue accents, dynamics and changes in tempo. In dance performances, drummers are the vital link between the dancers and other musicians. The lead drummer provides signals to other musicians that translate the detailed cues of the dancer's movements into musical gestures.

Many other types of *gamelan* continue to survive, and occasionally new ones are created. Some are used only in the context of religious ritual. One of the rarest is the *gamelan selunding*, a sacred ensemble with instruments of iron keys suspended over simple trough resonators. Special ceremonies and offerings must accompany it, as the iron keys are thought to be charged with great spiritual energy. Some *selunding* melodies are themselves sacred, not to be played or even hummed except during ceremonies.

Most bamboo *gamelan* ensembles, in contrast, evolved as vehicles for popular village entertainment. The most widely known is the *gamelan joged* which accompanies the flirtatious *joged* dance. As with bronze orchestras, bamboo ensembles are found in various sizes, styles and specific instrumentations. Some are composed exclusively of bamboo marimbas; others include non-pitched percussion instruments, such as cymbals and drums. Of all bamboo orchestras the most impressive is the *gamelan jegog*, which evolved in Jembrana, western Bali. It is named after the enormous bass instruments, *jegogan*, which use bamboo tubes up to 30 cm in diameter and 3 m in length. Struck with large, padded mallets, they produce bass tones of awesome power.

Sonority, structure, and dance

The music of the Balinese *gamelan* is, at its most characteristic moments, a densely patterned, contrapuntal web of sound, based in duple meters. The texture is made more complex by the "paired tuning" system, in which each tuned key and gong is paired with another, tuned slightly higher or lower. When struck simultaneously, the two tones produce a rapid beating as a result of the difference in frequency that creates the shimmering sound quality characteristic of the Balinese *gamelan*. Some observers have compared the sound to the nightly choruses of crickets and frogs in the rice fields.

Though some music experts use a written notation, which supplies a skeletal outline of the trunk melody and punctuating gong tones, its function is only for documentation or study. In day-to-day performance practice no notation is used; everything is learned by imitation from a teacher's model. A teacher repeats each musical fragment until the players master it, a time-intensive but satisfying rehearsal process. Once mastered, a piece is further honed and shaped according to the group's individual character and skills, making it their own. This is brought about through subtle shadings of dynamics and tempo, as well as stylistic variations characteristic of that group and/or region.

This direct and interactive approach is also important in learning the complex interlocking parts (*kotekan* or *kilitan*) for which Balinese music is renowned. Two complementary parts are woven together to form a complete melody; they fit together in perfect rhythmic tandem as two pieces of a puzzle. Aside from the pure fun of fitting the parts together, the technique of *kotekan* enables musicians to play at dazzling speeds, much faster than could be done alone. The collective Balinese spirit and finely tuned sense of musical interaction enable *gamelan* musicians to scale heights usually reserved for the most accomplished of virtuosi in other musical cultures.

—*Wayne Vitale*

A Unique Vision of the World

Wayang kulit, the shadow theater of Bali, is one of the longest running theatrical spectacles the world has known. For centuries it has survived changes in politics, ideology, and fashion, continually renewing itself and providing the Balinese with a unique vision of the world and of themselves.

The elements of the performance are simplicity itself: a white screen, a flame, music, and flat puppets that move and tell a story. Balinese audiences delight in seeing their favorite characters in familiar predicaments. There is the braggart caught in his own lies, the old fool who isn't so foolish, the invincible hero who needs to be rescued, the gods needing help from humans, and of course the beautiful princess, abducted, rescued, and stolen back again.

The shadow puppets are made of rawhide, carved and perforated to create lacy patterns of light and dark. The puppets and screen are flat, but when all elements of a performance are in place—flickering firelight, *gamelan* music, voice, and movement—they take on an unearthly dimension.

A new type of puppetry has come to the forefront this century called *wayang listrik* or electrified *wayang*, named for the use of electrical light bulbs and projected Power Point images on the screen replacing the traditional oil lamp. This is coupled with live dancers performing on both sides of the screen and makes for quite an innovative and entertaining show. New puppets are being made out of mirrored glass, paper, and plastic.

The characters are all recognizable at a glance by their headdresses, costumes, and facial characteristics. There are two main types: *alus* and *kasar*. *Alus* means refined and controlled. *Kasar* is vulgar and quick to

Flickering shadow puppets transport the audience to an ancient world of heroes and villains, where good ultimately triumphs over evil.

anger. *Alus* is not necessarily good nor *kasar* bad; what is admired is the right combination of attributes at the right place and time.

A performance is usually a kind of offering that marks the completion of a ceremony. The occasion could be a wedding, a funeral or any other major event in the life of the individual or community. In urban areas, a performance may be two hours long. In rural areas, expectations are greater and work schedules more flexible, so a performance is likely to begin after 10 pm and last three to five hours. Farmers often go directly from the performance to the fields.

Most puppeteers, or *dalangs,* in Bali specialize in *wayang parwa* stories from the *Mahabharata* myth cycle about two families in conflict over succession to the throne. Although each side has valid claims, one operates from greed and self-interest, while the other is more altruistic. The five Pandawa brothers struggle to assert their best qualities, pitted against the 100 Korawas, who lust for power.

An apprentice *dalang* will spend years following his father or teacher from one performance to another. Gradually his understanding of composition, rhetoric, and humor become instinctive. He is expected to improvise in several languages, to give convincing and inventive explanations of local customs and events, and to be adept in the use of proverbs and slapstick comedy.

The performance

The shadow play group usually arrives several hours before the performance. As they chat with their host and exchange gossip, the *dalang* will listen for ways to adapt the story for his audience. He never announces which story he is going to perform, reserving the right to change his mind.

In a given performance, 30 to 60 puppets are used. While the musicians play the overture, the *dalang* makes his selection. Antagonists are placed to his left, protagonists to his right. Major characters are placed closest to the *kayon,* the "tree of life" puppet that marks the beginning and end of major scenes. The shadows are purposely indistinct at this point, symbolizing that the creation of the story has begun, but that like a child in the womb, no one knows what it is going to develop.

There is singing as each character is presented. The first scene is the meeting scene, where problems central to the night's episode are introduced. It is entirely in Kawi, the ancient language of poetry, religion, and theater. Then there is a sound like someone clearing his throat, followed by a slow, deliberate laugh. A hush settles over the audience as a large figure moves ponderously across the screen and bows. This is Tualen, and for the first time, Balinese is spoken.

Tualen is one of four *punakawan,* advisors and servants to the king, and interpreters for the audience. They are the only puppets with lips; when the *dalang* pulls a string attached to their jaws, it looks as if they are talking.

During the initial scene it might be revealed that an army is gathering to attack; that someone is missing, kidnapped, or stuck in a dream; that a rare object is needed to complete a ceremony, or that everyone is invited to a marriage contest. There are hundreds of possible openings. They all end with a decision to solve the problem.

In pursuit of their goal, they might journey through a forest filled with dangerous animals, visit a hermit in his cave, enlist the help of an ally, climb mountains, or cross an ocean. There will be a meeting between the two sides, ending with sharp words and a battle. There might be a romantic interlude as one of the Pandawas and a beautiful enemy princess fall in love.

Ultimately, fighting ensues and magical weapons fill the air. Eagles fight snakes. Fire fights rain. Ogres change shapes, fly, and become invisible. The *penasars* are everywhere, fighting, arguing, joking, dodging weapons and providing a commentary which gives the musicians a chance to rest.

The *dalang* works furiously. His assistants try to second guess him and hand him the right puppet when he needs it. The musicians pay close attention, emphasizing each arrow shot with a resounding chord. The audience cheers, laughs, and groans, gripping each other in anticipation of what is to follow.

When the *dalang* feels the audience is satisfied, he will play a rousing battle scene ending in victory for the right side. This is not so much the ultimate triumph of good over evil as the re-establishment of a balance between the two. The clowns have a last word, then the *kayon* appears at the center of the screen, and the *dalang* utters the words: "Though the fighting is over, the stories go on forever. We apologize for stopping so soon."

—*Larry Reed*

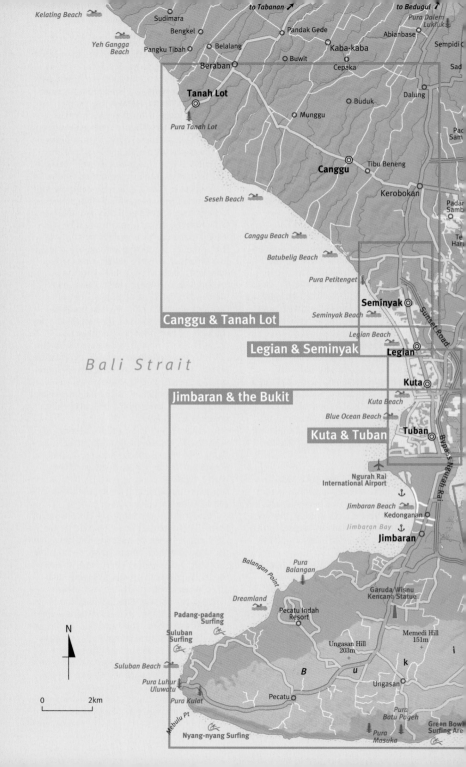

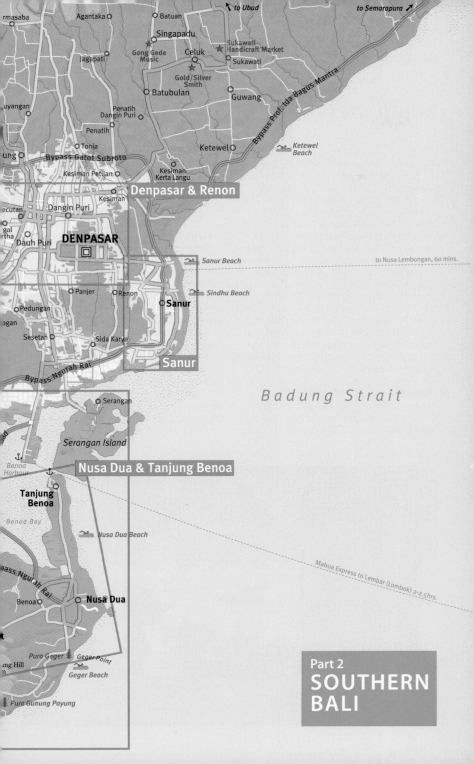

INTRODUCTION

Southern Bali

Fabulous beaches, magnificent sunsets, crashing surf, exclusivity and food, fun, and shopping galore make Bali's southern beaches the island's main tourist destination. Unless arriving by sea from Java to the west, from Lombok to the east or via cruise ships dropping anchor at Benoa in the south, all visitors enter Bali via Ngurah Rai International Airport where immediately upon disembarking the heat and humidity and occasional ocean breezes mark the beginning of holiday adventures for as many as 20,000 people per day. As such, the infrastructure is far better developed here than elsewhere on Bali, and whether being greeted by a resort representative or arranging accommodation and transportation on-the-spot, getting from the airport to the first stop of the day is relatively easy.

Choosing a base of operations
The most difficult decision for many travelers is where to stay. With so many choices — ranging from low-cost digs to ultra-lux resorts — budget is often the main criteria. Past that, ambience is the second priority. While **Kuta Beach** is the island's most famous and has the largest concentration of budget accommodations, many people are now discovering that they can enjoy the day- or night-time scenes there but base themselves in less crowded areas.

Tuban, south of Kuta (where the airport is actually located), has morphed into a more upscale version of its former self, with medium-range to expensive hotels. North of Kuta is **Legian**, attracting a slightly older crowd than Kuta. **Seminyak**, **Petitenget**, and **Kerobokan**, north of Legian, cater to families and well-off beautiful people who reject the crowds, traffic, and hubbub of its neighboring beaches. Kerobokan and further northwest to **Canggu** are rural areas adored by those seeking a more natural experience but who still enjoy being in close proximity to the shopping, restaurants, and bars of the main southern beaches. On the east side of Southern Bali is **Sanur**, well-established and

Kuta Beach has long been a haven for surfers and beach bums.

more staid than its other southern counterparts. It is favored by families and quiet resort-seekers.

Heading south past the airport is the "chicken's egg" part of the island, jokingly referred to for the way it looks on a map, with the mainland shaped somewhat like a mother hen. The geography, climate, and atmosphere here are entirely different than the rest of Southern Bali. Tourism development began in this area in the 1970s with the establishment of an exclusive resort enclave on the east coast at **Nusa Dua**, which remains an upmarket, secured, isolated community today. North of Nusa Dua is **Benoa**, formerly only housing the island's major harbor and now lined with a string of resorts featuring water sports of every description that attract a younger, more independent crowd.

On the opposite side of the peninsula is **Jimbaran**, featuring luxury resorts perched atop limestone cliffs overlooking crashing surf. South of Jimbaran is **Bukit Badung**—called the Bukit—a plateau dotted with opulent resorts specializing in serenity, total privacy, and personalized service.

Denpasar, the provincial capital and Bali's major city, attracts few overnighters other than those who are passing through from other areas of the island and have business to attend to in the financial district.

Growing in popularity are the Nusas—Penida and Lembongan—two small islands off the southeast coast. Formerly visited primarily by day-trippers for diving, snorkeling, surfing, and other water sports, Nusa Lembongan has experienced a great deal of development in recent years allowing sun and surf seekers the pleasures of gorgeous beaches formerly only known in the Kuta area in a less-crowded environment, with the bonus of excellent diving. Nusa Penida remains very rural, but its 2011 recognition as a national marine reserve is certain to attract the attention of future investors.

Southern Bali excursions

Beach activities or resort life, perhaps interspersed with a round of golf and a massage or two, are the agendas for many visitors who require nothing more to make their holiday ideal. But there are also several half- or full-day trips worth taking if the spirit is moved to get out and about, and all of them can be done from anywhere in Southern Bali.

Reconstructed in the 16th century and

The famous rock islet of Tanah Lot is one of Bali's holiest sites.

renovated in the late 19th century, **Pura Luhur Uluwatu** is the Bukit's most sacred temple. Firmly implanted at the top of one of Bali's most perilous cliffs overlooking one of its hottest surfing beaches far below, it is a pilgrimage site for many Balinese. A walkabout around the temple compound can be accompanied by a drive around the Bukit's majestic south coast, stopping in at one of its luxury resorts for a spa treatment, lunch, or cocktails.

Pura Tanah Lot is another of Southern Bali's sacred temples and is particularly beautiful at sunset, when it can be very crowded with tourists. For more peaceful viewing, go during the day and combine the visit with a drive through the countryside at Canggu, where there is an equestrian resort, a cricket club with swimming pool and spa, and an 18-hole golf course.

Denpasar has many interesting cultural and historic sites—museums, **Puputan Square** and several old temples—not to mention the bustling traditional marketplaces **Pasar Kumbasari** and **Pasar Badung.** Also check schedules locally to see what events are being held at the expansive **Werdhi Budaya Art Center**, whose calendar usually includes art exhibitions and cultural performances.

For more time on the azure coastal waters, several boat companies offer a variety of day trips: sail to **Nusa Lembongan** for lunch and snorkeling, returning at sunset; take a dive cruise to **Nusa Penida**; arrange a romantic dinner cruise; or take in some deep-sea fishing.

If all else fails, head to **Seminyak**'s streetlong "boutique row" and shop for designer goods, stopping at any one of its many restaurants or coffee shops when the feet start complaining.

—*Linda Hoffman*

KUTA AND TUBAN

Kuta Beach: Bali's Tourist Epicenter

For many years, **Kuta Beach** was Bali's best-known tourist destination. Bounded on the north by Legian and on the south by Tuban (where the airport is actually located), Kuta is living proof that one man's hell is another man's paradise. This bustling beach resort spontaneously burst onto center stage of the international tourist scene in the 1970s, after first being discovered by European backpackers travelling to the East in the 1960s. It is here that many visitors form their first (if not only) impressions of what Bali is all about. Many are shocked and immediately flee in search of the "real Bali" elsewhere on the island.

The truth is, however, that certain souls positively thrive in this labyrinth of boogie bars, beach bungalows, DVD shops, and honkytonks, all part of the Kuta lifestyle. What then is the magic that has transformed this sleepy fishing village overnight into an overcrowded tourist haven with no end in sight to its haphazard expansion?

Before tourism came to the area, Kuta was one of the poorest places on Bali, plagued by poor soils, endemic malaria and a surf-wracked beach that provided little protection for shipping. In the early days, it nevertheless served as a port for the powerful southern Balinese Badung kingdom, whose capital lay in what is now Denpasar.

Rice, slaves, and booty

Though Bali was never very trade-oriented, it did supply neighboring islands with several commodities, mainly rice, and notably slaves. Also, the booty salvaged from shipwrecks provided an occasional bonanza for the hardy inhabitants of this coastal outpost.

After an earlier Dutch trading post had been abandoned as commercially unviable (even the illegal trade in slaves proved disappointing), there arrived in Kuta a remarkable Dane mounted on a proud stallion, the likes of which the Balinese had never seen. Mads Lange, as he was called, had the audacity to march straight to the palace of the *raja* of Badung and demand an audience. Despite his bravado, Lange had in fact recently been a victim of his own intrigues on the neighboring island Lombok, where he had aided the wrong *raja* in a war and lost all. As fate would have it, Lange not only survived his move to Bali, but prospered, building here an extensive new trading post, coconut oil factory and luxurious residence stocked with wines and other delicacies.

Within the walls of his fabled Kuta residence, Lange wined and dined a succession of visiting scholars, adventurers, princes, and colonial officials. During the tumultuous 1840s, he repeatedly played a critical role in mediating between the Balinese rulers and the Dutch. Today, his grave can be seen in a Chinese cemetery at the center of Kuta, not far from a Buddhist temple and the crumbling remains of his once-regal house.

A tourist caravansary

It took a young Californian surfer and his wife to first notice Kuta's tourism potential. The year was 1936. Robert and Louise Koke decided to leave Hollywood and start a small hotel on Bali. In Louise Koke's book, *Our Hotel in Bali*, she describes their discovery of Kuta as follows: "The next day we cycled ... to the South Seas picture beach we had been hoping to find. It was Kuta ... the broad, white sand beach curved away for miles, huge breakers spreading on clean sand."

The hotel they founded was called the Kuta Beach Hotel, naturally. It was a modest establishment, but things went reasonably well in spite of an occasional malaria attack and a run-in with a young and fiery American of British birth by the name of Ketut Tantri, who managed to stir up controversy wherever she went during her 20-odd years in Indonesia.

After World War II, tourism in Bali all but disappeared. And when the first tourists began to trickle back during the 1960s, Kuta was all but forgotten. Suddenly and without warning, however, a new kind of visitor began

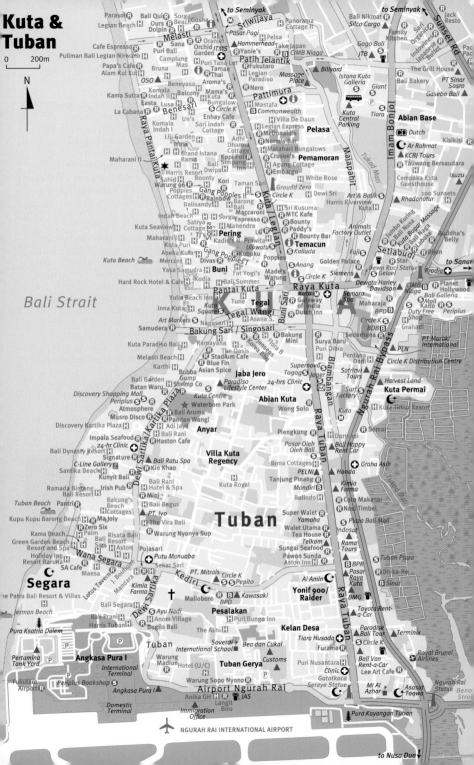

to frequent the island during the 1970s, and their preferred abode on Bali was Kuta beach

Nobody quite knew what to make of the first long-haired, bare-footed travelers who stopped here on their way from India to Australia, nobody, that is, except for the enterprising few in Kuta who quickly threw up rooms behind their houses and began cooking banana pancakes for this nomadic tribe.

The main attraction here was and still is one of the best beaches in Asia, and the trickle of cosmic surfers and space age crusaders in search of paradise, mystical union, and good times soon turned into a torrent, as tales of Bali spread like wildfire on the travelers' grapevine. Stories of a place where travelers could live out extravagant dreams on one of the world's most exotic tropical islands—for just a few dollars a day—seemed too good to be true.

Within the space of a few years, Kuta's empty beaches and back lanes began to fill up with homestays, restaurants, and shops. Most visitors stayed on as long as the money lasted, and many concocted elaborate business schemes that would enable them to come back, investing their last dollars in handicrafts and antiques before leaving.

In Kuta, the clothing or "rag trade" developed rapidly. Fortunes have been made and a handful of young entrepreneurs who began by selling batiks out of their backpacks have made it big. With the new affluence came a lifestyle of flashy villas and sultry tropical evenings beneath moonlit palms.

By the end of the 1970s, nobody knew quite what was going on. Upscale tourists were mixing in increasing numbers among the "hippie travelers", and deluxe bungalow hotels were popping up between $2-a-night homestays. With them came the uncontrolled proliferation of shops and bars and tourist touts lurking on every street corner. By the 1980s, Kuta was no longer a secret.

Kuta's reincarnation

Many changes, good and bad, have come to Kuta over the years. The good includes excellent food, great shopping, and a vibrant nightlife; the bad includes mundane problems such as traffic jams, pollution, and dirty beaches and escalates to the devastating terrorist bombings of 2002. Next to the Balinese who lived and worked in the affected areas, Australian tourists—who once dominated the Kuta scene—were the largest number of casualties. For several years thereafter, many Australians avoided Bali altogether, further demolishing Kuta's tourism-based economy. By 2008, Kuta had made a remarkable recovery—perhaps due to the speedy arrests and trials of the perpetrators and the

Kuta is Bali's most popular beach scene, attracting a younger set.

Kuta's accommodation ranges from budget to mid-range and is generally quite inexpensive.

world's view that terrorism occurs not only in isolated spots, but across the globe—and today it is truly international, the spectrum of visitors ranging from macho Brazilian surfers to prim Japanese secretaries. There is a **memorial** to the bombing victims on Jl. Legian at the former site of Paddy's Bar and opposite the Sari Club site where the 2002 explosion took place. Each year on the anniversary—October 12—there is a ceremony attended by Balinese and international visitors to mourn the lives lost as well as those changed forever.

After the bombings, an equally rapid rise in domestic tourism began, with the Jakarta central government's appeals to Indonesia's wealthier citizens to holiday at home rather than abroad, and in particular to support Bali and to show international travelers that it was safe to return. Large numbers of out-islanders have also settled here, opening businesses or simply hanging out in this Indonesian version of a gold-rush boom town. The impression visitors may get is that the local Balinese have become a minority in their own community.

For many, this litany of change reads as an indictment of yet another paradise lost. Certainly for those who knew Kuta in an earlier, more innocent state, the new Kuta is often difficult to accept. But what of the local Balinese; what do they think of all this? The most common answer is that despite the changes, the Balinese community remains strong, if wary. The traditional ceremonies are still being held, so there is as yet no need to worry, they feel. One need only witness the powerful *calonarang* dance in Kuta beneath a full moon to understand this. While we despair the loss of Kuta's village past, we cannot condemn all that is new. In fact, goods and services have improved, and Kuta enjoys a standard of living higher than almost anywhere else in Indonesia.

Above all, though, Kuta beach has become a major cross-cultural international meeting spot with few peers. Love it or leave it, only one thing is definite: the old Kuta has passed away, and nobody knows what the future may bring.

Kuta sights

The biggest tourist attraction at Kuta is, of course, its **beach**, which first attracted backpackers and surfers five decades ago. With no dangerous rocks or corals, it remains a good place for beginners to try their luck. There are several surfing schools that will happily teach novices the ropes. Boards are also available for rent on the beach, with local dudes standing by offering basic lessons. As there are some very strong currents here, stay between the flags when swimming. There are trained lifeguards on duty to keep the oblivious in safe areas and to assist those in trouble.

The major drawback to Kuta beach are the tradespeople who annoy sunbathers into submission to have their nails manicured or hair braided, get a massage, or buy a souvenir. If uninterrupted solitude—or pristine sands—are desired, skip this beach. However, these irritants don't deter the young and young-at-heart.

Shopping opportunities are perhaps Kuta's second biggest draw, its streets and alleys lined with kiosks and stores selling T-shirts, sarongs, cheap jewelry, sandals, and souvenirs. On the north end of Jl. Kartika Plaza, **Kuta Square** is only the beginning of a long line of more upscale shops selling surfwear and fashions.

At the end of each day, twilight is celebrated with beachside **sundowners** to watch fabulous sunsets. Following darkness, the **partying** begins and progresses from one watering hole to the next until the wee hours of the following day.

Kuta's southern neighbor

Considered by most outsiders to be part of Kuta, **Tuban**—often called "South Kuta" or "New Kuta Beach"—is actually a separate community with its own characteristics. The label "new" is more descriptive than not, as that's exactly what much of it is. Following a devastating wave that eroded much of the beach-front here, the land has been reclaimed, the beach is back where it's supposed to be, and a new walkway now hugs the shore. Several formerly damaged hotels and restaurants have also received facelifts and have reopened their doors with a fresh new look. Some of them have emerged in elegance, perhaps giving more upscale Seminyak a run for its money because the traffic is so bad there. The area's development began in the mid-1970s when Kuta started rising to international fame, spilling over into Tuban. Although travelers may not really care where Tuban ends and Kuta begins, knowing its unique personality can help them make more informed decisions about where to base themselves and how to plan their precious holiday time.

Tuban begins at its north where Jl. Bakung Sari, heading west toward the sea, turns south and then becomes Jl. Kartika Plaza (also called Jl. Kartika). Another tip: when traveling south on Jl. Legian, the long stretch of road that runs parallel to the coastal Jl. Raya Pantai Kuta, Jl. Legian's name changes to Jl. Raya Tuban south of the police station.

Souvenir shops abound on every street corner.

Not as frenzied as Kuta, Tuban is a good place to stay for those who want to play in Kuta, just a short walk away, but don't want to sleep there. The beach is not as crowded here, and the street traffic is not quite as congested.

Accommodations begin in the medium priced category and go up to expensive. Whereas in Kuta, the "beachfront" properties are actually on busy Jl. Raya Kuta, in Tuban, most hotels literally open up onto the sand. The other notable thing about Tuban is that it is peppered with independent restaurants serving a variety of cuisines.

Tuban's most prominent landmark is **Ngurah Rai International Airport**, coded DPS, for Denpasar, in the airline world. A lot more fun than the airport is the wild and wet **Waterbom** on Jl. Kartika Plaza. Highly successful in its 19 years on this spot, it continually adds new thrills and provides something for absolutely everyone in the family. After trying all 17 exhilarating waterslides, the nerve-mangling Climax and the Smashdown—a 25 m (80-foot) tall ride with a ground speed upwards of 70 km/h (43 mph)—wet and wild ones can relax and float down the Jungle River surrounded by tropical foliage. The kids can splash around in a supervised play area, while mom and dad have a massage at the spa or sip a cocktail at Splash Bar.

Across the street from Waterbom is **Discovery Shopping Mall**, sprawling along prime beachfront property. Along with up-market department stores Centro and Sogo, it also has a *pasar* of sorts in the basement selling low-quality handicrafts and souvenirs, and several DVD shops. On the top floor is a food court with many choices of inexpensive Asian food; primarily in the corners of the mall are the ubiquitous fast food chains. In between are shops of all sorts normally found in malls, such as sportswear and eyeglasses.

—Bruce Carpenter & Linda Hoffman

VISITING KUTA
(TELEPHONE CODE: 0361)

The 5-km-long arcing white sand stretching north of the airport is still arguably the best beachfront on Bali, although the vendors remain annoying. The villages along the coast are far from being the fishing communities they once were: the area is now a booming Pacific resort and its streets are clogged with tourists and traffic, particularly during the peak holiday seasons.

Kuta Beach is practically a household name around the globe, but it's not for the fainthearted. It's a rabbit's warren of cheap accommodations and eateries, bars, and souvenir kiosks, jam-packed with people from every corner of the world. But there's no denying that sunset on Kuta is fabulous. Those who love it often return many times and wouldn't think of going anywhere else.

See map, page 71.

ORIENTATION
The area often referred to collectively as "Kuta" is actually three separate beaches and communities, each with its own personality and attracting a certain type of clientele. They are:

TUBAN Often referred to as "South Kuta", Tuban begins south of Bali's Ngurah Rai International Airport at Jimbaran, with its northern boundary at the top of Jl. Kartika Plaza, now also called Jl. Dewi Sartika. The southern beaches' bigger resorts and hotels are here, including Discovery Kartika Plaza, Bali Dynasty, Kupu Kupu Barong, Holiday Inn Resort Baruna Bali, and Ramada Bintang Bali.

KUTA Kuta's southern boundary begins north of Jl. Kartika Plaza (Jl. Dewi Sartika) and stretches to Jl. Melasti in the north. It includes Jl. Legian and Jl. Pantai Kuta (the beachfront drive) and the little lanes in between, extending east past Jl. Imam Bonjol out to Jl. Sunset. Jl. Legian is the commercial artery of Kuta and the location of many of its restaurants, shops and nightspots. Another line-up of seaside resorts starts at the corner of Jl. Pantai Kuta with the Hard Rock Hotel all the way to Alam Kul Kul with the Harris Resort Kuta Beach in between.

At Kuta, many ladies offer massages on the beach. In response, certified masseuses have banded together in an association identifiable by name tags and same-colored T-shirts. Although they may not be as good as the ones in the five-star spas, most travelers report satisfaction. Note: Massage on Bali has nothing to do with sex. The local euphemism for the latter is "jiggy-jig".

LEGIAN Legian is the northern extension of Kuta proper, beginning north of Jl. Melasti as its southern boundary to Jl. Arjuna (formerly called Jl. Double Six) at its north, where many of the expat designers and long-stay tourists live. There are three ways to reach Legian and Seminyak: north on Jl. Pantai Kuta then turn east on Jl. Melasti, then north; from Jl. Imam Bonjol, turn west on to Jl. Patih Jelantik at the gas station; or from the north via Jl. Kerobokan, taking the bypass road.

Note that even though it's a bit further, it's faster to travel from Kuta and Legian to Seminyak by using Jl. Sunset Road instead of traffic-packed Jl. Raya Seminyak/Legian.

GETTING THERE & GETTING AROUND
Perama (Jl. Legian 39, tel: 751-551, www.perama-tour.com), with its convenient location and fast and efficient service, is Kuta's most active travel agent. Perama also has daily shuttle buses to Candidasa, Lovina, Padangbai, Sanur, and Ubud. Inquire about hotel pickup.

ACCOMMODATIONS
Kuta has thousands of rooms, ranging from tiny $10 a night concrete boxes in a Balinese family compound deep in the back lanes to the upmarket Hard Rock Hotel.

The choice of where to base yourself is relatively easy: if you want action, stay in Kuta; if you want relative quiet, try Canggu further to the north; if you want a mix, stay in Sanur, and if you want top-end luxury, head for Tuban in the south or Seminyak or Petitenget in the north. Each area has advantages and disadvantages. The main hassle north of Seminyak is a lack of public transport.

The best way to find a room that suits you is to shop around. There are several online booking services. Try www.agoda.com for good prices. Otherwise, grab almost any old place the first night, then hit the ground the next morning and upgrade yourself. If you're in a hurry, you can book through the hotel association counter at the airport. The recommendations here are intended to give some points of reference.

Hotels are often fully booked during the peak seasons (Christmas–New Year, July–August, and during Ramadan), so make a reservation for a day or two and look around if the hotel is not to your liking. In the low season most hotels offer discounts of up to 40 or even 50 percent. As part of your bargaining stance, request that children under 12 sharing their parents' room be allowed free of charge. Bear in mind that in many accommodations throughout Indonesia, KITAS holders (temporary residents) and Indonesian citizens are usually given discounts.

There are literally hundreds of *losmen* or homestay "inns" scattered throughout Kuta. The rooms are basic, usually concrete blocks thrown up in a family compound. A breakfast of fruit salad or toast and tea or coffee is almost always included.

For a bit more money, you can get a larger room or private bungalow with AC nearer the beach. Rates are negotiable, particularly in the off-season and for longer stays.

Balisandy Cottages, off Gang Poppies II, tel: 753-344, fax: 750-791, www.balisandy.com. 55 nicely-furnished rooms with AC, tv, private bath, hot water, around a lawn and a big pool. Though close to the beach, it's quiet and near excellent eateries. From $20.

Kedin's II, Gang Sorga (north of Gang Poppies I), tel: 763-554. Clean rooms in a two-story block, cold water, fans. Attractive garden, low-decimal surroundings for Kuta. From $10.

Komala Indah II Sunset, Jl. Pantai, tel: 751-670, www.komalaindah2.baliklik.com. Unpretentious, clean, fan or AC rooms with hot water. In a quiet area under palms, a skip away from the beach. **Komala Indah I** is on Jl. Benasar. Same owner. From $10.

Sorga Cottages, Gang Sorga (off Gang Poppies II), tel: 751-897, fax. 752-417. Nicely furnished basic rooms, some with AC, in a 3-story building. Small pool, restaurant. Good value. From $15.

Yulia Beach Inn, Jl. Pantai Kuta 43, Kuta, tel: 751-893, fax: 751-055, www.yuliabeachinns.com. 34 rooms. Good reputation; one of the original Kuta places; only 5 minutes from the beach. Also has an inn in Ubud. $45–85.

Fat Yogi's, Gang Poppies I, tel: 751665. Set back down an alleyway 300m from the beach is this laid-back and very central surfie's place with pool. 26 clean AC rooms, hot water, private bath, private balcony. No tv but free WiFi. $35–40.

Taman Sari Cottages Bar & Restaurant, Gang Poppies II. A cluster of bungalows 300m from the beach. 20 twin and double AC rooms surrounded by tropical gardens. Hot water, fridge, private balcony, or terrace. Pool, restaurant, bar. $30–35.

Tune Hotels Kuta, Jl. Kahyangan Suci (off Jl. Pantai Kuta), www.tunehotels.com. A new concept hotel designed for budget travelers in a modern hotel building. 139 basic rooms with AC, elevator, concierge, hotel/airport transfer, bicycle rental. Internet rates as low as $30.

There's a whole new type of intermediately priced hotels in Kuta. Built in 2009 and 2010, most are not on the beach and cater to business travelers and folks who need a place to stay near the airport. Fully furnished with kitchenettes and kids' facilities, they also appeal to families and long-term stays. They're clean, modern, great value, but not much charm.

100 Sunset Boutique Hotel, Jl. Sunset Rd No 100, tel: 847-7360, fax: 847-7329, www.100sunset.com. Managed by Aston, a modern minimalist boutique hotel with 28 rooms and 17 short-term and long-term apartments. All rooms have kitchenette, AC, tv, WiFi, sound system. Spa, 24-hr on call doctor. $68–108.

Harris Resort Kuta Beach, Jl. Pantai Kuta, tel: 753-868, fax: 753-875, www.harris-kuta-bali.com. Located around a free-form swimming pool overlooking gardens, 191 guestrooms and suites in simple modern style. Each room equipped with satellite tv, mini-fridge, AC, WiFi. Dino Kid's Club. Restaurant serves Italian cuisine. $75–80.

Note that this hotel is in the process of being engulfed by the Sahid Kuta Lifestyle Resort, a huge new development stretching 250m along the beachfront road. The project will include a new 5-star Sheraton Bali Kuta (scheduled to open in 2012), with a total of 5,000 hotel rooms and over 200 stores and eateries and parking space for 1,000 vehicles. Attached "Beachwalk" will be a lifestyle center for hotel guests as well as other visitors.

Harris Riverview Kuta, Jl. Raya Kuta 62A, tel: 761-007, fax: 761-006, www.harris-riverview-bali.com. Located 15 minutes from Kuta beach, 184 one- and two-bedroom rooms and residences. 4 swimming pools, Harris Café, Harrissimo Italian cuisine, Dino Kid's Club. Spa and reflexology, meeting facilities, free WiFi. $60–90.

Aston at Grand Kuta Hotel & Residence, Jl. Dewi Sri No 8, tel: 300-0888, fax: 300-0999, www.grandkuta.com. A short drive to the beaches, 1-, 2- and 3-bedroom leisure apartments. 3 swimming pools, BBQ area, kids' playground. Gym, sauna, and gardens. Wide selection of shops, restaurants, and cafes on the first floor, ample underground parking. $80–140.

Poppies Cottages, Gang Poppies 1, tel: 751-059, fax: 752-364, www.poppiesbali.com. A long-time Kuta favorite, it includes 20 quaint cottages in secret tropical gardens in the heart of Kuta. Natural swimming pool and Jacuzzi; 5 minute walk to Kuta beach. Open-air restaurant serves good international food. $75–100.

Luxury ($100–up)

The accommodations in this category are listed here because of their prices, but don't be shy about looking at their online rates, where they become much more affordable.

Alam KulKul Boutique Resort, Jl. Raya Pantai Kuta, tel: 752-520, fax: 752-519, www.alamkulkul.com. A 4-star newly refurbished boutique resort across the road from Kuta Beach. Tropical gardens and cascading pools surround thatched roof villas and spacious rooms. Antique furniture and local handicrafts in contemporary facilities. $160–220.

Hard Rock Hotel, Jl. Pantai Kuta, tel: 761-869, fax: 761-868, www.balihardrockhotels.net. 418 rooms and suites adorned with images celebrating artists from the '50s to the late '90s. Facilities include Boom Box Recording Studio, free-form swimming pool, Rock Spa, 5m rock-climbing wall, gym, sauna steam room, and of course Hard Rock Café. $240–630.

Kuta Seaview Cottages, Jl. Pantai Kuta. 82 AC rooms and cottages with tv, fridge, hot water tub and shower, private balcony. Rossovivo Restaurant and Lounge next to the pool overlooking the ocean serves Italian and Indonesian cuisine. Live music every night. $175–335.

Ramayana Resort & Spa, Jl. Bakung Sari, tel: 751-864, fax: 751-866, www.ramayanahotel.com. Good location on the border of Kuta and Tuban, just a short walk to the beach and Kuta Square, one of southern Bali's largest shopping complexes. Six categories of rooms; resort club. $191–300.

Villa De Daun, Jl. Raya Legian, tel: 756-276, fax 750-643, www.villadedaun.com. 12 villas designed to capture the spirit of a traditional village in 3 different categories, each with its own garden compound, full-length pool, outdoor leisure space, kitchenette. Butler service. Award-winning Dala Spa (www.villadelaspa.com). Restaurant serves Indonesian cuisines. $300–700, including breakfast.

DINING

The entire beach area from Tuban all the way north has become a culinary paradise. New places open frequently and competition is fierce. Most don't last for long. The ones which do have great food at unbeatable prices. Seafood and Asian dishes are your best bets. Or try Mexican, Indian, Japanese, Mediterranean, or Moroccan. The more well-known places are mentioned below, plus some promising newcomers. Ask around for the latest "in" spots. Look for discount coupons in tourist literature.

"Halal" on menu means it is food acceptable to Muslims.

An invaluable source of sound dining information is restaurant critic Jerry William's irreverent and perspicacious website www.balieats.com. His reviews of an eating establishment's food quality and overall value for money are based on actual visits to the restaurants without their knowledge or support.

American

Hard Rock Café, Jl. Pantai Kuta, tel: 755-661, www.balihardrockhotels.net. Dine-in rocks with great music, memorabilia ambiance. International food. Terrace is loungy and acts as a stage for local DJs and first-class Indonesian artists, who play after sunset as well as for events. A hang-out spot for local youth as well as tourists. Happy hours 5–7 pm daily, as well as food promos.

Planet Hollywood, Bali Galleria Shopping World, Jl. Bypass Ngurah Rai, tel: 757-827, fax: 765-848, www.planethollywoodbali.com. Burgers and grills with a long drinks list, cinematic memorabilia with surround tv and excellent children's play area.

Balinese & Indonesian

Padang. Everyone's favorite Indonesian regional cuisine from West Sumatra is served out of a great number of *warungs* along Jl. Legian to service the large non-Balinese population. Ten or more different dishes will be served upon seating, all of it fiery hot. You're charged only for what you eat.

Plengkung, Jl. Raya Kuta 90, tel: 757-393. This no-nonsense good-value eatery is located on the way to the airport, two-thirds of 1 km (1 mile) south of Bemo Corner. Specialty is *ikan bakar* (grilled fish). Also try their *gurami goreng* (fried *gurami* fish) Popular, above-average Indonesian food with a nice atmosphere.

Delicatessens

Bali Bakery, Jl. Raya Kuta 65, tel: 755-149, fax: 767-340, www.balibakery.com. Patisserie and café; purveyor of all things bread and pastry, expanded into a restaurant serving a vast variety of food. Function room, catering service, WiFi, inside-outside seating. Also has outlets in Denpasar and Seminyak. Open 7:30 am–10:30 pm for breakfast, lunch, and dinner.

Dijon Food Specialties, Kuta Poleng Blok A1-2, Jl. Setiabudi, tel: 759-636, 759-638, fax: 759-783, www.dijonbali.com. Just off the Jl. Bypass roundabout, has a surprisingly wide range of imported foodstuffs from Aussie meat pies to cold cuts and French cheeses. Also has a café across the parking lot from the shop serving make-your-own sandwiches on a variety of breads, fresh salads, soups, pastas, and other hot meals. Try their smoothies. Also does home and villa deliveries.

Fine dining

*Kori's Restaurant & Bar, Gang Poppies II, tel: 758-605, fax: 752-510, www.korirestaurant.com. Since

1998, fantastic interior and idyllic garden setting. Extensive international menu with western favorites, such as bangers and mash and roast beef with Yorkshire pudding. Also try the giant seafood kebab for two and reasonably priced imported and local wine, chilled cocktails, or ice cold beer to wash it all down. Lively poolside bar with regular cocktail promotions. Always busy. Wednesday is Ladies' Night, with 50 percent off margaritas. Cigar salon, pool table and valet parking are extra touches. Reservation recommended during peak seasons. Open 11 am–midnight.

Poppies Restaurant, Gang Poppies I, tel: 751-059. An old favorite in downtown Kuta with an upmarket atmosphere and menu. Specialties: fresh seafood, steaks, shish kebabs, as well as salads, a selection of Indonesian dishes and an extensive wine list. Advance bookings are a must during the high season.

German

Mama's German Restaurant, La Walon Shopping Center, Jl. Legian (near the junction with Jl. Tanjung Mekar), tel: 761-151, www.bali-mamas.com. Since 1985, the place for homemade sausages from their own butchery (the owner is from Hamburg) and yummy German dishes. Sandwich corner. Free WiFi. Open 8 am–4 pm.

Indian

Kama Sutra Bali Restaurant, Club & Lounge, Jl. Pantai Kuta. tel: 761-999. A combination nightclub and restaurant serving tasty and well-presented food. Exotic décor.

International

Kopi Pot Café & Bar, Jl. Legian, Kuta, tel 752-614. New full restaurant menu, outrageous homemade cakes, fine coffees from around the world. Stylish new Lone Palm Bar serves the coldest beers on Jl. Legian. Top sporting events via satellite tv; ample off-road parking.

Made's Warung I, Jl. Pantai Kuta 16A (near Bemo Corner), tel: 755-297. A reliable old-time favorite and popular hangout for people-watching and great food (Indo-International). Specialties include Thai and Vietnamese salads, prawns in chili sauce, squid fillet, black rice ice cream, and cappuccino. Has a breakfast special that includes fruit juice, eggs, bacon, toast, fresh fruit yoghurt, and frothy cappuccino. Also has an outlet in Seminyak.

The Balcony, at Un's Hotel, Jl. Benasari 16, tel: 757-409. This stylish restaurant has long been a standout for its excellent European-style food and service. It is best known for its variety of brochettes, juicy meat, and seafood skewers. Special offers available every day of the week. Un's Hotel also offers rooms.

Italian/Mediterranean

Because of the large and steady numbers of southern European visitors and residents, there are many Italian restaurants in Bali's cities, and Italian dishes are also found on the menus of almost every tourist restaurant.

Nero Bali Mediterranean Restaurant & Lounge, Jl. Legian Keloid No 384, tel: 750-756, www.nerobali.com. A high-class restaurant and bar serving excellent Greek and Italian food. Stunning interior. From outside it looks expensive but it's not. Modern, simple, exquisite, delicious.

Papa's Café, Jl. Pantai Kuta (in front of Alam KulKul Boutique Resort), tel: 755-055, fax. 750-751, www.papascafe.com. Facing the beach, this alfresco-style restaurant is among the island's very best for Mediterranean/Italian cuisine. Known for its inspired fresh seafood dishes, superb coffee drinks, and good service. Check out the Volcano Pizza.

Warung 96, Gang Poppies II. Probably the cheapest crispy wood-fired pizzas in town. High-quality Italian and international cuisine, fresh salads and Indonesian classics: *gado-gado*, curries, *nasi goreng*. Extremely good value. Worth the walk or the drive, as you can't go wrong eating here.

Japanese

Café Take, Jl. Patih Jelantik, Komplex Sriwijaya, tel: 759-745. Pronounced *tar-key*, meaning "bamboo" in Japanese. Try their special tepanyaki menu of lobster, sirloin, and chicken. Other specialties are sushi, sashimi, Robatayaki, and shabushabu. VIP tatami room available.

Mexican

TJ's, Gang Poppies I, tel: 751-093. Authentic and delicious enchiladas and margaritas. The nachos and salsa are perfect with a cold beer. Try a frozen strawberry margarita. Smart garden interior. Open 9 am–11 pm.

Organic food

Sari Organics, in Little Tree Green Building Supplies and Lifestyle Center, Jl. Sunset 112X, Kuta, with another outlet at Ambengan, Ubud, tel: 780-1839. Fresh organic, healthy food.

Vegetarian

Aroma's, Jl. Legian (north of Jl. Benasari), tel: 751-003. This haven for vegetarian food has for years delighted both vegetarians and non-vegetarians. The menu is extensive, the portions generous. Check the boards for the ever-changing daily specials. Great drinks and desserts. The laidback garden setting makes it a pleasurable dining experience. Open 7 am–11 pm.

NIGHTLIFE

The best way of keeping up with what is going on at night in southern Bali is to get a hold of any of the tourist magazines.

Bali's nightlife is legendary and these days there are two very different "scenes": the young boisterous crowd that dominates the Kuta circuit and a cooler, slightly older expat Euro and Jakartan crowd that frequents the beach cafes and chic restaurants of northern Legian and Seminyak.

When the sun begins to set, the whole southern Bali coastal strip from Tuban to Canggu comes to life. There's no dress code in Kuta. Get down in board shorts and T-shirts or get all gussied up.

From 9 pm–11:30 pm, on the **Hard Rock's Centerstage,** local and international bands play in an unplugged format each night of the week—and no cover charge! Look out for big national and international acts from 11 pm–2 am. **Macaroni Club,** Jl. Legian, has strong cocktails and is a good spot to start evening forays. **Planet Hollywood,** Bali Galleria Shopping World, has live music every night with special big acts occasionally.

As the night wears on, some heavy-duty action seekers move to other spots further north, but there is still some action in Kuta. Along Jl. Legian there is plenty of action and many spots change over time. Be prepared for heavy security, ID checks, ladies beckoning passersby inside clubs, traffic jams, and parking problems. Also be wary of cheap liquor sold on the streets. Several locals and tourists have died recently from drinking *arak api*, which is locally made and contains other ingredients—sometimes even gasoline—to give it an extra kick.

Some of the current ear-splitting rowdy faves are **Apache** (across the street from Macaroni), with live reggae music. **Bounty** is on a pirate ship (honestly) in the middle of a shopping area, but is expected to move its frenzied clientele to a new location soon. Embargo sends gangsta rap into the air, and there's also Brandy's HipHop Club, Sky Garden Lounge, Red Room Discotheque, Eikon… the list goes on.

Away from Jl. Legian, try **Twice Bar** on Gang Poppies II for punk. **The Wave** beachfront on Jl. Pantai Kuta is part of an odd assortment of entertainment that contains Sailfin fine dining restaurant, The Coffee Bar al fresco café and beach bar and The Club, a disco. For something more soothing, Gabah Terrace Lounge in the Ramayana Resort & Spa on Jl. Bakungsari has jazz.

SHOPPING

Kuta is a shopper's dream. This is partly because it's an important manufacturing center of summer wear, jewelry, decorative handicrafts, and home-wares, which are exported all over the world. Most of the goods are designed by expatriates from Europe, the US, and Japan.

The best areas for shopping are Jl. Legian, Jl. Bakungsari, Jl. Melasti, and nearby back lanes such as Poppies I and II. Some bargains, though, can still be struck as far away as Seminyak and Kerobokan. Before buying, check wares carefully because goods are not returnable.

There are two shopping malls in Kuta: Carrefour Plaza on Jl. Sunset, with an excellent Periplus book-shop and a giant Carrefour supermarket. **Bali Galleria Shopping World** is on Jl. Bypass Ngurah Rai with a large duty free shop in front favored by bus-loads of Asian tourists. It also has a Periplus book-shop and a Gramedia book store outlet.

The best for one-stop-shopping are the **Matahari** stores, with their huge selection of goods from clothing to homewares. There is one in Kuta Square. Their supermarket is a good source of snacks, dry goods, and processed foods.

Clothing & fabrics

A whole range of clothing prices and styles can be found in Kuta, from gaudy T-shirts to exclusive designer labels. Always check the quality of costly items to ensure you don't get export remnants. Counterfeit branded goods are abundant. In small shops, bargain hard. The established manufacturers generally have more than one outlet in Kuta and Legian. Bear in mind that it would undoubtedly be less expensive and perhaps more satisfying to simply have your clothing made. Ask around for a good tailor or seamstress who can copy a favorite, perfect-fitting garment. Various shops can make almost anything to order for both men and women, from suits to shoes, from bathing suits to neckties. Tailors often have a large stock of different fabrics to choose from and offer speedy service.

Animale, Kuta Square, Jl. Pantai Kuta, tel: 753-830. A stylish ladies clothing store occupying 3 floors with sizeable collections of bright day, night, and beach wear, which for the most part appeal to a more mature clientele. Includes a range of French imports. Also plus sizes. Factory outlet at Jl. Raya Kuta No. 82.

Body & Soul, Kuta Square 32D, Jl. Pantai Kuta, tel: 755-227; Discovery Shopping Mall, tel: 769-751; and Bali Galleria Shopping World, 1st floor Unit 1A-39, Jl. Bypass Ngurah Rai, tel: 767-065, www.bodyandsoul-clothing.com. Trendy fashion lycra pants, shirts and bright prints aimed at the younger market. Other outlets in Seminyak, Legian, Nusa Dua. Factory outlets in Legian and Seminyak.

By the Sea, Jl. Legian 186, tel: 757-775. A striking range of cool leisurewear for the whole family.

CV Wira, Jl. Pantai Kuta (opposite Supernova), tel: 753-253. A department store that stocks a limited but stunning range of local fabrics, crisp cool cotton, *kebaya* (ceremonial blouses) and stunning silk batik clothing.

Milo's, Kuta Square, tel: 754-081, www.milos-bali.com. One of the original overseas designers to discover the artistry of Balinese batik workers and translate it into Western styling, this 3-story boutique stocks a wonderful and tactile range of expensive silks. Also has outlets in Seminyak.

Children & teens

Colorful children's wear is popular throughout Kuta. Quality fabrics and trendy styling means that when you get back home, the gear will hold up. Stock up on basic playwear such as jeans and T-shirts at a quarter of the prices abroad.

Indigo Kids. 6 stores in Kuta, Legian, Seminyak, and Nusa Dua selling a great collection of children's wear for kids aged 3 months to 12 years. Established in 1983, also sells wholesale. Australian designs manufactured throughout Indonesia. Reliable quality, affordable prices. Specializes in fine handicrafted details. Also sells children's accessories.

Kahuna Surf Kids, Jl. Legian Kaja 476, tel: 755-927. Kid's colorful surf wear.

Kids A Go Go, Jl. Legian, tel 751-957. Presents a bright and fun collection of brilliant batiks that have been inspired by kids themselves.

Kidz Station Bali, Bali Galleria Shopping World, Jl. Bypass Ngurah Rai. Mostly imported toys, gifts, costumes, computer games. One of the island's best selections.

Rascals. Two stores located on Kuta Square Block D-6, Jl. Pantai Kuta, and Jl. Legian 86, tel: 461-357. Cute range of kid's swimwear and accessories styled in traditional batik that look good on and off the beach.

Furniture, antiques & reproductions

There's a plethora of "antique" stores in southern Bali. Be wary: many objects aren't genuine and are cleverly aged and reproduced. Most authentic pieces were bought up years ago, but with luck it's still possible to buy the genuine article between 25 and 40 years old from Bali, Java, Kalimantan, and Nusa Tenggara. Make sure any furniture bought here has been kiln dried so that the wood won't crack in drier climates when you get it home.

Hishem Furniture, Jl. Sunset 86C, tel:/fax: 737-441, 731-868, www.hishem.com. Manufacturer of synthetic rattan furniture.

Homewares & interiors

Frangipani Bali Interior Workshop, Jl. Mertasari IV/8, Jl. Sunset, Kuta, tel: 847-7488, www.frangipanibali.com. A wide range of well-designed soft furnishings and home accessories: curtains, bedding, cushions, sofas, and floor coverings made from cotton, silk, linen, woven fabrics, Sunbrella fabric, rattan, and sea grass. Also paintings from talented young Balinese artists.

House of Yanie, Kuta Square, tel: 758-048, www.houseofyanie.com. Over 3 floors brimming with a selection of fine gifts and homewares, both domestic and international, selected by Yanie during her travels in Indonesia, Asia, and abroad. From traditional to contemporary fashion, souvenirs, toys, and ornaments—retail or wholesale—can be found in this eclectic treasure trove.

DOUBLE TROUBLE

Getting your bearings in the small but traffic-congested and crowded beach areas is difficult enough without the additional challenge of streets bearing more than one name. Several street names have been changed, some of them more than one time. The problem is that not all of the ads in tourist magazines—or the shops and restaurants themselves—have conformed to the new monikers.

Below are the confusing names most commonly encountered:

New name	Former name(s)
Kuta:	
Jl. Singosari	Jl. Bankung Sari
Legian:	
Jl. Blue Ocean	Jl. Pantai Legian
Jl. Werkudara	Jl. Pura Bagus Taruna; Jl. Rum Jungle
Jl. Yudistira	Jl. Padma
Seminyak:	
Jl. Arjuna	Jl. Double Six
Jl. Abimanyu	Jl. Dhyanapura; Jl. Camplung Tanduk; Jl. Gado-Gado
Jl. Kayu Aya	Jl. Laksmana; Jl. Oberoi
Jl. Raya Basangkasa	The northern stretch of Jl. Raya Seminyak
Tuban:	
Jl. Dewi Sartika	Jl. Kartika Plaza

Jewelry

Most large hotels have upmarket jewelry shops. Attractive accessories such as bracelets, earrings, and brooches can be found in many of these shops.
Jonathon Silver, Jl. Legian 109, tel: 7542-09. Extensive range of well-presented silverware from simple silver rings to full silver coffee sets at affordable prices. Also has a store in Seminyak.
Mayang Bali Fine Jewelry, Kuta Square A 12, Jl. Pantai Kuta, tel: 752-902, fax: 752-736, www. mayangbalijewelry.com. Sterling silver jewelry set with many beautiful and unusual gemstones: diamonds, lapis lazuli, garnets, moonstones, labradorites, sapphires, and rubies set in over 500 different designs manufactured by their own craftsmen. Open 9 am–9 pm daily.
Suarti Design Collection. Factory and showroom are in Celuk (central Bali)—Bali's silver center—but Ibu Suarti's fashion jewelry is found in a large number of jewelry outlets in the major shopping centers in southern and central Bali. Offers unique designs executed by experienced craftsmen reflecting the culture and tradition of Indonesia.

Surfwear & Sporting Goods

Surfwear is ubiquitous in southern Bali. There's said to be over 800 surf shops, selling the latest boardies, bikinis, skirts, and tops of the surfing world.
Rip Curl, Kuta Square, Jl. Pantai Kuta, tel: 865-035, and 10 other outlets. One of the biggest surf gear shops on Bali. Stocks a full range of surf labels, both beachwear and gear. Open Monday–Saturday, 10 am–11 pm.
Surfer Girl, Jl. Legian 138, next door to Quiksilver surf shop. Bali's best all-girls surf shop and largest in the world. Complete collection of beach and resort wear.
Volcom, Kuta Square, Blok AII, tel: 752-711, www.vol-comind.com. Excellent selection of surf and skate gear and accessories. Open 9:30 am–11 pm. Opening times are subject to change; best to call ahead.

MONEY

Automated Teller Machines. ATMs are abundant and found at banks, Matahari Department Store on Jl. Legian and in Kuta Square, Jl. Pantai Kuta and in many other locations. Most accept bank cards linked to the Cirrus, Pulse, Visa and MasterCard international networks.
Moneychangers. Kuta has a great number of moneychangers. Most are open daily until late at night. Rates differ, so shop around. Only do business with "authorized" moneychangers (their signs will be marked) who do not ask for a commission, otherwise you're just asking to be ripped off. If the rates are too generous, be suspicious. Check the calculations yourself with your own calculator, get a receipt, and count your money before leaving.

COMMUNICATIONS

Internet

Charging Rp 400–500 per minute, cyber cafés that provide internet connections are found everywhere in the Kuta area. Recommended is the **Bali@Cyber Café**, 9 Kompleks Sriwijaya, Jl. Patih Jelantik, tel: 761-326, 762-290, ww.balicyber.net. With top computer gear, a good restaurant, and staff on hand to help the computer-illiterate and serve drinks while you tap away at the keyboard. Open 8:30 am–11 pm.

Post

The **Kuta Post Office** is located on Jl. Slamet, a small lane off Jl. Raya Kuta, open 7 am–2 pm Monday–Thursday, 7–11 am Friday, 7 am–1 pm Saturday. Many shops double as postal agents (look for the orange sign "approved by the post office") sell stamps, handle parcel shipments, and offer courier services.

VISITING TUBAN

(TELEPHONE CODE: 0361)

Tuban is the southernmost beach and is sometimes called "South Kuta". Its northern boundary is at the top of Jl. Kartika Plaza (also called Jl. Dewi Sartika) and it extends south of the airport, where Jimbaran begins. There are no budget accommodations here to speak of; there are primarily 5-star resorts. A new breed of hotels has crept in during the last couple of years, however, adding some medium-price range "apartments" away from the beach that could be attractive to longer-staying guests and those who need a quick overnight stay due to airport delays.

See map, page 71.

ACCOMMODATIONS

Moderate ($25–50)

Fave Hotel, Jl. Kediri No. 5, tel: 780-0535, fax: 767-323, www.favehotels.com. A new concept, all the amenities of an upmarket hotel with budget prices. All rooms have double or twin beds, tv, AC, WiFi. On-site parking. From $35.

Intermediate ($50–75)

Aston Inn Tuban, Jl. Kediri, tel: 762-828, fax 762 829, www.astoninntuban.com. 76 rooms and suites in a 3-star hotel within easy reach of the beach. Minimalist business hotel blended with resort ambience. Hula's Café & Pool Bar, Lomi Lomi Spa, pool and Jacuzzi. Business center, meeting rooms. Free airport transfers. $58–88.

Harris Hotel Tuban, Jl. Dewi Sartika (Jl. Kartika Plaza), tel: 765-255, 766-358, www.harris-tuban-bali.com. A friendly and efficient boutique business hotel, 5 minutes from Bali's airport, only 8 minutes walk to the beach. 66 rooms and suites, swimming pool. Quiet in spite of its busy location, it offers a plethora of business services from aromatherapy to Internet. Ideal for families and business travelers. Spa, reflexology, Harris Café. $55–95.

First Class ($75–100)

Bali Garden Hotel, Jl. Dewi Sartika (Jl. Kartika Plaza), tel: 752 725, fax: 752-728, www.baligardenhotel. com. A 4-star hotel in 2 ha of tropical gardens directly across from Waterbom Park. Restaurant, café and bar, coffee shop, pizzeria, billiard bar, pool bar, outdoor theater. Tari Spa and Oolala Spa. Swimming pool and kids' pool. WiFi. $96–513.

Luxury ($100–up)

Aston Kuta Hotel & Residence, Jl. Wana Segara No. 2–5, tel: 754-999, fax 765-506, www.astonbaliho-tels.com. A contemporary hotel a short walk from the beach. 209 rooms, banquet and meeting facilities, business center. Gym, pool, spa, 24-hr room service. 5 minutes from airport. Restaurants, rooftop lounge. $115–212.

Bali Dynasty Resort, Jl. Kartika Plaza, tel: 752-403, fax: 752-402, www.balidynasty.com. 312 rooms. Recently completely renovated with all new bathrooms and furnishings, AC and soundproofed patio doors. Fresh modern design, LCD tvs, DVD players, WiFi throughout. 3 pools, spa, dedicated clubhouse, 4 bars and 6 restaurants, including a superlative Cantonese/Sichuan, lively Irish game pub, sumptuous breakfast buffet. Focus is on families, one child under age 12 stays free in room with parents; plus waterslide and games arcade. $142–300.

Bali Rani Hotel, Jl. Kartika Plaza, tel: 751-369, fax: 752-673, www.baliranihotel.com. 104 rooms, including 2 suites, in a 3-story building overlooking a lotus pond or swimming pool. All rooms have AC, balcony, private bath, tv, mini-bar. Lobby inspired by a traditional Balinese water palace. $130–240.

Discovery Kartika Plaza, Jl. Kartika Plaza, tel: 751-067, fax: 752-476, 754-585, www.discoverykartika-plaza.com. Room blocks, suites, and beachside villas with complete facilities. Awarded the prestigious Green Globe Benchmarked Silver status for operating according to the world's highest environmental standards. $220–1,000.

Holiday Inn Resort Baruna Bali, Jl. Wana Segara 33, Tuban, tel: 755-577, fax: 754-549. www.bali.holiday-inn.com. Guest rooms, suites and executive club level in line with Holiday Inn international standards. Palm Restaurant, Envy Restaurant, Chill Out Bar &

Restaurant beachfront. Health & fitness center renovated 2009. Rascals kids' club. Tea Tree Spa offers kids' and family spa treatments. $119–284.

Kupu Kupu Barong Beach Hotel, Jl. Wana Segara, tel: 753-780, fax: 753-781, www.kupubarongbeach.com. Sister to Kupu Kupu Barong Villas & Tree Spa in Ubud. 10 suites, 4 with private plunge pool, 2 with dining room, living room, and pantry. MaJoly Restaurant. Sunset Bar faces the Indian Ocean. $202–318.

Kuta Paradiso Hotel, Jl. Kartika Plaza, tel: 761-414, fax: 756-944, www.kutaparadisohotel.com. A luxury 5-star resort with 243 deluxe and superior rooms and suites arranged in 2 wings leading off the lobby. All rooms overlook the ocean and hotel's landscaped gardens. Bars, restaurants, bakery. $120–210.

Ramada Bintang Bali Resort, Jl. Kartika Plaza, tel: 753-292, fax: 753-288, www.bintang-bali-hotel.com. Rooms, suites, residences. Kids' playground, pool with cascading waterfalls and Jacuzzi, kids' club, restaurant inspired by Dutch colonial fine dining. Theta Spa (www.thetaspa.com) serves champagne on request. $140–1,400.

Risata Bali Resort & Spa, Jl. Wana Segara, tel: 753-340, fax: 753-354, www.risatabali.com. Rooms, suites and villas featuring modern home comforts and private balcony or terrace. Flat screen tv. Large swimming pool, kids' playground, pool table, gym. Wood-fired oven pizzas and Pandan Bali Restaurant. Sukha Spa. $154–183.

Santika Beach, Jl. Kartika Plaza, tel: 751-267, fax: 750-260, www.santikabali.com. 164 rooms, suites, and private bungalows. Swimming pools, tennis courts. 2-bedroom family units face a children's playground. Suite complex has private pool. $160–430.

The Vira Bali Hotel, Jl. Kartika Plaza No. 127, tel: 765-700, fax: 765-800, www.thevirabali.com. A chic 4-story, 4-star hotel with 56 rooms and suites. Contemporary minimalist design, Balinese hospitality, central and cozy. Swimming pool with waterfall and fountains, enhancing the hotel's tranquil atmosphere. $145–210.

DINING

American

Bubba Gump Shrimp Co., Jl. Kartika Plaza No. 8X, tel: 754-028, www.bubbagump.com. American chain restaurant decorated with paraphernalia from the movie *Forest Gump*. If you've seen the movie then you know it's all about shrimp. Dynamite Shrimp is popcorn shrimp with a spicy Thai-style glaze. Shrimper's Heaven is a multitude of different forms of shrimp. Casual. Excellent desserts and good drinks.

Chinese

Golden Lotus, Bali Dynasty Hotel, Jl. Kartika Plaza, tel: 752-403. Specializes in Cantonese and Sichuan cuisines, in particular Peking duck. Authentic dim sum lunch. Ornate décor reminiscent of a stylish Hong Kong restaurant. Private rooms. Everything on the menu is delicious. Surely one of the top five Chinese restaurants on Bali. Open for lunch and dinner seven days a week.

The Mandarin, at the Bali Rani Hotel, Jl. Kartika Plaza. Traditional Chinese cuisine—Cantonese, Szechwan, and seafood—at moderate prices. Open at lunch and dinner. Live music.

French & international

MaJoly, Kupu Kupu Barong Beach Hotel, Jl. Wana Segara, Tuban, tel: 753-780, fax: 753-781, www.ma-joly.com. French and international fine dining beachside with great wines and excellent service. Also serves fresh fish from Jimbaran. Sunset Bar serves fresh fruit juices, cocktails, and cappuccino.

Irish

Gracie Kelly's Irish Pub, Bali Dynasty Resort, Jl. Kartika Plaza, tel: 752-403. An Irish pub open for lunch and dinner. Friendly staff, warm atmosphere, an open brick fireplace. Typical home-cooked pub favorites (like in the old country) including fresh baked bread, Irish Stew, and a classic fish and chips. Pool tables, darts, karaoke, and jukebox. Live band every night.

Japanese

Blue Fin, Jl. Kartika Plaza 16, tel: 763-100. Japanese fusion cuisine. Recommended by local expats.

Pub food

Stadium Café, Jl. Kartika Plaza, Complex Kuta Sidewalk 5–8, tel: 764-100, fax: 763-200. Inexpensive food favored by—as the name suggests—the sports crowd, who flock here for live telecasts of international events. In addition to cold beer, recommended are nachos, pasta, and pub fare.

Thai

Kin Khao, Jl. Kartika Plaza 170, tel: 753-806. Authentic Thai food since 1994 ranging from *tom yum* soup to *khao neow mannuang* (sticky rice with mango). Homemade sauce has no msg added. Curry pastes, tea, and coffee imported from Thailand.

NIGHTLIFE

BuGils Bali, Jl. Dewi Sartika (Jl. Kartika Plaza), No. 1BB (opposite Harris Hotel Tuban, 300m from the airport), tel: 758-322, www.bugilsbali.com. By the same owners of BuGils, Cazbar, Eastern Promise, One Tree, and De HOOI in Jakarta, BuGils Bali is a combination of the best features of their Jakarta bars, including a professional all-female staff, lots of wood

and very cold beer, plus a relaxed holiday atmosphere. They suggest that if your flight is delayed, this is to place to wait it out. The local expats say it's a good spot to be in late at night.

Envy, at the Holiday Inn Resort Baruna Bali, Jl. Wana Segara 33, tel: 752-527, fax: 754-549, www.envy-bali.com. Divine pastas, calzones, and pizzas, steaks and seafood grills. Open lunch and dinner. At sunset, Envy is packed with the sundowner crowd, which goes on into the night. Entertainment ranges from the Balinese *kecak* dance to percussions.

Ocean's 27 Restaurant, Beach Club & Grill, Discovery Esplanade (Beachfront), Jl. Kartika Plaza, tel: 765-027, fax: 755-522, www.oceans27.net. One of the new beach clubs that has recently appeared on the scene, it's a place to loll around the pool or on the beach with food and drinks close at hand. Ocean's 27 Grill on the beach serves lunch and dinner daily. At sunset, the DJs begin to welcome the end of another day. Beach parties with live music attract clubbers by the hundreds. Open 11 am until late.

SHOPPING

Fabrics

Talimas, Jl. Raya 83 E, tel: 763-863. A textile wholesale and retail gallery offering a wide variety of woven, knitted, printed and dyed fabrics. A computer is available if you want to create your own designs.

Mall

Discovery Mall, Jl. Kartika Plaza, tel: 755-522, fax: 767-300, www.discoveryshoppingmall.com. This massive shopping mall is right on the beach—for better or for worse—squeezed in between 5-star resorts. Includes 2 large department stores (Centro and Sogo) and 98 shops, from Crocs to Nike. In the basement is a large handicrafts market. 19 food outlets. "Movie under the Moonlight" in the beachfront amphitheater every Saturday, 8 pm–midnight. Open Monday–Thursday 10 am–9 pm, Friday–Saturday 10 am–10 pm, Sunday 11 am–8 pm.

ACTIVITIES

Waterbom, Jl. Kartika, tel: 755-676, fax: 753-517, www.waterbom-bali.com. Great for the whole family—17 exhilarating slides, Pleasure Pool for swimming and volleyball, Jungle River relaxing float. supervised kids' area, Splash Bar, food court, massage. They're always adding something new to this ever-popular park, keeping the wet and wild endlessly entertained for 19 years. Open daily 9 am–6 pm, US$26/adult; $16/child (2–12 yrs). 2-day passes $31/adult; $17.50/kid.

LEGIAN, SEMINYAK, PETITENGET, AND KEROBOKAN

Trendy Beach Areas North of Kuta

Visitors will be forgiven if they are unable to determine where one village stops and another begins along the 5-kilometer stretch of beach that is often erroneously called "Kuta". There are no markers differentiating one from another, yet each has its own distinguishing characteristics; and less obvious is that each is governed by a different set of village leaders who attend to rituals, festivals, ceremonies, and tourism.

North of Kuta, Legian is slightly quieter than the central beach at Kuta, and it is difficult to tell where Kuta ends and Legian begins. However, north of Legian, Seminyak, Petitenget, and Kerobokan have decidedly different auras. Developing later than Kuta and Legian, these villages opted to appeal to higher-end travelers and those seeking a bit more peace and quiet.

Legian

As with Tuban, south of Kuta, Legian blossomed into action to cash in on Kuta's fame in the 1970s. At its southern boundary it begins just north of Jl. Melasti and in the north merges into Seminyak at Jl. Arjuna. Legian has historically attracted a slightly older crowd than Kuta's and for many years, expatriates on a budget who weren't into the beach scene at Kuta lived and gathered here. Many of those resident foreigners have now moved their homes and social lives elsewhere, but Legian remains a good location for kid-friendly, medium-priced accommodations, several bars that are not quite as frenzied as Kuta's and, of course, glorious beach life. The exception to this more sedate reputation is a gaggle of bars off Jl. Arjuna (formerly called Jl. Double-Six) on the beach, which are known to party hard until the wee hours.

Life in Legian revolves around the beach, and there's not a lot else to see here. **Surfing lessons** can be arranged from one of the reputable schools, or surfboards and boogie boards rented on the beach. On the northern stretch of sand south of Jl. Arjuna there are

Sunset on Legian Beach, where surfboards and body boards can easily be rented

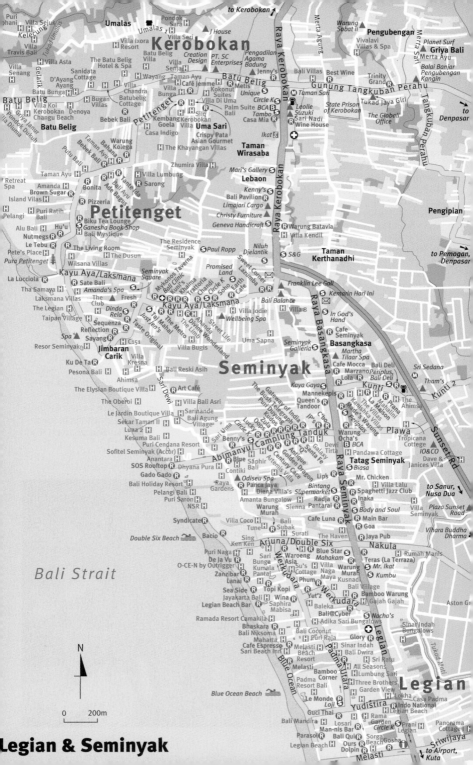

friendly **football games** every late afternoon, with both locals and visitors joining in the mayhem. On Saturday and Sunday evenings crowds gather here for jam sessions and everyone is invited to exhibit their talents. Some folks prefer to take the sidelines and enjoy both happenings at one of the beachfront cafes with a yummy fruit juice, cocktail, or an ice cold beer and a snack.

The only other pastime in Legian is **shopping**. From Jl. Arjuna in the north to Jl. Melasti at the southern boundary, all the side streets running perpendicular to the sea are filled with kiosks selling items Bali has always been known for: souvenirs, handicrafts, sarongs, and sportswear. An **art market** on Jl. Melasti near the beach will happily take any leftover shopping money.

A bit more exciting, however, is Jl. Legian from Jl. Padma as far north as weary feet can take shoppers. It has already happened in Ubud, and now it's happening here: shops filled with cheap trinkets and poor quality T-shirts are gradually being replaced by quality items that are practically irresistible even to the most nonchalant of buyers. As with accommodations and restaurants, further north toward Seminyak is where the more exclusive shops are, but in Legian there is a large enough variety to make a day out of it, or maybe even two. Look for **jewelry stores** showcasing gemstones, intricate designs, and the superb craftsmanship that Bali has

become known for internationally. Many of the garment businesses that formerly made clothing here but exported all of it abroad have at last set up boutiques in Bali, eliminating the markup that customers would pay in stores abroad. By the Sea has designs that are ideal for wearing on the beach while on holiday as well as for summer wear back home. **Interiors shops** have also sprung up along Jl. Legian featuring tableware, lamps, and other top-end accessories at much more affordable prices than in Western countries. The bonus is these boutiques are air-conditioned.

Seminyak

Expensive boutiques, spas, villas, restaurants, and nightspots proliferate in Seminyak. Inhabited almost completely by expatriates— a good many of whom either own export businesses or seem to do nothing at all— Seminyak and points north are the high end of the beach strip. Seminyak's southern boundary is Jl. Arjuna (formerly called Jl. Double Six), which becomes Jl. Nakula east off Jl. Raya Seminyak. Jl. Arjuna also divides some of the beaches' hippest nightspots, leaving the legendary, recently closed, Double Six Club—which gave the jam-packed, impossible-to-pass little street its former name— and its newer neighbor **Bacio** on the Seminyak side of the border and its sister and brother party-goers, **De Ja Vu** and **Zanzibar**, on the northern end of Legian.

Seminyak clubs rock until dawn.

Double Six beach in Seminyak at sunset

The beat goes on until the early hours and can even end with a bungee jump for those in the mood. If the choices are too many to coax a decision, simply stroll up **Jl. Laksmana** until something catches your fancy.

Petitenget

Actually an extension of the Seminyak beachside lifestyle, until fairly recently Petitenget was happy to be known as part of its southern wealthy neighbor, until village chiefs wisely decided that the village could establish a unique reputation of its own. With the dividing line between Seminyak and Petitenget being a major street filled with all sorts of tourist temptations — Jl. Laksmana — addresses are often listed in Seminyak when they are actually located in Petitenget. Which village is which actually makes no difference to visitors: just be aware that there might be confusion locating one area or the other near their boundaries.

The only cultural landmark in **Petitenget** is **Pura Petitenget**. Built in the 16th century, this temple was completed when the area was covered by dense jungle of a different type than the urban one of today, in honor of the Javanese priest Danghyang Nirartha, who constructed Tanah Lot further up the coast. There is a large parking lot where the trees once stood, serviced by men of the local community. It's wise to park here and walk down — or up — the beach to avoid Seminyak's horrendous traffic congestion.

The exclusive Seminyak beach's northern boundary can be confusing. Technically, at Jl. Kayu Jati and eastward in a zigzag fashion toward Jl. Raya Kerobokan (north of Jl. Laksmana), it becomes Petitenget and Kerobokan. Until fairly recently, few people knew or cared where the dividing lines were; however, now that Petitenget and Kerobokan are developing at lightening pace, the new establishments to the north are using the correct district names, while the old ones elsewhere still call the entire area "Seminyak".

Heavy duty, shop-'til-you-drop, your feet wear out, or your wallet is empty (or your credit card is maxed out) is the name of the game in Seminyak when the sun is too hot beachside to breathe. The day can be broken up with stops for a cappuccino, lunch, and high tea at any of a number of fancy cafes and restaurants, or a spa treatment or two before heading back toward the sea for a sundowner at the end of the day. When the sun has disappeared behind the horizon, then it's time to go back to the villa or five-star resort — there are no budget accommodations here — to freshen up for the evening's outings and activities.

Nighttime in Seminyak begins with scrumptious dining in whatever cuisine suits your fancy followed by after-dinner liqueurs, coffee, and perhaps a cigar while waiting for party time to begin. After 10 pm, many of the elegant restaurants let down their hair, and like the Pied Piper the DJs draw in the crowds with every sort of music, from R&B to punk.

Kerobokan

Without the Indian Ocean at its borders to lure visitors, inland **Kerobokan** is developing itself based on rice field views and serenity away from the noise and hubbub of the southern beaches. It is near enough to get to the shopping and nightlife, but the setting is rural. As with Petitenget and Seminyak, it is difficult for casual visitors to discern where one ends and the other begins, but if trying to locate an address, be aware that if you are driving through the countryside, there's a pretty good chance that you're in Kerobokan.

There are too many private villas in Kerobokan to count, and development has only just gotten started. Some villas are for rent, and most come with a cook and gardener and car and driver. Online research to find a rental agent, or word of mouth recommendations, are the best way of finding the perfect slice of heaven.

—*Linda Hoffman*

VISITING LEGIAN
(TELEPHONE CODE: 0361)

Legian is Kuta beach's a-bit-more-affluent sister to the north, beginning at Jl. Arjuna (formerly Jl. Double Six) as its northern point of demarcation to Jl. Melasti in the south, where Kuta begins. This area attracts those who want to have fun in Kuta, but prefer to sleep somewhere that's a little bit quieter.

See map, page 85.

ACCOMMODATIONS
Moderate ($25–50)
Bali Subak Hotel, Jl. Arjuna (Jl. Double Six), Legian, tel: /fax: 730-901. Standard and superior suites serving guests for over 10 years, constantly upgrading property and service. Swimming pool, restaurant, room service. From $42.

Sari Bunga Hotel, Jl. Arjuna (Jl. Double Six), Legian, www.balivillagehotel.com. 30 traditional style rooms and suites with queen-sized beds, AC and ceiling fan, tv, fridge, hot water, all with verandah or balcony overlooking pool and pool bar. Open-air restaurant serves Asian and European cuisine. $40.

Three Brothers Bungalows, down a small lane off Jl. Raya Legian Tengah, tel: 751-566, fax: 756-082, www.threebrothersbungalows.com. Bohemian-style, clean, surrounded by tropical gardens. Living room and semi-open baths on the ground floor and AC bedrooms on top floor, all with tv, fridge. Hot water. Large swimming pool and kids' pool. Restaurant and bar. Spa. $29–49.

Tune Hotels Legian, Jl. Arjuna (Jl. Double Six), Gang Villa Coco, www.tunehotels.com. 170 budget rooms with AC, WiFi, elevator, restaurant, hotel/airport transfer, spa. Internet rates as low as $28.

Intermediate ($50–75)
Hotel Kumala Pantai, Jl. Werkudara, tel: 755-500, fax: 755-700, www.kumalapantai.com. Rooms, suites, and a presidential suite in 3-story blocks designed in Balinese style around a garden filled with old trees and statues depicting Balinese culture. Olympic-sized pool, restaurant, and bar with mild jazz and contemporary music. Occasional dance and music performances, BBQs, and buffets. $80–265.

Legian Paradiso Hotel, Jl. Raya Legian No. 118, tel: 752-167, fax: 754-372, www.legianparadiso.com. 124 rooms in a Mediterranean-style building arranged around a central pool and gardens. $55–150.

Luxury ($100–up)
Legian Beach Resort, Jl. Melasti, tel: 751-711, fax: 752-651, www.legianbeachbali.com. Recently refurbished relaxing tropical thatched bungalow complex with hotel block facing the beach. 118 single-story cottages and 100 guest rooms, including 23 family rooms and 5 rooms catering to disabled travelers. Bale Banjar Restaurant, Iais Restaurant, Gino's Pasta & Pizza Corner. Ole Ocean View Patio beside the pool has great views and upbeat music. $174–525.

O-CE-N Bali by Outrigger, Jl. Arjuna No. 88X, Legian, tel: 737-400, fax: 737-408, www.outrigger.com. An "interesting" exterior of contemporary glass and metal seems odd in Bali but will appeal to some. 5 levels of AC rooms, 1-, 2- and 3-bedroom suites —some with kitchenettes—and villas; split-level penthouse suites with Jacuzzi on top floor. 2 pools, full service spa, free WiFi. Beachfront fine dining restaurant, seafood bistro, tapas bar. $198–416.

Padma Resort Bali, Jl. Padma No. 1, Legian, tel: 752-111, fax: 752 140, www.padmaresortbali.com. Newly renovated rooms, suites and chalets in a 5-star resort on 6.8 ha of gardens. Kids' club, games center, 5 restaurants, 3 bars, gym, sauna, steam room, spa. Free WiFi. $189–379.

Ramada Resort Camakila Legian, Jl. Padma No. 1, Legian, tel: 752-111, fax: 752-140, www.ramadaresortcamakila.com. 4 floors beachfront with 117 deluxe rooms and suites with a choice of views and private balcony. Azaa Restaurant, Salila Spa. $133.

DINING
Most of Legian's restaurants are found in hotels, but there are a few good independent establishments.

International
Indo-National, Jl. Padma 17, Legian, tel: 759-883, www.indonationalrestaurant.com. Owned by an Australian couple, long-time Bali residents. Good Western and Indonesian food and ice cold beers.

Lanai, Jl. Pantai Blue Ocean (at the end of Jl. Arjuna), tel: 731-305. Great views of the sea from terrace or beach seating. International and Asian dishes come in large portions. Open for lunch, dinner, and snacks in between.

Yut'z Place, Jl. Werkudara 521, tel: 765-047. Open all day, beginning with hardy breakfasts and serving generous portions of an unusual selection of European dishes, cold plates, appetizers, and Indonesian food, all at reasonable prices.

Italian
Teras (La Terrazza), Jl. Raya Legian 494, tel: 730-492. A rooftop restaurant with superb views of Legian at night. Imported grilled meat, wood-fired pizza,

and homemade pasta, and a wide assortment of alcoholic and soft drinks has made the Teras a favorite among old Bali hands for years. Lunch menu features light or full meals and snacks.

NIGHTLIFE

Legian flows into Seminyak at Jl. Arjuna (Jl. Double Six), with some of the hottest nightspots on the beach on both sides of the road. The Legian and Seminyak crowd tend to start the ball rolling with sundowners on the beach at **Benny's, Blue Ocean,** or **Zanzibar** at the bottom of Jl. Arjuna (Jl. Double Six), followed by dinner and further frivolity at nightspots on lively Jl. Abimanyu (Jl. Dhyanapura) in Seminyak.

Blue Ocean Bali, Beach Restaurant & Terrace, Jl. Pantai Arjuna (Jl. Double Six), tel: 747-2308, www. blueoceanbali.com. Opened in 1969, a favorite haunt for travelers from all over the world; specializes in fresh seafood at reasonable prices. Terrace has ocean views, with spectacular sunsets while enjoying coolers and cocktails. Free high-speed internet, backgammon boards, comfortable lounge. Every Friday presents some of the best bands on Bali. Shower available to wash off the sand.

De Ja Vu, Jl. Blue Ocean Beach/Arjuna 7 X, tel: 732-777. A spacious venue down from Benny's Café beach area next to O-CE-N. Comfortable lounge bar, comfy sofas and stools, impromptu parties, and some of the best cocktails and DJs on Bali every day of the week. Popular from about midnight 'til 3 am, when the all-nighters move on.

Red Square Bali, at Hotel Pullman Legian Nirwana, Jl. Pantai Legian, tel: 767-540, fax: 767-541, www. redsquarebali.com. Opened in 2009 after success in Jakarta, the Russian-themed vodka bar has award-winning vodka cocktails, Russian fusion cuisine, party lounge, DJ driven disco, new wave retro, and euro lounge chill-out music. Flair Show Bar features midnight shows daily. Caters to the cosmopolitan

and affluent. Open for lunch at 11 am, happy hours 4–9 pm, dinner 5 pm–midnight.

Zanzibar Beach Side Restaurant & Lounge, Jl. Arjuna (Jl. Double Six), tel: 733-529, www. zanzibarbali.com. On Double Six Beach, serves Mediterranean dishes and seafood as well as breakfast, lunch, daily finger food buffet and special drinks list, dinner. Semi-open with outside tables. A lively spot at night.

SHOPPING

Legian is not about shopping; it's about the beach and nightlife. However, there is an **Uluwatu** cut-lace women's wear boutique at Jl. Pengabetan, tel: 751-933, as well as other outlets in Kuta and Ubud. And of course there are **Rip Curl** surf gear and beachwear shops everywhere, including Legian.

The best for one-stop shopping are the **Matahari stores** with their huge selection of department store-type goods. There is one on Jl. Legian, in Legian Plaza. Their supermarket is a good source of snacks, dry goods, and processed foods.

There's a **Body & Soul Factory Outlet** at Jl. Raya Legian No. 386, tel: 754-412 www. bodyandsoulclothing.com, next door to their Legian store. They stock trendy fashion lycra pants, shirts, and bright prints that aim at the younger market. The factory outlet receives overruns of designs from export orders and incomplete styles from their main stores; also slightly damaged or discontinued items. Look for good bargains here.

Indigo Kids, Jl. Melasti, www.indigokidsglobal. com has 6 stores in Kuta, Legian, Seminyak, and Nusa Dua selling a great collection of children's wear and accessories for kids aged 3 mos. to 12 yrs. Established in 1983, it also sells wholesale. Specializes in fine handcrafted details. Australian designs manufactured throughout Indonesia. Reliable quality, affordable prices.

VISITING SEMINYAK, PETITENGET, & KEROBOKAN
(TELEPHONE CODE: 0361)

Seminyak is five-star luxury, nothing less will do, and is also home of some of the most vibrant, glittery nightlife in southern Bali. Petitinget and Kerobokan are in many ways more laid-back versions of their neighbors to the south; they are a bit quieter, less crowded and more suitable for longer stays. Get ready to shop to the point of exhaustion here. There are too many choices, and many are irresistible.

See map, page 85.

ACCOMMODATIONS

Although the resorts and villas in this area range from expensive to mega-expensive, check for Internet rates, making some of them a teeny bit more affordable, especially in the low season. Also look for packages that include spa treatments for better rates.

Luxury ($125–up)

Anantara Seminyak Resort & Spa, Jl. Abimanyu (Jl. Dhyanapura), Seminyak, tel: 737-7773, fax 737-772, www.bali.anatara.com. 59 suites with plasma screen tvs, contemporary Asian-inspired furniture, broadband Internet connection. Wild Orchid Restaurant, spa, 2 infinity-edge pools. $450–500; the Penthouse $2,900.

Oberoi Bali, Jl. Kayu Aya (Jl. Laksmana), Seminyak, tel: 730-361, fax: 730-791, www.oberoihotels.com. 74 cottages and villas, tucked between 6 ha of tropical gardens and the sea at the northern end of Seminyak beach. Traditional Balinese thatched-roof style villas have private pools, garden bathrooms, tv, DVD players; iPod in Luxury Villas. Pool faces the sea. Restaurants, bar, amphitheater, spa, and fitness center, WiFi. From $295.

Silq, Jl. Petitenget 27C, Petitenget, tel: 847-5461, fax: 847-5459, www.silqkerobokanbali.com. Luxury boutique hotel containing 17 private residences, each with Jacuzzi, infinity-edged pool, Villeroy & Boch bathrooms, flat-screen tvs, and teakwood 4-poster beds. Butler service. Spa. $500–2,000.

The Elysian Boutique Villa Hotel, Jl. Sari Dewi 18, Seminyak, tel: 730-999, fax: 737 509, www.theelysian. com. Recommended by Hip Hotels. Private villas each with a pool, super-sized bed, sunken bath, Apple tv system, iPods and Bose SoundDocks©, DVDs. Laptops available to all guests with resort-wide WiFi. Spa, gym, restaurant, bar, swimming pool. $320–600.

The Haven, Jl. Raya Seminyak No. 500, Seminyak, tel: 738-001. www.thehavenbali.com. 1- and 2-bedroom suites in earthy minimalist style overlooking 3 swimming pools. Also hotel and 7 villas, all with LCD flat screen tv, broadband, cable Internet service. Sabeen Restaurant serves organic ingredients, salad bar, pan-Asian, and international favorites. Spa. $150–625.

The Legian, Jl. Kayu Aya (Jl. Laksmana), Seminyak, tel: 730-622, fax: 730-623, www.ghmhotels.com. An all-suite hotel, 67 studio, 1- and 2-bedroom ocean-view units on private, quiet stretch of beach. Blu-ray disc player, tv, iPod, entertainment system, espresso machine, well-stocked pantry. The Restaurant on the ocean's edge. The Spa. Gym. Also **The Club at The Legian**, 11 private villas with pools and butler service and access to all The Legian facilities. The Club Lounge. From $578–1,748.

The Royal Beach Seminyak Bali, Jl. Camplung Tanduk (Jl. Abimanyu/Jl. Dhyanapura), Seminyak, tel: 730-730, fax: 730-545, www.theroyalbeachseminyakbali. com. 128 rooms on 4.5 ha of gardens, 2 pools, and 17 spa villas with private pool or Jacuzzi. Ballroom. Fitness center recently expanded and a new lounge added on the 3rd floor with reading area, Internet corner, tv, and games. Snack bar and drinks for guests. Cigar Terrace. From $200.

Villas

C151 Smart Villas, Jl. Laksmana No.151, Seminyak, tel: 739-151, fax: 737-258, www.c151.net. "An exclusive and intimate setting for guests seeking privacy and luxury in the center of all things uber cool." 1-, 2- and 3 bedroom villas, club villa, and presidential villa with plasma tv and DVD player. Bathrooms equipped with iSpa Jacuzzi with overhead tv, remote-controlled curtains, full AC. Kitchen with oven, grill, side-by-side fridge-freezer with ice maker. Finest china. Spa, private yoga sessions. $700–5,000.

Island Villas & Spa Bali, Jl. Raya Petitenget No. 469, Petitenget, tel: 736-487, fax: 736-658, www. islandvillasbali.com. 10 luxury 1-bedroom villas, each individually decorated with aesthetic design, include gourmet kitchen, dining and lounge area, sunken tub for two. Private pool and sundeck, rooftop terrace. Butler service, gym. Island Café or candlelight dinner or BBQ at your villa. Taman Merah Spa (www.tamanmerah.com). From $310.

Kanishka Villas, Jl. Kunti 8Y, Seminyak, tel: 733-870, fax: 738-144, www.kanishkavillas.com. 15 luxury pool villas down a quiet lane with tub, shower, Jim Thompson fabrics. Private pool, fully equipped kitchen, open dining, sundeck, tv, DVD, sound system, and high speed Internet. Butler and in-villa food and beverage service. Malkoha Spa. $450–600.

Sienna Villas, Jl. Raya Seminyak, Gang Keraton No. 5, tel: 734-698, fax: 732-585, www.sienna-villas.com. 3- and 4-bedroom villas, 2 with private pools and some in Mediterranean style on 2 levels with private lap pools. Use the modern kitchen or order from reasonably priced in-house menu. $495–880.

Uma Sapna, Jl. Drupadi No. 20 XX, Basangkasa, Seminyak, tel: 736-628, fax: 736-629, www.coconut homes.com. 20 secluded private villas with plunge or swimming pool. In-house chef can prepare high quality food for guests and their parties. Massage, meditation, wellness. $210–380.

Villa Bali Asri, Jl. Sari Dewi No. 29, Seminyak, tel: 735 444, fax: 737 508, www.villabaliasri.com. 11 private vacation villas on a quiet back road in the heart of Seminyak, in a wooded space surrounded by trees. Gym, spa. $265–1,200.

Villa Coco, Jl. Arjuna (Jl. Double Six), Gang Villa Coco, Seminyak, tel: 730-736, fax: 734-838, www.villacoco. com. Affordable 1- and 2-bedroom villas and pool villas and 4-bedroom luxury villa with private pool. All have private entrance and garden, kitchenette, fan, tv and DVD player, AC bedrooms. In-house catering, pool with pool bar. $160–465.

Villa Jodie, Jl. Laksmana No. 21, Seminyak, tel: 737-262, fax: 737-261, www.villajodie.com. 2- and 3-bedroom villas each with private pool, kitchen, dining and living areas, AC, soundproofed bedrooms,

DVD/CD stereo player, tv. At reception disc library, books, magazines, and tourist information. Private staff serves from your own dining area. $410–860.

DINING

Jl. Laksmana (also called **Jl. Oberoi**) is arguably Bali's trendiest restaurant strip, or "eat street", hosting a mind-boggling array of dining venues. Many of them experience a metamorphosis after dinner and transform into nightspots, where the beautiful people come to see and be seen. No T-shirts and boogie board pants here, please.

Asian

Antique Restaurant & Bar, Jl. Abimanyu Arcade No. 7 (Jl. Dhyanapura), Seminyak, tel: 730-907, fax: 485-501, www.antiquebali.com. Elegant establishment offering Southeast Asian fusion cuisine, a wide range of specialty coffee drinks and after-dinner cocktails. Same owners as Antique Spa, Villa & Gallery in Umalas. Open dinner only 6 pm–midnight, Friday and Saturday until 2 am.

Biku Tea Lounge, Restaurant, Antiques and Bookstore, Jl. Raya Petitenget No 888, Petitenget, tel: 857-0888, www.bikubali.com. Eat, drink, read, lounge, and shop, all in an historic 150-year old traditional teakwood *joglo* from East Java. Includes the **Ganesha Book Shop**. Lounge area with WiFi for reading or relaxing. Try the Asian high tea with scones, jam, fresh whipped cream, finger sandwiches and homemade cakes. Restaurant serves "tropical comfort food".

Crispy Pata Asian Gourmet, Jl. Petitenget No 27C, (near Silq Villas), Petitenget, tel: 847-5461, fax: 847-5459, www.crispypatabali.com. Crispy Pata is a dish from the Philippines, a generous serving of pork leg and trotter, slow simmered in a savory broth, air-dried to cure and deep fried to a crunch. Also serves a varied selection of Asian cuisine, including soups, salads, and other favorites. Open 7 am–11 pm.

Made's Warung II, Jl. Raya Seminyak, Seminyak, tel: 732-130. The second outlet for the ever-popular Made's Warung in Kuta, serves up high-quality Balinese/Indonesian food. Fried shrimp and *nasi campur* (rice, a vegetable, and meat) are signature dishes; outstanding Western food can be had as well. Great American breakfasts.

Belgian

Mannekepis Jazz & Blues Bistro, Jl. Raya Seminyak No. 2, tel: 847-5784; fax: 847-5785, www.mannekepisbistro.com. Belgian bar and bistro serving Belgium beer and other drinks, with jazz and soulful blues. Belgian specialties and international dishes: steak tartar, escargot. Open for lunch and dinner.

Continental

Art Café, Jl. Sari Dewi No. 17, Seminyak, tel: 736-751, www.iloveartcafe.com. Opened in 2009, serves up home-cooked continental and Indonesian meals in a warm atmosphere with adjoining art space. All day breakfast, starters and snacks, main courses, desserts and drinks. Live music 8 'til late, Monday, Wednesday and Friday; Sunday is Kids' Fun Day with arts and crafts from 11 am–2 pm.

Greek

Mykonos Taverna, Jl. Laksmana No. 52, Seminyak, tel: 733-253, www.mykonos-bali.com. A high quality chain that serves traditional authentic Greek cuisine. Renowned for its hearty home-cooked food at reasonable prices, including tangy dips, Greek salad, Gyros and Shoarma pitas and tender shish kebabs. Open 11:30 am–midnight.

Indian

Gateway of India, Jl. Abimanyu (Jl. Dhyanapura) No. 10, Seminyak. tel: 732-940, www.baliindianfood.com. Serves a wide selection of traditional Indian dishes for lunch and dinner. Try their famous lassies, *keema mater* and *kadai* (chicken). Popular with the Indian community.

O'India, Jl. Sunset Barat No. 3, tel: 847-6818. Managed by the Gateway of India chain, shares many of the same dishes, with a variety of traditional Indian dishes from across the subcontinent. Located at the 5-way intersection on Jl. Sunset, perfect for those who don't want to detour into the hectic Seminyak or Kuta traffic. Open air stage; VIP room.

Queen's Tandoor, Jl. Raya Seminyak No. 73 (Gallery Seminyak), Seminyak, tel: 732-770; fax: 732-771, www.queenstandoor.com. Another member of the Gateway of India empire. A 2 story building and a large outdoor patio. Serves classical Indian food from all 4 corners of India. Try their chicken *tikka*, *naan* (butter, herb, or cheese) or 20 different curries. Delivers to south beach area.

International

Café Jemme & Jemme Jewelry, Jl. Raya Petitenget 28, Petitenget, tel: 732-392, www.jemmebali.com. A place to wine, dine, and shop for exquisite jewelry. Good bar, fine dining, wine menu, affordable prices. Most dishes prepared with fresh seasonal vegetables from their own farm near Negara, western Bali. Free WiFi. Open daily 11 am–late.

FINE DINING

Chandi Restaurant, Jl. Laksmana No. 72, Seminyak, reservations tel: 731-060, www.chandibali.com. Pan-Asian cuisine using organic greens and spices from local farmers, imported meats, soy products made in Bali. Espresso Bar, some of Bali's wildest cocktails. Kitchen open noon–midnight, bar noon 'til late. Valet parking daily 6 pm–midnight.

Ku de Ta, Jl. Kayu Aya (Jl. Laksmana) No. 9, Seminyak, tel: 736-969, www.kudeta.net. Ocean-front venue, ultra-modern and elegant ambience, seductive music. Caters to the "beautiful people". Famous for not only its Australian-style cuisine but cocktails; the in-place for after dinner drinks. You may feel out of place if you don't dress smartly. Packed every night, dinner reservations essential. Lunch specials change daily and are easier on the pocketbook.

Lola Restaurant, Jl. Raya Kerobokan 58, Kerobokan, tel: 738-570, fax. 738-566, www.lolarest.tripod.com. French haute cuisine in an atmosphere of chic elegance. Minimalist style with art by Indonesian painter Krisyono. Genuine escargot, *foie gras*, and mouthwatering desserts, beautifully-presented. Open for lunch Monday–Saturday noon, open for dinner daily 6:30–11:30 pm.

Metis, Jl. Petitenget No. 6, Petitenget, tel: 737-888, fax: 847-5472, www.metisbali.com. Spirited haute cuisine Chef Nicolas "Doudou" Tourneville, formerly of all-time favorite Kafe Warisan, presents French-Mediterranean cuisine, personal attention, and flawless service. Reservations recommended for dinner. Gallery and boutique with contemporary fashions, hand-crafted jewelry, and unusual *objet d'art*. Also open for lunch with a lighter menu. Thursday jazz night in the lounge; Friday and Saturday, house and guest DJs.

Nutmegs, Jl. Petitenget, Petitenget, tel: 736-443, www.nutmegs-restaurant.com. Oddly enough, a culinary haven with candlelight in the hottest playground on the beach. Chef Philip Mimbimi says: "Every plate from the very first dish out of the kitchen has to be better than the last one." Lunches range from sandwiches and salads to Indonesian fare. Open 11:30 am–11:45 pm.

La Lucciola, Jl. Kayu Aya, at end of Jl. Laksmana, Seminyak, tel: 730-838. With its beach lounges and good service, this is a favorite spot for sunset cocktails. Indoor-outdoor seating right on the beach, delicious Italian and contemporary food. Friendly staff. Scrumptious Sunday brunch. Reservations recommended.

Sarong Restaurant & Bar, Jl. Petitenget No. 19X, Petitenget, reservations tel: 737-809, www.sarong-bali.com. Australian owner/chef serves "elegantly Asian" cuisine. Starters include salmon, chicken, or raw tuna with betel leaf and local spices, scallops, oysters, and Wagyu beef. Light dishes and salads.

The Living Room Fine Dining Restaurant & Lounge, Jl. Petitenget No. 2000X, Petitenget, tel: 735-735, fax: 735-736, www.thelivingroom-bali.com. Celebrated

its 10th anniversary in 2010, making it an icon among icons. Fine dining inside and outdoors features Pan-Asian flavors, elaborate flower arrangements, and hundreds of candles at night. Lounge music at the bar on Thursday, Friday, and Saturday, with international DJs attracting an eclectic crowd, 11 pm–3 am.

Japanese

Kuni's Jl. Laksmana, Seminyak tel: 730-501, www.kunisbali.com. A favorite among Japanese travelers, which testifies to its authenticity. Fresh food in subtly lighted, elegant surroundings.

Moroccan

Khaima Moroccan Restaurant, Lounge & Bar, Jl. Laksmana, Seminyak/Petitenget, tel: 742-3925, www.khaimabali.com. In a tent-like structure, a Moroccan restaurant, shisha lounge, bar. Moroccan afternoon teas, Oriental pastries. Open for lunch and dinner, belly dancer every Friday and Saturday 9 pm.

Organic & vegetarian food

Bali Buddha Café, Shop & Home Delivery, Jl. Banjar Anyar 24, Kerobokan, tel: 844-5936, 844-5935, www.balibuddha.com. Other outlets in Ubud and Uluwatu. Vegan, raw food, vegetarian dishes, salads, soups, pasta, chicken or fish burgers, super health drinks, healthy breakfasts, and yummy baked goods.

Earth Café, Jl. Laksmana No. 99, Seminyak, tel: 736-645, mobile: (62) 081-6470-8884, www.downtoearthbali.com. From the Down to Earth Organic Vegetarian Foods kitchen, Earth Café was born in 2006, focusing on working with the universe for healthier life. Supports local farmers and educating the community about the importance of kitchen hygiene and the use of unprocessed products. Gourmet vegetarian cooking classes. Also owns Zula.

Zula, Jl. Dhyanapura (Jl. Abimanyu) No. 5, Seminyak, tel: 732-723. Same owners as Earth Café, billed as totally vegan and features the highest quality ingredients, fresh organic produce, nutritional principles, and love. No MSG, preservatives, sugar, dairy or animal products. Mantra is "we do not use anything with a face or a mother".

NIGHTLIFE

Much of the Seminyak action happens in and around **Jl. Abimanyu,** Bali's party street. With its scores of cocktail bars and cafes, at night it's the busiest street in Seminyak and attracts droves of people, filling every establishment to the maximum until around 2:30 am, when they starting emptying and everyone starts heading to the few places still kicking (e.g., Bacio). Since Seminyak spills over into Legian at Jl. Arjuna (Jl. Double Six), also check Legian

"Practicalities" for more of the hottest nightspots on the beach.

Bacio, Jl. Arjuna (Jl. Double Six), tel: 733-607, www. bacioclub.com. A music, cocktail, wine, and fine gourmet tapas venue. DJ booth, upstairs lounge, catwalk. Caters to sophisticated ladies, expats, locals, and affluent tourists looking for entertainment in a safe, classy atmosphere.

Benny's Bistro, Jl. Dhyanapura/Abimanyu, Seminyak, tel: 732-917. Jam sessions with live salsa music. Good food and infectious rhythms.

Divine Wonderland, Jl. Laksmana opposite Trattoria Pizza, tel: 730-759, www.divinewonderland.com. Opened in 2010, an interesting-looking Melbourne-inspired Victorian, French Baroque, Alice in Wonderland decor with oversized chairs and carved chaise lounges, a piano, and pool table. Tapas served 'til midnight every night. DJs upstairs every weekend. Breakfast, lunch, dinner, and drinks.

Gado-Gado Restaurant & Bar, Jl. Camplung Tanduk (Jl. Dhyanapura/Abimanyu) No. 99, Seminyak, tel: 736-966, fax: 736-955, www.gadogadorestaurant. com. In business since the 1980s, this club's revamped beach lounge features the latest international music, fine dining, respectable wine list, flavorful coffee, inventive cocktails, great atmosphere, and an unbeatable view. Open for lunch and dinner seven days a week.

Hu'u Bali, Jl. Petitenget (Jl. Oberoi), Petitenget, tel: 736-443, www.huubali.com. Another Bali beach institution and a popular hangout for expats and tourists, who chill out on comfortable lounges or dance to the DJ turntable beats. Lychee martinis voted the best on the island. DJ shooter specials. Open 10 am–dawn.

Jaya Pub Bali, Jl. Raya Seminyak No. 2, Seminyak, tel: 735-310. Over 15 years in Bali, follows after its sister club in Jakarta. Cozy dining area serving Western and Indonesian food is separated from huge bar, lounge-loft overlooking the stage. Live bands every night, pool room. Open 5 pm–2 am daily.

Red Carpet Champagne Bar, Jl. Laksmana 42, Seminyak, tel: 737-889. A great little bit of chic in the middle of Seminyak, this over the top glam bar is the closest most people will come to posing for the paparazzi. Guests are escorted to their table, while champagne is the order of the day. It's open to the street, so a great place for people watching.

Santa Fe Bar & Grill, Jl. Abimanyu (Jl. Dhyanapura) No. 11A, Seminyak. Established in 1993 and open 24 hours/day. Wide selection of food and beverages, specializing in Mexican cuisine and pizza. Live band every night.

SOS Rooftop Lounge at Antara Seminyak Resort & Spa, Jl. Abimanyu (Jl. Dhyanapura), Seminyak, tel: 737-7773, fax 737-772. A casual and relaxed place to be at sunset. At night the DJs crank out the music and SOS transforms into a place to see and be seen.

SHOPPING

If you thought Jl. Laksmana was only for eating, watch out shopaholics as you may not be able to restrain yourselves. This listing is just a tease. There are more shops here than we have space for.

Fashions

Animale, Jl. Raya next door to Bintang Supermarket, Seminyak. A stylish ladies clothing store occupying 3 floors, with sizeable collections of bright day, night and beach wear, for the most part coordinating printed separates that appeal to a more mature clientele. Also a range of French imports and plus sizes. Factory outlet at Jl. Raya Kuta No. 82.

Bamboo Blonde, Jl. Laksmana 61, Seminyak, tel: 742-5290, www.tabootrading.com. Funky dresses, sexy shirts, crazy tops, and stunning accessories. Everything a girl wants and needs. Stores also in Kuta, Nusa Dua, Surabaya, and Jakarta.

Biasa, Jl. Raya Seminyak No. 34 & 36, tel: 730-766, 730-799, www.biasabali.com. Displays an excellent range of women's clothes with an emphasis on cool comfort in a variety of whites, pastels, and bright colors using Indian-style cottons and silks. Also men's and children's wear, shoes, bathing suits, and an innovative selection of homewares.

Body & Soul Factory Outlet Seminyak, Jl. Raya Seminyak No. 16C, Seminyak, tel: 733-011, www. bodyandsoulclothing.com. Stores also at Seminyak Square Unit A #7-8, Jl. Laksmana, tel: 736-439, and Jl. Raya Seminyak No. 11, tel: 733-564. In factory outlet, up to 70% discount on discontinued styles and clearance stock. Lycra pants, shirts, and bright prints aimed at the younger market.

C Boutique, Jl. Laksmana 8, www.cboutique.net. Extensive collection if imported swimwear, bags, shoes, jewelry.

Dinda Rella Fashion Boutique, Jl. Laksmana No. 45, Seminyak, tel: 736-953, www.dindarella.com. Also in Legian. Fashions created for women who love quality and glamorous dresses. Also exotic accessories.

Lily-Jean, Jl. Laksmana (next to Soho Diner), tel: 847 5678, www.lily-jean.com. Fashions, bags and shoes.

Milo's Bazaar, Jl. Laksmana No. 38, Seminyak, tel: 735-5551, www.milos-bali.com; also **Milo's at Made's Warung,** Jl. Raya Seminyak, tel: 731-689 and **Milo's Oberoi,** Jl. Laksmana No. 992, Seminyak, tel: 276-3115. One of the original overseas designers to discover the artistry of Balinese batik workers and translate it into Western styling, this boutique stocks a wonderful and tactile range of expensive silks. Also an outlet in Kuta Square.

Nico Perez, Jl. Laksmana No. 117X, Oberoi, Seminyak, tel: 738 308. Designer men's wear.
Paul Ropp, Jl. Laksmana, Seminyak, tel: 734-208, www.paulropp.com. Ethnic fashions using hand-woven materials. Other outlets in Jimbaran, Kerobokan, and Ubud.
Paul's Place, Jl. Laksmana (near Ku De Ta and Oberoi Hotel), tel: 736-910. Contemporary ethnic rayon and cotton clothing, with Asian accents for women 35 and older. Alternative "soft" dressing in sizes from regular to XXXL. Also home furnishings, choice arts, crafts, and artifacts.
Renegade Republic, Jl. Laksmana 69, tel: 276-3115, www.renegaderepublic.net. Hip fashions for men and women.

Children & teens

Dandelion Boutique for Boys and Girls, Jl. Raya Seminyak No 28, tel: 730 375, www.dandelionkid.com. For children ages 3–10 years. Easy to wear, easy care, from tank tops to party dresses.
Indigo Kids, Jl. Seminyak, Seminyak, www.indigokidsglobal.com. Great children's wear for ages 3 months to 12 years. Specializes in fine handicrafted details. Also sells children's accessories. Other stores can be found in Nusa Dua, Kuta, and Legian.
Kiki's Closet, Jl. Raya Seminyak, Seminyak. A trendy range of clothes for boys and girls who want to look grown up. Export quality.

Homewares, interiors & ceramics

DeLighting, Art of Illumination Gallery, Jl. Laksmana 20/14C, tel:/fax: 420-512, www.de-lighting.com. Designers and manufacturers of innovative quality lighting, furniture, and accessories. Also has office, showroom, and factory in Kerobokan.
Haveli, Jl. Raya Seminyak, tel: 737-160, www.havelishop.com. Art de la table, art de vivre, home decoration.
Mien, Jl. Petitenget 198X, Unit 3–4, tel:/fax: 735-964, www.mien-design.com. Antiques, art and accessories. Takes custom orders for villa styling, bed and bath, lamps, rugs, candles, glassware, and silver jewelry. Also in Jakarta.
Piment Rouge, Jl. Sunset 18, www.pimentrouge-lighting.com. Lights and lamps using a myriad of materials as a basis for innovative designs. Other stores in Ubud, Legian, and Kerobokan.
Platform 18/27, Jl. Kayu Aya No. 8A (opposite The Seminyak, between Ku de Ta and The Legian Hotel), tel: 738-746, www.platform.com. Homewares, furniture, tableware, jewelry, art, fashions.
Vinoti Living, Jl. Laksmana, Seminyak Square C 06–07, tel: 732 202, www.vinotiliving.com. Furniture, accessories, and artwork designed for great living.

Jewelry

Jemme Jewelry & Café Jemme, Jl. Raya Petitenget No. 28, Petitenget, tel: 733-508, www.jemmebali.com. Exporting to Europe and Australia for 25 years, opened Bali shop in 2007. Silver, 18K gold and white gold jewelry with semi-precious stones for men and women. Excellently designed and handcrafted in Bali and Java workshops. From $15–50,000. Open Monday–Saturday, 10 am–10 pm.
Jonathon Silver, Jl. Laksmana, Seminyak, tel: 780-2553. Extensive range of well-presented silverware from simple rings to full coffee sets at affordable prices. Also a shop in Kuta.

Souvenirs

Geneva, Jl. Raya Kerobokan No. 100, Banjar Taman, Petitenget. 3 floors of handicrafts from across the island selling in quantity for lower prices. Rattan table-ware, ceramics, incense, wood carvings, local textiles, pillows, stone carvings, furniture. No bargaining.

MARKETS

Bali Deli, Jl. Kunti 117 X, Seminyak, tel: 738-686. This is one stop shopping for the gourmet, from quality imported items and wine to a pet food section and fresh local foodstuffs—it's all here. Also a bakery, deli, and open-air restaurant. Delivery service. Open 8 am–10 pm. LeSpot Restaurant, open 7 am–11 pm.
Bintang Supermarket, Jl. Raya Seminyak, Seminyak, tel: 730-552. Shop in air-conditioned comfort. Wide choice of food, household items, art supplies, even children's toys (upstairs). On the outside is a newsstand and mobile phone vendors.
Circle K convenience stores, open around the clock, carrying essentials at outlets everywhere. If you don't see one, look instead for **Alpha Mart** or **Indomaret** mini-markets.
The Promised Land, Jl. Laksmana No. 99 (behind Earth Café), Seminyak, tel: 736-645, Mobile: (62) 081-6470-8884, www.downtoearthbali.com. Every 2 weeks hosts a market with other producers, suppliers, not-profit organizations, organic growers, healers, and new age crafts. Organic vegetarian food and healthy juices served. Arts and crafts workshops for kids featuring art from nature. Ear candling, tarot reading, flower healing, Reiki. Call for schedules, also for information on Earth Market, its organic supermarket.

SPAS, MASSAGE, YOGA & BEAUTY

There are several options in this category. Most of the larger hotels have their own spas, the majority of which also have a complete salon for hair treatments, facials, waxing, pedicures, and manicures.

AMO Beauty & Spa, Jl. Petitenget 100X, tel: 275-3337, 275-3338, www.amospa.com. A full-service beauty spa on 2 levels. Main floor has music, fashion tv, retail, WiFi. Upstairs are wet rooms, facial and waxing rooms, singles' and couples' massage rooms. Hair salon, manicures, reflexology. Walk-ins welcome.
Body Works, Jl. Kayu Jati, tel: 730-454, runs a very popular and sumptuous spa. Try the various treatments including body scrubs, massages, and cream baths, and a divine hair treatment that includes head, neck, and shoulder massage.
Disini Spa, Jl. Mertasari No. 28, Seminyak, tel: 737-537. www.disinivillas.com. Located within Disini Luxury Spa Villas. Morning, evening, and all-day spa sessions using organic ingredients.
Jari Menari ("Dancing Fingers"), Jl. Raya Basangkasa #47, Seminyak, reservations: 736-740, www.jarimenari.com. Massage menu includes Jari Menari Favorite Massage, Gentle Soul, Tibetan Singing Bowl, Gourmet Massage. Learn Massage every Tuesday. Open 7 days, 9 am–9 pm. Also in Nusa Dua.
Prima Spa at The Villas, Jl. Kunti 118 X (across the street from Bali Deli), tel: 730-840, www.thevillas.net. For something different try the luxurious Moroccan-style spa.
Yoga Shala, Jl. Raya Kerobokan Kelod 10, Banjar Taman, Kerobokan, tel: 735-202, www.bali-yogashala.com. Yoga classes for adults and kids, Hatha yoga, meditation.

ACTIVITIES/ENTERTAINMENT

Cocoon Beach Club & Restaurant, Jl. Arjuna (Jl. Double Six) Beach, Seminyak, tel: 731-266, www.cocoon-beach.com. Opened in 2010, a lá Mediterranean beach clubs, this is a place to hang out all day and play all night. Changing rooms for swimming in pool or sea, fine dining, great chill-out music on the terrace, a grass terrace for kids to play on, boutique carrying resort wear and gifts, amphitheater for events, luggage storage for airport delays, and shuttle to airport.
Horse Riding. Riding along Seminyak Beach at sunset is simply divine.
Umalas Equestrian Resort, Jl. Lestari 9X, Banjar Umalas Kauh, tel: 731-402, fax: 731-403, www.balionhorse.com, is a professional stable and equestrian resort with trainers and lessons. Over 30 horses and ponies; instructors are available for children.

ART GALLERIES

Biasa ArtSpace, Jl. Raya Seminyak No 34, tel: 847-5766, fax 730-766, www.biasaart.com. Founded in 2005, fosters some of the most significant new developments in contemporary Indonesian art, working closely with prominent emerging artists and curators.
Kendra Gallery of Contemporary Art, Jl. Drupadi No. 888, Seminyak, tel: 736-628, www.kendragallery.com. Opened in 2008, highlights both established and young artists from Indonesia, Europe, Asia, and the United States. Lectures, films, workshops, and performances.

MONEY

Be careful of unscrupulous money changers. Avoid anyone who charges a commission, use your own calculator to determine correct amounts, get a receipt, and count your money carefully before leaving. **PT Bali Maspintjinra** across the street from Bintang Supermarket on Jl. Seminyak has been there for many years and is "authorized", trustworthy, and honest.

CANGGU AND TANAH LOT

Gorgeous Beaches and a Famous Temple

Northwest of Petitenget and Kerobokan is a handful of villages collectively called **Canggu** by some, at least for now. As development continues everywhere in southern Bali, the trend is that new establishments are using the correct area names to distinguish themselves. However, more mature settlers still use the old names. In the not-too-distant future, the areas with hitherto unknown labels will be as familiar to travelers as Kuta and Legian are now, as the area continues to evolve. Get there by going north on Jl. Kerobokan (the road to Tanah Lot, which should definitely be avoided at rush hour times) until it becomes Jl. Raya Canggu. Then follow any of the real estate sales signs down little lanes west toward the sea.

The pounding waves along this coast originally attracted surfers and there are a few homestays, *warungs,* and board repair kiosks still here. The big shock, though, is the amount of construction equipment traveling up and down along the narrow country roads. Hotels and villas—some of which can best be described as mansions—are popping up everywhere on beaches named **Berawa, Canggu (Batu Bolong)**, **Echo (Batu Mejan)**, **Pererenan** and **Selasih**, stretching all the way from Kerobokan and Petitenget to the Tabanan Regency border northwest of Tanah Lot. Where there are tourists, there will soon be eateries, bars, and shopping, but for now rice fields still dominate much of the land.

Off the main road, small lanes lead to the various beaches. **Jl. Pantai Berawa** (also spelled Brawa), the road to Berawa Beach, is lined with rice fields—with enormous villas on the horizon—and is the location of the

The beaches west of Seminyak and Kerobokan near Canggu are quite deserted and good for surfing.

Pura Tanah Lot (Temple of the Land in the Sea) is one of Bali's most famous sights.

Canggu Club, a cricket club of sorts with swimming pool and spa. Day passes are available. Foreigners riding bicycles and motorbikes equipped with surfboard racks abound, as do construction sites. At the end of the road there is a *warung* offering surfing lessons, gear, board repair, and pizza in its garden café near **Legong Keraton Beach Hotel**—right on the beach—which undoubtedly attracts the new generation of more affluent surfers than those who stayed in cheap *losmen* in the past. Berawa Beach vendors gather here to sell sarongs and souvenirs to tourists.

There are not many villas yet along Jl. Pantai Batu Bolong (also called Jl. Canggu Beach) but there is a large parking area, as this beach has been attracting intermediate and experienced surfers for several years with its lefts, rights, sand bars, and reef breaks. Next to that is the long-established **Hotel Tugu Bali**. Filled with antiques and art, it is part museum, part art gallery, all packaged under the humble title "hotel".

Returning to the main street, Jl. Raya Canggu, the next small road to the sea leads to Echo Beach, also known as Pantai Batu Mejan. It is possibly the fastest growing development, with wall-to-wall private villas and more waiting for the contractors to get to them. Echo Beach has already earned a reputation for being a "happening" place. On Sunday afternoons the beach turns into a mini-Wood-stock with music and frivolity.

Down another small, badly broken asphalt road to the sea—Jl. Melayan—is **Canggu Tua** (Old Canggu), which still has glimpses of what the region must have been like before the foreigners with money started moving in. Further near the ocean, though, some of the most enormous villas yet loom where rice fields used to be, fronted by expensive cars and hoards of household staffs.

For a different look at the beaches, **Umalas Equestrian Resort**, Jl. Lestari 9X, in nearby Ulamas, offers horseback riding packages that include a two-hour ride on the beach and lunch at the resort.

A temple in the sea

All old Balinese realms have a mountain-to-the-sea axis, an ordering of the physical land-scape that mirrors the ordering of the cosmos, with major points marked by temples. Each former Balinese kingdom thus has six major temples, the *sad kahyangan*, consecrated to the six most significant features of the landscape: the forest, the mountains, the sea, the lakes, the earth, and the rice fields. Similarly, there are six cardinal temples for the whole of Bali. **Pura Tanah Lot** seaside sanctuary is one of them.

Continuing northwest on the crowded road leading to the Canggu beaches, at Baraban village there are good signs indicating the turnoff to majestic Pura Tanah Lot seaside temple. *Tanah* means earth and *lot* means south or sea (usually written *lod*), or "Temple of the Earth in the Sea". It is actually constructed atop a large, jagged outcropping of rock just off the coast and is accessible by footpath only during low tide. The temple itself is quite modest, consisting of two shrines with tiered roofs (seven and three), a few small buildings, and two pavilions.

Like so many other temples on Bali, Tanah Lot is connected with the Majapahit empire Brahman priest, Danghyang Nirartha, who fled from Java to Bali in the 16th century to escape Islam on his home island. On one of his journeys he decided to sleep in this beautiful spot, and then afterwards advised the Balinese to erect a temple here, which they did, making it one of the *sad kahyangan*, or six most holy temples for all of Bali.

Folklore has it that the poisonous, black-and-white sea snakes that live between the rocks surrounding the temple were originally Niratha's sashes that fell into the sea and became transformed. The snakes are said to guard the temple and keep evil away.

The *sad kahyangan* were meant to be in sight of one another, uniting all of Bali, and on a clear day Pura Uluwatu is barely visible to the south. Many Balinese—and tourists— enjoy sitting on the beach or on a bluff over-looking the temple in the late afternoon, watching the tides change and enjoying the silhouettes of the temple *meru* (pagodas) against the brilliant setting sun. Foreigners are forbidden to enter the temple, but still they come by the busloads, especially at sunset. Visit at any other time and the place will be empty, except for the vendors and *warungs*.

Just down the road is **Pan Pacific Nirwana Bali Resort**, featuring an award-winning 18-hole world class Greg Norman golf course.

—*Linda Hoffman & Hedi Hinzler*

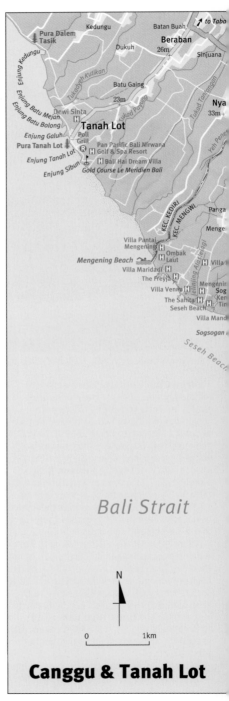

Bali Strait

Canggu & Tanah Lot

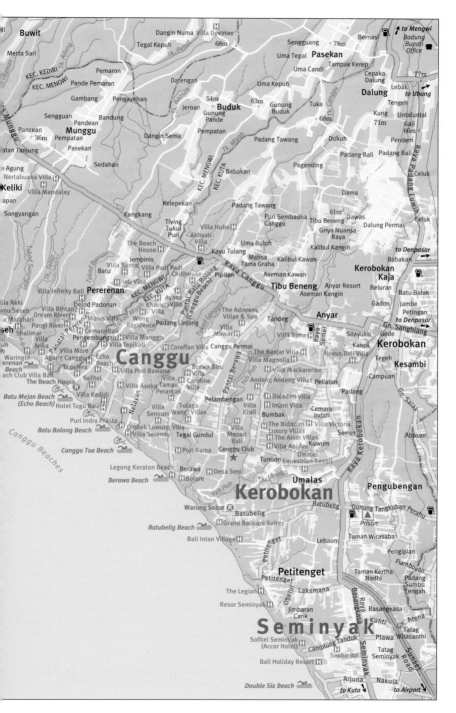

VISITING CANGGU
(TELEPHONE CODE: 0361)

The area called Canggu (pronounced *chang-gu*) is actually several small rural villages and six beaches which, until recently, had not seen many tourists. It begins at Jl. Petitenget to the north of Petitenget and Kerobokan and extends to Tanah Lot.

Canggu is in the beginning stages of tourism development. Holidaymakers who stay in this area generally are either surfers or those who want easy access to the southern beaches, shopping, and dining but prefer spending more time in the countryside than in the crowds. Enjoy it while you can. Canggu is growing like wildfire. There are a few homestays and *warungs* here catering to surfers, but now there is a plethora of expansive villas, some suites and a couple of resorts catering to the more affluent.

ACCOMMODATIONS
Budget (under $25)
Puri Rama, Jl. Pantai Berawa, Berawa beach. Simple rooms and a *warung*.

Wayan's Homestay, Jl. Pantai Berawa, Berawa beach. Locally owned simple homestay.

Moderate ($25–50)
Chillhouse, Bali Surf Retreats, in the rice fields near Canggu Tua, www.Chillhouse.at. Treetop loft, 5 bungalows with private gardens, single and multi-rooms, swimming pool, unlimited WiFi. Suitable for families. Surfguiding, lessons, private coaching, massage, meditation, yoga, and organic meals all day in the restaurant. Sleep and eat from $30, surfing packages. Another location on the Bukit.

First class ($75–100)
Balisani Padma Hotel, Jl. Batubelig Beach, Berawa, tel: 730-550, fax: 730-141, www.bali-sani.com. Bungalows in Balinese style, some with AC, tv, room service. Restaurants, bars, pool bar. $80–95.

Luxury ($100–up)
Desa Seni, Jl. Subak Sari (Jl. Kayu Putih) No. 13, Pantai Berawa, Canggu, tel: 844-6392, www.desaseni.com. Set in the middle of a rice field, an unusual collection of antique wooden Indonesian homes that have been restored and formed into a "village". The focus is an authentic Indonesian experience through exploring culture, religion, food, and complete wellness. 10 minute walk to Canggu beach. Yoga classes. Day guests welcome. From $150.

Grand Balisani Suites, Jl. Batubelig Beach, Berawa, tel: 730-550, fax: 730-141, www.bali-sani.com. Adjacent to Balisani Padma Hotel, 100 rooms and suites. Fine decor, notably Balinese hardwoods, local stone, hand-woven textiles and artifacts. Open-air restaurant, swimming pool, and an open-air library facing the beach. Restaurant, coffee shop, pool bar, lounge, open stage. $275–726.

Hotel Tugu Bali, Jl. Pantai Batu Bolong, Canggu Beach, tel: 731-701, fax: 731-708, www.tuguhotels.com. 21 thatched suites and pavilions amidst wild lotus ponds. Museum boutique hotel showcases a rare collection of over 1,000 pieces of Indonesian statuary, artworks, and unique Balinese and Javanese architecture. Each room is individually designed, all with oversized beds and private plunge pools. Spa. Luxury facilities. From $203.

Legong Keraton Beach Hotel, Jl. Pantai Berawa, Canggu, tel: 730-280, fax: 730-285, www.legongkeratonhotel.com. Right on the beach, several room categories and beachfront cottages. Swimming pool, meeting room, spa, and wedding facilities. $100–180.

Umalas Equestrian Resort, Jl. Lestari 9X, Banjar Umalas Kauh, tel: 731-402, fax: 731-403, www.balionhorse.com. 4 guest rooms and 1 suite on 1.6 ha of rice field land, all with private terrace, AC, mini-bar, cable tv. Lestari Grill & Pasta restaurant, saltwater pool with waterfall, kids' playground, gift shop, car rental. Babysitter on request, massage therapists. WiFi. Rooms from $110–230, riding packages for all levels of experience.

Villas
Antique Spa, Villa & Gallery, Jl. Dukuh Indah, Banjar Umalas, tel:/fax: 739-0840, www.antiquebali.com. A blend of modern and traditional elements, 2 private villas with AC bedrooms, outdoor bath, fully equipped kitchen, dining area, and private pool. Spa uses a special line of men's spa products. WiFi. Breakfast served in your villa. $250–300.

Canggu Club Bali, Jl. Pantai Berawa, Banjar Tegal Gundul, tel: 844 6385, fax: 844-6386, www.cangguclub.com. Luxury villas set on the grounds of the fabulous Canggu Club (see description in "Activities" below). $390–2,550.

SABA Villas, Jl. Subak Sari No. 30, Banjar Tegal Gundul, Canggu, tel: 738-058, www.sababali.com. Set in the rice fields near Berawa Beach, 5 luxury villas feature large bedrooms, garden baths, open air living, and dining pavilions; kitchens, pools, tv, and WiFi. Guests also have complimentary access to the Canggu Club. In-house chefs and butlers. From $195.

DINING
Bali Puputan, Tugu Bali Hotel, Jl. Pantai Batu Bolong, Canggu Beach, tel: 731-701, fax: 731-708, www.tuguhotels.com. This dining venue, full of museum

quality artifacts, serves a *rijstaffel* dinner in grand colonial-style on a giant marble-top table used in the Dutch governor's residence in Surabaya 150 years ago. Also in the same hotel is Waroeng Tugu, serving delicious traditional and authentic Javanese *warung* food (but not at *warung* prices).

Lestari Grill & Pasta, Umalas Equestrian Resort, Umalas, tel: 792-6375, www.lestari-bali.com. European food with a Swiss flair overlooking the swimming pool. Full European breakfasts with cheese-filled sausages, light lunches with a variety of international choices, pasta, risotto, and ravioli. Full dinner menu and delicious desserts. Takes credit cards.

Naughty Nuri's, Jl. Batubelig 41, tel: 362-2901. Thank goodness for miracles, Ubud's favorite hangout has opened a second location in the Canggu area. Nuri's famous ribs, salads, curries, and fabulous martinis, plus margaritas and bloody Marys without having to go up the hill. Hallelujah.

The Beach House Restaurant, Jl. Pura Batu Mejan, Echo Beach, tel: 747-4604, www.echobeachhouse.com. Popular with surfers and those who simply want to watch" both locals and tourists. Seafood BBQ and organic salads every night, live DJ music every Sunday night, fun for the family. Large bar. Free home delivery, catering at your villa. Free WiFi. Open breakfast, lunch, sunset, dinner, and party nights.

Warung Sobat, Jl. Batu Belig near Grand Balisani Suites, 91 m before the beach. Owned by a Balinese family who has farmed this land for generations, owner Made and his wife began selling food to construction workers, then later enlarged their dining area to cater to the new villa tourists.

MARKETS

Canggu Deli, near Canggu Club. Stocks cold cuts, cheese, salad items, ice cream, beer, and wine. Very handy to have in the neighborhood. Also includes The Loop Restaurant.

ACTIVITIES

Canggu Club Bali, Jl. Pantai Berawa, Banjar Tegal Gundul, tel: 844 6385, fax: 844-6386, www.cangguclub.com. A members-only club opened in 2006, contains swimming pool, kids' splash pool, gym, and some of the best sporting facilities on Bali. Tennis, soccer, gymnastic, and swimming academies, squash courts, Wellness center, restaurant, pub. WiFi, library. Emphasis is on family life. Day passes available for adults and families $30-65.

Umalas Equestrian Resort, Jl. Lestari 9X, Banjar Umalas Kauh, tel: 731-402, fax: 731-403, www.balionhorse.com. Opened in 1995 with 6 horses, today owner Sabine Kauffman has over 30 ponies, thoroughbreds, Arabians, Friesians, Australian stock horses, and mixtures, some stabled by private owners, and a staff of 40. Lessons, tours, stables, arenas, tack shop, restaurant, saltwater pool, souvenir shop. Lessons include beginner, dressage, and show jumping. Beach and rice field rides offered morning and afternoon, starting at $25. Pony rides for kids $5. Reservations requested to avoid disappointment.

VISITING TANAH LOT
(TELEPHONE CODE: 0361)

Shortly before Tabanan on the main highway west from Denpasar a signboard indicates the southwest turnoff to Tanah Lot. Alternative access is north of Legian, turning west toward Canggu, and then following the signs from there. There are a great number of shops and restaurants nearby. Tourists congregate at this Balinese landmark by the busloads at sunset.

ACCOMMODATIONS & DINING

Inexpensive eating *warungs* are around the parking lot, and both sides of the coastal path to the east and above the temple are lined with restaurants. Recommended is the open-air Dewi Sinta Restaurant inside the hotel by the same name. Several upscale dining outlets are found in the Pan Pacific Bali Nirwana Resort.

Dewi Sinta Hotel, Spa & Restaurant, Taman Wisata Tanah Lot, tel: 812-933, fax: 813-956, www.dewisinta.com. 27 rooms and suites. Spacious deluxe rooms in the back looking out on rice fields, All with AC, hot water, tv, and mini-bar. Clean, well-run, and friendly.

The pleasant restaurant serving Indonesian, Chinese, seafood, and European cuisine is a bonus. Swimming pool, open stage, convention facilities. Credit cards accepted; $45–55.

Pan Pacific Bali Nirwana Resort, Jl. Raya Tanah Lot, Tabanan, tel: 815-900, fax: 815-901, www.panpacific.com. Formerly LeMeridien Nirwana Golf & Spa Resort, a luxury hotel with an 18-hole world class Greg Norman golf course. 278 deluxe rooms, executive suites, presidential suite and villas set on 103 ha. Offers absolute privacy, 5 restaurants and lounges, a spa and 4 swimming pools. $117–380. Discounts for booking 2 weeks in advance. Packages.

SHOPPING

Numerous kiosks surround the entrance to the temple in organized market fashion. Aside from Balinese souvenirs, clothing, and novelties, there are plentiful counterfeit branded goods. Also money changers.

DENPASAR AND RENON

A Tour of Bali's "Big City"

Denpasar is a "village-city" with an aristocratic past. Born from the ashes of the defeated Pemecutan court following the *puputan* (suicide) massacre of 1906, Denpasar became a sleepy administrative outpost during Dutch times. Since independence, and especially after it was made the capital of Bali in 1958, it has been transformed into a bustling city of some 788,000 (2010 estimate) souls that provides administrative, commercial, and educational services not only to booming Bali, but to much of eastern Indonesia as well. Denpasar is Bali's largest city and the most dynamic one east of Surabaya.

Although not a tourist destination in its own right, it attracts visitors because — as the provincial capital — it has a large financial district (including many banks and ATM machines), airline offices, bus terminals, and all the other services normally found in large cities. The surrounding streets are filled with small shops, homestays, hotels, and eating establishments frequented by both foreign and domestic travelers. Traffic here is chronic during business hours, so be forewarned.

New city, old villages

Originally a market town — its name literally means "east of the market" — Denpasar has far outgrown its former boundaries, once defined by the Pemecutan, Jero Kuta, and Satriya palaces and the Tegal, Tampak-wangsul, and Gemeh brahmanical houses. Spurred in all directions by population pressures and motorized transport, urban growth has enveloped the neighboring villages and obliterated huge amounts of the surrounding rice fields, leaving a new metropolitan landscape in its wake.

To the east, urbanization spills across the Ayung River into the village of Batubulan, known for its *barong* dances. To the south, it reaches to Sanur and Kuta, while the Bukit further south has become a haven for foreign-owned villas and five-star resorts. To the west, it sprawls as far as Kapal, whose beautiful temple now has to be seen above the din and dust of suburban traffic.

This unchecked growth has swallowed up many old villages of the plain, yet in many ways they remain as they were, their architecture focused around open courtyards, their intricate temples and collective *banjars*. The power structure itself, although adapted to new urban tasks and occupations, has also not changed much. Local *satrias* (the warrior caste), be they hotel managers or civil servants, remain princes, still have control of land and territorial temples, and may mobilize their "subjects" for ceremonies. Local Brahmans are even more powerful, continuing to provide ritual services for their followers and occupying some of the best positions in the new Bali. Thus Denpasar is a showcase of Balinese social resilience: still "Bali" and worth a visit for its gates, its shrines, and its royal mansions.

But Denpasar is nevertheless a modern city. Shops, roads, and markets have conquered the wet rice field areas leased and sold by village communities. Here, urbanization has taken on the same features found elsewhere in Indonesia: rows of gaudily-painted shops in the business districts; pretty villas along the *protokol* streets; narrow alleys, small compounds, and tiny houses in the residential areas.

Experiment in integration

This new urban space continues to welcome waves of new immigrants, Balinese as well as non-Balinese. As such, it represents an experiment in national integration. Inland Balinese indeed make up the majority of the population. The northerners, southern princes, and Brahmans were here first. Beneficiaries of a colonial education, they took over the professions and the main administrative positions and constitute, together with the local nobility, the core of the native bourgeoisie. Their villas — with their roof temples, neo-classical columns, and Spanish balconies — are the modern "palaces" of Bali.

More recently, a new Balinese population settled here, attracted by jobs as teachers, students, nurses, and traders. Strangers among the local "villagers", these Balinese are also the creators of a new city landscape and architecture. Instead of setting up traditional compounds with their numerous buildings and shrines, they build detached houses with a single multi-purpose shrine. In religious matters, they are transients retaining ritual membership in their village of origin, praying to gods and ancestors from a distance through the medium of the new shrine. They return home for major ceremonies to renew themselves at the magical and social sources of their original villages.

There are also several non-indigenous minorities in Denpasar, comprising perhaps a quarter of the total population. Muslim Bugis came to Bali from Makassar as mercenaries as early as the 18th century. They have their own *banjar* in Kepaon village, where they live alongside the Balinese, speaking their language and intermarrying with them. Old men of Pemecutan can take visitors to a "Bugis" shrine in a small temple near the family cremation site.

The Chinese came early as traders for the local princes. They integrated easily, blending their Chinese and Balinese ancestry. They

The four-sided Catur Mukha statue stands in the middle of Denpasar's busiest intersection.

also have a shrine, the Ratu Subandar or "merchant king's" shrine up in Batur, next to the shrines of Balinese ancestral gods. Later, new Chinese, often Christians, arrived, attracted by Bali's booming economy.

There are also Arabs and Indian Muslims who came in the 1930s as textile traders and have since become one of the most prosperous local communities. They live in the heart of the city, in the Kampung Arab area, where they have a mosque.

Most migrants, however, are Javanese and Madurese, known collectively as *Jawa*. They fill the ranks of the civil service and the military (Sanglah and Kayumas areas) as well as the working classes, skilled, and unskilled (Pekambingan, Kayumas, and Kampung Jawa areas). Relatively new actors on the Balinese social stage, they introduced new habits, such as food-selling and peddling. They are also builders of new housing: shacks and tiny houses that bring Denpasar into line with other cityscapes of modern Indonesia.

Thus Denpasar is very much a place where the theme of nation-building is played out. It brings together within earshot of one another the high priest's mantra, the muezzin's call, and the parson's prayer. *Eka Wakya, Bhinna Srutti*—"The Verbs are one, the scriptures are many"—so goes the local saying. Balinese tolerance within a national tolerance.

Balinese city, Indonesian nation

Nation-building is also very much a Balinese concern. Denpasar is the center from which the national language, Bahasa Indonesia, is spread to other parts of the island, and people here speak Indonesian interspersed with Balinese words.

Denpasar is also the breeding ground for a revamped traditional culture. It is here that the concepts of Balinese Hinduism are being re-Indianized by the Parisada Hindu Dharma (Hinduism Religious Council), beyond the maze of Bali's old *lontar* manuscripts and oral traditions. The supreme god, Sanghyang Widhi Wasa ("All-in-One God"), assumes precedence here, relegating the ancestors to minor functions. New prayers are taught (*Tri Sandhya*) and new government priests officiate, called from Denpasar to the villages for the rites of official-dom and for inter-caste rituals. Reversing the old village-based trend, Denpasar is also home to the new arts. Modern dances and music are created and taught, spreading into the villages from the city.

Denpasar & Renon

Last, but not least, Denpasar is the home of a new breed of Balinese. Born to the sounds of contemporary music, raised in a world of new wishes and desires, taught in the words of a national language and culture, Denpasar's young are Jakarta-looking rather than Bali-oriented. Their thoughts take form in a world of Kuta discos and lavish Sanur villas. They are the avant-garde of the new, Westernized Indonesia. Resilience, renewal and decadence, Denpasar is the stage for modern Bali.

Modern city with a traditional touch

As a microcosm both of modern Bali and of present-day Indonesia, Denpasar is easier to understand than to see. Nevertheless, it awaits the intelligent traveler who wants to learn about Bali's future as well as the past, and who wishes to take home more than just a few images. So forget taking photos for a while. Forget the traditional village Bali; and have a look at the new urban Bali.

For a look at contemporary Bali, go first to **Puputan Square** in the center of the city, a large park commemorating the suicidal battle of the Badung kingdom against the Dutch in 1906. Bounded on the north by the main west-east artery, Jl. Gajah Mada, which changes names to Jl. Surapati east of the roundabout, this is a good orientation point as well as a nice spot, surrounded by gardens, to rest weary feet. On its northwestern corner is another landmark: the **Catur Mukha** ("God of the Four Directions") statue gazes impassively through one of its faces at the monument to the fallen of the *puputan*. Across the street to the northeast corner of the park on Jl. Surapati is the Tourist Information Office (closed weekends and public holidays). On the east side of the Square is Pura Jaganatha, Bali Museum, and the massive military headquarters.

The **Bali Museum** (closed weekends and public holidays) was established by the Dutch in 1932 and displays archeological finds, masks, weapons, dance costumes, handicrafts, paintings, and Ming ceramics. The main building represents the Karangasem palace (east Bali) architectural style featuring a wide veranda. The Tabanan palace style (west Bali) is represented by the windowless building on the right, and the brick building on the left resembles the Singaraja (north Bali) palace. On the north side of the museum is the Javanese-*pendopo*-styled governor's residence, **Jaya Sabha**. The Bali Arts Festival

procession held every June or July begins in front of this building.

Denpasar's temples and palaces

In the very heart of Denpasar, just behind Jl. Gajah Mada are many traditional compounds, their gates, shrines, and pavilions in among the multistory Chinese shop-fronts.

For a look at Denpasar's more typical villages, travel the streets of Kedaton, Sumerta, and particularly Kesiman villages, east of the city center, will do. **Kesiman** has some of the best examples of the simple, yet attractive Badung brick-style, a dying witness to a passing grandeur that is being replaced by the new baroque of the Gianyar style and the ugliness of reinforced concrete.

Of the temples, the most ancient is **Pura Moaspahit**, in the middle of the city on the road west to Tabanan (Jl. Sutomo). It dates back to the early Javanization of Bali in the 14th century. Every 15 days, at the full moon and the dark moon, Moaspahit is filled with young Balinese, who come to pray, often followed by evening *wayang kulit* (shadow puppet) performances. No less interesting, although more recent, are the temples of the royal families: **Pura Kesiman**, with its beautiful split gate, **Pura Satria** and the lively **Pasar Burung (Bird Market)** next door (north on Jl. Veteran), and **Pura Nambangan Badung** near the Pemecutan and Pemedilan princely compounds.

A "modern" temple also worth a visit is **Pura Jagatnatha**, the temple of the "Lord of the World", in Puputan Square. Its tallest building is a big *padmasana* lotus-throne shrine and has a gilded statue of the supreme god, Sanghyang Widhi Wasa.

Among the palaces, the most typical is **Jero Kuta**, north on Jl. Setiabudi, which still has all the functional structures of a traditional princely compound. The **Pemecutan Palace** on Jl. Imam Bonjol has been transformed into a hotel. The **Kesiman Palace**, a private mansion, houses an elaborate family temple. Now consisting of two buildings on Jl. Supratman northeast of the city center, one of them is open to tourists.

Other sites

The vast **Werdhi Budaya Art Center** on Jl. Nusa Indah in the Sumerta area east of the city center is not only a cultural venue dedicated to visual and performing arts, it is a monument to Balinese temple and palace

Denpasar's two main markets, Pasar Kumbasari and Pasar Badung, are separated by a river.

architecture. Its large grounds house three art galleries, exhibition space, and several performance venues, including the grand **Arda Candra Amphitheater**. Check schedules on arrival for exhibitions and performances. There is always something—painting, photography, or textile exhibitions, or performances —going on here. Next to the Art Center is **Indonesia Institute of the Arts Denpasar** (ISI Denpasar), an accredited state university offering Bachelor and Master of Arts degrees in both traditional and contemporary arts.

A visit to Denpasar would not be complete without some shopping, and the best places to do that are where the locals go. **Pasar Kumbasari** on Jl. Gajah Mada is a beehive of activity that is a combination of traditional morning market on the first floor, selling everything from farm-fresh vegetables to live chickens, spices and offering flowers, and an open-air "shopping mall" the rest of the day. The second level sells handicrafts, clothing, and art, and on the third floor are traditional cooking utensils and ceremonial temple accouterments. Across the river to the south is **Pasar Badung**, which is similar to Kumbasari, minus the handicrafts and art shops. Don't forget to bargain. Both are open until 10 pm. South of the markets is a nice shop-lined street with wide sidewalks and potted plants, unlike any other Indonesian city.

Amidst large bank buildings on Jl. Gajah Mada and on Jl. Thamrin are a myriad of small stores selling many different items,

such as textiles. **Jl. Hasanudin** is locally known as the "gold street", where 18-22K gold jewelry is bought and sold at current market prices, which are posted and updated each day. Nearby **Jl. Sulawesi** is a haven for fabric lovers. **Pasar Satria**, north of Jl. Gajah Mada on the corner of Jl. Veteran and Jl. Nakula, is smaller than Pasar Badung, but also sells handicrafts on the second level with a traditional market on the ground floor.

Renon

Travelers in need of embassy services must make their way south of Denpasar city and then east to **Renon**, a "new" town built to house governmental offices and the main financial district, passing the impressive **University Udayana** on a modern four-lane boulevard en route. Tribute must be paid to the Balinese architects who designed this town.

Foreign embassies and consulates dominate the main west-east street, **Jl. Puputan**, passing Renon's own version of Puputan Square. Side streets to the north are lined with large, shady trees that look anything but new, and the offices here are stately and handsome, unlike the stark, unimaginative government buildings found elsewhere in Indonesia. The area is surrounded by department stores, doctors' offices, mobile phone shops, and fast-food outlets, making Bali Province's civic center an oasis at the outskirts of a bustling city.

— *Jean Couteau*

VISITING DENPASAR
(TELEPHONE CODE: 0361)

Denpasar is the bustling commercial heart of Bali. At its center is a grassy town common, Puputan Square, the city's best known landmark. Jl. Gajah Mada is the main street, running east–west. Its name changes to Jl. Dr. Wahidin to the west and Jl. Surapati to the east. The center of commercial activity is Jl. Diponegoro and the streets around Puputan Square. The government administrative district and many consulates are in Renon to the southeast.

ACCOMMODATIONS
Denpasar has two hotels of historical and cultural note—**Inna Bali Hotel**—and the **Pemecutan Palace Hotel**. There are also several quite comfortable 2- and 3-star business hotels that appeal to conferences and business travelers. There are also many *losmen* here catering to domestic tourists, backpackers, and overseas students. If you're on a tight budget, these can be a great bargain. During the Indonesian holiday seasons (June–August, Ramadan, and Christmas/New Year), all classes of accommodations throughout the country fill up, so make reservations in advance if traveling during those times.

Budget (Under $25)
Adi Yasa, Jl. Nakula 23B, tel: 222-679. Though becoming a bit tattered at the edges, this is an old reliable standby that has served travelers from as far back as the 1970s. Friendly, central, simple but spacious rooms. Internet. From $6.

Dharmawisata, Jl. Imam Bonjol 125 (south of the Taman Suci Hotel), tel: 484-186. 34 rooms, 7 with AC and 27 with fan and clean and pleasant Indonesian-style bathrooms. Swimming pool.

Merta Sari, Jl. Hasanudin 24, tel: 222-428. 5 rooms in clean bungalows. Centrally-located, a couple of minutes walk south from Paputan Square. Helpful staff. Excellent value. $9.

Nakula Familiar Inn, Jl. Nakula 4 (across the road from the Adi Yasa), tel: 226-446, www. nakulafamiliarinn.com. 8 large, modern rooms, each with balcony and shower, choice of fan or AC. Friendly atmosphere. From $10.

Taman Wisata, Jl. Nangka 98A (off Jl. Gatot Subroto), tel: 236-015. 41 comfortable, clean rooms in Dutch colonial style, some with AC. From $10.

Moderate ($25–50)
Alinda Hotel, Jl. Karna No. 8, tel: 240-435, fax 2235-997. Standard AC rooms from $25.

Inna Bali (ex-Natour), Jl. Veteran 3, tel: 225-681, fax 235-347, www.innabali.com. 70 rooms. This hotel's claim to fame is that it was Bali's first, built by the Dutch in 1927. Authors Miguel Covarrubias, Colin McPhee, and others stayed here when they first arrived on Bali. These days it's a government-owned business hotel with conference facilities. Good central location. Swimming pool. Restaurant serves *rijsttafel*. $35–76.

Pemecutan Palace Hotel, Jl. Imam Bonjol & Jl. Hasanudin, tel: 423-491. Formerly the palace of one of the royal families, located near Puputan Square. Unique traditional Balinese traditional architecture, constructed in the 16th century.

Taman Suci Hotel, Jl. Imam Bonjol 45, tel: 484-445, fax: 484-724, www.tamansuci.com. 45 rooms. Clean, comfortable accommodation with 24-hr coffee shop, bar, and live music; WiFi, ATM. From $40 (includes American or Continental breakfast).

Intermediate ($50–75)
Aston Denpasar Hotel & Conference Center, Jl. Gatot Subroto Barat No. 283, tel: 411-999, www. astondenpasar.com. From the Aston chain, newly built 3-star hotel. Over 300 rooms and suites, large ballroom, restaurant, entertainment, meeting rooms, shopping in the same complex. From $80.

FaveHotel, Jl. Teuku Umar No. 175-179, tel: 842-2299, www.FaveHotels.com. Opened in 2010, a new 2-star concept by the Aston group, FaveHotels offer contemporary facilities and amenities at affordable prices. Deluxe room $40.

Hotel Nikki, Jl. Gatot Subroto IV No. 18, tel: 413-888, fax: 412-333. 78 rooms, Chinese restaurant, lounge bar, pool with bar and Jacuzzi, business center with Internet, tour counter, fitness club, sauna, jogging track, salon and spa, meeting rooms. Caters to business travelers and conventions. $46–64.

DINING
Denpasar is a great place for all styles of Indonesian and Chinese food and every other cuisine imaginable. Prices are very reasonable. For an authentic local experience, check out the **night markets (***pasar malam***)**, where you sit out under the stars and eat at small open-air food stalls. Open from sunset to 10 pm. The biggest is at Kereneng terminal, another is outside the Kumbasari Shopping Center, Jl. Hayam Wuruk/Jl. Kamboja. The food is mostly Javanese and Balinese, but there's also Chinese, fiery Padang, and Muslim goat and chicken satay with sauces, and plentiful sweets like fried bananas (*pisang goreng*) and *kue putu* (green *pandan* cakes) smothered in coconut shavings.

For the whole range of local food in a cleaner, if less exotic, environment try the food centers, often air-conditioned, located in the city's big shopping centers, where a vast array of Indonesian, Chinese, and ethnic cuisines are sold at unbeatable prices in cool and clean surroundings. A bonus is watching the spectacle of mall life.

Coffee lovers shouldn't miss **Kopi Bali (Bhineka Jaya Kopi Bali)**, Jl. Gajah Mada 80, tel: 222-053. Forget Starbucks, this is the biggest producer and distributor of coffee on Bali. You can order your favorite brew here and also buy beans from Sumatra, Sulawesi, Java, and of course Bali. Balinese coffee make great souvenirs too.

Mei 88, at No. 88, has delicious and very economical Chinese dishes, such as meat balls.

Bakwan Surabaya, Jl. Teuku Umar No. 54X, tel: 224-478, 742-9650. Meatball soup (*bakwan*) with noodles that's perfectly cooked. Choose your own meat or tofu.

Bali Bakery, Jl. Hayam Wuruk No.181, Tanjung Bungkak Denpasar, tel: 243-147, fax: 243-145, www.balibakery.com. An expat favorite bakery and café for lunch, teatime, or dinner serving a large variety of western and local foods.

Dapur Bebek, Jl. Teuku Umar, tel: 784-2525, 871-8580. Delicious Balinese duck (*bebek*) crispy fried or grilled with choice of rice.

Hongkong Restaurant, Jl. Gajah Mada 99 (near Badung Market), tel: 233-296. A local favorite for Chinese food with small, medium, and large sized portions. Karaoke in the evenings.

Kak Man, Jl Teuku Umar 135, tel: 227-188, fax: 238-597, www.kakmanrestaurants.com. Excellent Balinese food and art collection.

Ozigo Country Restaurant & Bar, Jl. Moh, Yamin No. 859, Renon, tel: 241-570, fax: 264-648, ozigo.country@gmail.com. Good restaurant serving international and local food. Downstairs is a bar with live country music several nights/week.

Rasa Sayang, Jl. Teuku Umar 243. tel: 262-006. A popular place for Chinese fare, particularly seafood, in a cool and clean environment.

Samudra Seafood Restaurant, Jl. Teuku Umar 69, tel: 221-758. Good quality food at very reasonable prices. Fully AC, 100% *halal*, parking. Get the chili crabs; choose live seafood from their aquariums. Condiments are free.

SHOPPING

Denpasar is a great place to shop. Store hours generally follow the 9–5 Western format, but some still close at 1pm for lunch.

In addition to the treasures to be found at the **traditional markets**, also try the **arts and craft shops**

on Jl. Sulawesi and Jl. Gajah Mada. The **handmade wooden furniture center** is along Jl. Bypass Ngurah Rai, particularly around the Sanur Bypass area, as well as in Batubulan.

Mega Art Shop, Jl. Gajah Mada 36, tel: 462-555 has a wide range of Balinese arts: jewelry, leather, puppets, paintings, ceramics, and fine textiles, including reasonably priced framed weavings from Timor, and *ikat* from Sumbupen, 9am–4pm.

Jl. Hasanuddin, near the city's massive traditional market, is lined with **gold shops**; a few others are found on Jl. Sulawesi. The gold is 18–22K.

There are 4 stores selling handicrafts, sarongs, T-shirts, trinkets and many other souvenirs found in tourist areas. The difference is that these items are sold in bulk so are cheaper. Two good options are:

Krisna, Jl. Nusa Kambangan 160A, tel: 084-235-373 and Jl. Nusa Indah No. 77, tel: 262-365.

UD. Erlangga I, Jl. Nusa Kambangan No. 28B, tel: 221-281 and Jl. Nusa Kambangan No. 137, tel: 229-860.

Textiles & fabrics

Jl. Sulawesi, beside Pasar Badung, known locally as "Kampung Arab", is the street for contemporary and traditional textiles, especially Indian or Muslim-style fabrics. A number of shops also carry batik, *ikat*, and traditional *songket* cloth (woven with silver strands). A good tip is to buy cloth by the meter and have dresses and shirts made by local tailors, leaving a perfectly fitting garment to copy.

Duta Silk, next to Matahari, tel: 232-818. A reliable outlet for luxury fabrics including high-quality silks, linen, cotton, lace, wool, and velvet. Mostly imported stock, prices are fair, and you won't be ripped off.

Kencana, Jl. Imam Bonjol 169, tel: 483-695, 480-178. The definitive fabric store of Denpasar: cotton, velvet, rayon, curtain, and other decorative materials. Wide selection, good prices.

Pasar Kumbasari, on the west bank of the Badung River (opp. Pasar Badung) has a wide variety of batik and *songket*.

MEDICAL

Toko Sentosa, Jl. Gajah Mada, tel: 222-812, is a wonderful traditional Chinese apothecary that carries everything from ginseng root to Ho Shou Wu. Open 8:30 am–3:30 pm.

SPAS

Rei Wellness Spa, Jl. Griya Anyar, Br. Kajeng Pemogan, tel: 847-3320, fax: 847-3319, www.reiwellness.com. An holistic wellness facility that adheres to the positive principles of Feng Shui; a journey of self-awareness. Treatments $85–200.

SANUR

A Beach Resort with a "Checkered" Past

The black and white checkered cloth—standard of Bali's netherworld—is nowhere more aptly hung than on the ancient coral statues and shrines of Bali's largest traditional village, Sanur. This was Bali's first beach resort, a place of remarkable contrasts.

Sanur is a golden mile of "Baliesque" hotels that has attracted millions of paradise-seeking globetrotters. And yet, within the very grounds of the 10-story **Inna Grand Bali Beach Hotel**—originally funded by war-reparations from the Japanese—is the sacred and spiky **Ratu Ayu** temple of Singgi, the much feared spirit consort of Sanur's fabled Black Barong. The district is legendary throughout Bali for its sorcery. Black and white magic pervades the coconut groves of the resort's hotels like an invisible chess game. And yet the community is modern and prosperous.

Sanur is one of the few remaining Brahman *kuasa* villages (controlled by members of the priestly caste) on Bali and has among its

Traditional fishing boats at Sanur Beach

charms some of the handsomest processions on the island, Bali's only all-female *keris* dance and the island's oldest stone inscription. Even the souvenirs sold on the beach—beautifully crafted kites and toy outriggers—are a cut above those found on the rest of the island.

Traditional Sanur

Just a stone's throw from any of Sanur's beachside hotels lies one of a string of very ancient temples. Characterized by low coral-walled enclosures sheltering platform altars, this style of temple is peculiar to the white sand stretch of Sanur coast from its harbor in the north to **Mertasari Beach** in the south. Inside, the altars are decorated with fanciful fans of coral and rough-hewn statuary, often ghoulishly painted but always wrapped in a *poleng* checkered sarong.

The rites performed at the anniversary celebrations of these temples are both weird and wonderful, the celebrants often dancing with effigies strapped to their hips, while the priests are prone to wild outbursts, launching themselves spread-eagled onto a platform of offerings and racing entranced pell-mell into the sea.

The area, with traditional Intaran village at its heart, has evidently been settled since ancient times. The Prasasti Belanjong, an inscribed pillar here from A.D. 913, is Bali's earliest dated artifact, and is now kept in **Pura Belanjong** temple in south Sanur. It tells of King Sri Kesari Warmadewa of the Sailendra Dynasty in Java, who came to Bali to teach Mahayana Buddhism and then founded a monastery here. It may be presumed that a fairly civilized community existed then, as the Sailendra kings built Borobudur in Central Java at about the same time.

It is interesting that the Intaran village square is almost identical to that of Songan village on Mt. Batur's crater lake, particularly the location and size of the *bale agung* (great meeting hall), the *wantilan* community hall and associated buildings. The priests of Sanur-Intaran are often mentioned in

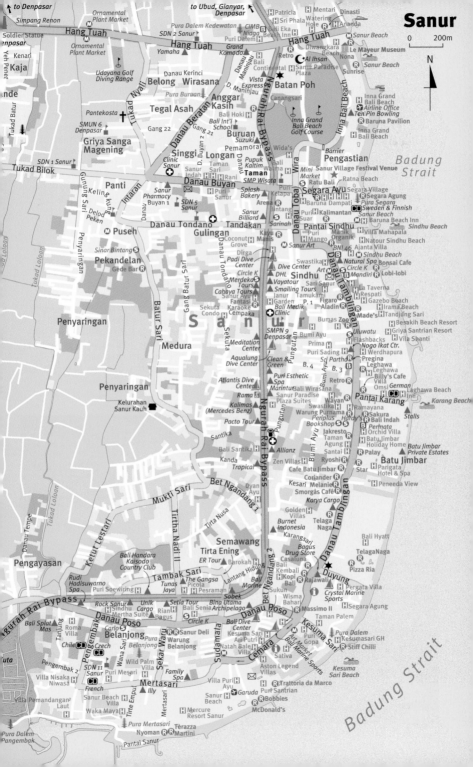

Sanur

0   200m

to Denpasar
Simpang Renon

to Ubud, Gianyar,
Denpasar

Ornamental
Plant Market

Soldier Statue
Kenari

Hang Tuah

Hang Tuah

Pura Dalem Kedewatan

SDN 2 Sanur

Patricia   Mentari   Dinasti

Sri Phala Watering
Hole   Ananda

Hang Tuah

Yeh Penet

Ornamental
Plant Market

Yamaha

Grand
Komodo

Bali Eka

CIMB
Niaga

Puri Dalem

Diwangkara

Al Ihsan

Sanur Beach

Le Mayeur Museum

Sanur Beach

Kaja

Udayana Golf
Driving Range

Belong Wirasana

Retro

Vista
Express

Continental

Sanur Beach

Sanur Beach

N

Inde

Tukad Batur

Pantekosta

Tegal Asah

Danau Kerinci

D. Maninjau

Batan Poh

Manjan

Sanur
Maninjau

Canangsari

Samm Paradise
Plaza

Sunrise

Inna Grand
Bali Beach

Nona

SMUN 6
Denpasar

Anggar
Kasih

Bali Int'l
School

Gang 22

Gang 21

Buruan

Inna Grand
Bali Beach
Golf Course

Wida's

Airline Office
Ten Pin Bowling

Baruna Pavilion

Griya Sanga
Magening

Singgi

Longan

Bali Hoki

Pemamoran

Inna Grand
Bali Beach

SDN 1 Sanur

Tukad Bilok

Panti

Clinic
Sanur

Taman
Sari

Pupuk
Kaltim

Pengastian

Barrier

Mini
Market

Sanur Village Festival Venue

Badung
Strait

Gunung Sari

Keling

Sanur
Pharmacy
Buyan 1

Danau Buyan

SMP Wisata

Ratna Beach

Segara
Village

Intaran

Delod
Peken

Rani

SDN 5
Sanur

Taman

Segara Ayu

Segara Agung

Puseh

Danau Tondano

Tandakan

Splash
Bakery

Arena

Sanur
Puri

Sanur
Billiard

Ketapa

Bintang

Baruna Dampati

Suar

Kalimantan

Pura Segara

Sweden & Finnish
Sanur Beach

Baruna Beach Inn

Sindhu Beach

Pekandelan

Sinar Bintang

Gulingan

Gede Bar

Penyaringan

Penyaringan

Medura

Penyaringan

Sekuta
Condo

Coconut
Grove

Padi Dive
Center

Circle K

Merdeka
Tours

Cahaya Tours

Fantasi
Karaoke
Cempaka

Meditation
Center

Aqualung
Dive Center

Atlantis Dive
Center

Diirga

Dive Center

DHL

Vayatour

Smailing Tours

Garden

Bali Medik
Clinic

SMPN 9
Denpasar

Bumi Ayu

Prima

Puri Sading

Clean &
Green

Puri Esthetic
Spa

Marintur

Sanur Paradise
Plaza Suites

Kalimas
(Mercedes Benz)

Pacto Tour

Santika

Bali Santika

Kanda

Tropical

Sanur Art

Kayu
Manis

Mango

Janur

Sari Sanur

Aladin

Bumas Zoo

Kesari

Smorgas Café

Karya Cargo

Pantai Sindhu

Pura
Organik

BNI 46

Mandiri

Circle K

Art

Swastika

Tamukami

Tigaro

Uluwatu

Sri Partha

B.4

Warung Purnama
Periplus
Bookshop

Jakresto
Taman
Agung

Zen Villas

Cafe Batu Jimbar

Coriander

Melanie

Golden
Villas

Burnet
Indonesia

Telaga
Naga

Natour Sindhu Beach

Villa Mahapala

Sindhu Beach

Ajanta Villa

Natural Spa
Bonsai Cafe

Lobi-lobi

La Taverna
Respati

Gazebo Beach

Irama Beach

Tanjung Sari

Besakih Beach Resort

Griya Santrian Resort

Vila Shanti

Flashbacks

Nogo Ikat Ctr.

Werdhapura

Pregina
Leghawa

Billy's Cafe

Omsi

German

Laghawa Beach

Pantai Karang

Karang Beach

Ramayana

Sakura

Bali Indah

Permata
Orchid Villa

Batu Jimbar
Holiday Home

Palay

Batu Jimbar

Batu Jimbar
Private Estates

Santai

Ryoshi

Star

Peneeda View

Semawang

Tirta Ening

ER Tour

Barokah

Karangsari
Bagus
Drug Store

Casaluna

Bali
Kembali
Kopi
Bali

Sukun

Wisma
Bahari

Telaga Naga

Bali Hyatt

TelagaNaga

Pizza Ria

Segara Agung

Taman Palem

Duyung

Crystal Marine
Sports

Pergata Villa

Pengayasan

Rudi
Hadisuwarno
Spa

Bali Handara
Kaisodo
Country Club

Tunas
Jaya

The Gangsa
Picola

Bali
Marine

Lantang Hidup

Pesraman

Nguerah Rai Bypass

Bali Splat
Mas

Rock Sanur

Unik
Cargo

Mertha Suite

Rian
Bagus

Circle K

Setia Tour

Bina Utama

Bali Senia

Archipelago

Massimo II

Rajawali

Aji Marine Sports

Segara
Sari Beach

Roma
Villa

Danau Poso

Carlo

Chile

Czech

Belanjong

Pura
Belanjong

Sanur Deli

Warung
Belanjong

Danau Poso

Bali Deluxe
Center

Kesuma Sari
Ari Putri

Sudamala

Cemara

Sativa

Aston Legend
Villas

Kesuma
Sari Beach

Stiff Chilli

Pura Dalem
Kesumasari GH

Pura Dalem
Gopa

Villa Nisaka
Niwasa

SDN 11
Sanur

Puri Mesari

Family
Spa

Villa Puri
Ayu

Garuda

Puri Santrian

Bobbies

French

Illy

Sanur Beach
Villa

Waka Maya

Mertasari

Tirte Empul

Sanur
Beach

Trattoria da Marco

McDonald's

Villa Pemandangan
Laut

Pura Mertasari

Nyoman

Terazza

Martini

Mercure
Resort Sanur

Pura Dalem
Pangembak

Pantai Sanur

Badung Strait

historical chronicles dating from Bali's "Golden Age", the 13th to the 16th centuries. However, it was not until the early 19th century that the king of the Pemecutan court in Denpasar saw fit to place his *satria* prince-lings outside the village's medieval core.

Before that, Sanur consisted of Brahman *griya* (priestly mansions) in Intaran and several attendant communities, among them the Brahman **Anggarkasih** *banjar,* **Belong** fishing village (which still holds a yearly *baris gede* warrior dance at the **Pura Dalem Kedewatan** temple near the Inna Grand Bali Beach Hotel), and **Taman** village, whose Brahmans have traditionally served as the region's chief administrator, or *perbekel.* Taman is also home to an electric *barong* troupe with an impish *telek* escort, a *pas de deux* by the freaky *jauk* brothers and a spine-tingling last act featuring the evil witch Rangda, all amidst fluttering *poleng* checkered banners.

Westerners in Sanur

In the mid-19th century Sanur was first recorded by Europeans as more than just a dot on the map. Mads Lange, a Kuta-based Danish trader of the time, mentioned the special relationship that the Sanur *perbekel*

enjoyed with his great friend the king of Kesiman, Cokorda Sakti. In a less flattering light, it was also a Sanur *perbekel* who turned a blind eye to the landing in 1906 of Dutch troops on their way to the massacre of the Pemecutan royal house, one of the most ig-noble days in Dutch colonial history. The full story was immortalized by 1930s Sanur resi-dent Vicki Baum in her book, *A Tale of Bali.*

In another international nod to Sanur, the BBC produced a film of a local trance medium "possessed" by the spirit of a beer-swilling English sea captain to whose semi-divine memory a trance *baris* dance, called Ratu Tuan, is performed by Banjar Semawang. The costume consists of Chinese kung-fu pajamas of black-and-white checkered cloth.

The first half of the 20th century also saw Sanur's emergence as prime real estate for the Bali-besotted. Beach bungalows in what Miguel Covarrubias referred to as "the malarial swamps of Sanur" were built by, among others, Dr. Jack Mershon and his choreographer wife Katharine (inventor, with Walter Spies, of the *kecak* dance), writer Vicki Baum, anthropologist Jane Belo (author of *Trance in Bali*) and art-collector Neuhaus, who was killed by a stray bullet during a skirmish

Sanur Beach is far quieter than Kuta (photo courtesy: www.bali-travel-life.com).

between local guerillas and Japanese occupation forces in 1943 while playing bridge on the verandah of his home.

Belgian impressionist Adrian Jean Le Mayeur arrived on Bali in 1932 and at the age of 55 married a 15-year old Balinese *Legong* dancer, Ni Polok. His former studio-home is now **Le Mayeur Museum** on Jl. Hang Tuah (tel: 286-201), beachside north of the Inna Grand Bali Beach Hotel. Le Mayeur's heavenly courtyard was the inspiration for his breasty, nymph-filled paintings, mostly of his wife. The house remains much as it was before his death in 1958, its gardens filled with statues and carvings, a living memorial to days gone by.

These early "Baliphiles" hosted a steady stream of celebrity visitors during the 1930s, including Charlie Chaplin, Barbara Hutton, Doris Duke, and Harold Nicholson. It was probably more from the travel reports of these sophisticates than from the movie with a sarong-draped Dorothy Lamour that Bali's fame spread abroad.

Bali's most famous expatriate of the era, artist-writer-musician Walter Spies, was a frequent visitor to Sanur's shores, but his aversion for coastal Bali can be traced to one particular visit. It was the day of a lunar eclipse and the birthday of Spies' young nephew, who was visiting him in Bali. A soothsayer warned the boy not to go near the water that day, but he defied the warning and swam at Sanur, where he was taken by a shark. A weird coincidence: the Balinese symbol for an eclipse is the giant-toothed mouth of the demon spirit Kala Rauh devouring the moon goddess.

Australian artists Ian Fairweather and Donald Friend, whose marvelous books and paintings have inspired a generation of Australians, also chose picturesque Sanur for their Bali retreats. Donald Friend lived here in imperial splendor with an in-house *gamelan* and Bali's finest art collection within the grounds of his home, north of the Bali Hyatt.

20th century Sanur

At about the same time, two Sanur Brahmans were leaving their mark on the community. The first, high priest Pedanda Gede Sidemen, was entering the twilight of a prolific career that spanned 70 years as south Bali's most significant temple architect, healer and classical scholar. His life and the pride he brought to his native home inspired a generation of local Brahmans, who may otherwise have contemplated abandoning

their Vedic scriptures for a different life.

The second, Ida Bagus Berata—nephew of Pedanda Sidemen—insisted during his tenure as mayor of Sanur from 1968 to 1986 that the area should be economically as well as culturally autonomous. To that end Ratu Perbekel, as he was affectionately known, established a village-run cooperative that to this day operates several businesses and owns land in Kuta and Denpasar. This strident new economic approach provided a friendly environment for the establishment of many other Sanur-based tourist businesses.

By the 1980s the writing was on the wall. Sanur's bread and butter (but not its lifeblood, its culture) was mass tourism. The Intaran Brahmans are now hotel owners, their "serfs" are building contractors and room boys, and the farmers of the area have become taxi drivers and art shop owners. Beachside there is no land left, and the ribbon of "Bali Baroque" mansions is thick along the highway. Sanur's Brahman priests are met at dawn by convoys of limousines, their schedules of incantations and blessings as busy as those of any senior statesman or tycoon. The proud heritage of yesterday is gone and forgotten, and the new generation of rich and famous are obsessed more with diet and commerce than with intrigue and traditions. But late at night, when the cash registers are asleep under their batik cozies and the mobile phones are turned off, Ratu Ayu steals from her throne into the night to a temple near you. Sanur's checkeredness is not a thing of the past.

Modern Sanur

Today, Sanur's glory as the island's most upscale resorts has been replaced by even more luxurious properties throughout the island, yet it remains the favorite of many returning guests who appreciate its mature, upmarket ambience, wide selection of restaurants and accommodations, and its reef-protected beach that is safe for swimming, thus attractive to families. While the cheaper lodgings in Kuta attract the often-noisy younger set and expensive Seminyak is home to many affluent foreigners, Sanur remains stable and relaxed.

Water sports are a key activity in Sanur. Practically all varieties are available here, from parasailing to kite surfing and from sea-kayaking to waterskiing; ever present is the hum of jet skis. Although surfing is not a prime attraction (there are better sites elsewhere on Bali), from October to March there are good breaks. Boards can be rented on the beach. A **beachfront walk** runs for 4 km (2.5 miles), and is ideal for jogging or simply strolling. During the months June through August, watch for the giant kites—some measuring 10 m (32 ft) long and taking five or six men to launch—that are flown here, capped off by a huge **International Kite Festival** in August, part of the month-long **Sanur Village Festival**.

On an entirely different note, the Sanur-based **PPLH Foundation** (Pusat Pendidikan Lingkungan Hidup, Jl. Hang Tuah No. 24, tel:/fax: 288-221, www.pplhbali.or.id), is a non-government organization established in 1997 to focus on environmental issues and community empowerment. Their programs include organic farming, house waste management, and a Green School, and they have published several environmental education manuals for teachers to use in classrooms concerning air and water quality, protecting coral reefs, preserving of mangroves, protecting sea turtles and their habitats, and waste management and recycling. The center has a library and visitors are welcome.

Serangan's Turtle Temple

Serangan (locally known as "Turtle Island") is a classic example of tourism development gone *amok*. A small island lying just off Bali's southern coast near Sanur, it has an area of only 72.8 ha and once had a population of about 2,500. Being too dry for wet rice farming, its residents grew corn, maize, peanuts, and beans and made shell trinkets to sell to the tourists. However, their main source of income was the trade in endangered sea turtles, as many Balinese are fond of turtle meat, which is also eaten at certain ceremonial occasions.

The most popular edible species is the Green Turtle *(Chelonia mydas)*, and in addition to buying them from fishermen, Serangan residents caught the cumbersome reptiles when they swam ashore to lay eggs in a shallow pit in the sand before returning to the sea. The eggs are also considered a great delicacy, and were dug up immediately and sold in local markets.

In an environmental nightmare that turned out to be a very dark cloud with a silver lining, in a scheme to convert the island to a tourist resort that failed due to the Asian economic crisis of 1997, the entire island was flattened, "reclaimed" land was added, and a causeway

was built connecting it to the mainland, forcing the fisher families who lived there to leave.

Although not a tourist destination today by any stretch of the imagination there are two things of interest on Serangan. One is the **Turtle Conservation and Education Center** (tel: +62 (0) 813-3841-2716), which has a hatchery and also cares for injured adults until they can be returned to the sea. Its biggest tasks, though, are reeducating many Balinese that the consumption of turtle meat is not a good practice, and protecting an historic hatching site from settlers, who are now returning to live on stretches of abandoned land along the coasts.

Manis Kuningan festival

The other reason to visit Serangan is that annually on the holy day Manis Kuningan in the 210-day Balinese calendar thousands of worshippers wearing their colorful finery flock to **Pura Sakenan** temple for the anniversary of its founding by Mpu Kuturan, which, according to the Prasasti Belanjong inscription, occurred during the 10th century. The Sakenan complex consists of two *pura* on the north coast of the island just west of Dukuh, a small fishing village that survived the destruction. The festival lasts for two days, beginning on the last day of *Kuningan wuku* (week) and ending on the first day of *Langkir wuku*.

Inside the first *pura* there is only a single shrine in the form of a *tugu* or obelisk. This is the seat of Dewi Sri, the goddess of prosperity and welfare. In the second and larger part of Pura Sakenan there are typical Balinese-style shrines for the *prasanak*, relatives of Sri who come to visit the temple on its anniversary day. On arrival, worshippers pray at the shrine of Dewi Sri to ask her for a prosperous year in the fields or in business.

Mangrove restoration

Thanks to funding by the Japanese government, 600 ha southwest of Sanur were set aside for mangrove restoration to protect part of the eastern coastline from erosion and pollution. At the **Mangrove Information Center** (Jl. Bypass Ngurah Rai, Km 21, tel: 726-969, fax: 710-473), educating school kids and visitors about the environmental dangers of losing mangrove forests is a top priority. The first stop is the visitors' center to learn about mangrove inhabitants, followed by a stroll on one of two boardwalks through the forest.

— *Made Wijaya & Nyoman Oka*

VISITING SANUR
(TELEPHONE CODE: 0361)

Sanur is where Bali's first luxury beach hotel was built 50 years ago and subsequently it became the prime spot for 5-star seaside accommodations. Although there are now even more elegant accommodations in other areas, Sanur's 5-km stretch of beach remains a favorite of many due to its location and relaxed pace. Many foreigners have lavish villas and bungalows here and it is the preferred upmarket place—especially in the Batujimbar and Belanjong areas—for many who stay long-term.

The main attraction here is the white sand beach bordering a reef-sheltered lagoon. The beach stretches south from the Inna Grand Bali Beach Hotel and ends up in the mangrove marshes opposite Serangan Island. Due to the protection of the lagoon, it is one of the safest beaches on the island, and thus ideal for families. There is no surf apart from out on the reef, and swimming isn't possible at low tide, but at other times this is the best place in Bali for windsurfing and sailing.

ORIENTATION

Sanur can be divided into several sub-areas, running north–south:

Batan Poh is west of the large Inna Grand Bali Beach Hotel gardens and golf course. This northern section of Sanur is popular with local crowds, particularly on Sunday afternoons.

Sindhu is east of Jl. Bypass Ngurah Rai and south of Jl. Segara Ayu, extending south to the first stretch of Jl. Danau Tamblingan. This area is classier, with good hotels on the beach, night and art markets, as well as good local restaurants.

Batujimbar is further south in central Sanur with fewer hotels. The beachfront here is the location of the affluent expatriate and Indonesian community. Exclusive beaches and properties are reached via small lanes.

Semawang in south Sanur stretches south from the Bali Hyatt Hotel to the Sanur Beach Hotel and beyond. It is the locale of both some of the priciest hotels and restaurants, as well as the red light district.

MONEY

A word of caution: moneychangers in Sanur are notoriously shifty. Use only "licensed" outlets, take your own calculator, ask for a receipt and count your money carefully before leaving. There are ATM machines everywhere.

GETTING THERE & GETTING AROUND

Along Jl. Danau Tamblingan—Sanur's main street —are many car, motorbike, and bicycle rental outlets. Bemos can also be found here. Sanur is also small enough for walking around. Jl. Bypass Prof. Ida Bagus Mantra along the eastern coastline is still under construction, causing many delays as queues of vehicles wind their way through detours. Along the road going northeast are many signs announcing villas for sale, indicating that once the highway is completed it will open up new beach destinations.

ACCOMMODATIONS

The choice of accommodations in Sanur ranges between the superior service and extensive facilities of the larger luxury establishments to the intimacy and personal attention of smaller bungalow-style hotels and guesthouses. Make your choice based on location rather than the number of stars. Some hotels do not charge extra for two children under 12 years old occupying the same room with parents.

An alternative to hotels is to rent luxury bungalows owned by foreign residents. These can work out relatively reasonably if accommodations are needed for a large number of people and if food and drink are bought at supermarket prices. Prices range from $250/day for a villa for two to $1,500/day for a two-hectare beachfront estate with 14 staff, an archery range, and use of a game fishing boat. For villa rentals browse Sanur villas online, where there are many options.

Budget (under $25)

Even budget homestays in Sanur provide laundry service, though prices are a bit higher than in Kuta and Ubud. Most places offer AC, Western-style toilets, showers, guided tours, and airport transfers.

The budget end of town is along Jl. Hang Tuah in northern Sanur (Sanur Kaja)—handy for restaurants and other services and only a short walk to the beach and the brilliant promenade. There's a whole cluster of cheapies opposite the entrance to the Inna Grand Bali Beach Hotel.

Ananda Beach Hotel, Jl. Hang Tuah, tel: 852-8521, www.anandabeachhotel.com. Family-owned basic rooms on good surfing beachfront on the north end of Sanur. Fan or AC rooms, all with full bath and morning tea service. Restaurant and bar, Internet. Near boats to Nusa Lembongan. $23–40.

Flashbacks, Jl. Danau Tamblingan 110, tel: 281-682, fax: 281-699, www.flashbacks-chb.com. Bungalows, rooms, suites, and guesthouse rooms. Small saltwater swimming pool. The Porch café is open 7 am–11 pm. $15–45.

Kesumasari Guest House, Jl. Pantai Kesumasari, Semawang, tel: 807-0181, www.kesumarihotel.com.

On the beach near shops and market, restaurants and bars. Thatched roof Balinese-style cottages with private balconies, AC and ceiling fan, hot water, fridge, tv. Restaurant, café, and bar. Family atmosphere. From $30.

Puri Mango Guesthouse, Jl. Danau Toba 15, tel: 281-293, fax: 288-598, www.purimango.com. A popular budget accommodation with swimming pool, restaurant, and bar. From $20.

The Watering Hole, Jl. Hang Tuah 37, tel: 288-289, www.wateringholesanurbali.com. This two-floor hotel with restaurant is a traveler's place par excellence with in-depth library, big inner courtyard, and quiet common areas. From the spacious balcony, a nice view over the Inna Grand Bali Beach gardens. From $7.

Moderate ($25–50)

Sanur has a great selection of intermediate range hotels, with the only significant difference in price being proximity to and view of the ocean. Most have AC, hot water, and private verandas.

Palm Garden Hotel (Hotel Taman Palem), Jl. Kesumasari 3, Semawang (southern Sanur), tel: 287-041, 288-026, fax. 289-571, www.palmgarden-bali.com. Including a first-class continental breakfast, this is one of the best deals in Sanur. Only 16 rooms, very personal, friendly staff; comfortable, peaceful and just a 2 minute stroll to the beach and its outstanding seafood restaurants. All rooms with bathroom and adjoining living room. From $29.

Prima Cottage, Jl. Bumi Ayu 23, tel: 286-369, fax: 289-153, www.primacottage.com. Small, cozy hotel with Balinese-style architecture. Rooms and bungalows a few minutes from the beach in a quiet neighborhood. Restaurant, café, bar, fresh water swimming pool. $27–75.

Intermediate ($50–75)

Laghawa Beach Inn, Jl. Danau Tamblingan 51, Batujimbar, tel: 288-494, fax 282-533, www.laghawa beach.com. A small hotel on 2 beachfront ha with hand-carved doors, windows and sculptures, Balinese antique furniture and beautifully land-scaped grounds. Modern facilities; courteous and efficient staff. The Laghawa Grill specializes in steaks and seafood. $50-170, breakfast included.

Peneeda View Beach Hotel, Jl. Danau Tamblingan 89, mobile: 0813-3753-6464, www.peneedaview beachhotel.com. 56 rooms on 1.5 ha beachside with expansive gardens and open-air facilities, beachside restaurant and bar, 3 swimming pools. From $60.

Sativa Sanur Cottages, Jl. Danau Tamblingan, tel:/fax: 287-881. 10 two-story cottages on the beach with Balinese atmosphere, handcrafted wood furniture, local art, tv, mini-fridge, AC and in-house movies. Restaurant, bar, pool. $50–96.

Sekuta Condo Suites, Jl. Sekuta 12, tel: 287-727, 289-032, fax: 286-723, www.sekutacondosuites.com. Fully furnished condos, each with living room, dining room, and kitchen. The Cavern Bar restaurant, swimming pool, massage, room service. $50–75.

Vila Shanti Beach Hotel, Jl. Danau Tamblingan 47, tel: 852-8521, www.vilashantisanur.com. Beachfront property. All rooms have AC and private terraces overlooking gardens. Seaside restaurant and pool, coffee shop, 24-hr room service. $60–97.

First class ($75–100)

Batu Jimbar Holiday Home, Jl. Danau Tamblingan 87, tel: 282-697, www.btjbali.com. A leafy private estate near the beach, shops, and restaurants. Rooms have private balcony and kitchenette. $280-330/week; $890–1,050/month.

Gazebo Beach Hotel, Jl. Danau Tamblingan 35, tel: 361-0840, www.gazebobeachhotel.com. On the beachfront, Balinese style architecture, pool, fitness center, library/lounge, art gallery, restaurant, and bar. Piazza Bakery & Deli. $75–142.

Hotel La Taverna, Jl. Danau Tamblingan 29, tel: 288-497, fax: 286-165, www.latavernahotel.com. 36 rooms in 2-level buildings with Mediterranean stucco and Balinese thatched roofs. White sand beach, swimming pool. Rooms are furnished with antiques. Isola beachside restaurant serves Italian dishes, pizzas, and Indonesian favorites. Room service, tv, WiFi. Swimming pool, spa. $75–290.

Sanur Paradise Plaza Hotel, Jl. Bypass Ngurah Rai 83 (intersection Jl. Bypass Ngurah Rai and Jl. Hang Tuah), tel: 281-781, fax: 281-782. 329 rooms in a low-rise complex set around a serpentine landscaped swimming pool and lush gardens. A 4-star hotel with 3 restaurants, bar, spa, kids' club, fitness center, and tennis courts. This hotel is not on the beach but is within walking distance. Request a room away from noisy Jl. Bypass. From $95.

Luxury ($100–up)

Most of the hotels in this category have their own beachfront and provide swimming pool(s), bar and lounges, cafes and restaurants, shops, rooms with private verandahs, AC, hot water, fridge, tv, video, telephone, and dazzling evening entertainment. (Major credit cards accepted.) Some of the older hotels are in need of sprucing up. While they qualify as "Luxury" because of their rates, some of them definitely aren't.

Bali Hyatt, Jl. Danau Tamblingan, Semawang, tel: 281-234, fax: 287-693, www.bali.resort.hyatt.com. 390 rooms. One of the island's first international-standard hotels, which just marked its 30th anniversary and is starting to look worn. With thatched-roof and terracotta-tiled lobby, open, relaxed feel and magnificently landscaped gardens, this is not your typical luxury chain hotel. Complete repertoire of indoor and outdoor high-class restaurants. Complete sports facilities, 2 large pools, plus waterfall, Jacuzzi, and cold dip. Spa. From $120.

Inna Grand Bali Beach, Jl. Hang Tuah 58, tel: 288-511, fax: 287-917, ww.innagrandbalibeach.com. 523 rooms. The first luxury hotel in Sanur, constructed with war reparation funds from Japan in 1966 in the classic "Waikiki" high-rise style. Today it is owned by the Indonesian government. Rooms in tower, low-rise block, or cottages. Beauty salon, spa, pool, mini golf. From $110.

Mercure Resort Sanur, Jl. Mertasari, tel: 288-822, fax: 287-303, ww.mercureresortsanur.com. 189 guest rooms in 41 thatched roof cottages on 5 ha of beachfront gardens. 2 pools, tennis court, spa, supervised Kids' Club. From $270.

Natah Bale Villas, Jl. Cemara 32, mobile: +62 813-3735-3646, www.natahbalevillas.com. Four 1- and 2-bedroom villas, each with private entrance, open living room, dining room, fully-equipped kitchen, outside-inside bathtub, and shower. Peacefully private. Beach is only a few meters away. Restaurant, swimming pool. WiFi. $100–244.

Sanur Beach, Jl. Mertasari, Semawang, tel: 288-011, fax: 287-566, www.sanurbeach.aerowisata.com. 425 rooms in a 4-story block, one of Sanur's older beachfront hotels known for its friendly service. Restaurants, bars, fitness center, spa, cultural performances. From $105.

Segara Village Hotel, Jl. Segara Ayu, tel: 288-407, fax: 287-242, www.segaravillage.com. 120 renovated guest rooms in a 4-star beachfront property with 5 distinct "village" areas. 3 swimming pools. The Beach Restaurant and Bar has Indonesian and international menu. Jacuzzi Bar serves cocktails while being soothed by water jets with ocean views. Spa. $118–186.

Tandjung Sari Hotel, Jl. Danau Tamblingan, Batujimbar, tel: 288-441, fax: 287-930, www.tandjungsari.com. 26 beachfront bungalows built in 1962; charming decor, tranquil, elegant. The bungalows are reminiscent of those found in the pleasure gardens of the Balinese rajas. Swimming pool, restaurant, bar. $230–340.

Villa Mahapala, Jl. Pantai Sindhu, tel: 286-222, www.villamahapala-bali.com. A luxury resort with 20 villas, each with private pool and featuring the 12 signs of the zodiac. Restaurant and bar, swimming pool, spa, fitness center. $275–375.

Waka Maya, Jl. Tanjung Pinggir Pantai 41, Sanur, www.wakaexperience.com. Deliberately located away from crowds and shops, Waka Maya is all about seclusion. 7 Balinese-style villas with 2 or 3 bedrooms and kitchen; 7 luxurious bungalows, some with private swimming pools. Facilities include swimming pool, spa, beach club, and restaurant. From $160 for lanai; from $210 for villas.

DINING & DRINKING

Sanur's fine dining international and specialty restaurants run the gamut from affordable classic French and Indian to nouveau cuisine and Italian. Many offer free pickup and drop off in the Sanur area.

The hotels have a wide variety of restaurants, buffets, and coffee shops. Restaurants outside the hotels offer a greater variety of food in a broad price range. Most close at 10 pm.

Jl. Danau Tamblingan has many bars serving cocktails and cold beer.

Local food

The cheapest and most colorful food spot at night is the **Sanur Night Market**, located in the Art Market at the north end of Jl. Danau Tamblingan. The food is spicy, but nothing is cheaper.

Moderate restaurants

Arena Cafe, Jl. Bypass Ngurah Rai 115 (near McDonald's), tel: 287-255. An Australian-owned pub atmosphere, much loved by local and foreign residents. Big screen tv for sport events and generous servings of European-style home-made food. Ribs are worth raving about. Billiards. Open 4 pm–2 am.

Elang Laut, Jl. Danau Tamblingan 188, southern Sanur, tel: 282-552. Offers Dutch specialties such as *bitter ballen, krokets,* and *utsmeyer*. The bar is very comfortable and convivial. Friendly service.

Kalimantan Bar & Restaurant, Jl. Pantai Sindhu 11, tel: 289291. Those looking for breakfasts, sandwiches and burgers should try this cozy restaurant among the trees down beside the Segara Village Hotel. It has a loyal following among local expats. Bob, the owner, is an old-time Bali resident with a voluminous store of knowledge about the island and an avid golfer.

Massimo Il Ristorante, Jl. Danau Tamblingan 206, tel: 288-942. Using only the finest imported ingredients, the menu blends the taste of good old-fashioned Italian home cooking with a warm and friendly atmosphere. The Italian ambassador is a regular here. Excellent wine cellar. Open 11 am–9 pm. Also delivers to homes and villas.

Sanur Deli, Jl. Danau Poso 67, tel: 270-544. One of the best handmade sandwich (whopping big!) shops in Bali. Also sells baguettes, foccaccia, Aussie meat pies, quiche, pastries, salads, and iced drinks. Pleasant patio café.

Warung Blanjong, Jl. Danau Poso 78 (corner of Jl. Buyan and Jl. Danau Poso), tel: 285-613. This open-air Indonesian-style restaurant serves a classic Balinese *nasi campur*, a complete meal of rice accompanied by meat and a vegetables for only Rp15,000. Or try their *ayam betutu*, roast chicken, tender and succulent, with a delicious stuffing. Also a full selection of dishes from other islands, all cooked with great attention to the authentic flavors. Because of their low prices and free home delivery, very popular with local expat community, who know where all the bargains are. Open 8 am–10 pm.

Organic restaurants

Café Batujimbar, Jl. Danau Tamblingan 152, tel: 287-374, www.cafebatujimbar.com. Sanur's "in" place. Its hanging vines, open-air seating and sturdy furniture gives it the look of a Riviera cafe. This is the haunt of the local expat community, many of whom live in the Sanur area. The café offers light, healthy mixed cuisine, organic food, great salads, and daily specials. Coffee and baked goods are their specialties. Newspapers, magazines. Open 7 am–11 pm.

Manik Organik, Jl. Danau Tamblingan 85, Sanur, tel: 855-3380, www.manikorganikbali.com. In addition to being a vegetarian café serving healthy foods and promoting natural health remedies, Manik Organik's community health center hosts an organic vegetables night market, yoga, meditation, and *qigong* sessions.

Luxury restaurants

The majority of fine dining restaurants offer similar fare and prices; menus generally feature grilled seafood. Many also stage dance performances and offer pick-up services.

Some of the best places for those who want to dine in luxury are found in hotels, such as **La Taverna** (good seafood, brick-oven pizza) and **Tandjung Sari**, known for its Indonesian *rijsttafel* and its Balinese palace atmosphere. Dine to the strains of a bamboo *tingklik* orchestra while looking out to sea, or have a drink in the seaside bar. A romantic spot for dinner by moonlight.

Kayu Manis, Jl. Danau Tamblingan, tel: 289-410. Delicious international food at great prices. Popular with expats. No credit cards.

Pala Restaurant & Wine Bar, Jl. Bypass Ngurah Rai 121XX, tel: 283-835. Splendid retro-French, 2-course dinners and 1-course lunches. Contemporary brassier-style interior, warm atmosphere, in-house bakery, ample parking. Menus change every week. Be prepared for such culinary delights as *canard a'l'orange*, salmon *tartar*, tenderloin *aux poivres*, and mousse *au chocolat*. Lunch starts 11:30 am, dinner 6 pm. Wine bar open 'til 2 am. Closed Monday nights.

Resto Ming, Jl. Danau Tamblingan No. 105 (457 m south of Bali Hyatt), tel: 281-948, tel: 286-079, fax: 270-805. A wonderful restaurant where the French-speaking owner, Mr. Ming, and staff fall over themselves trying to please. Great upbeat atmosphere. Sophisticated menu is delicious and extremely good value.

Ryoshi, Jl. Danau Tamblingan 150, tel: 288-473. An island-wide favorite for dependable authentic fresh sushi and typical Japanese fare. Good value. Open noon–midnight.

Smorgås Café, Jl. Danau Tamblingan/Pantai Karang II, tel: 289-361. Owned by a Swedish family, great freshly made Swedish food and good coffee.

Stiff Chilli, Jl. Kesumasari 11, Semawang Beach, tel:/fax: 288-371, www.rjhgroup.com. Part of a chain. Good Italian food made with important ingredients, organic salads, gelato. Does anything else need to be said?

The Village Restaurant & Bar, Jl. Danau Tamblingan 66, tel: 285-035. Open breakfast, lunch and dinner, innovative cuisine that ranges from New Orleans Creole to Italian, seafood, and vegetarian dishes. 8 am–midnight daily.

Treo Beach Café, Mertasari Beach, tel: 921-8588, www.treosanur.com. Open for breakfast, lunch, and dinner. International and local dishes made from fresh local fruit and vegetables. Fruit juices and lassies, cappuccino, espresso, and very cold beer.

SHOPPING

At the end of Jl. Danau Toba in north Sanur, the **Sanur Beach Market** has a wide range of stalls selling inexpensive gift items. Jl. Danau Tamblingan has scores of shops selling local handicrafts, homewares, textiles, carvings, paintings, leather, and silver goods. Also check out **Pasar Sindhu** at the north end of Jalan Pungutan and the **Art Market** at the end of Jl. Hang Tuah.

Otherwise, go to the arcades in the main hotels for high quality goods and no bargaining or to the many designer boutiques opposite the souvenir kiosks. Some other interesting shops are:

Ceramics

Gudang Keramik, Jl. Danau Tamblingan, tel: 289-363. Open daily (except Nyepi), 9 am–6 pm. Gudang Keramik ("Ceramics Warehouse") is a treasure trove of tableware and accessories that are seconds from the fabulous (and expensive) Jengala Ceramics in Jimbaran. On some items the flaw may be so tiny that you have to squint to see it.

Clothing & textiles

Mama & Leon, Jl. Danau Tamblingan 99A, tel: 288-044. A long-established designer very popular with fashion hounds who want something out of the ordinary.

Nogo Bali Ikat Center, Jl. Danau Tamblingan 100, tel: 288-765, www.nogobali.com. Traditional hand-woven textiles from throughout Indonesia made into modern clothing. They also take special orders.
Uluwatu, Jl. Danau Tamblingan, tel: 751-933, fax: 287-054, www.uluwatu.co.id. A beautiful collection of clothing and sleepwear in crisp cotton and silky rayon finished with handmade Balinese lace. Also has attractive homewares. Other boutiques are in Nusa Dua, five locations in Kuta, one in Seminyak and one in Ubud.

Food
There are mini-markets throughout Sanur selling snacks, beer, cold drinks, toiletries, and the like. For something more substantial, try:
Hardy's Supermarket, Jl. Danau Tamblingan 193, tel: 28191, has everything anyone could ever need, including wine and spirits.

Home furnishings and accessories
Carlo Innovative Furnishings, Jl. Danau Poso 22, tel: 285-211, fax: 281-923, www.carloshowroom. com. Carlo Pessina's unique designs in furniture, furnishings, and accessories focus on natural materials. Found in many of the world's great resorts, they are now available in this Sanur showroom.

ACTIVITIES
Golf & art
Inna Grand Bali Beach, Jl. Hang Tuah 58, tel: 288-511, fax: 287-917, www.grand-balibeach.com, has a well-maintained 9-hole course for those interested in a quick round. It is also home to **Maha Art Gallery**, in the Club House (tel: 872-8866, fax: 285-488, www. mahaartgallery.com). An art space in an unusual location, whose goals include creating an interaction between artists, collectors, and art lovers while improving general education about the arts.

WATER SPORTS
Almost any water sport imaginable is available in Sanur. Most of the facilities are right on the beach around the Art Market and in front of the big hotels. Sanur's diving and snorkeling is not the best on the island, but there are several agents that organize trips to better underwater sites. The surfing is not great at Sanur, either, but there is one spot with good breaks during the rainy season; boards are available for rent on the beach.

Boats to Nusa Lembongan depart several times daily from the beach at the end of Jl. Hang Tuah, near **Sanur Beach**.

Diving
Atlantis International Bali Diving, Jl. Bypass Ngurah Rai 350, tel: 284-312, Mobile: 081-2380-5767, fax: 282-824, www.balidiveaction.com. Has operated in Bali, the Maldives, and the Philippines since 1996. Small groups only.
Bali International Diving Professionals (BIDP), Jl. Danau Poso 26, tel: 285-065, fax: 270-760, www. bidp-balidiving.com. More then 25 years diving experience in the Indo-Pacific region. Provides day trips, safaris, and courses for all levels of skill and experience. Small groups only. Dive masters and guides speak several languages.
Baruna Adventurer, Jl. Bypass Ngurah Rai 300B, tel: 753-820, fax 753-809, www.komodo-divencruise. com. Has beach booths in front of the Inna Grand Bali Beach and the Bali Hyatt, offering diving tours to Komodo Island on its live-aboard boat for a minimum of 5 people. Also has non-dive trips.
Crystal Divers Scuba Centre, Crystal Santai Hotel, Jl. Danau Tamblingan 168, tel:/fax: 286-737, www. crystal-divers.com. Owned by a PADI Course Director, in business since 1997. Dive safaris and day trips on their own boats. PADI courses and non-certification courses. "Explore Dive" program lets divers who have discovered a new spot name the site. Retail shop.
Ena Dive Center & Marine Adventures, Jl. Tirta Ening No. 1, tel: 288-829, fax: 287-945, www.enadive. co.id. In business for 25 accident-free years and a 5-Star Gold Palm PADI Resort recipient. Has friendly English-, Japanese-, and Indonesian-speaking guides and staff. PADI instructions, diving packages in Bali and beyond.

Other water sports
Blue Oasis Beach Club, Sanur Beach Hotel, Jl. Danau Tamblingan, tel: 288-011, fax: 288-106, www.blueoasis.com. Excellent and professional, has a good dive site in front of a protective reef, kitesurfing in the nearby lagoon, as well as windsurfing, sailing, kayaking, waterskiing, and wakeboarding. Also offers PADI certification and dive tours. Pro shop with new and secondhand equipment.
Bali Kitesurfing, Jl. Cemara No. 72, tel:/fax: 284-260, www.bali-kitesurfing.org. Established in 1999, specializes in board- and kitesurfing (also called kiteboarding), combining the speed of windsurfing, the tricks of wakeboarding and the jumps of surfing. Rental equipment and lessons. Website has good information on Bali and other Indonesian islands, including wind and wave forecasts.

JIMBARAN AND THE BUKIT

Southern Bali's Cliff-faced Shores

At Bali Island's southernmost point is a shoe-shaped peninsula, Bukit Badung ("Badung Hill"), and the "leg", the isthmus that connects it to the mainland, is Jimbaran.

Since in the past, visitors only went to the peninsula for Nusa Dua stays, traveling along the eastern mudflats and mangrove swamps, the west coast went unnoticed by everyone except extreme surfers until 20 or so years ago. Before that, there were no hotels or homestays, no tourist restaurants, no shops, few artists, and not many English speakers. All that has changed, though, and the fine beaches at Jimbaran and the Bukit, as it is familiarly called, now have the largest concentration of luxury hotels and villas along their edges than anywhere else on the island. And after nearly two decades of having the isolated Four Seasons and InterContinental as its only resorts, it is currently experiencing yet another growth spurt.

This region also has places of cultural significance, the most renowned being Uluwatu Temple (Pura Luhur Uluwatu).

Bali's fishing center

Jimbaran encompasses the area on the isthmus just south of Bali's international airport. Most of its 12,000 or so inhabitants live in a cluster of traditional *banjar* neighborhoods at the narrowest part of the isthmus, but the Jimbaran area also includes the sparsely populated northwestern corner of the Bukit plateau.

Jimbaran village is unique in that it borders two separate coasts lying less than 2 km (1.2 miles) apart, each of which has a markedly different geography. To the west is the broad expanse of Jimbaran Bay and the Indian Ocean. To the east is a tidal mudflat enclosing the shallow and sheltered Benoa Harbor. The ecosystems of the two strands, and the occupations of villagers who live on them, differ dramatically.

Salt making and lime production are the principal livelihoods on the eastern side, while fishing is the main industry on the west. The salt is made by sloshing seawater onto the flats, to be dried by the sun. Villagers then rake up the salty dirt and evaporate the solution over wood fires in shallow metal pans. The abundance of coral fragments provides the raw materials for the lime industry. (Note: you will have to ask directions if you want to see salt and lime workings; these areas are only accessible via a rabbit's warren of unpaved tracks.)

Jimbaran's lovely western beach is protected from larger waves by a fragmented reef behind which lies shallow water, an ideal anchorage for large fishing boats. However idyllic it may appear during the dry season, the beach is often rather unpleasant from about November through March, when high waves assault the shore, and the sand becomes littered with flotsam of every description.

Fishing is the principal activity all along the bay, not only in Jimbaran itself but also in Kedonganan and Kelan villages to the north. Kedonganan's catch always surpasses that of Jimbaran. The fishermen—who are mostly Javanese—use large, motorized *prahu* made in Madura to catch enormous quantities of fish with huge purse-shaped seines. They depart in the late afternoon and return just after dawn to sell their catch to wholesalers at the Jimbaran **fish market** (*pasar ikan*).

In contrast to those in Kedonganan, almost all fishermen in Jimbaran are local Balinese who use *jukung* (small outrigger boats) and fish with gill or large, round cast nets. The gill nets are set out in the bay in the late afternoon and the catch is collected early the next morning. During the fishing season there is a lot of interesting activity just after sunrise when the boats go to the market from both areas to sell their catch. An early morning trip to Jimbaran's *pasar ikan* is certainly well worth waking early, to see fish being unloaded and iced down, ready to make their way to smaller markets and restaurants throughout southern Bali. Also, Jimbaran's **produce market** is located on the northeast corner of the main crossroads in the village, just across the street from Pura Ulun Siwi.

There are no handicrafts sold specifically for tourists, but there is a considerable variety of local products, including baskets and mats produced by the weavers of nearby villages such as Ungasan and Pecatu. Look for the chefs of Bali's best restaurants doing their daily shopping. The market is open daily, and activity is greatest early in the morning, almost ceasing by noon.

Today, Jimbaran is best known to travelers as the home of magnificent seafood dinners, thanks to three clusters of about 50 restaurants right on the sand that draw those who love great food and eye-popping sunsets. The first group is just south of the *pasar ikan*, the second is near Jimbaran's main intersection, and the third is just before reaching Four Seasons Resort Jimbaran. The setting sun, the lights of fishing platforms twinkling across the horizon, the candlelit tables overlooking the beach, and the barbecue racks billowing smoke all make for an enchanting atmosphere. Be advised to arrive early—around 5 pm—to select a restaurant and grab a ringside seat.

The **swimming** is also good in Jimbaran Bay, which is protected by a reef system, whereas further south crashing waves and strong undertows make it too dangerous to swim. However, the primary pastime in Jimbaran is relaxing and luxuriating in one of the area's divine resorts.

Pura Ulun Siwi

Pura Ulun Siwi (or Ulun Swi) is Jimbaran's best-known "sight" for the Balinese as well as for tourists. This large temple lies at the northwestern corner of the principal crossroads, across the street from the market. It is unusual for several reasons. First, it faces east, rather than south. During prayers, the worshippers face west, rather than to the north to Gunung Agung, as is the usual practice. This is attributed to the fact that the temple, once a primitive shrine, was "converted" to Balinese Hinduism fairly early, in the 11th century. At this time, the Javanese holy man who founded the temple, Mpu Kuturan, still followed the custom of his homeland in orienting his temples toward holy Mt. Semeru, in East Java. It was only much later that Gunung Agung became the focus of Balinese Hinduism.

The temple has only two courtyards, instead of the usual three. The spacious interior courtyard measures 66x30 m (210x100 ft) and is dominated by an enormous 11-tiered *meru* tower that is more massive than artistic. The temple has been periodically renovated but remains simple and rustic, lacking the ornate *paras* stone carvings that characterize Gianyar's temples to the north.

The principal gate, a *kori agung* with wings, is very similar in construction to that of Pura Uluwatu on the Bukit, except that it is made of brick instead of coral stone. There is a close connection between these two temples, and it is said that one should pray at Pura Ulun Siwi before proceeding to Pura Uluwatu.

Ulun Siwi is unusual in yet another way. It is the principal temple in Bali dedicated to the welfare of both wet and dry rice fields, and the spirits which live in the temple are thought to control the mice and insects that periodically infest the fields. Farmers regularly come to Pura Siwi to get water, which they then take back home and sprinkle on their fields, either to protect them from these pests or to rid them of those already present.

Lesser-known temples

Jimbaran also has the usual three village temples, the Pura Dalem (called Pura Kahyangan locally), Pura Puseh and Pura Desa. The latter two are combined into one enclosure, as occurs in many villages. These tend to be overlooked in favor of the more spectacular and better-known Pura Ulun Siwi, but each is interesting in its own right.

Pura Kahyangan lies just to the west of the cemetery. **Pura Puseh** and **Pura Desa** are about 50 m (160 ft) northeast of the market. It is interesting to note that the *odalan* or anniversary ceremonies of these three temples, and of Pura Ulun Siwi, all occur within four days of each other, commencing on the third day after Galungan, which is the biggest holy day in the traditional Balinese calendar. Jimbaran becomes a beehive of ritual activity at this time of year.

One of the most important ceremonies in Jimbaran is the exorcistic Barong procession. The Barong is a mythical beast that acts as protector of the village and its people, represented by a huge masked effigy that is paraded through the area during ceremonial occasions. Jimbaran's inhabitants spare no expense to support the Barong, making offerings to it, praying, and performing the ritual. Appearances of the Barong on Jimbaran's main street between Pura Ulun Siwi and the market are always accompanied by the evil witch Rangda and her two cohorts, and by a

Jimbaran & the Bukit

0   1km

N

Bali Strait

Tuban Beach
Holiday
Resort Bar

The Pat
Ba

Jimbaran Bay

Muaya Be

Pura Tegal Wangi

Four Seasons
Resort

Batu Layah
Beach

Balangan Point

Ayana Resort
& Spa

Gending Kedis

Balangan Beach

Kesambi Kembar

Bukit
Jimbara
Villa Jimbaran
High Land

Dreamland Beach

Hole 17 Villas

Dusun Trafalgar
Square Estate

Bukit Hijau

Blok James
Cook Village

New Kuta
Condotel

**Pecatu Indah
Resort**

Puri Gading
Raya Gading 1

Bingin Beach

Dusun Chiyoda
Town

Impossibles Beach

Kesuma Sari

Cengiling

Frangipani Villa
138m

Anantara Uluwatu
Resort & Spa

C151 Smart Villas
Dreamland

Blok Natural
Residential

Padang Padang
Beach

Villa Capung
Bali

Tundun Penyu

Griya
Permata

Suluban
Surfing

Blue Point Bay
Villas & Spa

Labuan Sait

Bangket

Blok
Natural
Residential

+76m

163m

+ 156m

The
Pondok

Suluban
Beach

The Dreamland
Luxury Villas

Bingin

Umpeng
Padang Padang

Blok Nuri

+ 166m

Dreamland Luxury
Villas & Spa

Ungasa
Simpan

Uluwatu
Surf Villas

Les

Padang
Padang

Indah Manis
Villa Bali

152m

Bakung Sari

The Istana

Emma

62m

133m

166m

Blok Sahadewa

198m

Wana Giri

Surf Maniac
Camp

+61m

142m

U

164m

Suluban

Kulat

B

Temu Dewi

Sarikaya

60m

64m

Song Bintang
+109m

Dauh Puseh

Raya Uluwatu

Kertha Lestari

Pura Luhur
Uluwatu

Pagpagan

Pecatu

+210m

+144m

107m

Bustegeh

115m

Karang Bromo

173m

Bangbang Kembar

153m 140m

Mebulu Point

Puri Bali Resort

Giri Sari Selonding

213m

155m

Wijaya Kusumah

Nyangnyang
Surfing

Tirta Bali

145m

Raya Uluwatu
164m

Pulukpuluk

165m

Alila Villas
Uluwatu Bali

Tembiyak

Karma
Kandara

Bany
Tre

Aisis Luxury
Villas Bali

160m

Bulgari
Resort

The Edge
Villas Bali

Alila Uluwatu

Pura Masuka

Karang Mas sejahtera

Tukad Batu Mejan

Gua Ringdig

Tukad Bugbug

Tk. Serna

Tuksd Balongpule

Tk. Songkhung

Tukad Pangpang

Kulumbung

Tukad Klimpif

Uluwatu Pt.

Mata Uluwatu

retine of about a dozen other dancers. Trance plays an important part in a Barong performance, and the actions of the trance dancers who try to stab Rangda are bizarre and unforgettable to any foreign visitor.

A limestone plateau, luxury villas, and a surfer's paradise

South of Jimbaran, the road climbs steeply up several switchbacks onto Bukit Badung plateau, offering dramatic panoramas back up the beach to the ricelands and the volcanoes on a clear day and of the pounding surf far below.

The first noticeable thing about **Bukit Badung** is that the landscape is totally different from most of the rest of the island. A large part of Bali is volcanic, rich soils watered year-round by runoff from mountain lakes and streams that support dense, tropical vegetation. In contrast, the Bukit is a non-volcanic limestone plateau which has its own unique ecology.

The Bukit has an ecosystem characterized by its lack of surface water. The soil lies on a base of cracked, porous limestone, and any rainfall quickly seeps through fissures into a very low water table. The area is thus ill-suited to agriculture during the dry season, when the scrubby vegetation looks more Mediterranean than tropical. During the rainy season, however, the region becomes quite lush, and crops of soybeans, sorghum, cashew nuts, manioc, beans of various sorts, and corn, flourish.

The plateau, which constitutes most of the peninsula, rises abruptly to about 200m (650 ft) above sea level, and is ringed on all sides by steep cliffs. Many lovely beaches line the shores of the peninsula and the isthmus, although access is often difficult. The biggest beach is at Jimbaran Bay, on the western coastline south of the airport, but more secluded and equally beautiful sands are found further to the south along the south-western shores of the Bukit plateau.

The whole area has a host of natural attractions for those willing to invest the time to explore. Grand, gray-white cliffs overlook long, white rollers that are world famous among surfers. Graceful fishing boats sway at anchor in tranquil Jimbaran Bay. The quiet, empty bush areas of the elevated plateau are ideal for experienced hikers, though few good maps of the area are available.

All around the western and southern edges of the plateau, limestone cliffs tower above the pounding surf 70 m (230 ft) below, where some of Bali's best surfing is found. Heading south from Jimbaran, **Balangan** is the first of a string of rare white sand beaches on the west coast favored by surfers during the dry season (April–October). Skipping the fabled, once-beautiful **Dreamland**, which has now been decimated by a resort development, the next idyllic spot is **Bingin**, followed by **Padang Padang**, and **Suluban**, further south. Of them all, the most famous by far is **Uluwatu**, with its seven breaks that have

Sunset at Pura Luhur Uluwatu, which is perched atop a cliff facing west

attracted surfers for four decades. Most of these beaches are difficult to access, but the reward of a deserted, unblemished beach is worth it for sunbathers and sand-and-surf enthusiasts.

A glimpse of the past

The Bukit bears witness to a long history. There are limestone caves throughout the area, and evidence of prehistoric human occupation has been found in a cave called Gua Selonding. Before Uluwatu became a Hindu temple, it was the site of worship for more ancient cults. The foundation of the temple itself is dated by Balinese tradition to the 11th century.

The poverty of the soil and its geographical isolation have shaped the social landscape of Bukit Badung. There was never any wet-rice farming here, and other crops and cattle breeding did not feed the population. So those who could not subsist in traditional ways looked to the sea for salt, lime, and fish, while others migrated to rice-growing areas. Old men of Sukawati once talked of Bukit peddlers exchanging betel lime and salt for gleaning and accommodation rights in other parts of the island.

Bukit Badung is also known as a region where the overlords of the Mengwi and Badung kingdoms banished malcontents and defaulting debtors. Nowadays the population is growing, the region having become a major focal point of Bali's relentless tourism boom.

Uluwatu

The Bukit's most famous landmark is **Pura Luhur Uluwatu**, an exquisite monument situated on a headland at the westernmost tip of the peninsula. The carvings which decorate the temple are very well preserved in comparison to many of Bali's temples, due to the extremely hard, dark gray coral stone used in its construction.

Uluwatu was reputedly built by the priest Mpu Kuturan in the 11th century as one of the six major *sad kahyangan* territorial temples of the island. The reformer priest, Pedanda Wawu Rauh, rebuilt it in its present state in the 16th century. He is said to have attained his *moksa* (release from earthly desires) here. The temple is home to a large colony of monkeys who have caused some damage to the temple over the years, but still retain their protected status as sacred creatures. It is advised to remove all eye-

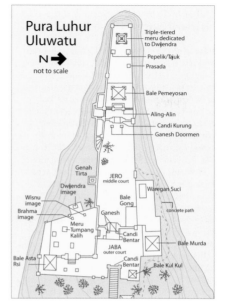

glasses and jewelry before entering the temple and to hold tightly to purses and bags. They can expertly swoop down, grab anything that attracts them quickly and be out of sight before you can say "naughty monkey".

The temple's structure follows the tripartite pattern of godly, human, and demonic courtyards. The outermost entrance is a *candi bentar* split gate shaped as a set of carved Garuda wings—an unusual feature as they are usually left smooth. Inside the temple, a second gate is capped by a monstrous Kala head guardian figure. At the foot of the gate are two Ganesha "elephant god" statues. The temple underwent renovations in the late 19th century, again in 1949, and more recently in the 1980s, and some parts are actually as new as they look. Despite its mixture of old and contemporary, it is a breathtakingly beautiful spot, especially when the sun begins to set.

The island's south coast

Continuing east from Uluwatu along the Bukit's southern shoreline are resorts so opulent that remoteness, serenity, personalized service, and complete and total privacy don't do them justice. The grandest of them all, **The Bulgari Resort Bali,** even offers trips to neighboring islands and volcano-viewing by helicopter.

—*Fred Eiseman & Jean Couteau*

VISITING JIMBARAN & THE BUKIT
(TELEPHONE CODE: 0361)

Located on the isthmus 2 km (1.2 miles) south of Ngurah Rai International Airport and—after being interrupted by the runways—a continuation of the soft white sands of Kuta Beach, Jimbaran Bay is one of Bali's most underrated resort areas. Tranquil compared to Kuta, and popular with the Balinese, Jimbaran still retains much of its fishing village charm. With its shallow water and lack of sharp corals, Jimbaran is particularly ideal for families. The area also remains free of aggressive vendors.

Jimbaran's lively *pasar ikan* (fish market), actually located in Kedonganan at the northern end of the beach, is where nearly all of south Bali's restaurateurs come to buy their seafood. It opens for business at 4 am. As any housewife will attest, the market sells the highest quality and freshest seafood in all of south Bali, and at very good prices.

The peninsula at Bali's southernmost tip is Bukit Badung, locally referred to as "the Bukit" (meaning "the Hill"). Until the 1970s only known by surfers for its outstanding breaks on the west coast, this formerly dry and barren land has now, together with Jimbaran, mushroomed into Bali's largest concentration of high-end resorts and luxury villas.

See map, pages 122–123.

GETTING THERE & GETTING AROUND
Ojek motorcycle taxis can be found around the Jimbaran market. Bargain first, based on the distance you want to cover.

ACCOMMODATIONS
Except for some budget accommodations near the surfing beaches and a few intermediate-range places inland, most visitors stay in Jimbaran and the Bukit for their exclusive resorts and villas. Most offer free shuttles to Kuta.

To find one of the many privately owned villas available for rent, browse the Internet for villas in Jimbaran, Uluwatu, or Bukit Badung and you'll get a dizzying array of agents and information.

Intermediate ($50–75)
Puri Bambu, Jl. Pengeracikan, Kedonganan (north Jimbaran), tel: 701-468, fax: 701440, www.puri-bambu.com. Set in Kedonganan village, 45 rooms and 3 suites 180 m from the beach, each furnished with modern ethnic furniture. All have AC, tv, hot water. Pool with sunken bar, performance stage. Free airport and Kuta transfers. $65–112.
Udayana Eco Lodge, Jimbaran Heights, tel: 747-4204, www.ecolodgesindonesia.com.

A Green Globe hotel set in a conservation area for birds and butterflies on 30 ha of bush land overlooking Mt. Agung, Jimbaran, and Benoa Bay. Primarily frequented by visitors to Udayana University and people working on Bali. All rooms have AC and fans, garden showers. Restaurant, swimming pool. Home of the Udayana Cricket Club. Free WiFi. Ask Meryl about the butterflies and Alan about the birds. Also inquire about packages to other Eco Lodges in some of Indonesia's remote national parks. $70–75. Family rates available.

Luxury ($100–up)
Ayana Resort & Spa Bali (formerly Ritz-Carlton), Jl. Karang Mas Sejahtera, tel: 702-222, fax: 701-555, www.ayanaresort.com. 368 guest rooms, 78 ocean-front and ocean view villas, and 71 club rooms on 77 ha. Overlooks a rugged bluff and the sea; beautiful, secluded surroundings with two-tiered swimming pool, 18-hole golf putting course, Aquatonic© Seawater Therapy Pool, tennis courts, kids program and pool, 6 restaurants, beach club. From $197.
Bali InterContinental, Jl. Uluwatu 45, tel: 701-888, fax: 701-777, www.bali.intercontinental.com. 418 luxury rooms on 14 ha, each designed to give clear views of Jimbaran Bay, water features, or the wide-open landscaping. The quintessence of a tranquil, easy-going holiday resort with a full athletics program, jogging/bike path, as well as 5 pools, and an incredibly long beachfront. Spa, Planet Trekkers. From $182.
Blue Point Bay Villas & Spa, Jl. Labuan Sait, Uluwatu, Pecatu, tel: 769-888, fax: 769-889, www.bluepoint-bayvillas.com. 30 villas and 30 deluxe rooms atop a cliff overlooking the Indian Ocean. All villas include AC, Jacuzzi, mini-bar, some with WiFi. 3 swimming pools. Surfboard rental and lessons. $150–680.
Four Seasons Resort at Jimbaran Bay, Jl. Bukit Permai, tel: 701-010, fax: 701-020, www.fourseasons.com. 156 elegant villas and private residence rentals, each comprised of 3 Balinese-style pavilions for sleeping, bathing, and living, a courtyard, and plunge pool. Arranged in "villages", each with its own staff and service center. Stunning sunset views. Ganesha Art Gallery. Indonesian spa offers massages, body, facial, and Avuryeda-inspired treatments and salon services. Dramatic hilltop and oceanside dining. From $680.
Gending Kedis Luxury Villas & Spa Estate, Jl. Karang Mas Sejahtera 100Y, Jimbaran Bay, tel: 708-906, fax: 708-905, www.gendingkedis.com. 19 luxury 1-, 2-, 3- and 4-bedroom villas, each with its own pool, kitchen and spacious living areas. New clubhouse

with gym, Spa, salon, gym, Alcedo Restaurant, and cocktail lounge, lagoon swimming pool. $450–1,110.

Jimbaran Puri Bali, Jl. Uluwatu, tel: 701-605, fax: 701-320, www.jimbaranpuribali.com. An Orient-Express resort. 32 garden cottages, 8 beachfront cottages and 22 new luxury villas. Cottages attractively designed with thatched roofs, private open-air baths and verandahs. Swimming pool and children's playground. The beachfront restaurant is a marvelous spot for lunch. Spa, café, and bar. From $295.

Kayumanis Jimbaran, Jl. Yoga Perkanti, tel: 705-777, fax: 705-101, www.kayumanis.com. Spacious 1- and 2-bedroom villas hidden among swaying coconut palms. 24-hour butler service. Serenity and privacy. Tapis Restaurant serves Indonesian cuisine. Kayumanis Spa. From $499.

Keraton Jimbaran Resort & Spa, Jl. Majapati 1, Jimbaran, tel: 701-961, fax: 701-991, www.keraton-jimbaranresort.com. Located next to the fish market along the beach. 102 rooms, 3 suites and 6 villas, all with private bath and balconies, AC, tv, and fridge. Palm-shaded garden. The lobby is designed like a *keraton* (palace). $150–500.

Pat-Mase Villas at Jimbaran, 2 minutes from Jimbaran beach, www.pat-mase.com. Twenty 2-, 3- and 4-bedroom villas with private pools. Bedrooms have private bath, tv, AC. Fully fitted kitchen with fridge and coffee maker. Each cluster of 4 or 6 villas also has access to a larger pool. Free shuttle service to Jimbaran beach and Kuta. Spa. $395–650.

Villa Balquisse Boutique Hotel, Jl. Uluwatu No. 18X, Jimbaran, tel: 701-695, fax: 703-087, www.balquisse. com. A boutique hotel 300 m (330 yds) from the beach with superior and deluxe rooms and a family bungalow. Exotic furnishings featured in interior decoration and travel magazines. Natural stone swimming pool, Henna Spa, dining. $130–165.

DINING

Stretching all along beach from the Jimbaran *pasar ikan* (fish market) south is an ever-burgeoning and very affordable selection of 50 or so sand floor **seafood beach restaurants**. Coming alive after sunset, these smoky, palm-thatched, open-air establishments grill the choicest prawns, squid, snapper, and lobster over coconut husk fires. The setting is unbeatable. Choose your fish from big ice boxes, pick a table and enjoy. This is definitely a must-do while on Bali.

The fresh catch of the day comes with an array of special spices, *sambal* (a spicy mixture of chilies, onions, and garlic) and a tomato and cucumber salad. These eateries are super popular at sunset time, so arrive by the late afternoon to get the best ringside tables.

There are three main concentrations, all with good parking: one small strip close to the road on the way to PJs at the Four Seasons, another longer row if you turn west towards the sea at Jimbaran's main intersection, and yet another cluster up north on the way to Jimbaran's fish market. It is currently generally considered that the best group lies between the Bali InterContinental and PJs. Because the staffs are current or former employees of the nearby starred properties, more care goes into the food's preparation and presentation.

Other than the fish restaurants, the best cuisine in Jimbaran is prepared in resort kitchens. The following are recommended by local residents who know great food.

Dava, Ayana Resort & Spa Bali (formerly Ritz-Carlton), Jl. Karang Mas Sejahtera, tel: 702-222, fax: 701-555. Asian fusion cuisine in an ultra-modern setting overlooking a floating garden. Indoor AC dining or outdoor terrace. Martini & Oyster Bar for pre- and post-dinner refreshments. Open for breakfast 7–10:30 am; dinner 6:30–11 pm.

Honzen Japanese Dining & Grill, Ayana Resort & Spa Bali (formerly Ritz-Carlton), Jl. Karang Mas Sejahtera, tel: 702-222, fax: 701-555. Spectacular Japanese cuisine in a contemporary setting. Sushi & Sashimi Bar, Teppanyaki, Japanese Barbecue and Grill, private Tatami rooms. Also has an a la carte menu. Indoor and outdoor seating. Open for lunch 11:30 am–3 pm; for dinner 5:30–11 pm.

Kisik Bar and Grill, Ayana Resort & Spa Bali (formerly Ritz-Carlton), Jl. Karang Mas Sejahtera, tel: 702-222. An exotic restaurant with stunning views serving excellent super-fresh grilled seafood. Choose your favorite from an iced display and the chefs will prepare it to your specification. Organic salad bar. Dining is on the sand surrounded by tiki torches. Open 6–11 pm.

Ko Japanese Restaurant, Bali InterContinental, Jl. Uluwatu 45, tel: 701-888, fax: 701-777, www.bali. intercontinental.com. Authentic Japanese cuisine in a variety of settings. The Sushi Lounge & Bar serves drinks and light snacks, sushi, sashimi, yakitori, and robotayaki skewers, tempura, noodle and rice dishes. Or be seated at one of the teppanyaki tables to watch the chefs' performance as they prepare the food. Also offers al la carte menus.

PJ's at Four Seasons Resort at Jimbaran Bay, Jl. Bukit Permai, tel: 701-010. This outstanding seafood restaurant on the bay also serves superb pizzas, *foie gras*, green tea soba sushi rolls, Australian sirloin, and couscous salad, to name a few. Romantic setting on the seashore includes 25 canopied dining-beds on the beach. Delicious food and casual seaside atmosphere makes it worth the drive out there. Kids', children's, young adults', and vegetarian menus.

Dress: smart casual. Reservations recommended. Open for lunch 11 am–6 pm, dinner from 6 pm.
Padi, Ayana Resort & Spa Bali (formerly Ritz-Carlton), Jl. Karang Mas Sejahtera, tel: 702-222. An open-air Asian restaurant surrounded by terraced lotus ponds. Chefs from Thailand, Indonesia, and India create favorite dishes from their home countries with flair and fast-paced action. Open 6:30–10:30 am for breakfast; dinner 6:30–11 pm.

Taman Wandlan, Four Seasons Resort at Jimbaran Bay, Jl. Bukit Permai, tel: 701-010. Italian-influenced cuisine, such as roasted mahi-mahi fillet and braised duck leg with spinach, truffled mashed potatoes, wild mushrooms, and crispy shallots. Children's and young adults' menus. Live music 6–11 pm. Open for breakfast 6:30–11 am, dinner 6-10 pm. Reservations recommended for non-resort guests.

Wawasan Café, Jl. Four Seasons, Muaya Beach, Jimbaran, tel: 703-580. The freshest seafood from the Jimbaran fish market selected daily. Beach chairs for relaxing in the daytime with fresh juices or cocktails. Music at night and dancing on the beach 'til sunrise.

SHOPPING

Jenggala, Jl. Uluwatu 2, tel: 703-310, www.

jenggala-bali.com. A state-of-the-art manufacturing facility producing a stunning range of simple, elegant ceramics with fine finishings. The showroom (open 9 am–6 pm) displays not just artistic ceramics, but glassware and homewares as well. Though individual pieces are designed in-house, much of their work is custom-made, marrying an Eastern aesthetic with a Western twist. Demonstration areas, evening events. Café/Art Gallery serves light meals, freshly brewed coffee and tea (9 am–5 pm). A boon to parents is Jenggala's Paint-A-Pot program for kids of all ages (9 am–5 pm).

Jimbaran Gallery, Jl. Bypass Nusa Dua 99 X (if coming from the west, beside Bali Taxi on the left side of the road), tel: 774-957. Extensive and eclectic range of paintings, statues, lighting, furniture, handicrafts, antiques and interiors. A treasure trove for the bargain hunter.

Lotus Gourmet Garage, Jl. Bypass Ngurah Rai, Jimbaran, www.lotusfood.com, tel: 705-848, fax: 701-007, www.lotusfood.com. Wide selection of local as well as imported food, including an excellent selection of fresh fruit, vegetables, cheese, meats, and deli items. Cookbooks, kitchenware, and spa products. Also has a café.

VISITING ULUWATU
(TELEPHONE CODE: 0361)

ACCOMMODATIONS
Luxury ($100-up)

Alila Villas Uluwatu, Jl. Belimbing Sari, Banjar Tambiyak, Pecatu village, tel: 848-2166, fax: 848-2188, www.alilahotels.com. 84 villas designed and constructed to follow an environmentally sustainable framework, each with private pool and cabana overlooking the Indian Ocean below the limestone cliffs. Personal butler. Fine dining and traditional *warung*-style restaurants, cliff top pool and bar, spa, gallery, library. WiFi. From $550.

Banyan Tree, Jl. Melasti, Banjar Kelod, Ugasan, tel: 300-700, fax: 300-777, www.banyantree.com. Cliff top living with magnificent ocean views, privacy, comfort. All villas have infinity outdoor jet pools, living and dining areas, gardens. Resort has a private beach. (Note that swimming is not allowed for the safety of guests.) Bambu restaurant has indoor/outdoor cooking stations, sushi counters, grill, and barbecue. Themed buffet dinners with traditional performances on selected days. From $620.

Karma Kandara Resort, Jl. Villa Kandara, Banjar Wijaya Kusuma, Ungasan, tel 848-2200, fax: 848-2244, www.karmakandara.com. 46 private beach villa residences, each comprised of 2 or 3 pavilions with living, dining, and lounging areas and fully

equipped kitchens. Restaurant de Mare, Temple Lounge on the rooftop, Karma Spa & Wellness, all suspended on rocky outcrops 270 ft (85 m) above the surf. From $735.

The Bulgari Resort Bali, Jl. Goa Lempeh, Banjar Dinas Kangin, Uluwatu, tel: 847-1000, fax: 847-111, www.bulgarihotels.com. Fifty-nine 1-, 2- and 3-bedroom villas 150 m (500 ft) above the sea with a 1.5 km (1-mile) beach accessible only through the resort's inclined elevator. Luxurious interiors and amenities expected of the renowned Italian jewelry designer, including a collection of Balinese antiques and exotic art pieces. Il Ristorante, bar, spa, private beach club. Day trips to neighboring islands and volcano visits by helicopter are available. $750–6,500.

DINING
Organic & vegetarian food

Bali Buddha Shop & Home Delivery, Jl. Raya Uluwatu (from Denpasar, before Pecatu Indah Resort), Pecatu, tel: 701-980, www.balibuddha.com. Serving healthy meals since 1994, Bali Buddha uses chemical-free produce and meats where possible. Vegan, raw food and vegetarian, as well as yummy baked goods. Other outlets in Kerobokan and Ubud.

NIGHTLIFE

There is virtually no nightlife outside the resorts in Jimbaran and the Bukit. However, two establishments do standout.

The Rock Bar, Ayana Resort & Spa Bali (formerly Ritz-Carlton), Jl. Karang Mas Sejahtera, tel: 702-222, www.ayanaresort.com/rockbarbali. Literally on a rock 14 m (45 ft) above the Indian Ocean, this is one of the most glamorous night spots in Jimbaran. Opened in 2009, it has already extended the bar and added a second one. DJ booth carved into the cliff-face. Chic casual dress. Beverages and snacks 4:30 pm–1 am.

Nammos Beach Club at Karma Kandara Resort, Jl. Villa Kandara, Banjar Wijaya Kusuma, Ungasan, tel: 848-2200. Styled after similar clubs in the Greek islands on the Aegean Sea, set on a lagoon reachable 100 m (330 ft) below by the resort's private inclinator. Serves signature cocktails, Mediterranean menu, oyster bar, wood-fired pizzas, freshly caught seafood farmed in the lagoon (you can even catch your own). Champagne and ice-cold beer. Daybeds and water sports. Cool DJ music at night with a vibrant ambience.

ACTIVITIES

Cultural performances. Many of the resorts present cultural performance. Inquire upon arrival about times and locations. Pura Uluwatu presents *Kecak* ("Monkey") dances every evening 6–7 pm.

Spas. Although all the resorts have fabulous spas, there is one independent one that is also recommended. **Henna Spa** at Villa Balquisse, Jl. Uluwatu No. 18X, Jimbaran, tel: 701-695, fax: 703-087, www.balquisse.com. A sanctuary for mind, body, and soul. Massage, spa, and ritual treatments of ancient island cultures.

Surfing. There are a couple of good breaks south of the airport. Charter a boat from Jimbaran Bay if interested. The Bukit area south of Jimbaran is sacred to the world's surfers. Favored during the dry season (April–October) are Balangan, Bingin, Padang Padang, Suluban (called Blue Point by the surfers), and Uluwatu. For tips on finding the best spots, contact the surf shops in the Kuta/Legian area, at your hotel, or inquire at the surfing beaches, which you can reach by taking side roads off the main road to Pura Uluwatu. There are simple accommodations and basic *warungs* at most of the beaches. Although difficult to reach, sunbathers and beach lovers swear it's worth the effort.

Uluwatu is Bali's most famous surfing spot, but only for experienced surfers, as the rocks and sharp corals can be dangerous.

NUSA DUA AND TANJUNG BENOA

A Well-Manicured and Gated Resort

Although some people call the Bukit's east coast and the stretch of land that juts out into the sea above it "Nusa Dua", the two regions—Nusa Dua and Tanjung Benoa—each have their own attractions.

Geologically, the area is quite different from the rest of Bali, and even from the rest of the Bukit peninsula of which they are a part. Instead of rice fields or limestone cliffs, the soil reaches down to a long, picture post-card sandy beach protected by a reef. Coconut palms are everywhere, as Nusa Dua was once a huge coconut plantation. The climate here is also drier than the rest of Bali, freshened by mild ocean breezes.

The genesis of a beach resort

Once upon a time, so the story goes, the Balinese giant and master builder Kebo Iwa decided that the Tanjung Benoa marshes should be transformed into rice fields, so he went to the Bukit and picked up two scoops of earth. While shouldering them along the coast, his pole broke, dropping the earth into the sea. Two islets appeared in front of where the Bali Collection shopping complex is now: the "**Nusa Dua**" ("Two Islands").

The marshes were never to become rice fields; the bay remained a bay with a long cape, Tanjung Benoa jutting into it. Nevertheless, the mythical Kebo Iwa, who created the area, became engaged in another venture: luxury hotel development.

Making Nusa Dua into a tourist paradise was a consciously implemented government effort designed with the help of the World Bank in the early 1970s. Two main concepts underlay the project: to develop as a revenue-earning industry an up-market tourist resort, beautiful, secure, easy of access, with the most modern facilities, while keeping the disruptive impact on the natural and social

An aerial view of the hotel developments lining the beach at Nusa Dua

Nusa Dua & Tanjung Benoa

Serangan Island

0   0.5km

N

Benoa Bay

Nusa Dua - Benoa Toll Road

Denpasar, Sanur, and Airport

Mutiara Bali

Mumbul

Puri Mumbul Permai

Griya Mandiri

Extreme Toys
Rahayu Clinic

Bypass Ngurah Rai

Ellie's
Sonni Putera
Sama Sama
Circle K

Giri Puspa

Taman Mumbul

Taman Sari Royal Heritage Spa

Villa Diamond Star
Hill Resort & Spa

Real Estate Taman Mumbul

Taman Yasa

Arah Restu
Bali Garden Villa
Swiss Belhotel Bay View
Goodway (Putra Bali Hill Village)

Giri Hill Terrace

Taman Mumbul Indah

Global Village
Putra Bali Hill

Wisma Nusa Permai

Kampial Indah

Kampial Permai

Darmawangsa

Setra Gede Bualan Kampial

Menesa
Ocean Blue Hotel Bali

Kampial Permai

Raya Kampial

Buala River
Toya Spa

Puri Nusa Dua

Hardy's Nusa Dua
Night Market

Swiss Bel
hotel
Nusa Dua

Global Village

Puja Mandala
Nusa Dua Hill Resort

Koki Loka
Bualu

Keruksetra 3

Siligita

Bypass Ngurah Rai

BCA
Tragia
Fukutaro

Celuk
Bali Tourist Board
Warung Agung

Lotus Garden

Pratama Raya

Dieba Cafe
Bukit Sari
Car Rental

Bali Gonzago

Kayu Manis Villa

Piasan

Bali Desa
Nusa Dua Beach

Bali International Convention Centre

The Westin Resort & Spa

Bali Desa Suites

Museum Pasifika

Tata Laguna Resort

Melia Bali

Peken

Wirayuda

Village Market

Nusa Dua Main Gate

Garuda Airlines

CD Spain

Nusa Dua Sogo

Kura Kura

Mount Agung View

Nusa Gede Island

Nusa Dharma Island

Bualu Indah

Pande Penyarikan

Siligita

Nyoman's Beer Garden
Bali Star Resort

Grand Hyatt

Kriya Spa
Pura Segara Nata

Pantal Peminge
Pantal Mengiat

Ming Garden
El Pirata

South Gate

Inna Putri Bali

The Ayodya Resort

Water Blow

Nusa Dua

BALI COLLECTION & ENTERTAINMENT COMPLEX

Bali Griya Shanti
Swiss Grand Bali

Bali Golf & Country Club

Bualu Village Resort
Novotel Bali Nusa Dua

Peminge

Amanusa Golf

The Italian

AMANUSA

Sekar Nusa

The Bale
Bliss

Nusa Dua Selatan

The Mulia

Bousen Villa

Sawangan

Nusa Dua Selatan

Bali Golf & Country Club 18 Holes

St Regis Resort Residences

Mengiat Fishing Boat Station

Geger Beach

Pura Geger

to Pecatu, Bali Cliff

Tanjung Benoa

Fish Market
Klenteng Tanjung Benoa
Benoa Cape

Panca Bineka

Purwa Santi

RAV

Kerta Pascima

Mujahidin
Princess Nusa Dua
Pondok Agung
Sorga Nusa Dua
Ramada Resort

Taman Sari Marine Sport
BNB Watersport
Mekar Sari Watersport
Art Market

Nusa Dua Beach
Century
Baruna Dive
Leo's Watersport
Pura Dalem Setra
Panca Sari Dive
Muslim Cemetery
Virgo Watersport

Tanjung Benoa Anyar

Rasa Dua
Asuna

Nusa Pudut I.

Tengkulung

Nina
Nelayan
Rasa Sayang

Puri Panca Setra
Setra Ganda
Mayu Padma
Nosea Garden
Warung Sate
Nugras
Jukung

Rumah Bali
Coco Bistro
Mandollow
Telaga Sari

Casabela
Kazunoya
Circle K
Maxi Boga

Terora

Bali Reef Resort
Novotel Benoa
The Bali Khama Beach Resort & Spa
Mahalaya Spa
Grand Mirage Resort
Thalassa Spa
Club Bali Mirage
Pacific Marina
Kinds Villa
Bintang Resort
Peninsula Beach Resort
Aston Bali Resort & Spa
The Oasis
AJB Grace
Matahari Terbit
Warung Nyoman
Bali Royal Water Sport
Dive Centre
Cafe Hamburg
Puri Tanjung
Bali Becik

Tanjung Benoa

Pendidikan
Hemingways
Rawabang
Tamansari Spa
Megumi

Bahari Mas
Bali Royal Int'l
Conrad Bali Resort
Spice
The Benoa
Hindu Cemetery
Vilastra Dive

Beringin 59
Arena
Sari Agung

Wiaste
Management System B7DU

Art Market
Multi Art

North Gate

Puri Joma
Nusa Dua Beach
Bali Tropic
Cafe Gong Bali
Melia Benoa
Segara
Samuh
Pura Samuh
Club Mediterranée

Badung Strait

Nusa Dua's hotels are luxurious and self-contained.

environment as low as possible. Also unique for its time was the collaboration between Suharto's government and the private sector. It was hoped that this isolation of tourism into one area of formerly unproductive land would shield the rest of Bali from the impact of the anticipated onslaught of visitors and serve as an example for tourism development while retaining the cultural aspects of other Indonesian islands.

Bualu, an excruciatingly poor area whose residents subsisted on copra, fishing, and coral collection, was chosen for this ambitious project, both for its scenic location and for its relative isolation from densely populated areas. By 1971, a master plan designed by a French consulting firm was ready. Infrastructure construction began in 1973. With many challenges to overcome, it was projected to take 20 years to complete: a water supply system, electricity, sewage treatment, and waste disposal plants, storm water drainage and irrigation systems, telecommunications and roads. And a highway had to be built connecting Denpasar and the airport with Nusa Dua. The first order of business was to get the Hotel and Tourism Management Training Center (BPLP) up and running, which opened in 1978. It was a 50-room training hotel that gave priority to

people from Bualu and Benoa villages. Eventually it expanded to include language labs and Bachelor and Master of Arts degree programs, and has since been relocated and accepts students from throughout the nation. The first hotel, Garuda Indonesia airlines' 450-room Nusa Dua Beach Hotel, was inaugurated in 1983.

The early days

The project did have its teething pains. Farmers and fishermen had to be relocated and trained for other jobs, investors were reluctant to spend their hard-earned cash on such a pie-in-the-sky scheme, and then there were all the temples. These obstacles were all eventually settled: tenants got land, fishermen started taking tourists sailing for a fee, the investors eventually came through, and the temple festivals continued.

The entrance to the complex consists of a tall *candi bentar* split gate. Facing it 200 m (650 ft) away is a modern-style *candi dwara pala pada* fountain-gate surmounted by a monstrous *kala* head. The outer split gate separates while the inner gate unites; the cosmic complementarity of Bali and tourism in a nutshell.

The hotels are landmarks of the new Balinese architecture. The design committee specified that buildings be no higher than the coconut trees and that their layouts be based on Balinese macro- and micro-cosmic models. Thus, the Club Med was constructed with its head in a Padmasana shrine to the northeast and its genitals and bowels in the discotheque (naturally!), with the kitchen to the southwest. Open modular architecture was required and the use of indigenous building materials was encouraged. Roofs had to be made of terracotta. Land use had to be low-density (limited to 50 rooms per hectare), and buildings had to be set back from the beach by 25 m (80 ft), and could only cover 30 percent of each lot.

Nusa Dua today

Today's Nusa Dua is exactly what its designers, planners, and instigators dreamed it would be, an exquisite self-contained resort, perfect in almost every way, housing some of the world's finest resorts and attracting travelers who want to escape from reality, if only just for a little while.

The area had, and keeps, very special features. Its best known ritual is an appeasement of the sea to protect the land from any incursion by the fanged monster lurking beyond the waves—Jero Gede Mecaling—harbinger of death and illness. People present him with offerings in his many shrines along the coast. The area sea temples are still tended by villagers, with the nearby resorts assisting in whatever way they can, and *pengelem* duck sacrifices to the sea are offered under the eyes of passing tourists. Pura Bias Tuget on the southern of the "two islands" is the site where the 16th century Javanese sage Pedanda Sakti Bawu Rau composed poetry.

The outstanding **Bali Golf & Country Club** has done more than its share to attract the type of tourists that Nusa Dua was created for. Its championship 18-hole course hosts international tournaments and professional golfers. In front of the Westin, the Bali International Convention Center is a venue used for a variety of events, bringing large groups to the area.

The impressive **Museum Pasifika** is a collaboration between a foreigner and an Indonesian, both art collectors, and focuses on Indonesian, European, Asian, and Polynesian artists with both permanent and rotating exhibits. A gigantic shopping and entertainment complex—**the Bali Collection**—houses the up-end Sogo department store, designer boutiques, cafes, restaurants, and bars without the traffic and hassle of the Seminyak area.

In addition to practically every imaginable water sport being available within walking distance of luxury suites and villas, there are other more relaxed opportunities to enjoy nature. The water management system north of Nusa Dua where it connects with Tanjung Benoa was lovingly designed to be camouflaged from the public and to be environmentally sound. Its carefully planned greenery is now a wonderful spot for birdwatching, attracting both local and migratory birds. There is a 7 km (4.3 mile) long **walking path** that stretches from the Ayodya Resort at Nusa Dua to the Grand Mirage on Benoa that is pleasant for strollers, particularly early mornings and late afternoons.

Tanjung Benoa: a revamped port

For centuries, and particularly after Bali's major harbor was moved from Singaraja to **Tanjung Benoa** in 1953, the natural means of communication between this area and the rest of Bali was by boat from the northern tip

of the peninsula, as this was easier than the overland route via Jimbaran. Tanjung Benoa was in fact a trading port for Badung and eastern Bukit, with a world outlook extending across the archipelago. Its population bears traces of this mercantile past. Chinese have lived here for centuries: a **Ratu Cina shrine** in the local temple bears witness to their long presence. Although most families have moved to Denpasar, there is still a Buddhist *klenteng* temple here, where local fishermen now inquire about the secrets of the stars with a Chinese abbot. There is also a **Chinese cemetery** about mid-way up the peninsula. Benoa village also has a Bugis quarter with a small **mosque**, and there's a **Muslim cemetery** across from the Tanjung Mekar Hotel and a Christian cemetery further south.

The **harbor** itself is worth seeing. On a given day there may be Navy vessels, native fishing boats, cargo vessels, oil tankers, public ferries and private yachts at anchor. Many leisure expedition and livaboards are berthed here, offering dive trips and excursions to Nusa Penida and Lembongan, day trips, dinner cruises and extended trips to other Indonesian islands. There are also high-speed boats to the Nusas and to Lombok here. Many have comfortable departure lounges, where guests can sip cocktails or cold fruit juices while waiting to board. **The Royal Bali Yacht Club** (www.theroyalbaliyachtclub.com) is also here and was the receiving end host of the Fremantle to Bali International Yacht Race in April 2011, an event last held in 1997.

The main reason travelers choose to stay on Tanjung Benoa is for the total beach experience. Although it is also almost exclusively populated by luxury resorts and villas, it has a much more laid-back ambience than its sister to the south. Every **water sport** in the world is available here: ocean kayaks, windsurfers, paddle boats, boogie boards, Hobi cats, banana boats, jet skis, parasailing, water skiing, glass bottom boat excursions, diving and snorkeling, as well as offshore fishing trips, to name a few. Although they're not the best on the island, there are a couple of breaks, one in front of the Club Med on Nusa Dua and another off of nearby Serangan (Turtle) Island to accommodate surfers. Even though the same activities are available at Nusa Dua, the bonus is that Tanjung Benoa's multicultural village life—absent in Nusa Dua—reminds visitors that they're having a holiday on Bali.

—Jean Couteau

VISITING NUSA DUA & TANJUNG BENOA
(TELEPHONE CODE: 0361)

Nusa Dua's luxurious resorts are geared to opulent travelers, attendees of international meetings and conferences, groups and beach lovers, and each has its own combination of first-class leisure and business facilities. Located in a large, landscaped, self-contained park, the complex is also home to a giant international convention center, a championship 18-hole golf course, a luxury shopping center, and an amphitheater for music and dance.

Tanjung Benoa is a narrow cape consisting of a strip of more up-end resorts, restaurants, and water sports operators and hotels. Its white sand beach, stretching for 4 km (2.5 miles) the whole length of the coast up to the fishing village at the tip of the peninsula, is particularly popular with watersports enthusiasts. In the service community, Bualu, just outside the Nusa Dua main gate, there are additional facilities.

NUSA DUA

You've come to the right place for beach relaxation. Nusa Dua's beach resorts front a shoreline of sugary white sand with gentle waves. In perfect keeping with the resort's exclusivity and environmental correctness, boats are only allowed to pick up passengers at designated jetties, and barriers have been constructed to protect the swimming environment, moving the surf quite a distance from shore.

The beach in south Nusa Dua, in front of the Ayodya all the way to the Nikko, is far superior to that in the north. It's clean, free of stones, and the swimming area is wider (the reef starts further out). As you walk north and hit the Grand Hyatt, there are more rocks and coral in the water.

There's a lovely **seaside park** south of the Westin, with a picnic rest area and nearby rocky outcroppings with spectacular blowholes created when waves blow up through fissures in the coral. This is also a great birdwatching area.

A **walking path** connects Nusa Dua to Tanjung Benoa, beginning at the Ayodya and ending at the Grand Mirage on Benoa.

ACCOMMODATIONS

The coastal road, where most of the resorts are located, has no official name. Some resorts are beginning to list their addresses as Jl. Raya Nusa Dua, while others show *Kawasan Pariwisata* (Tourism Area), which is what the area was called on the original master plan in the 1980s. To find actual locations, check the map on page 131. Note that *Selatan* on some of the addresses means "south".

LUXURY ($100–up)

Amanusa, Jl. Amanusa, Nusa Dua, tel: 772-333, fax: 772-335, www.amanresorts.com. 35 thatched-roof suites offering the very highest standards of luxury. Magnificent monumental architecture with commanding views of the golf course and the ocean. Every suite has a queen-size four poster bed, outdoor patio, and garden shower. Spa, Reiki, reflexology. Tennis center, gym. The Terrace restaurant, The Beach Club, pool, library, boutique. WiFi. $800–1,600.

Ayodya Resort Bali, Jl. Pantai Mengiat, tel: 771-102, fax: 771-616, www.ayodyaresortbali.com. Formerly the Bali Hilton, 541 rooms, each with private balcony, flat screen tv, Internet connectivity. Also a selection of cottages and luxury suites built around 11.5 ha of quiet gardens. Free-form swimming pool that stretches all the way to a luscious 300-m (100-ft) long beach, all-weather tennis courts, squash courts, health club, gym, and spa. 18-hole golf course next door. Water sports facilities: surfing, snorkeling, diving, parasailing, and wind surfing. Camp Anada for kids. Accessible rooms for the disabled. No Pets Policy. From $300.

Grand Hyatt, Nusa Dua, tel: 771-234, fax: 772-038, www.bali.grand.hyatt.com. Conceived as a water palace with lakes, gardens, and 5 lagoons, 648 rooms, suites and villas, most with private balconies or gardens. Club rooms. Camp Nusa for kids. Kria Spa; 5 restaurants, 2 bars; Pasar Senggol, a lively night market and shopping experience open daily, 7–11 pm. Cultural performances. 5 outdoor pools, water sports. $165–610.

Melia Bali Villas & Spa Resort, Nusa Dua, tel: 771-510, fax: 771-360, www.meliabali.com. Awarded the Best Hotel of the Year 2009 at Bali's Tri Hita Karana Award Presentation. 484 rooms and suites and 10 secluded private villas with plunge pools on 10 ha of gardens. Spanish management and ambience. Lofty, open-air lobby and fountains, 4 restaurants. Popular with tour groups. Tennis and squash courts, fitness center with indoor pool, spa, large lagoon-style outdoor pool, children's playground. $128–600.

Nikko Bali Resort & Spa, Jl. Raya Nusa Dua Selatan, tel: 773-377, fax: 773-388, www.nikkobali.com. 389 rooms perched atop 40 m (130 ft) high cliffs on Nusa Dua's southern tip. Commands stunning panoramas of the Indian Ocean. 5 restaurants, luxurious spa, wide choice of recreational activities, nearby secluded white sandy beaches. $135–1,950.

Nusa Dua Beach Hotel & Spa, PO Box 1028, Denpasar, tel: 771-210, fax: 772-617, www.nusadua-hotel.com. 381 guestrooms and suites set in 4-story buildings with views of 9 ha of tropical gardens or

150 m (500 ft) of beachfront. Nusa Dua's oldest property, rooms and spa renovated in 2010. New rooms conceptualized by Tierra Design of Perth. Blends trendy amenities with traditional Balinese architecture. Awarding-winning spa, classes, full gym and squash courts, 3 bars, 5 restaurants. $118–305.

The Bale, Jl. Raya Nusa Dua Selatan, south of Bali Golf & Country Club, tel: 775-111, fax: 775-222, www.thebale.com. 20 single, deluxe and double private "pavilions", each with their own pool and fashionable interiors, all within sight of the sea. A member of The Small Luxury Hotels of the World; a charming little jewel dedicated to revitalizing your soul. Spa treatments, wellbeing programs and organic produce served in restaurants. $600–950.

The Laguna Resort & Spa, Kawasan Pariwisata Nusa Dua, tel: 771-327, fax: 771-326, www.starwoodhotels.com. Formerly the Sheraton Laguna Nusa Dua, 271 newly-refurbished rooms and suites with butler service. Surrounded by lush tropical gardens, blue lagoons, and cascading waterfalls. Fully equipped health club, spa, tennis courts, and water sports center. 3 restaurants. $205–305.

The St. Regis Bali Resort, Kawasan Pariwisata Lot S6, Nusa Dua, tel: 847-8111, fax: 847-8099, www.starwoodhotels.com. 123 suites and villas on 8.8 ha adjacent to the Bali Golf & Country Club with handcrafted Balinese art, balconies, and Butler Service. Reméde Spa, swimmable sand-beach lagoon, pools. Sports center can arrange snorkeling, kayaking, windsurfing, canoeing, or kite surfing at the resort. Dining, cocktails, fitness center, library, LaBoutique. WiFi. Uses environmental practices. $486–1,915.

The Westin Resort Nusa Dua, tel: 771-906, fax: 771-908, www.westin.com. 334 rooms with Heavenly Beds® for a guaranteed good night's sleep; high-speed broadband Internet access in each room. The hotel's lagoon meanders through 7 ha of landscaped grounds with a large free-form pool with waterfalls. Recreation: peaceful beachfront, 3 pools, a variety of water sports, 4 floodlit tennis courts, fitness center. Spa and kids' club. Note that guest rooms were revitalized May 2010–May 2011. From $340.

DINING

Nusa Dua's five-star resorts contain a great number of high-standard restaurants (with matching prices) serving international, European, Chinese, Balinese, and Indonesian cuisine. Generally, the restaurants of Tanjung Benoa have greater variety and are better value.

Worthy of particular mention is the Grand Hyatt's **Pasar Senggol,** a brightly-lit and sprawling affair that recreates a native "night market" where guests wonder among open-air artisans' and food stalls with the deep notes of a monstrous bamboo tube *jegog gamelan* orchestra resonating in the air. **The Boneka** at The St. Regis has a marvelous Sunday brunch. **Faces** in The Bale has raw and vegan dishes.

Cheaper eateries are found on Jl. Bypass Ngurah Rai beyond the Nusa Dua main gate, where Koki Loka, Lotus Garden, and Fukutaro are located. All offer free transport to and from area hotels.

The Lotus Garden Restaurant, Jl. Bypass Ngurah Rai, tel: 773-378, www.lotus-restaurants.com is one of the successful Lotus restaurants found elsewhere on the island. Reminiscent of its Ubud café, it seems to float on a large lotus pond and is decorated with antiques from throughout Southeast Asia. The focus is Mediterranean cuisine. Free WiFi. Open for lunch and dinner.

Indian Dhaba, Jl. Bypass Ngurah Rai No. 123, tel: 910-9000, is managed by the Gateway of India conglomerate, which always serves reliably good authentic Indian food.

Along **Jl. Pantai Mengiat** just outside Nusa Dua's south gate, is another string of restaurants. Everyone seems to gravitate towards the two **Ulams,** which serve bland and overpriced tourist food. A far better choice is **Mentari Ming Garden** (tel: 772-125), which is superior in service, attitude of the staff, and especially in the quality of the food. **Nyoman's Beer Garden** (tel: 775-746) is popular because of its broad menu of consistently good Western, Indonesian, and Asian food and friendly staff.

The **Bali Collection shopping center** has numerous eateries covering a wide range of flavors, from Asian and Italian to grills and bars.

NIGHTLIFE

Nusa Dua is a resort for short to medium stays, conventioneers, and families who generally don't go out at night. If you want to go nightclubbing, head over to Jimbaran or the Kuta, Legian, Seminyak area. The naughtiest it gets in Nusa Dua is live music in a café or a trio playing Top Forties in an open-air barbecue by the pool. In Nusa Dua this is deliberate; people come here to get away from all that.

SHOPPING

Bali Collection shopping center, Kawasan Pariwisata Nusa Dua, tel: 771-662, fax: 771-664, www.bali-collection.com. A shopping, entertainment, and dining complex containing the island's most up-market shops, away from the traffic and hassles of southern Bali. Top-end designer shops such as Body & Soul, Indigo Kids, Coco. Restaurants, lounges, brasseries, and cafes. Health and beauty spas, children's playground, and entertainment. There are also handicraft and art shops and an excellent Periplus book store. A supermarket, a pharmacy and a Garuda Indonesia airlines service center are also here.

MARKETS

Daily Market, Perumahan Taman Griya, Jl. Danau Batur Raya, Nusa Dua, tel: 771-844, 772-455, www. pepitosupermarket.com. This supermarket offers a wide selection of fresh produce and groceries as well as delicious prepared meals, salads, and sandwiches.

ACTIVITIES

Bali Golf & Country Club, Kawasan Wisata, Nusa Dua, tel: 771-791, fax: 771-797, www.baligolfandcountry-club.com. Designed by Robin Nelson and Wright, a championship 18-hole course that has hosted international golfing stars. Club facilities include a driving range, putting and chipping greens, pro shop, restaurant, bar, clubhouse, swimming pool. Club and shoe rentals. Pick up and drop off from surrounding hotels. Also has 3- and 4-bedroom fairway-view villas nestled around the 9th hole with kitchen, chef, staff, and personal butler. Villa guests have priority tee-off times. **Museum Pasifika,** in front of The Laguna Resort & Spa, www.museum-pasifika.com, is a world class institution in the heart of Bali featuring Indonesian, Asian, European, and Polynesian artists. Permanent collection and revolving exhibitions. Open daily 10 am–6 pm.

WATER SPORTS

Most resorts offer water sports or you can find them along the beach: ocean kayak, windsurfer, paddle boats, boogie boards, Hobi cats. Speed boats, banana boats, jet ski, parasailing, water ski, glass bottom boats, and snorkeling, to name a few. Enquire at your accommodation or book directly on the beach. Prices are fairly consistent (about $25–30 for most activities), so choose the outfit you feel most comfortable with.

Diving

Nusa Dua Dive Center, Jl. Pratama No. 37 XX, tel: 774-711, fax: 778-073, www.nusaduadive.com is a well-established PADI International Resort Association member offering PADI courses and dive safaris throughout Bali. It also does reef dives just a few minutes by boat from Nusa Dua for $45/1 dive, $65/2 dives, and $65/night dives.

Surfing & public beaches

At nearby Serangan (Turtle) Island, there's a left and right reef break. Sri Lanka is in front of the Club Med in Benoa and is a short right-hander reachable from the beach. Between the two small islands on the east coast of Nusa Dua in front of the shopping mall is a nice beach that is a good picnic spot for families who want to escape the resorts for a bit. South of that, surfers gather in the wet season in front of the Ayodya Resort and further south is lovely Geger Beach, where the eatery of choice is Nusa Dua Beach Grill.

TANJUNG BENOA

ACCOMMODATIONS

Budget (Under $25)

Rasa Sayang Beach Inn, Jl. Pratama 88 X, tel: 771-268. 19 rooms. The best value accommodation on the peninsula, patronized by budget travelers and Indonesian businessmen attending Nusa Dua conferences. This 2-story *penginapan*-style hotel has very simple rooms with terraces. Comfortable, though it can be a bit noisy. $8–15.

Moderate ($25–45)

Ellie's at Bali Sari, Jl. Tanan Lawangan 1, Banjar Mumbul, Bypass Ngurah Rai, tel: 781-6841, mobile: 0819-3305-5350, fax: 770-517, www.ellies-bali.com. A real treasure: 1 hill-facing, 3 sea view and 2 pool-side rooms, each decorated in contemporary, chic style. AC, tv, DVD player, mini-bar. Small outdoor restaurant and bar, rooftop terrace, DVD library, reading spaces. Can arrange car and motorbike hire, guided tours, diving, and whitewater rafting. Free WiFi. $45–50. Does not take credit cards.

First Class ($75–100)

Aston Bali Resort & Spa, Jl. Pratama 68 X, Tanjung Benoa, tel: 773-577, fax: 774-954, www.astonbali. com. 187 newly refurbished rooms and suites with a wide range of choices in décor and style. 3 high-quality restaurants, large swimming pool, gymnasium and a very popular spa. The beach out front is wide and clean with great views. $88–498.
Kinds Villa Bintang, Jl. Pratama, Tanjung Benoa, tel: 772-631, www.villabintang.com. 54 renovated rooms, suites with balconies, and villas furnished with traditional Balinese woodcarvings and fabrics. Snapper Restaurant and Suisen Restaurant, Lembongan Pool Bar, spa, business center, swimming pool. $88–489.

Luxury ($100–up)

Conrad Bali Resort & Spa, Jl. Pratama No. 168, Tanjung Benoa, tel: 778-788, fax: 773-888, www. conradhotels.com. The casual chill-out atmosphere of this property with its clean, contemporary minimalist design caused a lot of buzz on Bali when it first opened, and it's still impressive today. 360 rooms and suites with private patio or balcony featuring striking tribal Indonesian art. Suites guests' receive exclusive access to the Conrad Suites Lounge, Beach Club and pool, among other amenities. Spa, gym, floodlit tennis courts, 5 restaurants.

Swimmable lagoons, pool, and a range of water sports and cultural programs. Kura Kura Kids' Club. $215–505.

Grand Mirage Resort, Jl. Pratama 74, Tanjung Benoa, tel: 771-888, fax: 772-148, www.grandmirage.com. 248 rooms spread over 5 ha on the beach. Offers fun, activities, entertainment and sports without formality. Kids Fun Club, 2 floodlit hard court tennis courts. Bicycle tours and rentals, table tennis. Aerobics, jogging and power walk. Pool, beach games, water sports, water volleyball. Kids club and game lounge. $135–690.

Hotel Novotel Bali Benoa, Jl. Pratama No. 70, Tanjung Benoa, tel: 772-239, fax: 772-237, www. novotelbalibenoa.com. A 4.5-star resort with 187 rooms and villas, each with unique coconut wood interior design. 3 restaurants and bars, 3 pools, golfing facilities, tennis court, fitness center, spa. Water sports include water skiing, glass bottom boat, diving. Free for 2 kids under 16 sharing parents' room. $108–380.

The Royal Santrian, Jl. Pratama, Tanjung Benoa, tel: 778-181, fax: 776-999, www.theroyalsantrian.com. A collection of 20 villas designed for seclusion and comfort on 2.5 ha of gardens sloping to a sparkling white sand beach. Private pools, open-air gazebos with dining and living areas. ocean-view restaurant and wine cellar, teppanyaki and sushi bar, martini bar, cigar lounge. Public pool. Water sports can be arranged. WiFi. $440–640.

DINING

A great variety of good restaurants are found on both sides of Jl. Pratama, the main road, all the way from the turnoff to Nusa Dua to Benoa village. Many restaurants offer free pick-up for Tanjung Benoa and Nusa Dua areas.

Beachfront restaurants with romantic ambience in each of the premier hotels, all with clear views of the white cliffs of Nusa Penida, present seafood barbecues several times weekly. Menus are a mixture of European, Indonesian, and Asian-fusion. Theme night entertainment such as South Seas, Barong, or Monkey Dance usually takes place 7 pm–10 pm. Check upon arrival for current schedules.

Bumbu Bali, Jl. Pratama, Tanjung Benoa, tel: 774-502, www.balifoods.com. Voted by the readers of the 2009–2010 Miele Guide as one of the 5 best restaurants in Indonesia. Set in the open-air courtyard of a Balinese home, Bumbu Bali is one of the prizes of Nusa Dua. Balinese home-cooking the way the Balinese themselves enjoy it. Dependable quality, generous portions, clean environs, and affordable prices. The service by waiters dressed in Balinese attire is impeccable. The sumptuous *rijstaffel* is exceptional value. Cooking class, sea turtle protection project. Open for lunch and dinner

11 am–11 pm. Dinner reservations recommended.

Eight Degrees South at the Conrad Bali Resort & Spa, Jl. Pratama No. 168, tel: 778-788. A first-rate beachfront restaurant with gourmet pizzas, pasta, lobster, and seafood. Create your own organic salad. Candlelit dinners include Mediterranean specialties. Soothing DJ music from 4:30–6:30 pm.

Nelayan Seafood Restaurant, Jl. Pratama No. 101, Tanjung Benoa, tel: 776-868, www.nelayanbali.com. Across from the Novotel and established in 2000. Moderately-priced, comfortable and centrally-located with fresh fish, steaks, curries, Indonesian food, pizza, and sandwiches. Free transport to and from area hotels.

Suku at the Conrad Bali Resort & Spa, Jl. Pratama No. 168, tel: 778-788. Balinese and Asian- inspired cuisine served al fresco with views of the Indian Ocean. Nightly cultural performances. Open for breakfast, lunch, and dinner.

The Tree, Jl. Pratama in front of Peninsula Beach Resort, Tanjung Benoa, tel: 773-488. New restaurant, a sister to the popular Nyoman's Beer Garden in Nusa Dua. Balinese and European food, seafood, pizza, vegetarian. Cocktails, wide wine selection. Daily entertainment, Free WiFi. Highly recommended. Open 10 am–midnight. Free transport in Nusa Dua/Benoa area.

ACTIVITIES

Cooking School

Bumbu Bali Cooking School, Jl. Pratama, Tanjung Benoa, tel: 774-502, www.balifoods.com. Bumbu Bali restaurant has an enormous following, even among affluent Balinese, who know what authentic Balinese cuisine should taste like. Run by flamboyant chef Heinz von Holzen, the cooking school begins early with a trip to the morning market to select the day's catch and the freshest vegetables available. After creating the day's masterpiece, you get to eat it for lunch. A delightful way to spend a day. Classes held Monday, Wednesday and Friday 6 am–3 pm. $75. Reservations recommended.

Massage

Jari Menari ("Dancing Fingers") massages, opposite The Conrad, Benoa, tel: 778-084, fax: 771-584, www. jarimenari.com. Opened in August 2010 after success in its Seminyak outlet, massage menu includes relaxing and rejuvenating Dancing Fingers Massage, I Love Back Massage, Massage for Kids, and Cool Stone Massage. Professionally trained, all-male practitioners are dedicated to massage as a healing art. Retail boutique. Open daily 9 am–9 pm.

WATER SPORTS

The mantra for Tanjung Benoa is marine sports. Water sport company offices and dive shops line the entire strip, facing a gentle and shallow shoreline on the peninsula's eastern side. People complain about the noisy jet-skis, water scooters, motorboats, and banana boat rides, but eco-friendly recreation is also available. At generally less expensive prices than Nusa Dua, enthusiasts may enjoy parasailing, scuba diving, snorkeling, water-skiing, wakeboarding, glass-bottom boats, speedboats, reef fishing, and trawling expeditions. The intensive training for parasailing takes all of 120 seconds.

It is advisable that you use only a reputable professional marine sports agency who can provide adequate insurance coverage.

Adi Dive & Marine Sports, Jl. Pratama No. 105, Tanjung Benoa, Mobile: 0812-390-6032. Seawater adventures include jet ski, banana boat, flying fish, snorkeling, parasailing, diving, fishing, glass bottom boat, and Turtle Island Tour.

C-Trex Sea Trekking, Mawar Kuning Wisata, Jl. Pratama, Tanjung Benoa, tel: 804-9400, fax: 750 637. Sales office Jl. Kubu Anyar No. 17, Kuta. Accompanied by PADI certified divers, walk on the sea floor wearing a diving helmet and see the coral reefs up close, 10 m (30 ft) below sea level. Suitable for ages 5 years and above. Also offers underwater photo shooting, parasailing, rolling doughnuts, flying fish, jet ski, water ski, diving, and snorkeling.

Tirta Harum Dive & Water Sport, Jl. Pratama No. 36X, tel: 775-575, www.tirtaharum.com. More than 15 years experience in the marine sport business, a member of PADI and of the Indonesia Marine Tourist Association. In addition to diving and snorkeling, they offer jet skiing, parasailing, banana boats, wake boards, knee boards, waterskiing. Their Dive Walker is a walk among the fish on the sea floor wearing a helmet connected to air by a hose and accompanied by a professional diver. They also have Flying Fish, the newest water sports "toy" on the market.

Yos Marine Adventures, Jl. Pintas Tanung Benoa No. 3, tel: 773-774, fax: 775-439, www.yosdive.com. Highly respected marine business operator for nearly 20 years and a PADI International Resort Association active member. Yos Marine Adventures has been appointed by many leading hotels and resorts in Bali to teach introductory Discover Scuba Diving at their pools to augment and enhance their existing In-house recreational programs. PADI dive courses, daily dive trips, dive safaris. Also offers boat charter, snorkeling, dolphin tours, water sports, and fishing. Dive trips to Komodo and Lembeh (north tip of Sulawesi). Branches in Candidasa, east Bali and Pemuteran, north Bali.

SAILING EXCURSIONS

At the northernmost tip of the peninsula is a busy working harbor servicing all sorts of vessels from fishing boats to Navy ships. It is also the home of the Royal Bali Yacht Club as well as many cruise companies that offer diving and sailing excursions to nearby Nusa Penida and Lembongan, up the east coast of Bali, and further east to remote Indonesian islands. Below are some of the other boats that berth there.

Adelaar, mobile: +62-81-2383-7898, www.adelaarcruises.com. Owned by a German doctor and his American wife, this wonderful boat has recently been completely refurbished to provide en suite bathrooms in private cabins as a liveaboard. Sailing and diving charters to Nusa Penida and Nusa Lembongan, as well as along the east Bali coastline and to Menjangan Island in the West Bali National Park. Also to Lombok and to Komodo Island.

Bali Hai Cruises, Benoa Harbor, tel: 720-331, fax: 720-334, www.balihaicruises.com. This outfit puts together a variety of fun, family-oriented, and romantic sailing excursions and packages that deliver an unforgettable experience. Their motto is "100% holiday in just one day". See Nusa Lembongan Practicalities for their "Island Beach Club Cruise".

Bounty Cruises, Bounty Cruises Private Jetty, Benoa Harbor or Jl. Wahana Tirta 1, Denpasar (both open daily 7:30 pm–9 pm), tel: 726-666, fax: 726-688, www.balibountygroup.com. 600 passenger 3-deck catamaran with cruising speed of up to 30 knots and state of the art equipment. Offers Nusa Lembonan transfers, day cruises, dinner cruises, offshore night cruises, and party charters.

Sea Safari Cruises, Jl. Dermaga II, Pelabuhan Benoa, tel: 721-212, fax: 723-363, www.seasafaricruises.com, www.divingseasafari.com. Specializes in leisure expeditions on custom-built *phinisis* (traditional Sulawesi sailing rigs). Destinations include Lembongan island, Komodo Island, Labuanbajo (Flores), and Sumbawa Island. Also does private dinner cruises. Live aboard dive trips to Raja Ampat (Papua).

Seatrek Sailing Adventures, tel: 283-358, fax: 283-357, www.seatrekbali.com. Includes a fleet of 3 schooners—*Ombak Putih*, *Katharina*, and *Atasita*—and a 23 m (75 ft) yacht, the *Merrymakin*. The *Katharina* and *Ombak Putih* have scheduled "leisure expeditions" departures to the islands east of Bali and to Papua, Ambon, and the fabled Spice Islands. The liveaboard *Atasita* specializes in diving cruises, and the *Merrymakin* is available for private charters.

Waka Dinner Cruise, Benoa Harbor, www.wakaexperience.com. Relax under the stars on a harbor dinner cruise aboard Waka Experience's luxury 16 m (52 ft) catamaran. Excellent cuisine in an intimate setting. After a delicious meal of local seafood, meats, and salads—your choice of International or Indonesian meals—relax with a liqueur or cognac. $2,200/2–10 people.

Bali's "Sister Islands": Another World!

Nusa Penida, Nusa Lembongan, and Nusa Ceningan are Bali's three "sister islands" situated in the deep, whirling straits separating Bali from Lombok. Nusa Ceningan, the smallest of the three, is little more than a tiny rock with a single village that snuggles cozily between the massive highlands of Penida to the east, and Lembongan's coral beaches to the west. The three islands differ radically from the rest of Bali, consisting of barren limestone highlands covered by cacti and shrubs. Physically, they have much more in common with the southern Bukit Peninsula and the islands to the east of Bali.

The magic of seaweed

Nusa Penida (usually called just "Nusa") has 16 government-run villages and another 40 *desa adat* that still operate under traditional laws scattered along its shores and in the highlands. Its main town is **Sampalan**, where the government offices are located and the island's biggest market is. Great improvements to the roads have been made in the past decade. They are now paved with asphalt from one village to the other; however, narrow, but good roads covered with limestone lead to smaller hamlets.

Everything that comes from and goes to the Bali mainland is done by boats. Among Nusa Penida's exports are cattle, free-range chickens, seaweed—which is the main

Many villagers on Nusa Penida and Nusa Lembongan earn a living by farming seaweed.

income for most families—and some traditional *ikat* textiles. Unlike the rest of Bali, fish are available year-round. Water is scarce here, so imports include vegetables and rice—which are rarely grown—as well as other items, such as cooking oil, that are not produced on the island. The advent of regular ferry service in 2006 has also facilitated the arrival of other interesting items. At times of traditional or temple festivals, it is common to see expensive cars on the roads brought over by the more affluent "natives" who now live off the island.

Houses built with limestone blocks in the Balinese style are quickly being replaced by modern constructions, which are much cheaper to build. **Toyapakeh**, Nusa Penida's second most important town because of its harbor, has a mosque and is primarily populated with non-Balinese Muslim immigrants, primarily Sasak from Lombok and some Bugis from Sulawesi, many of whom believe they were here before the Balinese came. The local people call Toyapakeh "Kampung Muslim", or Muslim Village.

In the past, highland farmers worked in terraced dry fields and bred cattle, which were taken to market aboard *jukung* (outrigger boats) to be slaughtered in Denpasar. However, the success of early seaweed farmers on the coast lured many away from the hills, as one *are* (10x10 m/ 32x32 ft) of seaweed generated six to eight times the income in only 45 days than the same amount of farmland did in twice the amount of time. The seaweed—the large, green *Kotoni sp.* and the smaller, red *Spinosum sp.*—is exported to other Asian countries for use in the cosmetics industry.

Women who formerly helped their husbands in the fields now have more time for weaving *ikat* textiles, called *cepuk*. While in the past produced exclusively with hand-spun cotton and natural dyes on back-strap looms, many weavers today use foot-treadle looms and chemical dyes. They also produce *endek*, a non-ceremonial cloth.

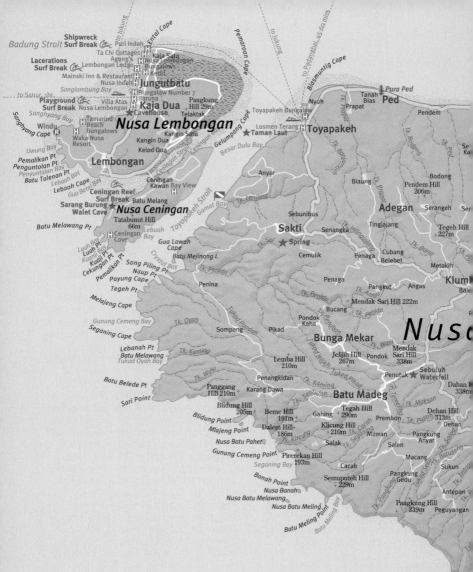

Badung Strait

Shipwreck
Surf Break

Lacerations
Surf Break

Playground
Surf Break

Pulau Jukung

Entai Cape

Pemaroan Cape

to Jukung

to Padangbai 45-60 mins

Biasmuntig Cape

Puri Indah
Ta Chi Cottages
Agung's
Lembongan Lodge
Mainski Inn & Restaurant
Nusa Indah
Bungalow Number 7
Baruna
Nusa Lembongan
Tamarind
Beach
Bungalows
Waka Nusa
Resort

Kaja Satu
Nusa Lembongan
Bungalows
Ketai

Jungutbatu

Pangkung
Hill 29m

Telaktak

Pura Ped

Tanah
Bias
Prapat

Ped

Pendem

Nyuh

Kaja Dua
Cavehouse

Nusa Lembongan

Toyapakeh Bungalow

Losmen Terang
Taman Laut

Toyapakeh

Windu
R

Sanghyang Cape

Sanglambung Bay

Sanghyang Bay

Uwung Bay

Pemalikan Pt
Penuntolan Pt
Penyuntalan Bay
Batu Talenan Pt

Lebaoh Cape

Lebaoh Bay

Gua Betei Bay

Sarang Burung
Walet Cave

Batu Melawang Pt

Lembongan

Kangin Satu

Kelod Dua

Ceningan
Kawan

Bay View

Ceningan Reef
Surf Break

Batu Melang

Nusa Ceningan

Tatabunut Hill
66m

Ceningan
Cove

Luoh Pt
Luoh Pt
Kuonji Pt
Kuoji Pt

Cekungan Pt
Pemalikan Pt

Song Piling Pt

Naup Cape

Payung Cape

Tegeh Pt

Melajeng Cape

Gunung Cemeng Bay

Seganing Cape

Lebanah Pt
Batu Melawang
Tukad Oyah Bay

Batu Belede Pt

Sari Point

Lebuah
Bay

Crystal Bay

Gua Lawah
Cape

Batu Mejinong I.

Gamot Bay

Toyopakeh Strait

Ceningan Strait

Gelumpang Strait

Besar Dulu Bay

Anyar

Tk. Lanjing

Sakti

Spring

Sebunibus

Senangka

Cemulik

Penina

Sompang

Penina

Tukad Pandan

Pikad

Pondok
Kaha

Bucang

Tk. Penida

Tk. Penida

Biaung

Penaga

Cubang
Belebet

Mendak Sari Hill 222m

Tk. Oyah

Tk. Kaming

Tk. Wali

Lemba Hill
210m

Karang Dawa

Tk. Kaming

Penangkidan

Panggang
Hill 210m

Blidung Hill
205m

Blidung Point

Mlajeng Point

Nusa Batu Pahet

Gunung Cemeng Point

Banah Point

Nusa Banah

Nusa Batu Melawang

Nusa Batu Meling Point

Beme Hill
191m

Dalen Hill
186m

Gahing

Klicung Hill
210m

Salak

Pirerekan Hill
193m

Seganing Bay

Cacah

Semuputeh Hill
229m

Batu Meling Point

Batu Meling bay

Bunga Mekar

Jelijih Hill
267m

Tukad Pikad

Batu Madeg

Tegah Hill
290m

Prembon

Mawan

Salen

Pondok

Penutuk

Mendak
Sari Hill
338m

Sebuluh
Waterfall

Tk. Moksan

Dehan Hill
313m
Dehan

Pangkung
Anyar

Macang

Pangkung
Gedu

Antepan

Pangkung Hill
239m

Peguyangan

Sukun

Pendem Hill
206m

Bodong

Adegan

Tingjájang

Tegeh Hill
227m

Serangeh

Metakih

Klum

Bale

Angas

Nus

Dahan
338m

Pehikan Point

INDIAN OCEAN

Marta Point

Nusa Batu Jinengan

The relative wealth brought to the island by seaweed farming has improved life for many. Electricity is now available in most areas, and in the north there is mains water. In the south, however, rainwater is collected in huge tanks for supply during the dry season, and on Penida's southern cliffs a spectacular bamboo stairway has been constructed to gather water from natural springs just above the sea. Education, job, and entertainment opportunities are scarce.

The cursed islands

All kinds of appalling myths have always been attached to Nusa Penida due to its former gloomy atmosphere and unrewarding conditions. Black magic is said to flourish here. In all actuality, however, even though the Nusa Penida people do practice magic, the same is true of other remote areas in Indonesia. All evil affecting Bali — especially floods and diseases during the dry season — is said to come from Nusa, brought by the giant demon king Jero Gede Mecaling (also called Ratu Gede Nusa), its former ruler and the leader of 500 *wong samar*, invisible spirits whose status is lower than that of humans and who inhabit only dark places.

The story goes that the *wong samar* were created by the venerable Danghyang Nirartha, who came to Bali from east Java to spread the Hindu religion. Some people believe that Nirartha was actually Syech Siti Jenar, one of the holy *Wali Songo* who spread Islam on Java. However, he did not practice all elements of Islam. It is said that Nirartha's daughter — Dewi Melanting — was cursed by Naga Basuki, who made her physical body disappear. In order to keep her from being lonely, the loving father Nirartha transformed some of his followers into invisible spirits to keep her company. Throughout Bali, Dewi Melanting is revered as the protector of economy, and every traditional market has a shrine dedicated to her.

Jero Gede Mecaling was a very powerful magician and could change his looks from being handsome and charming to very scary with big fangs; he is still today thought by Balinese outside of Nusa Penida to spread disease and evil. In order to avoid sickness — which logically comes about by climate changes during the transition in seasons — ceremonies are performed in many mainland areas. In Badung and Gianyar Regencies — once conquered by Jero Gede Mecaling and

his men — the giant and his troops are particularly feared and are said to cross the straits and land at Lebih, where they are met and expelled by exorcistic *sanghyang dedari* trance dances.

Formerly, all three islands were part of the Klungkung kingdom, which used Nusa Penida as a place of banishment, thus stripping the exiled and their descendants of their noble titles, Dewi or Sri. Therefore, most inhabitants are commoners and only a few bear those titles.

Visiting Nusa Penida

Nusa Penida is the ideal place to get off the beaten track, and to seek quietude and authenticity. The inhabitants here speak Balinese with a local accent peppered with old Balinese words no longer used in the modern language. Some also understand the Lombok language, Sasak, because of family ties to that island. From the mid-17th century until the early 1890s Balinese kings ruled neighboring Lombok.

On Nusa Penida, there is almost no mass tourism yet; only a few foreigners venture this far off the beaten track. The largest number of visitors are Balinese who come here on ceremonial occasions to make pilgrimages. It is wonderful to walk, ride on *ojek* motor-cycle taxis, or drive through the villages in the highlands and along the shore to experience the island's rough beauty. It is also a rare chance to experience spending the night in a local home, as locals are very welcoming.

Several sights are worth visiting, such as the sacred **Gua Karang Sari** (also called **Goa Giri Putri**) cave near Suana, a limestone tunnel with dripping stalactites that leads through a hill, emerging on the other side. Before going inside the cave, a purification ritual must be performed; then it is entered via a small opening leading into a vast cavern that was once used by the local people to hide from the Japanese when they arrived here during World War II. The cave itself is considered to be female (*putri*) and to house a manifestation of Siva. Its many Hindu and Buddhist shrines are visited by Balinese asking for prosperity. Because of vast amounts of incense burned here on ceremonial occasions (every five, 15, and full moon days), the aroma of bat dung is barely noticeable. The local people believe that Pura Puncak Mundi is the father of the island, this cave is the mother, and Ratu Jaro Gede Mecaling is the son.

The **Sebuluh Waterfall** near Batu Madeg (300+ m/ 980 ft), where there is a beautiful cliff, is surrounded by forest with a natural pond, Pasiraman Dedari, where only men can swim. For ladies there is a spring-fed pond nearby. It is about a 1-hour walk from Dimel Bali/Pedukuhan Sekar Jepun. The island's most interesting—and very large—temple is Jero Gede Mecaling's **Pura Penataran**

Agung Ped (also called **Pura Ped**), 3 km (2 miles) west of Toyapakeh, also about the same distance from the ferry harbor at Mentigi, and less than 3 km (2 miles) from Buyuk harbor, where the speedboats land. It consists of four sections: Pura Dalem Segara for cleansing and for blessing the ocean, Pura Beji also for cleansing and for prosperity, Pura Ratu Gede in honor of the ruler, and the

THE BALI STARLING CAPTIVE BREEDING PROGRAM

The Friends of the National Parks Foundation (FNPF) was founded by a young Balinese veterinarian, Drh. Bayu Wirayudha, in 1998 after helping to rescue animals in a devastating forest fire in Tanjung Puting National Park, central Kalimantan. Embarrassed that so many foreigners were involved in the effort and so few of his countrymen, he set about trying to do whatever he could to demonstrate that Indonesians do indeed care about their own environment. After initially engaging fellow-Balinese veterinarians and later other volunteers in orangutan rehabilitation, reforestation, and community development

The magnificent Bali Starling is successfully bred and released into the wild on Nusa Penida (photo courtesy: www.fnpf.com).

programs were established in Tanjung Puting. Over time these projects began to attract international attention and funding, allowing FNPF to expand into other areas.

Although the first Bali Starling Project in Indonesia was established in 1983 in West Bali National Park, it has never been successful. In nearly three decades since the program was instituted there are still only 10 birds in the park—the only place on earth they were hitherto known to exist—perhaps even fewer. Believing a fresh approach was warranted, in 1999 Bayu engaged the assistance of Bradley and Debbie Gardner, then owners of a luxury resort on Bali, and after establishing the Begawan Foundation they purchased two pairs of Bali Starlings from England. The first of Bayu's "babies", 25 micro-chipped birds, were released on Nusa Penida in 2006. His breeding theories were correct. Starting with only two pairs, 82 chicks have been hatched in the last decade, and as of mid-2010, eight wild pairs have been recorded on Nusa Penida and Nusa Lembongan, meaning that the birds are now established on three islands. The Bali Starling's survival from virtual extinction in the wild is almost assured.

This captive breeding program has been a success for two reasons: one man's dream, intelligence, and experience were turned into action, and the cooperation of the local people. Appealing to the leaders of the 41 traditional villages on Nusa Penida, Bayu was able to enlist their help by implementing ancient laws requiring them to protect nature. In the four years that FNPF has been established on the tiny island, they have an active land rehabilitation program, seedling propagation, and reforestation sites, a bamboo project where carbon sequestering research is ongoing, and of course the birds are monitored daily. In addition to traditional dance classes for children, FNPF also provides scholarships for local students to attend high school and the Veterinary Faculty at Bali's Udayana University.

For more information about FNPF's work and how to donate to its projects, visit www.fnpf.org.

— Linda Hoffman

female Penataran Agung, which is visited by those who can see the invisible world. In the smaller sanctuary here, a strange tree composed of three entangled ones grows, and from the trunk a stone mouth protrudes, believed to be that of Mecaling's minister. The temple *odalan* (anniversary) falls on Buda Cemeng Kelawu. Every three years on the fourth full moon (*Purnama Kapat*), a great festival (*usaba*) is held, during which pilgrims from throughout Bali come to pray at Pura Ped.

The sacred *Gandrung* dance, performed by two pre-pubescent boys clad in women's attire, is still practiced on Kajeng Kliwon, Purnama, and Tilem according to the Balinese calendar. In the past this dance was traditional in other parts of Bali, but it was performed by girls and women. *Baris Pati* is performed in cemeteries at the time of cremations, in simpler costumes than on Bali. *Baris Gede* is danced at the *odalan* at Batu Maulapan. *Sanghyang Jaran* exorcistic dances are held in times of crisis in Kutampi and Sakti, as well as in other areas.

Pura Banah in the southern part of the island is a little-visited *sad kahyangan* temple, meaning it is not dedicated to the function of a particular village or district, but is open for all who want to come there to pray, and there are many other *sad kahyangan* temples on the island, as well. Pura Banah was founded, it is said, because a fisherman was once stranded there due to bad weather, so he climbed up the nearly-vertical cliff looking for help. When he reached the top, the only thing he could find to eat was a *banah* plant, which does not normally have a tuber. However, this one did and the plant is now considered to be magical, with supernatural powers that can protect against harm from any weapon. Out of respect for this great gift, the fisherman built a temple on this site. Today, this temple is seen by some as a *pura segara*, dedicated to fishing and boats, while others view it as a *pura subak*, honoring agriculture. During temple festivals, the local people bring offerings from their crops and take blessed agricultural offerings back to their farms to make the land more fertile.

Two particularly scenic spots are the **cliffs** on the south coast, with awe-inspiring drops into the sea far below, and **Puncak Mundi** (549 m/1,720 ft), Nusa Penida's highest point, where a wind farm generates electricity with solar-powered turbines.

There's excellent snorkeling in almost complete privacy at **Crystal Bay** near Sakti village, which is fringed by an almost perfect white sand beach, rare for Bali. Diving is also good at Crystal Bay as well as at **Big Rock**, **Pura Ped**, **Manta Point** and **Batu Aba**. Relatively new on the scene is deep sea fishing by catamaran. In 2010 Nusa Penida was named an Oceanic Conservation Area by the Indonesian government.

The endangered Bali Starling

Bird and nature lovers will want to stop by the **Friends of the National Parks** (FNPF) office in Ped village (tel: 977-978,) to learn about and see the results of their work. Together with The Begawan Giri Foundation they are breeding and releasing the critically endangered Bali Starling (*Leucopsar Rothschildi*) at the sanctuary they established there. With the vast majority of Bali Starlings (perhaps as many as thousands of them) owned by collectors throughout the world, they are endangered because of poaching, with one breeding pair being valued at US$5,000 (seven years' salary for an uneducated worker), creating a lucrative black market for them. In 2005, there were fewer than 10 individual birds in West Bali National Park, the only place they were known to be in the wild. A highly controversial undertaking—as other breeders believed it impossible for the rare bird to survive outside the park—it was the cooperation of all 40 traditional villages and one *kampung Bugis* on the island which signed bird protection laws and are thus sworn to stop the illegal trade that made this program possible. Not only has the release program worked, by June 2010, 82 chicks had successfully hatched, and at least 100 birds were flying free at their new Nusa Penida and Nusa Lembongan homes. With the assistance of funding generated by FNPF there are also reforestation, education, and scholarship programs, creating jobs for the local people and habitats for the birds, as well as nurturing children to become the future caretakers of their own environment.

Nusa Lembongan

Nusa Lembongan is a small island covered with coconut trees, mangrove forests, and small farms, and is surrounded by coral reefs. The island's population is split between two villages, Jungutbatu and Lembongan. About 75 percent of its population is involved with seaweed farming. The relaxed atmosphere on the island is synchronized with the cycles of the tides.

What began as a well-kept secret, one of several on Indonesia's south coast circuit, is now a full-blown tourist destination catering to beach and water sports lovers of all budgetary requirements. Many opt to take **day cruises** from the mainland, going to Nusa Lembongan in the morning and returning around sunset. Others loll about in luxurious surroundings or base themselves in less expensive bungalows. But what all visitors have in common is that they're attracted by the relaxed world that's so near yet so far from the frenzy that southern Bali has become.

Extreme surfers are here when the southeast winds bring great breaks at **Shipwreck**, **Lacerations**, and **Playground** beaches, April to September. Divers of all levels can explore flat reefs and walls populated seasonally with giant sunfish (*mola-mola*) and manta rays year round at Blue Corner, Jackfish Point, and Ceningan Point. Note that the currents here can be tricky, making it imperative to be accompanied by a reputable dive operator who knows these waters intimately. Snorkelers can paddle happily at Mushroom Bay or hire a *jungkung* to take them to several other sites.

Nusa Lembongan is a prime surfing and diving destination away from the noise of southern Bali.

For everyone else there is parasailing, wakeboarding, jet skiing, banana boat rides, and sea kayaking, or exploring the mangrove forests on the northern shore by outrigger boat.

Nusa Lembongan also offers excellent **walking** opportunities. Its many footpaths invite the intrepid to stroll around coastlines, around coves or over Devil's Tear on the southwestern coast. Next to Devil's Tear is Sunset Beach, with a cave carved out of the adjacent limestone cliff. Near **Lembongan** village, see the seaweed farmers at work planting, harvesting, drying, and replanting the crop that sustains them. South of Lembongan, **Dream Beach** is ideal for simply relaxing and enjoying the scenery. The currents can be very strong here and swimming is not advised.

Of course no Bali visit is complete without visiting at least one temple, and **Pura Puncak Sari** north of Lembongan village awaits. Two not-to-be-missed experiences: crossing a narrow, creaky 1-km (1,000-yard) **suspension bridge** connecting to sister island Nusa Ceningan (birdwatchers should check out the cliffs here) and **sunsets** from anywhere on the island that affords a mainland Bali backdrop.

Nusa Ceningan

Wedged in between its two sisters, tiny **Nusa Ceningan** is relatively undeveloped, but for bicyclers and trekkers there are some scenic roads and rough paths. The first thing to notice is the bamboo frameworks for seaweed farming in the lagoon below the suspension bridge, which you can walk, bicycle or motorbike across. At 65 m (210 feet), the island's highest hill holds some stunning views. There's a surf break at Ceningan reef, but most of the action takes place at Jungutbatu on Nusa Lembongan.

Community empowerment and conservation activist group **JED (Jaringan Ekowisata Desa) Village Ecotourism Network** based in Seminyak offers a tour to Nusa Ceningan using grassroots techniques and local guides. Planned and managed by the community in each village, JED tours are designed to raise funds for cultural and conservation activities and to instill pride amongst villagers. For other information, visit www.jed.or.id.

—Agnès Korb & Veronica H. Long;
extensively rewritten by Linda Hoffman
with information from Bayu Wirayudha,
Founder of FNPF

VISITING THE NUSAS: PENIDA, LEMBONGAN & CENINGAN
(TELEPHONE CODE: 0366)

Of the three Nusas—Penida, Lembongan, and Ceningan—only Lembongan has been fully developed for tourism. Penida and Ceningan remain off-the-beaten-path destinations, but both offer a unique serenity and beauty. Boats of all sizes, shapes, and speeds ply the routes to the islands from Sanur and Benoa and from Padangbai in eastern Bali. As the Nusas continue to develop, more transportation options will likely arrive, some will go by the wayside, and departure times and prices will change.

The best way to find out current schedules and rates for any transportation needs throughout Bali is to begin by asking at your accommodation. If they don't have them at their fingertips, they can find out quickly or can point you to an agent. Here are some tips to help you decide how to get to the Nusas.

At certain times of the year the sea can be treacherous, full of strong currents and even whirlpools. Ask locally about current conditions. During these periods, the voyage is not advisable in small boats; it's safer to take one of the large excursion boats. You will have to wade through the water to get on and off smaller boats, and you may get splashed during the crossing, so pack everything in plastic bags and keep a waterproof handy.

Other useful hints: there are no ATMs on the Nusas and money changers, only found in hotels, charge unfavorable rates. Bringing enough cash in rupiah to last throughout your stay is a good idea.

The same treacherous seas that change boat schedules can also affect water activities. Mushroom Bay is sheltered and safe for swimming; however, swimmers should avoid Dream Bay and Sunset Beach. Surfing on all four breaks at Lembongan is not recommended for beginners.

GETTING THERE
From Padangbai

There are private boats to Nusa Penida and Nusa Lembongan available for charter, departing from the beach just east of the big ferry terminal. Prices—determined by the size of the engine—are negotiated on the spot (around $10). There's also a public boat to Nusa Penida ($3 per person), which is scheduled to leave at 9 am, but note that it won't depart until the boat is full. Travel time: 1 hr.

From Sanur

Boats depart from Sanur beach at the end of Jl. Hang Tuah. Departure times are generally around 8 am and 10:30 am and in the afternoon 2–3 pm. Check schedules for exact times. Some make hotel pick-ups, so be sure to inquire.

"Regular" boats take 1–1.5 hrs to cross to Lembongan; fast boats take 30–45 mins, depending on currents. Some make return trips on the same day; some don't. Some also offer day cruises; some continue on to Lombok.

Public boats—the ones with the cheapest fares—can get overcrowded. It's a good idea to make advance reservations on smaller capacity cruise boats.

Some of the privately-owned boats are:
Perama, Warung Pojok, Jl. Hang Tuah.
Scoot Cruise, next to Dunkin' Donuts, Jl. Hang Tuah, tel: 285-522.
Tamarind Jaya Express, tel: 857-2572.
The **Tanis Lembongan Express**, tel: 743-2344.

From Benoa
Lembongan Island Fast Boat, tel: 361-0840.

NUSA PENIDA
GETTING THERE
On Nusa Penida, the drop-off points are Toyapakeh (passengers and cargo from Sanur, Kampung Kusamba, Banjar Nyuh, and Banjar Bias, plus speedboat passengers from Buyuk) and Sampalan (cargo and passenger ferries from Mentigi). Nusa Ceningan is reachable by suspension bridge from Nusa Lembongan.

GETTING AROUND
In Toyapakeh, take a *bemo* 9 km (5.5 miles) to Sampalan terminal (under $1) where you can charter another *bemo* for an island tour ($15–$20 unless you are very good at bargaining). Far better to rent a motorbike for $8–12/day; your *losmen* can help you find one. To go to Jungutbatu on Nusa Lembongan either charter a private *jukung* (about $10) or take a public *jukung* (under $1). Nusa Penida is not suitable for bicycling, as it's hilly and paths can be rocky.

ACCOMMODATIONS
There are only simple accommodations on Nusa Penida, all of them on the northern shore between Toyapakeh and Sampalan. Outside those areas, the only other option is staying in homes of the local people. Ask the *kepala desa* (village head) upon arrival for permission and recommendations.
Losmen Kaswari, near Pemda Bungalow on the beachfront at Sampalan, mobile: 0813-3803-2369, contact: Ketut Sudarta. 10 rooms, all with fans, $4–8.
Made's Homestay, Sampalan, mobile: 0852-3764-3649. 4 rooms in a family-run homestay with a pleasant garden. $13.

Nusa Boga Losmen and Restaurant, in front of Pura Penataran Agung Ped, mobile: 0828-367-4049, contact: Wayan Tisna. 4 rooms, all with twin beds and fan, 2 with private bathroom and 2 with shared bathroom. The only restaurant on the island with freshly-cooked hot meals. $5–6.

Nusa Garden, Banjar Sampalan, mobile: 0813-3801-7173, contact: Dewa Ketut Rai. 140 km (150 yds) from the main road, accessible by car. One bungalow with 2 rooms with en suite baths; other rooms have private bathrooms with twin or king sized beds and fans. Can provide meals for groups on request. $8–10.

Penginapan Ibu Sri, near the main market and the ferry harbor fence, Sampalan, tel: 23592, contact Ibu Ketut. 6 rooms, 2 with shared bath, standard bed, fan ($3); 2 with private bath, twin bed, fan ($5); and 2 with private bath, twin bed and AC ($10).

ACTIVITIES

Friends of the National Parks (FNPF), Ped village; main office: Jl. Bisma 3, tel: (0361) 977-978, www.fnpf.org. Runs a very important Bali Starling breeding and release program on Nusa Penida, which could very well save the species from extinction in the wild. Drop by their office and inquire about treks around the island, birdwatching, their bird sanctuary, reforestation project, and *ikat* weaving in Tanglad village. They also have guest facilities, which may be available if not in use by researchers or volunteers.

DIVING

Many dive operators in Bali offer trips to Nusa Penida, where the main attractions include seasonal oceanic sunfish (*mola mola*) and manta rays year round. Because of the swift currents, drift dives for the more experienced are favored. There is only one diving center permanently based on Nusa Penida:

MM Diving Resort, Toyapakeh, mobile: 0813-3707-7560, 0813-3702-2676, 0813-503-3027. A Czech-owned diving center offering not only snorkeling and dive trips to areas with ocean sunfish, manta rays, stingrays, sharks, and well preserved coral reef, but also motorcycle trips, hiking excursions, and accommodations with families. Café and library.

NUSA LEMBONGAN

Promoted as Bali's weekend getaway, Nusa Lembongan has become an aquatic playground, attracting day-trippers as well as longer-stay folks with its stunning coral reefs, sandy beaches, and lively surf breaks. In the budget category at Jungutbatu—first "discovered" by surfers—bungalows facing the beach are the most expensive but have the best views. Electricity is only available from 5–7 pm. Upmarket hotels and resorts are found

around Mushroom Bay (Tanjung Sanghyang) southwest of Jungutbatu, with other accommodations stretching the length of the beach in between.

Incoming boats stop either at Jungutbatu or Mushroom Bay, and some stop at both.

Nusa Lembongan is small—only 4x1.6 km (3x1 miles)—so distances aren't great. From Jungutbatu it is 5–7 mins to Mushroom Bay and 10–15 mins to Sunset Beach on the southwest tip of the island.

GETTING AROUND

Both bicycles and motorbikes are available through accommodations. Alternatively, hop on the back of an *ojek* (motorbike taxi) for a small fee. Local boats can be hired to take you from one end of the island to the other, one-way or round-trip, also for a small fee ($3–5).

JUNGUTBATU

Budget (under $25)

Bungalo No. 7, Banjar Lelod Desa, Jungutbatu, www.bungalo-no7.com. 13 rooms on the beach. Family owned since 1982, named after the patriarch's boat. Bapak and Ibu (pop and mom) take care of guests and tend the gardens. 3 types of rooms. $20–30.

Bungalow Ketut Losmen, Jungubatu, tel: (0361) 747-4638, mobile: 0813-3784-6555, www.ketut.net. Family-run, clean, private 2-story bungalows with 12 rooms, all with fan and hot water, some with AC. $20–60.

Linda Bungalows, Jungutbatu, mobile: 0812-360-0867, www.lindabungalows.com. 12 comfortable, clean rooms. Also Kainalu 2-bedroom villa. World-classing surfing, stunning sunsets, good Western food. $15–45.

Pondok Baruna Guesthouse, Jungutbatu, tel: 366-24486, mobile: 0812-3900-686, www.worlddiving.com. Clean fan rooms with bamboo furnishings and balconies facing the beach and new AC garden bungalows next to the swimming pool. Friendly staff, restaurant, and also the office of World Diving Lembongan. $10–40.

Moderate ($25–50)

Secret Garden Bungalows, Jungutbatu, mobile: 0813-3809-8815, www.bigfishdiving.com. 9 clean rooms with fan and semi-outdoor bathrooms. Double and twin rooms each have verandahs. Shaded by palms, frangipani, and mango trees, only 50 m (160 ft) from the beach. Good tourist information from friendly staff. Weekly movie night. Big Fish Diving Center. $32–57.

Intermediate ($50–75)

Coconuts Beach Resort, Jungutbatu, tel: (0361) 413-538, www.coconutbeachresorts.com. 18 large bungalows with fan or AC, hot water, tv, right on the beach. 2 large pools, restaurant, bar, Internet. Explore the island, swim, snorkel, kayak, surf, dive, banana boat. $58–110.

Mainski Lembongan Resort, Jungutbatu, tel: (0361) 923-7322, mobile: 0815-5828-9123, fax: 24481, www.mainski-lembongan-resort.com. Boutique accommodation with choices of fan, AC rooms, or 3-bedroom villa. Infinity pool on the beach with a poolside games area. Restaurant uses the freshest ingredients. Bar has extensive cocktail list, wines, and cold beer. WiFi. Range of water and land activities can be arranged. $28–140.

Shipwrecks Beach Villa, Gang Shipwrecks (Gang Puri Nusa), Jungutbatu, mobile: 0813-3803-2900. A villa a few meters from the beach with 3 rooms (1 master and 2 standard), each with king-sized 4-poster beds, AC, ceiling fans. Shared main pavilion has living and dining rooms and kitchen. Separate AV room with tv, DVDs, CD player, board games. A smoke-free property; adults only. Unsuitable for those with mobility difficulties. $55–68.

Luxury ($100–up)

Indiana Kenanga Villas, Jl. Jungutbatu Beach 56, tel: 24471, Mobile: 0819-1674-6593, 0812-3644-3503, 0812-3793-3452. www.indiana-kenanga-villas.com. 6 one-bedroom suites and 2 two-bedroom villas; French-owned; restaurant, pool, spa. $130–340.

MUSHROOM BAY (TANJUNG SANGHYANG) & TAMARIND BEACH

Moderate ($25–50)

Lembongan Beach Retreat Bungalows, Tamarind Beach, mobile: 0878-6131-3468, www.lembongan-beachretreat.com. 6 rooms on the beach in front of Shipwrecks surf break, all with ceiling fan, mini-fridge, cold water private bathroom, and balcony or verandah with sea or garden views. $32–57.

Tamarind Beach Bungalows, between Playgrounds surf break and Mushroom Bay, tel: 857-2572, www.balitamarind.com. 6 rooms, all with ocean view, ceiling fan, shower, and tub. Adult and kids pools, bar and restaurant. $40–50.

Intermediate ($50–75)

Nanuk's Bungalows, Tanjung Sanghyang Bay, tel: (0361) 852-8521, www.nanukbungalows.com. About 180 m (200 yds) from Mushroom Bay and Secret Bay, clean fan rooms, family owned. Swimming pool, restaurant, bar. $55–95.

The Tanis Villas & Lembongan Express, Mushroom Bay, tel: (0361) 743-2344, fax: (0361) 292-441, ww.tanisvillas.com. Rooms, suites and villas, some

with fan and others with AC, mini-fridge. Pool, restaurant, and pool bar, Internet. Snorkeling gear provided. Also owns Lembongan Express fast boat. $55–145.

Ware Ware Surf Bungalows, overlooking Sanghyang Bay, mobile: 0813-3753-6464, www. warewaresurfbungalows.com. 8 standard rooms and 1 family room with ceiling fans and AC, furnished with antique beds with mosquito nets. Restaurant, lounge bar, tv and video lounge, pool, library, art gallery, spa. $56–84.

First class ($75–100)

Rickey Lembongan Beach Huts, Tamarind Beach, mobile: 0878-6132-3761. Small beachside accommodation with rooms, huts, and family options, all with hot water and ceiling fans. Restaurant and beach umbrellas. $85.

Victory Shine Lembongan Bungalows & Spa, mobile: 0878-6132-3761, www.victoryshinelembongan.com. Superior rooms with AC, bathtub, shower, tv, DVDs. Ocean views and beach access. Motorbike, snorkel gear, boats available. Daily breakfast, lunch, and BBQ dinner on beach. $95–120.

Villa Atas Nusa Lembongan, Tamarind Beach, www.nusalembongantravel.com. Overlooks Playgrounds and Lacerations surf breaks with views as far as Shipwrecks, a villa that sleeps 4 with AC bedroom, plunge pool, indoor/outdoor living and dining. Hot water. From $95.

Luxury ($100–up)

Batu Karang Lembongan Resort & Day Spa, Tamarin Beach, tel: 24880, www.batukaranglembongan.com. 23 luxury rooms, all with king-sized beds, outdoor baths, mini-fridge, AC, Internet. Muntigs Restaurant & Bar, spa, 3 pools, steam room, gym, wedding pavilion, sweeping views. $210–750.

Villa Shambala, Jl. Sunset, Mushroom Bay, www.villashambala.com. Secluded villa with private pool. 2 bedrooms. Near beaches, restaurants, and water activities. $150.

Waka Nusa Resort, Tanjung Sanghyang Bay, tel:/fax: 24477, www.wakanusa.com. 10 romantic bungalows. Activities include sailing on a traditional *perahu* (fishing boat), glass-bottom boat rides, snorkeling, canoeing, boogie boarding, and a games room. Swimming pool, restaurant and spa center. $170. Discounted Internet rates available. Dive packages of 3 days/2 nights $311.

OTHER AREAS

Dream Beach Huts, Dream Beach (south coast), tel: (0361) 743-2344; fax: (0361) 292-441, www.dreambeachlembongan.com. *Lumbung*-style simple huts of various sizes on the beach with balconies, king-sized beds. Pandan Cafe on the beach has relaxed atmosphere. Motorbike rental, mini-library. $75–125.

DINING & NIGHTLIFE

Almost all accommodations have their own eateries, primarily serving seafood, so just wander around until you see one you like and give it a try. Almost all serve beer and the larger places have cocktails. Among the few independent cafes are:

Cafe Bali, on Mushroom Bay, mobile: 0828-367-1119. Serves seafood, pasta, and pizzas.

Ketut's Warung, in Jungutbatu, mobile: 0813-3784-6555. Family-owned restaurant serves Indonesian and Thai food.

Scallywags Bar & Grill, on Sunset Beach, mobile: 0828-9700-5656. Serves breakfast, lunch and dinner. Indonesian and European food with wine cellar, great cocktails, icy beers. Freshwater pool for long, lazy lunches and free pick-up around the island.

Scooby Doo Beach Bar & Cafe, Jungutbatu, mobile: 0812-3622-9776, has a beachside bar where surfers hang out from dusk 'til 10 pm or so. Serves burgers and pasta; sports shown on communal tv.

Warung Sunset, on Sunset Beach on the southwest coast, open for breakfast, lunch, and dinner. Call mobile: 0812-362-1633 for free area pick-up.

WATER ACTIVITIES

Most people visit these islands to surf, scuba dive, or snorkel. The **snorkeling** here is excellent. Diving and snorkeling equipment can be rented from your hotel: snorkeling trips (around $15), scuba diving ($40 per dive). For experienced divers, there are exciting drift dives at Nusa Penida. There are three **main surf spots** just offshore from Jungutbatu: Playground, Lacerations, and Shipwrecks (the most notorious and has the best breaks). Not recommended for beginners; bring your own surfboard.

Other water activities:

Bali Hai, Benoa Harbor, tel: (0361) 720-331, fax: (0361) 720-334, www.balihaicruises.com. "Island Beach Club Cruise" is a full day of marine activity at Nusa Lembongan, including ocean kayaking or rafting, snorkeling, reef pontoon, sailing, banana boating, PADI certified diving. Also village tours, swimming pools, massages, dolphin sightseeing, and beach club. Departure 9:15 am, returning 4:15 pm. $75 includes snorkel equipment, hotel transfers, continental breakfast, BBQ lunch.

Bounty Cruises, Bounty Cruises Private Jetty, Benoa Harbor or Jl. Wahana Tirta 1, Denpasar (both open daily 7:30 pm–9 pm), tel: (0361) 726-666, fax: (0361) 726-688, www.balibountygroup.com. 600 passenger 3-deck catamaran with cruising speed of up to 30 knots and state of the art equipment. Nusa Lembonan transfers, day and dinner cruises, offshore night cruises, and party charters.

The Pamela Catamaran, tel: (0361) 780-0293, 730-023, fax: (0361) 730-022, www.sailboatbali.com. Deep sea fishing (trolling and bottom) with heavy and light fishing tackle in the crystal waters between Bali and Nusa Penida on a 9-m (30-ft) catamaran powered by two eco-friendly engines. Full day cruise includes snorkeling, sundeck, Italian and Mediterranean cuisine lunch and snack. Two cabins for resting and transport to and from hotel.

The Waka Sailing Catamaran, tel: (0361) 723-629, mobile: 081-715-010, fax: (0361) 722-077, www.the-waka.com. "The Waka Sailing Cruise" aboard a 16-m (50-foot) catamaran is available every Wednesday and Saturday from Benoa, arriving at Waka Nusa Resort on Nusa Lembongan. Program includes lunch at the resort, seaweed farm tour, snorkeling, glass bottom boat, volleyball, chess or backgammon, before returning to Benoa in the afternoon. The catamaran is also available for private charters: fun fishing, cocktails, dinners, or sightseeing. $94/person.

Diving

Fed by deep ocean waters, the waters around the "Sister Islands"—Nusa Penida, Nusa Lembongan, and Nusa Ceningan—are excellent for snorkeling and diving. Numerous dive sites have been recorded in this area, including Lembongan Bay, Blue Corner, Mangrove Point, Ceningan Wall, Gamat Bay, Crystal Bay, Toyapakeh, Pura Ped, Sental Point, Buyuk Point, and Manta Point.

Bali Diving Academy, Bungalo No. 7, Jungutbatu, head office: Jl. Danau Tamblingan 51 (Ruko Laghawa), Sanur, tel: (0361) 270-252, fax: (0361) 284-431, www.scubabali.com. In business since 1991, offers day trips for divers and non-diving companions. Visits over 15 dive sites.

Big Fish Diving, Secret Garden Bungalows, Jungutbatu, mobile: 0813-5313-6861, www.bigfish-diving.com. Uses Seaquest Wave BCDs with Aqualung Calypso regulators, 5mm full length wetsuits, a variety of masks available, all equipment in prime condition. Rents boats from local families to support the community. Emergency oxygen, life jackets, and fully stocked first aid kit accompany every boat.

World Diving, Jungutbatu, mobile: 0812-390-0686, fax: 24486, www.world-diving.com. A UK-managed 5-Star PADI international resort opened in 1998, visits 18 different dive sites with more opening in the future. Professional staff, offers first class diving in spectacular and exciting environments.

Sanda

Kebon Pad...

Kebon Padang

Mundeh

Belimbing

Sarinbuana

Wanagiri

Lumbung

Pupuan Sawah

Tiying Gading

Gunung Salak

Dalang

Selemadeg

Megati

Antosari

Bajera

Bantas

Serampingan

Meliling

Beremberg

Antap

Mambang

Tegal Mengkeb

Soka Beach

Tangguntiti

Baturiti

Tista

Belumbang

Kerambitan

Beraban

Tibubiyu

Pasut Beach

Kelating

Kelating
Penarukan
Beach

Sudimara

Yeh Gangga Beach

Around Tabanan

Bengkel

Beraban

Buwit

Tanah Lot

Pura Tanah Lot

N

0   5km

Wongaya Gede

Tengkudak

Penebel

Penatahan

Hot Spring

Jegu

Rejasa

Kesiut

Timpag

Riang Gede

Sembung Gede

Batuaji

Subamia

Denbantas

Samsam

Dajan
Peken

Delod Peken

Dauh
Peken

Tabanan

Gubug

Bongan

Kediri

Pejaten

Nyitdah

Pandak
Gede

Nyambung

Buduk

Canggu

Tibu Beneng

Seseh Beach

Canggu Beach

Batubelig Beach

Pura Petitenget

Seminyak

Seminyak Beach

Legian

Legian Beach

Kuta

Kuta Beach

Rice Fields
& Vista

Hot Springs

Angseri

Pura Luhur
Batukaru

Jatiluwuh

Senganan

Apuan

Mekar Sari

West & North of Ubu...

Luwus

Peta...

Babahan

Mengesta

Tua

Persiapa...
Sulanga...

Persiapa...
Pangs...

Biaung

Pitra

Payangan

Perean

Pura
Yeh Gangga

Petiga

Petiga

Buruan

Marga

Caubelayu

Margarana
Memorial

Tunjuk

Butterfly Park

Wanasari

Buahan

Selanbawak

Kuwum

Sembung

Monkey Fore...
Pura Bukit S...

Tegaljadi

Tar...

Batan Nyuh

Werdi
Bhuana

Peken

Reptile
Park

Ayunan

Sangeh

Sobangan

Pung...

Kukuh

Beringkit

Baha

Dauh Yehcani

Blahki...

Abianse...

Monkey
Forest

Pura Taman
Ayun

Mengwi

Gulingan

Penarungan...

Mar...

Banjar Anyar

Abiantuwung

Cokorda's Palace
Carved Bell Tower

Gedong Marya
Theater

Cattle
Market

Mengwi Tani

Kapal

Sibang

Kekeran

Lukluk

Sibangge...

Pandak
Bandung

Kaba-kaba

Abianbase

Pura Dalem
Lukluk

Darmasaba

Sempidi

Sading

Dalung

Munggu

Kerobokan

Padang Sambian

Tegal
Kertha

Pemecutan

Dauh Pu...

Tegal
Harum

Dauh Pu...

Peguyanga...

Ubung

Tor...

Dar...

Pedur...

Pemogan

Sesetar...

Carangsa...

Dance
Performances,
Palaces

Kekeran

Wongaya Gede

Cepaka

Tiying Gading

Gadungan

Belimbing

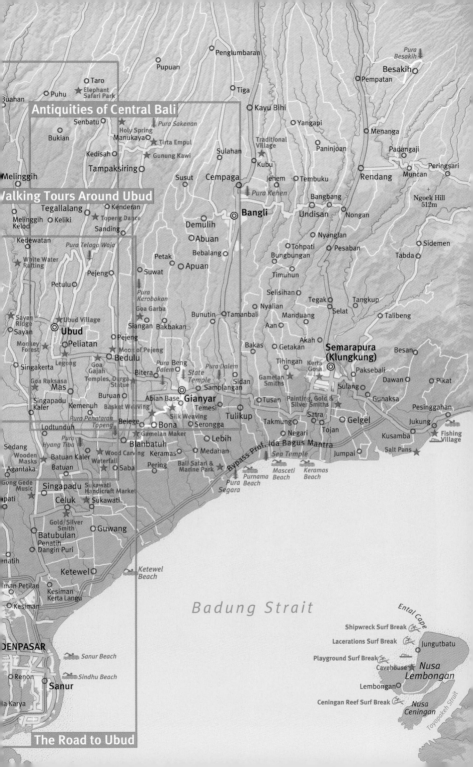

INTRODUCTION

Central Bali

Central Bali's Ubud is Bali's second largest tourist destination, with many holiday-makers electing to divide their time between the Southern beaches and this beautiful hillside community. A prime destination for backpackers in the 1960s and 1970s featuring only basic accommodations and amenities, over the years it has evolved into a high-end resort area, its streets lined with designer boutiques, upscale restaurants, and a plethora of spas, wellness centers, and yoga studios focusing on well-being. The art galleries, handicrafts shops, and a few budget- to medium-range accommodations and cafes are still there, but instead of everything being concentrated in "downtown" Ubud as it once was, surrounding villages have also undergone development. Nowadays, most travelers elect where to overnight based on their preference of accommodations, secure in the knowledge that most offer shuttle services to and from the main Ubud town.

The Ubud area is an ideal base for excursions into the countryside to other cultural and historic sites and activities, passing through scenic plantations, farmland, and rural communities en route. The only drawback is traffic, as roads are narrow and serpentine. Although distances from one point to another may not be great, don't expect to travel at high speeds. Allow more time than you think is actually needed and be prepared for inevitable delays.

The road to Ubud
The Central Bali experience usually begins with a drive north into the hills from the airport or beaches in Southern Bali, along the way pausing for shopping and sightseeing. However, if in a rush to get up the mountain, allow plenty of time on the way back down to see some of Bali's most skilled handicraft makers and performers at work. **Batubulan** is home to the island's stone carvers, their work

Young dancers performing at a full moon ceremony in Bedulu village, near Ubud

The rice terraces of Central Bali are truly amazing.

most often seen in statues and elaborate temple entrances. The small village is also the base for five of Bali's best Barong Dance troupes. **Celuk** is a center for silver and gold-smithing, with shops selling fine jewelry and other handicrafts. At **Singapadu**, stop by GEOKS performing arts venue, showcasing contemporary music, dance, and puppetry and the shops of excellent wood carvers.

Continuing north on the road to Ubud is **Sukawati**, an ancient court center with magnificent temple complexes. Its shadow-puppet masters (*dalang*) are known throughout the island. Bali's only zoo is also located here. Further up the road, **Batuan** was a 19th century court center. Today it maintains its regal status through dance performances. In the art world, the "Batuan style" of painting is well known and can be seen in the town's many galleries. The last stop before Ubud is the woodcarvers' center at **Mas**, whose shops feature statues, furniture, carved doors, and bric-a-brac. Also drop by the House of Masks and Puppets to see a private collection of over 6,000 pieces from throughout the world.

Ubud town itself deserves at least one day of strolling in and out of shops —and eating in its fine restaurants —with avid art aficiona-dos, wellness seekers, and certainly shoppers needing more time to pursue their passions. There are also a number of walking tours into rural central Bali that begin from Ubud and don't forget to allocate some evening hours for dance performances either in Ubud proper or in neighboring villages.

Sites north of Ubud

There are many sites that can be easily visited in a day from the Ubud area, even taking into consideration holiday sleep-in time. Distances

are short, the only hindrance being traffic and the amount of time spent at each stop.

Northwest of Ubud there are historic sites at **Mengwi**, and nearby are **Sangeh monkey forest** and the **Butterfly Park** in Wanasari, south of Marga. At Marga is the **Margarana Memorial**, commemorating the final battle of Lieutenant Colonel I Gusti Ngurah Rai and his men, who in 1946 fought Dutch colonial forces to their deaths rather than surrender. There is a particularly scenic drive from Marga to **Tabanan** town, an artistic center.

For a closer look at Bali life, spend a half-day in a family compound west of Marga. At **Taman Sari Buwana**, visitors can try their hands at plowing a field or planting rice, making offerings, cooking, or simply strolling around soaking in the culture, followed by lunch. Several **outdoor adventure** outfitters offer a variety of activities nearby, including all-terrain vehicle or cycling treks through fields and villages, tubing and white-water rafting. Round off the day with a healing dip in the hot water springs at **Yeh Gangga** ("Waters of the Ganges").

Northeast of Ubud, the **Elephant Safari Park** at Taro could easily consume a whole day, as could any of the rafting, kayaking, and trekking tours offered by the park's owners. For more animal adventures, the **Bali Bird Park** is a lovely way to spend a few hours. A great way to start the morning is by strolling through the park early, before the heat sets in, and finishing the tour with breakfast at its café alongside a flamingo pond.

Alternative journeys

Heading southeast from the Ubud area, visiting the antiquities in **Gianyar** regency could take an entire day, beginning with a stop at **Goa Gajah**, the ancient Hindu-Buddhist "Elephant Cave" excavated in 1923. From there stop to see the 14th century stone re-liefs at **Yeh Pulu** before continuing on to **Pejeng**'s large bronze kettledrum, 11th century statues, and several temples. In the same area are a collection of 17th century *topeng* masks housed at **Pura Penataran Topeng** in Blahbatuh and the carved **Pura Dalem** at Sidan. North of Sidan is Bangli and one of Bali's most beautiful temples, **Pura Kehen**.

Near Bali's southeast coast, a full day adventure awaits at **Bali Safari & Marine Park**, with animal shows, cultural perfor-mances, a water park, and eateries.

—Linda Hoffman

THE ROAD TO UBUD

Batubulan, Celuk, and Singapadu: Surprising Art and Craft Villages

Neighboring Batubulan, Celuk, and Singapadu villages are the first in a series of impressive art and craft centers that are encountered going north along the main road from Denpasar toward Ubud. These villages have garnered fame for a variety of skills: Batubulan for its *barong* dance and stone carving, Singapadu for its *gong saron* and *gong gede* music, and Celuk for its silver- and goldsmithing.

Batubulan: home of the Barong
Ten kilometers (6 miles) north of Denpasar, **Batubulan** is known throughout Bali for its ornate door-guardian statues, carved of soft *paras* volcanic tuff. Until these became popular for secular use earlier in the 20th century, the carvings were only used in temples or palaces, but this art form has spread widely in

recent years and is today found in many homes and public buildings. The families of Made Leceg and Made Sura, two of the most famous carvers of the area, continue the legacy of their mentor, the late Made Loji. Both have shops on the main road, where carvings can be purchased and packed and shipped home. Roti Adhe is another well-known carver and his shops are on the Batubulan and Singapadu main road.

Batubulan is also home to five famous **Barong dance troupes** that perform five times a week at 9:30 am on their own stages before busloads of enthralled tourists. The development of these groups parallels that of tourism in Bali, but even so the Batubulan *barong* troupes are relatively young. The first, the Den Jalan Barong Group, was established in 1970, while the Tegaltamu, Puri Agung, Sila

Batubulan village is known for its excellent barong *troupes.*

Budaya, and Jambe Budaya groups were formed later. These troupes perform on stages that were constructed for this purpose.

While in the neighborhood, **Pura Puseh Batubulan** is well worth visiting. Four statues of Wisnu poised on carved pedestals embellished with *Tantri* tales guard the temple. If you care to shop, Galuh Art Shop offers an extensive range of Balinese batik and weavings, and Kadek Nadhi's Antique Store has many antiques, from *krises* (ceremonial daggers) and masks to carved doors. Seraya Art Shop also has fine carved doors and carvings. All three are on the main road, Jl. Raya Batubulan.

Just north of Batubulan on the way to Singapadu is the wonderful **Bali Bird Park** (**Taman Burung Bali**) where over 1,000 birds of 250 species are housed amidst 2,000 types of tropical plants. See the rare Bali Starling (*Leucopsar Rothschildi*), walk through the free-fly aviary, and have photos taken with a Brazilian Macaw. A café serving excellent food overlooks a pond of flamingos.

Next door, the **Rimba Reptile Park** (**Rimba Reptil**) houses 20 different species, including Komodo dragons, a 8 m (26 ft) reticulated python, water monitors, and crocodiles. An open-air area houses some of the tamer species, while the Serpent Cave holds deadlier creatures such as king cobras, mambas, and vipers.

Celuk: silver and jewelry

Although many arts and crafts have prospered in **Celuk**, the village has evolved into a center for silver and goldsmithing. Almost every home in the village contains small-scale production facilities, filling orders placed by large shops and exporters. Bracelets, rings, earrings, and brooches, to name a few of a wide range of products fashioned here, are made by special order for the export market.

The silver and gold craft trade was pioneered by the Beratan clan of smiths (*pande*). Nowadays most Celuk residents, whether or not they are members of the Pande clan, have become gold- and silversmiths. Wayan Kawi and Wayan Kardana are among the better craftsmen.

Along the main road between Batubulan and Celuk are over 50 shops, most of which sell **gold and silver jewelry**. Keraton Gold and Silver Collection, Celuk Silver, Dede's, and Semadi Gallery have particularly good selections. Other shops, such as Wirama

The Road to Ubud

Antiques and Modern Art and Bali Souvenir, sell masks, statues, old basketry, and textiles, among other things.

Singapadu: village of the "twin kings"

The history of small **Singapadu** village, just up the road from Batubulan, goes back to the reign of I Dewa Kaleran, a king of Kalianget who assisted the ruler of Sukawati, I Dewa Agung Anom, in defeating the Mengwi king with the aid of two powerful *krises*.

As an expression of gratitude and to strengthen family ties, I Dewa Agung Anom offered his sister to be Dewa Kaleran's bride. Impatient at the long wait for his sister's pregnancy, I Dewa Agung then presented another princess to Dewa Kaleran, this time one who was already pregnant. This princess gave birth to a boy, called I Dewa Agung Api. Meanwhile, Dewa Agung's first wife also became pregnant and gave birth to another son, Dewa Kaleran Sakti. With the birth of both sons, two princes had rights to the throne, and the name *singha-padu,* meaning "twin lions", was given to the place.

Some believe that Dewa Kaleran's sacred *kris*, Sekar Sandat, possesses creative powers and has therefore helped dance, music, and carving to flourish in the area. In the past Singapadu was known as a center for dance and music. Unfortunately, these groups have largely withered away. However, *barong* and *arja* groups continuing the traditions of the

past can be found in Banjar Sengguan. Apart from the *gong gede,* a type of *gamelan* which most *banjars* in Singapadu possess, two *banjars,* Apuan and Seseh, have an older type of *gamelan* known as the *gong saron.* This is mainly used to accompany death ceremonies, as the tones produced are thought to express sadness and sorrow. The seven-key xylophones of the *gong saron* differ from the 10-key *gangsa* of a typical *gamelan.*

Many well-known dancers have come from Singapadu: Wayan Griya, Ketut Rujag, Wayan Kengguh, Made Kerdek, and Ni Ketut Senun. Today, there are many good ones left, such as Nyoman Cerita, Ketut Kodi, Ni Nyoman Candri, and Ketut Rumita. Made Raos, another prominent dancer, is one of Singapadu's best *barong* (*bapang*) dancers. Two other prominent figures in the field of dance, Dr. I Made Bandem and Dr. I Wayan Dibia, both deans at ISI (Indonesia Institute of the Arts) in Denpasar, are also natives of Singapadu. Dibia has created a new performing arts venue called **GEOKS** in his home village, which showcases contemporary music, dance, and puppetry.

The late Cokorda Oka's mastery of *topeng* and *barong* mask-making has now been handed down to his pupils, I Wayan Tangguh, Cokorda Raka Tisnu, and Nyoman Juala. Wayan Pugeg and Ketut Muja also exhibit great talent in carving wood statues.

— *I Made Suradiya*

There are many fine silver- and goldsmiths in Celuk village.

SUKAWATI VILLAGE

An Ancient Court and Bali's Best *Dalangs*

Located midway between mountain slopes and the sea on the main road north of Denpasar to Ubud, **Sukawati** is a modest town of few tourist attractions, yet it has a lot to offer in rich cultural traditions. At one time, Sukawati stood with Klungkung as one of the two great *negara* or kingdoms of Bali. From Tegallalang to Ubud to Singapadu, *topeng* mask dancers still interpret the history of the old Sukawati realm before rapt audiences. The arts have remained vital here thanks to royal patronage and commissions from other parts of the island.

"My heart's delight"
Early in the 18th century the Sukawati region, formerly known as Timbul, came under the influence of an evil sorcerer, Ki Balian Batur. His enemies all became violently ill due to his powerful black magic. Seeking to pacify Timbul, the raja of Mengwi, Angelurah Agung, sought help from I Dewa Agung Anom, son of the raja of Klungkung. Together they defeated the sorcerer with magic weapons brought from the Klungkung court. Ki Balian Batur is still remembered today in the name of nearby Rangkan village, which means "place of the evil man". As a token of his gratitude, the raja invited I Dewa Agung Anom to build a palace and live there.

I Dewa Agung Anom dreamed of creating an ideal kingdom based on the example of Majapahit in East Java. From Klungkung he brought attractive men and women who were talented in the arts and were representative of the important lineages. Once in Timbul, they built the Pura Penataran Agung as a central shrine and the Puri Goro Gak as a residence for I Dewa Agung Anom and his family.

Lavishly embellished with carvings, the beauty of the great *pura* was enhanced through the addition of fabulous gardens and pools. Every night, the sensuous sounds of the *gamelan* were heard wafting from an enormous *bale* pavilion covered with gold leaf. The marvels of Timbul invariably caused visitors to exclaim "*sukahatiné*", which means "my heart's delight", and gradually the town became known as Sukawati.

Popularly known as Dalem Sukawati, the first raja, I Dewa Agung Anom, enjoyed a long reign. Eventually wearying of political life, he retired to meditate in Petemon, near Bedulu. Meanwhile, his sons grew fond of gambling and broke up a magic *kris* belonging to the palace to be made into spurs for fighting cocks. Dalem Sukawati, despairing of his sons' inability to rule, declared that upon his death, whichever son would dare to take the deceased Dalem's tongue into his mouth would inherit the kingdom.

Following the Dalem's death, his corpse became so swollen and repulsive that his sons were unwilling to perform the odious chore. This fell to a relative, the raja of Gianyar. Miraculously, when the raja took the hideously protruding tongue into his mouth, the corpse shrank to normal size and emitted a wonderful perfume. This failure of the sons, however, together with the loss of the protective *kris*, caused the heirs of Dalem Sukawati to be defeated in war by Gianyar, and subsequently the palace was abandoned.

Bali's finest *dalangs*
Sukawati residents are proud that their town has a complex of temples unrivaled outside of Besakih. Represented here is the complete *sad kayangan* group of six temples — Pura Desa, Pura Puseh, Pura Dalem, Pura Melanting, Pura Ulun Siwi, and Pura Sakti — symbolizing Bali's sacred mountains.

Pura Penataran Agung, at the center of Sukawati, is a pilgrimage site for all members of the surrounding area's royal houses: Tegallalang, Ubud, Peliatan, Batuan, Mas, Negara, and Singapadu. Destroyed in an earthquake in 1917, the temple was rebuilt on a smaller scale, which has in no way affected its importance. Next door to the temple is the **Pura Kawitan Dalem Sukawati**, which has panel-carvings of *Tantri* tales and several unusual statues in the outer courtyard. Further to the south in Ketewel village is

Pura Payogan Agung, where it is said that the original Legong dance originated.

The **Pura Desa**'s massive *candi bentar* gate on the northeastern corner of the town is a tribute to the continuing excellence of local craftsmen. Also known throughout Bali are the *tukang wadah*, craftsmen of the great cremation towers required for royal funeral ceremonies, and the *tukang prada*, makers of gold-painted costumes and umbrellas.

Sukawati is best known, however, for its many shadow-puppet masters, or *dalang*. As many as 20 of these artists and their troupes are available for hire for ceremonial occasions, and they travel throughout Bali to perform. The Balinese say that Sukawati's *dalangs* are the best on the island because of many generations of experience.

Two renowned *dalangs* originated in Banjar Babakan: I Wayan Wija (who currently lives in Banjar Kalah, Peliatan), known for his unusual *wayang tantri* and innovative glass puppets, and I Wayan Nartha. Both can be contacted to commission a shadow play or a special set of puppets. Their nephew, I Wayan Mardika, who works in the Department of Culture and Tourism, can also be commissioned to perform a *wayang* in English. Anyone in the *banjar* can direct you to their houses.

A scholar and member of the *sangging* caste of artisans, I Nyoman Sadia turned from his family tradition of stone carving to making fine jewelry. His house and shop are just off the main road at Jl. Sersan Wayan Pugig No. 5.

The commercial center of the town is the *Pasar Seni* or **Art Market**. With patience and a sense of humor you can find bargains here on everything from woodcarvings to paintings. Just west of this market is the **wood-carving market**, which is only open from 7–10 am, and there are some choice bargains there. Along the main road, shops cater to local needs, such as baskets and ceremonial umbrellas. Directly across the road is an open-air produce market.

Wildlife conservatory

On Jl. Raya Singapadu in Sukawati is the **Bali Zoo (Kebun Binatang Bali)**, which is privately owned and is Bali's only zoo. Set in 4.86 ha of lush tropical gardens, it includes an animal petting area, walk-through bird aviaries, Komodo dragons, and African lions in an open-range den. The purpose of the zoo is to preserve Indonesian and other wild animals and to encourage an educational experience.

— *Tom Ballinger*

The "Art Market" (Pasar Seni) in Sukawati is famous as a place to buy souvenirs.

BATUAN VILLAGE

A Village of Famous Painters

For over 1,000 years **Batuan** has been a village of artists and craftsmen, old legends and mysterious tales. Batuan's recorded history begins in A.D. 1022 with an inscription that is housed in the main village temple, **Pura Desa Batuan**.

The name "Batuan" or "Baturan" mentioned here prompts villagers to joke about being "tough as stone" or "eating rocks", as *batu* means "stone" in Indonesian. But it likely refers to an ancient megalithic tradition in which standing stones served as meeting places and ceremonial sites for the worship of ancestral spirits.

Famous families

Batuan's central location in south Bali is the primary reason for its historical importance. Besides the ancient village temple, **Pura Gede Mecaling** is also here, which is said to be on the site of the old palace of the demon king Jero Gede Mecaling, whose name the Balinese are afraid to even utter. He is

supposed to have moved from here to Nusa Penida Island, where his spirit still resides. In the 1600s, Gusti Ngurah Batulepang's family dominated south Bali, living as prime ministers based in Batuan. They remained prime ministers until the early 1700s, when a branch of the Klungkung royal family was established at nearby Sukawati. At that time the chief centers of the kingdom were Sukawati, Batuan, and Ketewel village nearby. Batuan still has ritual links with Ketewel that commemorate that era.

The Batulepang family scattered to the far corners of Bali in subsequent centuries as the result of a priestly curse, but a small temple for Gusti Batulepang remains on the site of his palace. The Buddhist priests, or *pedanda boda*, who later made Batuan a great spiritual center built a house, the **Griya Ageng**, on that part of Batulepang's temple where death rituals were once held. They then marshaled powerful Tantric forces here.

Brahman majority

Because Batuan became a center from which Buddhist priests and Brahmans spread to the south Bali main court centers, the village has an unusual preponderance of Brahmans living here. DeZoete and Spies, in their book *Dance and Drama in Bali*, describe it as almost entirely a Brahman village. This is not really true, but much of the village near the main Denpasar to Ubud road is inhabited by the extended family of the Buddhist Griya Ageng and of a smaller number of Siva-worshipping Brahmans who came later to Batuan. The other main high caste family are the Dewas, related to the Batuan *puri*, or extended palace family, who are in turn closely related to the Gianyar royal family. Batuan is unusual in that commoners actually form a minority in the center of the village.

The western area of Batuan, known as Negara, was a separate village and court center in the 19th century. It grew so powerful that it revolted against the main house of Gianyar in 1884, destroying the kingdom and

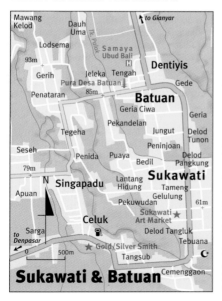

Sukawati & Batuan

setting south Bali on a path of internal conflict which opened it up to Dutch conquest. In 1900, when the Dutch took over Gianyar, Negara was incorporated within Batuan. Similarly, the adjacent area, Puaya, an important center for dance and theater ornaments, puppets, and other objects made from hide, is regarded as being quite separate.

Dancing ancient tales

The Batuan Buddhist Brahmans, in concert with the former king of the village, Anak Agung Gede Oka (1860–1947), were responsible for making Batuan the island's center for the most courtly and elegant of all Balinese dance forms, the *gambuh*. In all of Bali, it is only the troupes from Batuan that continue to preserve this tradition and still perform this theatrical presentation of tales of ancient princes and princesses on a regular basis. Performances are held on the 1st and 15th of every month.

One of these troupes is led by I Made Jimat, one of Bali's most celebrated dancers of modern times, whose genius never fails to leave his audiences breathless. His son, Nyoman Budiawan, has formed a group, Yayasan Tri Pusaka Sakti, which puts on performances featuring multiple generations: Jimat, his son, his grandchildren, and his mother, Men Cenik, who, until she passed away in 2010 at the age of nearly 90, could still command an audience.

Another troupe consists of the extended family of the greatest dancer of the generation preceding Jimat—the late I Nyoman Kakul—who passed on the skills and techniques of *gambuh* and of the other important dance forms, such as the masked *topeng* plays and the operatic *arja* theater. Ketut Kantor, Kakul's late son, led the troupe until his death in 2008. Today, Ketut Wirtawan, Kantor's son, carries on the tradition.

A third troupe, formed with assistance from the Ford Foundation, was founded in 1993 and is a community-based group comprised of dancers from all *banjars*. They train young dancers weekly and perform at the Pura Desa on the 1st and 15th of every month.

In his day, Kakul was able to call on the mask making skills of Dewa Putu Kebes, whose *topeng* masks were charged with the spiritual forces of kings and heroes from the Balinese past. Since his death, his son Dewa Cita and grandson Dewa Mandra have

maintained the combination of immaculate skill and divine inspiration which made his work so powerful. Two of the family's pupils, Made Regug of Negara and Nyoman Medor, also uphold the fine carving tradition.

In addition to the dances, performed in the central part of the village, Batuan is also respected for its *wayang wong*, masked performances of stories from the *Ramayana*. This is exclusively performed in **Banjar Den Tiis**.

The "Batuan style" of painting

From Den Tiis also came the inspiration for the modern Batuan style of painting. In the 1930s, two brothers, I Ngendon and I Patera, began experimenting painting with ink on paper. The result was powerful black-and-white images of magic and of Balinese life. The families of these two artists are still influential in the village, and now own the **Artshop Dewata** on the main road leading to Ubud.

Ngendon and Patra originally studied under a painter living to the east of the palace, but from them the painting tradition spread back to the main part of the village, where it was enthusiastically embraced by a number of their fellow villagers. The present-day generation of artists includes Made Tubuh, Wayan Rajin, Ida Bagus Putu Gede, Made Budi, and Made Bendi, and the latter two have become loved through their humorous and insightful depictions of tourists in Bali.

Aside from painters, Batuan has also given birth to one of Bali's most easily recognizable contemporary musicians, I Wayan Balawan, who is known for his "tapping" technique on his double fretted guitar. Along with his group, **Batuan Ethnic Fusion**, he performs not only throughout Bali, but around the world.

Bali Fun World

On the lighter side, there is an indoor playground for kids in Batuan, **Bali Fun World,** that makes for a wonderful half day outing for young ones. Open Tuesday–Sunday from 9:30 am–9:00 pm, this new arena provides an area for toddlers, another one for under 12s and plenty of games for teens and adults, including Sumo wrestling in big plastic suits. Everything here is made from rubber and plastic, including the rock climbing wall. Best to go in the mornings when it's cooler as it is not air-conditioned.

—*Adrian Vickers*

MAS VILLAGE

A Brahmanical Woodcarving Center

Mas village lies on the main road 20 km (13 miles) north of Denpasar and 6 km (3.7 miles) before Ubud, in a hilly countryside covered with rice fields irrigated year-round by the Batuan and Sakah rivers.

Today, the village appears as a succession of palatial art shops, as **Mas** is a flourishing center for the woodcarving craft. It is difficult to imagine what it was like before dozens of tourist buses started to drop in every day, yet Mas (which means "gold") actually played an important role in Balinese history. During the 16th century, it was the place where the great Javanese priest Danghyang Dwijendra (also called Nirartha), had his hermitage (*griya*).

Descendants of holy priest

The holy man, known locally as Pedanda Sakti Wau Rauh (literally "The Newly Arrived High Priest"), came to Bali from Kediri in east Java after the fall of the powerful Majapahit kingdom, and was invited to Mas by prince Mas Wilis (Tan Kober). Here the *pedanda* acquired great fame through his teaching and gathered many disciples. His son by Mas Wilis' daughter is the forebear of one of Bali's four important *brahmana* clans, which to the present day traces its roots back to the village.

The priest's fame reached the Dalem Waturenggong court in Gelgel, who, impressed by Danghyang Dwijendra's superior wisdom, appointed him the king's counselor and court priest in 1489.

Based upon his instructions, many temples were built, especially after his *moksa* (holy death). His belongings—*bajra* (holy bell), black shirt, mattress, and staff—are now kept in the Mas *griya*, and the Pura Taman Pule temple was built on that site.

Realm of blessed craftsmen

The gods are also said to have bestowed talents on two of Mas' houses: the skill of the shadow-puppet master to Griya Dauh, and the skill of woodcarving to Griya Danginan. At first, the woodcarvers (*sangging*) were all

brahmanas who worked only on ritual or courtly projects. Their disciples (*sisya*) learned the craft from them, and woodcarving skills were transmitted from father to son. The traditional *wayang* style prevailed, featuring religious scenes and characters from the *Ramayana* and *Mahabharata* epics.

During the 1930s, under the influence of Walter Spies and Pita Maha, a new style of woodcarving developed here. The motifs were more realistic, and inspired by everyday scenes featuring humans and animals. Several of these early works are on display in

The galleries of expert woodcarvers line the roads in Mas village.

Ubud's Puri Lukisan museum. During this period, woodcarvings began to be appreciated and purchased by foreigners, but only after 1970 did the real boom take place. The first art shops in Mas were those of Ketut Roja (**Siadja & Son**), followed by Ida Bagus Nyana and his son Ida Bagus Tilem, and Ida Bagus Taman (**Adil Artshop**). At first, they all produced works of quality in limited quantities, mainly working with locally-available woods. A more abstract style was later developed by Purna and Nyana, featuring elongated, curved lines and woods such as ebony and sandalwood. One of Tilem's best students is I Wayan Darlun, whose work is shown at **Baris Gallery** on Jl. Raya Mas. Later on, in Pujung and Tegallalang, Cokot began to carve roots into demonic figures.

In the 1980s, many realistic, brightly painted animals and fruit trees (known here as *pulasan*), based on European designs, appeared on the market. First created by Togog in Pujung, much of the production is now of questionable quality, but the prices are very low.

Later, brightly painted and "batiked" masks were created by the now late Ida Bagus Ambara and family. **Wayan Muka**, Banjar Batan Ancak, Mas (tel: 974-530; mobile: 081-239-12902) and **I. B. Anom**, whose shop flanks the northern border of the football field in Mas, carve excellent *topeng* masks.

Woodcarving shops

Bidadari Art Shop on the main road features very fine modern woodcarvings. There are also a few shops that prepare huge slabs of wood to be used for exquisite tables and doors. One of them is **Bidadari Workshop** on the small road that goes east just 100 m (320 ft) south of their shop.

To see craftsmen at work, stop by any of the galleries where there are workshops. The system is paternalistic; the shop owner gives work to his craftsmen according to their skills, the price being settled after the fact based on the final result. They work on the spot or at home. Skill is learned at an early age inside the family; tools used are still quite traditional: various types of axes, chisels, and drills made by local blacksmiths. Prices are very high, and are often in U.S. dollars. They can sometimes handle special orders. Nyoman Tekek Manis carved a giant Christ that was placed on the Cengkareng

Church altar in Jakarta, and inaugurated by Pope John Paul II in 1989.

A relatively new phenomenon that has cropped up in Mas is furniture shops. Showrooms now display all types of settees, chairs, and carved doors. Before purchasing, make sure the wood has been properly dried, and the only way to ensure this is to bring your own gauge.

Located 100 m (320 ft) from the road on the east side, **Pura Taman Pule** does not take its name from the holy *pule* trees growing behind it, but means "Beautiful Garden". Danghyang Nirartha is said to have planted a purple flowered *tangi* tree there— still growing behind an altar in the *jaba tengah* (middle court)—from which a golden bud sprouted, giving Mas its name. At the back of the main temple, a *padmasana* surrounded by a pond is said to have been the place of Nirartha's hermitage. People from throughout Bali come here to pray, not only *brahmanas* but also commoners of the Pasek Bendesa Mas clan, especially on its five-day *odalan,* falling on Kuningan Day (Saturday).

The **Wayang Wong Ramayana troupe** is still very much alive in Mas. It was revived by artist Walter Spies, and its 22 sacred masks are now kept in the temple. A performance is held on Kuningan eve, and three more on Kuningan day, as ritual contributions (*ayahan*).

Talented *dalangs* such as I. B. Geriya and I. B. Anom usually perform ritual *wayang lemah* on Kuningan night in the Taman Pule area.

Setia Darma House of Masks and Puppets

The **Setia Darma House of Masks and Puppets,** Jl. Tegal Bingin, Banjar Tengkulak Tengah, Kemenuh (tel: 977-404) was initiated by Hadi Sunyoto, a businessman and cultural enthusiast who has collected masks and puppets from different regions in Indonesia since 2003. This space, completed in 2006, is dedicated to collecting, preserving, and disseminating knowledge of these two art forms. The collection of over 6,000 pieces—and still growing—including a *wayang golek* (wooden puppet) of Barack Obama, are housed in four old Javanese *joglo* (traditional wooden houses). There are masks and puppets from all over the world, but the main emphasis is on Indonesian forms. Exhibitions, seminars, and performances are held here on a regular basis.

—Agnès Korb

PELIATAN VILLAGE

Home of the Legendary Legong Dance

Peliatan, a small village of 8,000, is often overlooked, though it lies just 2 km (1.2 miles) south of Ubud on the main road. Rich in the arts, and not as packed with tourists as Ubud, it is definitely worth a visit, particularly for those who are interested in dance and music.

"That which is seen"

The Peliatan court actually preceded the one in Ubud. Although the dates are unclear, the 17th century *Babad Dalem Sukawati* (a chronicle of the Sukawati court) recounts an argument between two princes—I Dewa Agung Gede and I Dewa Agung Made—that resulted in two separate dynasties.

The former ran off to Blahbatuh and the latter to Tegallalang, taking with him a sacred heirloom, the Segara Ngelayang spear, which is now kept in the Peliatan palace. I Dewa Agung Made later moved to Peliatan to be closer to his ancestral home in Sukawati.

His children then set up palaces in Ubud, and to this day Ubud royalty still pay homage to their cousins in Peliatan.

Peliatan literally means "that which is seen", and according to some accounts this refers to the fact that Sukawati is within view down the road. Others claim that a former king of Peliatan was given religious instruction here by a priest and was therefore able to "see" **Pura Gunung Sari** before it was built. Today, this temple is a favorite with dancers and musicians who come here in search of *taksu* (inspiration).

Bali's most notable Legong

Peliatan is best known for its Legong, a graceful dance traditionally performed by two pre-pubescent girls in glittering costumes (see "Balinese Dance and Drama", page 57). In fact, the first Balinese dance troupe to travel abroad was a *legong* group from Peliatan that performed at the Paris

Peliatan village is known as the center for training young legong *dancers.*

Exhibition in 1931 under the leadership of Anak Agung Gede Mandera (affectionately known as "Gung Kak"), a man who excelled in both music and dance. The group's performances created a sensation, and it was then that French actor Antonin Artaud first witnessed the Balinese *barong*. In 1952, the renowned Sampih and Gusti Raka performed on the American Ed Sullivan TV show. Gung Kak's descendants and students still carry on the tradition; a 1989 tour to the United States included many of his family members, who continue to dance around the globe.

Traditions of dance and music in Bali are passed from teacher to pupil and parent to child. Some teachers become very well known, such as Peliatan's Gusti Biang Sengog, who, in her prime, was recorded for posterity in the film *Miracle of Bali: Midday Sun* teaching young women who have all become prominent dancers today.

To see Peliatan's young *legongs* in action, travel east from Peliatan to Teges Kanginan, one of the few places on Bali where the dancers are still trained in the traditional manner. The teacher at Yayasan Polesseni, Sang Ayu Ketut Muklin, is from neighboring Pejeng village and is of the same age and caliber as Gusti Biang Sengog.

Even though the standard of music here is quite good, with a proliferation of *gamelan* groups, there really are no individuals that match the skill of the musicians from the 1930s, such as I Made Lebah, his son I Wayan Gandera, and I Made Grindem, all long gone.

Peliatan today is home to 15 *gamelan* groups, including *gong kebyar, gong semar pegulingan, gong angklung,* and *joged bumbung*. Almost every *banjar* owns at least one set of instruments and the haunting sounds of the *gamelan* can be heard in the Peliatan area nearly every night, whether in rehearsal or performance.

In 1987, Peliatan's women's *gamelan*, **Mekar Sari**, was begun under the tutelage of Gung Kak. Now the group performs weekly in Banjar Teruna. The dancers are all under 12 years old. The **Gong Kebyar Gunung Sari** also puts on a dazzling show at Puri Agung. The more lyrical sounds of **Tirta Sari Semar Pegulingan** (with two different *legongs*) can be heard on Friday night at Balerung Stage, with a younger group, Genta Bhuana Sari, performing every Tuesday night. One of the better commercial *kecak* troupes, **Semara Madya**, performs at Puri Agung every

Balinese children learn to play the gamelan *from a very young age.*

Thursday night. **ARMA Museum** has numerous performances, including the rarely seen Wayang Wong on Saturdays and Cak Rina every new and full moon. Check the Ubud performance schedule for complete details.

The traditional and the modern continue to flourish side-by-side here. Anak Agung Oka Dalem, one of Gung Kak's children, excels in the *kebyar* styles that Peliatan put on the map 40 years ago. In 1982, he founded Padma Nara Suara (PANAS for short), a dance group that fuses modern choreography and costuming with traditional Balinese dance movements. It could be said that PANAS is the Busby Berkeley of Bali.

Carving and painting

Peliatan is also the home of many carvers and painters. Orchids, fruits, frogs, ducks, and birds—all favored by tourists—are fashioned out of wood throughout the village. Two of the more exceptional carvers are I Wayan Pasti—whose life-size horses and dogs inspire double-takes—and I Nyoman Togog (the original "fruit man"), a Presidential awardee.

I Ketut Madra of Banjar Kalah is an excellent painter in the traditional *wayang* style. He is not a businessman by nature and does not have a gallery, but likes to show his work to visitors and accepts special commissions.

To see the classical painting style of the 1930s, visit I Gusti Made Kuanji in Banjar Teruna and I Nyoman Kuta in Banjar Tengah. For an overview of Balinese painting, pop into the **Agung Rai Gallery** on the main road, one of the best collections on the island, as well as his museum, ARMA, on Jl. Made Lebah, where you can also relax in the garden or the **ARMA Café** after seeing the exhibition.

— *Rucina Ballinger*

INTRODUCTION TO UBUD

A Village Haven for the Arts

Ubud was once known as a "quiet" haven for the arts. Set amidst emerald green rice paddies and steep ravines in the stunning central Balinese foothills some 25 km (15.5 miles) north of Denpasar, the village was originally an important source of medicinal herbs and plants. "Ubud" in fact derives from the Balinese word for medicine, *ubad*. However, since the 1990s massive changes, including an influx of foreign investors, expats looking for peace and yoga, and the inevitable traffic jams that large buses bring, have made Ubud a tourist mecca, albeit with a much larger concentration of artists than perhaps anywhere else in the world.

It was here that foreign artists such as German painter Walter Spies settled during the 1920s and '30s, transforming the village into a flourishing center for the arts. Artists from all parts of Bali were invited to stay here by the local prince, Cokorda Raka Gede Sukawati, and Ubud's palaces and temples

German artist Walter Spies was very influential in creating what is recognized today as the modern "Balinese" painting style.

are adorned by the work of Bali's master artisans as a result.

According to an 8th century legend, a Javanese priest named Rsi Markendya came to Bali from Java and meditated in Campuan (*Sangam* in Sanskrit) at the confluence of two streams, an auspicious site for Hindus. He founded **Pura Gunung Lebah** here on a narrow platform above the valley floor, where pilgrims seeking peace came to be healed from their worldly cares. To get there, follow a small road to the Warwick Ibah Hotel on the western outskirts of Ubud, then take the path down toward the river.

An important 19th century court

In the late 19th century, Ubud became the seat of *punggawa* or feudal lords owing their allegiance to the Gianyar rajas. All were members of the *satria* family of Sukawati and contributed greatly to the village's fame for performing and other arts. The Gianyar kingdom was established in the late 18th century and later became the most powerful of Bali's southern states. And while elsewhere the Dutch conquest had such disastrous consequences for the Balinese royal houses, in Gianyar, for the most part, the raja and his subjects benefitted from a Dutch administration that brought improved roads, irrigation networks, healthcare, and schools. The period between 1908 and 1930 brought significant changes to the area, and toward the end of the 1930s Ubud was prospering as a budding tourist resort due to the flowering of the arts in the area.

In the late 19th century, Cokorda Gede Raka Sukawati established himself in Ubud and was instrumental in laying the foundations for the village's fame. The area was at this time bereft of remarkable cultural features. It was in the interest of Cokorda that various artists and literati sought refuge here from other kingdoms. Ubud slowly accumulated specialists and evolved into a cultural center, with resident artists and *lontar* (palm leaf book) experts.

A prime example is the case of the young I Gusti Nyoman Lempad who, with his father, a noted writer, sought and found refuge in Ubud from the king of Bedulu. In gratitude, the young apprentice sculptor helped to decorate the **Puri Saren Agung** palace in Ubud and carved statues and ornaments on the main temple—**Pura Puseh**—of the noble family, north of the palace. He also carved the temple of learning, **Pura Taman Saraswati**. His work can still be seen on location, and some of his statues can be admired in Ubud's museum. At an advanced age he turned to pen and ink, working consistently until his death in 1978 at the age of 116.

A flowering of the arts

Between the World wars, Ubud's *punggawa*, Cokorda Gede Raka Sukawati, was a member of the Dutch colonial government's *Volksraad* (People's Council) in Batavia and was already interested in the "arts and crafts movement" spreading from Europe to Asia and Japan. He encouraged Walter Spies to settle in Ubud, thus provoking a growing tide of visitors to this enchanting village.

At the turn of the century, painting in Bali was integrated into religious, or *adat*, ceremonies with the themes being taken from classical Balinese tales that were well known from *wayang* performances. Inspired by the foreign artists who settled in Ubud, Cokorda Gede Raka Sukawati gradually developed this tradition. This unique mélange of traditional Balinese and modern Western art forms came to be associated with Ubud.

In the late 1920s and early 1930s Ubud became the focal point for foreign artists and other creative people gathering around Spies, a highly gifted and versatile German artist. A painter and a musician by training, Spies heard of Bali on reading Jaap Kunst's *Music of Bali*, published in 1925, in which the Dutch musicologist highly praised the village of Peliatan for its *gamelan* orchestra. His work on and anecdotes about Bali fascinated Spies, who was then director of the sultan of Yogyakarta's European orchestra.

Many other talented foreigners were also attracted to Ubud at this time. Among others, Miguel and Rosa Covarrubias discovered the hitherto unknown beauty of Bali upon seeing Gregor Krause's magnificent photo album, published in 1925. Krause had worked as a doctor in Bali around 1912. After living in Ubud and Sanur, Covarrubias wrote his *Island*

of Bali, one of the classics on Bali to this day. Rudolf Bonnet, the Dutch painter, was told of Bali's breathtaking beauty by etcher and ethnographer W. O. J. Nieuwenkamp in Florence and went there to seek inspiration in the late 1920s. Colin McPhee arrived to join Spies' experiments in musical traditions, which were at this time very dynamic, with new creations springing up overnight. They worked together with the legendary Anak Agung Gede Mandera of Peliatan, and McPhee later published a book on Bali's musical traditions as well as an account of his experiences here, *A House in Bali*.

Ubud rapidly became the village *en vogue* for many of these visitors, based on insider tips from the many musicians, painters, authors, anthropologists, and avant-garde world travelers who passed this way, especially after Spies settled in **Campuan** next to Ubud, on what is now the site of the Tjampuhan Hotel & Spa.

Spies and Bonnet both encouraged local Balinese artists, each in his own fashion. In 1936 they founded the Pita Maha, an artists' organization, together with Lempad, Sobrat, and I Tegalan, among many other excellent Balinese artists. This association was to guarantee and promote high artistic standards among its more than 100 members.

Ubud since independence

The Pita Maha movement did survive the vagaries of the Japanese occupation and the Indonesian struggle for independence. However, Cokorda Gede Agung Sukawati, assisted by Bonnet, later founded the Palace of Arts Museum (Puri Lukisan Museum) in 1953 to provide a retrospective of local achievements. Balinese artists thus continued to work together, sparking a renewal of artistic activity in the 1950s.

In the early 1950s, Dutch painter Arie Smit founded the Young Painters School of naive painting in Penestanan with Cakra. This style, free of any philosophical or abstract influence, led to uninhibited young school children using bright chemical colors to produce two-dimensional landscapes depicting daily life. Their work reflects the changing vision and lifestyle of young Balinese during the post-war period.

Han Snel was a young Dutch soldier who left the Dutch Colonial Army and "vanished" into Bali after his military service, finding his way to the hills around Ubud. His work captured the imagination of both foreigners and Balinese alike with its invigorating synthesis of both cultures. Following his marriage to a Balinese girl, Siti, he built a studio in a secluded spot in Central Ubud. Antonio Blanco, another Western painter, settled with his Balinese wife and five children on the Campuan heights bordering Penestanan. This eccentric even had one of Ubud's first telephones, a link between paradise and the madding crowds abroad.

The tourist boom

In the 1970s and 1980s the hotel and catering industry implanted itself in Ubud — modestly enough compared to how it had taken firm control of Kuta–Legian — but this idyllic village did nevertheless witness an ever-accelerating flow of visitors, who came to indulge in the arts and to escape from the daily grind. In short, tourism knocked gently but insistently on Ubud's door. The advent of mass tourism in the 1980s provided many young inhabitants of the area with stable employment rather than farming the fertile rice fields in the surrounding hills. Land reform and hereditary laws, in any case, had led to a scarcity of arable land.

It is therefore with mixed feelings that the visitor will notice how "business-like" the Ubudians are, although their artistic talents are still being cultivated. But modern times bring progress, which is not to be stopped in the name of nostalgia. Ubud's inhabitants retain their individuality and generosity of spirit through all the changes, leaving travelers wondering how these charming people can manage to deal with the dizzying alterations in the village structure resulting from the modernization of social, economic, and perhaps occasionally spiritual factors. This must be one of the world's most closely guarded secrets, or perhaps it is only a special peace of mind that comes from such a beautiful environment and a mild climate. The unruffled calmness of Ubud has soothed many a visitor, while the extraordinary beauty of the surroundings still inspires the creative to work.

Nowadays, the fruits of that extraordinarily prolific period of pre-World War II Ubud are still on display through dance, music, painting, and sculpture. Dance performances are given daily in at least three places, including the main palace. Ceremonies still abound where various dance or shadow puppet performances and excellent *gamelan* music are practiced. And painters, sculptors, writers, and creative designers continue to seek inspiration in the special atmosphere of Ubud, Campuan, and nearby Sayan.

— *Kunang Helmi Picard*

Dance performances happen nightly in several venues in Ubud.

A TOUR OF UBUD

On the Gallery and Temple Circuit

It is dawn and Ubud is awakening. The air is fresh, mixed with the heady scent of flowers and the incense of offerings. There are so many ways to spend a day here: visiting galleries and artists' studios, sipping drinks in garden cafes, and enjoying long strolls through the countryside. Below are a few of the "must sees".

Ubud highlights

No visit to Ubud is complete without a stop-over to the **Puri Saren Agung** palace at the main crossroads, with its maze of family compounds and doorways richly carved by Lempad. The royal family temple, **Pura Pamerajaan Sari Cokorda Agung**—a storage place for the family *pusaka* (regalia)—is next door.

To the west behind a lotus pond by the **Puri Saraswati** palace (now a hotel), lies the superbly chiseled **Pura Taman Saraswati** temple of learning, a *clin d'oeil* dedicated to Ubud's artistic past. From the crossroads here, walk north to Ubud's "navel" temple, **Pura Puseh**, with its delightful sculptures.

Next stop is the **Puri Lukisan Museum** to relish the paintings and sculptures and the peaceful garden. The museum was founded in 1953 by surviving members of Ubud's famed Pita Maha movement. Painted panels that Lempad executed 50-odd years ago depict the Balinese agrarian cycle.

There are numerous studios and shops in the center of town. Look for Prada and Starbucks competing with the **traditional market**, on the corner of Jl. Ubud Raya and Jl. Monkey Forest, and tiny souvenir shops selling everything from the ubiquitous T-shirt to hand-carved coconut spoons. Opposite the *wantilan* or community hall, check in with the

Pura Taman Saraswati, Ubud's temple of learning, is surrounded by a lotus pond.

Bina Wisata Tourist Office for local performances and festival schedules.

Ubud's best commercial galleries are scattered throughout the town. Suteja Neka, whose father was a painter, is the foremost dealer and collector on Bali, and is also the founder of the **Neka Art Museum**, a bit away from the town center to the west, on Jl. Raya Ubud. Ubud's most famous artist was Lempad, and the best places to see his delicate erotic pen and ink drawings are in the Puri Lukisan, Neka, and ARMA museums.

Contemporary art can be found at the **Komaneka Gallery**, established by Neka's son, on Jl. Monkey Forest, and there are numerous artist studios all vying for attention throughout the town. East of the Post Office are **T Art**, a modern structure that has rotating exhibitions, and **Pranoto's Art Gallery**, where the husband and wife team Pranoto and Kerry Pendergrast hold shows of charcoals, water colors, and nudes. Traveling west along the main road across the bridge to Campuan is the museum of the late eccentric Filipino-American painter **Antonio Blanco**, with his extravagant nudes, now run by his son Mario.

Every **handicraft** imaginable is available in the traditional market — watch out for pickpockets and don't forget to bargain — or in many shops. Some of the more upscale (but not hard on that wallet) are Bojog on Jl. Monkey Forest, Murni's west of the market, Alam Asia Crafts, Kuluk, and Celeng in Lungsiakan. Threads of Life on Jl. Kajeng No. 24 (tel: 0361 972-187, fax: 976-582, www.threadsoflife.com) features exquisite hand-woven textiles from throughout Indonesia; profits are plowed back into community projects.

Mischievous monkeys

Another of the major "sights" of Ubud is the **Monkey Forest Temple**, actually Padangtegal village's Pura Dalem Agung, 2 km (1.2 miles) to the south. If for no other reason, stroll down Jl. Monkey Forest to have a look at all the shops and restaurants. Before entering the forest (there is a small admission fee) itself, however, put away all edibles, eyeglasses, or any shiny jewelry, and hold on tight to your bags. These daring rascals are rapacious thieves and can be dangerous if provoked.

For those interested in a unique collection of books, **Ganesha Bookshop** on the main road (Jl. Ubud Raya) next to the Post Office

A denizen of Ubud's "Monkey Forest" temple.

is worthwhile. With both new and used books (and probably the best collection on the island of contemporary and historical works on Indonesia), music, knickknacks, and daily newspapers, this is a bookshop you won't want to miss. **Periplus** has a number of shops in Ubud, featuring large format books, a travel and cooking section, and novels. Ubud's only **library** at Pondok Pekak on the football green has a decent collection of all types of books, including a separate children's library. It also offers lessons in mask making, *gamelan*, and Indonesian language. Courses in all forms of Balinese arts, including offering making, are held at Puri Lukisan Museum and the ARMA Museum.

Nyoman Suradnya, Nirwana Homestay, Jl. Gautama (tel: 975-415), teaches **batik** with great humor and Cokorda Agung Pemayun in Pejeng gives lessons on batik using natural dyes. For **silver jewelry making**, try Studio Perak. Budding chefs will revel in the number of **cooking schools** here: Casa Luna on Jl. Ubud Raya, Laka Leke in Nyuh Kuning village behind the Monkey Forest, Taman Rahasia in Penestanan village, and Mozaic on Jl. Raya Sanggingan.

Other highlights on the must-do list are **nightly performances** at the palace and at other venues around Ubud; artists studios, boutiques, and eateries; or venture into the side alleyways, where the "old Ubud" still exists.

Aside from the arts — and the fantastic shopping — be sure to visit the **Ubud Botanic Gardens**, tap into your inner self at **The Yoga Barn**, or rejuvenate with a massage in one of the area's many **day spas**. However, be forewarned that because of the traffic, it's best to travel around Ubud by motorbike, bicycle, or on foot.

—Kunang Helmi Picard & Linda Hoffman

"New Age" Ubud

The Green Revolution of the 1970s introduced new strains of rice to Indonesia and the rest of Southeast Asia. Due to the intense development on Bali as well as a new awareness about environmental issues, a re-greening of the island has taken place, both environmentally and spiritually. The Balinese have always lived close to nature, and their philosophy of *Tri Hita Kirana* (literally "The Three Causes of Happiness due to Humanity's relationship to Nature, God, and Community") reflects this. More and more farmers are using permaculture, Sustainable Rice Intensification (SRI), and organic farming methods. Coral restoration and reforestation is taking place. Hotels and villas are installing waste water systems, using LED lighting and solar powered electricity, and of course offering health and spirit rejuvenating spa and yoga programs. These positive actions are coming just in time, as the island has absorbed about as much development as it can take.

The organics
There are two **organic farmers' markets** operating: Manik Organik in Sanur on Thursday afternoons and Ubud Farmer's Market in Ubud on Wednesday and Saturday mornings. For greens already prepared, many of Bali's cafes and restaurants now serve **organic** and **raw foods**: Como Shambhala, Little K, Kafé, Sari Organics, Down to Earth Café, Bali Buddha, and The Fivelements. Batujimbar Café in Sanur was the first to offer organic foods from their own hilltop gardens, and Sunday lunch packs in the locals and expats alike.

Ubud herb walks
Ni Wayan Lilir and I Made Westi of **Ubud Herb Walks** are a young couple who grew up in healer families. Their love of plants and what plants can do for good health inspired them to lead visitors on three-hour daily herb walks through the rice fields and plantations around Ubud. They offer the opportunity to learn firsthand about the healing properties of local plants, and they also offer classes on making *jamu*, or traditional herbal health and beauty concoctions.

Kneading those aching muscles
Spas and reflexology centers are almost as ubiquitous as Internet cafes and mobile phone shops on Bali. For under ten dollars, shopping-tired feet can be treated to a rigorous session of reflexology. What Indonesians call "spas" are usually places to get massages, facials, cream baths (heavenly hair, scalp, and neck treatments) and mani/pedicures. These range from a decent **massage** in rustic surroundings (Sara Spa in Ubud), to wondrous atmospheres (Spa Hati and Bali Botanica) to luxurious settings in a lush environment (Fivelements Puri Ahimsa and Bagus Jati Resort). Other five-star resorts also know what international visitors expect and offer a wide variety of packages.

Fivelements is the latest independent player in the wellness trend. The brainchild of Chicco and Lahra Tatriele, it opened in July 2010. Fivelements Puri Ahimsa is a healing center located in Mambal along the Ayung riverbank and offers Balinese Healing, Living Foods, and Sacred Arts in an exquisite atmosphere. The bamboo hall is worth visiting on its own. Their spa has Watsu and many other types of massage, and their dining room serves vegan raw foods.

Downward facing dogs beware
The world's **yoga** explosion has hit Bali in a big way. Well-known practitioners from around the world hold workshops here, and classes are offered in nearly every upscale hotel. In addition, there are many independent yoga studies; some of the leaders are Yoga Barn and Intuitive Flow in Ubud, Desa Seni in Canggu, Yoga Shala in Kerobokan, and Zen Resort in Ume Anyar village, north Bali.

Learning from bamboo
The Green School, an international school spearheaded by jewelry designers John and Cynthia Hardy, is set in small Sibang viillage. With nearly everything made of bamboo, the school's 75 buildings are cooled and powered with renewable energy sources, such as micro-hydro power, solar power, and bio-diesel, its main focus being to mould its students into ecologically responsible citizens. Tours are available.

Ubud has recently reinvented itself as a healing and wellness center, especially since the "Eat, Pray, Love" boom created by the book and film.

The Hardys' fascination with bamboo as a sustainable resource also inspired them to create a new business, **Ibuku**, designing furniture and architecture and selling organic bamboo home-building supplies, such as flooring, roofing, and poles. Their products—even adhesives and finishes—are free of petro-chemicals, and designs require no metal screws or nails.

Linda Garland of Nyuh Kuning village was one of the first on Bali to make furniture for export out of giant bamboo. She started the **Environmental Bamboo Foundation** in 1993 to protect tropical forests by promoting and demonstrating the many conservation and development opportunities that bamboo offers. She now works with the East Bali Poverty Project, where a sustainable **Bamboo Research and Development Centre** has been established.

Eco-tourism

Bali is filled with activities that fall under the umbrella term "eco-tourism". Rafting, hiking, water sports, elephant rides, and safari parks, to name just a few, are all here. There are some that stand out for their heartfelt approach to the true spirit of eco-tourism. **JED** (Village Ecotourism Network) offers day and overnight trips to villages where travelers eat and interact with villagers and go on locally-guided hikes. Tours are organized and managed by the village and all proceeds go to them. **Sarinbuana Eco-Lodge**, in the midst of the Batukaru mountains, offers over a dozen workshops in a tranquil and isolated location. **Puri Lumbung** in Munduk, located high in the hills of Buleleng Regency coffee growing country, is an ideal spot to relax, hike, or take classes in offering-making, dance, *gamelan*, and other Balinese cultural arts.

To see a sampling of the many natural building materials available on Bali, head down to **Little Tree Green Building and Lifestyle Centre** on Jl. Sunset in Kuta, and while there, have a healthy lunch at the Sari Organic Café branch inside.

—Rucina Ballinger

WALKING TOURS AROUND UBUD

Breathtaking Glimpses of Village Bali

Ubud's surroundings offer many rewarding walks and excursions up hill and over dale, with breathtaking vistas and many surprising glimpses of rural, unspoiled Bali. To get a glimpse of what Ubud used to be like at the turn of the last century, hire a car, scooter, or bicycle or go by foot and visit some of the surrounding villages. Each one has its own charm. Don't hesitate to wander off the main roads and explore.

What follows is but a short list of suggested itineraries. Many more could easily be added.

Hike 1: The "high road" to Kedewatan
This is an easy, half-day hike west of Ubud up along the road through Campuan and over to Kedewetan. Get an early start at the Campuan Bridge and stop in to see the **Pura Gunung Lebah** temple that nestles in the gorge. Rsi Markendrya founded it at the confluence of these rivers in the 8th century. Follow the main road up a steep hill past the **Neka Art Museum**. Along the way are delightful views and a chance to stop in at the studios of famous artists like **Antonio Blanco** and **Ngurah KK**, to name a few. Be sure to stop in at Neka Museum, too, to see the works of a veritable who's who of Balinese painters, past and present.

After Neka's, the road takes a sharp turn to the left with **Ulun Ubud Resort & Spa** on the right. Inside, there is a small gallery belonging to Ida Bagus Tilem, Bali's best-known wood-carver. Continuing up the main road, you'll eventually reach the Payangan–Kedewatan T-junction. Turn right, and after a few hundred

Spectacular green rice terraces surround Ubud in every direction.

meters is **Kedewatan** village, with its extraordinary rice terraces stepping down to the Ayung River below. Look for Pura Telaga Waja, a temple with multi-tiered *merus*. Afterwards, travel by *bemo* back to Ubud.

Hike 2: To Petulu, where egrets nest

A fairly easy, half-day hike north and east of Ubud, start around lunchtime at the main Ubud crossroads in front of the Puri Saren palace, and go north along Jl. Suweta. The road is paved all the way past **Pura Puseh** (Ubud's temple of origin, with carvings by Lempad), about half a mile from the crossroads. Continuing straight ahead, you emerge in open rice fields with spectacular views of Mt. Agung on a clear day. After about an hour, you reach **Bentuyung** village. From here, either take the road back south to **Tegallanting** and **Taman** *banjars*, their temples tucked in the midst of family compounds at the crossroads.

Alternatively, turn to the right (east) through **Junjungan** to **Petulu** to see white egrets hovering over the village as they alight in lofty trees at sunset. Every evening around 6 pm hundreds of graceful egrets and a few herons make their way back to nest in the trees lining the streets, making them look like cotton-studded greenery. Local folklore has it that these birds only started coming to Petulu post-1965, and that the birds are the souls of the unpurified dead who were massacred in 1965 and placed in a mass grave here. Mention any of the above places, and locals will point the way. From Petulu, take a *bemo* or walk back to Ubud. However, be aware that *bemos* do not run after dark.

Hike 3: To Penestanan

Penestanan is just west of Ubud. To get there, go past the Campuan bridge and take the 54 steps to walk through the rice fields. Once on the paved road, turn right and follow it until to Penestanan, where there are lots of small shops selling beadwork. Have a drink and a massage at Taman Rahasia or spa treatment at The Mansion before heading back into town.

The following hikes will be a stretch for all but the hardiest trekkers because of their distance but can also be done by car.

Hike 4: To Nyuh Kuning

To get to **Nyuh Kuning** village—known for its wood carvers—from the center of Ubud go south on Jl. Monkey Forest, cutting through the forest to the opposite side. (Note that they charge a small entrance fee. Alternatively, you can go through the parking lot and follow the one-lane paved path on the east side of the forest entrance at no charge.) Nyuh Kuning, where the path ends, is a tiny two-street village that houses an Ayurvedic healing center, two yoga studios and an alternative healing center, a gallery selling hand-woven textiles from throughout Southeast Asia, Linda Garland's Bamboo Foundation, a locally-run orphanage, and Bumi Sehat Birthing Clinic.

Many expats have made this village their home. After a cooking class or a divine lunch at Laka Leke Restaurant, indulge in rejuvenating bodily delights or pick up a souvenir.

Afterwards, continue to the main road and turn right. Go over the bridge, and at the next major road turn left to get to **Singakerta** village to see the daily life of local farmers. Coming back, go due east toward Pengosekan, and turn left onto Jl. Hanoman and back into Ubud. This expedition will take at least half a day—without stopping for lunch and spa treatments—and is not on the *bemo* routes.

Hike 5: To Pengosekan

Colorful fish and birds are what makes the **Pengosekan** (pronounced: *pongo-SAY-kan*) painting style distinctive. The aristocrats of neighboring Mas were somewhat put out when Queen Elizabeth insisted on being taken to low-caste Pengosekan in search of a painting in 1974; and the villagers themselves were disappointed that she had forgotten to wear her crown.

In 1979 they established the island's first artists' cooperative, exhibiting and selling together and supporting each other with raw materials (in the days when the cost of a tube of imported acrylic paint would feed a large family for three weeks). Incorporating elements of traditional Balinese communalism, they called themselves the **Pengosekan Community of Farmers and Artists**, led by *mandala* painter **Dewa Nyoman Batuan**. Painters to look for: Batuan himself, his brother Mokoh, Putralaya, Kobot, Barat, and Sena.

This village is also home to jewelry designers, *gamelan* musicians, and dancers, as well as incense and basket makers. The **Cudamani Summer Institute of Gamelan and Dance** is here as well, as is the home of **Ketut Liyer**, the toothless healer from the movie, *Eat, Pray, Love.*

— *Kunang Helmi Picard*

VISITING UBUD
(TELEPHONE CODE: 0361)

While it's possible to visit Ubud in just one day, such a short trip would barely touch the surface of this extraordinary village, which in the span of just a few decades has become renowned for its art and culture. An interesting mélange of rural Balinese life and modern services co-exist here. Only 60 minutes from Ngurah Rai airport (on a good traffic day), Ubud is close to many of Central Bali's major historic and cultural sights.

Visitors usually outnumber residents during peak periods in July and August, and tour buses jam the narrow streets. However, for the rest of the year, Ubud retains the atmosphere of a small country town and the pace can be very relaxed. It's a great place to tour on foot or by bicycle, and there's a wide range of facilities for tourists of all budgets. For those who enjoy being in the epicenter of Balinese arts and culture, yet within easy reach of creature comforts and natural surroundings, Ubud is ideal.

ORIENTATION
The crossroads in front of Puri Saren palace is the "navel" of Ubud—its cultural, historical and commercial focal point. The main street, Jl. Raya Ubud, is lined with restaurants, mini-markets, shops, and galleries, stretching all the way from the T-junction at the eastern end of Ubud to the Campuan Bridge in the west. Small lanes with homestays, hotels, *warungs*, souvenir shops, and Balinese compounds extend north and south from the main road.

Jl. Monkey Forest, branching south from "downtown" Ubud is lined with hotels, restaurants, cafes, artists' studios, and boutiques for a distance of some 2 km (1.2 miles). A parallel road south, Jl. Hanoman, just to the east of Padangtegal is similar, though less congested. Away from these main streets, Ubud is still relatively quiet.

Roads radiate west out of the main town to Campuan (also spelled Campuhan and Tjampuhan), Payangan, Kedewatan, Penestanan, and Sayan. To the south is Batuan, Nyuh Kuning ,and Pengosekan. To the east is Peliatan, Tegas, and Bedulu, where Goa Gajah (Elephant Cave) is located. To the north is Sanggingan and Petulu.

Bemos can be flagged down in the daytime on the main road and charge according to the distance traveled. Ubud to Campuan, for example, costs Rp 2,000.

TOURIST INFORMATION
For information on nightly performances, transport schedules, temple festivals, and special activities, inquire at the **Ubud Tourist Information Center**,

Bina Wisata, Jl. Raya Ubud, tel: 973-285, on the southwest corner of the main intersection, across the street from the Ubud traditional market.

GETTING THERE
Ubud is 60 minutes by car from the airport and southern beach resort areas and 40 minutes from Sanur on good traffic days. Note that the roads to Ubud are narrow and winding and if an accident should occur or a ceremonial procession is in progress, travel times can be delayed. Be sure to allow plenty of travel time, particularly if airline departure times are an issue.

Taxis from the airport cost Rp 200,000. The taxi windows at both the domestic and international terminals are to the left after emerging from the baggage claim area.

From Denpasar, take a *bemo* from Kereneng Terminal to Batubulan Terminal, then transfer to Ubud (Rp 10,000). Chartering a *bemo* from Denpasar costs about Rp 125,000 after bargaining. Alternatively, hop on one of the shuttle buses which depart Kuta for Ubud at 6 and 10 am and 1:30 and 4:30 pm (Rp 50,000). Call **Perama Tour**, Jl. Legian, Kuta, tel: 751-875 or Jl. Pengosekan, Ubud, tel: 973-316 for further information regarding schedules and pick-up locations.

GETTING AROUND
Although it's easy to walk around Ubud, renting a **bicycle** can save time and effort. Bikes can be rented everywhere for around Rp 20,000–30,000 per day; motorbikes (100cc) cost Rp 50,000–80,000 per day. Both are also easily available from most *losmen* and homestays.

Taxis don't exist in Ubud, but—as you'll soon find out, walking the main streets—there are plenty of private cars which you can "charter". Look for the circular yellow "E" logo on the windshield certifying them as Ubud Transport Association members. A Suzuki jeep costs around $12/day; it will be cheaper by the week or month.

These **private vehicles** also take the place of taxis for short hauls. Their drivers line the main streets and offer "transport" to whomever passes by. Ask at your accommodation the current rate for the distance you're going and settle on a price before getting in. The drivers will, of course, attempt to secure longer trips by asking what your "program for tomorrow" is, and many of them actually make good guides.

Buy **shuttle bus** tickets to Kuta (Rp 50,000) and Candidasa (Rp 60,000) from the many travel agencies in the town.

Shuttle buses to Sanur, Kuta, and the airport depart at 8:30 and 10:30 am, 12:00, 3:00 and 6:00 pm. The direct shuttle bus to Ampenan on Lombok leaves at 7 am.

ACCOMMODATIONS

Though you'll find the full gamut from $5/night home-stays to luxurious $1,000/night suites and villas, on the whole Ubud's accommodations have gone dramatically upmarket in the past several years; hot water, AC, telephones, WiFi service, and swimming pools are now widely available. A number of Bali's most exclusive hotels, including The Maya, Amandari, and Four Seasons Bali at Sayan are also located here.

Decide on the area you want, then look around. Signs pointing the way to small hotels in the inter-mediate range line Jl. Raya Ubud and Jl. Monkey Forest and offer lovely bungalows set in gardens with pools for $20–50/night. Balinese-style homestays provide charming rooms with private bathroom, fan, and hot water for only $5–10. Most are easily reached on foot from the town center.

Travel out of Ubud in almost any direction and you'll find little homestays and bungalows tucked away among the rice fields, some with dramatic vistas. If you stay out in the paddies, it's handy to take along an electric anti-mosquito device (buy one in any local mini-market), as well as a flashlight.

Pengosekan, just south of Ubud, is cheaper and quieter. **Penestanan** and **Campuan** to the west are lovely villages where farmers still work the fields. The area is lusciously green, with bungalow complexes, private villas, shops and bamboo restaurants everywhere. Most rooms have private bathrooms and rates include a breakfast of toast, coffee/tea, and fruit salad.

Further west, the more upmarket hotels in **Sayan** and **Kedewatan** offer luxury rooms, suites, and villas overlooking a spectacular river gorge with great views up to the volcanoes and down to the coast.

Budget (under $25)

Budget accommodations are Balinese homestays in family compounds or small bungalows in the paddies built specifically for tourists. Simple and clean, many have attached bathrooms, hot water, and fans. A simple breakfast is always included and children are welcome. Homestays are clustered in well-defined areas: Jl. Bisma, Jl. Hanoman, Jl. Kajeng, and Jl. Tebesaya. As there is little difference in the level of comfort, the choice is really between experiencing the intimacy of a family compound, the quality of the breakfast or other amenities, or the proximity to the daily rhythms of the rice fields. For cheaper places and longer stays, look around Peliatan, Penestanan, and Nyuh Kuning.

CENTRAL UBUD

Family Guest House, Jl. Sukma 39, Tebesaya, tel: 974-054. In a family compound.

Gusti's Garden Bungalows, Jl. Kajeng 27, tel: 361-0840. Balinese-style rooms with hot water.

Jati Home Stay, Jl. Hanoman, Padangtegal, tel: 977-701. A compound belonging to a family of artists. Rooms in all natural materials, such as bamboo.

Ketut's Place, Jl. Suweta 40, tel: 975-304. Stay with a delightful Balinese family. Great dinner and cooking classes.

Matahari, Jl. Jembawan, behind the post office, tel: 975-459. 6 rooms near a deep ravine looking out onto a bamboo forest. A Japanese-style hot tub is available. Rooms with hot water, $25/single, $35–40/double.

Oka Kartini Bungalows & Gallery, Jl. Raya Ubud (opposite the BCA Bank in Padangtegal), tel: 975-193. Restful Balinese-style bungalows with hot showers are surrounded by pool and gardens, but the best thing about staying here is the charm, grace, and liveliness of Ibu Oka's company.

Rumah Roda, Jl. Kajeng 24 (northwest of Ubud palace), tel: 972-187, www.rumahroda.com. Excellent location. Newly built 3 stories behind the home of a Balinese family that has been welcoming travelers into their fold for many decades. You won't find a more accommodating place than this. $15–20.

WEST OF CENTRAL UBUD

Penestanan Bungalows, Jl. Penestanan, tel: 975-604, fax: 288-341. 12 rooms. Climb the steep stairs on the left off Jl. Campuan, 100 m (320 ft) past the Campuan Bridge, and follow the signs. Lovely garden setting with stunning views over the rice fields. Restaurant, hot water, and a swimming pool. Friendly, helpful staff. $25 with fan.

SOUTH OF CENTRAL UBUD

Guci Guest Houses, Jl. Pengosekan, tel: 974-974, www.guci-bali.com. Tucked away off the road, 5 charming bungalows offer quiet; good breakfasts.

EAST OF CENTRAL UBUD

Villa Bhuana Alit, Banjar Kalah, Peliatan, tel: 971-561, www.bhuananalitvilla.com. At the southern end of Peliatan village, this small hotel has rooms (some with AC) as well as houses to rent. Pool. $25–40.

Moderate ($25-50)

This category has the widest selection, the most scenic locations, and the best value. Most have pools. Reservations recommended during the high seasons (June–August and December–January).

CENTRAL UBUD

Nick's Pension & Restaurant, Jl. Bisma, tel: 975-636, www.nickspension-bali.com. Also accessible through their restaurant on Jl. Bisma. 24 quiet cottages on a terraced hill, bridging a stream. $28–80.

Okawati's, Jl. Monkey Forest, tel:/fax: 975-063. 19 rooms with attached baths and fans. Pool and restaurant. A nostalgic favorite. Ibu Okawati opened the first restaurant in Ubud. $33–55.

WEST OF CENTRAL UBUD

Ananda Cottages, Jl. Raya, Campuan, tel: 975-276, fax: 975-375, www.anandaubud.com. 45 rooms set in rice fields near the Neka Art Museum. Older clientele, families with children. Verandas and garden bathrooms. Pool. $40–70.

Melati Cottages, Penestanan, tel: 974-650, www.melati-cottages.com. Clusters of bungalow-type rooms with rice field views far from the madding crowds, but walking distance to Ubud. Yoga pavilion. $30–45.

SOUTH OF CENTRAL UBUD

Bali Breeze Bungalows, Jl. Pengosekan, tel: 975-410, fax: 975-546. 9 *lumbung*-style bungalows. Bedroom upstairs, toilet and sitting room downstairs. Well-designed. $30–45.

Kebun Indah, Jl. Pengosekan, tel: 973-366, reservations: tel:/fax: 974-629, www.alamindahbali.com. Owned by the Café Wayan-Alam Indah family, this was their first guesthouse. Set back down a path about 130 m (140 yds) from the road, a peaceful oasis attracting many repeat and long-term guests. 2 garden rooms and a Tea House, spacious 2-bedroom suite, 2 rooms in the Big House by the pool. Delicious breakfasts from Café Wayan. Alam Asia Crafts shop roadside supports artisans in Southeast Asia; little Kebun Indah Spa. $40–80.

Pondok Saraswati, Lod Tunduh village, 6 km (3.7 miles) south of Ubud, tel: 974-172. 5 rooms. If you want peace and quiet in a pleasant setting, this is it. Hot water showers and mosquito nets. Simple furnishings, and the view and the breeze from the upstairs rooms are refreshing. $40.

Tegal Sari, Jl. Pengosekan, www.tegalsari-ubud.com. Set in the middle of rice fields but an easy walk to Ubud, these 21 rooms offer great value. Pool and fitness area. $35–65.

Villa Kerti Yasa, Nyuh Kuning, tel: 971-377, www.villakertiyasa.com. Small inn with garden setting in village on the other side of the Monkey Forest. Pool, small meeting room. $45–80.

Intermediate ($50–75)

These hotels have either individual bungalows or 2-story buildings of 4 units, each with phone, fan or AC and a bathroom with hot water. Most have swimming pools, restaurants, and pleasant views of gardens, valleys, or rice fields. Credit cards usually accepted. Many are located away from the center of town, so a car is recommended.

CENTRAL UBUD

Anom Cottages, Jl. Raya Sanggingan, tel: 852-8521. Fabulous ridge view in 6 bungalow-style rooms with kitchen facilities. $50–60.

Puri Saraswati, Jl. Raya Ubud, tel: 975-164, www.purisaraswati.com. Smack dab in the center of town, these 18 rooms offer convenience in the royal palace compound. $57–65.

Murni's Houses, Jl Raya Ubud (up the ramp opposite Pura Dalem on the main street, left at the top, 2nd gate on the right), tel: 975-165, www.murnis.com. 4 delightful units, a 5-minute walk from the center, peaceful, traditional, clean, and very reasonably priced. Beautifully furnished by Murni in Balinese style. Well-kept gardens and the excellent Tamarind Spa in the grounds. Pick up, drop, activities, tours, and classes can all be arranged. $60–115, includes Murni's Big Breakfast.

WEST OF CENTRAL UBUD

Sayan Terrace, Jl. Raya Sayan, Kedewatan, tel: 974-384, fax: 975-384, www.sayanterraceresort.com. 10 rooms with teak parquet floors, wrap-around windows, hot water, and spectacular views across the Ayung River. Great value. $50–100/rooms; $125–242/villas.

Tjampuhan Hotel & Spa, Jl. Raya Campuan, Campuan, across the bridge and just up the road on the right, tel: 975-368, fax: 975-137, www.indo.com/hotels/tjampuhan. 63 rooms set on terraced gardens overlooking the Campuan River and temple. Spring-fed swimming pool and tennis court. Built on the site of Walter Spies' compound of the 1930s. Many steps! $70–115.

SOUTH OF CENTRAL UBUD

Alam Indah, Nyuh Kuning, tel:/fax: 974-629, www.alamindahbali.com. 10 rooms. Owned by the Café Wayan family, this small, exquisite hotel is a gem. All rooms have hot running water, 2 with AC, the rest have ceiling fans. Rooms are large and airy, and most have rice field views. Family suite has upstairs bedroom, 2 bathrooms. Superb, pampering service. Free transport to and from Ubud center. Pool. $75–125.

Across the road are **Alam Shanti** and **Alam Jiwa**, owned by the same family, as is Laka Leke Restaurant nearby. All are highly recommended and enjoy many repeat guests.

Villa Sonia, Nyuh Kuning, tel: 971-307, www.villa-sonia.nl. 9 private garden villas in a quiet village setting $75–125.

First class ($75–100)
EAST OF CENTRAL UBUD
Tepi Sawah Villas & Spa, Jl. Raya Goa Gajah, Banjar Teges, Peliatan, tel: 970-388, fax: 970-377, www.tepisawahvillas.com. Owned by a Balinese art collector, this property began as a gallery, a restaurant was added, then 12 modern thatched-roof villas. Fabulous rice field views in the gorge below, excellent restaurant is a good lunch stop serving fresh food not found in the eateries where tour buses normally stop. Swimming pool, spa, art gallery, satellite tv, WiFi, butler service. Offers classes: painting, woodcarving, and offering making. Discounted Internet rates; packages $95–275.

NORTH OF CENTRAL UBUD
Alam Sari, Keliki, Tegallalang, tel: 981-420, www.alamsari.com. 12 AC rooms set high above the road with sweeping vistas, this hotel offers courses, village walks, fitness, and pool; Internet. Popular with student groups. $98/room; $180/family suite.
Murni's Villas, Ponggang, Payanagan, a 15–20 minute drive from Ubud, tel: 972-146, www.murnis.com. 3 luxury villas, stunning infinity pool, amazing, picture-perfect views of rice terraces, hills, and forests. Beautifully furnished by Murni. Lovely staff. Ideal for weddings and honeymoons. All meals can be provided by an excellent cook. Good discounts for longer stays. Pick up, drop, activities, tours, and classes can all be arranged.

Luxury ($100 & up)
Spacious Balinese-inspired bungalows, villas, or suites. AC, mini-bar, private pool, and balconies overlooking private gardens are standard features in this category. Weddings are often done in these venues. Airport transfers are usually included. Major credit cards accepted.

CENTRAL UBUD
Komaneka Resort, Jl. Monkey Forest, tel: 976-090, www.komaneka.com. In the heart of Ubud; the perfect base from which to explore the town's shops and markets. Set in rambling gardens with a beautiful swimming pool. From $220/suite room, $250/villa. Also check out their sister property, Komaneka Suites, tel: 978-123, overlooking a luxuriant valley in Tanggayuda village, Kedewatan, to the west.

WEST OF CENTRAL UBUD
Alila Ubud, Desa Melinggih Kelod, Payangan, tel: 975-963, fax: 975-968, www.alilahotels.com.

60 rooms and suites. Tranquil, secluded hillside retreat at the end of a quiet country road overlooking a magnificent valley. Rich wood interiors, private gardens. From $200/deluxe; $350/suite.
Amandari, Kedewatan, Sayan Heights overlooking the Ayung River, about 3 km (2 miles) west of Ubud, tel: 975-333, fax: 975-335, www.amanresorts.com. 30 private pavilions designed by Australian architect Peter Muller; one of Bali's most exquisite hotels. Each villa is nestled in its own private walled compound, and several have private swimming pools. Service is exemplary. Jaw-dropping view over the Ayung River Gorge. $800–1,200.
Bumbu Indah, Banjar Baung, Sayan, tel: 977-922, 974-357, fax: 974-404, www.bambuindah.com. 15 minutes south of central Ubud, a compound of historic Javanese teak cottages that have been lovingly restored, with public buildings created from bamboo based on traditional Sumatran architecture. Each house is unique and is decorated with collections from the global travels of famed jewelry designer John Hardy and his wife Cynthia, who live next door. Modern amenities, such as AC and light switches, have been cleverly camouflaged to blend in with the eco-friendly concept. $210–310. Special Internet rates available.
Four Seasons Bali at Sayan, on the Sayan Ridge south of the Amandari, tel: 701-010, fax: 701-020, www.fourseasons.com. 47 rooms and villas in a labyrinth of extraordinary architectural innovations of a giant lily pond topping the restaurant, stairways, interior rivers, and waterfalls. Superb food and guest service, as is always expected of Four Seasons Resorts. From $460/standard room to $3,500/3-story villa with private swimming pool.
Pita Maha, Campuan, tel: 974-330, www.pitama-ha-bali.com. Set in the upland hills above Campuan with incredible river gorge views. Each villa has its own plunge pool, hot water, AC, and the utmost privacy. $393–580.
Royal Pita Maha, Kedewatan, tel: 980-022, www.royalpitamaha-bali.com. 20 minutes outside of Ubud. Overlooking the Ayung River, these luxury suites bring tranquility and serenity. Spa on grounds. $376–433.
The Mansion, Jl. Penestanan, Sayan, tel: 972-616, www.themansionbali.com. 10 eco-friendly villas and 12 deluxe rooms with plunge pools and Jacuzzis within a private courtyard, a perfect choice for discerning travelers and honeymooners. $330–1,780.
Ubud Hanging Gardens, Buahan, Payangan, tel: 982-700, www.ubudhanginggardens.com. Each of the 38 luxury Balinese private villas hug the hillsides and surrounding rice terraces, offering an uninterrupted peaceful view of the ancient Pura

Penataran Dalem Segara temple on the opposite hillside. Quite a way out of Ubud; perfect for honeymooners. $455–605.

Warwick Ibah Luxury Villas & Spa, Jl. Raya Campuan, Campuan, tel: 974-466, fax: 974-467. www.warwickibah.com. Managed by Paris-based Warwick Group, 17 uniquely designed villas offering every amenity in luxurious and stylish surroundings. Saltwater swimming pool, 2 plunge pools, restaurant, spa, library, only a 5-minute walk from Ubud center. Opened in 2010 is "Treetops", 6 suites in a single structure, with jungle canopy views and sounds from the river far below. $245–445.

EAST OF CENTRAL UBUD

Maya, Jl. Gunung Sari Peliatan, tel: 977-888, fax: 977-555, www.mayaubud.com. A luxurious 5-star property on the Petanu River with a mix of modern materials and charming antiques. 3 different classes of rooms from urban-style to villa and deluxe villas. Take the lift down to the spectacularly situated spa and relaxing River Café. $270–900.

The Chedi Club, at Tanah Gajah, tel: 975-685, www. ghmhotels.com. 20 luxuriously appointed suites set in the middle of 5 ha of paddy fields just outside of Ubud, near Goa Gajah. Offers serenity surrounded by Javanese antiques. Spa, fitness, tennis. From $360/standard bungalow to $970/2-bedroom villa.

NORTH OF CENTRAL UBUD

Bagus Jati Resort, Banjar Jati, Desa Sebatu, Tegallalang, tel: 978-885, fax: 974-666, www. bagusjati.com. After about 3 km (2 miles) of bad country road passing through villages and forests, arrive at this serene, isolated residential health and well-being center, organic gardens, and gourmet restaurant. 8 deluxe and 10 superior villas with private spa facilities set on 5 ha of hillside gardens. Offers a global palate of world-class health and well-being programs: nutrition, detox, yoga, meditation, stress relief, anti-aging, nature trekking, fitness center, cooking workshops. From $260, includes all wellness programs. Internet rates and additional tours available.

Bali Elephant Safari Park Lodge, Jl. Elephant Park Taro, Taro village, tel: (0361) 721-480, fax: 721-481, www.elephantsafariparklodge.com. A 25-room luxury boutique resort inside the Elephant Safari Park set on 3.5 ha. Elephants roam around the grounds and guests are encouraged to interact with them as a way to learn more about them. Elephant chauffer pick-up from rooms, exclusive pachyderm bathing sessions and access to baby nursery and four shows daily, in addition to swimming pool, spa, fitness center, and viewing terrace usage. A variety of room types, starting from $225.

Kamandalu Resort & Spa, Jl. Andong, Banjar Nagi, tel: 975-825, fax: 975-851, www.kamandaluresort. com. 56 villas in a 5-star boutique resort designed in Balinese village style with a touch of the contemporary; set on curving ridges overlooking the Petanu River. Relaxed atmosphere; friendly staff. Pool with swim-up bar, kids' pool, WiFi, complimentary shuttle to Ubud center, restaurant, lounge, spa. $280–440. Internet specials and packages available.

The Viceroy Bali, Jl. Lanyahan, Banjar Nagi, tel: 971-777, www.viceroybali.com. In a tiny village far north of Ubud, this is luxury incarnate. 15 rooms, each with its own pool and all the amenities expected in this type of establishment. Cascades Restaurant. $800–2,000.

Waka di Ume Resort & Spa, Jl. Sueta, Banjar Sambahan, 2 km (1.2 miles) north of Ubud, tel: 973-178, fax: 973-179, www.wakadiumeubud. com. Winner of Bali's Tri Hita Karana Emerald award for 5 years of living in harmony with the spiritual, environmental, and social community, also Asia Green Hotel award, 2010–2011. Bungalows, suites and villas, one with a private pool, overlooking rice fields. Architecture is in *lumbung* style to blend in with surroundings. The floor above the spa is perhaps the most ethereal meditation room in Bali. Terraced swimming pool; regular shuttle buses to Ubud. From $244/room, $303/suite, $357/villas.

DINING

Ubud has an incredible variety of places to eat. The simple *warungs* serving *nasi campur* and satay are still around, but now there is also everything else. Today, Ubud offers a choice ranging from American burgers and steaks, to country-style Japanese, sophisticated Italian pastas, and globally-acclaimed haute cuisine. A few restaurants stand head and shoulders above the crowd for the quality and originality of their food. The following is just a sampling of the area's better restaurants.

CENTRAL UBUD

Ary's Warung, Jl. Raya Ubud, tel: 975-053, www. dekco.com. Located in the heart of Ubud, Ary's is known for its friendly service and great food. Inspired by the Slow Food movement, contemporary Balinese-Asian cuisine; tasting menu offering several courses. Wine cellar, cigars and freshly brewed *kopi luwak* coffee are features. Pricey.

Batan Waru, Jl. Dewi Sita, south of the football field, tel: 977-528, www.baligoodfood.com. Mixed/ Western. Best place in town for breakfast; check out the ginger pancakes and the Florida lime pie. Chili crab on Tuesday nights. Extensive Indonesian menu without the fire. If you want it spicy hot, request it. Open 8 am–11:30 pm.

Bebek Bengil (Dirty Duck Diner), Padangtegal, tel:/fax: 975-489. Arguably one of the largest and most beautiful restaurant environments on Bali, offering a highly creative, cheeky menu. The specialty of the house is Balinese crispy fried duck. Low tables with cushions create a cozy atmosphere, and the food is wholesome. Local expats swear by the salads, pastas, and vegetarian dishes. Daily specials and a great selection of desserts.

Black Beach, Jl. Hanoman 5, tel: 971-353. Italian-owned and operated; Italian home-cooked meals. Sunset Terrace rooftop café. WiFi. Art films on Wednesdays and Thursdays.

Café des Artistes, Jl. Bisma 9X, tel: 972-706, www.cafedesartistesbali.com. Belgian cook. Wonderful steak dishes.

Café Lotus, Jl. Raya Ubud, tel: 975-660. While still one of the most beautiful settings in Ubud (in front of the royal family's clan temple and a huge lotus pond), the food and service are lackluster, but there are homemade pastas and fabulous desserts. Pricey.

Café Wayan, Jl. Monkey Forest, tel: 975-447. One of the best places to eat in town, Ibu Wayan has cooked in California and Thailand and loves to travel; the menu reflects her diverse culinary background. On Sunday nights they put on an extravagant Balinese buffet. Death by Chocolate Cake is just that. Packed at dinner; not so crowded at lunch.

Casa Luna, Jl. Raya Ubud, tel: 973-283. In the center of town, 2 floors of spacious dining with an eclectic menu ranging from Western standards to Indonesian favorites. Just inside the entrance is an excellent bakery with fresh baked breads and cakes. Highly regarded **cooking school** offers workshops Monday-Wednesday mornings.

Cinta, Jl. Monkey Forest, tel: 975-395, www.baligoodfood.com. Grilled foods and ribs are the order of the day here. Happy hour 2-for-1 mojitos.

Ibu Oka's Babi Guling (Roast Suckling Pig), Jl. Suweta and Jl. Raya Mas. Ibu Oka's is an Ubud institution. People come from miles away to eat her crispy pig skins. You can get a huge plateful for about $1 here.

Juice Ja, Jl. Dewi Sita, tel: 971-056. Located in the heart of Ubud, a comfortable, unpretentious café on 2 floors serving wholesome and delicious breakfast, lunch, and dinner. Emphasis is on using organic and local ingredients to produce salubrious meals and baked goods for the café and for the local farmers' market.

Kue, Jl. Raya Ubud, near the post office, tel: 975-249. For a chocolate fix or a birthday cake, this is the place. International menu. Open 9 am–10 pm.

Lamak, Jl. Monkey Forest, tel: 974-668. A back-to-the-future restaurant with a physical space beyond compare. The scallops appetizer served on green tea noodles has perhaps the most tender melt-in-your-mouth scallops on the island. Also a wonderful risotto. Upbeat, elegant atmosphere, AC lounge, good music, trippy toilets, and a great wine list.

Nomad's Restaurant, Jl. Raya Ubud, tel: 977-169, fax: 975-115, www.nomadbali.com. An old institution that has been rejuvenated. Western, local, and Asian fusion cuisine since 1979. Open breakfast, lunch, and dinner. Packed nightly. Try the Balinese tasting menu or the grilled fish.

Terazo, Jl. Suweta, about 100 m north of the Ubud Palace, tel: 978-941, www.baligoodfood.com. Enjoy a wonderful Tuscan Pie, lamb shanks or stiff cocktail in this trendy bistro with a smart, upmarket Mediterranean ambience.

Warung Igelanca, Jl. Raya Ubud, mobile 0815-877-1465. A fantastic new little restaurant run by 3 women a 1-minute walk from the post office. Wonderfully tasty food, great prices, and friendly vibes. Ask for the daily specials, usually under $3. Next door is a very reasonable *nasi padang* restaurant, **Puteri Minang**, also popular with travelers.

Warung TutMak, Jl. Dewi Sita 97, tel: 975-754, 975-209. Set right on the football field, this popular café serves international fare and the best coffee in town, roasted in their own kitchen.

WEST OF CENTRAL UBUD

Fly Café, Jl. Raya Lungsiakan, Kedewatan, tel: 975-440, www.fly-cafe.com. Ribs and more. Friday night quiz; match your wits against the local expats.

Murni's Warung, Campuan, tel: 975-233, www.murnis.com. An old favorite, on the Ubud side of the Campuan bridge overlooking the stunning rainforest and Wos River. This multi-storied restaurant, decorated with Asian antiques from Murni's collection, is where the eclectic menu mix of Western, Indonesian, and Balinese favorites got its start in 1974. Murni's menu and dishes have stood the test of time and the satay, *gado-gado*, and grilled fish are delectable. The Lounge Bar, loved by expats, plays soft jazz. The lower dining areas offer tranquility, with only the sound of the river accompanying the peace. Outstanding desserts and freshly-squeezed fruit juices.

Naughty Nuri's, Jl. Raya Lunsgsiakan (across from Neka Art Museum), Kedewatan, tel: 977-547. An Ubud institution, this is where you come to get ribs and other grilled delights, down some great margaritas, and rub elbows with the local expat crowd, who quaff the excellent martinis by the gallons. Thursday night specials. Open 10 am–10 pm.

SOUTH OF CENTRAL UBUD

Kokokan Club, Jl. Bima, Pengosekan, tel: 973-495. Mainly traditional Thai cuisine with a full bar downstairs and an elegant restaurant upstairs. Curries are unparalleled on Bali.

Laka Leke, Nyuh Kuning, tel: 977-565, www. lakaleke.com. Set right in a rice field, delicious Balinese food presented elegantly. Excellent cooking school. Weekly performances at 8 pm.

Pak Sedan's Warung, Jl. Bima, Pengosekan. Next door to the petrol station, this small *warung* is always packed. Lunch for under $1. Vegetarian dishes, too.

Pizza Bagus, Jl. Pengosekan, tel: 978-520. Italian delicacies and pizzas. Fast WiFi. Open 8:30 am–10:30 pm. Delivery available.

EAST OF CENTRAL UBUD

Warung Teges, Jl. Raya Peliatan. Look for this simple *warung* as the road from Peliatan to Mas opens onto fields. One of the best *nasi campur* (pork or chicken with rice and a vegetable) on Bali, served with a wonderful *sambal matah* (fresh hot chili sauce) in an attractive garden courtyard. The place hasn't changed in over three generations.

NORTH OF CENTRAL UBUD

Kampung Café & Cottages, Tegallalang, tel: 901-201, fax: 901-202. The latest in nouveau Indonesian cuisine, this gem overlooks the incredible sculptured rice fields and tropical forests of Ceking. The pastas and salads are divine, and the daily specials will impress with their innovativeness and freshness of ingredients. The chocolate brownies will keep you going all day. Service is slow, but the price is right. Open 8 am–9 pm.

Mozaic, Jl. Raya Sanggingan, tel: 975-768, www. mozaic-bali.com. Award-winning French-American chef Chris Salens' masterpiece, set in lush gardens. Food, presentation and service here are flawless. Try the 6-course Tasting Menu, the Veal with Cactus Flower Sauce, tender grilled prawns, Duck Foie Gras Ravioli with bacon and caramelized onions or Moroccan-style Rack of Lamb. Open daily 5:45–9:45 pm. Pricey.

Attached is a **kitchenware shop** selling everything from cutlery and other tableware, ceramic vases and matching glasses, to picnic baskets, linens and napkins, all elegantly displayed in a variety of themed presentations. Also has a **cooking school**.

West End Café, Jl. Raya Sanggingan, tel: 978-363. Scrumptious afternoon tea, complete with scones. Open 9 am–6 pm, closed Sundays.

Organic food

Bali Buddha Café, Shop & Home Delivery, Jl. Jembawan 1, across from the post office, tel: 976-324, 978-963, www.balibuddha.com. Also has outlets in Kerobokan and Uluwatu. Try the cooling drinks, like Tamarind Fizz or yogurt smoothie, a bagel smeared with sundried tomatoes and cream

cheese, and read a magazine left behind by another patron. Well-stocked health food store and bakery on ground floor.

Fivelements Puri Ahimsa, Banjar Baturning, Mambal village, tel: 469-206, www.fivelements.com. Offers raw foods in the spiritual setting of a healing center.

Kafé, Jl. Hanoman 44, Padangtegal, tel: 970-992. This little treasure is a magnet for yogaphiles. An array of healthy foods, exotic blender drinks, and desserts. Free WiFi. Open 7:30 am–11 pm.

Little K, Jl. Pengosekan (at Yoga Barn), tel: 970-992. Same owner as Kafé. Awesome fresh and raw foods set below the Yoga Barn. Free WiFi. Open Tuesday–Sunday 9 am–4 pm.

Sari Organics, Ambengan, tel: 780-1839. At the Campuan bridge, follow the signs up through the rice fields, a lovely 15-minute walk. Also has an outlet in Little Tree Green Building and Lifestyle Center, Jl. Sunset 112X, Kuta. Reasonably priced, delicious organic and raw foods from their gardens. Homemade wines.

NIGHTLIFE

Ubud's nightlife has taken a turn for the better in recent years with a small but lively scene and more late night bars opening. Start the evening at **Naughty Nuri's**, Jl. Raya Campuan (opposite Neka Art Museum), tel: 977-547. A busy local hangout with lots of character, a Balinese *warung* with a touch of New York. The relaxed atmosphere may well be due to the epic martinis, but the real drawing card are the barbecue nights: tuna night is on Thursdays, but there are also steak, ribs, sausages, and lamb chop nights.

For a laidback drinking atmosphere, try the downstairs cocktail bar at **Ary's Warung**, Jl. Raya Ubud, tel: 975-053.

The **Jazz Café Tebesaya** on Jl. Sukma in the eastern part of town, tel: 976-594, offers live jazz nightly, except Sundays and Mondays from 7–10:30 pm. Ubud's original jazz club with an easy-going atmosphere, they also serve unique snacks, lunch, full dinners, fine wines, and creative stiff drinks.

Other nightspots to drop in on are **Flava Bar** on Jl. Bima in Pengosekan, where local and expat musicians jam several nights a week. **Bunute**, Jl. Dewi Sita, tel: 972-177, has live music every Thursday–Sunday (you can often catch hot guitarist Balawan here). **Café Havana** on Jl. Dewi Sita has salsa lessons and live music for dancing on Sundays.

ACTIVITIES

Several restaurants offer **cooking schools** and two museums host **cultural courses**, so be sure to check all the sections of this and other listings for the many activities options.

Bamboo Wonders, The Green School, Sibang Kaja, tel: 469-875, http://greenschool.org, is an international school spearheaded by jewelry designer John Hardy and his wife Cynthia. With nearly everything made of bamboo, the school's 75 buildings are cooled and powered with renewable energy sources, its main focus being to mould its students into ecologically responsible citizens. Tours are available. Visit http://bambooleague.com to learn how to join the program and create environmentally friendly life skill curricula in schools in your area.

The **International Network for Bamboo and Rattan**, www.inbar.int has information on improving the social, economic, and environmental benefits of using bamboo and rattan.

European designer Linda Garland of Nyuh Kuning village was one of the first on Bali to make furniture for export out of sustainable giant bamboo. She started the **Environmental Bamboo Foundation** (tel: 974-028, fax: 974-029, www.bamboocentral. org) in 1993 to protect tropical forests by promoting and demonstrating the many conservation and development opportunities that bamboo offers. She currently works with the East Bali Poverty Project, where a **Bamboo Research and Development Center** has been established.

Bali Bird Park (Taman Burung Bali), Jl. Cok Ngurah Gambir, Singapadu, tel: 299-352, fax: 299-614. Located on a back road between Ubud and Batubulan, it houses over 1,000 birds as well as Komodo dragons within a beautifully maintained garden. Well worth a visit. Excellent restaurant overlooking flamingo pond. Unique gift shop. Open 9 am–5:30 pm daily.

Bali Birdwalks, Campuan, reservations tel: 975-009, mobile: 0812-391-3801. Three-hour guided tours for bird lovers and anyone who appreciates the outdoors: butterflies, trees, and brilliant scenery. Combines exercise, nature, and cultural observations. Meet at 9 am in Murni's Warung by the Campuan Bridge. After a coffee or tea, the group sets out, getting back at around 1 pm for lunch. Of the 100 species of native birds found around Ubud, expect to see 30 or so, as well as some quite abrupt alterations of habitat. $37; includes guided bird walk, binocular use, lunch, bottled water, coffee/tea.

Bali Elephant Safari Park, Jl. Elephant Park Taro, Taro village (head office: Adventure House, Jl. Bypass Ngurah Rai, Pesanggaran), tel: 721-480, fax: 721-481, www.baliadventuretours.com. Jungle rides, Night Safari, daily shows, botanical gardens, museum, restaurant overlooking the lake, and shops. A member of the World Zoo Association, follows all global animal care guidelines. Established in 1996 to save endangered Sumatran elephants; has successful breeding program and manure

processing plant to recycle elephant dung into eco-fertilizer. Prices begin at $16/adults, $8/kids, $4/ infants. Family rates and packages are available.

Bali Safari & Marine Park, Jl. Bypass Prof. Dr. Ida Bagus Mantra Km 19.8, Gianyar, tel: 950-000, www. balisafarimarinepark.com. A world-class animal park with fun for the whole family: animal rides and shows, cultural performances, amusement park and water park. A tram ride goes through natural habitats. Open 9 am–5 pm weekdays, 8:30 am–5 pm weekends and holidays. $59/adults; $39/kids 3–12 years. Park also has Elephant Safari Jungle Lodge.

Bali Theater in the Park, Jl. Bypass Prof. Dr. Ida Bagus Mantra Km 19.8, Gianyar, tel: 751-300, www.bali-theatre.com. Opened in 2010, a 1,200-seat indoor mega-stage located inside Bali Safari & Marine Park. 150 dancers, musicians, shadow-puppet masters, animals—including elephants, camels, eagles, and tigers—perform. Sumptuous costumes complement the dynamic collaboration of Balinese *gamelan* with western orchestral music wedding modern theatrical technology with authentic Balinese culture. Performance 2–3 pm daily except Mondays.

Bali Zoo, Jl. Raya Singapadu, Sukawati, tel: 249-357, fax: 298-608, www.bali-zoo.com. A privately-owned conservatory set on 4.86 ha of beautifully landscaped ground. Includes walk-through bird aviaries, Gibbon islands, Komodo dragons, and free-range African Lion area. Open daily except Nyepi (Balinese day of silence) 9 am–6 pm. $24/ adults; $12/kids 2–14 yrs. Family passes available.

Cycling tours. Bali Budaya Tours, Jl. Raya Pengosekan, tel: 975-557. Cycle downhill and see the real Bali on an eco-educational guided cycling tour from mountainous Penelokan down into the Batur caldera, then roll through the agricultural heartland of Bali via secret back roads to Ubud, with stops at cultural sites along the way. $42, all inclusive.

Sobek Batur Cycling, tel: 768-050, fax: 768-090, www.sobek.com. Using new mountain bikes and safety equipment, take a downhill trail from Mt. Batur through sleepy villages along little-used roads and tracks, stopping frequently to see aged temple compounds, shady plantations, and the daily lives of local people. Half-day trip. $79/adults, includes lunch, hotel pickup, insurance, English-speaking guides. (Some guides speak other Asian languages.)

Green Camp, tel: 469-875, mobile: 0813-3726-9727, www.greencampbali.com. Geared for 5–14-year-olds, kids may sign up for any number of days Monday-Friday and stay in eco-yurts on overnight programs. Activities begin at 9 am and end at 6:30 pm and include fun and educational themes such as Eco-living (e.g. All Natural Wearable Arts), Teambuilding and Leadership (e.g. Balinese Amazing Race), Environmental Education (Coconut

Conversations anyone?), Sustainable Agriculture (plant your own rice and learn about Bali's unique communal subak irrigation system), and Art and Culture (e.g. Mask Making). The kids would probably be much happier here than tagging along on shopping forays, and they might even learn something really cool.

Pondok Pekak Library & Learning Center, on the east side of the football field off Jl. Monkey Forest (tel: 976-194), maintains a lending library full of holiday reading in various languages, and literature on Indonesian and Balinese culture. There's also a huge children's library upstairs with books in English and Indonesian. The house is full of kids, students, and adults of various nationalities. They also serve food and drink, provide e-mail service and teach Indonesian language courses. An excellent place for families to hang out.

Music lessons. Learn to play gamelan or flute or learn notation, composition, and music theory with one of Ubud's master musicians and directors, English-speaking **Tjokorda Raka Swastika** in Ubud's Puri Saren (royal palace) on Jl. Raya Ubud (tel: 975-753, Mobile: 0812-3980-111). Lessons are tailored to individual interests, whether a skilled musician or a beginner, adult or child. $15 for a 2-hr lesson. $50 for an 8-hr package (4 lessons for 1 or 2 persons). Classes are usually from 9–11 am.

Performances are staged nightly at the Ubud Palace (Pura Dalem Ubud), in scattered locations around central Ubud, and in nearby villages. Check with the Ubud Tourist Information Center (**Bina Wisata**) at the main crossroads for schedules and special events. Regularly held are: Legong, Barong, and Keris dances; Ramayana Ballet, Kecak Fire and Trance dance, Frog dance and *jegog* (bamboo *gamelan*) performances. Most begin at 7:30 pm. Tickets are around $10 and include transportation to village venues, where applicable.

There's an **all-women Kecak Fire Dance** troupe— **Kecak Srikandhi**—that performs on Wednesdays at 7:30 pm, Pura Batu Karu, Jl. Suweta, reservations: mobile: 0811-393-686. Rp 75,000.

Rimba Reptile Park (Rimba Reptil), Jl. Cok Ngurah Gambir, Singapadu, tel: 235-600. Next door to Bali Bird Park, home to venomous snakes, water monitors, crocodiles, and Komodo dragons. An open-air area houses friendlier creatures, allowing visitors to interact with them. $8/adults; $4.50/kids.

Smithing courses. Studio Perak, Jl. Hanoman, tel: 974-344, Jl. Dewi Sita, tel: 780-1879, Jl. Raya Ubud, tel: 973-371, and at the north end of Jl. Gautama, mobile: 0812-361-1785. Learn the basics of Balinese silversmithing and take home a ring of your own design at the Hanoman venue. They also offer 2- and 5-day courses teaching more advanced techniques

such as transferring designs onto silver and setting stones. Reservations recommended. $12 for half-day course, all materials included.

Surfing & beach-bumming. The secret that top world surfers have kept since early 2000 is out of the bag: **Keramas Beach** on the east coast has Bali's most perfect righthander, according to experts, and is now on world-circuit surfing competition tours. To get there, take the Jl. Prof. Ida Bagus Mantra By-Pass northeast from Sanur until you see a small sign directing to a dirt road that leads to the beach. Best surfed from mid to high tide; the action is hot early mornings in the dry season (June to October). There's a beachside restaurant there where international and local pro surfers hang out, owned by an Italian expat, if you're hungry.

Other beaches along the east coast, going from south to north are Ketewel, Purnama, and Masceti. Past the turnoff to Bali Safari & Marine Park are more: Tegal Besar and Lepang in Klungkung Regency. This area may be unknown to all but hard-core surfer dudes now, but there are villas popping up where fields used to be and "land for sale" signs everywhere. With the opening of the new bypass, it won't be long until this stretch of countryside becomes a Sanur suburb.

Ubud Botanic Gardens, Jl. Raya Kutuh Kaja, tel: 780-3904, www.botanicgardenbali.com. Lovely gardens with a vast variety of plant life, including orchids. Open 8 am–6 pm daily. $6.

Walking tours. Keep Walking Tours, Jl. Hanoman 44 (next to Tegun Gallery), Padangtegal, tel: 973-361, www.balispirit.com offers above-average guided cultural and ecological walks (minimum 2 persons; $45/pp) as well as sunrise climbs up Mt. Batur $55.

Ubud Herb Walks, mobile: 0812-381-6024, 0812-381-6020, www.baliherbalwalk.com. Owners are a young couple who grew up in healer families. Their love of plants and what plants can do for good health inspired them to lead visitors on 3-hr daily herb walks through the rice fields and plantations around Ubud. Tours include the chance to learn about the healing properties of local plants. They also offer classes on making *jamu*, traditional herbal medicinal and skin care ointments and tonics.

White water rafting. Bali Adventure Tours (head office: Adventure House, Jl. Bypass Ngurah Rai, Pesanggaran), tel: (0361) 721-480, fax: 721-481. www. baliadventuretours.com. Manager of Bali Elephant Safari Park & Lodge, this company began in 1989 as a white water rafting provider. In addition to the Safari Park and rafting on the Ayung River, it offers mountain-biking and trekking. Each guest is insured and safety is guaranteed. See website for packages combining Elephant Park and adventure activities, as well as off-peak rafting trips at reduced prices.

Sobek Rafting, tel: 768-050, fax: 768-090, www. sobek.com. Ayung River white water rafting through an amazing gorge. Half day trip, Class 2 river, 25 rapids, all safe and fun for ages 7 to 65. See animals and birds living along the river and pass 10 spectacular waterfalls falling into the river, which runs past steep stone cliffs and tropical rainforest. $79 includes lunch, hotel pick-up, insurance, and highly trained English speaking guides (some guides speak other Asian languages). Ask about children's rates. Many steps.

SHOPPING

There's a surprisingly sophisticated range of shopping in Ubud. A good place to start are the major streets: Jl. Raya Ubud, Jl. Hanoman, Jl. Dewi Sita, and Jl. Monkey Forest, where there are scores of shops selling fashions, antiques, artifacts, souvenirs, and a great variety of Bali memorabilia. Shops are generally open 9 am–9 pm.

The more adventurous can find a cornucopia of handicrafts in many of the less-visited villages surrounding Ubud. Check out Mas village, south of Ubud, for masks, arts and crafts, and furniture.
Shipping: To get all the good stuff back home, packing and shipping agents are abundant in Ubud. One of the best is **Bisama Group**, Jl. Raya Ubud 33X, tel: 975-520. Provides full documentation including export visa, textile quota, ocean freight consolidation, FCL LCL insurance; provides pick-up, handling, and even packing of goods; also serves as a purchasing agent for handicrafts, furniture, and garments.

Antiques, Arts & Crafts, Gifts

Belaga village near Blahbatuh specializes in bamboo tables, chairs, and other furniture made of attractive spotted bamboo. Next door is **Bona**, with a large bamboo and rattan furniture collection.

For something different than the tired old souvenir schlock found around Ubud, look for primitive art, high-fired functional ceramics (tiles, tableware, homewares) and *lontar* palm-leaf books (masterpieces of art and calligraphy).
Murni's Warung Shop, at Murni's Warung, Jl Raya Ubud, beside the Campuan bridge, tel: 972-146, www.murnis.com. Traditional arts and crafts from all over the archipelago, as well as overseas, assiduously collected by Murni who has formidable fine arts credentials and seasoned, sophisticated taste. If she's around, Murni will sign the best-selling *Secrets of Bali, Fresh Light on the Morning of the World* by Jonathan Copeland and Ni Wayan Murni. You can download her e-book *Murni's Very Personal Guide to Ubud* from her website.
Bojog Gallery, across from the football field on Jl. Monkey Forest, tel: 971-001. Two stories of antique

furniture, textiles, puppets, masks, wood carvings, and more from Sulawesi, Sumatra, Java, Bali, and the rest of Indonesia.
Celeng Gallery, Jl. Raya Lungsiakan, Kedewatan, tel: 898-9488, mobile: 0811-396-860. Specializes in antique furniture, stone carvings, and ritual artifacts from throughout Indonesia. Ask to visit the warehouse for wholesale prices on old furniture and custom orders made from recycled teak.
Kuluk Gallery, Jl. Raya Lungsiakan, Kedewatan, tel: 975-833. Indonesian art and antiques, specializing in museum-quality ritual artifacts and antique textiles and jewelry. Also has an extensive library for research and authentication.
Tegun Folk Art Gallery, Jl. Hanoman 44, Padangtegal, tel: 970-581, www.tegun.com. An Aladdin's Cave of lovely, unique, and very well-selected gifts, keepsakes, and other paraphernalia gathered from all over the archipelago. One-stop shopping for fantastic gifts, handmade and antique flutes, some jewelry, in every price range. Run by American Megan Peppenheim and her Balinese husband I Made Gunarta.

Books

Ganesha Bookshop, just off Jl. Raya Ubud (on the same lane as the post office), tel: 970-320, fax: 973-359, www.ganeshabooksbali.com. An intriguing selection of used and rare books and an Indonesian studies section, with many book selections not readily found in other bookstores. Also maps, cards, attractive stationery, exotic gifts, CDs, and musical instruments.
Periplus Tino Ubud, Jl. Monkey Forest, on the upper stretch, tel: 971-803, http://periplus.com. A wide and varied selection of travel guides, coffee table books, novels, cookbooks, non-fiction, and books on Bali and Indonesia.

Fashion

Animale, Jl. Raya Ubud, tel: 978-549. A wide range of fashions and coordinating prints that appeal to more a mature clientele.
Goddess on the Go, Jl. Dewi Sita and Jl. Pengosekan, tel: 976-084, www.goddessonthegobali.com. Brightly dyed beech cloth, perfect for traveling. Eco-friendly Travel & Leisure Clothing in 16 colors to reflect individual personalities. Silky smooth, lightweight, wash and wear. Versatile pieces for every occasion from bed to ballroom.
Bamboo, Jl. Jembawan. Men's ikat shirts, well made.
Uluwatu, Jl. Monkey Forest, tel: 977-557. This boutique showcases beautifully handcrafted Balinese crisp cotton and silky rayon lace clothing and sleepwear. Also bed linens and tableware, plus a superb collection of Balinese *ikat*.

Homewares

Hananto Lloyd, Jl. Raya Sayan, tel: 742-9337, www.hanantolloyd.com. Home deco, antiques, designer jewelry, and interior design.

Toko East, Jl. Raya Ubud, tel: 978-306, fax: 978-359, www.dekco.com. Contemporary Indonesian exterior and interior homewares. Features stoneware, ceramics, table top accessories, unique decorative items, and garden lamps.

Jewelry

Bloomz, Jl. Hanoman 44a, tel: 780-2401, www.bloomzbali.com. Silver jewelry from Camenae set in a unique flower shop.

Jean Francois, Jl. Raya 7, Pengosekan, tel: 972-078, www.jf-fcom. Exquisite artistry using gold, gemstones and carvings by Jean Francois Fichot. Jewelry and homewares.

Runa House of Design and Museum, Lod Tunduh. Ibu Pilar Runi is a Javanese silver jewelry designer who has turned her Bali home into a museum. Open daily 9 am–5 pm.

Treasures, Jl. Raya Ubud (next to Ary's), tel: 976-697. Features the work of a number of exclusive designers based in Bali and abroad. Upper echelon quality and originality. Precious metals (gold, white gold, silver) and precious stones are a specialty. With its works of art displayed behind glass, Treasures looks like the kind of place that needs armed guards in front of it. Popular with movie stars, such as Goldie Hawn.

Textiles

Alam Asia Crafts, Nyuh Kuning (at the entrance of Alam Indah hotel) and Jl. Pengosekan (at the entrance of Kebun Indah hotel), tel: 971-130, carries hand-woven textiles and gifts from throughout Southeast Asia. Supports disadvantaged artisans, primarily women weavers.

Buddhas and Silk, Jl. Pengosekan, tel: 973-336, www.buddhasandsilk.net. Luscious textiles, sacred images, unique jewelry, and homewares.

FNPF Visitor's Center, Jl. Bisma 3, tel: 977-978, www.fnpf.org. While this is mainly a center for the Friends of the National Parks Foundation, it is also an outlet for hand-dyed batik fabrics made by Cokorda Agung Pemayun.

Threads of Life, Jl. Kajeng 24 (northwest of the Puri Saren Palace), tel: 972-187, fax: 976-582, www.threadsoflife.com. A truly amazing collection of museum-quality *ikat* textiles. Group strives to preserve Indonesia's many traditional hand-woven cloth cultures. Promotes use of natural dyes only if sustainably harvested. Organizes educational exhibits, courses, cultural events, and supports traditional weavers on many Indonesian islands, especially the more endangered textile traditions.

Wardani Shop, Jl. Monkey Forest, tel: 975-538. Bolts and bolts of hand-woven *ikat* that can be made into clothing.

Wood & Stone Carvings

For lower prices on wooden handicrafts in all imaginable sizes, shapes, and colors, head up the hill to **Tegallalang**, **Pujung**, and **Sebatu**, all northeast of Ubud. In these crafts villages are a bewildering number of shops, mostly for export purposes. Bali's modern-day center for stone carving is **Batubulan** village, halfway between Ubud and Denpasar.

For high-quality **dance masks**, the most accomplished carvers are Ida Bagus Anom in Mas (next to the football field), whose innovative designs are everywhere in Bali, and Ida Bagus Alit in Lod Tunduh, just south of the junction at Mas and Lod Tunduh. Other preeminent mask makers in the area are I Wayan Tangguh, Cokorda Raka Tisnu, and I Wayan Tedun of Singapadu, and Ida Bagus Oka and I Wayan Muka of Mas.

The wood carvers in **Nyuh Kuning**, south of Ubud's Monkey Forest, are known for their lifelike animals carved out of *waru* wood.

MARKETS

Pasar Ubud (Ubud traditional market), Jl. Raya Ubud, central Ubud. A must for shopaholics. Wander around for any imaginable craft, household item, sarong, fruit, or spice. Also good selection of silver jewelry, carvings, paintings, textiles, bedcovers, clothes, pajamas, unusual souvenirs, as well as aromatherapy oils and incense. All at reasonable prices if you bargain hard. Similar to the Sukawati market, the Ubud market is smaller and pricier.

Pasar Tegallalang, north of Ubud. This area is where wholesalers buy their goods. Find an interesting-looking shop or showroom, pick out your item, then ask for "a sample" or the "business" (wholesale) price. Woven handbags that sell for $10 on Jl. Monkey Forest go for only $5 here.

Pasar Seni Sukawati (Sukawati Art Market), Sukawati. Down the road about 5 km (3 miles) from Ubud in the Gianyar District fabric and craft center, this maze-like 2-story building and its surrounds are a hive of activity for shoppers: masks, statuary, clothes, local traditional and modern textiles, basketry and ceremonial accoutrements, such as umbrellas. Bargain hard for everything at stalls stacked nearly to the ceiling. Also check out the street beside and in back of the market where even better bargains can be found. Take note of the long line of tour buses from Java. Sukawati is where Indonesian tourists shop.

Ubud Organic Farmer's Market, www.indonesia-organic.com, at Pizza Bagus, Jl. Pengosekan,

Saturdays 9:30 am–2:30 pm. At ARMA Museum parking lot, Jl. Bima, Wednesdays 9:30 am–2:30 pm. Support local farmers by buying organic produce and rice, condiments, jams and more, and feel healthier in the process. Win, win, win.

SPAS, MASSAGE & WELLNESS

Most—if not all—of the upmarket resorts have their own spas with the full range of amenities, but there are also many independent ones in the Ubud area, some better than others. Below are some of the better independents.

Bagus Jati Resort, Banjar Jati, Desa Sebatu, Tegallalang, tel: 978-885, fax: 974-666, www.bagusjati.com. A stunning property offering residential health and well-being programs ranging from 2–10 nights. Packages include New Start spa treatments, Ayurvedic, detox, yoga, meditation, nature walks, and aqua aerobics.

Bali Botanica Day Spa, Jl. Raya Sangginan, tel: 976-739, www.balibotanica.com. Have a fabulous 1-hr massage or an all-day blitz for under $100. Therapy rooms overlook the rice paddies. Free transport within the Ubud area.

Como Shambhala, Banjar Begawan, Desa Melinggih Keloid, Payangan, tel: 978-888, fax: 978-889, www.comoshambahala.como.bz. Adopting a holistic approach to wellness, this is a residential health retreat that offers guests new challenges and inspiration. Therapies include massage, bodycare, Ayurvedic, and facials. Activities include yoga, fitness, martial arts, Pilates, and outdoor adventure.

Fivelements Puri Ahimsa, Banjar Baturning, Mambal village, tel: 469-206, www.fivelements.com. Opened in July 2010, this is a healing center in an exquisite atmosphere located along the Ayung River whose specialties are Balinese healing, living foods, and sacred arts. The bamboo hall is worth visiting on its own. Spa has Watsu and many other types of massage, and their dining room serves vegan raw foods.

Sara Spa, Jl. Monkey Forest (behind Gang Lotus), tel: 868-8206. A funky little house with great massages. The price is unbeatable at under $10.

Spa Hati, Jl. Andong (past Delta Supermarket), tel: 977-578, www.spahati.com. Jacuzzi, steam room, and lap pool. Part of proceeds go towards the upkeep of Bali Hati Primary School.

Ubud Bodyworks, Jl. Hanoman No. 25, tel: 975-720, 971-393, www.ubudbodyworkscentre.com. Under the direction of healer Ketut Arsana, this center offers some of the best massages in Ubud.

Tamarind Spa at Murni's Houses, Jl Raya, Ubud (up the ramp opposite Pura Dalem on the main street, left at the top, 2nd gate on the right), tel: 970-923, www.murnis.com. Murni's extremely popular new spa shot to the top of Trip Advisor within weeks of its opening. Rave reviews. Many repeat guests,

including masseurs, say it's the best they've ever experienced. Well-kept gardens, fountains, sounds of running water, soothing music, healthy lunches. Reasonably priced.

YOGA, MEDITATION & FITNESS

Intuitive Flow Sanctuary for Yoga and Healing, Penestanan, Ubud, tel: 977-824, mobile: 0812-392-4649, www.intuitiveflow.com. Regular weekly yoga classes.

The Yoga Barn, Jl. Pengosekan, tel: 971-236, www.yogabarn.com. Set in wonderfully serene surroundings, packages include group and private yoga classes, organic food and detox, spa therapies, and eco-tours. Workshops in dance, meditation, yoga, and Pilates. Open 7 am–9 pm.

Ubud Fitness Club, Jl. Jero Gadung, Kutuh, tel: 975-804. Behind Bank BCA in Padangtegal (east Ubud) on the way to Peliatan. Ubud's most complete fitness center. Offers aerobics daily except Sunday 5–6 pm. Yoga classes on Sundays. Also squash courts and a terrace café. Open 6 am–9 pm. $6/day drop-in rate. $40/month.

Also visit www.balispirit.com for events, non-profits, fair trade handicrafts and clothing, and a listing of other meditative retreats in Bali.

FOOD SHOPS & BAKERIES

Bali Buddha Café, Shop & Home Delivery, Jl. Jembawan 1, across from the post office, tel: 976-324, 978-963, www.balibuddha.com. A bakery and holistic food and health products outlet. Packs a lot of high-quality (both prepared and processed) healthy and organic food into a tiny space. Health-food café on the upper level. Open 6 am–10 pm daily.

Bintang Supermarket, Jl. Raya Sanggingan 45. Very well-stocked supermarket, Open 8 am–10 pm.

Café Moka, Jl. Raya Ubud. An array of baked goods. Breakfast and lunch specials.

Delta Mart and **Circle K mini-markets** are every-where and are open 24/7. Standard convenience store products.

Delta Dewata, Jl. Raya Andong 14 (opposite Spa Hati), tel: 973-049. Lays claim to being the most complete supermarket in Ubud with good quality goods at reasonable prices, plus a respectable wine room. Open 8 am–10 pm. Other branches on Jl. Monkey Forest, tel: 972-760 (open 24 hrs) and Jl. Hanoman, tel: 972-767 (open 24 hrs).

Honeymoon Bakery at Casa Luna Restaurant, Jl. Raya Ubud, tel: 973-282. Home-baked breads, brownies, and cakes.

Kakiang, Jl. Pengosekan, tel: 978-984. Some of the best desserts in town, as well as breads. Danish pastries and good coffee.

MISCELLANEOUS

Post Office, Jl. Jembawan, up the small road opposite Neka Gallery. Open Monday–Saturday 8 am–2 pm, Friday 8–11 am, Sunday 8 am–noon. Regular, airmail, and express service.

Toya Clinic, Jl. Bima, Pengosekan. Dr. Susila is an excellent diagnostician. There are overnight services here as well.

Ubud Music, Jl. Raya Ubud, tel: 971-837 and Jl. Monkey Forest, tel: 975-362, does CD burning and photo processing. Also sells a large selection of CDs and DVDs. Also a book store.

MUSEUMS & GALLERIES AROUND UBUD

(TELEPHONE CODE: 0361)

There is often a fine line separating museums and fine art galleries which sell paintings. Many museums also call themselves galleries and almost always have a commercial showroom on the premises. Most museums and galleries open at 8 am and many remain open on demand through the early evening.

ART MUSEUMS

ARMA (Agung Rai Museum of Art), Jl. Bima, Pengosekan, tel: 976-659, www.armamuseum.com. This monumental structure houses the private collection of the highly-regarded collector, Agung Rai, who had his humble beginnings flogging paintings on the hot sands of Kuta Beach over 35 years ago. See originals by famous painters such as Spies, Bonnet, Hofker, Affandi, and many others. Rotating exhibits. Bookshop, nice gardens, and shop. Offers **cultural workshops**: *gamelan*, dance, architecture, traditional healing, and offering making. Open 9 am–6 pm. Entrance Rp 25,000. (See below for art gallery listing.)

Blanco Renaissance Museum, Campuan, tel: 975-502, www.blancomuseum.com. World-renowned gallery set in tropical gardens featuring Antonio Blanco's risqué paintings (none of which are for sale) with their elaborate frames, and paintings by his son Mario Blanco (very much for sale). Open 9 am–6 pm. Entrance Rp 50,000.

Museum Puri Lukisan, Jl. Raya Ubud, tel: 975-136, www.mpl-ubud.com. Founded under the auspices of the royal family in 1953, 5 separate pavilions represent the whole evolution of modern Balinese painting from its inception in the 1930s until the present. Originally catalogued by Rudolf Bonnet, the current trustees continue to maintain the same standard through a continuous program of acquisitions. Tranquil setting in lovely gardens. Also offers painting, dance, and carving workshops. 8 am–4 pm. Admission fee Rp 20,000.

Neka Art Museum, Jl. Raya Campuan, Kedewatan village (on the main road 1.5 km west of Ubud), tel: 975-074, fax: 97563, www.museumneka.com, Neka is Ubud's foremost art dealer and patron.

Five traditional buildings house Neka's private collection by Bali's most revered artists: Lempad, Spies, Covarrubias, I Bagus Made, and Made Wianta. Great areas for just sitting and passing the time. Open 9 am–5 pm, Sundays noon–5 pm. Closed on public holidays. Entrance: Rp 20,000. (See gallery location below.)

Museum Rudana, Jl. Cok Rai Pudak 44 (the main road from Mas to Peliatan), tel: 975-779, www.museumrudana.com. Important permanent collection of contemporary Indonesian art and commercial fine art housed in a monumental marble building. Open 9 am–5 pm. Admission: Rp 40,000.

Sakti Dharma House of Masks and Puppets, Jl. Tegal Bingin, Mas, tel: 977-404. Thousands of puppets and masks from all over Indonesia fill 4 traditional Javanese houses. Even Barack Obama is made into a wooden puppet here. Performances and events are held in the large wantilan (pavilion) on the landscaped grounds. Open daily 8 am–4 pm.

ART GALLERIES

There are hundreds of "art shops" selling paintings in the Ubud area and dozens of so-called galleries selling similar types of paintings of dubious quality. However, there are also a number of art galleries that showcase the best of Balinese, Indonesian, and expat artists. Below is a selected list.

Adi Art Gallery, Jl. Bisma 102, Ubud, tel: 977-104. Features upcoming artists; changes shows frequently so there is always something new to see. Open daily 10 am–5 pm.

ARMA (Agung Rai Museum of Art) Art Gallery, Jl. Cokorda Rai Pudak. Peliatan, Ubud, tel: 976-559, www.armamuseum.com. One of the first art galleries to sell museum quality paintings. Afternoon painting sessions for local kids are fun to watch. Open daily 9 am–6 pm. (See above for museum listing.)

Bidadari Art, Jl. Raya Mas, Mas village, www.bidadari.com. For one-of-a-kind woodcarvings that are well-displayed, this is the place to come. Open Monday–Saturday 8:30 am–5 pm.

Gaya Fusion Art Space, Jl. Raya Sayan, Sayan, tel: 979-253, 979-252, www.gayafusion.com. Features avant garde and contemporary art. Real Italian gelato on the grounds.Open daily 9 am–9 pm.

Hanna Artspace, Jl. Raya Pengosekan, Peliatan, tel: 978-216. Located on the grounds of the Pertamina petrol station, features young and upcoming artists.

Komaneka Fine Art Gallery, Jl. Monkey Forest, Ubud, tel: 976-090, fax: 977-140, www.komaneka.com. Managed by Koman Neka, the son of Pande Suteja Neka, this gallery has revolving exhibitioins of contemporary artists. Wife Man Sri also has high quality textiles for sale here.

Neka Art Gallery, Jl. Raya Ubud (opposite the post office), Ubud, tel: 975-034.The Neka Art Museum put Balinese art on the map.This is its gallery outlet. Open daily 9 am–5 pm. (See above for museum listing.)

Pranoto's Art Gallery, Jl. Raya, Teges-Goa Gajah, Tengkulak Kaja, Ubud, tel: 970-827, www.age.jp/~pranoto. A lively, active gallery in the heart of Ubud run by two artists, Pranoto and Kerry Pendergrast. It hosts life-drawing model sessions, exhibitions, and a large fine art collection of paintings by Indonesian and international artists. Ubud Life Model Sessions Wednesdays and Saturdays, 10 am–1 pm.Open daily 9 am–5 pm.

Rio Helmi Photography, Jl. Suweta No. 5, Ubud, tel: 972-304, www.riohelmi.com. Indonesian photographer Rio Helmi has been capturing images of his homeland for decades. His gallery features both his photographs and prints. Open 10 am–8 pm.

Seniwati Gallery of Art by Women, Jl. Sriwidari 2B, Ubud, tel: 975 485, www.seniwatigallery.com. Seniwati supports and showcases women artists. Their mission is to "expose the world to the long understated brilliance of Balinese women artists, encourage Balinese girls creativity and assist talented women to market their art". Open Tuesday–Sunday 9 am–5 pm.

Sika Contemporary Art Gallery, Jl. Raya Campuan, Ubud, tel: 975-084, www.sikagallery.info. Provides a venue for young creative artists, both local and international. Holds regular temporary exhibitions and events. Open daily 9 am–5 pm.

Tanah Tho, Jl. Raya, Lod Tunduh, www.tanahtho.com. Contemporary artists showcased here.

Tilem Art Gallery, Jl. Raya Mas, Mas village, tel: 975-099. Ida Bagus Tilem and his father Ida Bagus Nyana brought innovation to the world of carving. Still using traditional themes and everyday scenes, their inspired pieces are masterpeces. Their own work is on display and their students' pieces are for sale at the gallery.

Tony Raka Gallery, Jl. Raya Mas No. 86, Mas village, tel: 781-6785, www.tonyrakaartgallery.com. Probably the most innovative art gallery around, the exhibits here feature fresh and often wacky art.

UBUD DANCE PERFORMANCES: A WEEKLY SCHEDULE

The weekly traditional dances schedule below is based on the Ubud Tourist Information Center listing.

MONDAY

Sadha Budaya, Ubud Palace (Raya Ubud): Legong Dance, 7:30 pm, Rp 80,000.

Krama Desa Adat Junjungan, Junjungan Village: Kecak Fire (Monkey Chant Dance), 7:00 pm (transfer to venue 6:30 pm), Rp 65,000.

Sandhi Suara, Wantilan (Hanoman): Barong and Kris Dance, 7:00 pm, Rp 75,000.

Krama Desa Ubud Kaja Pura Dalem Ubud, Jl. Raya Campuan: Kecak Ramayana and Fire Dance, 7:30 pm, Rp 65,000.

Luh Luwih Bale Banjar Ubud Klod, Jl. Monkey Forest: Women's Performance, 7:30 pm, Rp 75,000.

TUESDAY

Bina Remaja Ubud Palace, Jl. Raya Ubud: Ramayana Ballet, 7:30 pm, Rp 80,000.

Semara Ratih Jaba Pura Desa Kutuh, Kutuh Village: Spirit of Bali, 7:30 pm, Rp 75,000.

Shandi Suara Pura Taman Sari, Jl. Hanoman: Kecak Fire and Trance Dance, 7:30 pm, Rp 75,000.

Genta Bhuana Sari Balerung Mandera, Peliatan: Legong Dance, 7:30 pm (transfer to venue 6:45 pm), Rp 75,000.

Sekaa Gong Karyasa Pura Dalem Ubud, Jl. Raya Campuan: Legong Dance, 7:30 pm, Rp 65,000.

Chandra Wati Ubud Water Palace, Kajeng: Women's *Gamelan* with Children Dance, 7:30 pm, Rp 80,000.

Nrita Dewi Bale Banjar Ubud Kelod, Jl. Monkey Forest: Trans Culture, 7:30 pm, Rp 75,000.

Semara Kanti Padangtegal Kaja, Jl. Hanoman: Barong and Keris Dance, 7:30 pm, Rp 60,000.

WEDNESDAY

Panca Arta Ubud Palace, Jl. Raya Ubud: Legong and Barong Dance, 7:30 pm, Rp 80,000.

ARMA Group ARMA Museum, Jl. Raya, Pengosekan: Topeng Jimat, 7:30 pm (transfer to venue 6:45 pm), Rp 75,000.

Yamasari Stage, Peliatan: Legong Dance, 7:30 pm (transfer to venue 6:45 pm), Rp 75,000.

Trene Jenggala Padangtegal, Jl. Hanoman: Kecak Fire and Trance Dance, 7:00 pm, Rp 75,000.

Yoana Swara Pura Dalem Ubud, Jl. Raya Campuan: *Jegog* (Bamboo *gamelan*), 7:00 pm, Rp 75,000.

Krama Desa Adat Taman Kaja Pura Dalem Taman Kaje, Sandat: Kecak Fire and Trance Dance, 7:30 pm, Rp 75,000.

Krama Desa Ubud Tengah Batukaru Temple, Suweta: Kecak Fire and Fire Dance, 7:30 pm, Rp 75,000.

Suara Guna Kanti Abangan Bale Banjar Ubud Kelod, Jl. Monkey Forest: Legong and Barong Waksirsa Dance, 7:30 pm, Rp 75,000.

THURSDAY

Panca Arta Ubud Palace, Jl. Raya Ubud: Legong Trance and Paradise Dance, 7:30 pm, Rp 80,000.

Semara Madya Puri Agung Peliatan, Peliatan: Kecak (Monkey Chant Dance), 7:30 pm (transfer to venue 6:45 pm), Rp 75,000.

Ananggga Sari Jaba Pura Desa Kutuh, Kutuh: Legong Dance, 7:30 pm (transfer to venue 6:45 pm), Rp 75,000.

Raja Peni Pura Dalem Ubud, Jl. Raya Campuan: Barong and Keris Dance, 7:30 pm, Rp 60,000.

Cenik Wayah Ubud Water Palace, Jl. Raya Kajeng: Spirit of *Gamelan* (Barong and Child Dance), 7:30 pm, Rp 80,000.

Sandhi Suara Pura Taman Sari, Jl. Hanoman: Kecak Fire and Trance Dance, 7:30 pm, Rp 75,000.

Krama Desa Adat Sambahan Batukaru Temple, Suweta: Kecak Fire and Trance Dance, 7:30 pm, Rp 75,000.

Puspa Kirana Bale Banjar Ubud Kelod, Jl. Monkey Forest: *Wayang Wong* Dance, 7:30 pm, Rp 75,000.

FRIDAY

Abasan ARMA Museum, Jl. Raya, Pengosekan: Barong and Keris Dance, 6:00 pm (transfer to venue 5:45 pm), Rp 75,000.

Shada Budaya Ubud Palace, Jl. Raya Ubud: Barong Dance, 7:30 pm, Rp 80,000.

Tirtasari Balerung Mandera, Peliatan: Legong Dance, 7:30 pm (transfer to venue 6:45 pm), Rp 100,000.

Padang Subadra Pura Padang Kerta, Jl. Hanoman: Kecak Fire and Trance Dance, 7:00 pm, Rp 75,000.

Suara Sakti Bentuyung Village, Suweta: *Jegog* (bamboo *gamelan*): 7:00 pm (transfer to venue 5:30 pm), Rp 80,000.

Krama Desa Ubud Kaja Pura Dale Ubud, Jl. Raya Campuan: Kecak Ramayana and Fire Dance, 7:30 pm, Rp 65,000.

Pondok Pekak Padang Teagal Kaja, Jl. Hanoman: Frog Dance, 7:30 pm, Rp 75,000.

Kidulling Swari Bale Banjar Ubud Kelod, Jl. Monkey Forest: Legong Dance, 7:30 pm, Rp 75,000.

SATURDAY

Bina Remaja Ubud Palace, Jl. Raya Ubud: Legong Dance, 7:30 pm, Rp 80,000.

Gunung Sari Puri Agung Peliatan, Peliatan: Legong Dance, 7:30 pm (transfer to venue 6:45 pm), Rp 75,000.

Trene Jenggala Padangtegal Kaja, Jl. Hanoman: Kecak Fire and Trance Dance, 7:00 pm, Rp 75,000.

Chandra Wirabhuana Ubud Water Palace, Kajeng: Legong Dance, 7:30 pm, Rp 80,000.

Semara Ratih Pura Dalem Ubud, Jl. Raya Campuan: The Beauty of Legong, 7:30 pm, Rp 60,000.

Krama Desa Adat Taman Kaja Pura Dalem Taman Kaja, Sandat: Kecak Fire and Trance Dance, 7:30 pm, Rp 75,000.

SUNDAY

Abasan ARMA Museum, Jl. Raya, Pengosekan: *Wayang Wong* Dance, 7:00 pm (transfer to venue 6:45 pm), Rp 75,000.

Jaya Swara Ubud Place, Jl. Raya Ubud: Legong of Mahabrata, 7:30 pm, Rp 80,000.

Trene Jengala Padangtegal Kaja, Jl. Hanoman: Kecak Fire and Trance Dance, 7:00 pm, Rp 75,000.

The Peliatan Master ARMA Museum, Jl. Raya Pengosekan: Legong Dance, 7:30 pm (transfer to venue 6:45 pm), Rp 75,000.

Cahya Warsa Ubud Water Palace, Kajeng: *Janger*, 7:30 pm, Rp 80,000.

Suara Sakti Bentuyung Village, Suweta: *Jegog* (bamboo *gamelan*), 7:00 pm (transfer to venue 6:45 pm), Rp 80,000.

Krama Desa Sambahan Batukaru Temple, Suweta: Kecak Fire and Trance Dance, 7:30 pm, Rp 75,000.

Pondok Pekak Bale Banjar Ubud Kelod, Jl. Monkey Forest: Legong Dance, 7:30 pm, Rp 75,000.

Sekaa Gong Wanita Mekarsari Balerung Mandera, Peliatan: Dancer and Musicians of Peliatan (women's group), 7:30 pm, Rp 75,000.

EVERY 1ST AND 15TH

Pura Desa Batuan, Jl. Raya, Batuan: *Gambuh* Dance, 7:00 pm (transfer to venue 6:45 pm), Rp 75,000.

EVERY FULL MOON AND NEW MOON

ARMA Museum, Jl. Raya, Pengosekan: Kecak Dance, 7:00 pm (transfer to venue 6:45 pm), Rp 100,000.

Scenic Drives Around Ubud Provide a Bit of History and Lots of Fun!

If based in Ubud, there is a wide array of activities to choose from when you're ready to venture out and have a nice drive through the countryside, soak in a little more history or culture, or have a full day dedicated to simply having fun.

The "Baliwood Hills"

Sayan, **Kedewatan**, and **Payangan** villages constitute what expats call "Baliwood Hills". Many four- and five-star resorts are on this stunning ridge overlooking the Ayung River. *Bemos* are available on market days (*pasah*), but otherwise you'll need your own transport. From the furthest south lies the **Kayumanis Resort**, followed by **Four Seasons Resort**—an excellent lunch stop at its PJ's Restaurant—and then the **Amandari**, the first luxury hotel in the Ubud area, with a superb chef. In between is the **Gaya Fusion Gallery**, which has periodic films, seminars, and exhibits and some of the best homemade gelato on the island. Continuing further north on the main road is **Kupu-Kupu Barong**, the **Royal Pita Maha**, and finally the **Alila Ubud**. Take the left turn at Payangan near Pura Air Jeruk to see the super-lux **Ubud Hanging Gardens**. All have stupendous views.

White water rafting

Two reliable outfitters offer white water rafting tours on the breathtakingly scenic Ayung River north of Ubud. The adventure takes novices and experienced oarsmen of all ages, led by trained guides, over Class II and III rapids through gorges flanked by magnificent waterfalls and paddy fields. Rafting expeditions with Bali Adventure Tours (www.baliadventuretours.com), manager of the Elephant Safari Park, can also be packaged with Park entrance and mountain cycling. Sobek (http://balisobek.com) has an almost identical white water rafting tour, an equally impressive safety record, and also offers mountain cycling.

Folktales in stone

South and west of Ubud there is a quiet, beautiful road that passes through **Mambal**, **Abiansemal**, and **Blahkiuh** villages, renowned for their stone sculptors. All of the temples, *kulkul* (bell) towers, and palaces along this road—beginning further south at **Sibanggede**—have beautiful sculptures, reliefs, and stone ornaments.

Many temples in this area were restored or refreshed after the 1917 earthquake, followed by another restoration boom during the 1930s. Reliefs with scenes from the Tantri stories, of Indian origin, were favorite subjects. In these legends, animals teach people how to live and about the good and evil they can expect from life, depending on their behavior.

One of them tells of the lion-king of the forest and the bull, the ruler-to-be, who must choose to either have a peaceful conversation, face-to-face, or fight to the death. Another tells of two thoughtful geese holding a pole with a tortoise atop while flying away to a safe place and two greedy jackals devouring the absent-minded tortoise, who fell off the pole.

Then there is the story of the wicked heron Baka, surrounded by the bones of a fish he promised to take to a better lake, but then ate it instead. Baka wanted to take a crab also, but the clever crustacean discovered the heron's dishonorable intentions and pinched its head off.

Yet another saga is of a grateful crab and the Brahman who rescued it. Later, the crab rescued the Brahman from an evil bird and snake in gratitude.

A few kilometers before Sangeh at Blahkiuh is a huge, holy *waringin* **(banyan) tree** on the eastern side of the crossroads. In 1989 the temporary market stalls at the foot of this tree were replaced by a concrete structure. In order to do this, part of the aerial roots had to be cut, which could only be done by a specialist with enough magic power to protect himself.

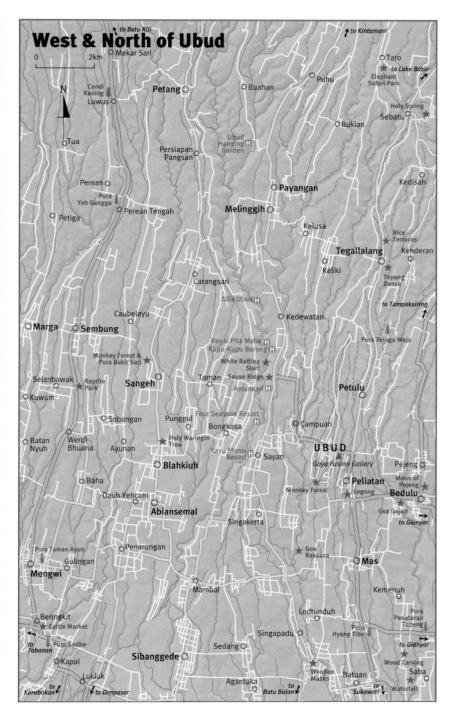

West & North of Ubud

↑ to Batu Riti

↑ to Kintamani

Mekar Sari

0   2km

N

Candi Kuning
Luwus

Petang

Buahan

Puhu

Taro

↗ to Lake Batur

Elephant Safari Park

Holy Spring

Sebatu

Tua

Persiapan Pangsan

Ubud Hanging Garden [H]

Bukian

Kedisah

Perean

Pura Yeh Gangga

Perean Tengah

Payangan

Melinggih

Petiga

Kelusa

Rice Terraces

Tegallalang

Kenderan

Keliki

Topeng Dance

Carangsari

Alila Ubud [H]

to Tampaksiring ↑

Caubelayu

Kedewatan

Marga

Sembung

Royal Pita Maha [H]
Kupu-Kupu Barong [H]

Pura Telaga Waja

Monkey Forest & Pura Bukit Sari

White Rafting Start

Selanbawak

Reptile Park

Sangeh

Taman

Sayan Ridge

Amandari [H]

Petulu

Kuwum

Sobangan

Punggul

Four Seasons Resort [H]

Campuan

UBUD

Pejeng

Batan Nyuh

Werdi Bhuana

Ayunan

Holy Waringin Tree

Bongkasa

Kayu Manis Resort [H]

Sayan

Gaya Fusion Gallery

Moon of Pejeng

Blahkiuh

Baha

Dauh Yehcani

Monkey Forest

Peliatan

Legong

Bedulu

Abiansemal

Singakerta

Goa Gajah

to Gianyar →

Pura Taman Ayun

Penarungan

Goa Raksasa

Mas

Gulingan

Mengwi

Mambal

Kemenuh

Beringkit

Cattle Market

Lodtunduh

Pura Penataran Topeng

to Tabanan

Pura Sadha

Sedang

Singapadu

Pura Hyang Tiba

to Gianyar

Kapal

Sibanggede

Agantaka

Wooden Masks

Batuan

Wood Carving

Saba

Lukluk

to Kerobokan ↓

↓ to Denpasar

to Batu Bulan ↓

to Sukawati ↓

Waterfall

Sangeh's Monkey Forest Temple

In **Sangeh**, 15 km (9 miles) beyond Mengwi, is the fabled **Monkey Forest** and **Pura Bukit Sari** temple. This small temple may date from the founding of Mengwi, although it is also said that it existed in the 17th century. There is an old statue here of Garuda, the mount of Wisnu, who is also associated with the search for the magic elixir (*amreta*) to release his parents from their torments in hell.

The temple is surrounded by tall nutmeg trees with grayish-white trunks, which are very rare on Bali, so they must have been planted deliberately. Many monkeys roam about in the forest. Although sacred to Hindus, they are quite a nuisance, so be sure to remove eyeglasses, jewelry, and watches and hold on tightly to handbags before entering the forest. It is said that some of the monkey-general Hanoman's primate troops fell on Sangeh with the top of Mt. Mahameru when he tried to crush the evil demon king Rawana with it, and that their descendants remain in the forest to this day.

Sebatu's sculpted terraces

Northeast of Ubud is **Sebatu**, which can be done all or in parts by car or *bemo*. From the traffic light with the archer statue at the eastern end of Ubud, head north past the police station and the Delta supermarket along a crowded, paved road that passes through **Petulu** and **Tegallalang** villages toward **Pujung**, a distance of some 16 km (10 miles). The road rises gradually, reaching cooler air, and passes through verdant rice fields and coconut groves. Notice the many assembly-line woodcarvings being produced in small workshops along this road: all sorts of colorful fruit trees and animals. At Pujung, turn right to reach a holy spring at Sebatu, about 800 m to the east, where you can cool off in deliciously fresh pools. From Pujung, a small road continues north to Kintamani past some of Bali's most dramatic rice terraces.

Elephants, trekking, cycling & rafting

North of Ubud on 3.5 ha of land near **Taro** village, west of the road to Mt. Batur via Tegallalang, there are elephants. Established in 1996 to give "jobs" to Sumatra's vanishing pachyderms, the **Elephant Safari Park** has been rescuing and protecting elephants ever since, with a successful breeding program begun in 2006. Managed by an Australian and his Balinese wife, Bali Adventure Tours invites guests to interact with these mammoth creatures — ride, play with, and feed them — as a means to developing an understanding about one of the world's most endangered species. A member of the World Zoo Association, the Park meets international standards for animal care. Programs also include a Night Safari and an elephant talent show.

— Linda Hoffman

Visitors can enjoy themselves at the Elephant Safari Park while helping conserve this endangered species.

The dramatic terraced ricefields in Tegallalang are one of Bali's most photographed sights.

THE ANCIENT MONUMENTS OF CENTRAL BALI

A Tour of the Many Antiquities Found in the Ancient "Land Between the Rivers"

The narrow strip of territory lying between the Petanu and Pakrisan rivers—extending from Mount Batur in the north to the sea in the south—forms a natural replica of the Hindu-Balinese cosmos. It is no wonder, therefore, that the steep ravines, rock river-beds, and cascading streams of this area were the sites of some of the earliest king-doms and religious settlements on Bali, as evidenced by the great wealth of antiquities found here. The major ones lie along the "Kintamani Tour" route and can be seen in a day, but many more days may easily be devoted to an exploration of the other interesting sites.

Inscriptions from this area date from the end of the 10th century. In the beginning it was ruled by Hindus and Buddhists, religions probably introduced directly from India. After the end of the 10th century, as the result of a marriage between Balinese Prince Udayana and a Javanese princess, East Javanese cultural influences appeared in Bali, and the language of the inscriptions changed from Old Balinese to Old Javanese. Kings are mentioned in many of them, and there seems to have been a court center located some-where in the vicinity of Bedulu or Pejeng.

Myths and legends

Numerous myths are connected with this region, many of which concern demonic kings who lost their realms as the result of bad marriages or wicked behavior. Their palaces, battlefields, and sacred landscapes are often connected with archaeological sites. Such a king was Maya Danawa. His story is told in the 16th century *Kakawin Usana Bali*, a poem about Bali's ancient history. The center of his realm was Balingkang, close to modern-day Teges or Bedulu.

Maya Danawa was in fact the son of god-dess Dewi Danu of Lake Batur. He defeated many kings in order to extend his realm, and the god of the lake, Batara Danu, granted him a boon: he was allowed to take a Chinese Buddhist wife. She did not feel at home in Bali, however, and soon fell ill. Maya Danawa went to the sanctuary at Tolangkir to ask for assistance, but the god did not favor someone with a false religion. Maya Danawa was so angry that he forbade the Hindu gods to be venerated, and dictated that he should be worshipped instead.

After some time his Chinese wife died, and Maya Danawa remained alone in his palace, enriching himself at the expense of his people. Twelve years later he was defeated by the god Indra, who tapped the ground at Manuk Aya (near Tampaksiring) whereupon a magical spring appeared. His warriors drank from it and received great strength. When they killed Maya Danawa, blood spouted from his mouth like a stream of gold, becoming the accursed river Petanu. Those who bathed or drank here encountered misery. The gods then bathed in a spring called Air Empul (now Tirta Empul), and from that time onward, the Hindu religion was restored and good kings reigned over Bali.

One of these kings was the Bedulu ruler, who was endowed with great magical powers. He would sit and meditate, legend has it, removing his head to reach the beyond. On one such occasion, an unnatural disturbance occurred and the king was forced to get a new head quickly. A pig happened by, and its head was taken and placed on the neck of the king. Therefore the king's name became Beda-Hulu ("he whose head is severed"). Some versions state that the king's real head fell to earth where Goa Gajah is now.

The king and his courtiers were ashamed of the pig's head, so they constructed a tower for him to live in, and his subjects were not allowed to look up, but had to kneel so they would not see the king's head. Somehow this became known in Java and the ruler of Majapahit sent his prime minister, Gajah Mada, to Bali to determine if it was true.

Antiquities of Central Bali

0   1km

to Kintamani

Subilang · Bukian · Lebah A · Lebah B · Tatag · Ked · Dujung · Sebatu · Holy Spring · Tiingpuan · Tatag · Sacred Spring · Manukaya Let · Pura Sakenan · Belahan · Pangiangan · Lumbuan · Alis Binfang · Buungan Hill 624m

Pujung · Telepud · Pura Gunung Kawi Sebatu · Calo · Manukaya · Manukaya Anyar · Basang Ambu · Penendengan · Kikian · Bungkuan

Pumnan · Bersela · Pakudui · Bayad · The Presidential Palace of Tampaksiring · Tirta Empul · Manik Tawang · Selat Nyuhan · Tanggahan Pekan · Sulahan · Cekeng

Triwangsa Bersela · Gadungan · Kedisan · Melit · Peneka · Saraseda · Gunung Kawi · Mancingan · Pangsut · Kebon · Tanggahan Gunung · Jalanbau

Tanah Bias · Lumbung · Tegal Suci · Griya · Tampaksiring · Buruan · Tangkas · 513m · Tukad Siap

Kebon · Tangkup · Dlod Blumbang · Tengah · Kawan · Tampaksiring Kelodan · Selat · Susut · Manuk · Dukuh

Tangkas · Tengah · Bukit · Eha · Mangkuning · Juwuk Bali · Penglumbatan Lebah · Pura Dalem Purwa

Gagah · Cafe Lulu · Cebok · Pande · Pondoh · Sala · Demulih · Pura Kanginan

Rice Terraces · Pejengan · Kulub · Mantring · Bangli · Kawan · Pura Agung Pule

Kelusa · Yeh Tengah · Tegallalang · Tangkas · Tengah · Manca Warna · Melayang · Padpadan · Abuan Kauh · Kawan · Putra Bali

Keliki · Pacung · Triwangsa · Topeng Dance · Gunaksa · Triwangsa · Karang Anyar · Song Layung · Penyembahan · Abuan · Pulung · Sedit

Triwangsa Keliki · Tengah · Tegal · Padang Sigi · Sanding Gianyar · Siih · Benawan · Madangan · Bebalang · Gancam

Salak · Penusuan · Pinjul · Sanding Biangbasa · Sanding Serongga · Tegal Saat · Tengah · Pande · Apuan · Serokadan · Petak

Kelabang Moding · Dukuh · Pura Telaga Waja · Sanding · Kepitu · Sanding Bitra · Pangembungan · Sema · Bon Nyuh · Mulung · Petak · Tanggahan Tengah · Sembung · Gaga · Uma Anyar

Triwangsa Sebali · Abangan · Sapat · Kenderan · Sembuwuk · Musung · Uma Anyar · Petak · Cafe Jembatan · Pesalakan · Suwat · Siladan · Dadia · Kuning

Sebali · Junjungan · Putulu Gunung · Anahata · Tanah Merah Resort & Gallery · Triwangsa · Uma Anyar · Sadewa · Pende · Teruna

Junjungan Ubud Hotel and Spa · Bentuyung · Gentong · Melayang · Cemadik · Pura Krobokan · Purna Desa · Kabetan · Bangun Lemah · Babah · Taman Bali · Dadia

Kintamani · Ubud Botanic Garden · Petulu · Villa Sarna · Tarukan · Uma Kuta · Munduk · Abian Calak · Tanggahan Talang Jiwa · Taman Bali Raja · Bunutin

Tegal Lantang · Laplapan · Kutuh · Petulu · Cagaan · Uma Dawa · Buditirta · Betiting · Dukuh · Dadia Puri

Pondok Sakti · Ketut · Taman · Villa Sabandari · Padapdapan · Natura Resort & Spa · Sawa Gunung · Roban · Ngenjung Sari · Teruna

Puri Lukisan Museum · Katuh · Sala · Tatiapi · Guliang · Selat · Siangan · Bakbakan · Tanggahan Anyar · Selati · Guliang

Cok Putra S. · Ubud · Pande · Candi Tebing Kalebutan · Goa Garba · Sawan · Kelusu · Panglan · Teruna · Triwangsa · Sanding · Angkling · Gitgit · Blah Pane

Padang Tegal · Peliatan · Teruna · Dukuh Geria · Pura Pusering Jagat · Pejeng · Loka Serana · Pacung · Selat · Sidan

Monkey Forest · Legong · Yangloni · Pura Kebo Edan · Intaran · Puri Saron · Dauh Uma · Beng · Bukit Batu · Jage Perang · Bukit Sari

Arsana · Kalah · Tengah · Goa Gajah (Elephant Cave) · Museum Gedong Arca (Archaeological Museum) · Roban · Triwangsa · Bukit Jangkrik · Dukuh · Pura Dalem

Pengosekan · Open Air Stage · Teges · Tengkulak · Marga Bingung · Sukawati · Mas · Sengguan · Pande · State Temple · Sampiang · Samplangan · Views

bian Semal · Mas · Batu Lumbang · Bedulu · Wanayu · Sema Baung · Batur Sari · Sema · Pura Dalem · Astina Utara · Puri Agung Palace · Astina Timur · Pegesangan

Tengah · Kumbuh · Yeh Pulu Reliefs · Tengkulak Kelod · Temples, Durga Statue · Kutri · Tegal Lingah · Marga Sengkala · Candi Baru · Teges · Patuluan

Satria · I. B. Sutarja · Njana Tilem · Adil · Tengkulak Mas · Bangun Liman · Celuk · Gianyar · Pasdalem · Triwangsa · Temesi · Menak

Kelingkung · Ary Pudja · Kawan · Tarukan · Juga · Buruan · Silk · Abian Base · Tegal Abian Base · to Semarapura Kaja Kauh

mi Ubud Resort · Tantra & Raka · Siadja · Taman Arum · Getas Kawan · Basket Weaving · Sangging · Pratama

Wismaya · Bangkilesan · Pondok Mas · Manis · Lumbung Mas · Getas Kangin · Bono · Serongga

Lodtunduh · Puri Mas · to Denpasar, Sanur · Sumampan · Artha Agung · Darma Tiaga · Babakan · to Denpasar, Sanur

By means of a ruse (drinking water from a pitcher with a long spout), the visitor managed to discover the king's secret and caused his downfall.

Another story is that of Kebo Iwa, which literally means "bull" but was also the title of a court functionary in ancient Bali. Kebo Iwa was a princely giant in some versions, King Bedahulu's minister in others. He scratched rocks with his fingernails, creating many of the rock-cut monuments and reliefs found here today, for example Goa Garba and Yeh Pulu (see below). In some versions, he was killed when invited to the Majapahit court in East Java.

Goa Gajah

The first major site encountered coming from the south or from Ubud, just 2 km (1.2 miles) east of the Teges intersection, is the complex known as **Goa Gajah**, the "Elephant Cave". It overlooks the Petanu River and consists of a Siwaitic cave carved out of the rock, a bathing place, a monks' chamber, a number of Buddhist stupas and statues, and several foundations. It received its name from the archaeologists who discovered it in 1923 because there is a giant head with floppy ears

above the entrance, which was at a first glance thought to represent an elephant.

The entrance to the cave itself is 2 m (6.5 ft) high and 1 m (3 ft) across, with a head sculpted above it that in fact resembles a man with bulging eyes, hairy eyebrows, protruding teeth, and a long moustache. He is surrounded by sculpted ornaments in which little creatures — men, animals, and gruesome heads — are depicted. It is as if they refer to a story, but it is not known which tale this could be, although some say they are running from an earthquake.

The grotto inside is T-shaped, containing 15 niches hewn out of the cave walls, which may have served as benches to sleep or meditate on. For this reason, it is thought that the cave once served as a hermitage. A four-armed Ganesha (the elephant-headed son of Siva) and a set of three *lingga,* each surrounded by eight smaller ones representing the eight points of the compass and the center, were found at the ends. The cave may date from the second half of the 11th century. There are pavilions to both sides of the entrance, in which ancient statues have been placed. One is Hariti, the Buddhist goddess of fertility and protector of children.

The cave temple Goa Gajah (Elephant Cave) houses statues and scriptures of Hindu and Buddhist origin.

The bathing spot behind the cave consists of three compartments which were discovered and excavated only in 1954. The central one is small and holy, the left one is for women, and the right one is for men. They are all sunken, flush against a wall, the top of which is level with the courtyard in front of the cave. Each side basin has three statues of women holding urns, from which water pours into them. There may have been a statue in the central basin as well, but it has disappeared.

Behind the complex are three remarkable carved stupas: a large one in the center and two smaller ones that look like branches coming together in one main trunk. Two sitting, meditating Buddhas, probably from the 8th century, have been found here as well. To the right of the entrance, further down, are the remains of a hermit's cave with a small pond in front.

Yeh Pulu

A couple of kilometers to the east in the direction of Bedulu just off the main road are the **Yeh Pulu** antiquities dating from the late 14th century. These consist of reliefs cut out of the rock and a sacred well. The reliefs are in a naturalistic style; horsemen, men carrying animals hanging from a pole, a sitting Brahman who holds an offering spoon, sitting women, an ascetic, a man carrying two large pots on a pole over his shoulder, the entrance of a cave or a hut, are among the figures which are depicted. So far, however, nobody knows what story is represented and what is meant by it. About 200 m north of Yeh Pulu is another, small bathing place consisting of two basins with naturalistic reliefs of men cut in niches in the rock at the back.

Southeast of Bedulu, in Kutri village, lies the **Pura Pedarman** temple with its 2.2 m (7 ft) high stone statue of the six-armed goddess Durga, the spouse of Siva. She has the outward appearance of a demoness and is killing an ogre cursed to take the appearance of a bull. It is said that the statue represents Prince Udayana's Javanese wife, the mother of Airlangga. An oral tale says that Udayana was allowed to marry her provided he did not take other wives; however, he did not keep his promise. The princess became very angry and turned to black magic.

The Moon of Pejeng drum

The area north of Bedulu, around **Pejeng** and Intaran, contains many antiquities. The most important is **Pura Penataran Sasih**, which forms part of a group of three temples. *Sasih* means "moon" and refers to the "Moon of Pejeng", a giant bronze kettledrum decorated with geometric patterns, ogres' heads, and stars kept high up in a shrine in the temple. According to some stories, it is the ear jewel of Kebo Iwa; others say that it is the chariot wheel of the Moon God which fell in a tree in Pejeng and has been kept in the temple ever since. At first it was bright and shiny; however, a thief tried to steal it and was disturbed by the radiance of the "wheel", so he urinated on the object. As a result, it lost its luster and turned green. The thief was punished for this deed and died immediately.

Bronze kettledrums have been found throughout eastern Indonesia, and on Bali other, smaller drums have been found as well. Even a mould has been excavated, which proves that such drums were manufactured here. Kettledrums date from the Bronze Age, but it is difficult to determine how old the Pejeng Moon is. They were symbols of prosperity and fertility, and in eastern Indonesia form part of the dowry. Apart from the drum, the temple possesses a number of 11th century stone statues, among them a Siva and *lingga*.

The "Navel of the World"

This area of Bali was also once considered the "navel of the world" and there is a temple bearing this name, **Pura Pusering Jagat** in Pejeng. It contains several interesting Hindu antiquities, probably dating from the 14th century, which are now placed in shrines.

Two statues, 1 m (3.2 ft) and 0.52 m (1.7 ft) high, in naturalistic style, are particularly attractive. They each contain four figures. In the taller statue there are dancing demons with bulging eyes, huge teeth, and moustaches grouped around a *lingga* in the center. The smaller one represents four gods, each with four arms holding various attributes, corresponding with the four quarters of the compass. Their heads are surrounded by a nimbus. There is also a shrine with a large *lingga*.

In a special pavilion, a 0.75 m (2.5 ft) high stone vessel is venerated. It has reliefs in a naturalistic style representing a group of gods and demons holding two snakes wound round a cylindrical mountain with trees. Animals and birds fly around it. This

The rock-cut Hindu temples of Gunung Kawi, the "mountain of the poet".

represents a story from the *Mahabharata* called the "churning of the ocean" in which gods and demons search for the elixir of life. They do so with a tip of a mountain (Mt. Mandara, sometimes also Mt. Meru); a snake (on Bali, two snakes) is used as a rope. In the beginning nothing happens. Then a magic horse with seven heads, an elephant with two pairs of tusks, a beautiful lady and a jewel emerge and, finally, a vessel with the elixir. This story fits well with the usage of the vessel as a container of holy water. It is dated with a chronogram corresponding with A.D. 1329.

Another temple in Pejeng, **Pura Kebo Edan**, includes the statue of a standing giant 3.60 m (11.8 ft) tall. He is called Kebo Edan, "the Mad One". The figure has a huge penis with four "penis pins" pierced through it right under the glans. The use of such pins to increase a woman's sexual pleasure is an old custom known throughout Southeast Asia. The giant stands in a dancing position and tramples a human figure, its face covered with something which may be a mask, as it is tied with ribbons at the back. The figure might represent a demonic manifestation of Siva as a dancer. There is another statue representing a fat, crouching demon holding

a big skull upside down in front of his chest. The demon is wearing a diadem decorated with small skulls on his curly hair. The style of these statues points to the 13th-14th centuries.

While in the Pejeng area, stop in also at the **Museum Gedong Arca**, located just 2 km (1.2 miles) north of Bedulu on the main road. Displayed are quite a number of stone sarcophagi, Neolithic axe heads, bronze jewelry and figurines, and Chinese ceramics.

Coffee break

On the road from Pejeng to Tampaksiring, in Banjar Seribatu, is **Buana Amertha Sari Coffee Farm**, where there are free samples of plain tea, lemon tea and ginger tea, as well as coffee and hot chocolate (cocoa), all grown on the property. Guided strolls through the landscaped gardens also make a nice road-trip break. Also available is *kopi luwak*, coffee made from coffee berries eaten by the Asian palm civet (*Paradoxurus hermaphroditus*), then passed through its digestive tract. It is said that the digestive juices in the cat's stomach renders the beans "special".

Rock-cut caves

From Pejeng the road begins a slow but steady ascent toward Mt. Batur. Northeast of Pejeng,

Goa Garba lies on the western side of the Pakrisan River. The complex can be entered via steep steps through a gateway at the back of the Pengukurukuran temple in Sawah Gunung village. There is a hermitage here consisting of three caves with slanting roofs, and there is an inscription in Kadiri square script in one of these saying "*sri*", a lucky sign. On the basis of the script, the complex may be dated to the late 11th century. Water basins with spouts are hewn in front of the niches. There are several pedestals with fragments of stone statues and a *lingga*. In the temple above, there are two stone Ganeshas, a *lingga*, and a winged stone snake with an inscription dated A.D. 1194.

Mountain of the poet
About halfway to the top, just near the source of the Pakrisan River, are two sites of great antiquity. The first, near Tampaksiring, is a complex of rock-cut monuments dating from the late 11th century and known as **Gunung Kawi**, the "mountain of the poet". The poet in this case is none other than the god Siva. In the ravines, on both sides of the river, royal tombs, a hermitage, and monks' caves have been cut out of solid rock. The main entrance to the site can be reached via a steep footpath that begins by a large parking lot lined with souvenir stalls on the east side of the road.

Upon entering the site, to the left is a rock-cut monument consisting of four facades suggesting the shape of temples. Each is surrounded by an oval-shaped niche about 7 m (23 ft) high; the reliefs are covered with a kind of plaster. On the other side of the ravine are five niches with similar facades carved in the rock. In the bases of all these, holes have been made that once contained stone boxes divided into nine squares, corresponding to the eight quarters of the compass and the center. The monuments are connected with the youngest son of the powerful East Javanese King Airlangga, who lived in the 11th century and was of Balinese descent via his father, Udayana. It is known that he issued edicts between A.D. 1050 and 1078. The central monument of the five may be devoted to him because there is an inscription in Kadiri square script at the top reading: "The king monumentalized in Jalu", which may refer to the name of the site.

Next to the monuments is a rock-cut monastery complex consisting of several caves with a free-standing building hewn out of the rock in the center. Characteristic are the large, rectangular apertures and oval-shaped entrances, with overhanging roofs, now overgrown with grass.

The sacred spring
In an inscription dated A.D. 960 discovered in **Pura Sakenan** temple in Manukaya village, mention is made of a double pool dug around a well near the source of the Pakrisan River. The king transformed this into a holy bathing place. This is the present-day **Tirta Empul**, one of Bali's most sacred spots. It lies just north of Tampaksiring along a well-marked road.

The sanctuary consists of an outer courtyard with a basin for public use and a central courtyard with two adjacent, rectangular pools (for those who fought Maya Danawa and were cleansed by the god Indra) containing clear, transparent water, all surrounded by a low wall of recent construction. There are 15 spouts in these pools. The inner court has two pavilions, one of which is for the god Indra (Maya Danawa's adversary), and more than 20 small shrines with newly-carved and wooden doors decorated with reliefs. Among these is one devoted to the rice goddess Dewi Sri, one to the Lord of Majapahit, and one to Mt. Batur.

— *Hedi Hinzler*

Devotees purify themselves at Tirta Empul spring.

KAPAL, MENGWI, TABANAN, KERAMBITAN, AND BATUKARU

Sights of the Old Kingdom of Mengwi

The Mengwi rulers were well known for their temples. The oldest of these is **Pura Sadha**, a few hundred meters south of the main road in **Kapal**, about 16 km (10 miles) northwest of Denpasar. The name *sada* may derive from the Old Javanese and Sanskrit term *prasada*, meaning "a tower temple". There is indeed a huge shrine in the shape of a tiered tower in the inner court. The local inhabitants call this temple a *candi*, a funerary monument for a deceased king.

According to the chronicles of the Mengwi rulers, the son of the first Cokorda or Lord of Mengwi, I Gusti Agung Panji, received a shrine in this temple after his death around 1710. The divinity of the temple is Bhatara Jayengrat, the Divine World Conqueror.

Kapal

At present the complex is venerated and maintained by the people of Kapal, irrespective of their caste or kin group. It was severely damaged during the earthquake of 1917 and was restored in 1950. The leader of the team of Balinese craftsmen was I Made Nama, and it is said that the construction of the tall tower was quite a challenge for him and his men.

The forecourt of the temple is large and spacious; a big tree grows at the center. The temple complex is surrounded by a wall of red brick constructed in the traditional way, without mortar. By rubbing one stone against the other, a fine powder crumbles from the surface layers. When water is added to it, the stones can be simply stuck together.

A split gateway on the west side leads to the central courtyard. A second, closed gateway with a three-tiered roof on the west gives way to the inner court, where there are 16 shrines. Right in front of the gateway is the *prasada* and behind it a square pedestal with 54 little stone seats. These are shrines for the *satya*, the servants, and facing them in one shrine in the south are the three *mekel satya*, their leaders.

The following story is connected with these shrines. A long time ago, when a king of Majapahit in East Java died, he was cremated and his ashes were carried by 54 men towards the sea in a bamboo tower (*bukur*) with a tiered roof. The tower was placed on a little boat (*kapal*), on which were seated the 54 followers (*patih*) of the deceased and three leaders (*mekel*). The boat, however, was stranded at sea.

This episode has been transposed to the temple and is symbolized in the stone tower at the center and in the pedestals with the 54 and three stone seats the tower being a replica of the bamboo cremation structure. Close to it, to the south, is a shrine with an 11-tiered roof, called "little garden with a pond" (*taman*). During the temple festival on Tumpek Kuningan, its "water" is used to bathe the god of the tower. This is in fact very convenient, because then a long tour outside the temple to a bathing place is not necessary.

Replicas of mountains that are important for south Bali (Mts. Agung, Batur, Sekanana, and Batukaru) are found in shrines in the north and the east of the inner court, which has a tiered roof in the *meru* (pagoda) style. The number of tiers is always odd, the highest being 11, which is only suitable for the most important peak. In this case it represents Mt. Agung.

There are more shrines in the north and the east devoted to various divine kings, including a *padmasana* seat in which the god Siva in his manifestation as Surya is venerated, and a little building in which a *barong* mask is kept.

Kapal to Mengwi

Along the north side of the main road in Kapal, a grand *pura puseh* temple includes relief panels on its outer wall depicting scenes from the *Ramayana*. The long *bale gede* pavilion is clearly visible from the road.

In **Mengwi** town, once the political center of the region, is the stately **Pura Taman Ayun** surrounded by tall walls with a bell tower bearing lovely carvings in the northern corner. "Taman Ayun" refers to a huge open space

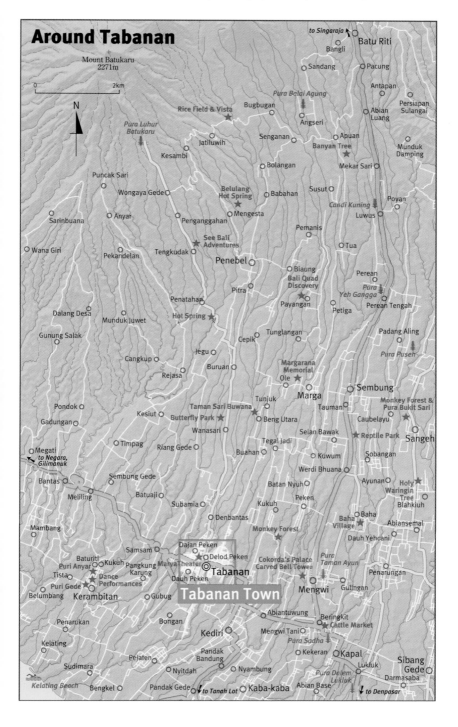

Around Tabanan

to Singaraja

Mount Batukaru
2271m

0   2km

N

Batu Riti

Bangli

Sandang   Pacung

Antapan

Persiapan
Sulangai

Pura Balai Agung

Rice Field & Vista ★   Bugbugan

Angseri   Abian
Luang

*Pura Luhur
Batukaru*

Jatiluwih   Senganan   Apuan   Munduk
Damping

Kesambi   Banyan Tree

Bolangan   Mekar Sari

Puncak Sari   Belulang   Babahan   Susut

Wongaya Gede   Hot Spring ★   *Candi Kuning*   Poyan

Mengesta   Luwus

Sarinbuana   Anyar   Penganggahan   Pemanis

Wana Giri   Pekandelan   Tengkudak   See Bali ★   Tua
Adventures

Penebel   Biaung

Bali Quad   Perean
Discovery   *Pura ₮
Yeh Gangga*

Dalang Desa   Pitra   Payangan   Perean Tengah

Penatahan   Petiga   Padang Aling

Gunung Salak   Hot Spring ★   Cepik   Tunglangan   *Pura Puseh*

Munduk Juwet

Jegu

Cangkup   Buruan   Margarana
Memorial

Rejasa   Ole ★   Sembung

Pondok   Tunjuk   Marga   Monkey Forest &
Pura Bukit Sari

Kesiut   Taman Sari Buwana ★   Tauman   Caubelayu

Gadungan   Butterfly Park ★   Beng Utara   Reptile Park ★   Sangeh

Wanasari   Selan Bawak

Timpag   Riang Gede   Tegal Jadi   Sobangan

Megati
to Negara,
Gilimanuk   Buahan   Kuwum   Werdi Bhuana   Ayunan   Holy ★
Waringin
Tree

Bantas   Batan Nyuh   Blahkiuh

Meliling   Batuaji   Peken   Baha

Subamia   Kukuh   Baha ★
Village   Abiansemal

Mambang   Denbantas   Dauh Yehcani

Monkey Forest

Samsam   Dajan Peken

Baturiti Kukuh   Pangkung Mahya Theater   Delod Peken   Cokorda's Palace   *Pura
Taman Ayun*

Puri Anyar   Karung   Carved Bell Tower

Tista   Dance
Performances   Dauh Peken   Tabanan   Penarungan

Puri Gede   Mengwi   Gulingan

Belumbang   Kerambitan   Gubug   **Tabanan Town**

Bongan   Abiantuwung   Beringkit
Cattle Market

Penarukan   Kediri   Mengwi Tani

Kelating   Pejaten   *Pura Sodha*

Pandak
Bandung   Kekeran   Kapal   Sibang
Gede

Sudimara   Nyitdah   Nyambung   Lukluk   Darmasaba

*Pura Dalem
Lukluk*

Kelating Beach   Bengkel   Pandak Gede   to Tanah Lot   Kaba-kaba   Abian Base   to Denpasar

Pura Taman Ayun near Mengwi town.

Brahman priest prepares holy water during temple festivals (*bale pawedan*) is decorated with a relief series focusing on Arjuna, who meditated to receive a grant from the gods, who sent nymphs to seduce him as a test. On the wooden wall of the *bale murda* pavilion is a colorful painting.

Today the family of Puri Gede Mengwi still maintains the temple, assisted by a committee of local traditional leaders. In 2010, vehicle traffic in front of the temple was redirected to a new parking area and the former road made into a pedestrian walkway to accommodate the large number of people who visit Pura Taman Ayun each day.

Held every Wednesday and Sunday at the **cattle market** in **Beringkit**, northwest of Kapal, herds of buffaloes and cows crowd the road and often block traffic along the Denpasar highway. Also traded are goats, chickens, and ducks, with a vibrant traditional market selling everything from clothes to flowers and agricultural equipment.

Tabanan town and the arts

Tabanan Regency is Bali's verdant "rice bowl". Medium sized and bustling, **Tabanan town** is the administrative center of the regency. Although it appears rather nondescript and has not much of a reputation among tourists, the arts are actually well represented here. At the end of the 19th century, Tabanan already had skilled woodcarvers, and there were (and still are) many good *juru basa*, or bards, who recited fragments of classic poems (*kakawin*) at festive occasions and during *Bebasan* recital club contests. Also, among the Regency's citizens are award-winning artists in literature, painting, traditional Balinese architecture, dance, and puppetry.

Bali's best known dancer, the late I Ketut Marya (also spelled "Maria" but pronounced, and frequently written as "Mario") is also connected with Tabanan. He was born at the end of the 19th century and died in 1968. Although he was actually born in Denpasar, he was raised in Tabanan under the guardianship of Anak Agung Ngurah Made Kaleran of the Puri Kaleran palace.

Marya performed as one of the dancers representing the female pupils of the witch Calonarang with the Gong Pangkung music club, founded in 1900. The Gong Pangkung, named after a village quarter in Tabanan, also possessed a set of *tingklik* instruments, bamboo replicas of a *gamelan* orchestra.

(*ayun*) representing a garden (*taman*). It was constructed under the first raja of Mengwi, I Gusti Agung Putu, in 1634 as a royal family temple in which to worship ancestors, and was damaged by a violent earthquake in 1917. Repairs were done in stages to return the temple to its original condition.

Surrounded by a moat filled with lotuses — a concept duplicated from Kertha Gosa in the mighty Klungkung kingdom — it seems to "float", representing the heavens, where divine nymphs and ancestors relax in similar pavilions, enjoying themselves.

The temple complex consists of a forecourt, a central court, and a spacious inner court. A tall stone gateway with wooden doors leads into it. The inner court has rows of shrines on the north and east sides, and carved stone pedestals with wooden pavilions to the west. The total number of structures is 27. Apart from the divine ancestor of the dynasty, the mountains so important to Mengwi (Agung, Batur, Batukaru, Pengelengan, and Mangu) are represented here by shrines with slender tiered roofs in the north and the east. Replicas of temples founded by the Mengwi rulers atop these mountains (Pura Pucak) and bordering the sea (Pura Ulun Siwi), and of state temples built by former Mengwi rulers (Pura Sada, Pura Bekak) are also here. The basement of a pavilion in which the

Together with three fellow dancers, Marya experimented widely with this orchestra and traveled throughout Bali, giving *gandrung* (transvestite) performances. Marya's troupe also refined the lively *kebyar* musical style that had been invented in north Bali around 1900, and he developed a number of new dances for the ensemble. The most popular is the Trompong dance, in which the performer dances in a squatting position and plays the *trompong* (a row of 10 bronze kettledrums). Marya also created the Kebyar Duduk (sitting *kebyar*), in which he crouches while dancing and sensuously flirts with one of the musicians. In the late 1920s and 1930s, these dances were already well known to tourists, and painter Walter Spies made superb photos of them for the book *Dance and Drama in Bali*, which he produced with Beryl de Zoete in 1935–36.

Marya was also a teacher of many dancers who would later rise to fame, in particular I Gusti Ngurah Raka from Batuan. He was a very strict mentor and only accepted the very best pupils. Although he taught them the same dances, he assigned each pupil slightly different movements, to enable him or her to

have something characteristic. To remember this dancer and teacher who put Tabanan on the map among the Balinese, a statue was erected in 1974 of the two dancers in front of the **Gedong Marya Theater**. A plaque on its base honors the beloved "Mario". Although the memorial is beautiful, the building—now covered with graffiti—is nothing special to see and serves as a community recreational hall and gathering spot instead of a proper theater. However, dance and other cultural performances are still held here. Check schedules locally upon arrival, if interested.

Just outside of town to the southeast is the **Subak Museum**, containing tools and implements connected with irrigation and agriculture. In the same complex is **Uman Bali**, a replica of a traditional thatched-roofed Balinese farmhouse.

Rich artistic traditions

Several villages southwest of Tabanan town are especially rich in dance and art traditions. **Kerambitan** (meaning "beautiful place") in particular, is noted for its *tektekan* performance, a procession of men wearing giant wooden cow bells with huge clappers around their necks

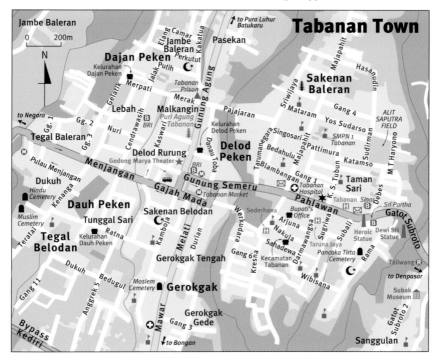

and carrying bamboo split drums. They traditionally marched around the village during an epidemic or great drought to chase away the evil spirits and bring fertility to the area.

There are two palaces here, belonging to branches of the Tabanan royal family. **Puri Gede**, built in 1650, is home of the descendants of the first generation. **Puri Anyar** was erected in 1750 for second generation families and can arrange events for visitors upon prior request. "Puri Night Dinner" includes a candlelit evening meal at the palace with a *tektekan* performance. There's also a guest house here open to tourists.

In nearby **Tista** village, just 0.8 km (0.5 mile) west of Kerambitan, special versions of the *legong kraton* dance, called *leko* or *adar*, are performed. This is a dramatized adaptation of a classic tale (the *Ramayana*) danced by three young girls: a *condong* (female attendant) and two *legong* (princesses). They change roles during the performance, but wear the same costumes. The Tista group was founded in 1989 under the guidance of two respected dancers from the 1920s era.

Just over 1.6 km (1 mile) south of Kerambitan, **Penarukan** village has many good sculptors —both Brahmans and *jaba* (*sudras*)— working in wood as well as in soft volcanic *paras* stone. The village is also known for its *tektekan*, and for the painter Ida Bagus Nyoman Cekug from the Griya Gede Brahmans, who was a pioneer in the use of modern elements in his works.

Butterflies galore

Under 5 km north of Tabanan town on the scenic road to Mt. Batukaru is the **Bali Butterfly Park (Taman Kupu-kupu Lestari)** in **Wanasari**. A center for breeding, research, and education, it is home to rare and endemic species, including spectacular Birdwings (*Ornithoptera, Trogonoptera,* and *Troides*) and Swallowtails (*Papilionidae*). See a magnificent display of nature at its best when hundreds of colorful butterflies are released to fly each day. It's best to visit on sunny days, when they are most active.

A famous native son

West of Sangeh near Marga is the modern temple-like **Margarana Memorial** that's somewhat of a national shrine. About 15 km (9 miles) northeast of the town is the spot where Lieutenant Colonel I Gusti Ngurah Rai, commander of the Balinese nationalist forces fighting the Dutch, was killed, along with his 94 freedom fighters, on November 20, 1946. Greatly outnumbered by Dutch forces and under attack by land and by air, they fought to the death rather than surrender, reminiscent of the *puputan* of the Badung ruler and his family in 1906. The heroic death of Ngurah Rai is commemorated not only in this temple, but also in a poem, *Geguritan Margarana*, written a short time afterwards by a fellow nationalist fighter. His name has also been given to Bali's international airport. The memorial itself contains a stone tower, or *candi,* in which a replica of the famous letter containing his refusal to surrender is carved. Placed in rows outside are 94 pointed stone pedestals representing his fellow martyrs, bearing the names and villages of each.

Spend the day as a villager

Nearby, 15 families from one ancestor in Banjar Beng Utara, Desa Tunjuk, have cleverly developed an opportunity for travelers to spend some time with them to see how rural Balinese actually live. They call themselves **Taman Sari Buwana**, and everyone is involved, from the smallest child—who demonstrates his growing prowess at cock fighting (just for fun, of course)—to his grandpa, who chuckles with delight. Walk around the compound and identify the buildings housing the various family groups, see where the pigs and chickens are kept, and stroll through the vegetable and flower gardens. Learn to make offerings and decorations out of palm leaves (grandma and the aunties will demonstrate) and be refreshed with *kelapa mudah*, young coconut picked fresh from the tree while you watch (or participate). Mama cooks lunch, and accepts any help offered, serving it on banana leaf-lined rattan plates. This can be followed with a trip to the rice paddy to try your skills at plowing and planting, assisted by papa and the uncles.

Visitors also drop by the village school, where part of the proceeds of this excellent sustainable tourism program go to teaching the younger generation computer, English, math, and positive thinking skills. A day in the village can also include a 2–3 hour trek through the rice fields to a *subak* temple and to see how Balinese ingenuity manages life-giving waters.

More adventures

East of Penatahan, Payangan village is the base of two other adventure travel groups, **Bali Quad Discovery** and its sister company, **Bali Canyon Tubing**. Traveling over small paths used by villagers via customized ATVs (semi-automatic all-terrain vehicles) or 4-wheel motorcycle buggies—either solo or in tandem—tours stop at a traditional house to taste Balinese coffee, pass forests, and climb hills. White-water rafting trips conquer the Siap River, watching monkeys play and rare birds flying in surrounding forests.

Tabanan antiquities

Only a few antiquities have been discovered in Tabanan Regency. One lies in **Perean**, west of the main road to Bedugul. This stone shrine, discovered here in 1920, consists of a square basement with panels and a temple body with niches on three sides, an entrance on the fourth and a mock door with a kind of lock carved in stone. Porcelain plates of various sizes are mounted in the temple body on both sides of these niches and the entrance. The temple now has a thatched roof with seven tiers.

There are also remains here of three small, ancient buildings. The complex is surrounded by a wall with a split gateway. Inscribed stones discovered nearby bear the dates A.D. 1339 and 1429.

East of Perean, on the other side of the road, is **Pura Yeh Gangga** ("Waters of the Ganges") hot water springs.

Hot springs and ATV adventures

Further north, the **Penatahan** hot springs near **Penebel** and the rice terraces at **Jatiluwih** make the slopes of Mt. Batukaru well worth visiting. These areas can be easily reached by *bemo* on the road directly north out of Tabanan town.

Northwest of Penebel, **Tengkudak** village is the home of **See Bali Adventures** and their innovative way to visit small communities and enjoy the scenery while simultaneously getting an adrenalin rush. Exploring by ATVs, guests travel to surrounding villages and interact with local people, passing through rice fields and cacao plantations. The group also offers eco-mountain cycling trips and an Outbound Fun Learning Program.

A temple on high

The highway that passes through Wanasari ends at **Pura Luhur Batukaru** about halfway up the slopes of towering **Mt. Batukaru** (2,276 m/ 7,467 ft), nominated as a UNESCO world heritage site in 2007. An unusual complex of shrines and a pool are set amidst dense tropical forests. The main enclosure lies at the northern end of the complex with two smaller temples, Pura Dalem and Pura Panyaum, to the south. A manmade lake to the east completes the "cosmic" design.

This was the state ancestral temple of the Tabanan court, and each of the shrines represents a different dynastic ancestor. Di Made, ruler of Gelgel between about 1665 and 1686, is represented by a shrine with a seven-tiered roof, and Cokorda Tabanan by one with a three-tiered roof. All of the shrines are very modest, without much ornamentation, which gives a great feeling of unity to the complex.

The nearby pond is fed by the river Aa (pronounced "ehe"). In the center are two pavilions on a little isle, one for the goddess of Lake Tamblingan and one for the Lord of Mt. Batukaru. The sacred peak thus surrounded by waters can be compared with the mythical Mt. Meru where the gods reside, enjoying themselves in floating pavilions.

East of here from Wongaya Gede, a small, rural road leads through some of the most spectacular rice field panoramas anywhere via Jatiluwuh, **Senganan**, and **Angseri**, where there are well-signposted hot springs. If continuing north to Bangli or the Bedugul Highlands (refer to p. 260 for more information about the Bedugul highlands), or back to Ubud, the country road continues until it meets the main north-south, Denpasar to Singaraja highway.

Climbing Mt. Batukaru

Only doable in the dry season (April–October), climbing Mt. Batukaru is a treacherous undertaking requiring an experienced guide, which can be arranged through most accommodations or at Pura Luhur Batukaru. It is partly covered by dense forest, and the trails can be extremely dangerous when it rains. Three trails start from Wongayagede, Sarinbuana, and Sanda and connect at Munduk Nyanggang. From there it is 2–3 hours of arduous climbing. The route from Sanda is the most difficult (7 hours to the summit) and from Sarinbuana is the easiest. Camping is allowed, except near Pura Luhur. Local guides can also lead nature lovers on less strenuous treks.

—*Heidi Hinzler; revised by Linda Hoffman*

VISITING TABANAN TOWN
(TELEPHONE CODE: 0361)

Tabanan town itself is not a usual overnight destination for travelers, with western Bali's south coast beaches nearby. However, as a Regency capital, it does have banks, ATMs, and a post office as well as a large Hardy's supermarket on the main road, which might be useful to those traveling further afield where such amenities are scarce. There is a guesthouse at the Puri Anyar palace for those who need to stay in town.

GETTING THERE & GETTING AROUND
The town's center is just off the main east-west highway that eventually curves south to the coast. Most visitors are just passing through on the way to other destinations in their own vehicles, but *bemos* departing from Denpasar's Ubung terminal arrive at Tabanan's Pesiapan terminal on its northern outskirts on their way to Gilimanuk (under $1). Once here, *bemos* run throughout the town en route to nearby villages.

ACTIVITIES
Puri Anyar, mobile: +62 (0) 812-392-6720, one of the royal palaces, can arrange a "Puri Night Dinner" at the palace with candlelight and a cultural performance. Prior reservations are required. There's also a guesthouse here open to tourists.
Subak Museum, Jl. Raya Kediri, tel: 810-375, contains agricultural tools and implements connected to Bali's unique irrigation system (*subak*). In the same complex is **Uman Bali**, a replica of a traditional thatch-roofed Balinese farmhouse.

TABANAN REGENCY
The interior of Tabanan Regency is Bali's agricultural heartland. The fabled rice terraces so often photographed are only the beginning, as at their edges are plantations bearing many types of fruits— *salak*, durian, and mangosteen —and spices, such as cloves and nutmegs. There are also cacao and coffee plantations that often have small shops offering tastes of their harvests.

The panoramas alone are worth a day trip from Ubud, but there are also adventure activities among the villages and a butterfly park.

ACCOMMODATIONS
Cempaka Belimbing Villas, Banjar Suradadi, Belimbing, tel: 745-1178, fax: 745-1179, www.cempakabelimbing.com. On the slope of Mt. Batukaru surrounded by mangosteen, clove, nutmeg, *salak*, durian, and cacao trees, as well as

rice fields. The design is Balinese architecture using local materials; 6 suite villas with garden views, 4 deluxe villas with rice field views, and 6 valley view villas. All have a large bedroom, verandah, tv, fridge, fan, and AC. Swimming pool, outdoor Jacuzzi, spa. Can arrange bicycle hire and trekking (4 routes). Winner of several awards, including the Tri Hita Karana Emerald award for incorporating the Balinese philosophy of balancing humanity and God, environment and other humans. Rates begin at $100. Internet booking discounts available.
Prana Dewi, 6 km beyond Penatahan in Wongayagede village, tel: 736-654, mobile: 0812-383-4757, www.balipranaresort.com. Peaceful mountain bungalows deep in the Tabanan countryside amidst organic rice fields, water and fern gardens. 13 rooms, each with a terrace or deck and *bale* (pavilion), perfect for yoga, meditation, or just relaxing. Restaurant overlooking giant bamboo and virgin tropical rainforest serves organic foods and vegetarian. From $55. Special packages for yoga retreats.
Puri Taman Sari, Dusun Umabian, Desa Peken, Marga, tel: 742-1165, 747-3783, fax: 747-2420, www.balitamansari.com. Stay in a traditional Balinese compound owned by a member of the Mengwi royal family. Surrounded by rice fields and coconut groves with three rivers running through. A traditional family compound, some of the pavilions have been converted into deluxe rooms and junior suites. Guests are encouraged to become involved with local life from the time *nenek* (grandma) wakes them with morning tea, through offerings, prayers, and mealtimes. Dance and *gamelan* lessons also available. Rates from $55/standard room, including breakfast. High season surcharge.
Tabanan Homestay, Banjar Ngis Kelod, Jegu village, Penebel, mobile: +62 817-0671-788, www.balihomestay.com. A chance to live simply with a Balinese extended family and become immersed in nature and culture. The program includes visits to Bedugul further north near Lake Bratan, to fish or wander; temple visits to Tanah Lot, Batukaru, and Ulun Danu; and traditional arts at Krambitan village. Rates include non AC rooms, all meals, guided tours, airport transfer. From 3 days/2nights $130/pp.
Villa Kembali, Cepaka, Tabanan, mobile : +61 418 325055 or +62 818-344-967, www.bali-villakembali.com. Located northeast of Tanah Lot, a private residence set among ancient trees and towering palms and overlooking a graceful river. 4- or 5-bedroom villa with Bulgari bathroom accessories, full kitchen, and East meets West menu in dining

pavilion. Bar, bar snacks. Private yoga, riverside spa treatments. Fully trained manager, drivers, chefs, and bar staff. $550–1,200.

Yeh Panes Natural Hot Springs and Spa, Jl. Batukaru, Penatahan, tel: 271-296, 484-052, mobile: 0823-617-338, 0812-463-3623, or 0816-573-279. An open-air resort consisting of 16 rooms on a hillside set over rice fields and a rushing river. A selection of 4-, 6- and 8-person natural spas are fed by a natural hot and healing mineral water springs. Big swimming pool and kiddie pool. The facility is set in a completely natural environment. Balinese, Chinese, and Western cuisine served in a riverside restaurant. $53 (Internet rate), includes breakfast and full access to the spas and pool.

DINING
A dining experience

Big Tree Farms (www.bigtreebali.com), head office Jl. Bypass Ngurah Rai, Denpasar Timur, tel: 461-978, (0541) 488-5605. Markets its organic products made from 80 different varieties of vegetables and fruits, vanilla, coffee, and oranges from throughout the world. Offers a "Firefly Supper Series", with elegant dinners on its farm in Jatiluwih, over 1,000 m (3,000 ft) high on the slopes of Mt. Batukaru. Deep in the uplands of Tabanan, this area is known for its sweeping panoramas, cool air, and great natural beauty.

The dinners take place in a rustic dining pavilion in a coffee plantation with hundreds of coconut torches lighting pathways; occurs every 2–3 weeks during the dry season (roughly May–September). Contact Big Tree Farms for rates, which include hotel pick-up, dinner, and wine.

ACTIVITIES

Bali Butterfly Park (Taman Kupu-kupu Lestari), Jl. Batukaru, Banjar Sandan Lebah, Wanasari (6 km/ 4 miles north of Tabanan town), tel: 814-282, 814-283, or 873-1414; fax: 814-281; http://balibutter-flypark.itrademarket.com. Encounter rare and endemic butterfly species from throughout the world released to free-fly each day. Among them are spectacular Birdwings and Swallowtails. Open daily 8 am–5 pm, last entry at 4 pm. It's best to visit on sunny mornings when the birds are most active.

Taman Sari Buwana, Balinese Traditional Farming, Ketut Buana, Br. Beng Utara, Desa Tunjuk, Tabanan, Bali, tel: (62-361) 722-388 or 742-5929; fax: 722-388; mobile: 0812-391-5655, www.balivillagelife.com. Highly recommended program designed by a large extended Balinese family. Spend the day in a tradi-tional housing compound walking through rice fields, learning to make palm leaf decorations, cooking cassava, scaling a coconut palm, or learning

to plant rice or plow the field. The whole family is involved and are very welcoming. Part of the proceeds goes to village kids to learn computer, English, math, and positive thinking skills. $59–66/ pp with English speaking guide. Can also organize cycling trips through paddies to meet local farmers.

MT. BATUKARU AREA
ACCOMMODATIONS

Sarinbuana Eco Lodge, Mt. Batukaru, www.baliecolodge.com, 4 hand-crafted bungalows located at 700 m (2,300 ft) on the slopes of Mt. Batukaru 10 minutes from protected rainforest. Surrounded by organic gardens producing vegetables for the lodge's kitchen, vanilla plants, coffee, coconut, and cacao trees. Activities include nature walks, edible garden tour, trekking, massage, yoga, and simply relaxing. Holds cultural and eco workshops; contributes to local projects. Owners also do eco-tour consulting. $139–209, plus one budget homestay room $26–35.

Sanda Boutique Villas & Restaurant, Sanda village, on the western slopes of Mt. Batukaru, mobile: +62 (0) 828-372-0055, +62 (0) 813-3851-8836, www.sandavillas.com. Set in an old coffee plantation, spacious, luxuriously appointed rooms with AC, ceiling fan, tv, mini-fridge, room service, and large private balconies with breathtaking views. Swimming pool, restaurant. Happy Hours 5–6 pm serving free Colonial pink gins. Can arrange tours and trekking. From $99.

ACTIVITIES

Climbing Mt. Batukaru. As Mt. Batukaru is not climbed by the masses, the trails are not clear in some areas, pass through dense forests, and are usually wet in the humid mountain atmosphere. A climb to the summit should only be undertaken by the physically fit, in the dry season. Locate an experienced guide through most accommodations or at Pura Luhur Batukaru, and expect to pay $80–100 for the trip up and back. Camping is permitted. Take plenty of food and water, as none are available on the mountain.

Waka Land Cruises, www.wakaexpericnce.com. A land cruise to Jatiluwih and Mt. Batukaru by air-conditioned, customized Land Rover that seats 6 to Waka Experience's private restaurant deep in a bamboo forest on the slopes of Mt. Batukaru. Tour includes expert guide through scenic countryside and visiting the unusual and traditional, such as a stone quarry, temples, shrines, and small villages. Stop to see—and taste—vanilla, coffee, and cacao grown on local plantations. $93/adults, children 5–10 half-price, kids under 5 free.

Mount
Tengayang
1117m
Mount Mengandang
+ 1363m
Pangejaran
Selulung
Dausa
Bantang
Pura Tegeh
Kuripan
Sukawana
Mt. Penulisan
1746m
Pinggan
Belandingan
Tambakan
Catur
Belantih
Daup
Serahi
Kintamani
Songan A
Songan B
Mount Batur
1412m
Lake Batur
Toya Bungkah
Lake Batur
Trunyan
Bali Aga Village,
Pura Gede
Pancering Jagat
Belanga
Awan
Batur Utara
Pura Ulun
Danu Batur
Batur Selatan
Hot Spring,
Volcanic Lake
Batukaang
Gunung Bau
Manik Liyu
Penelokan
Pura Jati Batur
Mountain
View
Jati
Mount Abang
2151m
Binyan
Ulian
Belancan
Batur Tengah
Kedisan
Belok Sidan
Mengani
Lembean
Bayung Cerik
Banyung
Gede
Buahan
Pelaga
Bunutin
Mangguh
Katung
Bonyoh
Sekar Dadi
Suter
Abang Tudinding
Langgahan
Abuan
Sekaan
Abang Songan
Kerta
Pengotan
Tapis Hill
1608m
Pupuan
Penglumbaran
Pempatan
Besakih
Pura
Besakih
Elephant
Safari Park
Taro
Tiga
Buahan
Puhu
Holy Spring
Yangapi
Menanga
Padangaji
Petang
Bukian
Senbatu
Manukaya
Traditional
Village
Paninjoan
Muncan
Peringsari
Persiapan
Pangsan
Kedisah
Tirta Empul
Pura Sakenan
Gunung Kawi
Sulahan
Kubu
Rendang
Ngoek Hill
512m
Melinggih
Tampaksiring
Susut
Cempaga
Jehem
Tembuku
Bangbang
Iseh
Kelusa
Rice Terraces
Kenderan
Bangli Town
Demulih
Pura Kehen
Undisan
Nongan
Sidemen
Tegallalang
Keliki
Topeng Dance
Petak
Bangli
Kawan
Nyangian
Pesaban
Tabda
Carangsari
Kedewatan
Pura Telaga Waja
Sanding
Abuan
Bebalang
Tohpati
Sayan
Ridge
Suwat
Petak
Apuan
Bungbungan
Timuhun
White Water
Rafting
Taman
Pejeng
Semarapura (Klungkung) Town
Selisihan
Tegak
Bongkasa
Petulu
Pura Kerobokan
Bunutin
Nyalian
Manduang
Selat
Tangkup
Talibeng
Punggul
Sayan
Ubud Village
Goa Garba
Bakbakan
Tamanbali
Aan
Besan
Singakerta
Ubud
Peliatan
Siangan
Gianyar Town
Bakas
Getakan
Akah
Kertha
Gosa
Semarapura
(Klungkung)
Dawan
Monkey
Forest
Legong
Pejeng
Moon of
Pejeng
Beng
Sidan
Tihingan
Gamelan
Smiths
Paksabali
Sulang
Pikat
Goa
Raksasa
Bedulu
Goa
Gajah
Bitera
Pura
Dalem
State
Temple
Samplangan
Tusan
Painting, Gold &
Silver Smiths
Gelgel
Gunaksa
Pesinggahan
Mas
Temples, Durga
Statue
Buruan
Gianyar
Pura
Segara
Temesi
Tulikup
Takmung
Satra
Tojan
Kusamba
Fishing Village
Mambal
Singapadu
Basket Weaving
Belege
Serongga
Lebih
Negari
Jumpai
Sedang
Lodtunduh
Kemenuh
Bona
Gamelan Maker
Medahan
Salt Pans
Sibang Gede
Wooden
Masks
Batuan Kaler
Batuan
Blahbatuh
Wood Carving
Waterfall
Saba
Pering
Keramas
Bali Safari &
Marine Park
Jl. Bypass Prof. Ida Bagus Mantra
Sea Temple
Masceti Beach
Keramas Beach
Klotok Beach
Agantaka

0   5km

N

nyar Barat
Tianyar Tengah
Salt Panning
ianyar
Pejukung
Ban
Sukadana
Batu Ringgit
Salt Panning
Kubu
Diving WW II
"The Liberty" Wreck
Dukuh
Tulamben
Tulamben Marine Reserve

Tulamben

Batu Niti Point

Laba Sari
Amed Area
Purwakerthi
Salt Panning
Datah
Amed
Jemulak
Bunutan
Culik
Keresek Hill
238m
Kertamandala
Lipah

Pura Pasaran Agung

Mt. Agung
2567m

Pidpid
Tista
Bangle
Mount Nampu
729m
Abang
Rice Terraces
Mt. Lempuyang
1065m
Ababi
Pura
Selang
Tirta Gangga
Lempuyang
Mount Seraya
1238m
Seraya Timur
ebudi
Basangalas
Tiyingtali
Duda Utara
Pura Tirta
Bukit
Amlapura
Telaga Tista
Jungutan
Seraya
(Karangasem) Town
Dudaputung
Budakeling
Padangkerta
Tegallinggah
Seraya
da Timur
Bebandem
Sibetan
Amlapura
Tangkuh Hill
623m
Tumbu
Seraya Barat
Bungaya
Karang Asem
Ngis
Subagan
Ujung Water Palace
Selumbung
Ujung
(Taman Sukasada)
Tenganan
Jasri
Salt Panning
Manggis
Tenganan
Pertima
Ujung Beach
Ulakan
Bugbug
Perasi
ang
Song Kidu
Nyuh Tebel
Candidasa
Buiton
Mulu Point
Marine Reserve
Candidasa
Marine
Kuan Island
ntiga
Reserve
Amuk Bay
Marine Reserve
Iti Point
Pura Silayukti
Around Amlapura
angbai
Baong Penyu Point
Marine Reserve
Padangbai Harbour
Lawah
Bungsil Point
(Cave Temple)
Padangbai

Gili Bia/Kambing Island

Lombok Strait

Sukadana Point

INTRODUCTION

Eastern Bali

E astern Bali's allure is its laid-back atmosphere. Far less hectic than the south, its beaches and cultural attractions can also be crowded during the holidays, but when compared to Southern Bali, even at the height of the busiest tourist seasons its aura and people elicit an easygoing pace. Many travelers now elect to spend their entire vacations here, combining snorkeling and diving with countryside sightseeing, as reducing the hours spent travelling means more time for doing what Bali holidays are meant for: chilling out and soaking up the atmosphere. All of the area's most visited sites are reachable in day-trips from Eastern Bali's three beach areas.

Choosing a base camp

Deciding where to stay is strictly a matter of personal preference, as each of the east coast's beach resorts has its own personality.

Padangbai, the closest to the Ngurah Rai airport, has retained a distinctive 1970s "flower child" feel. Most of its accommodations are directly across the street from an azure-watered bay rimmed by a pleasant white beach. With loads of budget inns and open-air cafés from which to choose, the only exception is an eco-friendly luxury villa compound on a hilltop overlooking Blue Lagoon at the west end of the main beach. Snorkeling is good here, with shallow waters in the sheltered lagoon being attractive to beginners and families with children. Dive shops offering PADI courses and excursions abound, most of which are run by foreigners.

The small town's only cultural attractions are three temples, one dating to the 11th century, which attract multitudes of devotees during ceremonial occasions. Padangbai's unique feature is ferry and chartered boat services to Lombok and to Nusa Penida, both of which lure snorkelers and divers.

Further up the coast, **Candidasa** was the favored base camp location of divers in the 1980s and 1990s. Since that time a great development in and around the main town has resulted in renovations to budget

The scenic coastline at Bunutan, near Amed, with Mt. Agung towering in the background

bungalows as well as new intermediate, first class, and luxury accommodations, villas, and dive resorts. Candidasa's plethora of dive centers cater to the majority of visitors, many of whom return every year.

Formerly almost unreachable by all but the foolhardy, the area known as **Amed** is further north, on Bali's northeast coast. The area called "Amed" is actually a very long stretch of beach bordering seven individually-named villages, and it ranges in terrain from dry flatlands where villagers distil salt from seawater to staggering cliffs overlooking a gorgeous bay. Even with a new road leading into the area, village life here is relatively unchanged with the exception of the addition of moderate, intermediate, and a couple of first class-priced accommodations to the few bungalows that have been there for over a decade. Snorkeling in protected bays, diving, and total relaxation in relative isolation are the name of the game here. Amed's wide range of overnight choices also make it attractive to divers who count the *USS Liberty* wreck at nearby Tulamben on their must-do lists.

Area sightseeing

Based in Semarapura town, **Klungkung**—once the most powerful kingdom in Bali—is closest to Padangbai but is easily reached from Candidasa. Overnighters heading for Amed can stop by to see the interesting Kertha Gosa Hall of Justice, Bale Kambang floating pavilion, and a small museum en route. Adjoining Semarapura is **Kamasan** village, an ancient artistic center known for its distinctive painting style and silversmiths. Visitors are welcome to stroll through workshops to see the artists at work, and one even offers courses.

Tenganan, one of Bali's few remaining Bali Aga (traditional) villages, is nearest to Candidasa but is an easy day-trip from Padangbai or can be visited on a stopover to Amed. Like Klungkung, an hour or two is sufficient to stroll through the historic village to observe a way of life that is completely different to that of its neighbors. However, textile and handicrafts lovers may want to allocate more time to watch the artisans at work and to shop.

Amlapura and Tirta Gangga can both be done in one day. The Karangasem palace at **Amlapura** affords an interesting glimpse into the lives of Balinese royalty, with its eclectic blend of European, Chinese, and Balinese

Pura Besakih, on the slopes of holy Mt. Agung, is Bali's largest and most sacred temple complex.

architecture. Also in this area is Taman Sukasada Ujung, a bathing pool complex constructed by the last Karangasem raja, which has been restored after being reduced to a shambles by multiple earthquakes and Mt. Agung eruptions. It is a tranquil place worthy of a leisurely stroll around the massive grounds while imagining how life must have been in days gone by.

The bathing pools at **Tirta Gangga**, 15 km (9 miles) north of Amlapura on the way to Amed, are a totally different experience. Its lush gardens, untouched by natural disasters, are the result of the constant care over the decades by descendants of the Karangasem royal family. The waters here are believed to be holy, and devout Balinese Hindus are often seen bathing or circumnavigating rock paths through the ponds. On a cliff above is a fine restaurant serving international and Indonesian food, making it a good lunch stop. Several treks can be done from here—some easy and others more strenuous—and guides can be hired on-the-spot.

An alternate route from Amlapura to **Pura Besakih**, Bali's "Mother Temple", is particularly scenic, passing through plantations, over mountains, and into valleys studded with verdant green rice fields. The multitude of steps reaching the upper levels of Besakih are steep and the compound can be crowded if rituals are taking place, warranting extra time for a careful inspection of its many shrines and vistas.

From Besakih, the road leads north to the **Kintamani highlands**: Mt. Batur, its crater lake, and Trunyan village, a Bali Aga settlement with a mysterious tomb.

—Linda Hoffman

GIANYAR TOWN

A Palace and a Sacred Banyan Tree

The *bemo* men on the roads from the south yell "*nyar, nyar, nyar*" in loud nasal tones, delighting in stretching the syllable as long as they can. *Nyar* is short for Gianyar, once a center of royal power, priestly learning, and the arts. Today this political and administrative capital has been passed over by the tourist boom, but in one area of creative endeavor it still reigns supreme: **Gianyar** has Bali's best **roast pig,** or *babi guling*. This most exquisite and festive of Balinese dishes can be had in a number of stalls in the market or near the main square, though everyone you ask has their own favorite and will argue its merits against all comers.

Despite the absence of tourists, the town and its surrounding districts are full of places of interest. This can be a good place to get a feel for Balinese history and culture in a non-touristed atmosphere. The heart of

Gianyar is the **Puri Agung Palace**, one of the best preserved of all Bali's royal houses, and home of Anak Agung Gede Agung, heir to the throne of Gianyar, former Foreign Minister, ambassador, and a prominent political leader in the 1940s and '50s.

Unfortunately, the splendors of the palace are not open to casual visitors. But from outside the walls, the majesty of an ornamented observation pavilion overlooking the garden near Gianyar's main crossroads are visible. *Tantri* animal fables are depicted in carvings on the lower part of the outside wall at the crossroads. This palace is also one of the few in Bali to maintain the *waringin*, or **sacred banyan tree**, which was the symbol of Balinese and Javanese courts. Gianyar's still stands in the open town square across from the palace, preserving somewhat the feel of a 19th century royal town.

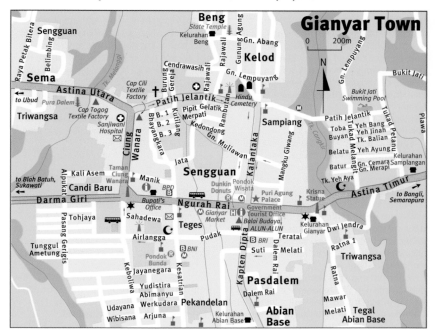

The Gianyar palace was founded in the 18th century, but rebuilt in a more splendid style when the Gianyar dynasty was restored at the end of the 19th. The original palace was said to have been constructed on the site of a priest's house or *griya*. The name "Gianyar" is in fact an abbreviated form of *griya anyar* or "new priest's house."

Just next to the palace is **Pura Langon**, the "Temple of Beauty", which is the major temple for the extended royal family and one of Gianyar's state temples. Further to the west is the **Griya Sidawa**, home of the area's major priestly family and one of Bali's important centers of learning and priestly tradition.

Other state temples are nearby at Beng to the north, and to the south on the coast at Lebih. The temple at **Beng** is for the descendents of Dewa Manggis, who founded the royal line. At **Lebih**, a few miles to the south of Gianyar town, is the **Pura Segara** or "Sea Temple", which is visited in the course of many different festivals that occur throughout Gianyar Regency. The temple is situated where the land meets the sea in sight of the "demon's island", Nusa Penida, and is regarded as a "hot spot", a place where magical forces can be harnessed.

On the road going south from the Gianyar town square to Lebih stands a **Chinese temple**, one of only a handful found on Bali. There is another, smaller temple on the road to the west of Gianyar, just past **Kemenuh** village, hidden below the road in a ravine. Nineteenth century visitors remarked on the strong Chinese presence here, stating that it was once one of the wealthiest states on Bali and a center for trade. The temples recall the strong links that once existed between the trading community and the Gianyar royal family, who were their patrons. When the palace was rebuilt at the end of the 19th century, the Chinese community contributed to the work, and many of the buildings show a Chinese roofing style.

To the west of the town is the adjoining **Bitera** village where, on the southern side of the main road, is the **Pura Dalem** or "death temple" beside a river and beneath a spreading banyan tree. Also on the western side of the town are the main cotton and silk *ikat*-weaving centers. A number of entrepreneurs turned their traditional expertise into an industry that previously thrived; however as with many that depended on foreigners as their major buyers, business fell after the 2002 bombings in Kuta. Their workshops are open to visitors, and income from tourists helps them rebuild. The fine cotton *ikat* produced here is used not only for the traditional *kain sarung* but for interior decoration as well.

Southwest of Gianyar lies the former **Keramas** court center, now known for its dancers, particularly of the operetta *arja*. Keramas is one of Gianyar's many theater and music centers, lesser known only because it is off the tourist path. Keramas was a major power in the area before Gianyar, and its princes are supposedly descended from the great rebel Gusti Agung Maruti, who in the 17th century brought down the Gelgel kingdom. Oddly enough, today Keramas is better known for its world-class surfing beach than for its history.

Keramas is also near another old mini-kingdom, **Blahbatuh**. The rulers of Blahbatuh were descendants of Gusti Ngurah Jelantik, Gelgel's prime minister, known for a military campaign he led against Java in the early 17th century. One of the souvenirs of that expedition was a set of masks which are said to be the prototypes for all Balinese *topeng* dance-drama masks. These are still kept in a temple near the Blahbatuh palace, **Pura Penataran Topeng**. In the 19th and early 20th centuries Blahbatuh was home to some of the greatest court dancing in Bali. **Bona**, between Blahbatuh and Gianyar city, is now known for two of Bali's younger innovative artists, puppeteer I Made Sidia (son of I Made Sija) and musician Gung Alit, as well as its bamboo and rattan industries.

On the eastern side of Gianyar is **Sidan** village, just north of the Bangli intersection. Sidan has an interesting **Pura Dalem** that can be viewed from the road, featuring a series of carvings on the outer tower showing the semi-divine hero Bima fighting with the God of Death.

Near the east coast is the **Bali Safari and Marine Park**, a sister to Taman Safari Indonesia parks on Java. Fun for the whole family includes camel, elephant, and pony rides, themed exhibits for Komodo dragons and white tigers, cultural performances, and animal shows featuring birds, elephants, and orangutans. There's also an amusement park with kids' rides and a water park. New in 2010 was an indoor theater featuring a contemporary theatrical and musical performance that has proved popular.

—*Adrian Vickers*

BANGLI

A Sleepy District Capital

Bangli is a small, sleepy town lying on the border between central and eastern Bali. It seems at first to contain nothing but concrete buildings and empty streets, which only become crowded on market and festival days. But **Bangli** is an old city, which may have been founded as early as A.D. 1204, judging from a stele in important Pura Kehen temple.

The market lies at the center of the town, surrounded by shops. On market days, the stalls spill into the street and customers flock here from the surrounding area to buy produce and manufactured goods. Opposite is the bus station, flanked by a row of shops owned by Chinese and Balinese merchants.

For most Balinese, Bangli is in fact the object of some ridicule; when someone says "I come from Bangli", everyone immediately

bursts into laughter. The reason is that there is a psychiatric hospital here, a pleasantly-situated institution with beautiful grounds that was established by the Dutch.

Physically and socially, the town is dominated by the *puri*, **palaces** of the royal family. The Bangli courts established their independence from Klungkung in the 19th century and played an influential role in Balinese politics through to the post-independence era. Eight royal households are spread around the main crossroads. The most prominent is the Puri Denpasar, the palace of Bangli's last raja. Much of the palace has been restored by his descendants. The royal ancestral temple lies just to the north of the crossroads, on the western side. Huge ceremonies are held here, attended by all descendants of the royal house, including many who live in other parts of Indonesia.

Temple of the hearth

One of Bali's most beautiful temples, **Pura Kehen**, stands at the northeastern boundary of the town, seemingly erected in the midst of the forest long before the town itself. Three copper steles testify to its antiquity and importance. The earliest one, with Sanskrit writing, is dated from the 9th century and mentions the deity Hyang Api (the "God of Fire"). The second is in old Balinese, and the third is in old Javanese, the latter already mentioning Hyang Kehen and indicating eight villages around Bangli that worshipped the deity. The name Kehen is actually a variant of *kuren*, which means "household" or "hearth". The reference to Hyang Api as a symbol of Brahma may mean that there once existed a cult to the god that worshipped him with a rite called *homa*, in which offerings were burned on a small hearth. At some point, it seems that Hyang Api became Hyang Kehen, the "God of the Hearth".

Pura Kehen is the state temple of the old kingdom. It is constructed on a number of levels, after the manner of ancient animistic sanctuaries that are built into the southern slope of a hill, much like Besakih. There are

There are many beautiful rice terraces in the Bangli area.

eight terraces: the first five are *jabaan* or outer courtyards, the sixth and seventh ones are lower and upper middle courts or *jaba tengah*, and the eighth one is the sacred, inner *jeroan*. A flight of 38 stairs adorned with *wayang* statues on either side leads to the main entrance, and a frightening *kala makara* demon guardian is carved on the gateway.

In the outer courtyard stand a huge old banyan tree and a three-tiered pagoda with two *kulkuls* drums inside, as well as a flat stone for offerings. The *kulkuls* represent male and female and were used to signal war in the past. Today, their role is to announce ritual ceremonies. The walls are inlaid with Chinese porcelain, a common feature of ancient temples and palaces. The temple has 43 altars, including one 11-roofed *meru* (pagoda) to Hyang Api. Several are dedicated to the ancestors of *sudra* commoner clans, such as the Ratu Pasek and Pande, which means that worshippers from all over Bali come to pray here, especially on its *odalan*, or anniversary. The huge three-compartment *padmasana* throne in the northeastern corner has beautiful carvings at the back.

Warriors of the mountain

In the Bangli area, various types of ritual *baris* dances have developed that are typical of mountain regions, such as the *baris jojor* (eight men in a line with spears), *baris presi* or *tamiang* (eight men in a circle with leather shields), and *baris dadap* (men in pairs with bat-shaped, curled shields made from holy *dadap* wood). They are performed especially at *odalan*. One of the biggest *gamelan* orchestras in Bali can also be found in the Bangli region. It was captured from the Klungkung dynasty by the Dutch, who gave it to Bangli.

The natural scenery around Bangli is impressive. Cool air and quiet paths lead to breathtaking panoramas. About half a mile west of the town on the road toward Tampaksiring, northwest of Bangli, is a huge ravine with springs and a number of bathing pools and irrigation works sponsored by the former mayor of Bangli. Bathers and visitors must descend a long flight of steps to reach the springs, but the beauty of the spot warrants the effort. This is a favorite meeting spot for flirtatious young locals.

Bukit Demulih, literally the "hill of no return", is located farther west, about an hour's walk from Bangli on the southern side of the road. A small temple stands atop the hill, offering a magnificent vista to the west. On the way, in a landscape of bamboo clusters and farmland, there is a holy waterfall.

To the east of Bangli, there is another lovely road meandering through spectacular rice terraces and across deep ravines. It emerges finally on the main road to Besakih, just near Rendang. This road runs just south of the transitional zone between wet-rice and dry-rice cultivation, which form the two main ecological specializations in Bangli.

— *Agnès Korb & Linda Connor*

SIGHTS OF SEMARAPURA (KLUNGKUNG)

The Palace of Bali's Most Illustrious Kings

S emarapura (formerly called Klungkung town) centers around **Puri Semarapura** or "Palace of the God of Love", former home of Bali's most illustrious line of kings. So great was their power that the Klungkung kings ruled all of Bali, with lesser rajas serving as their advisers. Unfortunately, all that remains now are the great gate and garden, and two pavilions with magnificently painted ceilings overlooking the town's main intersection, one of which is the **Kertha Gosa Hall of Justice** and the larger Bale Kambang (Floating Pavilion) just behind it.

The rest of this splendid complex was razed to the ground in 1908 during the royal mass suicide or *puputan* against the Dutch, removing the last obstacle to their domination of the island. A **monument** commemorating the *puputan* now stands across the road.

Inside Puri Semarapura, Kertha Gosa was a place for the monthly administration of traditional justice in pre-colonial times by a council consisting of the great Klungkung king and his priests, and was also used as a reception hall for visiting dignitaries. Every year on the full moon of the fourth month of the Balinese calendar, regional kings from throughout Bali came here to discuss the needs of the "confederation" of the Kingdom of Bali. After the Dutch defeated Klungkung, Kertha Gosa retained its status as a court of justice. One table and six chairs remain. The king's chair is adorned with a lion symbolizing his position as chief of the court. The chair with the cow image was used by a priest, who served as both lawyer and adviser to the king. A third chair, bearing a dragon, was for the secretary. A Dutch controller (high official) would sometimes attend trials.

The Kamasan *wayang*-style paintings on the ceiling tell of the punishments awaiting evildoers in hell, and of the delights of the gods in heaven. Different levels and stations in heaven and hell are described through the story of the hero Bima, who journeys to the underworld to save the souls of his parents. These scenes were used to alternately threaten and cajole anyone who appeared before the court. Interestingly, one section describes earthquakes and how they can foretell the future.

The elegant Bale Kambang (Floating Pavilion) of Semarapura

Semarapura (Klungkung) Town

Like the Sistine Chapel, the Kertha Gosa presents a whole complex of ideas on the workings of fate and the role of the divine in human affairs. The ceilings themselves have been repainted three times in recent memory. The last complete refurbishment occurred in 1960 under the talented artist Pan Seken, although in 1984, weather damage meant a number of panels had to be repaired.

The **Bale Kambang**, behind Kertha Gosa in the middle of Taman Gili ("garden in a pond"), was originally a smaller, lower structure with fewer pillars, and was the headquarters of the king's guards. The Dutch restored the building, remodeling it into its present form in 1942. The ceiling was painted by Wayan Kayun, and depicts episodes from the story written in 1365 of the Buddhist king Sutasoma, who defeated his enemies through passive resistance. Also portrayed is the story of the commoner Pan Berayut, a coarse man who received great spiritual blessings. Horoscopes are the theme of another section.

Palaces and priestly estates

Members of the royal family who survived the massacre of 1908 were exiled to Lombok. They returned in 1929 and settled in Puri Kaleran to the northwest of the old site on the other side of the street. Originally built 1715–1720, only one part of the old palace remains: when the family returned from Lombok in 1929, the king enclosed it in a new compound, **Puri Agung**. Notable among the last king's heirs was Dalem Pamayun, who became a priest.

Another son, Tjokorde Gde Agung, still lives in Puri Agung and is Klungkung Regency's *bupati* (regent). On October 10, 2010 in an elaborate ceremony attended by royal families from throughout Indonesia, Tjokorde Gde Agung was crowned the new king of Klungkung and was given the title "Ida Dalem Semarputra". A higher rank than "Cokorda" (Tjokorda) or "Anak Agung", "Dalem" can only be used by kings of Klungkung, as they are direct descendants of the Javanese ruler installed as Bali's king by Majapahit's illustrious Prime Minister Gajah Made when he conquered Bali in the 14th century. When Indonesia became a republic in 1945, the reigning sultans and rajas gave up their titles and no new kings have been crowned until recently. The reactivation of royal titles on Bali is seen by some scholars as a strengthening of ethnic identity. Well-traveled, with an excellent command of English, the new king welcomes visitors any time (except at midnight, he quips). Meetings can be arranged through the **Tourist Information Office**, which is located inside the Puri Semarapura compound. Beside the Tourist Information Office is the small **Semarajaya Museum**.

There is a small entrance fee to Puri Semarapura, and visitors are asked to don a sarong, which is provided. Next door is the large, impressive-looking **Bale Budaya**, where cultural and other performances are held. Check schedules on arrival.

To the north of the main crossroads, on the right side, is a set of beautiful and important royal temples, with an ancestral shrine dedicated to the great king of Gelgel, Dalem Seganing. Just next to it is the **Pura Taman Sari**, or Flower Garden Temple, with a moat surrounding a main pagoda. Until today, it remains a sacred place for praying and meditation. In the 19th century, a famous Klungkung warrior queen meditated and wrote poetry here. There are many priestly estates (*griya*) in Klungkung with long histories connected with the royal house. The best-known is **Griya Pidada Klungkung**, once home to the chief priests of the court.

To the east of the city is **Banjar Pande**, the blacksmiths' ward, and the long-established Muslim quarter.

The best time to visit Semarapura is every three days on the Balinese day known as *pasah*, when the **market** is in full swing. Tucked behind a row of shops to the east of Puri Semarapura, although it has lost some of its old atmosphere as a result of being re-housed in a new, multi-storied concrete structure, it offers a full range of local delights, including handmade homewares, baskets, flowers, vegetables, and the like.

For those interested in souvenirs, the row of **art shops** on the main road in front of the market is well-known to antique collectors. The astute old women who own them have been in business since the 1930s, although age is now thinning their ranks. They all complain, however, that nowadays they can only occasionally find the sort of valuable items which used to routinely fill their shops.

West of the town

To the west of Semarapura bordering Gianyar Regency is the fertile district known as

Banjar Angkan, separated from Semarapura by a spectacular ravine. This once served as a buffer zone between the two frequently warring kingdoms, and changed hands many times during the 18th and 19th centuries. Partly as a result, Banjar Angkan has developed its own unique identity quite apart from the rest of the region.

One of the objects of these frequent wars was the important **Pura Kentel Gumi** temple, "the Temple of the Congealing Earth", located on a bend in the main road west of Semarapura. The name of this temple indicates that it was a focal point around which the mystical and political forces of the former kingdoms moved.

Also to the west of Semarapura are the Tihingan and Aan villages. **Tihingan** is best known for its *gamelan* smiths or *pande gong*, who have been famous throughout Bali for centuries. **Aan** is known as the home of a learned high priest, Pedanda Aan, who advises people on the proper procedures for Bali's most important rituals. Between Banjar Angkan and Semarapura lies **Takmung** village, which also has many interesting temples, and is known as a center for the Resi Bhujangga sect, who are priestly worshippers of Wisnu.

Bali's original capital

The old court center **Gelgel** is situated 4 km (2.5 miles) south of Semarapura and actually comprises a number of distinct villages, notably Tojan and Kamasan. The entire area is filled with ancient and legendary sites from Bali's "Golden Age"—the 16th and 17th centuries—and this is the area to which all Balinese nobility and just about everyone else on the island trace their ancestry. The most important site lies at the very heart of Gelgel: the sacred **Pura Jero Agung** or "Great Palace Temple", which stands on the site of the former Gelgel palace. The temple is the ancestral shrine of the old palace, which was abandoned in the 17th century following a rebellion. Adjacent to it is the **Pura Jero Kapal**, all that remains of the second largest palace in Gelgel, that of the Lord of Kapal.

To the east of the Pura Jero Agung is an ancient temple, the **Pura Dasar** or "base temple", the lowland counterpart of Besakih providing a direct connection with the sacred "mother temple" up on Mt Agung.

The festivals held at Pura Dasar are spectacular, as all members of the royal family join in. It is here that the deified ancestors are worshipped. Inside are a number of stones set on a throne carved from rock, archaic symbols of ancestral worship. Nearby is the **Gelgel Mosque**, the oldest on Bali, which was established to serve the spiritual needs of Muslims who came from Java to serve the king in ancient times.

Further to the east of Gelgel is a large complex of graveyards and temples that are cited in the genealogies of many families from throughout Bali. Just north of this is a set of two unusual shrines, the **Pura Dalem Gandamayu**, which was the dwelling of Danghyang Nirartha, Bali's greatest priest and the ancestor of all Siva Brahmans on the island. He established this as a branch of the legendary graveyard of the same name on Java. One of the shrines at Gandamayu is dedicated to the descendants of Nirartha, while the other belongs to the *pande* or black-smith clan.

The present Gandamayu temple was restored in the 1970s after being partially destroyed by the 1963 eruption of Mt. Agung, which devastated the whole area. The adjoining **Tangkas** village was partially wiped out and many lives were lost, but it still maintains some of its famous musical traditions, particularly the ancient and rare ensemble called *gong luang*.

To the south of Tangkas, near the coast, is **Jumpai** village, which is a reputed powerful center for magic. The benevolent *barong* of

Jumpai is famous all over Bali, and there are stories of a powerful magician in the village who meditated and turned aside a lava flow that would have destroyed the village in 1963.

To the south of Gelgel is pleasant **Klotok beach**, an area of great importance in Balinese rituals. Processions to Bali's Besakih mother temple all pay a visit to Klotok to ritually bless their offerings.

Home of traditional Balinese painting

The adjoining village of **Kamasan** is a major artistic center, home of silversmiths and traditional Balinese painting. The many forms of painting found today in Bali all derive from the Kamasan or *wayang* style characteristic of this village, in which the figures depicted resemble two-dimensional shadow puppets. The style itself traces back to ancient Java, where similar figures are found on temple reliefs. The amazing thing is that this survives as a living art up until the present day on Bali.

Painters from Kamasan were once sent all over the island in the service of their royal patrons. The painters' ward is Banjar Sangging, but other parts of the village are known for their crafts as well. Nearby is Banjar Pande Mas, where gold and silversmiths work. The village also once provided dancers, musicians, and puppeteers to the court. Most of these activities have declined in recent years, but in the past they contributed to a lively creative atmosphere, providing inspiration for local painters.

A painting in the traditional Kamasan style

The presence of *dalang*, or puppeteers, in the village was particularly important. The iconography of the two art forms is the same, as are the stories depicted, great epics like the *Ramayana* and the *Mahabharata*. Scenes portrayed in the flickering shadows of the *wayang* are rendered in red, indigo, and ocher, arranged to show the workings of natural and supernatural forces.

Kamasan's foremost artist today is the relatively young Nyoman Mandra (b. 1946), whose work best captures the refinement of the tradition. Mandra heads up a government-sponsored school devoted to ensuring that village children will continue their 500-year-old traditions. Visitors to the school can see how beginners are trained.

In addition to Nyoman Mandra there are many other practicing artists here, such as Ibu Suciarmi, who continues the tradition of female painters in what was previously an all-male profession. Artists at Nyoman Mandra's studio and workshop, where there is a small exhibit of the materials and tools used for Kamasan paintings—surprisingly captioned in English as well as Indonesian—are happy to let visitors watch them work.

Since Kamasan is off the tourist track it is refreshingly free of art shops. Visitors can visit the homes and studios of the artists, where their crafts are also sold. Don't be put off by the initial hustle of sellers on the street; it is difficult for these artists to make a living. One compensation for the buyer is that any money spent goes directly to the artists and is not lost on middlemen.

To the magical east

From Kamasan, there is a good road to the east coast highway. Turn north to go to Klotok beach, Goa Lawah bat cave temple (10 km/6 miles), and to Candidasa via Padangbai. South will take you back to Denpasar (39 km /24 miles). Alternatively, go north through Semarapura to reach Besakih temple (22 km /13 miles) and the hinterland of eastern Bali.

Moving southeast from Semarapura along the main road toward the east coast highway, on the other side of the Unda River are a number of interesting villages, including Paksabali, Satria, and Sampalan.

Paksabali is renowned for its Dewa Mapalu or Pasraman Dewa festival, the dramatic "clashing" or "meeting of the gods". This is held during the annual Kuningan festival, when idols are borne from the temple aboard palanquins down a steep ravine to the Unda River to be ritually bathed and given offerings. As the palanquin bearers proceed back up to the temple gates, they are possessed by the gods they are carrying and race madly in circles, colliding against each other in an effort to get back into the temple compound.

The adjoining village of **Sampalan** is the home of one of Bali's foremost traditional architects, Mangku Putu Cedet, who is a builder of fabulous cremation towers and traditional houses. He is thoroughly steeped in the arts of healing and white magic as well. When the Klungkung royal family holds major ceremonies, it is he who is asked to perform a ritual to prevent it from raining.

An important village further to the east is **Dawan**, home of one of Bali's most famous high priests, Pedanda Gede Keniten. He is directly descended from the Gelgel court priest and is in great demand for major rituals. Adjoining Dawan is Besang village, known for its main temple, which has an ancient inscription under a giant pagoda. The Dawan area, situated among small hills, is another "hot spot" or center of natural and mystical power on Bali.

The main road meets the east coast highway at **Kusamba**, a fishing village with a dramatic black sand beach. For several decades in the late 18th century, the Klungkung palace was inhabited by a mad king, Dewa Agung Sakti, and Kusamba was the headquarters of his son and rival. At this time Kusamba was an important port; like Kamasan and Klungkung it was a center for blacksmith clans, whose skill in the manufacture of weapons was of crucial importance to any ruler. In 1849, when the Dutch conquered northern and eastern Bali, Kusamba was the site of a major battle in which a Dutch general was killed by order of the "virgin queen", Dewa Agung Isteri Kanya.

Not far beyond Kusamba is the unusual **Goa Lawah** bat cave temple, one of the state temples of Klungkung Regency. Legend has it that when Klungkung was ruled from Kusamba, a Mengwi prince sought protection here and entered the bat cave. He was not seen again until he emerged nearly 20 km (12 miles) to the north at Pura Besakih. It is rumored that no one has since tried to prove whether the cave really extends that far; the strong odor of bat droppings is no doubt a major deterrent.

—Adrian Vickers

Bali's Lofty "Mother Temple"

Driving up to Besakih from Menanga, Mt. Agung's silver-gray cone looms above, its summit still bare from the ravages of the 1963 eruption. At 3,142 m (10,308 ft), this is the highest peak on Bali, and a major focus of divine power in the Balinese cosmos. The huge temple located here, **Pura Besakih**, is the greatest of all Balinese sanctuaries, the most sacred and powerful of the island's innumerable temples. For this reason, it has always been associated with state power. It lies at an altitude of 900 m (2,950 ft) on the southwestern slope of the mountain, offering spectacular views over the whole of southern Bali.

Pura Besakih is not a single temple but a sprawling complex consisting of many separate shrines and compounds, united through ritual and history into a single sanctuary. There are 22 temples in all, spread along parallel ridges over a distance of almost 1.6 km (1 mile). The highest of these, Pura Pengubengan, lies amidst beautiful groves in a state pine forest. Most of

Pura Besakih, with sacred Mt. Agung behind

the temples, however, cluster around the main enclosure, Pura Penataran Agung.

In this same area there are many ancestral temples (*pura padharman*) supported by individual clans. Four public temples also form a distinct sub-group (*catur lawa* or *catur warga*) and are associated with certain kin groups. Local Besakih village extended families also have temples here.

Besakih is busy almost every day. Balinese often come in order to obtain holy water for ceremonies back in their home villages as a symbol of the presence of the god of Gunung Agung/Pura Besakih, which is required for most major rituals. They also come to Besakih at the end of the long series of funeral rites, after the post-cremation purification of the soul has taken place, to ready the soul for enshrinement in the family house temple. In all cases, the worshipper is sure to pay reverence at the triple lotus shrine of the Pura Penataran Agung.

The symbolic center

Pura Penataran Agung, the "Great State Temple", is the symbolic center of the Besakih complex. Originating probably as a single prehistoric shrine, its six terraces suggest a history of successive enlargements, the latest being in 1962. In all, there are 57 structures in the temple, about half of which are devoted to various deities. A study of these provides a glimpse of important developments in the temple's history.

The *meru* or pagodas were probably introduced no earlier than the 14th century, whereas the lotus throne (*padmasana*) dates from about the 17th or even 18th century. With the introduction of the *padmasana*, the ritual focus of the temple seems to have shifted from the upper terraces to the second lower terrace. The *padmasana* is now the ritual center of Pura Penataran Agung and of the Besakih complex as a whole.

The three seats in the lotus throne are dedicated to the godhead in his tripartite form as Siva, Sadasiwa, and Paramasiwa or,

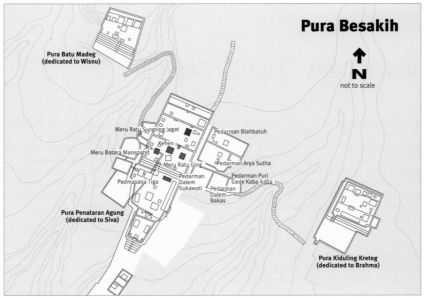

Diagram of temple

more commonly in the popular tradition, to Brahma (right), Siva (center), and Wisnu (left). These deities are associated with the colors red, white and black respectively. Behind the *padmasana* lies the Bale Pasamuhan Agung, where the gods of the Besakih temples take residence during major rituals.

Of all the present structures in the temple, only one or two predate the great earthquake of 1917. Although visitors are normally not allowed inside the main courtyard, there are several vantage points from where they can get good views of the shrines.

Temple categories

A dual structure underlies the Besakih sanctuary as a whole, through a division of the sacred areas into two parts. Pura Penataran Agung is the main temple "above the steps". Its counterpart "below the steps" is Pura Dalem Puri, the "Temple of Palace Ancestors". This small but very important temple, associated with an early dynasty of the 12th century, is dedicated to the goddess identified as Batari Durga, goddess of death and of the graveyard, as well as of magic power.

The Brahma, Wisnu, and Siva holy trinity is the basis of a three-part grouping that links the three largest temples. Pura Penataran Agung, the central temple, honors Siva; **Pura Kiduling Kreteg** ("Temple South of the Bridge") honors Brahma, and **Pura Batu Madeg** ("Temple of the Standing Stone") honors Wisnu. On festival days, banners and hangings in their colors represent these deities. Pura Batu Madeg in particular has a fine row of *meru*.

A five-way grouping links these three temples with two others, each being associated with a cardinal direction and a color. Pura Penataran Agung is at the center. Surrounding it are Pura Gelap (east/white), Pura Kiduling Kreteg (south/red), Pura Ulun Kulkul (west/yellow) and Pura Batu Madeg (north/black). This five-way classification, the *panca dewata*, is extremely important in Balinese Hinduism. At Besakih, however, it seems to have been a relatively late development, as it is not mentioned in Besakih's sacred charter, the *Raja Purana*, which probably dates from the 18th century.

The gods descend

The unity of the complex's 22 public temples becomes manifest, above all, in Besakih's great annual festival, the Bhatara Turun Kabeh or "Gods Descend Together" rite, which falls on the full moon of the tenth lunar month (*purnama kadasa*). During this month-long festival, the gods of all temples on Bali take up residence in the main shrine at Besakih. Tens of thousands of people from all over the island come to worship at the triple lotus throne, and solemn rituals are conducted by *brahmana* high priests.

In terms of numbers of worshippers, the annual ritual at Pura Dalem Puri is also quite remarkable. Within the 24-hour period of this festival, soon after the new moon of the seventh lunar month, vast crowds pay homage here, presenting special offerings with which to insure the wellbeing of family members whose death rites were completed the previous year.

But these great rituals are only the most important out of a total of more than 70 held regularly at the different temples and shrines at Besakih. Nearly every shrine in Pura Penataran Agung, for instance, has its own anniversary, almost all of which are fixed according to the indigenous Balinese *wuku* calendar. The most important festivals, however, follow the lunar calendar. These include rituals conducted by *brahmana* priests at four of the five main temples, and also a series of agricultural rites culminating in two of Besakih's most interesting ceremonies—the Usaba Buluh and Usaba Ngeed—which center around the **Pura Banua** dedicated to Bhatari Sri, goddess of rice and prosperity. With the exception of these *brahmana* rituals, most ceremonies at Besakih are conducted by Besakih's own *pemangku* (priests).

State and temple

The performance of rituals and the physical maintenance of the temples demand considerable resources, and throughout the temple's history these have been at least partly provided by the state. During pre-colonial times, the relationship between state and temple was expressed in a largely Hindu idiom of religion and statecraft, but in the course of the 20th century this changed to one couched in legal and constitutional terms.

Besakih's earliest history consists of legendary accounts that associate the temple with the great priests of the Hindu traditions on Bali, beginning with Rsi Markandeya. In the 15th century two ancient edicts inscribed on wood, now regarded as god-symbols of one of Pura Penataran Agung's important deities, indicate heavy state involvement.

The Gelgel and Klungkung dynasties (15th to early 20th centuries) regarded Pura Besakih as the chief temple of the realm, and deified Gelgel rulers are enshrined in a separate temple here, called **Padharman Dalem**.

Through the turmoil and shifting politics of the 19th century, which saw the rise of Dutch power on the island, the temple was seriously neglected. The great earthquake of 1917 completed its destruction, but at the same time galvanized the Balinese, who then rebuilt it with Dutch assistance. Control was maintained by the princely houses, which were responsible for rituals and maintenance. After independence, Bali's regional government took over responsibility. Only in recent years has the Hindu community itself taken on a greater share of the burden involved in the temple's upkeep.

Cosmic rites of purification

The involvement of the Balinese with Pura Besakih is at no time more in evidence than during the great purificatory rites known as Panca Walikrama and Eka Dasa Rudra. Ideally, these are held every 10 and 100 years respectively, but in practice they have been irregular. The Panca Walikrama was held in 1933, 1960, 1978, 1989, and most recently in 2009.

The Eka Dasa Rudra, greatest of all rituals known in Balinese Hinduism, is an enormous purification rite directed to the entire cosmos, represented by the 11 (*eka dasa*) directions. Rudra is a wrathful form of Siva, who is to be propitiated. It has been held twice this century: once in 1963, and again in 1979. The Eka Dasa Rudra of 1963, held at a time of great political tensions, was an extraordinary catastrophe, for right in the midst of the month-long festival Mt. Agung erupted with violent destructive force for the first time in living memory. Such a strange coincidence prompted various interpretations, the most common being that the mountain's deity was angry, perhaps over the ritual's timing.

According to certain sacred texts, the rite should be held when the Saka year ends in two zeros. Such was the case in 1979 (Saka 1900), and it was decided to hold the Eka Dasa Rudra once again. The mountain remained calm and hundreds of thousands attended the main day of celebration, including then-President Suharto. This marked Besakih's new-found status as the paramount Hindu sanctuary not only for Bali, but for all of Indonesia.

—*David Stuart-Fox*

PADANGBAI AND CANDIDASA

Bali's Eastern Beach Resorts

Candidasa is a beach resort located on Bali's southeastern black sand coast. Its biggest competition as a base for explorations of the area is Amed, further north on the east coast. Both are quieter alternatives to the southern tourist centers.

Following the main road east from Semparapura, the highway crosses the border into Karangasem Regency shortly after Kusamba village, and further north past Goa Lawah bat cave temple. Continuing eastward through coconut groves for several miles before reaching a turn-off; turn right to go to **Padangbai**, a major harbor for ferries and ships to Lombok and points east, as well as for smaller boats to Nusa Penida. It is worth the 2 km (1.2 miles) detour to see its picturesque, semi-circular hills surrounding a sparkling blue bay.

Padangbai

The village itself has many small hotels and restaurants; if you're looking to drop out for a few days and just hang by the beach, this is the place to do it. Padangbai's **Pura Silayukti** temple, where the Buddhist sage Mpu Kuturan is said to have lived in the 11th century, is also located here. Over 1,000 years

old and one of the four oldest temples on Bali, every six months a ceremony is held at Pura Silayukti that attracts more than a thousand devotees per day. Pura Tanjungsasi and Pura Telagamas are the village's other two temples, and each conducts its own rituals.

Padangbai has three **beaches**. The main beach, where the ferries and boats are anchored offshore, is not great for snorkeling, but the road is lined with accommodations and eateries, money changers and ticket booths, and practically everything else a traveler could need. While Bias Tugel is a white sand beach and good for sunbathing, the most popular is a small black sand beach called Blue Lagoon, which is excellent for snorkeling. There are also many dive shops in the town that will happily arrange expeditions to rocky outcroppings further out.

Back on the main road, continue to Manggis village a few kilometers to the east. There is a lovely path from here leading up to nearby **Putung** in the hills overlooking the coast. The path runs through woods and gardens and reaches Putung after a distance of some 5 km (3 miles), where there is a splendid view across the sea to the nearby islands. Another possible side trip is from

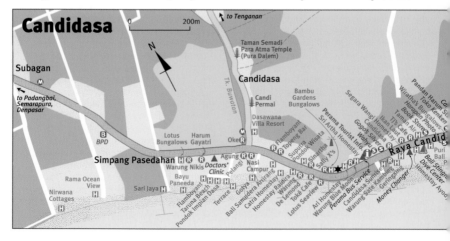

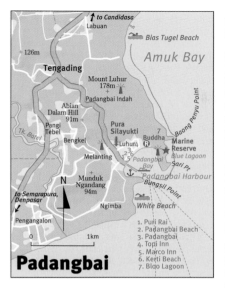

Padangbai

1. Puri Rai
2. Padangbai Beach
3. Padangbai
4. Topi Inn
5. Marco Inn
6. Kerti Beach
7. Blao Lagoon

mainly worshipped by childless parents who pray for fertility.

Toward the end of the 1970s the first bungalows appeared by the beach. From 1982 onwards a building frenzy set in; new hotels, shops, and restaurants seem to open almost weekly. Today's Candidasa and the surrounding area is more mature: a bustling seaside resort with the full range of hotels ranging from five-star properties to homestays, with moneychangers, shops, and restaurants. The main attraction of the area is as a base from which to visit neighboring Tenganan village, some 5 km (3 miles) away and further inland in east Bali, swimming (at high tide), snorkeling, and diving. Candidasa enjoys cool breezes and is a good resting point for trips to the east and north.

Bugbug and environs

Four kilometers (2.4 miles) to the east of Candidasa lies Bugbug, a sizeable rice-growing and fishing village that is the administrative center for the sub-district. Along the way, the road climbs the unexpectedly steep **Gumang Hill**. There is a beautiful panorama of the sea from the top, the Buhu River, rice fields, and Bugbug, with Lempuyang and Seraya mountains in the distance. On a very clear day Mt. Rinjani on Lombok is visible from here.

Bugbug and the surrounding villages are quite old-fashioned. Apart from the official village head, there is a council of elders responsible for all religious affairs. The elders are not elected, but enter the council on the basis of seniority. Another atypical feature of

Manggis east along a small road through isolated Ngis and Selumbung villages. The road finally rejoins the main highway in Sengkidu shortly before Candidasa. It is also possible to continue from Ngis on to Tenganan.

Candidasa town

Continuing east another 7 km (4.3 miles) past Ulakan and Sengkidu villages, the main road enters **Candidasa** just after the Tenganan turn-off. The name was originally applied just to two small temples, one for Siva and the other for Hariti, which overlook a beautiful palm-fringed lagoon by the beach. Hariti is

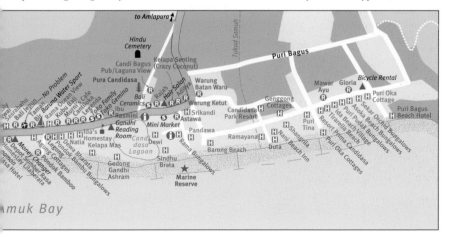

these villages is communal land tenure, and the presence of associations for unmarried boys and girls, which must fulfill duties in the context of village rituals.

Two rituals are especially important. The first takes place around the full moon of the first Balinese month. This ritual worship of the village gods is carried out in the central temple (*pura desa*), and lasts for several days. Most spectacular are the dances by unmarried boys (*abuang taruna*) clad in costumes of white and gold-threaded cloth, with headdresses and *keris*.

After the dance there follows the *daratan* ritual, in which older men in a trance carrying *keris* approach the main shrine of the temple to the accompaniment of special music. Three orchestras play simultaneously: the sacred *selunding* (iron metallophones), the gong *desa* with drums and cymbals, and a *gambang* ensemble which has bamboo xylophones and bronze metallophones.

During the same full moon period there are similar rituals in other nearby villages, such as Asak and Perasi. **Perasi** lies just east of Bugbug on the main road, and from its eastern end there is a nice walk through the hills to the beach. Swimming here is hazardous, since the beach is not protected by a reef.

A second major ritual occurs in Bugbug every two years on the full moon of the fourth month. Four villages (Bugbug, Jasri—also spelled Jasi—Bebandem and Ngis) participate in a ritual "war of the gods", which is in fact the enactment of an old legend.

The god of Bugbug had three daughters and one son. One of the daughters was to marry the god of Bebandem but she eloped with the god of Jasi. To appease the former, the god of Bugbug gave his second daughter and son to him, and the third daughter was married off to the god of Ngis. The war is to resolve the dispute, and the ritual battle takes place near the temple on top of Gumang Hill.

At Jasi there's an unspoiled beach, reachable by taking a rough road. Turn at the hand-painted sign on the right (going north) that says "White Sand Beach". The crystal clear water is ideal for snorkeling and swimming. Eateries there rent lounge chairs, offer outrigger rides, and provide massages. Activity prices arranged through the *warungs* are negotiable if you buy lunch there, too.

—*Danker Schaareman*

Waves roll over a dramatic black sand beach near Padangbai.

VISITING PADANGBAI, CANDIDASA & SURROUNDS (INCLUDES MANGGIS, SENGKIDU & JASRI)

(TELEPHONE CODE: 0363)

In addition to simply being a great place to drop out for a while, water sports lovers come to Bali's east coast beaches for snorkeling and diving. Padangbai and Candidasa are only two of the underwater wonderlands, with Amed, Tulamben, and Kubu/Seraya also ranking as top destinations for snorkelers and divers who delight in pristine reefs, drift dives, drop-offs, and the latest sensation, muck diving in the shallows for some of the world's most unusual sealife.

PADANGBAI

Upon arrival at Padangbai beach, don't be put off by the busy pier. Padangbai hides great coves and dive spots behind its hills. Quiet Bias Tugel lies behind a small hill to the west, while Padang Kurungan, or Blue Lagoon, lies to the north, nearer to the town center. Rows of colorful outriggers are lined up on the sandy beach, east of the pier.

TOURIST INFORMATION

Tourist information as well as tour and transportation ticketing (including shuttle buses to Ubud) are available at every accommodation and at kiosks along the main road.

GETTING THERE & GETTING AROUND

Padangbai, about 31 km (19 miles) from Denpasar, is a main departure point for Lombok and other islands to the east. Several ferries leave the harbor for Lombok every 1.5 hours, 24/7. Most popular is **Suranadi Express**. Prices are determined by type of ferry and class of service (about $3 for adults; $2 for kids), and tickets are purchased at the ferry terminal next to the huge parking lot, which is surrounded by a large, ugly fence to protect the town from queues of waiting vehicles. Note that there are two types of ferries: regular and high-speed. For safety reasons, it is advisable to have a look at all boats and ferries before buying tickets, as the waves in the area can be dangerous in certain seasons. Travelers can buy insurance at the harbor ticket office.

To go to **Lombok** and its **Gili islands**, the **Gilicat** is Australian-built to international standards, with fully accredited captains and engineers, state-of-the-art safety equipment; capacity 30, cruising at 30 knots. Departs Padangbai daily at 9 am, Gili Trawangan (Lombok) 8 am, and Teluk Kodak (Lombok) 8:20 am. There's a Gilicat kiosk on the main beach, or to book in advance, the head office is at Jl. Danau Tamblingan No. 51, Sanur, tel: (0361) 271-680, www.gilicat.com.

There are **private boats** to Nusa Penida for its temple, beach, cave, and waterfall and to Nusa Lembongan, popular with snorkelers and divers, available for charter departing from the beach just east of the big ferry terminal. Prices—determined by the size of the engine (up to 600 hp)—are negotiated on the spot (around $10). There's also a **public boat** to Nusa Penida ($3 per person), which is scheduled to leave at 9 am, but note that it won't depart until the boat is full.

The best way to explore the area's back roads is by car, motorbike, or bicycle, all of which can arranged through your accommodation. **Motorbikes** with manual or automatic gears go for about $10 for 12 hours; bargain for a lower rate for longer rentals. **Cars** with drivers for day trips run $3–10, depending on destination and type of vehicle.

ACCOMMODATIONS

There are many inexpensive places to stay just across the street from the main beach and a few further afield. There is also one place that's a step up from "Budget", and luxury privately-owned villas for rent up on the hill overlooking Blue Lagoon bay. All prices include breakfast.

Budget (under $25)

Dharma Homestay, Jl. Silayukti, Gang Tongkol 06, 50 m (150 ft) from the beach, tel: 41394. Nice upstairs rooms with AC or fan. Hot water. $8

Kembar Inn, Jl. Segara 6, tel: 41364. A cozy little inn on a side street. AC and fan rooms; hot water. Can arrange tours, transport, rental car, motorbike, diving, snorkeling, ticketing, trekking. $5.

Made Homestay, on the main beach, tel: 41441. A 2-story building with 8 rooms, all cold water. Café. $5.

Marco Inn, on the main street, mobile: 081-2466-0996. Budget rooms with sea views, roof terrace, yoga, Reiki, cold beer.

Padangbai Beach Homestay, on the main beach, mobile: 081-236-07946. Old and newer rooms with cold water. Nice gardens.

Pantai Ayu, on the hillside with beautiful bay views, tel: 41396. 10 rooms, some with hot water. Good café serves Indonesian and Western food. Can arrange tours. $5.

Parta Inn, downtown, tel: 41475. A 2-story building with choice of cold water and fan or hot water with AC rooms. The top room has the best views. $15.

Pondok Wisata Serangan I & II. Serangan I is located behind the *wartel* downtown; Serangan II is 300 m

(320 yds) back from the beach on Jl. Silayukti, tel: 41425. Budget accommodations with clean rooms, cold water, fan. $6

Puri Rai Hotel, Jl. Silayukti No. 7X, tel: 41385, www. baligotours.com. The only hotel in town (except the villas) with a swimming pool.

Topi Inn, Jl. Silayukti 99, at the end of the main street, tel: 41424, www.topiinn.nl. 3-story natural-style building with 5 budget rooms on the second floor and a dormitory on the top floor, sleeping 12. Asian toilets, cold water. Good café serves cappuccino, Internet, refills water bottles $1. Very cheap.

Moderate ($25–50)

Kerti Beach Inn, Jl. Silayukti, tel: 361 0840, www. kertibeach-inn.com. AC bungalows with a unique style located in the middle of the main beach. Comfortable. $31–36.

Zen Inn & Happy Resort & Le48 Restaurant, Jl. Raya Candidasa 48, mobile: 081-855-9307, www.zeninn. com. Located behind the ferry port, only 1 minute walk from the main beach. Rooms furnished in a funky, eclectic style, all with double beds, Western bathrooms, outside shower, and private garden.

Luxury ($100–up)

Bloo Lagoon Sustainable Village, on the cliffs above Blue Lagoon Beach, tel: 41211, mobile: 0817-474-5751. www.bloolagoon.com. For rental: 25 beautiful individually-owned ocean view villas with kitchens that share facilities and staff, lap pool, restaurant, lounge/library, spa, amphitheater, open-air deck pavilion suitable for yoga and other activities. Energy-saving technologies (composting, organic gardening, water recycling) employed. From $120 for 1-bedroom villa to $170 for 3-bedroom villa, including breakfast. High season (July 1–Aug 31 and Dec 20–Jan 5) surcharge $20 per room per night.

DINING

On Padangbai's main road is a plethora of eating establishments. Most serve seafood and simple Indonesian fare but a few have some international alternatives. Best advice is to walk down the street, peer in, have a look at their menu signboards, and chose the one that tickles your fancy.

Depot Segara, tel: 41443. Sandwiches, burgers, and yogurt drinks, also Balinese and fresh seafood. Try the fish satay, a specialty of eastern Bali.

Grand Café, on the main street, tel: 434-5043. Indonesian and Western food, including pizzas. Information about ferries and fast boats.

Le48 Restaurant, tel: 41177, mobile: 812 36 497 848, www.le48balic.om, has a well-stocked bar and serves Western and Asian food using the freshest local ingredients. Fan rooms from $15; AC rooms from $25.

Omang Omang Café, mobile: 081-23-38052, www. omangcafe.com. One of the few more upscale cafes in town, serves Western and Indonesian food. Has live music and dancing several nights a week.

Ozone, west from the cemetery, tel: 41501. Sandwiches, seafood, and pizza.

NIGHTLIFE

There are a couple of good places to hang out at night and hear tales from other travelers. Try **Babylon Bar**, open late, or **Joe's Bar**, on the main street next to Grand Café.

DIVING

At Blue Lagoon beach, shallow waters make excellent snorkeling for all ages. For divers, the white sand beach bottom slopes gradually to 22 m (70 ft), has scattered rocks, soft and staghorn coral, and a huge array of fish life: sea horses, turtles, moray eels, rays, and octopi. Easy diving and great for night dives. Watch out for stonefish. There are many dive shops in town, and all are foreign-owned except two.

Absolute Scuba, Jl. Panti Silayukti, tel: 42088, www.bali-dive.com. Tailor-made diving and accommodations. Prices range from $50/Blue Lagoon/2 dives; $70/Tulamben/2 dives; $75/Tepekong/Mimpang/2 dives; $80/Amed or Gili Biaha/2 dives; and $85/Nusa Penida/2 dives. Further out: $95/Crystal Bay/2 dives; and $115/Manta Point/2 dives.

Blue Lagoon Divers, Jl. Silayukti, on the beach just in front of the pier, mobile: 081-2361-9139; www. bluelagoondivers.com. Locally owned, safety and service is their motto. PADI dive courses; daily dive trips. Prices include $30/single dive, $35/night dive; $60/Padangbai, Gili Tepekong/Mimpang/Biaha, Tulamben/Kubu; $65/Amed; and from $75/Nusa Penida or Lembongan.

Geko Dive Bali, Jl. Silayukti, tel:/fax: 41516, www. gekodive.com. Full PADI courses, daily dive trips. $60/Introductory Dive, 1 half-day dive; $75/Discover Scuba Diving, 1 confined session plus 1 day dive; $400/PADI Open Water Course, 4 dives, 4 days; and $325/PADI Advanced Open Water Course, 5 dives, 2 days.

OK Dive Center, Jl. Silayukti, tel: 41790, mobile: 0811-385-8826, 0811-3858-823, www.divingbali.cz. Daily manta ray dives by the best dive boat in Padangbai. PADI dive courses $300 by European instructors in many languages.

Paradise Diving, Jl. Silayukti 9B, tel: 742-5801, mobile: 0811-393-515, www.divingbali.de, Deutsche Tauchschule. Scuba Diving $35; PADI Open Water Diver $180.

CANDIDASA

Candidasa is a good place to escape the bustle of southern Bali. Accommodations are good and relatively cheap, as is the food. There are few beach vendors, and aggressive hawkers are rare. Although the town has tripled in size in recent years, the surrounding area is still serene and very quiet. Everything is oriented along the main street that parallels the beach.

TOURIST INFORMATION

There's a Tourist Information Office on the main road across from the police station run by the PHRI (Indonesia Hotel & Restaurant Association), but don't expect it to be open on weekends or public holidays. Your accommodation is your best source of information.

GETTING THERE & GETTING AROUND

Candidasa is abour 45 km (28 miles) from Denpasar. Public *bemos* operate between Batubulan (Central Bali), Candidasa, and Semarapura (Klungkung) for a nominal fee. There are also direct shuttle buses from Kuta. Consult with ticketing area near your accommodation for schedules and prices.

The best way to explore the area's back roads is by car, motorbike, or bicycle, all of which can be rented at several outlets in Candidasa. **Motorbikes** with manual or automatic gears go for about $10 for 12 hours; bargain for a lower rate for longer rentals. **Cars** with drivers for day trips run $3–10, depending on destination and type of vehicle. These are easily arranged with the staff at your accommodation.

ACCOMMODATIONS

The Candidasa area has all types of accommodations, from simple bamboo cubicles at $5/night to the exclusive $2,900/night Amankila villas. There is little difference between bungalows going for $10 and $20, apart from the distance to the beach, the landscaping, and the bathrooms.

Depending on the place, prices may be 10–30 precent cheaper in low season or whenever there are fewer visitors. Most places offer discounts for stays of more than a week. Talk to the management upon arrival. Water sports, tours, treks, and transportation rentals are readily arranged at all places.

Many foreigners are currently investing in Bali real estate, and Candidasa is no exception. The listing below includes several privately-owned villas that are for rent.

Budget (Under $25)

Agung Cottages, Jl. Raya Candidasa, near the beach, tel: 41535. 16 bamboo cottages surrounded by tropical gardens, each with a verandah. Room furnishings are basic but clean. Fan rooms with hot water. $15, including breakfast.

Amartha Beach Inn Bungalows, Senkidu beach, Candidasa, tel: 41230. 10 bungalow-style rooms with fan, bathtub, outdoor shower, some with hot water. Restaurant serves Western and French food. Bar serves cocktails. From $21.

Anom Beach Inn Hotel, Sengkidu beach, Candidasa, mobile: 081-2391-4438, fax: (0361) 742-6261. A 2-star holel; comfortable guest rooms. From $22.

Dasa Wana Resort, Jl. Raya Candidasa, tel: 41444, www.dasawana.nl. Not directly on the beach but surrounded by forest and gardens. 4 superior rooms, 4 bungalows, all with verandah, small kitchen and fridge, tv, AC. Has a good restaurant, swimming pool. From $20.

Iguana Bungalows, Candidasa Beach, tel: 41973. AC and fan rooms with hot water shower or bathtub in some rooms. Swimming pool with ocean view. Restaurant. $20–30.

Kelapa Mas Homestay, Candidasa Beach, tel: 41369, fax: 41947, www.welcometokelapamas.com. A relaxing hideaway with grounds filled with coconut palms and gardens. Bamboo cottages with verandahs; some have views; others have hot water and AC. Offers friendly and efficient service in beautiful surroundings. Library, Gemini Shop, snorkeling, fishing, motorbike rental, car rental, tours, laundry, massage. $18–30.

Pandan Bungalows, Jl. Raya Candidasa, tel: 41541. 10 bamboo bungalows, each with a private terrace and garden. Open-air bathroom with bathtub, Ceiling fans, some with AC. Bar and restaurant. $23–34.

Puri Bali Bungalows, Jl. Raya Candidasa, mobile: 081-2391-4438, fax: (0361) 742-6261. Bungalows with king-size bed, kitchenette, fan, shower, bathtub, and mini-fridge. Panoramic view of the ocean's waves. $23–30.

Puri Pundak Bungalows, tel: 41978. 17 rooms in the banana groves east of town near the homes of local fisherman. Large bamboo rooms, Western bathrooms, some with bathtubs; some nice new 2-story bungalows right on the beach. Overlooks the bay. Good value. $15/ standard fan rooms, some with hot water.

Temple Café & Seaside Cottages, Jl. Raya Candidasa, tel: 41629, www.balibeach front-cottages.com. Beachfront cottages with AC and hot water, as well as budget cottages. Restaurant offers wholesome home-style Western and Indonesian food. $10–35.

Moderate ($25–50)

Bungalows are usually medium-size with verandahs and electricity. Higher-priced units include fan and reading lamp, sometimes AC. No room phones. Restaurant often attached to the hotel. Breakfast always included. The following are highly recommended.

Aquaria Waterside Apartments, Jl. Puri Bagus, Desa Samuh, tel: 41127, mobile: 081-7978-9574, www.aquariabali.com. A calm oasis by the sea. Newly renovated spacious, airy apartments using feng shui principles with clean architectural lines and cool colors, oversized terraces, sea or pool views, all on one level. Intimate restaurant, ionized water pool, refreshment for the soul. AC and fan rooms, apartments, villa. $40–150.

Fajar Candidasa Beach Bungalows, Jl. Raya Candidasa, tel: 41538, 41539, fax: 41538, www.fajarcandidasa.com. Traditional Balinese architecture combined with modern conveniences. Fan or AC bungalows, hot water. From $32.

Ida's Homestay, Jl. Raya Candidasa, tel: 41096. 6 rooms east of the town in a lovely setting on the beach. Private 2-story thatched bungalows in a large, grassy coconut grove. 2-story houses have upstairs bedrooms and wide ocean views. Beautiful open-air bathrooms. Carved furniture in some rooms. No hot water. $30.

Nirwana Cottage Resort & Spa, Jl. Raya Candidasa, tel: 41136, fax: 41543, www.thenirwana.com. 12 rooms in a small hotel with thatched roof bungalows surrounded by coconut trees and garden. Some fridges. Clean and quiet. Poolside restaurant. $30–$60.

Pondok Bambu Seaside Bungalows, Jl. Raya Candidasa, tel: 41534, fax: 41818, www.pondokbambu.com. A happy, tropical resort, all rooms have AC, fan, tv, mini-fridge, and bathroom. Terrace restaurant's kitchen has been upgraded to meet European standards. Tap water is drinkable, as the resort has its own water purification system. Seaside swimming pool. From $27–35.

Sekar Orchid Beach Bungalows, Jl. Raya Candidasa, tel: 41086. 5 seaside bungalows in Balinese style. Basic rooms surrounded by gardens. $35, includes simple breakfast.

The Natia, Jl. Raya Candidasa, tel: 42007, 42006, fax: 41889, www.thenatia.com. Within easy walking distance of the beach, has infinity swimming pool. Small, simple rooms furnished in traditional style. Limited facilities. From $42.

Intermediate ($50–$75)

The Candidasa resort area has a number of good first-class places. Most provide spacious rooms, western-style baths with hot water, IDD telephone and AC. The majority are beachfront, have seaside restaurants and safety deposit facilities. Those listed here are well-managed. Most credit cards are accepted. Up to 2 children sharing the same room with their parents can stay free of charge in some.

Bali Santi Bungalows by the Beach, Jl. Raya Candidasa, tel: 41611, www.balisanti.com. 9 individual bungalows, including 4 new ones with AC, fan, minibar, hot water, and garden showers. Also 5 larges rooms with new queen size beds, inside bathroom with hot water, AC, fans, both with tv, DVD, surround sound system. Tropical gardens with oceanside restaurant and bar. Infinity pool. Can arrange wedding ceremonies, include legalities. From $60, includes full Western or Indonesian breakfast.

Bali Shangrila Beach Club, Desa Samuh, Candidasa, tel: 41829, 41003, fax: 363 41622, www.balishangrila.net. Hotel units, studios, 1and 2 bedroom apartments, 24-hr security, poolside restaurant, in-room satellite tv/DVD, rooftop party location with Jacuzzi, beachfront massage pavilion, on-site fishing, snorkeling and **PADI scuba diving training center**. Boat trips on private 9 m (30 ft) boat, tour desk, car, and motorbike rentals; entertainment most nights at **Mr. Grumpy's**, off-site restaurant and sports bar. AC rooms with continental breakfast. From $59.

Kubu Bali Bungalows, Central Candidasa, tel: 41532, 41256, fax: 41531, www.kububali.com. 10 luxury standard and 10 deluxe suites, all with marble terraces and simple, elegant teak furniture. Pathways lead through garden of terraced ponds and waterfalls. AC, fans, hot water in open-air showers. $50–65.

Lotus Bungalows, Jl. Raya Candidasa, tel: 41104, www.lotusbungalows.com. A PADI 5-star dive resort with 20 bungalows, each with elegant furnishings, open-air bathroom, hot water, and a verandah overlooking the ocean. Swimming pool, open-air restaurant. Gunga Divers on site. $65–120.

Puri Oka Beach Bungalows, Jl. Puri Bagus, tel: 41092, fax: 42148, www.purioka.com. Offers a wide range of facilities to suit all budgets. Restaurant and pool. Friendly staff can arrange tours, boat trips, snorkeling, and diving. $25–65 rooms and bungalows. Also owns Ocean Wild and Ocean Island Villas.

Rama Candidasa Resort & Spa, Jl. Raya Sengkidu, tel: 41974, www.ramacandidasahotel.com. 72 AC rooms and bungalows decorated with contemporary Balinese décor. Secluded private balconies with ocean views, swimming pool, and private beach in a peaceful setting. Offers a full range of activities from water sports to mountain and village experiences. Garpu Restaurant. $65–195.

Resort Prima Candidasa, Jl. Pantai Indah No. 16, tel: 41373, fax: 41971, www.hotelprimagroup.com. 14 deluxe and 14 standard rooms, 1 family room, all within 50 m (160 ft) of the beach. AC, hot water. Swimming pool, poolside bar, beach restaurant, ice cream corner. Can arrange all water sports, tours, car rental. See website for spa, diving, and honeymoon packages. $65–280.

First Class ($75–100)

Bayshore Villas, Jl. Raya Candidasa No. 4 (next door to Bayside Bungalows), tel: 41232, www.bayshorevillascandidasa.com. Hidden from the main street, directly on the beach, 6 ocean front villas feature a mix of modern and traditional architecture. $75–250/deluxe rooms, suites, beach house.

Villa Dasarata, on the sea, Candidasa, contact: Cathy Eynaud, mobile: 0818-850-283, www.villadasarata.com. Beachfront villa with guest houses; sleeps up to 12 people, part of a small residential development of 5 houses. Access to the village is by private lane. Complex has its own water, electricity and back-up generator. European management and professionally trained Balinese staff. Large lagoon-shaped private pool. $350–1,350 per week.

Villa Gils, Dua Gils and **Rumah Kecil**, tel: 42155, www.eastbalivilla.com, Private 1-, 2- and 3-bedroom rental villas in a small enclave of 7 houses surrounded by banana and coconut groves. Villa Gils and Dua Gils are located one house back from the water on opposite sides of the lane. Rumah Kecil is opposite Villa Gils, on the water's edge. The road ends at Rumah Kecil, so there's rarely any traffic. Private white sand beach is accessible by a walkway. AC bedrooms. Restaurant or private in-house dining. Spa, free WiFi. 24-hr staff amd security. Complimentary evening child care. $85–325. Dua Gils has **Timur Restaurant@ Dua Gils**, by reservation only, mobile: 0812-387-9961. A quiet place to dine.

Villa Impi Yanya, on Candidasa beach, www.balibeachhouse4rent.com. Individualized luxury for 2–8 persons. Four 2-person bedrooms and 3 bathrooms, can be rented either partially or in total. Includes pool, sundeck, covered terrace. $100–200/3 days, lower rates for longer stays and renting the entire house.

Luxury ($100–up)

Alam Asmara Dive Resort, Jl. Raya Candidasa, tel: 41929, fax: 42101, www.alamasmara.com. Formerly Pandawa Resort, newly transformed into a "Romantic Dive Resort" with 12 deluxe bungalows, also an active PADI dive operator. Honeymoon and Romance packages available. Rendezvous Restaurant. $115.

Puri Bagus Candidasa, Jl. Raya Candidasa, tel: 41131, fax: 41290, www.puribagus.net. 50 rooms and suites decorated in traditional style, open-air showers. Large and children's swimming pools, dive center office, spa with steam room, hair and facial treatments. Restaurant overlooking the ocean serves Balinese and international cuisine and great seafood; snacks served throughout the day poolside. Exotic cocktails and wine. There are several other Puri Bagus resorts on Bali. Check website for details. $150–235, Internet rates available.

Ocean Island Villa and Ocean Wild Villa, Candidasa Beach, contact Mr. Simon Wild, tel: 41092, www.purioka.com. Newly opened in 2010 by the owners of Puri Oka Beach bungalows, both villas have ocean frontage, 3 large bedrooms, private plunge pool, full kitchen, maid, cable tv, WiFi. Ocean Island $160; Ocean Wild $200.

Villa Gita, tel: 0813-3862-9874, www.villagita.com. Brand new ocean-front villa for rent, 3 luxurious self-contained bedroom suites with en suite bathrooms. Private infinity pool and open-air Jacuzzi. Internet available. Fully staffed, including cook and 24/7 security. $350 during peak season (Aug 1–31 and Dec 21–Jan 8); discount during regular season. Check website for minimum stay requirements.

Villa Sasoon Bali, Jl. Puri Bagus, tel: 41511, fax: 41911, www.villasasoon.com, 4 luxury villas, each consisting of 3 pavilions, private swimming pool, courtyard, and entertaining area. Each has a fully-equipped kitchen with European appliances and "on-call" chef. Dining room open on 3 sides to a stone terrace. 1 and 2 bedroom villas $250–300/night.

Watergarden Hotel & Spa, Jl. Raya Candidasa, tel: 41540, fax: 41164, www.watergardenhotel.com. 12 rooms. A venture of TJ's restaurant in Kuta, designed with their usual attention to detail and quality. Gorgeous bungalows set in a network of cascading streams, pools, and elegant gardens. Mountain bikes, hiking maps, and information about local events and places of interest available. Swimming pool, spa. $151–387. Internet rates available.

Watergarden Kafe serves innovative food in a relaxing setting, including seafood and vegetarian BBQ; great cocktails. Free WiFi. Open 7 am–11 pm. Free transport in Candidasa.

DINING

Menus are similar in the eateries along Candidasa's main road and include various salads, Indonesian and Chinese dishes, seafood, sandwiches or pizza, and desserts. Some include steak, curry, pasta, and cakes. Prices are good, averaging $4–$5/person with drinks. Seafood can be a lot more expensive. Breakfast and lunch are available everywhere. Most places close by 10 pm. For a dinner splurge, try one of the upmarket hotel restaurants. Menu descriptions are usually available on their websites. The villages with five-star resorts are within easy driving distance of Candidasa. Recommended independent cafes and restaurants are listed below.

Candidasa Café, Jl. Raya Candidasa 80811, tel: 41107, www.candidasacafe.com. Delicious food and wine. International, Balinese and Indonesian cuisine. Free WiFi, Free pickup around Candidasa and Buitan areas.

Friends Bar & Restaurant, east side of Jl. Raya Candidasa, tel: 41655, www.friends-bali.com. A small, cozy restaurant with a fairly priced menu. Open daily. Lunch served from 11 am–2 pm. Dinner served until 10 pm; bar open late.

Lotus Sea View Restaurant, Jl. Raya Candidasa, tel: 41257, www.lotus-restaurants.com. Next to Toke Bar & Restaurant, but larger and more formal. Great seafood; location near the water. Part of the Lotus Ubud group.

Rendezvous Restaurant, Candidasa, tel: 41929. Turn right 100 yds east of Candidasa Lagoon. Free transport in Candidasa area. Intimate dining niche with sweeping views of neighboring Nusa Penida in the background. Open for breakfast, lunch, and dinner. Fresh home-made breads daily, guaranteed hygiene and sanitation, clean ice, all foods prepared without preservatives.

Toke Bar & Restaurant, Jl. Raya Candidasa, tel: 41991, www.tokebali.com. Opens to the beach on one side and to the main road on the other. Offers the best combination of Balinese ambience and Western intimacy. Great welcoming drink and good pasta for a couple of dollars. Indian, Balinese, and Western cuisine, great choice of international cocktails and wines. Free WiFi, Open 10:30 am 'til late. Takes credit cards.

Vincent's Bar, Lounge & Garden Restaurant, Jl. Raya Candidasa, tel: 41368, www.vincentsbali.com. International and Balinese cuisine, bar with wide range of international cocktails, relaxed atmosphere with modern art and Jazz music. Open for lunch and dinner, international wines. Open 10:30 am 'til late. Credit cards accepted.

NIGHTLIFE & ENTERTAINMENT

Most of the restaurants listed above have bars that stay open late. A few others offer entertainment. For further information about locations and schedules, call the numbers below or ask at your accommodation.

Candi Agung Bar & Restaurant, tel: 41672. Nightly *legong* dance.

Dewata Agung Bar & Restaurant, tel: 41204. Nightly *legong* dance.

Iguana Bar & Restaurant, on Candidasa beach, tel: 41973. Live music Tuesday, Friday, and Sunday.

Legong Restaurant, tel: 41052. Nightly *legong* dance or movie.

Malibu Café, tel: 42011. Live acoustic music Monday, Wednesday, and Friday.

Raja's Restaurant, right by the lagoon, tel: 42034. Nightly movie.

Wayan Café, tel: 41128. Nightly Balinese *legong* dance.

SHOPPING

Candidasa is not a great place for shopping, but kiosks along the main road sell sarongs, basic beachwear, sandals, and the like. There's a German bakery on the road just past Dasa Wana Resort and a mini-market next to Watergarden Hotel & Kafé that's handy for basic necessities and snacks.

The big find is in nearby **Tenganan** village, where most of the shops are actually the front room in people's homes. Their basketry is made from a special reed grown in the area and has decorated 5-star resorts and luxury villas throughout the world. They also sell hand-woven *ikat* textiles (you might get lucky and stumble upon some of the ladies weaving). The traditional double-*ikat gerinsing*— only woven in Tenganan and two other places in the world—go for very high prices for obvious reasons. The other specialty here is stories from the Hindu epics inscribed on leaves from the *lontar* palm, and young men can usually been seen in the village courtyard honing this craft. There's a small fee to enter the village.

ACTIVITIES

Diving

Candidasa is all about diving; even dive operators from south Bali offer trips to this area. Below are some of the locally-based outfits.

Bali Bubbles Dive Center, Jl. Raya Candidasa, tel: (0361) 923 0800, fax: (0363) 42196, www.bali-bubbles.com. Prices from $65/Padangbai to $115/Manta point, with Tulamben ($75) and Nusa Penida ($85) also on the menu.

Gangga Divers at Lotus Bungalows, Jl. Raya Candidasa, tel: 41104, www.lotusbungalows.com/diving. Packages from $240/4 day dives and 1 night dive to $1,030 for 22 day dives/2 night dives, all at various locations.

Shangrila Scuba Divers, Jl. Raya Candidasa at the Bali Shangrila Beach Club, tel: 41829, 41003, fax: 41622, www.divingatbalishangrila.com. Owner Graeme is a Master Scuba Diver Trainer. Offers PADI dive courses, daily fun dives, dive packages with accommodation. New dive gear for sale, private/small group dives. Safety, service, value stressed. From $75 Padangbai/2 dives to $130/Manta Point/2 dives.

Subocean Bali, Jl. Sengkidu, next to Rama Candidasa Resort & Spa, tel: 41411, fax; 42137, www.suboceanbali.com. A PADI certified diving center run by an international team. Packages can include air tickets, luxury hotel, diving, snorkeling, and fishing for all skill levels. On-site dive training for beginners.

Yes Dive, Jl. Raya Candidasa, tel: 41982, www.yes-dive.com. 15 years experience in Bali; top quality equipment, English and Balinese guides/instructors, PADI dive courses, daily fun dives. Personalized diving and quality service. From $70/Padangbai/2 dives to $130/Manta Point/2 dives.

Snorkeling

Snorkeling can be arranged almost anywhere. Prices for 1.5 hours of snorkeling (including roundtrip transport) at the islands just off Candidasa are around $5/person in a party of up to 3 people. If going out alone, expect to pay $6, which includes the price of the fins and mask. Watch out! The waves can be rough near the islands. Also, land on the beautiful beach at Pasir, east of town, for a swim.

Fishing

Early morning or late afternoon fishing trips on local dug-out fishing boats can be arranged through most accommodations.

Cycling

Many places rent bikes. **Kubu Bali** has 5- and 10-speed mountain bikes. **Watergarden Hotel & Spa** has mountain bikes and maps at similar rates. Count on paying Rp 10,000 per day. Be sure to test the brakes before renting. Cycling tours can be arranged through many hotels. Also check out **East Bali Bike Tour**, www.eastbalibik.com, mobile: 0862-3823-1850 or 0812-466-7752. Exhilarating and memorable bike tours in East Bali. Relaxed pace.

Hiking

A fine 3-hour, 6 km (3.7 mile), walk from Candidasa to Tenganan starts just east of Kubu Bali Bungalows. Follow the ridge-top trail and drop left into Tenganan just before the fourth major hill. Magnificent views, but start early to avoid the midday heat.

A shorter hike starts at the tip of the headland east of town: walk the hill due northeast down to a long, deserted black sand beach. Other hikes from Tenganan to Putung or to Bedabudug (Bandem) are also good.

MANGGIS & SENGKIDU

Manggis is a small fishing village on Teluk Amuk (Amuk Bay), west of Candidasa. Its name is the Indonesian word for mangosteen, the delicious hard-skinned purple fruit that grows nearby. (Look for the statue along the road.) The development began here with the super-exclusive Amankila and the Serai (now Alila Manggis Bali), and has blossomed from there. Sengkidu is a few kilometers east of Manggis on the same bay, followed by Candidasa further east. Clumps of trees separate the three areas, retaining their uniqueness.

ACCOMMODATIONS
Budget (Under $25)

Lumbung Damuh, Jl. Pantai Buitan Kelod, mobile: 0813-5312-5888, tel:/fax: 41553, www.damuhbali.com. Located between Manggis and Sengkidu, *lumbung* (traditional rice barn) style homestay right on the beach. 2 *lumbungs* sleep 2 people each and a third exclusive one is big enough for a small family. Owners live on-site. Hot water, mini-bar, fans. Tropical gardens. $25–40.

Luxury ($100–up)

Alila Manggis Bali, Buitan, Manggis, tel: 41011, fax: 41015, www.alilahotels.com. 53 rooms and 2 corner suites in 2-story thatched Balinese pavilions with private terrace or balcony. Spa. Check out their Organic Garden Breakfast ($40), served in their own garden 10 minutes away. Explore with their gardener; pick herbs to make your own tea blend. Restaurant also serves healthy menu breakfasts. $225–650, including a la carte breakfast and afternoon tea. Check website for Internet rates.
Amankila, Manggis, tel: 41333, fax: 41555, www.amanresorts.com. 35 individual suites, 7 of which have their own swimming pool. Located on a seaside hill. Extraordinary luxury, this is where movie stars stay thanks to the ultimate in privacy and security. $800–2,900.
Candi Beach Cottage, Mendira beach, Sengkidu, tel: 41234, fax: 41111, www.candibeachbali.com. 64 hotel and cottage rooms with satellite tv and mini-bar, each with its own verandah. Pool, spa, fitness center, tennis, open-water dive school. $193–254, breakfast not included. Check website for Internet rates.

JASRI

Northeast of Candidasa where the road turns inland to Amlapura is Jasri (also spelled Jasi), at the beginning of the easternmost edge of Bali Island. The area here and further east is only beginning to develop, as the coastal road on the peninsula is badly in need of repair. However, a couple of places are on the leading edge of the building trend.

ACCOMMODATIONS

Turtle Bay Hideaway, Jl. Pura Mascima, Jasi Kelod (also spelled Jasri), tel: 23611, fax: 23612, www.turtlebayhideaway.com. Surf, dive, snorkel, or just soak in the soothing breeze by the pool. Beautiful gardens, well-appointed wooden cottages. Experienced staff, massages, cultural experiences. Gourmet cuisine prepared from own organic gardens. WiFi $115–225.
Villa Matanai, Jasri Beach, mobile: 0813-3761-1010, www.villamatanai.com. 500 m (540 yds) from the Jasri surfbreak. Villa has 3 levels with 5 bedrooms, AC, above-average luxury, single, double, and triple rooms. Swimming pool, restaurant serving local and international food, cocktails. Internet available. $50–100.

TENGANAN VILLAGE

An Ancient Village and Exclusive Community of God's Chosen Ones

Time is reckoned differently in **Tenganan Pegringsingan**. Here, each new day begins with 21 deep, throbbing drumbeats and lasts until the same pulsating tones are struck the next morning. Tourists arrive when the sun is at its zenith and the valley is glowing with light. They leave towards evening, when the all-important religious ceremonies commence. A month in Tenganan lasts exactly 30 days. Modifications to the calendar are needed to adjust to the lunar-solar year; altogether 15 days are added every three years.

The ancient, ritualistic Bali Aga (original, pre-Hindu Balinese) society of Tenganan opened up a few decades ago and became accessible to non-Tengananese. Its festivals have been publicized, and the village itself has become known as a result of its proximity to the Candidasa beach resort. Gone are the days when it was isolated and difficult to access.

It is said that all footprints of visitors to Tenganan were once literally wiped out once they left. In this century, the village has faced new and different problems. More parking space for the cars, minibuses and limousines that tourism brings had to be added, and the art shops, which distort the community's divine plan, have been added.

Microcosm of the universe
The *desa adat* (traditional village) Tenganan Pegringsingan is a microcosmic reflection of the macrocosm, an *imago mundi*. According to this divine plan, it is arranged systematically both in its delimitation from the outside world, as well as in its separation into distinct private and public areas within the village precincts itself.

The village is laid out in a large rectangle measuring some 250x500 m (820x1,440 ft) (about 6 ha), encircled by natural boundaries and walls. Three public corridors rise in terrace-like fashion, allowing the rain to flow down, running along a north-south axis from the sea toward the sacred volcano Mt. Agung.

There are six lengthwise rows of compounds; the pairs located in the center and west are striking because of their closed fronts, which resemble palm leaf-covered longhouses.

The buildings and areas for public use are situated on the central axes of the central and western streets. There are a number of walled temple areas, longhouses, smaller pavilions, rice granaries and shrines here, all of which suggest a strong communal life with pronounced ritual ties. This is where the 300 inhabitants of Tenganan live.

In the eastern compounds of the *banjar pandé* (community) live those who have been banished from the village, together with those whose customs are more like the majority of Hindu-Javanized Balinese. Labor in the surrounding gardens and communal rice fields behind the hills is largely performed by tenant farmers from neighboring villages who receive half of the crop yield, leaving the Tanganese free to pursue their arts and rituals. Owning approximately 1,000 ha of arable land, Tenganan is one of the richest land-owning communities in all of Bali.

Divine origins
Unlike other Balinese villages, Tenganan traces its origins and its social institutions back to a written source, a holy book known as the *Usana Bali* (a chronicle of Bali). According to this text, the Tenganese have been chosen by their creator, Batara Indra, to honor his royal descendants through communal offerings and sacrifices. It states, furthermore, that descendants of the original villagers have been chosen to administer the surrounding lands, a consecrated place of devotion and ritual, and must use all available means to keep them pure.

The concept of territorial and bodily purity and integrity plays an exceedingly important role in the village culture. It is reflected not only in many important rituals (purifications and exorcisms), but also in the idea that only if a person is healthy, physically as well as mentally, may he or she take part in rituals. No one with a disability and no outsider can be admitted to the *adat* organizations of the village.

As a result of this divinely ordained scheme, the original layout and social organization of the village may not be changed. Houses, compounds, gardens, village council and youth groups are to be left as the gods have created them. Should anything be changed or taken away, the curse of the gods will fall upon the village, and its people will perish. Anyone guilty of not respecting the inherited order is banned from participating in village rites, and thus from sharing in communal property. In the gravest of cases, they are even banished from the village altogether. The *desa adat* is itself regarded as divine and almighty within the traditional social order.

Exclusive membership

It is not surprising that a community regarding itself as divinely blessed would strictly define its own members and place restrictions on outsiders. This exclusivity is expressed very clearly in the qualifications needed to enter the all-village council or *krama desa*. Only men and women without mental or physical defects who were born and live in Tenganan, having duly passed all ritual stages of initiation by the time they marry, are eligible to join the council. Although now more lenient, the practice of village endogamy (marrying within the village) also has had a restrictive effect until fairly recently. Women are now allowed to marry outsiders as long as they are from the upper castes, Brahma, Ksatrya, and Vaisya.

Newlyweds take their place at the lowest end of a hierarchical seating in the huge *bale agung*, the forum and sacred meeting pavilion of the village council. With the entrance of a new couple, the parents retire and everyone moves up a step, receiving new ritual responsibilities. The layout of the 50 m (160 ft) long hall is eminently suited to the numerous rites that bring together the gods, ancestors, and villagers. Here, members of the *krama desa* meet, dressed in ritual clothing, for communal meals with deities and ancestors whom they worship with prayers, offerings, dances, and music. In many cases, youths will take part in the performance of these rituals, either because the girls have been formally

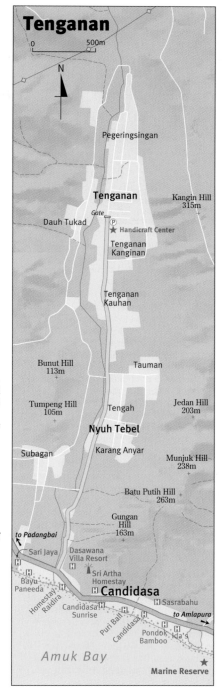

Geringsing, *double ikat ceremonial textiles, in Tenganan village (photo by Jonathan Copeland, www.jonathaninbali.com)*

invited by the married women to dance before the *bale agung,* or because the village council requires one of the sacred iron *gamelan* orchestras (*selunding*) maintained by the boys' organizations to be played.

For such a society to work, a long initiation period is needed, allowing its members to prepare for their complex ritual duties and activities within the village council. When children enter a youth club between the ages of six and eight, they go through a "school of life" in which the behavior required for participation in the *krama desa* is learned, and where the manual skills and esoteric formulas needed for rituals can be practiced.

The three boys' associations of the village are named after the location of their assembly houses, located on three consecutive terraces along the western street. There are also three girls' clubs, that adhere to strict and formal relationships concerning mutual help, exchange of gifts, offerings, meals, as well as entire rituals. A girl must be at least seven years old to join a *sekaha daha* or girls' club, whose meetings are held in the compounds of retired village elders.

Some years ago, the girls still brought their looms to the meeting houses so they could practice weaving. In the 11th month of the Tenganan year, they brought yarn to their clubhouses to undergo instruction in the exceedingly complex art of double *ikat.* Unfortunately, this custom, so vital to the preservation of the local textile craft, has been abandoned for several years.

The sacred *geringsing* cloths

Ritual clothing is an indispensable part of the sacred order of Tenganan. The double *ikat* cloths known as *geringsing* produced here rank among the masterworks of traditional textile art, providing a further sign of the divinely-ordained exclusivity of the society. The cloths are said to have been directly inspired by Batara Indra, the Creator, who was once sitting in a tree enjoying the beauty of the moon and stars. While contemplating the heavens, he decided to teach the women of Tenganan the art of *ikat* patterning. Since then, the community has obeyed a divine commandment to wear *kamben geringsing* or double *ikat* cloths. In this way, the villagers evince purity and the ability to perform rituals, qualities which these cloths protect from harmful outside influences.

Festival of the swings

Among the most important religious duties of Tenganan villagers is the festive reception of gods and ancestors, who from time to time descend to their megalithic thrones and altars in and around the inner village precincts. The presence of deities and ancestors is of great significance, above all during the fifth month of the Tenganan year, Sasih Sambah, for it is then that the universe, the village, and the religious community are renewed and given strength through the performance of extensive and solemn rites.

The ceremonies that take place then are reminiscent of old Vedic swinging rites performed during the *mahavrata* winter solstice celebration, which focuses on the god Indra. The swinging unites sun and earth, and together with textile techniques and recent genetic research, suggests that Tenganan may be connected with an immigration from east or southeast India during Vedic times.

In a legendary account, the people of Tenganan are said to have arrived here while searching for the king of Bedahulu's favorite horse. Although it was dead when found, the king showed his gratitude by promising to give the searchers all land in the area where the horse's decomposed body could be smelled. A representative of the court, accompanied by the village head, walked around the huge area that today forms Tenganan, finding that in fact the horse's flesh could still be smelled for quite a distance. After the court officer had departed, the cunning village chief pulled a piece of bad-smelling horse meat from under his waist-band. The remnants of the horse are believed to be scattered around the village as megalithic monuments.

There are other indications, too, that the Tenganan people have not always lived here. A copper inscription dated A.D. 1040 speaks of a relationship between the powerful governor from Java, a certain Buddhist reformer Mpu Kuturan in Silayukti (near Padangbai), and a nearby village named "Tranganan" that was then on the coast at Candidasa and later moved to the interior.

Proof that the Tenganan villagers moved from the seaside to their present location is provided in the design and placement of the original altars (*sanggah kamulan*) in the house compounds. In other parts of Bali this altar is always built in the corner facing east and toward the mountains. In Tenganan it is placed towards the sea.

When a member of the Tenganan community dies, his or her body is not cremated. Once the sun is past the zenith, the corpse is carried from the compound to the cemetery. At the grave the body is undressed, then it is returned to Mother Earth (Pertiwi), head seaward and face down.

Shopping in Tenganan

In addition to having an opportunity to see an ancient culture co-existing with the modern world, the other reason tourists flock to Tenganan is for their **handicrafts**, which are as unique as their culture. The Tengananese, particularly the younger generation, have

adapted very well to tourism, and they are shrewd negotiators. There are no bargains here. The front of practically every house is a handicrafts "showroom", their open doors inviting visitors to step in. On the village's main street are tables where men sit etching inscriptions on palm leaves, and there is a small market selling soft drinks and sarongs near the entrance.

The greatest treasures, of course, are the ***geringsing* weavings**. Produced in small villages in only two other countries—Japan and India—and nowhere else in Indonesia, double *ikat* involves the painstaking process of tying and dying both warp and weft threads to form a motif before the cloth is woven. Red, dark brown, blue-black, and tan are the predominant traditional colors here, and it has been said a drop of the dyer's blood is added to the colors to protect the wearer. Taking up to three years to complete one cloth, they are reserved for ceremonial occasions and are, needless to say, expensive, exacting anywhere from several hundred dollars to several thousand, depending on the size, motif and quality.

In ancient times throughout Bali, written records were inscribed on dried *lontar* (*Palmyra*) leaves. Tengananese men have revived this art, creating and selling ***lontar* leaf "books"** depicting stories, primarily from Hindu legends. Using a sharp knives, a lot of patience and extremely good eyesight, they etch illustrations onto the dried leaves, then rub candlenut over the surface to make them last. The leaves are bound between two pieces of split bamboo for easy carrying and storage. A superb five-page book takes about one month to complete and fetches a higher price than lower quality works.

In the early 1990s, Tenganan's especially fine **basketry** reached a frenzied level of popularity when new five-star resorts across the island decided to "go natural". Suddenly Tenganan place mats, urns, bowls, tissue holders, and boxes decorated every upmarket hotel, becoming something of a status symbol. Prices soared, quality dropped, and there was little left for tourists to buy. Nowadays, luxury resorts have moved on to other decors, making Tenganan's wonderful baskets available to the public once again. Made from the *ada* vine that grows only in this area, they are not only beautiful but they last forever, being much stronger than those made from rattan.

—*Urs Ramseyer*

AMLAPURA, TIRTA GANGGA, AND EASTERN BACK ROADS

Water Palaces and Bali's Most Scenic Views

Once the seat of the powerful Karangasem court, **Amlapura**, the district capital at the eastern end of Bali, is now an administrative town much like others throughout Indonesia. Formerly known simply as Karangasem, the town was given its present name after the Mt. Agung eruption in 1963 nearly wiped it out; black lava flows can still be seen from the road on the way into town. There are several interesting palaces here, and the surrounding countryside contains superb scenery, as well as some of the most interesting traditional villages in Bali.

The Karangasem palaces

Amlapura's main attraction is its several traditional palaces or *puri*. There is a western, a northern, a southern, and an eastern *puri* as well as several others, all still occupied by members of the royal family. Of these, only **Puri Agung Karangasem** (also called **Puri Kangin**, the eastern palace) on the main road

to the market in the center of Amlapura is easily visited. Built in the 19th century by King Anak Agung Gede Jelantik, this palace is worth a look, as it gives a vivid impression of how local royals used to live. It is an eccentric blend of details borrowed from the Hindu Balinese (statues and a bas relief), Chinese (window and door styles and other ornaments), and Europeans (the style of the main building and its large veranda) set in what is essentially a traditional Balinese compound, with several pavilions and rooms surrounded by pools and connected by walkways. There are three sections in the compound. The front was where traditional art performances were held and is called Bencingah. In the middle is a garden housing two very old lychee trees and the main palace building bearing the name "Maskerdam", adapted from "Amsterdam" when the king established friendly relations with the Dutch government. Another building in the rear is

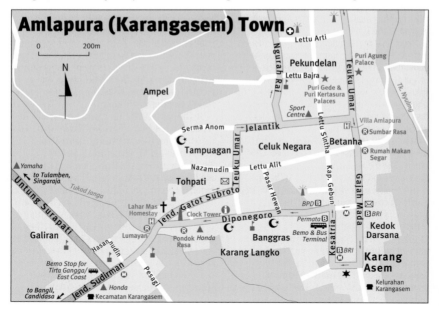

Many parts of eastern Bali offer gorgeous views of Mt. Agung.

the royal family's residence and is called "London", and the furniture curiously bears the crest of the British royal family.

The Karangasem ruling family traces its ancestry back to the 14th century Hindu-Javanese Majapahit empire, claiming to be direct descendants of a certain Batan Jeruk who was Prime Minister of Bali during the 16th century.

There is a tale concerning the dynasty's divine origin. A woman who lived near the palace was once overheard talking to a stranger in her house. When asked who it was, she replied that it was the god of Mt. Agung. After some time, the woman became pregnant, and not long afterwards a miraculous fire descended from the mountain to the woman's house. She soon gave birth to a son atop a hill to the east of the town. This son, the "god of the eastern hill", is said to be the founder of the royal Karangasem line.

Karangasem conquered Lombok in the 17th century and in turn became a vassal of the neighboring island in the 18th and 19th centuries. As a result, there are today several Sasak settlements in and around Amlapura, and these have had a significant influence on the culture of the area. Family and trading relations with Lombok still exist until the present day, and intermarriages are common. When Lombok was occupied by Holland in

1894, Karangasem was transferred to Dutch control as well. Nevertheless, the ruler of Karangasem was retained as "governor" of the region, and his status was confirmed in 1938 when the Balinese kingdoms were granted partial self-rule. After independence in 1945, these princely realms vanished and were replaced by the present-day *kabupaten* or regencies. Until 1979, however, the regent, or *bupati*, of Karangasem was a prince of the royal house and was still considered "raja" by most people in the area. Even today, members of the royal family participate in rituals held in the nearby villages.

Ujung and Mt. Seraya

In addition to being a man well-versed in letters, the last Karangasem raja, Anak Agung Anglurah Ketut (1909–1945), was also an assiduous builder of opulent pleasure palaces for his frequent excursions to the countryside with his wives and children. In fact, during his lifetime he built no less than three different "water palaces" — at Ujung, Tirta Gangga, and Jungutan — which he also used for receiving dignitaries.

Ujung, 8 km (5 miles) to the south of Amlapura, is a small fishing village with distinct Islamic and Hindu-Balinese quarters. The construction of the lavish complex here — three vast pools bordered by small

One of the many pools at Taman Soekasada Ujung (Ujung Water Park)

pavilions with a massive stained-glass and stucco bungalow in the center—began in 1901 and buildings were added until 1937. In 1963, thanks to a Mt. Agung eruption, followed by a 1976 earthquake, it was completely destroyed except for a watch tower overlooking the harbor. The ruins of this building were left untouched and still stand atop the hill as if guarding its charge.

Now officially called **Taman Soekasada Ujung**, rebuilding of the site using its original unique Balinese and European architectural styles began in 1998 funded by the World Bank, with Phase II beginning in 2001. It was dedicated in 2004. Today, the park is a heavenly garden; on a quiet day it is almost possible to imagine how it must have been in days gone by. In the center of the largest pool is a covered building, Bale Gili—actually part of a bridge from one side of the lake to the other—decorated with ornaments and statues. Other *bales* (pavilions), one reachable by 107 steps, were used as sitting areas from which to view the park below and for banquets. In the area to the north there are statues of a rhino and a bull that recycle water into the pools. The complex is surrounded by a stone wall, part of which is original, fringed by palms and flowering plants. One of the buildings can be rented for workshops and events. It is unfortunate that villas built by members of the royal family

who live in Jakarta block a dramatic backdrop view of Mt. Agung overlooking the serene gardens.

Just before Ujung there is a road to the left leading toward **Bukit Kangin** ("eastern hill") where there is a panoramic view of the area and a temple dedicated to the founder of the royal dynasty. On the full moon of the fifth month of the Balinese calendar, several villages with close ties to the ruling dynasty participate in a festival at this temple.

From the beach at Ujung, a new road heading east climbs up to **Seraya** village, perched on the southern flanks of Mt. Seraya, Bali's easternmost peak (1,175m/3,854 ft). This is one of the most arid areas in Bali, and the road here hugs the hills high above the coast, offering splendid panoramas of the surrounding terrain and across the sea to distant Lombok. From Seraya, the road continues around the mountain and descends gradually on the northern side to Amed. Though a distance of only about 30 km (18 miles), the entire drive takes several hours as the road is quite steep and winding. Therefore, most travelers choose the northern road to Amed via Abang, passing the Tirta Gangga water palace en route.

Refreshing pools at Tirta Gangga

If the Ujung water palace can be described as serene, the pools at **Tirta Gangga** are best

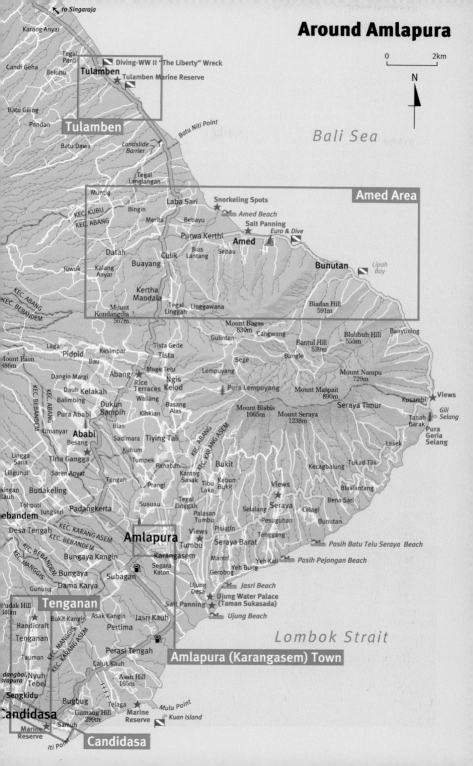

Around Amlapura

0   2km

N

to Singaraja

Karang Anyar

Candi Geha

Tegal Panti

Beluhu

Tulamben

Diving-WW II "The Liberty" Wreck

Tulamben Marine Reserve

Tulamben

Bali Sea

Batu Giling

Pandan

Batu Dawa

Landslide Barrier

Batu Niti Point

Tegal Langlangan

Muntig

KEC. KUBU

KEC. ABANG

Bingin

Laba Sari

Merlita

Bebayu

Snorkeling Spots

Amed Beach

Salt Panning

Euro & Dive

Amed Area

Purwa Kerthi

Amed

Datah

Culik

Bias Lantang

Sebau

Buayang

Kalang Anyar

Juwuk

Kertha Mandala

Tegal Linggah

Linggawana

Bunutan

Lipah Bay

Mount Kondangdia 567m

Biadan Hill 591m

Mount Bagas 830m

Cangwang

Gulinten

Bantul Hill 539m

Bangle

Bluhbuh Hill 555m

Banyuning

Laga

Mount Paon 886m

Pidpid

Kesimpar

Bau

Tista Gede

Tista

Sege

Lempuyang

Mount Nampu 729m

Kusambi

Views

Dangin Margi

Abang

Mage Telu

Ngis Kelod

Pura Lempuyang

Mount Maspait 890m

Gili Selang

Dauh Kelakah

Balimbing

Rice Terraces

Waliang

Basang Alas

Mount Bisbis 1065m

Mount Seraya 1238m

Seraya Timur

Tanah Barak

Pura Ababi

Dukun Sampih

Kihkian

Pura Geria Selang

Ababi

Bias

Sadimara

Tiying Tali

Kuhum

Bukit

Lesek

Umanyar

Besang

KEC. ABANG

KEC. KARANG ASEM

KEC. BEBANDEM

Lingga Sana

Liligundi

Tirta Gangga

Saren Anyar

Tengah

Tumpek

Prangi

Panaban

Karang Sasak

Tibu Laka

Kebon Bukit

Kecagbalung

Tukad Tiis

Blaslantang

Bena Sari

ingan Kauh

Budakeling

Jungseri

Padangkerta

Susuau

Tegal Linggah

Palasan Tumbu

Views

Seraya

Celagi

Bunutan

ebandem

Tohpati

KEC. KARANG ASEM

KEC. BEBANDEM

Desa Tengah

Pisiatin

Selalang

Pesuguhan

Tenggang

Bungaya Kangin

Amlapura

Karangasem

Segara Katon

Views

Tumbu

Seraya Barat

Mantri

Gerobog

Yeh Bung

Yeh Kali

Pasih Batu Telu Seraya Beach

Pasih Pejongan Beach

KEC. MANGGIS

Bungaya

Dama Karya

Subagan

Gunung

Ujung Desa

Jasri Beach

Ujung Water Palace (Taman Sukasada)

Ujung Beach

Pudak Hill 340m

Tenganan

Bukit Kangin

Asak Kangin

Jasri Kauh

Salt Panning

Lombok Strait

Handicraft

Tenganan

Pertima

KEC. MANGGIS

KEC. KARANG ASEM

Perasi Tengah

Amlapura (Karangasem) Town

Tauman

Caluk Kauh

dangbai, *arapura*

Nyuh Tebel

Sengkidu

Bugbug

Telaga

Asah Hill 165m

Mulu Point

andidasa

Gumang Hill 299m

Marine Reserve

Kuan Island

Marine Reserve

Samuh

Iti Point

Candidasa

called "lush". The gardens here are more mature and are bordered by forest and rice fields, with ocean views to the east and Mt. Agung to the north. The cool, spring-fed pools at Tirta Gangga—which literally means "Ganges Water" and refers to the sacred river of the Hindus—are located some 15 km (9 miles) north of Amlapura along the road to Amed. Although the water looks dirty and uninviting, it originates from sacred natural springs believed by the Balinese to be a precious gift from the gods. The waters here are thought to have medicinal powers, and those who bathe in them during the full moon will be healed and blessed with everlasting youth.

Constructed by Anak Agung Anglurah Ketut Karangasem in 1948, the palace buildings no longer exist. What visitors can see is 1.2 ha of gardens and ponds decorated with ornate water-spouting statues, meandering stepping stones across the holy water, and an 11-tiered fountain representing lotus blossoms. Descendants of the royal family still work and live on-site, and visitors are welcome to join villagers in processions to Tirta Gangga during ceremonial occasions.

A dip in the pools is deliciously refreshing after a long drive. The village itself is small and quiet, and is a good place to pause and rest for several hours, or even several days, to take advantage of the many delightful walks in the area. The entrance fee to the park is less than $1.

Trekking around Tirta Gangga

There are a number of excellent treks through the surrounding countryside, and local guides can be hired in the parking lot of the water palace. One of the most spectacular begins to the north in **Tanah Aron** village, quite high on the slopes of Mt. Agung. It is reachable on foot or by car. To get there, follow the main road north from Tirta Gangga in the direction of Amed for several kilometers, then turn left at **Abang** and follow a small climbing road up to the end. From here continue on foot, enjoying the broad panoramas in all directions and the thick, tree-fern vegetation. There is no shortcut back to Tirta Gangga, and it is best not to get too far off the main path, as the ravines are quite steep and dangerous.

Another, less taxing trek begins in **Ababi**, just 2 km (1.2 miles) north of Tirta Gangga on the main road. Turn left in this village and follow the road through Tanah Lengis to Budakling. On foot you can also reach this road by climbing the low hill behind the Tirta Gangga spring.

Ababi is an old-fashioned village, and in the fourth Balinese month a major ritual is

The Mahabharata pond at the water palace of Tirta Gangga

held in the village temple, an agricultural ceremony marking the end of the dry season. In Tanah Lengis, which is closely linked to Ababi, are several unusual music clubs. One is an *angklung* orchestra, an instrument comprised of lengths of suspended bamboo that produce various tones when stricken, and the other is a *cekepung* group.

Cekepung is a form of music known only in Karangasem and on Lombok, from where it originates, and is performed by a group of men. The leader begins by singing a text in Sasak (the Lombok language); this is then paraphrased by another man in Balinese. After a while the other men join in and perform a very rhythmic, interlocking song without words imitating the interplay, rhythm, and punctuation of a *gamelan* orchestra with their voices. Villagers drink palm wine during and in between the singing, making the festivities even livelier.

Budakeling village is situated on the other side of a broad river, which is almost completely dry during the dry season. This village is home to Buddhist priests, of whom there are only a dozen or so left on Bali (whereas their Sivaite colleagues number in the hundreds). It is also a renowned center for gold- and silversmithing, particularly high quality jewelry pieces that are occasionally offered for sale in Tirta Gangga. Budakeling also has several ironsmiths who produce household utensils and agriculture tools. To return to Tirta Gangga from here, turn left at the first crossroads in Budakeling and ask for directions to Padangkerta, a few miles south on the main Amlapura–Tirta Gangga road.

For a longer trip, continue westward to the important market village **Bebandem**. Entering from this direction, there are ironsmiths by the side of the road who usually work in the mornings on market days (every three days) producing cheap knives, *keris* daggers, and cock-fighting spurs. There is also a cattle market here. This is a beautiful area, with flowers grown for the offerings market. In Banjar Tilem, Bebandem, there's an unusual statue of an elephant with one foot on a human skull. Once back on the main road, you can choose to go back toward Tirta Gangga, south to Candidasa, east to Amlapura, or west to Rendang to continue on to Besakih.

A walk due east from Tirta Gangga through the rice fields brings you to **Pura Lempuyang**, one of the *Sad Kahyangan* or six main temples of the whole of Bali, perched at the summit of

A blacksmith at work in Bebandem village

Mt. Lempuyang (1,065 m/3494 ft). Pass Kuhum and Tihingtali villages and continue on to **Basangalas**. From here it is a strenuous climb up 1,750 steps to the temple. Basangalas can also be reached by car from the south at a turn-off to the north of Tirta Gangga at Abang. If coming from the north, pass through Culik to Aang. The lower temple is usually open, but to enter the upper one (at the top of the dragon staircases), ask around and someone will lead you to the keeper, who will unlock it for you. There are magnificent sunset views from here.

A large temple festival takes place at Lempuyang every 210 days on the Thursday of the week Dungulan. Ten days later, on Sunday of the week Kuningan, there are festivals in the temples of origin (*pura puseh*) in many villages around Basangalas, including Lempuyang. These feature fine *rejang* dances by the unmarried girls of the village, accompanied by various orchestras.

Traditional villages near Amlapura
Several neighboring villages—Subagan, Jasri, Bungaya, Asak, and Timbrah—just to the west of Amlapura—are all very traditional, resembling Tenganan, the classic Bali Aga village, in many ways. Asak, for instance, is a caste-less village. Bungaya, on the other hand, has groups of *brahmana*, but they do not take part in village rituals.

These villages may be reached quite easily by car or on foot. Coming from Candidasa and Bugbug in the west, turn left at Perasi village on to a picturesque back road leading to Bebandem via Timbrah, Asak, and Bungaya. Jasi and Subagan lie on the main road between Perasi and Amlapura. There is also a lovely backroad connecting Subagan with the Asak and Bungaya road.

Jasri (also spelled **Jasi**) village, close to the beach, is well known for its earthenware casks, bowls, and pots. They may be purchased locally as well as at the Amlapura and Klungkung markets. Subagan has an Islamic quarter that was completely leveled in 1963 when Mt. Agung erupted.

Timbrah, **Asak**, and **Bungaya** are villages with several interesting festivals. The biggest and best known is called *usaba sumbu*, held once a year, with certain variations in all three villages (as well as in Perasi, Bugbug, and Bebandem). This is an agricultural rite in honor of the rice goddess, Batari Sri, and the god of material wealth, Batara Rambut Sedana, as well as the deified ancestors and other village deities. It is held in Bungaya around the full moon of the 12th Balinese month, in Timbrah during the waning moon of the second month, and in Asak around the full moon of the first month. (Check a Balinese calendar for months compared to the Gregorian calendar.) Several exquisite dances are performed during the daytime. A *rejang* is performed by unmarried girls, an *abuang* by unmarried boys, and several different groups take part in mock-fight dances called *gebug*. The dancers are beautifully dressed in costly ritual costumes, and the gold headdresses of the girls in Asak and Bungaya are justifiably renowned throughout Bali.

The dances are accompanied by some very rare and unusual music. Especially noteworthy is the sacred *selunding* orchestra, consisting of iron metallophones that are rarely played, and then only for specific ceremonies. A particular *selunding* in Bungaya, for instance, is only struck once every 10 years during a huge temple festival held there. In Asak, Timbrah, and Bugbug, the *selunding* is played once every year during the *usaba sumbu*.

Other interesting festivals are held on Galungan in Timbrah, on Kuningan in Asak and Bungaya, and during the seventh and eighth lunar months in Asak and Subagan. New years' festivals are worth attending in any of these villages.

The spectacular backroad to Besakih

The back road leading from Amlapura up to Rendang and thence to Besakih is one of the most scenic in Bali. From Amlapura the first villages passed are Subagan and Bebandem.

Spectacular rice terraces spread out from one of eastern Bali's many backroads.

Shortly after Bebandem there is an intersection, and a turn to the right goes to small **Jungutan** village, site of the third Karangasem water palace. **Pura Tirta Telaga Tista**, its official name, is not so much a palace, actually, as a small complex of ponds situated in a quiet and relaxing setting; a nice spot to stop and stroll around.

Back at the intersection, the road continues west through **Sibetan**, known throughout Indonesia for its delicious *salak* (snakeskin fruit), a crisp, tart fruit encased in a brown rind that has the look and feel of snakeskin. The winding road through Sibetan is lined by densely-planted *salak* palms, and trucks may be seen loading them for market in the major harvest season, January–February, and again from August–September. Several varieties are grown here, some very sweet, and all very unique to Bali. The *salak* sold in *pasars* (markets) and supermarkets elsewhere in Indonesia come from Central Java, and contain more tannin. Peel the scaly skin and enjoy the crispy pulp wrapped around a large seed.

Much to the dismay of many *salak* farmers, the Sibetan area has been named one of Bali's "agro-tourism" destinations. There are a few homestays here, and investors have already begun snapping up land, so for better or worse, more development can be expected in the near future. Kiosks along the road sell products made from *salak*: syrup, chips, candied *salak*, and *dodol*, a sweet, sticky candy. Thickets of the thorny palms line the road, interspersed with coffee and cacao plantations and groves of giant bamboo. It's a completely different type of beauty than the by-now familiar rice terraces.

Soon after the *salak* plantations, a road to the left leads a short distance to **Putung**, and from there to **Duda**, at the foot of Mt. Agung. This village holds a large festival in the temple of origin on the full moon of the fourth month. There are a couple of *warungs* here for those interested in taking a break and soaking in the atmosphere. After Duda there is another intersection. Straight ahead goes west to Rendang and from there north to Besakih, but the road to the left goes through Sidemen to Semarapura.

En route to Sidemen the road passes through **Iseh** village. As the road crosses mountains and valleys and over meandering rivers the scenery changes here from the previous plantations to rice fields in the wet season and vegetables in the other months.

Sarong-clad women go about their daily chores. Iseh's claim to fame is that the renowned painter Walter Spies (1895–1942) once lived in a small hut here and it's said that he produced some of his best work during that time. Additionally, an early 20th century Swiss painter, Theo Meier, chose the community life of Iseh with Mt. Agung in the background, as one of his subjects.

Sidemen (pronounced *seed-a men*) is well worth a visit as well as a nice stay for a night or two for some commune-with-nature time. The scenery is gorgeous, surrounded by terraced fields growing traditional varieties of Balinese rice during rainy months and chilies and cassava in the dry season. Clove trees line the road, emitting a wonderful fragrance at harvest time. There is a good homestay with a magnificent view down across a valley of rice terraces to the sea and southern Bali, which would be a good base for rice field trekking outings. Close by is a weaving factory where high quality traditional textiles (*endek*) are produced. In Sidemen there are also several places where the costly *kain songket* is woven from silk, with gold- and silver-colored threads added to create the patterns.

The road onwards to Rendang leads first through an old village, **Selat**, in an area that suffered badly from the 1963 Mt. Agung eruption. It is possible to climb the volcano; a sign reading "Gunung Agung, 10 km" marks a turn-off where a road leads a good way up the sacred mountain. Don't attempt the climb unless you are well-prepared and have a guide. Reaching the summit requires an overnight stay en route. English-speaking guides are locally available, but be sure to bring along food, water and warm clothing for the steep climb to the summit. At 3,142 m (10,308 ft), this is Bali's highest peak and it gets quite cold. The climb should only be attempted between July and October.

The village just after Selat, **Padangaji**, is known for its *gambuh* association. *Gambuh* is a classical dance-drama with slow, stately music that is rarely performed these days. The road then continues on through **Muncan**, past one of the most exciting rice field landscapes in Bali. The terraces are at their most spectacular when flooded, just before the young rice is transplanted, making them look like fields of reflecting mirrors. Finally at Rendang is the main Semarapura–Besakih road—a right turn goes to Bali's "Mother Temple."

—Danker Schaareman

VISITING AMLAPURA, TIRTA GANGGA, SERAYA & SIDEMAN

AMLAPURA
(TELEPHONE CODE: 0363)

About 78 km (48 miles) from Denpasar, there's no reason to stay in Amlapura with Candidasa and Amed only 20 minutes away. For those looking to focus on inland trekking, Tirta Gangga or Sideman offer more options.

GETTING AROUND
Bemos run frequently between Amlapura and the surrounding areas, as it is a business and market center. *Bemos* to and from Ujung (water palace), Denpasar, and Singaraja leave from the terminal east of town. Fares are under $1.

TIRTA GANGGA
(TELEPHONE CODE: 0363)

North of Amlapura, Tirta Gangga is still a small hamlet, quiet by day and even quieter by night, a nice place for a few days of hiking and reading with periodic dips in the sacred spring-fed pools of the water palace. Reach Tirta Gangga from Candidasa by *bemo* via Amlapura or from Amed for less than $1.

ACCOMMODATIONS & DINING
There are a few small, simple lodgings near the water palace overlooking rice terraces that make a good base for trekking expeditions. Several *warungs* are in a little shopping arcade in front of the water palace.

Good Karma is a cheap homestay that serves Indonesian and Chinese meals. Alternatively, there's the international-standard Tirta Ayu Hotel (see below) and its outstanding restaurant within the palace grounds.

Dhangin Taman Inn, tel: 22059, 10 rooms, 2 with fans adjacent to water palace. Restaurant. English-speaking guide service and shuttle bus to north, east and south Bali, and Lombok. $9.

Kusuma Jaya Inn, tel: 21250. 16 relatively comfortable budget rooms with wonderful vistas on a steep hill above the pools. Take the steps on the left just past the bridge. Semi-open showers. From $9.

Tirta Ayu Hotel & Restaurant, inside the Tirta Gangga water palace, tel:/fax: 22503, tel: 21425, www.hoteltirtagangga.com. Located within the grounds of one of Bali's most treasured palaces

overlooking the ponds, towered over by Mt. Agung, with ocean and rice fields in the distance. Owned by members of the royal family and opened in 2003. Also has an upmarket restaurant serving a wide selection of dishes at high-quality prices. An excellent stopping point for a delicious meal in a breathtaking setting. Clean, modern restrooms at the restaurant open to the public are a bonus. From $150.

Villa Djamrud and **Villa Tirta Ayu**, inside the Tirta Gangga water palace, tel: 21383, www.tirtaganna-villas.com. Same owners as the Tirta Ayu Hotel & Restaurant. From $120.

ACTIVITIES
Trekking
Many people visit Tirta Gangga to take a dip in the healing waters of the sacred pools. (There's also a fresh-water spring by the bridge.) However, aside from the palace, there are some excellent walks here suitable for all levels of fitness. Guides can be hired in the water palace parking lot or from your accommodation in Amed or Candidasa. ($7–10/hr). Don't forget to bring a camera.

It is also popular to try one of the many walks through the rice fields surrounding the palace. Ask around or just keep to the wider, well-worn paths. There's a wonderful cascade of rice terraces, and steep hills drop down into **Culik** just north of Tirta Gangga. **Pura Lempuyang Luhur**, high on Mt. Lempuyang, also offers some good trekking. The areas around **Selat** and **Sideman** (off the main Amlapura–Rendang road) are especially good.

Cycling
This is probably the best area in Bali for biking. There are some steep hills but there are lots of great back roads. Rent a bike elsewhere and either ride it out or bring it on the *bemo*.

Cultural tours
JED (Jaringan Ekowisata Desa)—Village Ecotourism Network, Jl. Kayu Jati 9Y, Seminyak, tel: (0361) 737 447, www.jed.or.id, offers tours to Dukuh Sibetan village *salak* plantations, a program designed to help villages raise funds for cultural and conservation activities through tourism. Communities design and implement their own programs and receive all proceeds from JED tours, which include local guides and foods.

SERAYA
(TELEPHONE CODE: 0363)

Seraya is on the easternmost peninsula of Bali northeast from Jasri (also spelled Jasi). This area is only beginning to develop, as the coastal road is badly in need of repair. However, an enterprising foreigner has constructed villas here and other accommodations are sure to follow.

ACCOMMODATIONS
Seraya Shores, Seraya Barat, contact Amanda Pummer, mobile: 0813-3855-7433, 04228-77162, www.serayashores.com. 4 unique styles of thatch-roofed villas, timber decks, open bathrooms, stunning sea views. **Cliffside Sunset Restaurant** prides itself in its BBQ seafood buffet. **Hillside Pandan Restaurant** overlooks the beach below, with coconut timber decking, ideal for lunch. No menus; chef prepares meals from freshest ingredients available each day. Yoga Barn. Contact Amanda Pummer for rates.

SIDEMAN
(TELEPHONE CODE: 0366)

One of the most beautiful areas in all of Bali is the Sidemen (pronounced *seed-a men*) valley, northeast of Semarapura (Klungkung), and west of Amlapura. Take the road over the bridge east of Semarapura, going north through exquisitely beautiful scenery of sharp green hills and rice terraces interspersed with *kubu* (thatched huts for keeping tools and animals, or for taking a shaded rest). Sidemen and Iseh are renowned for their views from the jagged hills, plunging down to steep rice terraces in the near distance and soaring up again to Mt. Agung rising above it all. Sidemen is known throughout Bali for its *kain endek ikat* cloth and golden-threaded *songket* weaving. There are four artists' workshops in the Sidemen area where visitors can watch the workers weaving.

Bemos from Semarapura cost $1, a rather steep price since it's a comparatively seldom-used route.

ACCOMMODATIONS
Homestays and hotels are all owned by members of the local royalty, the family of Cokorda Dangin. If all rooms are full in one place, they can refer you to another. Prices can be inclusive of up to 3 meals a day, cooked at your homestay, since there are no restaurants catering to non-Balinese tastes in the area. There are no fans needed in the cool mountain air.

Pondok Wisata Pantai Kikian (Homestay), Sideman, tel:/fax: 23005. Follow the signs on the right side of the road just after Sideman heading northeast from Amlapura. Perched high in the hills surrounded by forest, superb panoramas and total serenity. Spacious Balinese-style brick bungalows with verandahs facing the rice fields under the watchful eye of Mt. Agung. Hot water, books in every room, small spa pool. Call first, as overseer Ida Ayu Mas Andayani is heavily involved with an arts program for local school kids. Staff takes guests on walks, introduces them to weaving of traditional *endek* and *songket* weaving, and proudly shows off photos of celebrities who have stayed here. $30–50, including 3 meals/day.

Sideman Homestay, tel: 23009, fax: 23015. This is the first homestay coming from the south, up the steps on the hill above the road, just before entering the village. Deluxe rooms and villas, $30–40, including 3 meals a day.

Subak Tabola Inn, Tabola village, tel:/fax: 23015, mobile: 0813-3715-3444, www.subaktabolainnbali.com. At the intersection in the center of Sideman, follow signs for 2 km (1.2 miles) south to Tabola. Extremely quiet and remote in the rice fields, with mountain and valley views. Rooms are clean with spacious porches. Prices depend on how many meals/day are required. Children under 12 receive 50% discount. Restaurant has the usual Chinese/Indonesia menu with Balinese specialties such as *betutu* (smoked duck) and *babi guling* (roast suckling pig). Airport pick-up and trekking trips can be arranged. $40–50.

AMED, TULAMBEN, AND BEYOND

Secluded Beaches and a Diver's Underwater Paradise

The area referred to as **Amed** actually comprises of six villages, Amed being the largest. Going east along the coastline, after Amed beach is Jemeluk, Bunutan, Lipah, Lehan, and Selang, stretching 10 km (6 miles) along Bali's northeastern coastline. The terrain ranges from the dry flatlands at Amed village to rugged cliffs between the beaches. There's a beautiful view of Jemeluk bay from up in the hills further east, making it one of the most photographed of the area's bays.

Bali's newest beach resort
As is evident when following the road north from Amlapura the landscape changes

dramatically before reaching the northeastern coastline. It is a very dry region unsuitable for farming, making it one of Bali's poorest areas. Until the last decade, lack of suitable roads into Amed virtually cut villagers off from the rest of Bali, leaving them little changed. A few foreign-owned bungalows popped up in the early 1990s, but only intrepid travelers came due to lack of public transportation into the area.

All that changed in 2000 when a new road was finally installed, beginning an onslaught of the bungalows, resorts, and villas that are now side-by-side along the entire stretch of beachfront, while more are

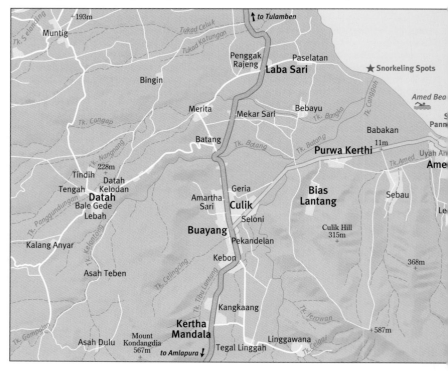

still being built. The surrounding villages seem unimpressed, however, and go about their business for the most part. This makes the Amed area a gem for those who wish to relax away from the crowds and experience a bit of the "real" Bali. With many of the inhabitants earning their livelihoods from fishing, double-outrigger boats line the beaches and can be hired for fishing expeditions early morning and late afternoon accompanied by local fishermen.

Other villagers are involved in salt-making, which can be seen at the bottom of the road near Amed. Working during the dry season, shallow flats of sea water are dammed up near the shore and are left to seep into the sand for one or two days. The water and a thin layer of sand are then placed into large baskets filled with stones held up by the wooden structures that are seen on this stretch of beach. More sea water is added and the filtered water pours into troughs, where it is dried in the sun until the salt crystallizes. It takes about a week to process the "sea salt", which is now popular among chefs in Western countries. The income from this relatively new product, together with tourism, has greatly improved the lives of the local people.

The Amed area is a divers' and snorkelers' paradise, with coral reefs just off the beach. It is also a good base for underwater adventures further afield. Tulamben and its World War II-vintage USS *Liberty* wreck is only 20 minutes away, with the Kubu dive sites a bit further north. There are cultural attractions nearby, too, in Amlapura. All accommodations can also arrange trekking adventure and most also rent bicycles and motorcycles for exploring back roads.

When it's time to depart, travelers can return to Amlapura and from there take the back road up to Besakih, or they can continue up the east coast road all the way to Singaraja, passing the lava fields of the 1963 eruption of Mt. Agung.

Tulamben

Tulemben, 30 km (18 miles) northwest of Amed, has attracted serious divers for several years. Its draw is the wreck of the US Army supply ship, the **USS Liberty**, which was torpedoed by Japanese invaders off the

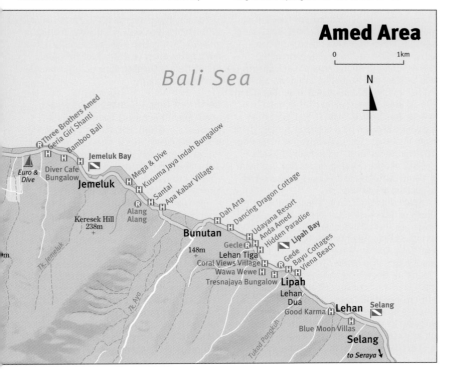

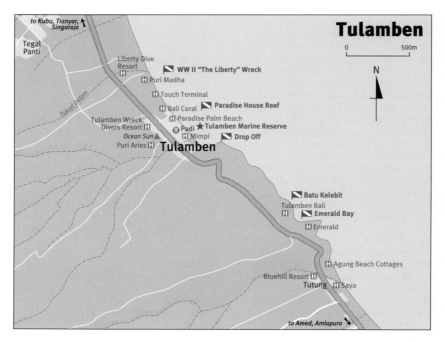

Lombok coast in 1942. Rendered useless, it was towed to Tulamben, unloaded, and left for salvage. When mother nature reared her ferocious head in 1963 in the form of the devastating Mt. Agung eruption, the *Liberty* was pushed back to sea by lava flows, where its 120 m (390 ft) hull rested at depths of 3 m (9.8 ft) at its highest point to 29 m at its lowest. It is located about 25 m (95 ft) from the shore and can be reached by a short swim from the beach. The amazing array of several hundred varieties of reef fish and 100 or so species of open-ocean pelagics that live there make it easily accessible, even to snorkelers, especially at low tide.

Apart from the *Liberty*, which draws hundreds of divers each day during high season, there are several other local dive sites worthy of exploration. Tulamben Wall, also known as the "Drop Off", is deeper, making it a favorite among technical divers. Seraya is a haven for "muck" divers who enjoy scrounging in the shallows for macro species such as tiny shrimp, beautiful crabs, and mimic octopi. Kubu is little visited and is home to several varieties of pygmy seahorse. Paradise Reef is an artificial reef project at a depth of only 3–4 m (10–12 ft), making it excellent for night dives.

For non-divers, there's little else to see or do in Tulamben. Basically, it's a small fishing village with a golden egg that sustains it for a few months every year. The best time for diving here is October–June or July, when the sea is usually calm.

Northwest from Tulamben to Singaraja

Just beyond Tulamben 15 minutes to the northwest is **Kubu**. Located on the opposite side of the *Liberty* wreck, it also caters to divers. Presently there are only a couple of dive centers and eateries there, but development is sure to come as Bali continues to attract more foreign investors looking for real estate.

The road further northwest from here eventually reaches Singaraja, hugging the coastline all the way, and the scenery is shocking. Everything in this area was completely wiped out by lava flows from the 1963 Mt. Agung eruption. The rice fields and plantations so typical of Bali are replaced by deep gashes in the earth and enormous black boulders. There's a salt panning area just outside of Tulamben, using a different system as the one in Amed.

Past this point there is not much else to see until Telakula, crossing into northern Bali.

—*Linda Hoffman*

VISITING AMED, TULAMBEN & KUBU/SERAYA
(TELEPHONE CODE: 0363)

With only 30 km (18 miles) separating Amed and Tulamben, deciding where to stay is a matter of personal preference. Hardcore divers interested in the USS *Liberty* wreck may choose to stay in Tulamben, but holiday-makers who indulge in the occasional dive might prefer the Amed area, where there is a wider choice of accommodations. Kubu and its sister village Seraya are northwest of Tulamben and are in the beginning stages of development. Therefore, there are presently not many options there, but that is certain to change in the not-so-distant future.

AMED

Amed is on the easternmost tip of Bali where some of Bali's most idyllic beaches are located. It is Candidasa's biggest competitor for east coast get-away spots, and while both offer relaxing seaside holidays among village folk, each has its own personality. The Amed area attracts snorkelers, casual divers, and beginners, families and folks just needing to drop out for a while. Like Candidasa, it offers a wide range of accommodations.

The nearest ATM is in Amlapura, 30 minutes away, where there is also a Hardy's shopping center carrying everything from groceries to souvenirs.

GETTING THERE & GETTING AROUND
Amed's beaches are about 2 hours from the Ngurah Rai airport and 60 minutes north of Candidasa. Note that even though the road along the beaches has been greatly improved, Amed is still relatively remote—which makes it quieter than other shorelines—and there is no regular transportation service that stops there. *Bemos* can, of course, be chartered from other areas, but the easiest way to get there is to hire a car and a driver, giving travelers the option of making stops along the way.

Taxis from the Denpasar airport cost about $40. **Motorbikes** are available for hire in many Amed locations for $5–8/day. Transport by **private car** and driver hire from Amed are roughly (in high season): $15–20 for trips within the Amed area or to Tirta Gangga, $25 to Amlapura, and $45 to Besakih and Mt. Batur. Further afield: $45 to Ubud and $40 to the Denpasar airport.

There's a new service, a high-speed transfer to the Gili Islands (Lombok) via the **Kuda Hitam** (Black Horse) operated by Eco-Dive. It leaves Amed at 8:30 am every day, arriving at the Gilis at 9:30 am, dropping off and picking up on all three islands. Final departure is from Gili Trawangan at 11 am, arriving Amed

at noon. $55/adults; $45/children. Bookings can be made at Eco-Dive in Amed or any of its local agents. Boat is 11 m (36 ft) long, seats 20, and is equipped with radio, GPS, and safety equipment.

ACCOMMODATIONS
Deciding where to stay is largely determined by the types of activities planned and gut instinct. If the place "feels" right, then that's the place for you. Generally speaking, the further east you travel along the coast, the more expensive resorts and restaurants become. Jemeluk beach attracts backpackers and budget travelers, with each subsequent beach becoming more expensive. Likewise, the beach at Amed village has coarse, black sand, and the further away from Mt. Augung (east), the softer the sand becomes. Most accommodations do not have in-room tv but have one for communal viewing in their eatery.

The six beaches that comprise "Amed" are: (from west to east) Amed, Jemeluk, Bunutan, Lipah, Lehan, and Selang.

Budget (under $25)
Bayu Cottages, Lipah beach, tel: 23495, www.bayu-cottages.com. 6 ocean-view rooms on a hillside with terraces or balconies. All have large, marble tiled bathrooms with hot water, satellite tv, AC, and fan. Free WiFi. Infinity edge pool with nearby restaurant. $20–35.

Eka Purnama Cottages, on the eastern-most end of Amed at Aas, Banyuning, mobile: 0828-372-2642, 0813-3757-8060, www.eka-purnama.com. Family-run quiet, remote resort. 4 cottages overlooking the sea with single and double beds, fans, Western toilets, restaurant. Budget.

Geria Giri Shanti Bungalows, Jl. Jemeluk, mobile: 0812-387-3866. Centrally located clean budget accommodation with 4 bungalows and nice gardens. Private baths have hot water. Café. From $10.

Kembali Beach Bungalows, Jl Jemeluk, Amed, mobile: +62 817-476-8313, www.kembalibeachbun-galows.com. 8 spacious bungalows with fan and AC, private bathroom, hot water, terrace. Pool overlooks the sea. Restaurant. $20–25, includes breakfast.

Moderate ($25–50)
Aiona Garden of Health, Bunutan, Amed beach, mobile: 0813-3816-1730, www.aionabali.com. Health resort, guesthouse, vegetarian restaurant, yoga, meditation. Shell Museum. Charming and odd, links holidays to healthy food from their own organic gardens. Guests' wellbeing is a top priority, to return visitors to their daily routines refreshed

and joyous a goal. From $25/standard room; $73/family house for 4.

Apa Kabar Villas, Bunutan, tel:/fax: 23492, www.apakabarvillas.com. Situated next to the Indian Ocean, 2 twin villas, 4 cottages, swimming pool, dive center, and open-air restaurant. $25–100.

Blue Moon Villas, Selang Beach, tel:/fax: 21428, mobile: 0812-352-2597, www.bluemoonvilla.com. Stunning ocean views. Luxury villas set in tropical garden. 2 pools. International restaurant and bar. From $35.

Double One Villas, tel: 22427, Amed beach, www.doubleonevillasamed.com. 3 oceanfront cottages with king size bed, AC, marble floor, corner tub and shower, rattan and bamboo furniture, private terrace. 2 cottages facing the sea with the same amenities. 1 garden view bungalow with ceiling fan and private terrace, 2 standard rooms with fan and terrace. Swimming pool, restaurant, bar, diving school. Restaurant has weekly live music. $35–65.

Kusuma Jaya Indah Homestay, Jemuluk, tel: 23488. 8 bungalows. Established in 1993 but spruced up annually, entrance is on a steep hill that slopes through a nice garden to a swimming pool and the beach beyond. Wonderful vistas. Both AC and fan rooms. Hot water showers. Decent restaurant. Interesting notice in rooms not to buy from beach sellers to avoid creating the aggressiveness found in Kuta and Lovina. Helpful staff can also arrange massages, fishing/sailing trips in local *jukung*, dives, snorkel equipment, trekking, transport, and motorbike rental. Beachfront bungalows $40, including breakfast and tax.

Sunshine Bungalows, Bunutan, tel: 23491. 2-story brick bungalows in Balinese style. Clean AC rooms with hot water, fridge. Swimming pool, 2 restaurants. $28–53.

Uyah Amed Hotel, Jl. Pantai Timur (the first hotel on the approach from Culik), tel:/fax: 23462, www.hoteluyah.com. 16 sea-view bungalows and 1 family villa. Swimming pool, Amed Dive Center, Café Garam serves Western and Asian cuisine. Tours and trips around East Bali, mountain bike rental. $25–50.

Vienna Beach Bungalows, Lipah, Amed, tel: 23494, fax: 21883. 12 rooms surrounded by coconut palms and exotic flowers. Restaurant serves Balinese dishes. Traditional music and dance some nights. $30–60.

Villa Coral Bungalows, Jemeluk, mobile: 0813-3852-0243, www.villacoral.com. 2 private beach-front villas facing a world-class reef, each sleeps up to 5 people. Behind the villas are 4 double rooms with AC, fan, hot water, and verandah. Restaurant. $35–75.

Intermediate ($50–75)

Anda Amed Resort, tel: 23498, www.andaamedresort.com. 1 bedroom villas with private garden, queen size bed, huge bathroom with tub and shower, AC, fridge. Family villa has 2 AC bedrooms and 2 baths. Large, airy bedrooms with sliding glass doors, providing sea views from the bed. Individual dining area, hot water, tv, DVD. Big infinity pool, restaurant, bar, massage, and spa treatments. $50–90. Check website for Internet specials.

Hidden Paradise Cottages, Lipah, Bunutan, Abang, tel: 23514; fax: 23555, 22958, www.hiddenparadise-bali.com. 16 cottages. Hot water, all rooms have AC. Complete facilities, sandy beach, bicycles, and water sports tours. Swimming pool has a water cascade. $70–120.

Puri Wirata Dive Resort, Villas & Spa, Bunutan, tel: 23523, www.puriwirata.com. A choice of deluxe or superior rooms, bungalows and 5 new villas built in 2009 on a slope ending at the beach. Great coral reefs right in front of the hotel. Dive center, spa, and 2 pools. From $50.

Santai Bungalows, Bunutan, tel: 23487, www.santai-bali.com. 10 simple thatched roof bungalows in Celebes style with Indonesian ethnic furniture made from products from local villages. AC, open bathroom, verandah. $70–115.

Villa Batu Tangga, Banyuning, mobile: 0813-3858-5993, www.batutangga.com. 8 bedrooms, 2 in the main house, 4 in the annex, 2 in charming guesthouse. Sitting and dining areas with AC and satellite tv, DVD. Staff of 7, pool with Jacuzzi, snorkel gear, car, bikes, access to the sea. From $62 for 1 room; $520/whole house.

Villa Flamboyant, Banyuning beach, mobile: 0828-9700-8353 or 0828-3722-636. Private villa with swimming pool located directly on the sea. 5 double-bed bedrooms, terrace, 5 person staff, and driver. From $55, breakfast included.

First class ($75–100)

Arya Amed Beach Resort, Jl. Raya Amed, Bunuatan, tel: 23513, fax: 21941, www.aryaamed.com. New in 2010, 6 ocean-view suites large enough to add an extra bed, giant bathtubs; 2 deluxe and 12 superior rooms without bathtub for families, each with 1 queen and 1 double bed. All have AC and outdoor shower. Infinity pool. $85-135

Life in Amed Bali, Leyan village, Bunutan, tel: 23152, Mobile: 0813-3850-1555, www.lifebali.com. 6 beach cottages decorated in Balinese and modern design, king size bed, fine linens. 2 villas ideal for families or romantic getaway. Restaurant serves organic salads. Can arrange tours. Large pool. $85–105. See website for Internet and low season rates.

Luxury ($100–up)

Jepun Bali Villas, Bunutan, Amed, contact Scott Swingle, tel: 081-337-577-083, www.jepunbalivillas.

com. Resort consists of 4 master bedroom AC villas on the beach with terraces, main villa with kitchen and living area, recreational villa with fitness center, dining pavilion. Teak furniture, artifacts chosen by owner for each villa. Private massage, cook, concierge, and security. Infinity pool with swim-up bar, tropical gardens with waterfalls and koi ponds. $7,500/week, e-mail for daily rates. Includes full use of resort, staff of 7, daily breakfast, special dinner with dancers, 4 massages, 4 diving sessions.

DINING

As the majority of accommodations in Amed have restaurants, they are not listed separately here.
Barong Café & Restaurant, mobile: 0818-0558-5010. Balinese, Indonesian, and international food. Call for free pick-up in Amed area.
Sails Restaurant, Leyan village, Bunutan, tel: 22006. Perhaps the only fine dining restaurant on the beach. Exceptional Indonesian, vegetarian, and Western food at surprisingly reasonable prices. Specialties: soups, pan fried mahi-mahi, prawn cutlets, slow-cooked chicken curry, pork spare ribs, tender fillet steak, sausage and mash, lamb medallions. Special desserts: heavenly crepes. Free water. Free pick up and drop off in the Amed area. Reservations recommended.
Sama Sama Café, mobile: 0852-370-5-8440. Midway up the stretch of beaches. Good grilled seafood. Cheap.
Warung Bobo II, Jl. Jemeluk, near Kembali Beach Bungalows. Reasonably priced seafood near the shore. Popular at sunset.
Warung Kadek, Lipah-Bunutan, opposite Coral View Hotel, mobile: 0852-3799-7885. Reasonable prices for Balinese, Chinese, and Western food. Scenic location.
Warung Kemulan, Selang, on the far eastern end of the beach on a hill with great views. Traditional food; cheap prices.

ENTERTAINMENT

Wawa-Wewe I & II, Lipah, Amed, tel: 23506 or 23522, www.bali-wawawewe.com. A bar and restaurant is attached to Wawa-Wewe I. Great menu, cocktails. Live music on Tuesday and Saturday nights, and Balinese dance performances on Wednesdays and Fridays that attract locals and foreigners.

DIVING

There is good diving with healthy corals at Jemeluk Bay, with a gentle slope from the shore quickly dropping off a 40 m (130 ft) wall, and good drift dives with schools of barracuda, giant barrel sponges, eels, and reef fish at Bunutan for experienced divers. Amed dive shops can also arrange dives in other areas of eastern Bali, including the *Liberty* wreck at Tulamben.

Amed Dive Center, in Uyah Amed Hotel, Jl. Pantai Timur, tel: 23462, www.ameddivecenter.com. Full range of PADI dive courses, snorkeling, sailing, and sunset tours. Packages. Guides speak English, French, and German.
Eco-Dive Bali, Jemeluk Beach, tel: 23482, www.ecodivebali.com. English, French, German, Dutch, Indonesian, and Japanese speaking guides. Owned and operated by a PADI Master Instructor with over 35 years diving experience, including 20 years in SE Asia. Daily dive trips to the best sites in Bali, full range of courses from Open Water to Instructor. $1 from every dive and $5 from every course goes to sponsoring local social and ecological projects. Rates from $75/Jemeluk/2 dives to $85/Gili Selang. Courses: Review (1 day/2 dives) $80; Divemaster (3–4 weeks) $750. All prices include hotel pick-up from Amed or Tulamben, full set of equipment, certification fees where applicable, and instructor/guide. Night-dives $45; Non-divers $15.
Euro Dive Bali, Hidden Paradise Cottages, Lipah, tel:/fax: 23605, www.eurodivebali.com. PADI dive center established in 1999. English, French, Hungarian, and Indonesian speaking guides.
Stingray Dive Center & Divers Café, tel: 23479, mobile: 0819-3656-9547. Dive courses, daily trips to Amed coral walls or US *Liberty* $50; bungalows, restaurant, swimming pool. Divers Café Bungalows, mobile: 081-3385-20243, www.ameddiverscafe.com.

SNORKELING

With a reef that follows the entire coastline, snorkeling is good everywhere; the only thing to watch is the tides. Ask at your accommodation for current tide times. Jemeluk has the best corals, and the waters can be rough at Lipah, but there's a small wooden shipwreck there. Snorkel equipment in good condition costs about $4/day.

OTHER ACTIVITIES

While diving and snorkeling—or simply hanging out—are the main draw, Amed is also a good base for day trips to **Tirta Gangga** water palace and **Besakih** temple, which can be arranged by all accommodations, as can **fishing** or **sailing** trips in double-outrigger boats, either early morning or late afternoon with local fishermen (about $14 for 2 hours). Mackerel is the preferred catch.

To climb **Mt. Agung** and reach the summit in time for sunrise, leave Amed at 2 am by car and stop at *pasar* Agung to get a guide. Parts of the climb can be quite strenuous.

For **Pura Lempuyung Luhur** visits (east of Tirta Gangga), be prepared to climb 1,750 steps up to the temple, which can be reached via Culik to Aang. After a left turn at Aang, follow the signs to the temple.

SHOPPING

Amed is not a shopping area *per se*, but an oddity possibly worthy of a visit is the **Shell Museum** on Bunutan Beach at the Aiona Garden of Health.

Crystal Mountain Jewelry, Jl. Raja Bunutan, Lipah Beach (opposite Coral View Villas) sells modern art jewelry, antique beads, and pearl beading.

TULAMBEN

With shallow fringe reefs, dramatic drop-offs, and the World War II *Liberty* wreck all attracting thousands of species of marine life at every site, Tulamben is one of Bali's most popular dive spots, and a huge draw. Underwater visibility is 2 m (6.5 ft) on average and up to 30 m (98 ft) in the dry season with the temperature a constant 28°C. Diving is relaxed and easy, suitable for all levels of experience, from beginners to advanced. The *Liberty* rests 40 m (130 ft) from shore and is 110 m (360 ft) long, at depths of 5–35 m (16–115 ft). Look for The Wall, a drop-off right off the beach, with spectacular coral formations at 30 m (98 ft). Tulamben is 15 minutes from Kubu.

GETTING THERE & AROUND

Reach Tulamben by *bemo* or bus from Candidasa via Amlapura or from Singaraja for about Rp 8,000. Hired cars from either town cost about $12.

ACCOMMODATIONS

Budget (under $25)

Bali Coral Bungalows, tel: 22909. 10 basic, clean rooms with AC or fan and modern bathrooms. Café. From $12.

Matahari Tulamben Resort & Tulamben Dive Center, tel: 22916, mobile: 0813-3863-6670, www. divetulamben.com. Accommodations for all budgets: bungalows and rooms, some without AC and hot water, owned by a Balinese family. Restaurant, pool. Dive Center managed by Putu, with over 20 years' experience. Offers PADI open water courses, introductory and fun dives. Rooms $15–60, including breakfast.

Tulamben Wreck Divers Resort, tel: 23400, www. tulambenwreckdivers.com. A wide range of accommodations to suit all budgets only 200 m (210 yds) from *Liberty* wreck site. Dive-and-stay packages; climbing tours. $20–120.

Colorful corals with the Liberty *wreck in the background, Tulamben*

Moderate ($25–50)

Liberty Dive Resort, tel: 23347, mobile: 0813-3776-2206, www.libertydiveresort.com. Located 300 m (980 ft) west of the *Liberty* shipwreck public car park entrance, 9 AC guest rooms with hot water, fridge, verandah. Restaurant serves continental breakfasts from 7 am, also lunch and dinner. Dive center opens at 7 am; dive trips can be arranged at short notice. $35–50.

Touch Terminal Resort, Tulamben beach, head office and reservations: Jl. Danau Tamblingan X/31, Jimbaran, tel: (0361) 774-504, (0361) 772-920, fax: (0361) 778-473, www.tulamben.com. German owned, directly on the beach, with the *Liberty* wreck only 200 m (650 ft) away. Completely remodeled in 2008, 2 bungalows, 23 rooms, 1 honeymoon suite, 1 family room. New 2-story restaurant, dive center, pool-beach bar. 2 pools, 1 for dive classes. $45–60.

The Toya Resort Bali, tel: +49 (0)1522 9567077, fax: +49 (0)3212 4451152, www.toyabali.com. An estate of 8 villas, each with its own garden and pool within swimming distance of the *Liberty* wreck. Villas designed using tropical materials and contemporary colors. Indoor-outdoor living at its best. From $50, reduced rates for weekly stays.

First class ($75–100)

Mimpi Resort Tulamben, tel: 21642, fax: 21939, www.mimpi.com. A sister to Mimpi Resort Menjangan near West Bali National Park, situated in front of the prime dive site. 12 patio rooms and 15 cottages with extremely tasteful architecture. Gorgeous pool and sensitive touches to rooms. All AC. Dive center, spa, restaurant. $90–175.

Luxury ($100–up)

Emerald Tulamben, tel: 22925, www.tulambenbali.com. Traditional Balinese style ocean view rooms, suite rooms, cottages, and villa with terrace, hot water, AC, fridge. Restaurant, coffee shop, bar, pool, helicopter pad, kids' room. Offers diving lessons and tours. From $126–366.

DINING

Tulamben's main street is lined with small eateries and most accommodations have restaurants, primarily serving average food.

However, there are a few independent eateries that are worthy of recognition. Try:

Safety Stop Bar & Restaurant, tel: 23593, www.safety-stop.com. Indonesian and international cuisine.

Warung Makan Komong, across the road from Wayan Restaurant & Bar and next door to Tulamben Wreck Divers Resort. Serves well-presented, large portions of good, fresh Indonesian and Western food at reasonable prices. Very clean.

Wayan Restaurant & Bar, on the main street, tel: 23406. Balinese and Indonesian food.

DIVING

There is a plethora of dive centers in Tulamben, most of them connected to resorts or other types of accommodations. In the high season (October–June or July), it's best to get started early if you want solitude, as the *Liberty* wreck can attract a hundred divers a day.

Bali Diving Academy Tulemban, head office and reservations: Jl. Danau Tamblingan 51, Sanur, tel: (0361) 270-252, www.scubali.com. Situated beachfront, offers macro lovers great dives along its house reefs. Day trips to Tulamben for divers and snorkelers. Night dives. The Diving Academy has PADI five-star facilities in 4 locations: Tulamben, Gili Trawangan (Lombok), Nusa Lembongan (Bali), and Pemuteran (North Bali). Australian owned and managed since 1990. Focuses on safety and service with style.

KUBU

Only 15 minutes northwest of Tulamben is the small fishing village of Kubu, located at the "other end" of the *Liberty* wreck. Kubu is in the beginning stages of development, but more is on the horizon as Bali continues to attract foreign investors. Kubu and neighboring Seraya are a macro paradise for divers. A black sand slope is covered with soft corals, pygmy seahorses, and other tiny rarities.

Scuba Seraya Resort, Kubu, tel: (0361) 283-922, fax: (0361) 281-347, www.scubaseraya.com. On Muntig Bay, thatched roofed villas and maisonettes with teak wood, marble, and natural stone acroutements from throughout Indonesia. Designed for style and serenity. Private black sand beach. $55–115.

Siddhartha Dive Resort & Spa, Kubu, tel: 23034, fax: 23035, www.siddhartha-bali.de. Built in 2009, a beautiful boutique hotel with ingenious architecture and interior design not usually associated with dive resorts, especially at such reasonable prices. 30 bungalows and villas (with private pools) set on 2.66 ha with 180 m (590 ft) of beachfront and Mt. Agung looming on the horizon. **Tantris Restaurant** serves high-standard Asian Fusion cuisine and wines with a themed menu each week. Can also cater special events. Pool-snack bar. Spa has "Six Elements" architecture. Includes **Werner Lau Diving Center**. Rooms from $57–128. Note that this resort is not suitable for children under age 8 years.

Bali Sea

Seririt & Munduk

Lovina Beach

Singaraja

Bedugul & Lake Bratan

Bungkulan Point

Penarukan Point

Pura Beji

Kubutambahan

Sangsit
Bungkulan

Buleleng Harbour

Kampung Baru
Penarukan
Jagaraga
Pura Dalem

Kampung Anyar
Banyuning

Lingga Beach
Banjarjawa
Jinengdalem
Bengkala

Singaraja
Penglatan
Menyali

Beratan
Pohborgong
Suwug

Sukasada
Sari Mekar
Alas Angker
Sawan

Pemaron
Panji
Sudaji
Bebe

Tegal Linggah
Pegadungan

Lovina Beach
Enjung Buntekan

Celuk Agung

Anturan
Ambengan
Silang Jana
Bukit Beb
4

Celuk Buluh
Kalibukbuk
Gitgit Waterfall
Pegayaman
Sekumpul

Enjung Sangiang
Kaliasem

Celuk Pengastulan
Gitgit

Celuk Labuhanaji
Temukus

Enjung Pengastulan
Sing Sing Waterfall
Kayu Putih
Lemukih

Celuk Ponjok Cukli

Pengastulan
Seririt

Ume Anyar
Sulanyah
Dencarik
Tiga Wasa

Patemon
Kalianget
Banjar Tegehe
Cempaga

Ringdikit
Hot Spring
Brahma Arama Vihara
Sidetapa

Ularan
Banjar

Views
Munduk Bestala
Pedawa
Mou Penggi 2153

Mayong
Bestala
Banyu Seri
Bali Handara Kosaido Country Club

Unggahan
Gunung Sari
Gobleg
Lake Buyan
Wanagiri

Busung Biu
Titab
Tirta Sari
Kayu Putih
Pancasari

Munduk Mengatang 884m
Kekeran
Pelapuan
Munduk
Lake Tamblingan
Candikuning
Mount Mangu Pura Puca 2020

Telaga
Kedis
Bengkel
Umejero
Gesing
Mount Tapak 1909m
Bali Botanical Gardens
Lake Bratan

Munduk Ngandang 944m
Subuk
Tinggar Sari
Mount Lesung 1865m
Pura Ulu Danu Bra

Sepang
Bantiran
Pura Gubug Tamblingan
Lubang Nagaloka
Bukit Mungsu Indah
Bedu Recre Park

Puncak Sari
Pupuan
Mount Pucuk 1629m
Bedugil

Bongan Cina
Munduk Pantas 762m
Pujungan
Mount Sengayang 2087m
Mount Pohen 2063m

Pajahan
Mount Batukau 2271m
Mount Adeng 1826m
Batunya

Munduk Temu
Batungsel
Baturiti

Tista
Kebon Padangan
Sanda
Rice Fields & Vista
Hot Springs
Angseri

Belatungan
Senganan
Jatiluwuh
Apuan
Mekar

Belimbing
Pura Luhur Batukaru
Wongaya Gede
Babahan
Lu

Pangeragoan
Sarinbuana
Mengesta
Tua

Wanagiri
Tengkudak
Penebel
Biaung

Mundeh
Pitra
Yeh Gang
Pet

Rando Hill 319m
Penatahan Hot Spring
Payangan

Pupuan Sawah
Gunung Salak
Dalang
Jegu

Lumbung
Rejasa
Buruan
Marga

Tiying Gading
Margarana Memorial
Tunjuk
Sembun

Gadungan
Kesiut
Butterfly Park

Singaraja to Tejakula

Kintamani & Mt. Batur

0   5km

N

Bukti

Pura Ponjok Batu

Pacung
Julah
Bondalem
Tejakula

Depeha
Tunjung
Sembiran
Les

ntinghing
Tajun
Sambi Renteng

akisan
Madenan
Penuktukan

Mendaa Hill
688m

Ngis Point

Kutuh
Subaya
★ Yeh Mempeh
Waterfall

Satra
Siakin
Tianyar Barat

ungan
Mount
Tengayang
+ 1117m
Tianyar Tengah

Ban

Mount
Mengandang
+ 1363m
Pangejaran
Dausa
Bantang
Pura Tegeh Kuripan
Sukawana
Pinggan
Belandingan

Selulung
Mt. Penulisan
1746m
Pejukung

Tambakan
Daup
Songan A

Mount Langlang
501m
Catur
Belantih
Serahi
Mount Batur
1412m
Songan B

Belanga
Awan
Gunung Bau
Kintamani
Batur Utara
*Pura Ulun
Danu Batur*
Toya Bungkah
Lake Batur
Lake Batur
Trunyan

Batukaang
Manik Liyu
Batur Selatan
Hot Spring,
Volcanic Lake
Bali Aga Village and
Pura Gede
Pancering Jagat

Binyan
Ulian
Belancan
Penelokan
Pura Jati Batur
Jati

Belok Sidan
Mengani
Lembean
Mountain
View
Kedisan
Mount Abang
2151m

Pelaga
Banyung Gede
Batur Tengah
Buahan

Bunutin
Mangguh
Katung
Sekar
Dadi
Abang Songan
Suter
Abang Tudinding
Tapis Hill
1608m

Langgahan
Abuan
Sekaan
Pengotan

ntapan
Kerta

Penglumbaran

Pupuan
*Pura
Besakih*

Elephant
Safari Park
Taro
Tiga
Pempatan
Besakih

tang
Puhu
Buahan
Holy Spring
Yangapi
Menanga

siapan
angsan
Senbatu
Manukaya
Pura Sakenan
Tirta Empul
Traditional
Village
Paninjoan
Padangaji
Sebudi

Bukian
Kedisah
Gunung Kawi
Sulahan
Kubu
Rendang
Muncan
Peringsari

erean
engah
Melinggih
Kelusa
Tampaksiring
Susut
Jehem
Tembuku
Bangbang
Nongan
Selat

Tegallalang
Rice
Terraces
Kenderan
Petak
Demulih
Cempaga
Pura Kehen
Undisan
Iseh

Carangsari
Keliki
Topeng Dance
Sanding
© Bangli
Kawan
Nyanglan
Pesaban
Sidemen

aubelayu
Kedewatan
Pura Telaga Waja
Petak
Abuan
Tohpati
Bungbungan
Tabda

Monkey Forest &
Pura Bukit Sari
White Water
Rafting
Pejeng
Bebalang
Timuhun

Sangeh

INTRODUCTION

Northern Bali

For many years, Lovina Beach was Northern Bali's prime tourist destination, luring to its shores those who wanted the beach life but rejected the crowds in the south. Apart from Lovina, little else was sufficiently developed to attract large numbers of tourists. As with several other formerly unexplored areas on the island, increased investment and improved infrastructure have brought about many changes, and nearly all of them benefit travelers by giving them a wider range of climates, terrains, and activities from which to choose during their Bali holidays.

A quick look at a map will reveal that the vast expanse that is Northern Bali is dominated by two volcanoes and their accompanying cool highland climes and a very long coastline. Thus, deciding where to stay is a relatively simple choice of sea or mountains, keeping in mind that it is completely doable to stay in both areas in one trip. For travelers who prefer to overnight where accommodations, food, and transportation are easily available, the selection can be narrowed down even more. The widest variety of accommodations for seaside life is still in and around Lovina; for the mountains it's the Bedugul Highlands. All excursions in Northern Bali can be made from either base in one day if a cursory glance is sufficient.

The north coast

The area called **Lovina** is actually a long stretch of beach passing through six villages with different names. Eateries, souvenir shops, and a complete range of accommodations line both sides of the highway. The younger crowd often chooses either budget homestays with Balinese families or the cheaper rooms in multi-storied hotels. Many of the hotels also have bungalows, which may be preferable for the more mature, although some return to foreign-owned homestays every year. Near the central beach at Kalibubuk village is the largest concentration of amenities; those who wish a bit of quiet

and countryside should go east or west from the main beach. West of Lovina south of **Seririt** is the Buddhist **Brahma Arama Vihara**, and in this area there are several wellness resorts and luxury villas. There are some stunningly beautiful drives through the countryside south of Seririt.

East of Lovina is **Singaraja**, the capital of Buleleng Regency and an historic port town. Several Dutch colonial buildings on the waterfront have been restored, as has a Chinese temple dating back to 1873. Standing in stilts in the sea opposite the temple is a compound of seafood restaurants, making a nice lunch stop. Also in Singaraja is Gedong Kirtya, a library/museum/research center containing ancient *lontar* (palm leaf) texts. Continuing east from Singaraja, there are some charming old villages and unusual temples, one with baroque architecture and the other with comic reliefs. Further east from Air Sanih hot springs, there are several spa and meditation resorts of varying prices.

Bedugul Highlands—Lake Bratan

Thanks to an increased number and a variety of accommodations, it is now comfortable to stay in the **Bedugal Highlands** for a few days to enjoy the scenery and fresh mountain air, and the number of available activities makes the region worthy of more than a mere day trip. If travelling to the highlands from Singaraja, the **waterfalls** at **Gitgit** are en route. South of Gitgit are the **Twin Lakes**, surrounded by clove, coffee, and tea plantations.

At the center of the Bedugul Highlands is **Lake Bratan**, where one of Bali's most photographed temples, **Pura Ulun Danu Bratan**, sits on its western shore. The lake itself is a recreation park offering waterskiing, parasailing, canoeing, and fishing. Another popular sport is golfing, playable year round at Handara Kosaido Country Club.

The area is surrounded by plantations of cool-climate fruits, vegetables, and trees,

Pura Ulun Danu Bratan on scenic Lake Bratan in the Bedugul Highlands

and most hotels offer guided walks and rent out bicycles, as many paths are sufficiently well-marked for individual explorations. More exuberant trekkers might wish to climb one of the area's three mountains. South of Lake Bratan is **Bali Botanical Gardens**, an extensive complex that also includes a **Treetop Adventure Park**. If time permits, from here Mt. Batukaru is easily accessible. See the Central Bali chapter for further information.

Kintamani Highlands—Mt. Batur

An exploration of the **Kintamani Highlands** can be a quick drive-through to see the gaping hole that is an ancient crafter and fabulous panoramic views, or a longer stop to soak in the wonder of it all at leisure. Surprisingly, there is one luxury property in the caldera, but more ubiquitous are budget accommodations, usually housing climbers who require an early morning start to summit **Mt. Batur**.

The great explosion that created the giant crater is thought to have occurred around 20,000 years ago. A drive or trek through the immense caldera floor reveals house-sized boulders ejected from the volcano and except for small patches of irrigated vegetable

farming and reforested sections it is barren and dry. **Lake Batur** is Bali's primary source of life-giving water. Isolated on the opposite side of the lake is **Trunyan**, a traditional village that some visitors find interesting. A regional guides association offers treks of varying durations and difficulty as well as climbs to the top of Mt. Batur.

Far above is **Penelokan** town, where several glass-fronted restaurants perched on the crater's rim have panoramic views, a particularly good choice for pausing to absorb this natural phenomenon on chilly days. There is also a museum documenting Mt. Batur's geological history.

Up the road from Penelokan is the large **Pura Ulun Danu Batur** temple complex dedicated to the lake, which was disassembled and moved here in 1927 following two devastating eruptions. Adjoining it is Pura Tuluk Biyu, relocated to this spot from active Mt. Abang.

The Kintamani people tend to be more aggressive than their gentle Southern and Central Bali counterparts, and on cloudy, windy days the weather can be bone-chilling, so be prepared.

—Linda Hoffman

KINTAMANI AND MT. BATUR

An Active Volcano and a Life-giving Lake

The focal point of the mountainous Kintamani region is spectacular Mt. Batur (1,717 m/5,633 ft) volcanic caldera with its deep crater lake, bubbling hot springs, and rugged, wild beauty. Wonderful mountain air and dizzying views in all directions, as well as several important temples, are what make Kintamani one of the most memorable stops on the Bali tourist itinerary.

Notice the architecture here. Absent are the walled family compounds with beautiful gardens seen in the south. Instead, the houses here are wooden or cement blocks with tin roofs, a primitive form of solar heating to soak up the sun's rays during the day to keep families warm in the cold mountain climate at night. The people here are different, too, being more aggressive and less gentle than the southern Balinese.

A drive-in volcano

Nearing Kintamani town, the land rises steadily toward an almost featureless horizon with only Mts. Agung and Abang in view to the east and northeast, respectively. Suddenly, the road crests a ridge, ending on the rim of a vast caldera measuring some 14 km (8 miles) across. Down in the crater sits Mt. Batur's blackened cone, surrounded to one side by the long, blue waters of Lake Batur and on the other by lava fields and cultivated vegetable patches.

The great size of the crater implies that **Mt. Batur** was once a much bigger mountain (as large perhaps as Mt. Agung), which blew its top as much as 20,000 years ago. The volcano is still active; the last serious eruptions occurred between 1965 and 1974,

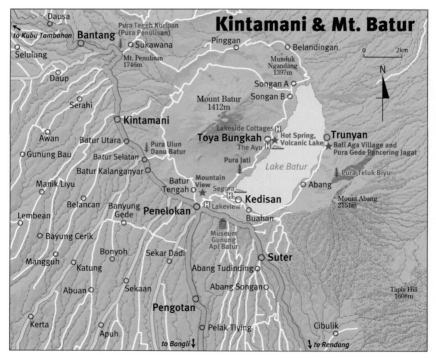

springing from the western flank of the mountain and leaving a vast field of black, needle-sharp lava rock. Much of the expansive crater is now being farmed and there have been reforestation efforts there for several years. Although rainfall is slight, farmers irrigate their crops with water from the lake.

Lake Batur, Bali's largest lake, is the source that feeds an underground network of springs throughout the southern-central flanks of the mountain. Homage is paid to the life-giving grace of the lake at Pura Ulun Danu Batur. The original temple is down by the lake, but during the 1920s, after two massive eruptions, what remained of the shrines was disassembled, moved piece by piece, carried uphill, and rebuilt on the western rim of the crater near Kintamani town.

There are six very old settlements around the lake, called *desa bintang danu* ("stars of the lake"): Songan, Abang, Buahan, Trunyan Kedisan, and Batur. People will tell you that these are Bali Aga villages, which some take to mean "original" (pre-Hindu) Balinese, while others say it refers to the myth of Markandya, a legendary saint-sage who led several bands of settlers to Bali from Desa Aga on Mt. Raung in East Java. In any case, the term is in popular use, and there are a number of **Bali Aga villages** throughout the mountains around Kintamani. They are distinguished by their unusual layout and the uniformity of the houses, as if they all adhere to a single design. The traditional mountain architecture is very interesting—steep bamboo shingle roof and walls of clay, woven bamboo, or wide wooden planks—but in many places this is disappearing as houses are rebuilt using modern materials.

A paved road follows the crater's rim around its southern and western circumference. From the south, the first stop is **Penelokan**, which means "lookout", and indeed the views from here are stunning. Enterprising citizens capitalize on the panorama, and there are swarms of peddlers and a string of shops, restaurants and small hotels all along the road to Kintamani town. The **Museum Gunung Api Batur** (Mt. Batur Volcano Museum), near the junction where the road from Bangli enters Penelokan, houses historical and archaeological data focused on Mt. Batur, an audio visual room presenting general information on the geology of volcanoes, a collection of volcanic rocks, and a telescope for better viewing.

Lake Batur as seen from Penelokan

The goddess of the lake

Going north from Penelokan toward Kintamani, the many *merus* (pagodas) of **Pura Ulun Danu Batur**, an imposing complex of nine temples, appear. *Ulun danu* means the "head of the lake", and the original site of this temple was at the lake's northeastern corner, the "holiest" quarter associated with the vitality of the sun as it approaches its zenith. Violent eruptions of the volcano in 1917 buried much of the area and took the lives of nearly a thousand people. Another serious eruption in 1926 forced the decision to rebuild the temple at its present site, high up on the rim of the crater. With help from the Dutch colonial government, the shrines were dismantled and transported across the lava-strewn landscape and up the steep sides of the crater, a staggering task, especially without roads or machinery.

People from the original Batur village, at the foot of the western flank of the volcano, also moved up to the new location, Batur Kalanganyar, to tend to the temple's maintenance and ceremonies. Lava from the 1917 eruption stopped only a few meters from the village, which somehow encouraged its citizens to rebuild it, damaged by tons of residual ash. The village remains just beyond the 1965-1974 lava fields.

Ida Batari Dewi Ulun Danu is the goddess of the lake. Myriad springs on the south side of the mountain feed the rich rice-growing Bangli and Gianyar districts, and Tirta Empul in Tampaksiring is one of the springs fed by Lake Batur. The various temples in the complex thus reflect a concern with not only the invisible world, but with the world of the living as well.

Ask someone to point the following major shrines out to you. **Pura Penataran Agung**

Batur is the principal temple, with five main courtyards. The dominant shrines are the *merus*, an 11-tiered one for the lake goddess and three nine-tiered ones for the gods of Mt. Batur, Mt. Agung, and Ida Batara Dalem Waturenggong, the deified king of Gelgel who is said to have ruled from 1460 to 1550. The Chinese-looking shrine to the northwest is for Ida Ratu Ayu Subandar, the patron saint of commerce. Another important shrine is the three-tiered *meru* to Ida Ratu Ayu Kentel Gumi, who protects crops from disease. This temple was built for the Chinese wife of the Kintamani king, and local lore has it that many of the names in this area, such as Pinggan village, are derivatives of her native tongue.

Penataran Pura Jati is related to the source temple on the western edge of the lake, while **Pura Tirta Bungkah** is linked to the hot springs at the water's edge. **Pura Taman Sari** and **Pura Tirta Mas Mampeh** are dedicated to agriculture. **Pura Sampian Wangi** is dedicated to crafts such as weaving, sewing, and the making of offerings and ceremonial cakes. **Pura Gunarali** is where adolescent boys and girls can invoke help to develop their natural abilities. **Pura Padang Sila** consists of 45 stone shrines for the gods and goddesses of Pura Ulun Danu Batur. The major *odalan* (anniversary) of the temple, attended by people from all over Bali, occurs sometime in March and runs for 11 days.

Pura Tuluk Biyu, just next to Pura Ulun Danu, is another relocated temple. "Tuluk Biyu" is the old name for Abang, the second highest mountain in Bali at the southern edge of the Batur crater. The original temple was at the summit of Mt. Abang, and is said to have been built by the sage, Mpu Kuturan.

Panoramic frontier town

Batur Kalanganyar village borders Kintamani town, the administrative center of Bangli Regency. This was formerly a way-station over the mountains that separate Buleleng (the old Dutch colonial headquarters) from the rest of Bali. The second hotel built in Bali was in **Kintamani**, but the place still looks like, and has the feel of, a frontier town. Notable are the delicious air and spectacular vistas: the crater to one side and all Bali extending to the sea on the other. Restaurants with panoramic views line the road and are especially crowded with local visitors during school and public holidays.

Up the road going north through Kintamani town is a market, busy every three

Pura Ulun Danu Batur in Kintamani, decorated for its anniversary festival

days on *hari paseh* of the Balinese calendar. This is interesting to visit to see the variety of produce from surrounding mountain farms: oranges and tangerines, corn and tomatoes, along with the usual vast array of scented flowers, dried fish, tools, livestock, pots, and baskets, plus a big clothing market. There are also men cuddling big furry Kintamani puppies, highly prized throughout Bali and often called into service for K-9 corps duty thanks to their outstanding intelligence.

A temple of ancient kings

Passing pine forests studded with the occasional giant poinsettia and fern tree a few kilometers past Kintamani town, on the right is the entrance to **Pura Tegeh Kuripan** temple, also called **Pura Penulisan** because of its location on Bukit Penulis (Writer's Hill) at 1,745 m (5,725 ft). Constructed around the ninth century, its location is between two mountain chains, more or less separating Northern and Southern Bali. From this point the road leads to Kubu Tambahan (1.5 hrs) and from there on to Singaraja.

Pura Tegeh Kuripan is a powerful place, ancient, royal, and remote. A long steep flight of stairs rises through the 11 terraces of the temple complex. The pyramidal form and the large stones that are still venerated there suggest that this place has been holy for many centuries. On the third level are Pura Panu and the temple garden; on the fourth tier is Pura Ratu Penarikan.

From **Pura Panarajon** on the uppermost terrace, the north coast of Bali and the mountains of East Java can be seen on a clear day. The proportions of the courtyard and various *balai* (pavilions) are modest, but the atmosphere is heavy with the solitude of hallowed kings. There are many sacred statues, including *lingga* (phallic symbols) and mysterious fragments housed in the open pavilions. Of particular interest is a royal couple bearing the inscriptions "Anak Wungsu" and "Bhatari Mandul", dated Saka year 999 (A.D. 1077). *Mandul* means "childless", and although it is impossible to know who this refers to, one interesting conjecture is that she was the Chinese Buddhist princess Subandar, whose shrine stands in Pura Ulun Danu, and that her barrenness was caused by a curse from a *siwaite* wizard.

While Pura Tegeh Kuripan sits atop Bukit Penulis, on its eastern slope is **Pura**

Balingkang Dalem. Balingkan means "king of Bali", and this temple served an 11th century royal family. The king, Sri Kesari Waradewa, had a Chinese wife who was a princess of the Chung Dynasty. Their marriage is depicted in the barong dance *ladung* that is still performed today. The Chinese influence is seen in the palace itself and also on old Balinese coins.

From **Sukawana**, just to the right of Pura Tegeh Kuripan's entrance, there is a paved road that arcs along the northern rim of the crater, offering splendid views of the lava fields below. A steep drop goes to **Pinggan**, overlooking the crater, with a road connecting it with Belandingan and Songan down by the lake.

The more usual approach to the lake is via a downward sloping road from Penelokan, descending to the water's edge at **Kedisan** and heading over to Toya Bungkah, where there is a hot spring believed to cure skin diseases. There are a number of simple hotels and restaurants here, and this is a good place from which to climb the volcano and to explore the lake area.

Along this road, men waving and shouting at the top of the road are not trying to collect a toll, but want to sell boat trips to Trunyan. Best to smile and keep going. Many of them have been known to cheat tourists by offering a low fare and then hold them hostage in the center of the lake until more money is paid.

At Kedisan at the bottom of the road you have to turn right or left. The right turn leads to a little port with boat-taxis to **Trunyan** and points around the lake; to the left is Toya Bungkah and Songan.

Of the lake villages, Trunyan is surely the most famous, but it is also notorious as a place to avoid. The village is virtually inaccessible except by boat, and on arrival the villagers wade out to meet visitors and clamor for money. In Trunyan, it's okay to beg, yet the prosperous residents have enough resources to have rebuilt their houses with modern materials (i.e., cement block and zinc). Traditional architecture is rare.

Still, the place has points of interest. In the **Pura Gede Pancering Jagat**—which is not open to tourists—is a unique, 4 m (13 ft) high guardian statue, Da Tonte, or Ratu Gede Pancering Jagat, but it is stored out of view in a closed *meru*. The Trunyan people do not cremate their dead, but place them exposed under a sacred tree by the lakeshore that has the remarkable property of preventing the decomposing corpses from smelling. Tourists are aggressively solicited to visit the grave-yard and see for themselves. This is further down from the village, and it is acceptable to ask to skip Trunyan and go directly to the gravesite (*kuburan*).

Continuing on the road along the lake to Songan, at its northeastern tip the landscape is barren and strange. An eerie feeling creeps in, knowing this is the caldera of the ancient, original volcano. Enormous boulders and craggy rocks protrude from the dry earth, surrounded by tall grasses with the remnants of the old Mt. Batur looming overhead. In some areas, patches of onions and corn grow in small fields between the rocks; other parts have the advantage of irrigation and sprout cabbage and tomatoes. There are several reforestation projects here funded not only by the Indonesian Forestry Department but also by foreign countries, such as Japan.

At **Toya Bungkah** is a small office marked **Association of Mount Batur Trekking Guides**, which offers several interesting expeditions. This is one of two headquarters for area licensed guides (the other is in Pura Jati), who stress heavily that only members of the association are permitted to operate here. There's a signboard listing the tours, level of difficulty, and prices. For example, "Mt. Batur Sunrise" and trekking around the main crater—their specialty, of course—are both moderate-to-difficult hikes. Mt. Abang and Mt. Agung are both marked "difficult", but there are also easy-to-moderate excursions around both craters.

The guides can also take visitors overland to Trunyan village, and customized treks can be arranged. Camping overnight is permitted. There are several well-marked approaches to Batur from Pura Jati and from Toya Bungkah, where the climb up and back takes about 2.5–3 hours. The latter route is appreciably easier.

Near the end of the road is **Songan**, an interesting village reminiscent of an Indonesian-style San Francisco, but with tiny shops and little houses perched on the sides of the hilly main street instead of grand old houses. It's a pretty area, with irrigated vegetable farms surrounding it. The site of the original **Pura Ulun Danu Batur** is at the northern tip, or "head" (*ulun*), of the lake.

Returning to the main road that passes the southwestern end of the lake, if planning a southward journey there are several options. One of them leads to Tampaksiring amidst coffee, vanilla, *salak*, and mangosteen planta-tions. Another goes to Bangli town via **Kubu**, a good road lined with jackfruit trees, poinsettias, and bamboo groves.

A side trip to the west of Kubu is **Penglipuran** Bali Aga village, with its unusual layout and singular house design using bamboo, wood, and thatch for construction. Home to less than a thousand people, there's a large gate at the entrance requiring visitors to pay an entrance fee before walking through (no cars allowed). Inside the village is a monument dedicated to the leader of the Bangli war against Dutch troops.

At the end of the road that runs in front of the hamlet is a fabulous "**bamboo jungle**" **tunnel**. The road is terrible, but it's worth the 10 minutes or so of bumping and grinding to experience the sensations of being completely surrounded by giant bamboo. The local people protect this forest using their *adat* (traditional) laws. For example, harvesting can only take place when necessary, and never on Sundays. Water is scarce here, so in late afternoons, villagers carrying buckets containing toothbrushes, toothpaste, and soap to the river to bathe.

On the way back to the main road toward Bangli town are fields of tall grasses, grown to feed the area's large population of cattle. There's a ginger plantation at **Susut** village (southeast of Tampaksiring) that grows a particularly large variety called *jahit gajah* (elephant ginger), primarily for export. Sai Land Agro Wisata at Banjar Teman, Susut, has a well-stocked gift shop selling attractively packaged hand-roasted coffee, cocoa mixes, gift oils, and creams.

From Susut, by going a little bit out of the way, there's an interesting drive south to Ubud by first going northwest to **Seribatu**, the heart of the "agro" district. Passing lem-ongrass gardens, mangosteen, and durian trees, suddenly the road is lined with shops selling natural herbs and spices, Bali coffee, and spa products. Look for *kopi luwak* signs, the coffee ground from beans defecated by civet cats that is something of a universal craze these days. There's also a yoga center, handicrafts, and a fine art gallery. As the road slopes down from the hills toward Ubud there are more agro-tourism centers and an art market selling kites and stove carvings.

—*Diana Darling*

VISITING KINTAMANI

(TELEPHONE CODE: 0366)

Kintamani is great for day trips, trekking, or simply for getting away from it all for a few days in Bali's high mountain climate. Penelokan offers heart-stopping panoramas of **Mt. Batur** set in a huge volcanic crater basin. Stop on the way to Singaraja to climb 333 steps to peaceful **Pura Tegeh Kuripan** in Penulisan, the highest temple in Bali. Try to arrive at Kintamani in the morning, as it is often overcast in the afternoon, particularly during the rainy season, and take a jacket, as it can get windy and chilly at the top of the mountain.

Penelokan and the crater villages are rather "un-Balinese" with aggressive vendors and people approaching visitors in the street to book accommodations. If you don't want to buy anything, don't show any interest whatsoever in the wares being offered.

There's a local charge of Rp 5,000 per person for any car with tourists crossing into the region. A similar fee is charged in lakeside Toya Bungkah.

GETTING THERE & GETTING AROUND

Kintamani is the end-point of several **tour itineraries** heading up from the southern rice plains. Most buses come up the excellent, scenic road via Tampaksiring, with stops on the way at Goa Gajah, Gunung Kawi, and Tirta Empul, then going back down through Bangli after seeing Pura Kehen.

But there are other interesting routes. One leads from Peliatan in the Ubud area through Tegallalang, Pujung, and Sebatu wood carving villages. The views along the way are superb. Other roads from Ubud to Kintamani run through Payangan or from Denpasar through the Sangeh Monkey Forest, Plaga, and Lampu, arriving to the north of Kintamani.

Public *bemos* to Kintamani are available from Ubud via Sakah (notable for its huge "baby" statue). They also run via Tampaksiring and Bangli. Shuttle buses which run between Ubud and Singaraja stop in Penelokan. Fares from Ubud $5–8, from Singaraja $15. From Denpasar, *bemos* leave for Kintamani from the Batubulan Terminal until late afternoon. The normal fare from Batubulan is around $5. From Singaraja, the *bemo* fare is $3.

Note if you choose to travel via *bemo*, it will be difficult to explore the entire Mt. Batur area, which is vast. Walking is possible, but distances are long and the descent into the crater is quite steep. Additionally, you'll miss many opportunities to take interesting scenic drives to and fro and stop for photo ops.

The best way to visit all of Kintamani is with your own transportation, **chartered car** or **motorbike**. Alternatively, day tours leave from all major tourist centers in Bali and include air-conditioned comfort and lunch (but book in advance). On such tours,

however, you will only see the view from the rim at Penelokan and then return, missing a visit to the caldera down the zigzagging 3-km (2-mile) road to Kedisan on the lake.

KINTAMANI TO BEDUGUL

There's a **beautiful drive** from here to Bedugul. From Kintamani town, follow the main road north until just beyond Penulisan and the Tegeh Kuripan temple. Take the small road that branches off to the left towards Belantih village, continuing west past Belantih to Lampu and neighboring Catur village, where the road bends south. Lawak village marks the beginning of the vanilla-growing region, where the harvest can sometimes be seen drying in shelters.

After Belok Sidan, keep right and head for Pelaga. Just before the village there's a sharp right turn that leads to a shortcut west to Lake Bratan, but in a few stretches the road is in poor condition. Avoid the shortcut and continue south, as the best has yet to come.

Beyond Pelaga and Kiadan, the elevated area around Nungkung and Sandakan is breathtakingly beautiful. A bit further ahead is Islamic Angan Tiga village, with its small mosque. The next village, Kerta, has a police station and even a bank. Pass the bank and turn right to Bedugul. (The road continues straight to Denpasar, which is only 32 km (20 miles) away.) From Kerta, the country road leads to the main highway at Luwus. Turn right for Bedugul or left for Mengwi and Denpasar. Both roads have beautiful panoramas.

TO TRUNYAN FROM KADISAN

Inside the caldera you can cross to the opposite side of the lake to Trunyan village either from Kedisan or from Toya Bungkah. Boatsmen here—and their "guides"—are notorious for the variety of rip-off scams they pull, even though attempts have been made in the past to set up a standard fee schedule that includes boat ride, "insurance", and village entrance fee. Once there, the Trunyan folk are not welcoming and in fact are aggressive beggars. If you want to visit, **Hotel Segara & Restaurant** in Kadisan at the eastern tip of the lake can arrange safe passage for $45 for 6 people. Reservations required.

If you are tired of bargaining hassles, simply hike around the crater to Trunyan to view the caldera from a new angle and also to see Mt. Abang. The **Mt. Batur Trekking Guides Association** offers guided tours departing from Sogan village.

ACCOMMODATIONS

There are two possible options for staying in the Mt. Batur area: up on the ridgeline or down inside the crater, and there are choices aplenty in both locations, particularly around the lake. However, most visitors who overnight here stay near the lake in order to climb Mt. Batur at dawn. The villages within the crater tend to have a rather scruffy appearance, but the people are eager to please their guests, and make a genuine effort to feed them well. The views are nothing short of stunning. Take a sweater, a blanket, and sheet if you're staying in a budget *losmen*. Phone to find out if they offer free pickup in Ubud. Several accommodations in Kedisan and Toya Bungkah offer Internet services, even to non-guests.

IN THE CALDERA
Budget (under $25)

Arlina Bungalows & Restaurant, on the main road, Toya Bungkah, tel: 51165. 11 bungalows with verandahs; the more expensive rooms have hot water. Very user-friendly, and a long-time favorite with budget travelers. From $10.

Lakeside Cottages & Restaurant, on the main road, Toya Bungkah, tel: 51249, fax: 51250, www.lakeside-bali.com. Until The Ayu was built, this was the top of the line place to stay on the lake floor, with large lakeside bungalows, fantastic views, hot water, tv. Also less expensive cold water garden-view rooms back from the lake. $10–35, including breakfast.

Segara Hotel & Restaurant, turn left before Kedisan if coming from Penelokan, tel: 51136, fax: 51212, www.c-bali.com/accommodation. Across the street from the lake. 30 rooms with private baths, some with hot water and tv. Pleasant open-air restaurant with varied menu, minibus with English-speaking driver for rent. Boat rental to Trunyan (reservations required), trekking guides. $15–32, including breakfast and tax.

Surya Homestay, Kedisan, tel: 51139. 10 bungalows with balconies on a hill. Spacious, clean Balinese-style rooms in a number of different classes with hot water. Fanciest room has bathtub and tv. $10–15 including breakfast and tax.

Under the Volcano, Toya Bungkah, tel: 51166, mobile: 0813-386-0081. 3 locations, all with 6 clean, well-designed rooms. Excellent food. Garden. This is the area's most service-minded establishment, run by Nyoman Mawa, who also has a tour agency and a shop. Around $7; some rooms have hot water.

Intermediate ($75–100)

Toya Devasya Resort & Spa, Toya Bungkah, tel: 51204, fax: 51205, www.toyadevasya.com.

Something out of the ordinary. Actually a luxurious natural hot spring swimming pool ($15 entrance fee includes welcome drink, locker, shower, and changing rooms, soap, shampoo, and towel). But it also offers "Camping Plus", tent camping on the grounds with spring bed or air mattresses, $75/2 people. Also has Lakeside Resto & Bar. The "Resort & Spa" part of the name are a bit misleading, as they are next door at The Ayu (same owner). Toya Devasya also offers outdoor adventure packages, including cycling and canoeing ($150/2 people) and trekking ($150/2 people), with English-speaking guides. All packages include dips in the hot spring pool.

Luxury ($100–up)

The Ayu, Toya Bungkah, tel: 52222, www.theayu.com. Completed in 2010, the newest and most up-market accommodation on the lake, undoubtedly appealing to the rich and famous only. 14 luxury suites, each with satellite tv, AC, 24-hour room service, WiFi, Jacuzzi and private pool, living room, dining room, and bar. All have been designed for lake views and to preserve original trees. Flamboyant Resto. Cultural performances under the stars on selected evenings. Ayurvedic Spa & Clinic offers treatments from head to toe. $935–3,100/night.

DINING

The better places are attached to the hotels in Penelokan up on the rim and down in Toya Bungkah by the hot springs. Penelokan has choices ranging from very simple inexpensive *warung* (eateries) with good local food, to big fancy restaurants with five-meter-long buffets catering to busloads of tourists coming from the swanky hotels on the coast. The local lake fish is a tasty variety, *mujahir*, available fried or grilled. It's best fried crisp, as more of the fish is edible.

Down in the crater at Toya Bungkah, most *losmen* have small *warungs*. The imaginative dishes served up on the high-end **Lakeside Cottages** are superb; also recommended is Nyoman Mawa's cozy **Under the Volcano** restaurant. His grilled lake fish (*ikan bakar*) with homemade *sambal matah* (hot, spicy chili sauce) is worth the trip to the mountains. As **The Ayu** is new, the successes (or lack thereof) of its **Flamboyant Resto**, serving healthy salads, wraps, snacks, low fat smoothies, and health drinks, as well as local and international cuisine, has not yet been reported, but judging by the price of the suites, the restaurant is bound to be expensive as well. **Toya Devasya's Lakeside Resto & Bar** next door, serving breakfast, lunch, and dinner, specializing in steamboat and cocktails, might be a more reasonably priced choice. Both are worth checking out when the daily consumption of *warung* food gets tedious.

TREKKING

If you've always wanted to walk around inside the crater of an active volcano, here's your chance. Mt. Batur is 1,717 m (5,633 ft) high, but the upper cone itself is only several hundred meters above the level of the lake and can be climbed and descended in just a few strenuous hours. At the top, there's a warm crust of ground over the cauldron. It's advisable to hire a guide in order to follow the protocol of the local guides association, as disputes have been reported from those who tried to venture out on their own or hire a guide who was not a licensed member of the group.

It's best to start while it's dark, very early in the morning, 3 am or at the latest 4 am; it's cool and you're likely to see a wonderful sunrise and avoid the mid-morning clouds. A guide will probably find you before you find him, or your homestay can recommend one.

Choose someone friendly who belongs to the **Association of Mount Batur Trekking Guides**, tel: 52362 (ask to see proof of membership), which has one small office in Toya Bungkah and one in Pura Jati. There are signboards in both offices listing the tours, their price, and level of difficulty, ranging from $30 per person to climb Mt. Batur for sunrise (4 hrs, moderately–difficult) to $60 (Mt. Batur Exploration, 6 hrs, moderately–difficult). Other climbing tours include Mt. Abang (hard climbing, $75), Mt. Agung on the southeastern edge of the outer caldera (overnight, difficult, $75), and further afield to Mt. Rinjani on Lombok. They can also arrange overnight camping on Mt. Batur for an extra fee. While these hikes are also available through travel agencies and hotels, note the prices will be higher because of commissions.

Take a hat and wear high-top shoes or boots: Mt. Batur's slopes are covered with fine dust in the dry season (April–September) and with mud in the rainy season (October–March). Other necessary supplies are drinking water and a snack or two. If you're fortunate, a great view stretching all the way to Lombok will reveal itself as the sun rises. On reaching the summit your guide will boil some eggs in the hot, volcanic sand and make coffee.

Going down is much easier and takes half the time than it does climbing up. It's possible to take another route down, through a shaded forest via the hot springs at Toya Bungkah. The other route crosses lava fields, which can get very hot during the day, so is best used on ascent. If you don't begin from one of the Trekking Guides Association offices, ask your guide to have his car or motorbike ready to bring you back to your original starting point once you get down. Climbing is not recommended during the rainy season.

There's a good road that circles the volcano rim from Penulisan east to Pinggan and Belandingan, where it comes to a dead end. Another route is to drive past Toya Bungkah to Songan and follow the signs west to Air Mampeh. The road leads to Penelokan through the caldera behind Batur. It is sometimes difficult to pass because of volcanic sand and stones.

Mountain trekking with a heart

If you'd like to have a view of Bali that few have ever seen and help villagers earn a sustainable income in the process, it's certainly possible. Several years ago a retired Swiss banker was setting up a water project in a particularly poor, dry area on the slopes of the mountains north of Lake Batur when he noticed the women of several villages—35 to be exact—were crossing the mountain to reach the road that would take them to the cities to beg for money.

Swinging into action, he established a Swiss-Indonesian non-profit organization, Future for the Children Foundation (Yayasan Masa Depan Untuk Anak-Anak). Under the program, village women have been trained to lead 3-hour treks beginning at **Songan** over mountain paths and through villages that are part of their daily lives—for which they are paid wages—giving visitors a rare opportunity to experience an entirely different side of Bali than they normally get to know.

Marketed primarily to Europeans by **Bali Rasa Sayang Tour and Travel**, mobile: 0813-3796-6240, prices range from $65–90, depending on the number of guests, and include pick-up and drop-off at your accommodation in Ubud, South, or East Bali, snack and water on the trail, lunch by the sea, experienced English-speaking guide, local village guide, and a contribution to the village children's fund. Trekking is moderate, suitable for those in good physical condition; not recommended for kids under the age of 10. For more information about the foundation and its many other Muntigunung Development Projects, visit www.future-for-children.com/en.

WHITE WATER RAFTING

Sobek, www.balisobek.com/twaja, well known for its outstanding safety record for its rafting trips on the Ayung River near Ubud, also has a similar program in Karangasem Regency called **Telaga Waja Experience**. The trip begins in the foothills of Mt. Agung, passes steep banks, terraced rice fields, and ancient trees, rafts straight through waterfalls, ducks overhanging obstacles, and navigates narrow gorges. Includes 2 exhilarating hours on the water plus an hour for lunch and a chance to change into dry clothes. Picks up at Nusa Dua, Jimbaran, Kuta, Sanur, and Ubud; $79/adults, $52/kids 7–15 years.

BEDUGUL AND LAKE BRATAN

Bali's Fertile Highlands and Sacred Lake

Heading south 30 km (18 miles) from Singaraja on the main north-south highway (Depensar-Mengwi-Singaraja) which traverses hill and dale, is the beginning of Bali's highlands in an area referred to as **Bedugal**. Southwest of long inactive Mt. Catur, it is a refreshing retreat from the beaches of the north and the overcrowded areas of the south. In the past, a lack of accommodations discouraged most tourists from spending more than just a few hours here, but as more resorts are developed highlighting delightful scenery, spectacular mountain walks and many other recreational opportunities, a new choice in experiencing all of Bali has emerged. Although crowded with tourists during local public and school holidays, it is a quiet refuge at other times.

The cool mountain retreats here are cradled in the crater of an extinct volcano and have been a popular getaway spot since Dutch

times. Here lies placid Lake Bratan (also spelled Beratan), source of life-giving water for the springs, rivers and rice fields below. Verdant tropical rainforests blanket the slopes of mountains rising 2,000 m (6,560 ft) above sea level, providing temperatures several degrees lower than the plains (11-30°C), so a jacket is advised in the evenings.

Waterfalls and lakes

Ten km (6.5 miles) south of Singaraja at the town of the same name is Bali's highest waterfall, **Gitgit** (Air Terjun Gitgit), looming 35 m (115 ft) above sea level. The road to Gitgit climbs steeply, offering fine views along the way. The waterfall, located about 500 m (540 yds) from the main road, is surrounded by lush, tropical vegetation. A fine, cooling mist hangs in the air, providing a refreshing welcome after the walk down. Dip your feet in the rushing river below. A rest area suitable

Gitgit waterfall, one of the most dramatic natural wonders of the Bedugul Highlands

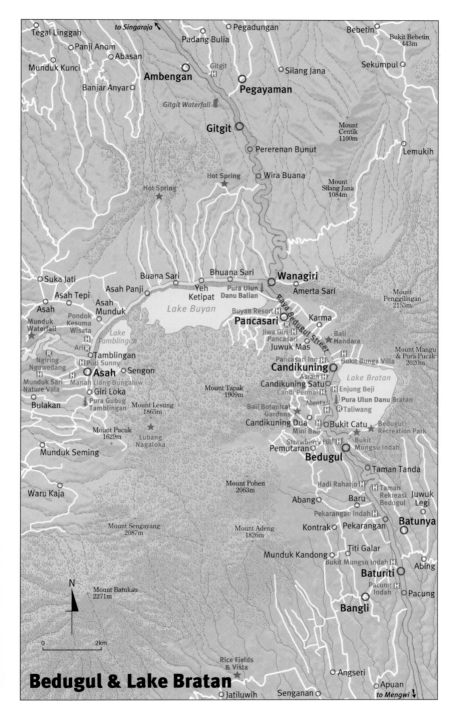

Bedugul & Lake Bratan

Pura Ulun Danu Bratan is one of the most photographed temples on Bali.

for picnics is near the base of the falls. There are three other waterfalls in this area, the most spectacular being Gitgit Twin Waterfall.

South of Gitgit, which is surrounded by clove plantations, the road goes downhill into the crater at **Wanagiri**, on the eastern border of the **Twin Lakes, Buyan**, and **Tamblingan**, about 6 km (4 miles) northwest of Lake Bratan. There are coffee and tea shops here, overlooking stunning panoramas. A good road with breathtaking scenery follows the northern shore of the two lakes to **Munduk**, where there's a little-visited waterfall, and from there west and north back to the north coast highway at Seririt. It is also possible to take a leisurely trek around Lake Tamblingan or in the Munduk vicinity.

Tropical golf

Continuing south on the Singaraja–Denpasar highway, northwest of Lake Bratan is **Pancasari** village, which is undergoing much tourist development, including new accommodations, villas, coffee plantations, jungle trekking, and fishing.

You have now crossed over into the northern reaches of Tabanan Regency. Shortly afterwards is the **Bali Handara Kosaido Country Club**, at an altitude 1,142 m (3,746 ft) above sea level, offering fresh air and cool temperatures. One of the world's most beautiful golf courses and considered one of the best in Asia, it was designed by famous golf architects Thompson, Wolveridge, and Fream. Its 18-hole masterpiece has lush, green fairways and the fastest greens found anywhere. Trees and beds of colorful flowers line the course, and there is a spacious clubhouse complete with pro shop, sauna, and fitness center, as well as a restaurant. Open to the public except on tournament days, the course is playable all year round.

Nature walks

For those who enjoy nature more without whacking a little white ball around, there are many delightful bush walks in the Bedugul vicinity. Guides are available at most hotels, and there are scheduled group departures from Bedugul Recreation Park (Taman Rekreasi Bedugul) and from the Bali Botanical Gardens.

One exhilarating hike is a 6-hour walk to the summit of **Mt. Mangu**, on the northeastern side of Lake Bratan. At the peak is an ancient temple, **Pura Pucak**, built by the first raja of Mengwi, I Gusti Agung Putu. The view is spectacular. Another walk begins at the northernmost end of the botanical gardens. There is a good wide path here, so it is safe without a guide. It leads across the foothills of **Mt. Tapak** to the northern end of the valley. The 8-km (5-mile) path emerges in the midst of vegetable gardens to reach the main road at Pancasari village.

There is a further walk passing up and behind Mt. Tapak through dense jungle to a waterfall on the other side. This is a long and steep climb and should only be ventured with a local guide and good footwear. Set off early and bring food. Nature lovers will find it well worth the effort.

It's a hearty climb starting from the Bedugul Recreational Park up **Mt. Catur**, at

2,096 m (6,876 ft). Accessible from the rim is a path leading to three 25-m (82-ft) deep caves, Goa Jepang, excavated by Indonesian forced laborers for the Japanese during World War II. It is also possible to trek the 25 km (16 miles) from Bedugul to Kintamani, heading east at Gitgit.

Lake Bratan

As the road winds up Mt. Bratan there are magnificent views stretching back over the lowlands to the coast and across to the misty peaks of Bali's volcanoes —Agung, Abang, and Batur to the east. To the west, deep gorges border tiers of jungle foliage below Mt. Batukaru's hazy peak.

Near the top of the hill the road suddenly branches to the right, sloping gently down, and a striking new panorama is revealed: sparkling blue waters backed by lush, green hills. Cottages dot the hillside down to the shores of the lake, and a pier provides a mooring for boats of all shapes and sizes. This is **Bedugul Recreation Park** (**Taman Rekreasi Bedugul**), a center for waterskiing, parasailing, canoeing, and fishing. Facilities include boat sheds, jumping ramps, slalom, and trick water ski equipment.

Oddly enough, on the western shore of the lake, keeping its dignity intact while all else around it indulges in fun, dramatic **Pura Ulun Danu Bratan,** one of the most photographed temples on Bali, projects into the water. A classic Bali icon, it appears on the back of the Indonesian 50,000 rupiah note. Here, local farmers make offerings to Dewi Danu, the lake goddess, who is much revered as a source of fertility. Built in 1633 by I Gusti Agung Putu, the king of Mengwi, it consists of four compounds, the two outermost of which are completely surrounded by water.

When the three-tiered Siwaitic *lingga petak* was restored, the builders discovered a bubbling spring and a big white stone flanked by two red ones, a phallic *lingga* representing the reproductive power of Siva as the god of fertility. Towering above this, on a separate islet, is a single shrine of 11 roofs dedicated to Wisnu in his manifestation as the lake goddess Dewi Danu, who protects all living creatures.

The main temple complex on the shore, **Pura Teratai Bang**, is a *pura penataran,* or temple of origin. Its many shrines are associated with different aspects of creation and are dominated by a large seven-tiered *meru* dedi-

cated to Brahma. The smaller **Pura Dalem Purwa** is dedicated to Dewi Uma Bhogawati, the goddess of food and drink.

Lush tropical gardens

In 1959, 50 ha of reforested land in the foothills of Bukit Tapak in **Candikuning** was set aside by the government as the **Bali Botanical Gardens (Kebun Raya Eka Karya Bali)**, and by 2001 the area had been increased to 154.5 ha. This extensive park is a popular place for weekenders, but during the week it is a haven of peace and solitude. A research center, it also serves educational and recreational functions. Recently added with garden grounds is the **Bali Treetop Adventure Park**. Suitable for all ages, visitors can test their skills in a series of circuits as they progress from treetop to treetop using eco-friendly bridges, nets, and cables.

More than 2,000 plant species representing flora from the mountain areas of eastern Indonesia are preserved at the Bali Botanical Gardens. Specialized collections include orchids, ferns, cacti, medicinal and ceremonial plants, roses, and aquatic flora. The library and herbarium are open to visitors and knowledgeable guides are on hand at the information center. In the forests both here and around Lake Bratan there is good birdwatching: blue-crowned barbets found only on Java and Bali, flycatchers, yellow-throated hanging parrots and Javan kingfishers, to name a few of the 97 species recorded.

The temperate climate, abundant rainfall, and rich volcanic soils make the surrounding crater ideal for market gardening. In the early 1970s most local farmers cut out their coffee gardens and started growing vegetables. Now Bedugul farms supply the huge Denpasar *pasars* (markets) and hotels with fresh cabbages, carrots, onions, strawberries, passion fruit, and other fresh produce. A stop at the **Candikuning** *pasar* (traditional market), Bukit Mungsu, will yield delicious rewards.

Flower growing has also proved profitable, and *bemo*-loads of freshly cut roses, lilies, gardenias, and gladioli are sent southwards at dawn each day. Nursery gardens and orchid shelters have sprung up all over the valley. Stop at the produce and plant market to see tier after tier of exotic flowering plants. Women here call out to passers-by in a new language: "Dendrobium? Azalea? You buy orchid, madam?"

—Sarita Newson & Hedi Hinzler;
revised by Linda Hoffman

VISITING BEDUGUL
(Includes Lake Bratan & Munduk)

The cool mountain climate and clean air of the Bedugul Highlands are an excellent base for exploring the surrounding area and as far south as Mt. Batukaru. From here, the north coastline is also easily accessible, as is Ubud.

THE BEDUGUL HIGHLANDS
(TELEPHONE CODE: 0368)

A pleasant climate, splendid views, water sports on scenic Lake Bratan, the botanical garden, fresh tropical fruits, and vegetables are but a few of the things that draw travelers to the Bedugul Highlands. With its highest peaks looming 2,000 m (6,561 ft) above sea level, it gets chilly by late afternoon, so bring a sweater. Thanks to a growing number of choices in accommodations, more tourists are discovering this scenic highland retreat than ever before. For nature lovers, it's a haven.

See area map on page 271.

ORIENTATION

Bedugal township is on the southwestern shore of Lake Bratan and houses a number of small hotels and restaurants, shops, a bank, moneychangers, a telephone office (*wartel*), and a small but colorful market, **Bukit Mungsu**, where local farmers sell fruit (including freshly-picked strawberries), spices in gift packs, plants (such as orchids), and handicrafts. Don't forget to bargain: starting at 50 percent of the asking price is acceptable. There's also a narrow road leading up to Bali's famed Botanical Gardens.

Beyond the village the road descends down towards the lake, turning left sharply at the **Ashram Guesthouse**. The road then continues north to Candikuning. On the right side is the entrance to the Pura Ulun Danu and other temples. A line of souvenir shops and a big parking lot indicate the way. A small fee (less than $1) is required to enter. The walk from the Bedugul market to Ashram Guesthouse takes about 10 minutes. The temples on the shore are another 10 minutes further. From the market to the entrance of the Botanical Gardens it takes about 15 minutes on foot.

GETTING THERE & GETTING AROUND

The Bedugul Highlands are situated on the main road connecting north and south Bali, 53 km (33 miles) north of Denpasar and 30 km (18 miles) south of Singaraja. It is the perfect place to stop for a night on an island tour or to use as a base to explore the Highlands and north coast.

To get to Bedugul from Denpasar, take a *bemo* from the Ubung Terminal. Past the Budugal Recreation Park turnoff, the road passes through Candikuning and Pancasari on the western shore of Lake Bratan. From there it climbs over the pass and begins to steeply wind down the mountains to the plains of the north.

From Singaraja, catch a *bemo* at its western bus station.

Once in the Bedugul area, **hire a car** and driver and wander through the area at your own pace. The brave may wish to **rent a motorbike** ($5–10/day), but be aware that road signs may be difficult to locate off the beaten path and roads may be winding, steep, and sometimes heavily trafficked.

At the Sari Artha Inn just below the market on the main road is a Perama office that sells shuttle bus tickets to other points in Bali, books tours and arranges charter transport.

Scenic drive To Bedugul from Kintamani

The Bedugul Highlands are also accessible from Kintamani on a circuitous route via Singaraja and the north coast. An alternative route used by very few people leads south through the mountains with spectacular scenery and a close view of the island's vanilla, clove, and coffee-producing plantations.

The road is good enough for cars or motorbikes, but it's best to allow half a day for the journey between **Kintamani** and **Luwus**, where it connects with the main road between Denpasar and Bedugul. Stop along the way, have a cup of coffee in one of the villages, and enjoy a leisurely ride.

From Kintamani, follow the main road north until just beyond Penulisan and the Tegeh Kuripan temple. Take the small road that branches off to the left towards Belantih village. Continue west past Belantih to Lampu and neighboring Catur village, where the road bends south. Lawak village marks the beginning of the vanilla-growing region, where the harvest can sometimes be seen drying in shelters.

After Belok Sidan (keep right) head for Pelaga. Just before the village there's a sharp right turn which leads to a shortcut west to Lake Bratan, but in a few stretches the road is in poor condition. Avoid the shortcut and continue south, as the best has yet to come.

Beyond Pelaga and Kiadan, the elevated area around Nungkung and Sandakan is extremely beautiful. A bit further ahead is the Islamic Angan Tiga village, with its small mosque. The next village, Kerta, has a police station and a bank. Past the bank take the right turn to Bedugul (the road continues straight to Denpasar, just 32 km (20 miles) away. From Kerta, the country road leads to the main highway at Luwus. Turn right for Bedugul or left for Mengwi and Denpasar.

ACCOMMODATIONS

Some hotels are in Bedugul proper overlooking Lake Bratan, while others are located on the upper slopes of Baturiti, south of Bedugual town, offering views over volcanoes, rice fields, and on a clear day, down to the sea. The best rooms afford fantastic views of the idyllic surroundings. Another option includes overnighting in Munduk, west of the Twin Lakes, en route back to the north coast. All accommodations can arrange trekking excursions.

LAKE BRATAN AREA

Budget (under $25)

Ashram Guesthouse, Jl. Danau Beratan, tel: 21042. 27 rooms 500 m (540 yds) from the traditional market. These cottages are clean, convenient, and overlook the lake. Private bathroom, hot water. Restaurant, large garden. Near the lake are great places to eat or just have a drink. Tennis court and table tennis. $8–16; includes simple breakfast.

Ibu Hadi Homestay, Jl. Kebun Raya, near the traditional market on the way down towards Lake Bratan. Basic accommodations in a 3-story homestay. Small restaurant. $8.

Lila Graha, between Candikuning and Bedugul, tel: 21446. 15 rooms across from Ashram Guesthouse. Pleasant individual bungalows. Very private. Go for the rooms overlooking the lake. From $10.

Pacung Indah Hotel, in Pacung, 10 km (6 miles) south of Bedugul, tel: 21020, fax: 21964, www.pacungbali.com. 8 bungalows and a restaurant with panoramic views surrounded by forest and rice terraces. From $23.

Penginapan Cempaka, on the entrance road to the Botanical Gardens, tel: 21042. Simple, clean guesthouse on 2 levels. Fans, some with hot water. $7.

Pondok Permata Firdous, Jl. Kebon Raya, tel: 21531. On the road up to the Botanical Gardens. Nice, clean basic rooms in peaceful location. From $8.

Sari Artha Inn, between the lake and the market, tel: 21011. Simple rooms, the more expensive ones have hot water. The Perama bus office is here. $10–15.

Moderate ($25–50)

Pancasari Inn, Jl. Raya Bedugul north of Lake Bratan, Pancasari, tel:/fax: (0362) 29195. 11 bungalows, each with 2 rooms. Tennis court. $40–$100.

Intermediate ($50–75)

Enjung Beji Resort, Jl. Raya Bedugul, Candikuning, mobile: +62 (0) 813-3751-5414, tel: (0361) 852-8521, www.enjungbejiresort.com. On the north side of Lake Bratan, 7 family cottages, 5 superior cottages, and 2 "penthouses". Hot water, satellite tv, restaurant and bar, tennis court, fishing pond. $50–138.

Lake Beratan Villa, tel: (021) 581-2220 (Bahasa Indonesia); +34 606 988-293 (English or Spanish), www.balilakesidevilla.com. 3 bedroom privately-owned villa at 1,110 m (690 ft) overlooking Lake Beratan and mountains. Peaceful, relaxing location. Sleeps 6 in 2 queen size bedrooms, dining room/ living room, kitchen, and bath on ground floor and master king size bedroom with tv above. Can arrange sightseeing tours. $65/night; weekly rates available.

Saranam Eco Resort, Jl. Raya Baturiti, Pacung, tel: 21038, fax: 21043, www.saranamresortbali.com. 35 rooms and 10 bungalows with good valley views. Can arrange a full range of activities in the central highlands. From $60.

Strawberry Hill Hotel, Jl.Raya Denpasar-Singaraja Km 48, tel: 21265, fax : 21442, www.strawberryhill-bali.com. 5 mins south of Bedugul town at the Km 48 marker. 5 new rooms have wood floors and walls. Cabins have cozy interiors and balconies, hot water. Restaurant serves Indonesian food plus soups, salads, chicken, burgers, and of course strawberries. Has a log-burning fireplace for cool nights.

First class ($75–100)

Bali Handara Kosaido Country Club, Pancasari, tel: 22646, fax: 23048, www.balihandarakosaida.com. 77 rooms on the slopes of Mt. Bratan. Cottages, suites, and villas with satellite tv, hot water, heaters, and fireplaces. Rooms in the newer wing are hotel style; older bungalows are scattered under the extensive garden. Restaurant, lobby, and snack bars, pub and karaoke. Conference facilities, spa treatments, tennis court, gym. Internationally renowned 18-hole golf course, listed among the world's top 50. From $75–200.

De'Kahyangan Spa, Restaurant & Villa, Jl. Raya Singaraja, Bedugul, tel: 21322, fax 21323, www. dekahyangan.baliklik.com. In the Baturiti area facing strawberry farms and vegetable plantations. Spa, restaurant. $90–165.

Pacung Mountain Resort, Jl Raya Baturiti, Pacung, tel: 21020, fax: 20143, www.pacungbali.com. 10 rooms and 10 bungalows 9 km (6 miles) south of Bedugul at the crossroads leading to Jatiluwih, Penebel, and Batukaru temple. Rooms with hot water on a hilly property. Impressive rice field and mountain vistas. Heated swimming pool, jogging track and 2 restaurants. $90–165.

DINING

There are only a few genuine restaurants in the Bedugul Highlands, but they cover a wide range of prices. There are good restaurants in the main hotels and at the Bali Handara Kosaido Country Club, which serves Indonesian, European, and Japanese food. The Country Club also has a Lobby Bar, Snack Bar and Pub & Karaoke lounge. Other independent eateries include:

Bedugul Lake View, between the Candikuning market and Lake Bratan. Indonesian food specializing in *ayam taliwang*, spicy chicken from Lombok. Open 11 am–9 pm.

Crackers Bar, Candikuning, tel: +62 (0) 811-388-697. Australian-owned sports bar and café at the back of the Candikuning market.

Roti Bedugul, Candikuning, tel: 21838. Offers freshly baked bread, croissants, and Danish pastries. Open 8 am–6 pm.

Strawberry Stop, on the road between Lakes Bratan and Buyan, tel: 21060. Snacks, milkshakes, and strawberries. Open 8 am–7 pm.

Warung Anugerah, Main Square, Candikuning. Good, cheap local food. Open 10 am–10 pm, one of the few open late.

ACTIVITIES

Bali Handara Kosaido Country Club, Pancasari, tel: 22646, fax: 23048, www.balihandarakosaida.com. Par 72 (36 out, 36 in) natural grass championship golf course, one of the most challenging in Asia. At an altitude of 1,142 m (3,746 ft) above sea level, surrounded by mountains, crater lakes, and ancient forests. Pro shop, lessons, halfway houses, rentals, carts. Accommodations and food and beverage outlets. Golf green fees for 18 holes: $100 weekdays and weekends.

Bali Botanical Gardens (Kebun Raya Eka Karya), Candikuning, Baturiti, tel: 22050, 21273, fax: 22050, 22051, www.kebunrayabali.com. Situated on 157.5 ha with temperatures of 17–25°C. Weather is unpredictable, so be prepared for rain and chill. More than 2,000 plant species, specializing in ferns, orchids, cacti, medicinal and ceremonial plants, roses and aquatics. Open 8 am–6 pm 7 days/week except for Nyepi (based on the Balinese calendar). Some areas (e.g., orchid gardens) may be closed at 4 pm for security reasons. Library, guides, accommodations, café, conventions, garden shop. Admission and parking less than $1. Cars can drive around the garden for an additional $1.50, but it's better to take a leisurely stroll.

Bali Treetop Adventure Park, tel: (0361) 852-0680, www.balitreetop.com. Located inside the Bali Botanical Gardens, 65 treetop challenges providing memorable experiences and great views. Trained Patrol Guides explain how each circuit and safety equipment works and will advise and assist. Suitable for all ages from 4 years up. Reservations advised.

Bedugul Recreation Park (Taman Rekreasi Budugul) on Lake Bratan has boats of every size and description from wooden *perahu* (canoes) to powerboats and covered boats. Water-skiing and parasailing. *Perahu* can be hired to paddle around the calm waters under shady trees. Fishing poles for hire and bait for purchase. The swimming is chilly, but early in the day in the dry season when the sun is out the waterskiing on the lake's glassy surface even attracts international competitions. Entrance fee to the park less than $1; boats $10–15, depending on type, for 30 minutes.

Bali's Historic Northern Port City

S ituated almost in the center of Bali's northern coastline, **Singaraja** is reachable from south or central Bali via the island's major north-south Denpasar-Singaraja thoroughfare, giving travelers an opportunity to experience vast changes in topography, agriculture, scenery, and climate. An east-west coastal highway also makes it easily accessible to other parts of the island.

Although Singaraja is not a tourist destination per se, it's interesting enough for a drive through and lunch stop-over or coffee break when traveling to other parts of the island.

Singaraja tour

The sights of Singaraja reflect the city's successive historical incarnations, first as a royal court center, then in the 19th century as the headquarters for Dutch commerce and administration for all of eastern Indonesia, and now as the modern capital of Buleleng Regency. Until 1953, when shipping was moved to Benoa Harbor, Singaraja remained Bali's most important port and its educational, business, and governmental center. Its population reflects its heritage as a busy trading center and includes descendants of Arab, Chinese, Buginese (from Makassar, in Sulawesi), and Javanese traders, some of whom live in areas near the harbor, which have names like Kampung Arab and Kampung Bugis. But before modern highways were built, passing through the highlands to reach Singaraja from other parts of Bali was difficult and time consuming, causing the central government to move the provincial capital to Denpasar in 1958, in the more accessible south. Today, Singaraja is an efficient and well-kept district capital with two universities, and it is Bali's second largest city after Denpasar.

Starting in the western end of the city, visit **Pantai Lingga** (**Lingga Beach**) just before the Banyusari *bemo* station. The road to Pantai Lingga ends at **Bukit Suci** ("sacred hill"), an old Chinese cemetery overlooking the sea. Now suffering from lack of care, some of the graves are most unusual, such as that of an illustrious member of the Chinese community. Surrounded by a rail, it is guarded by lions and two life-sized black guards swathed in white turbans and bearing lances. Walk through the cemetery to Pantai Lingga, a swimming spot much favored by locals.

From Pantai Lingga head east to a modern house at Jl. Dewi Sartika 42, the **Pertenunan Berdikari Handwoven Cloth Factory**. Specializing in textiles portraying traditional Buleleng motifs, it's one of the few places on Bali to see ladies weaving cloths. Using stand-up wooden looms, their unique designs feature characters from *wayang* puppet shows and one, called *naga candi,* depicts split-gate entrances to Balinese temples and *merus* (pagodas) bordered by two giant dragons.

East of the main crossroads of the town lies Singaraja's main **shopping district**, which includes a bank, a pizza place, a few tourist souvenir kiosks, and several silver and gold shops. The heart of the city is at the intersection of Jl. Gajah Mada and Jl. Jen. Ahmad Yani, where there are banks, a post office, and several small restaurants. The **Buleleng market**, **Pasar Anyar**, just off Jl. Gajah Mada, is down a narrow lane that runs behind a northeast group of buildings. From sunrise throughout the morning it is packed with sellers and traders buying meat and vegetables and offering flowers, clothes and homewares. Around dusk this area turns into an animated night market. Not to be missed.

From the main shopping district is just a short drive north to the **old harbor**, passing through streets lined with sadly deteriorating Dutch colonial buildings that are masked by large 21st-century signboards. Keep an eye out on Jl. Jen. Ahmad Yani, the main street, for an unusual **mosque** in the Dutch architectural style. Across a small bridge that was a gift from the Queen of Holland is the harbor, with a few restored buildings from the Dutch colonial period lining the now unused port, giving a glimpse into life as it must have

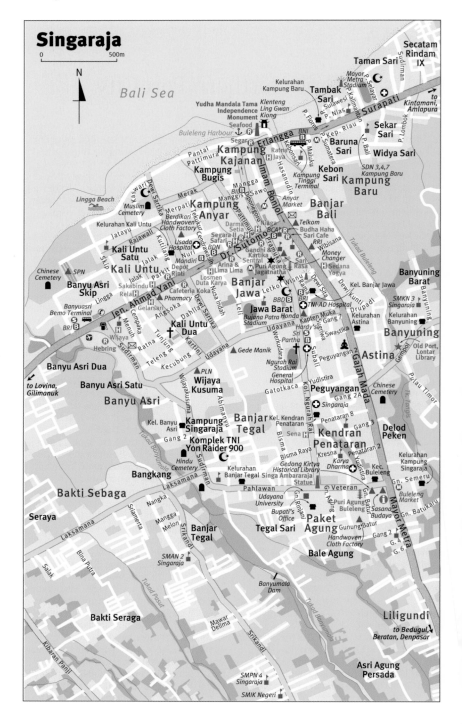

been when spices, vanilla, and tobacco were exported, and later, before the opening of Ngurah Rai Airport in the 1970s, when cruise ships landed here and all tourists to Bali entered through this port. Standing along the shoreline is a clutch of restaurants on stilts serving tasty grilled seafood, a pleasant interlude at lunch-time cooled by sea breezes. The gigantic **Yudha Mandala Tama independence monument**, with an Indonesian freedom fighter bearing a flag, looms over the harbor and has now been surrounded by decorative brick paving blocks to form a nice terrace.

Across the street from the monument is the **Ling Gwan Kiong Chinese temple** (*klenteng*), one of the few on Bali and evidence of this community's long presence in the town. Buddhism, Confucianism, and Taoism are all practiced here. Although the building has been restored many times and looks very new, with a precisely landscaped garden, the original ceiling, constructed in 1873, is above the inner altar. A large bell in the forecourt was brought over from England, and lamps from Holland are part of the old structure. The temple is open to everyone for prayer, and the English-speaking caretaker is happy to show visitors around.

At the southern end of Singaraja, overlooking the Jl. Ngurah Rai and Jl. Veteran junction roundabout, stands an imposing statue of Singa Ambararaja—a winged lion who gazes imperiously over the city. Another large monument on Jl. Veteran is of Ki Gusti Ngurah Panji Sakti, founder of the Buleleng dynasty. The name "Singaraja" means "Lion King".

Heading east from here along Jl. Veteran, stop in at No. 22. On the right-hand side is **Gedong Kirtya**, a library/museum/research center founded by the Dutch in 1928 for the preservation of *lontar* (palm leaf) texts collected in Bali and Lombok. Although the majority of real treasures are housed in Holland, a glass display case in the second room contains these traditional manuscripts, which are written in Balinese and Kawi (old Javanese) languages. The collection also includes books covering religion, architecture, philosophy, medicine, and black magic in Balinese, Kawi, Dutch, English, and German, as well as several *prasasti* (ancient copper plate inscriptions). You may be fortunate to see one of the employees copying an old *lontar* onto new palm leaves, or even the now rare art of making *prasati*.

Directly behind Gedong Kirtya is **Puri Kawan** (the "Western Court"), part of the former palace of the king of Singaraja. It is now the location of **Perusahaan Puri Sinar Nadiputra**, a textile mill where *sarungs* bearing Buleleng motifs were traditionally woven for the royal family and ceremonial occasions.

A few meters to the east is a major cross-roads with a market on the southeast corner. To the southwest is the **Sasana Budaya** (Buleleng Cultural Center), an exhibition hall where cultural performances, art exhibitions, and festivals are held. (Check events schedules at the Tourist Information Center on arrival.) **Puri Agung Buleleng (the Royal Palace)**, also called Puri Gede, is on Jl. Mayor Metra near the Cultural Center. It was built in 1604 by Raja Ki Gusti Anglurah Pandji Sakti at the beginning of his rule of the Buleleng Kingdom, which once extended from Java to Timor, in eastern Indonesian. Renovated several times, his descendants still live here and during limited opening hours, visitors may see the old house where kings once lived, historic family photos, and the Merajan Puri royal shrine. The last Buleleng raja, Anak Agung Pandji Tisna, ruled until 1950 and established the first tourist accommodation in what is now as Lovina.

—*Raechelle Rubinstein*

The Yudha Mandala Tama Independence Monument is situated in Singaraja's historic harbor, with seafood restaurants on stilts behind.

VISITING SINGARAJA
(TELEPHONE CODE: 0362)

While it's possible to make a day-trip to the north coast from southern Bali, it's a very long drive and you really need to stay longer to see the entire area. Best to base yourself either in the Lovina area, with its wide choice of hotels and restaurants catering to every budget, or in the cool climate of the Bedugul Highlands further south. From either location, the rest of northern Bali is easily accessible.

Even though Singaraja is Bali's second largest city, it hasn't quite gotten the hang of developing itself for tourism. However, that's not all bad. It's a pleasant place to visit, with a flavor somewhat more Islamic than Hindu. There are no traffic jams or pollution, and the majority of businesses are conveniently located on one main street, Jl. Jen. Ahmad Yani.

See map on page 278.

GETTING THERE & GETTING AROUND
Singaraja can easily be reached from all parts of Bali. From Denpasar, it takes 2–3 hours (78 km/48 miles) by car via the Bedugul Highlands. Another road, still more breathtaking, runs through Tabanan, Pupuan, and Seririt.

There are three terminals in Singaraja: Sukasada, Banyusari, and Penarukan. *Bemos* from Denpasar's Ubung terminal (about $3) and Kintamani arrive at Sukasada in the south of town, those from Gilimanuk (about $2) arrive at Banyusari to the west of town, while those from Amlapura (about $2) go to Penarukan terminal in the east of town. The fare from Banyusari to Lovina is under $1 and from Penarukan to Amlapura is around about $2.

ACCOMMODATIONS
As the Lovina strip starts only 6 km (4 miles) to the west of Singaraja, visitors tend to head there rather than stay here. If stuck in the city, however, give these two places a try.
Sakabindu Hotel, Jl. Jen. Ahmad Yani 104, Kampung Anyar, tel: 21791. Simple accommodations in the middle of the city.
Wijaya Hotel, Jl. Sudirman 74, Banyusari, tel: 21915, fax: 25817. Wide selection of relatively quiet, if ordinary rooms, conveniently located near Banyusari terminal. From $6.

DINING
Not particularly well known for its restaurants, either, the best option are the seafood eateries on stilts on the waterfront in front of the Chinese temple. Good food at reasonable prices; great seaside atmosphere.

ACTIVITIES
The Buleleng government has recently restored some Dutch colonial buildings at the old harbor and have added a nice terrace around the independence monument and the seafood restaurants, hoping to transform the area into a tourist attraction. They are also focusing on the buildings adjacent to the Gedong Kirtya library: the handwoven fabric factory (which was once part of the palace), the Buleleng Cultural Center, the Royal Palace, and a tourist information center, all in one location. Stay tuned; there may be some interesting changes to Singaraja in the near future.
Gedong Kirtya, Jl. Veteran, in the Sasana Budaya complex. Open Monday–Thursday 7:30 am–3:30 pm, Friday 7 am–12:30 pm, closed on public holidays. Established by the Dutch in 1928, this museum/library/research center houses valuable *lontar* manuscripts etched on palm leaves, *prasati* transcriptions on metal plates, and books in several languages that deal with many aspects of human life. Renovated in 2008, it was transformed from a musty old library to a full museum.
Puri Agung Buleleng (Royal Palace), Jl. Mayor Metra. Open 4–6 pm daily, closed on public holidays. Parts of the home of Buleleng kings since 1604 are now open to guests who want to know more about Singaraja's history. See the old house, historic family photos, and a royal shrine. Visit www.northbali.info for a sneak preview of some wonderful old family snapshots and a bit of history.
Sasana Budaya (Buleleng Cultural Center), Jl. Veteran. An exhibition hall where dance performances and art exhibitions are held. Check schedules upon arrival. Singaraja hosts two annual art festivals, with dancers, musicians, and other artists flocking to the city. The Bali Art Festival is held in May/June and the North Bali Festival in August.

TOURIST INFORMATION
Regional Tourist Office, at the corner of Jl. Veteran and Jl. Gajah Mada, tel: 25141 (near the museum). Visitor-friendly. Ask about dance performances, festivals, and other cultural events.

MEDICAL
Rumah Sakit Umum (General Hospital), Jl. Ngurah Rai, tel: 22046, is the largest public hospital in northern Bali. The city's **pharmacies** are concentrated along Jl. Diponegoro. The main **post office** is at Jl. Gajah Mada 156. Open Mondays–Thursdays and Saturdays 7:30 am–4 pm, Fridays 7:30–3 pm. Several banks change money and have ATMs.

Tranquil Beaches on Bali's North Coast

West of Singaraja is Lovina beach resort, which until fairly recent times was the main draw of Northern Bali. Formerly thought of as Bali's best snorkeling area, it also attracted those wishing escape from the over-crowded beaches of the south. Considered to be a quiet area with only basic accommodations in the 1980s, Lovina experienced a downturn in the late 1990s. More than decade later, with dolphin watching via local fishing boats added to its list of "must-do" activities, new resorts and spas are springing up along the shoreline, older hotels are being spruced up, and Lovina is now also a good base for exploring the fabulous scenery and outdoor activities available to its south and east. It can be very crowded in July and August, and during Indonesian school holidays, but apart from these times it's otherwise quiet.

Lovina Beach

Six kilometers (4 miles) west of Singaraja is **Lovina Beach**, a long stretch of black sand bordering the coastal villages Pemaron, Tukadmungga, Anturan, Kalibukbuk, Kaliasem, and Temukus. Numerous eating establishments and accommodations, ranging from backpacker homestays to luxury villas, line the coast for some 12 km (8 miles). The pace of life at Lovina reflects the calmness of the sea and its rural atmosphere. With coral reefs protecting the shore and blocking the undertows prevalent on southern beaches, a shallow sea near the shore and the water warm year round, this is an excellent spot for swimming. Snorkeling is good near the reef (local colorful fishing boats—*perahu*—are available for hire), and it is a good central location from which to explore northern and central Bali. The sunsets at Lovina are par-ticularly spectacular.

The name "Lovina" was coined by the last king of Buleleng. A convert to Christianity, he gave the name to a small tract of land that he purchased at Kaliasem, where he built the Tasik Madu ("Sea of Honey") Hotel in 1953 (which no longer exists). Some say the name Lovina signifies the "love" that is contained in the "heart" of all people. While the name originally applied to Kalibubuk, it has now been expanded to include four adjoining beaches, which are accessed by small lanes

Colorful fishing boats are lined up on beach at Lovina.

running perpendicular to the east–west coastal highway.

Kalibubuk village remains the center of Lovina, and north of the main road (Jl. Raya Singaraja-Seririt) is the largest concentration of nightlife, hotels, restaurants, shops, and money changers. Those who prefer a quieter retreat might be happier at either end of the beach—in Pemaron or Temukus villages—which border farmland and traditional villages. At the end of Jl. Binaria, on **Binaria Beach** is a **Dolphin Statue**, the "mascot" of Lovina and a gathering place for both locals and visitors. Its coconut palms, simple thatch-roofed *warungs*, and volcanic black sand are an ideal backdrop for romantic sunsets.

Dolphin sighting trips are offered at every hotel, as well as on the beaches. They depart every morning at dawn, and the hope is that there are more dolphins to see than tourist-filled *perahu.*

Further west

From Temukus at Lovina's western boundary it is 3 km (2 miles) to the twin villages **Dencarik** and **Banjar Tegeha**. Pass through Dencarik to neighboring Banjar Tegeha, home of the splendid Buddhist **Brahma Arama Vihara**, which plays a central role in Buddhist religious life and education. Opened in 1970 after 10 years of construction, it

replaces another founded in Banjar in 1958, which the followers merely outgrew. It combines architectural and iconographic elements found throughout the Buddhist world with a Balinese twist. Quiet, cool, and set high in the hills, it commands a view down to the ocean. The gardens and most of the compound are open to the public for meditation; however, the main building housing gold Buddhas and stupas is closed at night for security reasons. People from around the world and of all religions assemble here to practice meditation. Visitors are requested to dress in a respectful manner, to speak softly, and to remove their shoes before entering.

Banjar is also the site of the **Banjar Air Panas**, a sacred hot spring. In 1985 the sulfurous spring water was channeled into a public bathing area consisting of three pools, set in a tasteful blend of jungle and garden. The pleasant 38°C water, which is thought to have healing properties, pours forth from the mouths of eight *nagas* (mythical snake-dragon creatures) into an upper pool, and from there into another one below. Adjacent to these large pools is a smaller one with three upper level spouts, which do nicely for a strong massage. There are changing rooms, showers, toilets, and a restaurant. The best time to visit is early mornings, being careful

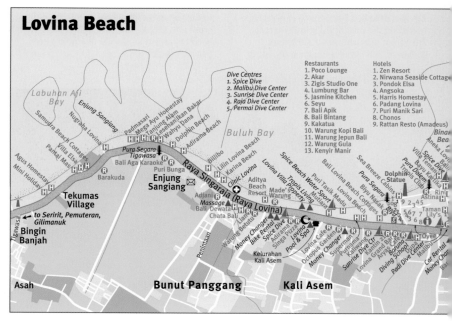

to avoid weekends and public holidays when the hot springs are crowded.

Just 3 km (2 miles) west of Banjar lies **Seririt**, the former commercial center of Buleleng Regency. It was devastated by an earthquake in 1976 and was subsequently rebuilt, but some of its Dutch colonial architecture remains. There's a lively night market in the center of town. Seririt does not in itself warrant a visit. However, if you have private transport, there are two scenic drives worth taking that commence there.

Turn south at Seririt and follow the road as it climbs through Bubunan, Petemon, Ringdikit, and Rangdu villages. The scenery along this road becomes increasingly impressive. At **Rangdu** a right turn at the T-intersection leads to Denpasar via Pupuan. Alternatively, the road continues from Rangdu to Mayong, Gunung Sari, Banyu Atis, and Kayu Putih. There are spectacular views of rice terraces, coffee, and clove plantations, the surrounding hills and, behind, the north coast. From Kayu Putih it is a further 13 km (8 miles) to **Munduk**, 1,200 m (4,000 ft) above sea level. The road between Kayu Putih and Munduk is a series of narrow hair-pin turns and should be traversed slowly and carefully.

From Munduk the road runs atop hills that surround two lakes, Tamblingan and Buyan.

Dolphin watching is a popular pastime at Lovina.

These lakes were one body of water until a landslide split them in 1818. The road then emerges at Wanagiri, just north of Bedugul.

A big surprise

Alternatively, continue going west to Pemuteran and the West Bali National Park. Along the beaches running parallel to the north coast highway across the border into western Bali are resorts—some of them dedicated to relaxation, meditation, and yoga—and sprawling complexes of foreign-owned luxury villas.

At Seririt the rice fields start blending in with a new crop that's more familiar to Europe than Asia: vineyards. Signs leading to resorts and villas begin appearing here. Suddenly along the coastline near **Ume Anyar** there is

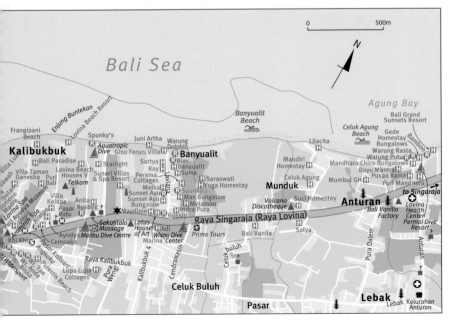

new development that seems so unlikely a spot that stumbling across it is nothing short of a big surprise. Tucked off the road toward the sea are a handful of resorts on the newly developed **Ume Anyar Beach**, and next to that is a sprawling compound of luxury villas owned by foreigners, who primarily live there only a small part of the year and lease them through rental agencies for the remainder. Street after street is filled with extravagant villas, with more under construction. For travelers who desire elegant living far away from mainstream tourist areas, this may be ideal.

—*Raechelle Rubinstein*

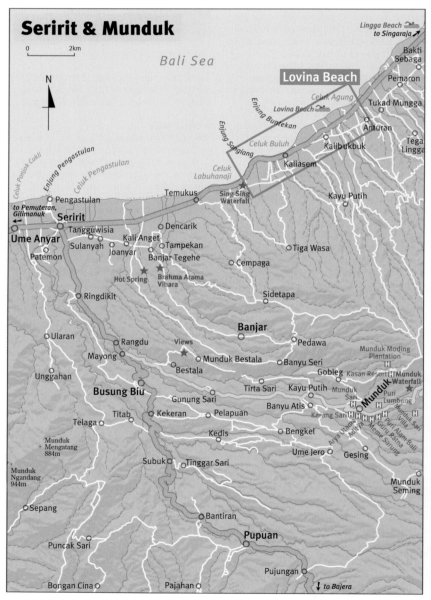

Seririt & Munduk

0   2km

N

Bali Sea

Lingga Beach
to Singaraja

Bakti
Sebaga

Pemaron

Lovina Beach

Celuk Agung

Tukad Mungga

Lovina Beach

Enjung Buleleng

Enjung Bupfekan

Anturan

Enjung Sangiang

Celuk Buluh

Kalibukbuk

Tega
Lingga

Celuk
Labuhanaji

Kaliasem

Celuk Pontjok Cukli

Enjung Pengastulan

Celuk Pengastulan

Temukus

Sing Sing
Waterfall

Kayu Putih

Pengastulan

to Pemuteran,
Gilimanuk   **Seririt**

Tangguwisia

Dencarik

Ume Anyar

Sulanyah   Kali Anget

Tampekan

Tiga Wasa

Patemon

Joanyar   Banjar Tegehe

Cempaga

Hot Spring   Brahma Arama
Vihara

Ringdikit

Sidetapa

Banjar

Ularan   Rangdu   Views

Pedawa

Munduk Moding
Plantation

Mayong   Munduk Bestala

Banyu Seri

Gobleg   Kasan Resort   Munduk
Waterfall

Bestala

Unggahan

Tirta Sari   Kayu Putih   Munduk
Sari

Munduk

Busung Biu   Gunung Sari

Banyu Atis

Puri
Lumbung

Munduk Sari

Titab   Kekeran   Pelapuan

Karang Sari

Puri Alam Bali

Telaga

Kedis

Bengkel

Arya Utama   Adtya   Meme Sarung

Puri Ratna
Meme Sarung

Munduk
+ Mengatang
884m

Ume Jero   Gesing

Munduk
Ngandang
944m

Subuk   Tinggar Sari

Munduk
Seming

Sepang

Bantiran

Pupuan

Puncak Sari

Pujungan

Bongan Cina   Pajahan

to Bajera

VISITING LOVINA
(TELEPHONE CODE: 0362)

The area known as Lovina comprises several villages along the coastal road west of Singaraja. From east to west they are: Pemaron, Tukadmungga, Anturan, Kalibukbuk (the original "Lovina") Kaliasem, and Temukus. All offer accommodations and many other tourist services.

It is quiet and rural at either end of the beach. Central Lovina (Kalibukbuk) can be crowded during holidays. The black sand beach is beautiful at sunset and sunrise. There's no surfing, but plenty of coral areas for snorkeling. Local fishermen can also be hired for early morning trips to see dolphins off-shore; arrange with the boatmen a day in advance. If you have had enough of the sea, the mountainous hinterland to the south is great for hiking.

GETTING THERE
Lovina is only 10 minutes from Singaraja, on a good road. **Public transport** runs from 6 am–9 pm. *Bemos* to Singaraja (Banyusari terminal) cost under $1. Just flag one down along the road. From Kuta to Lovina by *bemo* takes about 3 hrs; from the Denpasar airport or Sanur, about 2.5 hrs, traveling through the Bedugul Highlands.

There are direct buses to Java, usually traveling overnight. Buy a ticket at the Perama office, Jl. Raya Lovina in Anturan. Perama also sells shuttle bus tickets (or most accommodations can arrange them) to Bali's main resort areas: Candidasa $15 (5.5 hrs), Kuta $13 (3 hrs), Ubud $13 (2 hrs).

Tours of the area, as well as snorkeling, sailing, and dolphin trips can be taken care of by all hotels. The easiest way to arrange for bicycle (note that there are a lot of steep hills away inland), motorbike, and car rentals is also through local accommodations.

ACCOMMODATIONS
Having recovered from a downturn in the late 1990s, Lovina has sprung to life with a wide range of accommodations that include the *losmen* of yore, newly established boutique hotels and villas, and practically everything else in between. The biggest dilemma will be deciding which one is best for you.

Binaria Beach is at the end of Jl. Binaria. From here there's a path through a tree-lined area to Jl. Rambutan and Rambutan Beach. And from Rambutan Beach there's a trail to Kartika Beach, at the end of Jl. Kartika. Banyualit Beach is at the end of Jl. Laviana in the easternmost part of Kalibubuk, and is quiet and uncrowded.

Budget (under $25)
Some of the older hotels in this category are located right on the beach and are now well-established and have repeat clients. Newer places tend to be more spacious. Rates usually include breakfast. The highest concentration of budget places is on Jl. Binaria in "downtown" Kalibukbuk.

Angsoka Hotel, Jl. Binaria, Kalibukuk, tel: 41841, fax: 41023, www.angsoka.com. 44 comfortable rooms in 2-story bungalows and cottages, some with hot water. Pool and bar. Restaurant is popular with travelers; meals prepared in an open kitchen. $7–40.

Astina Seaside Cottages, Jl. Ketapang, Kalibukbuk, tel: 341-4118712. 16 rooms in a variety of categories, all with terraces, 20 m (65 ft) from the beach at the end of Jl. Mawar. A long-time Lovina favorite decorated with bamboo walls. Pool, restaurant, bar, garden. $7–40.

Deutsches Eck Rikesti & Restaurant, Jl. Raya Singaraja-Seririt, Temukus, mobile: +62 (0)812-3763-5475, www.wonderfulbali.com/rikesti. 2 clean guest-rooms on the outskirts of Lovina available for 1 night or for longer periods. The rooms are set in a large garden with a swimming pool. Poolside restaurant. Excellent traditional German, international, and Indonesian food at reasonable prices. $15.

Gede Homestay Bungalows, Lovina Beach, tel: 41526. Two rows of comfortable bungalows, some remodeled, in a fishing village. Enter via a narrow alley leading from the main road. Bungalows have combined living/bedroom and separate bathroom. Clean, family run. $10–12 with fan or AC.

Mas Bungalows, Banyualit Beach, tel: 41773, www. masbungalows.com. 8 bungalows in a tropical garden with Western bathrooms, verandahs, fan, and AC. Swimming pool and kids' pool. From $10.

Mega Ayu Homestay, Jl. Raya Singaraja-Seririt, Kaliasem, mobile: +62 (0)813-303-0275. www.biyu-nasakgallery.com. Situated in the center of Lovina just behind the Biyu Nasak Gallery on the main road near Jl. Binaria, which leads to the popular Dolphin Square and the beach. Within walking distance of ATMs, shops, bars and restaurants. US$5.

Puri Bali Lovina, Jl. Mawar, Rambutan Beach, Kalibukbuk, tel:/fax: 41485, www.puribalilovina.com. Popular with budget travelers, 30 clean rooms on 1.3 garden-filled ha in central Lovina, a 5 minute walk from the beach. A variety of rooms, some with AC, some fan; 2-bedroom suite for families has dining room, tv, hot water, fridge. Large pool, playground, basketball, and badminton court. Restaurant serves European, Chinese, and Italian food. Cocktails. Internet available. $18–70.

Rini Hotel, Jl. Ketapang, Kalibukuk, tel: 41386, www. rinihotel.com. Comfortable accommodation for every budget with a saltwater swimming pool. Popular with families with kids. From $20.

Sanders, beach-side, Kalibukuk. Clean rooms, but no hot water. One of the better budget accommodations in town. $5.

Suma Hotel, Kalibukbuk, tel: 41566, www.sumahotel.com. Economy, standard, and superior rooms, some with AC and hot water. Top-of-the-line "Luxe" room has both, plus mini-fridge. Restaurant, pool, playground, chess board with hand-carved wooden pieces. $15–71.

Sunset Ayu Bungalows, Jl. Laviana, Banyualit, Kalibukbuk, tel: 41054. Situated in central Lovina near the beach and a number of good international restaurants. 2 bungalows set in a lush tropical garden. $8.

Moderate ($25–50)

Intermediate-range hotels in the area are very pleasant, simple, and reasonably priced. Most consist of rows of bungalows on the beach. Nearly all serve a basic breakfast (coffee or tea with fruit salad, toast, and an egg). All rooms in this category have private bath. Always ask for a discount, particularly in the low season.

These hotels are all located right on the beach; facilities include swimming pools, bar, hot water, private bathrooms—some with bathtubs—and AC.

Adirama Beach Hotel, Jl. Raya Singaraja-Seririt, Kaliasem, tel: 41759, fax: 41769, www.adiramabeach-hotel.com. A uniquely located, cozy hotel on a quiet, long stretch of beach with ocean view. Standard rooms, suites, and family rooms. Restaurant has interesting menu. From $28. Discounts for bookings of 3 weeks or more.

Banjar Hills Retreat, Banjar Tegehe, (+62) 818-565-342, www.balibanjarhills.com. A small hotel overlooking the sea with twin and queen size bedrooms, all with garden bathrooms, hot water, AC, ceiling fans, and verandahs. Swimming pool, restaurant; Lovina and temple tours. $25.

Rambutan Beach Cottages, **Rambutan Boutique Hotel & Spa**, Jl. Mawar, Kalibukbuk, tel: 41388, fax: 41621, www.rambutan.org. Family run bungalows set around an attractive garden filled with fruit trees, some with unbeatable ocean views. Quiet, good service, kids' play area, restaurant, cocktails. Two pools, Internet, library, spa, billiard table, cooking classes. Family bungalows also available. From $28.

Intermediate ($50–75)

Aditya Beach Resort, Jl. Raya Lovina, tel: 41059, fax: 41342, www.adityalovina.com. 46 AC rooms and cottages with hot water, most with private verandahs, fridge, telephone, tv. 2 beach restaurants, pool, sunken bar, money changer, tour desk, doctor on

call. Credit cards accepted. Fishing, sailing, and scuba diving can be arranged. $55–73.

Bali Taman Lovina Resort & Spa, Jl. Raya Lovina, tel: 41126, fax 41840, www.balitamanlovina.com. Standard and deluxe rooms, suites, and family suite in Balinese architecture with landscaped gardens. Guest care is emphasized. Pool, garden, restaurant, Aruna Spa. $60–175. Check website for Internet rates.

Melka Excelsior Hotel, Jl. Raya Kalibukbuk, tel: 41562, 41552, fax: 41543, www.melkagroups.com. The only hotel in the world offering swimming with the dolphins in onsite saltwater pools; daily dolphin show. Zoo with a variety of animals. Butterfly garden, kids' club, spa. 63 rooms for a variety of budgets. $60–130.

Puri Saron (formerly Baruna Beach Cottages), Lovina Beach, www.barunabeach.com. On the beach with no other hotels in sight, yet 5 minutes from Lovina. 35 AC rooms with king-sized bed, hot water, fridge, tv, and deluxe room in Lombok style. Balcony Bar & Restaurant and Sea Cave Bar, Sun Deck Lounge, pool, massage, surf canoes, outrigger for hire, tours arranged. Credit cards accepted. $67–106.

Starlight Restaurant & Villas, Dusun Banyualit, Kalibukbuk , tel: 700-5271, www.starlight-bali.com. A new property with uniquely-styled cottages with AC, flat-screen tv, fridge, WiFi, with modern bathrooms. $55–100. See website for low season (Sept–May) and long stay rates.

First class ($75–100)

Bali Paradise Hotel, Jl. Kartika, Kalibukbuk, tel: 41432, www.baliparadisehotel.com. A small hotel with only 9 rooms, ensuring personalized service. Set in a rice field with no neighbors, you can watch the daily lives of farmers, mountain and ocean views from almost every room. Swimming pool, gardens, traditional Balinese massage, WiFi, dolphin tours. $86–145.

Nugraha Lovina Seaview Resort & Spa, Jl. Raya Lovina, tel: 41601, tel:/fax: 41605, www.nugraha-hotel.com. 17 AC ocean-view rooms set in a coconut grove along Lovina beach. Hot water, tv, fridge, private terrace or balcony. New suite rooms have private living room. Villa, for more privacy. Restaurant, spa, pool. $80–215.

Luxury ($100-up)

Aneka Lovina Villas & Spa, Jl. Raya Kalibukbuk, tel: (0361) 728-790, fax: (0361) 725-252, www.indo.com/hotels/aneka_lovina/index.html. A large new hotel on Lovina beach with 24 standard rooms, 35 villas, karaoke bar, spa, restaurant. $115–128.

Damai Lovina Villas, Jl. Damai, Kayu Putih, tel: 41008, fax: 41009, www.damai.com. 14 luxury villas with butler service in the hills 4 km (2.5 miles) inland from

Lovina. Award-winning restaurant serving organic vegetables and meats from their own farm and freshly caught fish. Spa offers therapeutic massage and body treatments using Balinese and other techniques. Check website for Internet special rates. Multi-night all-inclusive packages begin at $411/night for 2 people.

Puri Bagus Villa Resort Lovina, Jl. Raya Seririt-Singaraja, Desa Pemaron, tel: 21430; fax: 22627, www.puribagus.net. Highly recommended, well-run. 2 suites and 40 extremely comfortable AC Balinese-style beachfront villas with private pool and dining room, verandah, open-air shower, mini-fridge, tv. Beachside restaurant and bar, a great place for spectacular sunsets. Large pool. Offers water sports, land tours, and a sunrise breakfast tour on a private boat. Java Spa in a "floating" building. $180–370. Check website for packages.

Sunari Villa & Spa Resort, Jl. Raya Lovina, mobile: 0813-3753-6464, www.sunarihotel.com. 129 rooms, cottages, and recently renovated villas with private plunge pools and Jacuzzis, directly on the beach. Bar, restaurant, swimming pool, room service. $130–500.

Privately-owned villas

Villa Adirama, Kaliasem, tel: +31 (0)6 1888 2903. Built in 2007, a small Balinese villa suitable for 2 people in a quiet, green location about 2 km (1.2 miles) from central Lovina. $321/month. Minimum 1 month lease, but longer periods get cheaper rates.

Villa Merpati, in the hills at Kayu Putih, tel: 41883, mobile: +62 (0)813-3747-9329, www.luxury-villa-lovina-bali.com. 3 spacious luxury villas set in beautifully landscaped gardens in a quiet, private location above Lovina. Pool, room service. Water sports and land tours can be arranged. Free shuttle service to Lovina. $100–170. Minimum stay 4 nights.

Villa Santhi, Jl Pantai Segara Wangi 2, Tukad Mungga, tel: 41904, mobile: +62 (0)813-3717-5371, www.villasanthi.com. Set right on the beach in lush tropical gardens with a spectacular infinity swimming pool. A 3-bedroom private villa with contemporary design and uncompromising luxury and comfort. Beachfront setting. Friendly Balinese staff. A haven of tranquility and calm. Spa, dance performances, cooking classes, romantic dining. $552/night.

DINING

The highest concentration of food and beverage outlets are on Jl. Binaria, Jl. Pantai, and Jl. Rambutan, some serving international food. Food stalls on Binaria beach open around 4 pm and attract both local people and visitors with their simple, cheap fare. Nearly all hotels and some of the homestays in the area have restaurants. Below are some of the most popular independent eateries.

Adirama Beach Restaurant, Jl. Raya Singaraja-Seririt, Kaliasem, tel: 41759, fax 41769, www.adiramabeach hotel.com. Although in a hotel, we are listing Adirama Beach Restaurant because of its interesting menu, which includes Italian, German, Mexican, Indonesian, Chinese, Balinese, and vegetarian cuisine. Check out the cheese and paté platter. Small wine list.

Astina Bar & Restaurant, Jl. Rambutan, near the beach. Indonesian and Western food and large swimming pool for diners. Balinese dance performances on Saturday nights.

Barakuda Restaurant, Jl. Mawar, Kalibukbuk, tel: 41405, www.barakuda.baliklik.com. Popular restaurant specializing in seafood and Indonesian cuisine.

Barcelona, Jl. Mawar, Kalibukbuk. Reasonably priced Indonesian food.

Jasmine Kitchen, Gang Binaria, Kalibukbuk, tel: 41565. Thai cuisine in a 2-story building. Simple, pleasant setting, good service.

Kakatua Restaurant, Jl. Binaria, Kalibukbuk, tel: 41344. Varied menu, dishes made from fresh ingredients. Popular with tourists.

Kopi Bali, Jl. Binaria near the Dolphin Statue, Kalibukuk. Popular with backpackers, cheap Indonesian food.

Kubu Lalang Restaurant, Tukad Mungga. Beachfront, high quality food, high hygienic standards, friendly staff, and reasonable prices. Offers a wide variety of authentic local Balinese, Indian, Arabian, and European cuisines. Freshly baked bread daily.

Lovina Bakery, Jl. Raya Lovina, tel: 42225. Freshly baked breads, wine, and ice cream as well as Indonesian and European food. Open 7:30 am until late.

Lumbung Bar-Restaurant, Jl. Binaria, Kalibukbuk, mobile: 0877-6264-5167. Terrace seating and a bamboo bar serving cold beer, cocktails, juices, and coffee. Also has an inside bar and dining area with wide screen tv, pool table. Dutch, Indonesian, International, Italian cuisine. English-speaking staff can provide helpful tour information.

Sea Breeze Café, Jl. Binaria, Kalibukbuk, tel: 41138. Popular eatery west of the Dolphin Statue serving well-prepared entrees, fish, and vegetarian dinners, sandwiches, and desserts. Reasonably priced and good; weekends has live music.

Spice Café, west of Kalibukbuk, tel: 41969. The base for Spice Dive, the menu includes grilled seafood, snacks, Western, and Chinese cuisine at very reasonable prices. Live music on Friday nights. Fantastic beachside location.

Spunkey's Bar-Restaurant, Banyualit beach, Kalibukbuk, mobile: 0813-3736-5094. In a quiet beachfront location. Beer, cocktails, juices, soft drinks, and reasonably priced Indonesian, international and Australian cuisine.

Warung Aria, Jl. Raya Kalibukbuk. Very cheap Indonesian, international, Chinese, vegetarian, and seafood.
Warung Bambu Pemoran, between Singaraja and Lovina on the same road as the Puri Bagus, tel: 27080. Small, clean open-fronted restaurant on the beach with simple Indonesian and Balinese fare, congenial service, cold beer, unbelievably low prices. Specialties are the soups, *rijstaffel* and the Romantic Dinner. Balinese dance performances and cooking classes. Free transport in Lovina area.

NIGHTLIFE

After sunset, the *warungs* along Jl. Binaria are popular for beer and conversation. In addition to the restaurants listed above that offer music and dance performances, there are a few other places catering to late-nighters.
Jax Bar & Grill, Jl. Raya Lovina, Kalibukuk, www.jaxbar.150m.com. Open 6 pm–midnight. Live band every night, karaoke, pool room, darts, big screen tv for sports, dance floor. Also serves Chinese food.
Pashaa Lovina Nightclub, Jl. Raya Lovina, tel: 700-5272, www.pashaabalinightclub.com. Electro and sexy house music mixes from Balinese DJs, laser light shows, 3-D sound system, hot girls. All clubbers and holidaymakers over 20 years old welcome.
Triple 9 Grand Café & Lounge Bar, Jl. Rambutan, Kalibukbuk, mobile: 0813-3708-4318, www.triple9-lovina.com. Opened under the moniker "The Oldies" in 2008, changed to "The Duke" in 2009, now "Triple 9". Good food, cool cocktails, mellow background music of all genres.
Volcano Club, on the main road, Banyualit, tel: 412-222. Open 6 pm–late. An odd building on the highway shaped like a cave.

Zigiz Bar, Jl. Banaria, Kalibukuk (near the Dolphin Statue), mobile: 0852-370-29531. www.zigiz-bar.com. Open 4 pm–midnight. 2 floors containing downstairs and gallery seating. Big-screen tv for sports events. Large cocktail selection. Live acoustic guitar music nightly.

DIVING & SNORKELING

Lovina is a good base for diving and snorkeling excursions. Most hotels can arrange water sports, including snorkeling trips, not only for the Lovina area, but for Pulau Menjangan, 2 hours away in West Bali National Park to the west, and Tulemben and Amed to the east. There are two major dive operators in Lovina.

Usual rates: diving $55–75 per person to Menjangan or Tulemben or in Lovina area; snorkeling $5–7 per person in Lovina area; dolphin watching $6 per person; fishing trips $5–7 per person.
Lovina Dive, Jl. Banyualit, Kalibukuk, tel: 42319, 24997, mobile: + 62 (0)816-4700-936 or +62 (0)813-3866-8622, www.lovinadive.com. Operating since 1994, PADI dive center offering courses and fun dives to the major sites in north Bali. Dives tailored to individuals whether beginners, novices, intermediate, or experienced divers. Night dives.
Spice Dive, booking office: Jl. Binaria, main center: on the beach, Kaliasem, tel: 41305 or 41509, fax: 41171, www.balispicedive.com. Founded in 1989, well established PADI 5 Star dive center and the largest in Lovina. Awarded many certificates of excellence. Nitrox (enriched air) diving school. Offers day trips to all dive spots on north coast; highly trained instructor team speak several languages. Kids welcome.

VISITING SERIRIT & UME ANYAR
(TELEPHONE CODE: 0362)

Until relatively recently, few travelers noticed Seririt, even when they passed through it on the way from Lovina to West Bali National Park or going to the north coast on the road from Antosari in the south. Seririt has always been not much more than a good-sized market town, and still is. A few kilometers past Seririt heading west is Ume Anyar, which can be even more easily overlooked. However, a few years ago clever real estate developers found an untouched stretch of beach in the surrounding villages and *voilé*, there are now hotels, wellness retreats, and an enormous complex of

foreign-owned villas, beckoning visitors who want to be on Bali, but want to experience a completely new side of it.

SERIRIT
ACCOMMODATIONS

Bula Gallery, Jl. Samudra VI, Desa Tangguwisia, Seririt, www.villa-bulagallery-bali.com. Located on the Bali Sea, this villa reflects the owners' love of travel and abstract art. An oasis of rest in luxurious atmosphere and total privacy. Minimalistic décor.

WiFi, large verandah, private garden. $640/week.

Munduk Moding Coffee Plantation Nature Resort & Spa, Banjar Dinas Asa, Gobleg village, PO Box 123 PCS, Pancasari, tel: 700-5321, mobile: +(62) 81-1381-0123, www.mundakmodingplantation.com. A luxury boutique hotel on a working coffee plantation near the Munduk hills. Opened in 2009, 4 villas and 2 suites on 2.02 ha surrounded by forest, coffee, and fruit trees, rice fields. Activities include trekking, horse riding, plantation tours. Works closely with Puri Lumbung Cottages in Munduk, in the Bedugul Highlands. US$140-185/night.

Royal Residence Private Villas, Jl. Muntig, Rangdu (Seririt area), tel: 94783, mobile: +62 (0) 813-3784-4944, www.royalresidencerangdu.com. 6 luxury private villas in a serene environment bringing peace of mind and heart to all who enter. Natural environment, discrete personal attention, absolute privacy. Internet in villas, bar, massage, transport. $105/night.

Other privately-owned villas

To locate other privately-owned villas that are available for rental, simply do a web search for North Bali villas and an astonishing list of possibilities pops up, such as the following. These are all located in a compound in Dencarik village, between Lovina and Seririt.

Villa Agus Mas—www.villa-agusmas.nl
Villa Anais—villa_anais@yahoo.fr
Villa Bali Paradijs—villabaliparadijs@home.nl
Villa Buka Kecil—info@balibeachgarden.com
Villa Indah Bali—balivakantievillas@home.nl
Villa Insulinde—info@beachvilla-bali.com
Villa Sali—info@villasali.nl
Villa The Mango Trees—themangotrees@live.com

DINING

There is the usual variety of *warungs* in Seririt, but a huge surprise is that there's a bar-bistro-brasserie there. An easy drive from Lovina, vacationers who are hungry for authentic European cuisine will want give it a try.

Kwizien Restaurant, Jl. Raya Singaraja, Seririt, tel:/fax: 42031, www.balikwizien.com. Open daily 11 am–11 pm. Appealing primarily to the large number of expats who holiday in Lovina, Kwizien ("cuisine" spelled so everyone can pronounce it) is a Dutch-owned bar-bistro-brasserie. Wide price range, wine list, with different menus for lunch and dinner. For lunch, exquisite sandwiches and tasty salads. Steaks one of the main attractions at dinner. Menus change monthly so there is always something new.

UME ANYAR
ACCOMMODATIONS

Bali Nibbana Resort, Desa Ume Anyar, tel: (0362) 94567, 700-5198, mobile: 0815-573-4949, fax: 94567, www.balinibbanaresort.com, A new resort emphasizing the simple life in Bali, located at the top of the hill in Desa Ume Anyar, surrounded by vineyards and the sea. Tropical gardens. Hot water, AC, satellite tv, pool, Jacuzzi, yoga/meditation deck, bar, and restaurant. Room service, WiFi. $51–92.

Ganesha Bali Retreat & Villas, beachfront Uma Anyar, mobile: +62 (0) 813-5324-3307, www.ganesha-bali.com. A wellness retreat featuring spa, herbal medicine, acupuncture, massage, workshops, meditation, tai chi.

Shanti Loka Resort for Body & Soul, http://shanti-loka.com. A wellness facility near the beach for yoga, holistic health, spa treatments, massage, cleansing, and activities. A yoga hall and 10 beds in 5 bungalows. Restaurant serves breakfast with fruit salads, bread, and eggs. Delicious vegetarian meals for lunch and dinner, with a choice of fresh fish and chicken if requested. A Watsu pool and a second Yoga shala for groups were under construction in 2010. The soft opening prices for 2010 were: full room and board, yoga hall $40/person/sharing.

Zen Resort Bali, Desa Ume Anyar Seririt, tel: 93578, fax: 93578, www.zenresortbali.com. A luxury holistic boutique retreat to relax and rejuvenate physical, psychological, and spiritual wellness. Perched above the Bali Sea amidst rice terraces, vineyards, natural forest, and designer gardens. 14 villas, complete privacy, and attentive service. Spa, yoga. Teachers training at Zen Yoga Bali, c/o Zen Resort Bali, Desa Ume Anyar, Seririt, tel: 700-5305, www.zenyogabali.com.

Privately-owned villas

This is only a sampling of the villas available for rent; several more may be found by doing a web search for North Bali villas. Many of them are leased by agents who handle more than one property; if the chosen one is not available, ask for information about others with similar features.

Buddha Villa—www.buddhavilla.com
Loka Residence, Jl. Villa Mawar, Lokapaksa, tel: 81153, http://holidayhouseonbali.com
Villa Buddha, Jl. Mawar U11, Lokapaksa, www.villabuddha.com
Villa Frangipani, Jl. Mawar, Lokapaksa, mobile: 0813-3897-1823, www.balihuis.nl. In a villa complex near the Bali Nibbana Resort. Dutch owners also own Puri Ganesha Villas in Pemuteran.

VISITING MUNDUK
(TELEPHONE CODE: 0362)

Munduk village is located on a ridge along the mountain road leading from Wanagiri, just north of Pancasari to Mayong road. Overlooking coffee and clove plantations, there is pristine Lake Tamblingan with its traditional fishing community as well as forests, waterfalls, and some of the most beautiful views on the island.

Munduk is a perfect base for treks into the mountainous Balinese hinterland. Walk to Mt. Lesong (1,860 m/6,102 ft), around Lake Tamblingan, or visit the area's five waterfalls. Munduk has long been the center for an innovative community tourism development project, with the village setting up a number of activities for visitors.

GETTING THERE
Go from Bedugul to the Pancasari *bemo* terminal, then take a *bemo* to Munduk. Alternatively hop on a *bemo* at the Pempatan crossing. Each leg costs under $1.

If you hire a car or motorbike, drive cautiously on the road to Munduk; it's steep and tortuous.

The spectacular Munduk waterfall

ACCOMMODATIONS
Budget (under $25)
Guru Ratna Homestay, 200 m (650 ft) from the Munduk market, Munduk, tel: 92812, mobile: +62 (0) 813-3852-6092. 5 rooms in Dutch colonial style houses, some of them with verandahs and great views into the valley. Dining room also has good views. Ecologically concerned. Activities: cooking classes and offering making with the owner's family, plus excursions. Babysitting is available. $15.

Moderate ($25-50)
Meme Surung Homestay, Munduk, tel: 701-2887, fax: 700-5267, mobile: +62 812-387-4042. 10 rooms with attached bathrooms in a Balinese home environment featuring a combination of Dutch and Malay architecture. Located at a quiet spot, off the road and up a hill in the middle of the village. Restaurant $25–30.

Intermediate ($50-75)
Lumbung Bali Cottages, above Puri Lumbung Cottages, Munduk, tel: 92818, www.lumbungbali.com. 7 cottages surrounded by gardens. Restaurant, yoga, massage, trekking, and hiking programs. From $70.
Munduk Sari Villa, Munduk, tel: (0361) 747-5473, fax: (0361) 298-1246, www.munduksari.com. An eco-friendly, privately-owned villa in a village surrounded by coffee, clove, vanilla, and cacao plantations. Offers mountain, rice terrace, and waterfall treks, massage, cooking classes, yoga.

Puri Lumbung Cottages, Munduk village, tel: 701-2887, fax: 700-5267, mobile: +62 (0) 812-387-4042, www.purilumbung.com. 1 villa and 15 antique traditional Balinese *lumbung* (rice granaries) made of thatch, matting, and wood converted into comfortable rooms with hot water that sleeps 2. In a compound honoring Balinese traditions and providing jobs for villagers, encouraging forest and water preservation. Restaurant, spa, yoga, and trekking programs. Works closely with Munduk Moding Coffee Plantation Resort (see previous page). $72–245.

First Class ($75–100)
The Kalaspa Health Retreat, Banjar Asah Panji between Lake Tamblingan and Munduk. 6 private luxury villas and 2 family villas in Balinese design tucked in a rainforest at an altitude of 1,200 m (3,930 ft). Great views of 2 lakes below. Spa. $145–195.

DINING
Ngiring Ngewedang, mobile: +62 (0) 812-480-7010, fax: 41840, www.ngiringngewedang.com. From Wanagiri north of Lake Buyan, take the main road west toward Munduk. After Lake Tamblingan Ngiring Ngewedang is about 2 km (1.2 miles) before Munduk village. An interesting lunch stop for Balinese, Indonesian, and European food and a tour of their coffee roasting facility. Fabulous views are a bonus. Open 10 am–5 pm.

Baroque Temples and Playful Reliefs

The area east of Singaraja is noted for its ancient villages and unique temple architecture, especially those found around the coastal area from Singaraja to Kubutambahan and the region to the south. Time and again visitors have labeled this style of architecture "baroque", as the temples are so heavily adorned with reliefs that it seems no piece of stone has been spared the chisel. Another feature of this style relates to the carving of the heads and hands both of temple statues and of characters in reliefs: they protrude to such a degree that it seems as if the figures lie in wait to pounce upon unsuspecting passers-by.

Singaraja to Air Sanih (Yeh Sanih)

Not far east of Singaraja are some fine examples of charming old villages set amid lush vegetation: Sinabun, Suwug, and Sudaji, reached along a scenic road by turning right at the T-intersection prior to Sangsit.

The best example of Buleleng baroque architecture is encountered at **Pura Beji** in **Sangsit** village, 8 km (5 miles) east of Singaraja. A small sign on the left-hand side of the road announces the location of the temple. If you subscribe to the view that once you have seen one temple you have seen them all, then cast this misapprehension aside; Pura Beji is a work of art.

The baroque Pura Beji temple is highly decorated with Hindu stone carvings.

Pura Beji is a *subak* temple, that is, it belongs to a rice field irrigation association. The path leading to its great, arched entrance is flanked by two serpents. The front of the arch overflows with floral motifs interspersed with demon heads. Its reverse is adorned with mask-like *garuda* heads and floral ornamentation. The main shrines have been carved just as elaborately. The beauty of this soft-pink sandstone temple is augmented by the large, gnarled frangipani trees growing in its courtyard. Note the faded paintings on two pavilions, clearly the work of master craftsmen.

Further examples of old and interesting villages are found not far to the south of Sangsit at **Jagaraga**, **Menyali**, and Sawan. To get there, return to the main road and take the right-hand fork at the next T-junction.

Jagaraga, the site of fierce fighting between the Dutch and Balinese in the late 1840s, bears no obvious signs of this struggle. Visit its **Pura Dalem** dedicated to the dead and filled with statues depicting horrifying figures, the main one being of the Goddess Durga. The foreign presence in Buleleng Regency has also been captured with great humor here. See, for example, the relief of a European riding in a car held up by a knife-wielding bandit. However, such caricatures are few; this temple is dominated by the terrifying widow-witch Rangda.

From Jagaraga, drive through Menyali and follow the road as it climbs to **Sawan**, home of a well-known *gamelan* and ironsmith who can be watched at work. Head for the center of Sawan and ask for directions. His specialty is *gong kebyar*, the frenetic *gamelan* music heard throughout Bali. South of scenic **Sudaji** village at **Lemukih** are five dramatic waterfalls.

Back on the coast road, 3 km (2 miles) past the Jagaraga turn-off is old **Kutumbahan** village, best known for its **Pura Meduwe Karang** temple, which is perched high up on the left side of the road. Dedicated to the Lord of Dry Fields, although its style is more restrained than Pura Beji, it is impressive.

Three tiers of stone statues that are said to represent 34 figures from the *Ramayana* epic are positioned outside the temple. The walls are dominated by floral motifs. Renowned among the reliefs is an old one of a Dutch man riding a bicycle, its back wheel a lotus flower. It is located on the northern wall of the inner shrine.

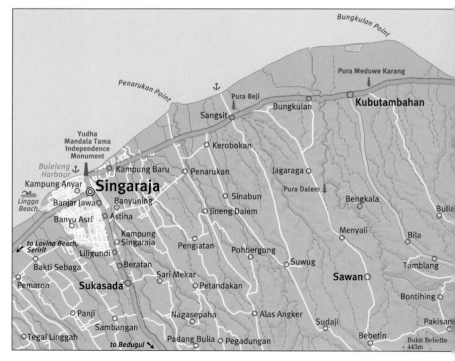

Seventeen kilometers (10 miles) east of Singaraja is the **Air Sanih (Yeh Sanih)** beach resort. Its main attraction is not its beach but rather a natural swimming pool located near the shore. Its icy water originates from a spring and is said to flow at a rate of 800 liters per second. Not as popular with visitors as Lovina (and therefore less crowded), the growing number and variety of accommodations in Air Sanih make it a serene base for trekking through rice terraces and plantations, swimming along the 5 km (3 mile) coastline, snorkeling 500 m (540 yds) out, and expeditions to mounts Batur or Agung or to the waterfalls further south. On the hill above, **Pura Taman Manik Mas** offers stunning architecture.

Air Sanih to Tejakula

Situated on the coast 7 km (4.3 miles) east of Air Sanih is the important temple, **Pura Ponjok Batu**, constructed entirely of stones. Built atop a hill, it affords a fine view of the ocean and some splendid frangipani trees. Cross the road to the small fenced-in shrine that encloses a number of stones. It is said that the 16th century priest Nirartha, drawn to the site by its immense beauty, sat on one of these stones as he composed poetry. For a change from Hindu Bali visit the Bali Aga village **Sembiran**, 6 km (3.7 miles) east of Pura Ponjok Batu. A steep, narrow winding road brings you into Sembiran. The layout of the village differs from that of predominantly Hindu villages. However, Hindu influence is nowadays visible in the form of temples. The village appears poor with its many mud-brick dwellings roofed with zinc sheets. There are excellent views back to the coast.

Tejakula, 3 km (2 miles) past the Sembiran turn-off, is the last important port of call in eastern Buleleng Regency. Stay in a seaside villa and simply enjoy being away from the crowds while watching local fisherman in outrigger dugouts set sail every morning and evening. Otherwise, use it as a base for exploring more of off-the-beaten track Bali. Visit **Banjar Pande**, the silversmiths district, and watch them at work as they produce Balinese religious items and jewelry. Also be sure to see the **horse bath**. To get there, turn south at the T-junction. This large, elaborate structure with its graceful arches has been turned into a public bathing area.

— *Raechelle Rubinstein*

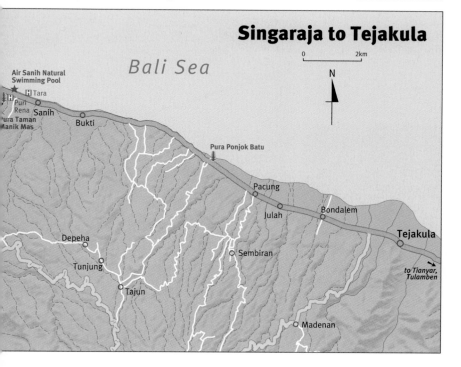

Singaraja to Tejakula

Bali Sea

Air Sanih Natural Swimming Pool

Tara
Puri
Rena · Sanih
Pura Taman Manik Mas · Bukti

Pura Ponjok Batu

Pacung
Julah · Bondalem
Depeha
Sembiran
Tunjung · Tejakula
Tajun
to Tianyar, Tulamben
Madenan

0   2km

N

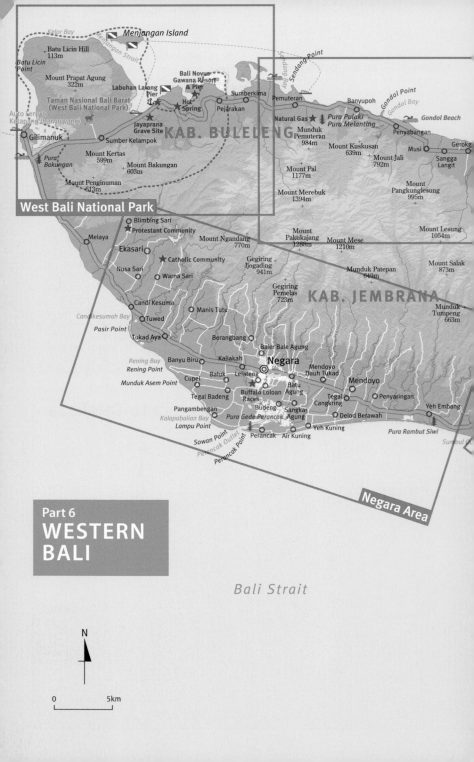

Kelor Bay

Menjangan Island

Batu Licin Hill
113m

Batu Licin
Point

Menjangan Strait

Mount Prapat Agung
322m

Labuhan Lalang
Pier

Bali Novus
Gawana Resort
& Pier

Sumberkima

Pemuteran

Banyupoh

Gondol Point

Gondol Bay

Taman Nasional Bali Barat
(West Bali National Park)

Hot
Spring

Pejarakan

Natural Gas

Pura Pulaki
Pura Melanting

Gondol Beach

Jayaprana
Grave Site

Auto Ferry to
Ketapang (Banyuwangi)

Gilimanuk

Sumber Kelampok

KAB. BULELENG

Munduk
Pemuteran
984m

Mount Kuskusan
639m

Penyabangan

Musi

Gerokg

Pura
Bakungan

Mount Kertas
599m

Mount Bakungan
603m

Mount Jali
792m

Sangga
Langit

Mount Penginuman
613m

Mount Pal
1177m

Mount
Pangkunglesung
995m

Mount Merebuk
1394m

West Bali National Park

Blimbing Sari
Protestant Community

Melaya

Mount Ngandang
770m

Mount
Pakukajang
1288m

Mount Mese
1210m

Mount Lesung
1054m

Ekasari

Catholic Community

Gegiring
Ijogading
941m

Munduk Patepan
640m

Mount Salak
873m

Nusa Sari

Warna Sari

Gegiring
Pemelas
723m

KAB. JEMBRANA

Munduk
Tumpeng
663m

Candi Kesuma

Canakesumah Bay

Tuwed

Manis Tutu

Pasir Point

Tukad Aya

Berangbang

Rening Bay
Rening Point

Banyu Biru

Kaliakah

Baler Bale Agung

Munduk Asem Point

Cupel

Baluk

Lelateng

Negara

Mendoyo
Dauh Tukad

Mendoyo

Tegal Badeng

Buffalo Loloan
Races

Batu
Agung

Tegal
Cangkring

Penyaringan

Pangambengan

Budeng

Sangkar
Agung

Yeh Embang

Kalapabalian Bay
Lampu Point

Pura Gede Perancak

Delod Berawah

Sowan Point

Perancak

Air Kuning

Yeh Kuning

Pura Rambut Siwi

Lampu Point

Perancak Outlet

Perancak Point

Sumbul Ot

Negara Area

Part 6
**WESTERN
BALI**

Bali Strait

N

0   5km

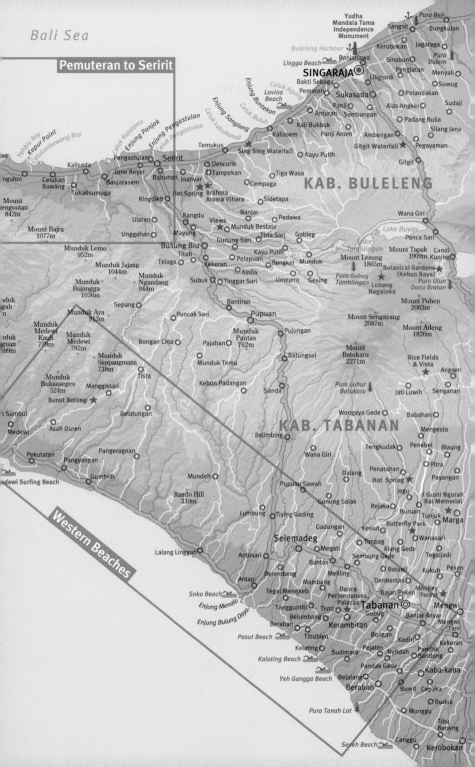

INTRODUCTION

Western Bali

Except for a handful of extreme surfers and some national park aficionados, until the past few years few tourists bothered to venture into Western Bali. While there is some interesting scenery along the highway running from Denpasar to Gilimanuk, where boats depart for East Java, this is a different sort of beauty. Most of Western Bali is extremely dry and unsuitable for farming, its population is relatively small, and in the past poverty was widespread. The inhabitants here are a mixture of Javanese —who migrated to the area to escape overcrowded conditions in eastern Java —and Balinese, with a healthy dose of those from Karangasem Regency, who moved hearth and home here after Mt. Agung's great eruption in 1963.

Without the undulating rice fields and lush gardens of Balinese housing compounds seen in the south, and due to the lack of infrastructure, Western Bali has been of little interest to tourists in the past. All that is rapidly changing, however, and the region is blossoming —not only as a water sports and nature destination, but also as the island's most environmentally concerned area, where eco-tourism in its purest form actually exists.

A few years ago, small-scale investors, both foreign and local, recognized that the vast expanses of undeveloped land in Western Bali and its unique ruggedness were excellent opportunities to develop a new "green" tourism, and they set out to lure travelers away from the overcrowded south and Ubud. Reef restoration and conservation dominate the coastlines, local families invite travelers into their homes to see how they live — sharing knowledge and earning much-needed incomes in the process —and forest preservation is taken seriously. In the west, there's a whole new side of Bali awaiting exploration.

There are two distinctive areas where travelers set up housekeeping for their stays in Western Bali. Generally speaking, surfers and beach lovers flock to its southern coastline, while divers and trekkers cling to

its north shores; there are several deluxe hideaways on both coasts.

Western Bali's southern beaches

Starting from Southern Bali, the highway west goes inland north of Pura Tanah Lot, through lush rice fields near Tabanan, then turns into a coastal road south of Antosari at **Soka Beach**, where the terrain and climate begin changing to the aridness of the west. Small roads lead from the highway to the sea between Tanah Lot and Soka Beach, where there are a number of budget- to medium-priced lodgings and at least one ultra-luxurious resort catering to get-away-from-it-all guests.

West of Soka Beach, the next resort area is at Lalang Linggu's **Balian Beach**, where development is just beginning. Already there are villas, inns, and resorts here, one of them specifically attractive to surfers, as it sits on the sea where waves crash to shore.

Moving further west, **Medewi Beach** still has its budget surfer digs at the eastern end, but new resorts are popping up along this long stretch of beach and old ones are being renovated. Rather than attracting surfers only, these accommodations are full-service facilities suitable for families with spas, restaurants, dance performances, and innovative tour services.

Local culture

Further west is **Negara**, the only town of any size in Western Bali, and the capital of Jembrana Regency. East of Negara is **Pura Rambut Siwi**, one of several great "sea temples" constructed by the priest Danghyang Nirartha in the 16th century. Magnificently perched on a cliff overlooking the ocean is a small temple said to hold the hair that Danghyan Nirartha gave the villagers to show his appreciation for their hospitality.

Negara is known throughout Bali for its **water buffalo races** held between July and October annually. Visitors are welcome to attend Sunday practice heats. Two unusual

Snorkeling and diving are favored pastimes at West Bali National Park's Menjangan Island.

villages lie north of Negara, one almost entirely inhabited by Protestants and the other by Catholics, the latter with a charming church in the midst of vegetable fields.

This area is also known for its unique form of *gamelan*, called *Jegog*, the largest instrument in the ensemble being made of giant bamboo emitting deep, resonating tones. *Jegog* performances can be complemented by other instruments or by dancers. Hotels on Medewi Beach either offer performances in-house or can arrange trips to village festivals, as well as tours to sites around Negara.

West Bali National Park

At the far western end of the island and encompassing a great deal of the interior is **West Bali National Park**. The primary attraction here is superb diving at **Menjangan Island** off the northwest shore. The park also offers some excellent trekking programs with trained guides, which are particularly favored by birdwatchers in search of the elusive Bali Starling. Treks range from short to long over a variety of terrains, and customized expeditions

can be arranged. The only accommodations in the park area are three high-end resorts, causing many travelers on smaller budgets to overnight in nearby Pemuteran.

Western Bali's northern coast

Pemuteran is the first town east of the park with a full range of accommodations. It still has a village feel to it even though there are three luxury resorts here, one of which has won awards for its conservation efforts and tranquility and another that was named one of the World's Best Hideaways by *Travel+Leisure* magazine and serves organic food in its restaurant. There are also plenty of budget- and medium-priced accommodations in Pemuteran. The diving and snorkeling are excellent here, and any one of the several dive shops can arrange packages that include Menjangan Island, macro diving, and safaris. Not-to-be missed is an underwater temple complex, ship graveyard, and "BioWreck" structure. There is also a turtle hatchery project protecting endangered sea turtles.

—Linda Hoffman

WESTERN BEACHES

New Beach Resorts and Surf Breaks

In a couple of spots along western Bali's southern shoreline, hard-core surfers have been following the waves from eastern Indonesia to Bali for several years, staying as long as there were breaks and moving on to the next beach when they abated, leaving entire areas practically empty the rest of the year. In the process, a few low-budget home-stays and *warungs* sprung up to accommodate them. Some of those long-established accommodations remain, but what's new is they have been joined by hotels, private villas, and five-star resorts, some of them owned locally and some by foreigners. This relatively new phenomenon opens up a whole new variety of choices to travelers, which is always good news for Bali beach lovers. Even better is that

where the stretch of western beaches begins is only one hour from the Denpasar airport, so those preferring to skip the crowds of the south can escape them quickly.

Hideaway beaches

Only 20 minutes from Pura Tanah Lot, **Pantai Yeh Gangga (Ganges River Beach)** is the beginning of a long stretch of shoreline that is broken up into segments due to the absence of a coastal highway. A local driver who is knowledgeable about the area will know the small roads from Pandak Gede, north of Tanah Lot, west through Pejaten and then south through Sudimara. However, self-driving first-timers might find it more expedient to head south from Tambanan town

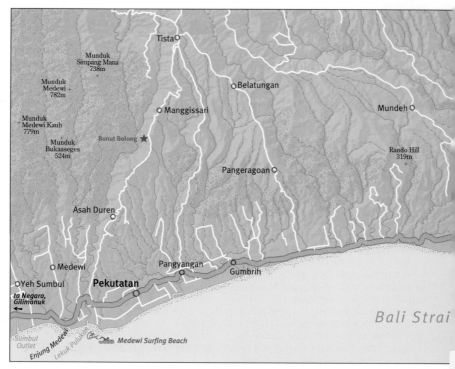

on the road that goes directly to Sudimara. Until relatively recently, Yeh Gangga was a "secret" coastline known only to intrepid travelers. Out in the middle of nowhere, and reachable by negotiating really bad roads, is a gaggle of homestays and bungalows that have been there for a very long time, and which are still going strong—some are undergoing renovations to meet the new tourism demand after a long dry spell. There are several dirt roads along the coast to these accommodations, and clever villagers have set up "toll booths" on some of them to take advantage of the growing tourism. In the midst of this is a surprising complex of luxury villas built by a developer, primarily for foreigners. Down the road a bit further is a busy horse riding stable that's been there since 1994, while near Sudimara village is the **Waka Gangga resort**, one of the award-winning Wakka group of properties that specializes in blending in with the natural environment. Further development of this shore—which is already underway—will open all sorts of alternatives for Bali beach lovers, especially if the local infrastructure is improved.

At the western end of this length of broad, black sand is **Pantai Kelating (Kelating Beach)**. To reach it, go back to the east–west road at Pejaten, and go west to the south turnoff to Kelating village. This long, once-deserted strip of paradise is now home to a super-luxe resort, **Alila Villas Soori**, a hideaway for lovers of fine sand, pounding surf, and stunning views down the coast as far as the eye can see.

A burgeoning cottage industry

Pejaten village is worth a stop. Practically everyone here is involved in making terra cotta roofing tiles, possibly thanks to the area's construction boom. Made individually by hand, and dried over fires fueled with coconut husks, one worker revealed that she made 100 roof tiles a day, but that she was just a beginner. The streets of the entire village are lined with stacks of the roof tiles and of coconut husks ready to be collected and transported either to worksites or to the port at Gilimanuk for export.

At one time, Pejaten was also known for its pale green decorative pottery, and today a few

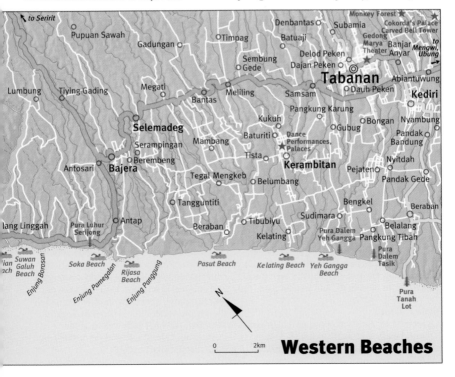

Western Beaches

artists still make it and offer it for sale along the town's main road.

Balian Beach

To get to the next beach—**Balian** (also called **Pantai Lalang Linggha**)—return to the Denpasar–Gilimanuk highway and turn west to **Selemadeg**, then south through Antosari to join the coastal road at **Soka**, where there is a **Taman Rekreasi (Recreational Park)** with a large tour bus-type restaurant, accommodations, river rafting, and a large shop selling *oleh-oleh* (souvenir snacks).

Continuing west on the Java–Bali highway, about 5 km (3.2 miles) away is the beginning of Jembrana Regency. The terrain and climate begin to change here and it gets increasingly drier to the west.

To get to Balian Beach take a small road south through Lalang Linggha village, slowly sloping down to the sea. Except for a couple of older *losmen* (homestays), the majority of accommodations here are new, they are owned by foreigners and, interestingly, they are far more upscale than is expected from a surfing beach. One explanation is that the surfing population is maturing, has more expendable income, and also bring family members who don't surf but refuse to be left at home. Another is good business sense: in order to survive when the surfers move on, large investments must provide something else to attract guests.

The sounds, smells, and sights of Indian Ocean waves crashing up on the beach are stunning here, and the rowdy beer-drinking crowd that is usually associated with surfing communities is isolated into one area, leaving the rest of the beach a quiet, peaceful place to drop out for a while to marvel at the over-whelming natural beauty of the area.

"Balian" derives from the Balian River and a mystical trance healer of the same name. Local legend has it that the mythical healer resided in the river, drawing villagers there to bathe in order to reap the benefits of its curative properties. Even today residents of five villages come here periodically to be cleansed and blessed, particularly teenage girls as a rite of passage into womanhood.

Medewi Beach

An interesting side trip between Balian and Medewi beaches is about 10 km (6.5 miles) north from **Pekutatan** to **Manggissari** to see **Bunut Bolong** ("Hole in the Banyan Tree"), a sacred tree so large that it forms a tunnel with the road passing through it. A shrine on its right side is often visited by travelers who stop to ask permission to pass through. The scenic mountain road passes clove, coffee, cacao, and rambutan plantations, and at the top overlooks a forested gorge.

Banyans are one of three tree species considered to be holy by the Balinese, and are believed to house spirits that must be appeased and treated respectfully. These trees are rarely cut, and if it becomes necessary to do so, a series of rituals is performed to ask for permission and pardon. One explanation is that the reason the forests in this area remain untouched is because the Dutch colonial administration were clever. They simply placed large boulders or trees along the boundaries of areas they wanted protected and the Balinese set up shrines at these landmarks and were afraid to enter for fear of angering the spirits. True or not, this tale emphasizes the complex relationship between the Balinese and nature.

Back on the Denpasar–Gilimanuk highway, **Medewi Beach**, beginning at Pekutatan, has a much different feel to Balian. At much smaller Balian Beach, most of the resorts and home-stays are on one road, whereas here several roads leave the main road to get to the long Medewi shoreline, all of them packed with different types of accommodations, ranging from simple *losmen* that have been around a long time to upmarket properties. There is a lot of renovation going on here as well as new construction. Only the future will tell if Medewi is making the same overdevelopment mistakes as its southern counterparts.

One particular area of Medewi near the river mouth has been well-known among hard-core surfers for a few years. Its long, left-hand breaks occur for two to three months of the year, but the swells are sufficient on the rest of the beach year round for beginners and families. From here almost to Pura Rambut Siwi, the coast is rapidly developing as a resort area specializing in beachside relaxation and day trips into the countryside to experience outdoor activities and culture. In addition to diving lessons, tour programs offered by most hotels include the temple, water buffalo races in Negara, West Bali National Park trekking and snorkeling, fishing, cultural performances, and village visits.

—*Linda Hoffman*

VISITING THE WESTERN BEACHES
Kelating, Yeh Gangga, Balian (Lalang Linggha) & Medewi

In the past, surfing, surfing, and more surfing, caring little about where to sleep, eat or anything else was the name of the game on the southern beaches in Western Bali. The extreme breaks are still there, and they still beckon enthusiasts, but what's blossoming are new higher-end resorts catering to couples and families. One parent can relax, have a massage, or take the kids touring while the other parent surfs, making everybody happy. Better yet, the whole family can learn to surf together on calmer beaches.

The surfer-families head to **Balian** (Lalang Linggha), where there's a consistent left-hander, and to Medewi, where the surfing is best near the river mouth in July and August, and thus the most crowded those months. The rest of Medewi can entertain beginners and beach-loving families all year round.

The exceptions to the surfing draw are **Kelating Beach**, where the mood is utter relaxation at the super deluxe Alila Villas Soori, an exclusive hideaway with all the amenities expected of a 5-star resort, and more; and at **Yeh Gangga**, where there are bungalows and the environmentally-friendly Wakka Gangga resort.

Rip Curl posts important surf news weekly at: www.swellforcast@ripcurl.com.

GETTING THERE & GETTING AROUND

West Bali's Denpasar–Gilimanuk south coast highway (also called the Java–Bali highway) is the main thoroughfare for traffic and trucks coming from and going to the ferry terminal at Gilimanuk, so traffic can be heavy at times. On a good day, though, it takes about 3 hours from Denpasar to Gilimanuk, passing through Tabanan, Negara, and points in between.

Because this is such an important route, there are many buses running from the south to Gilimanuk, stopping at major towns en route. Check schedules locally and book one day ahead.

As west Bali tourism is still developing, there's not much here in the way of **transportation** from the major towns to the beaches, so it's best to rent a car or motorcycle in the south. However, there are some **motorbikes** for rent at Medewi beach for scooting around locally.

From here, there is a beautiful scenic drive to the north coast, starting at Antosari via Pupuan to Seririt.

KELATING & YEH GANGGA BEACHES
(TELEPHONE CODE: 0361)

The Yeh Gangga area, a little known getaway on the south coast, is surrounded by working rice fields, lush green terraces tumbling down to a beach hammered by big unsurfed waves. Located just several kilometers northwest of the Tanah Lot sea temple and only 12 km (8 miles) south of Tabanan, here at last is utter solitude without the remoteness.

Not exactly a beach chair-war kind of place, it's not uncommon in the late afternoons to see **horseback riders** galloping along Yeh Gangga's stretch of glistening black sand. At night, a long almost unbroken line of lights from fishing platforms stretches across the whole horizon.

At the west end of this shoreline, accessible via Kelating village, is Kelating Beach (Pantai Kelating) and the exclusive Alila Villas Soori.

ACCOMMODATIONS

There are a number of privately-owned villas under construction in this area. Browse the Internet (search West Bali or South Bali villas) for details.

Budget (Under $25)
Bali Wisata Bungalows, Yeh Gangga Beach, Sudimara, tel: 261-354, fax: 810-212, www.bali-wisatabungalows.com. An affordable, ultra peaceful and laidback seaside hotel run by a pleasant Balinese family. 4 ocean view and 4 garden view bungalows, 4 standard rooms. European food served in its family-style restaurant. Swimming pool. From $20.

Luxury ($100–up)
Alila Villas Soori, Kelating Beach, tel: 894-6388, fax: 894-6377, www.alilahotels.com. Only 20 minutes from Tanah Lot temple, the infinity pool in the open-air lobby seems to spill into the Indian Ocean. Elegant minimalist design throughout. An all-villa resort, the most exclusive of which has 4 bedrooms, indoor and outdoor living areas with private infinity pool, and pathway to the beach. Comes with cook, driver, and butler. Less costly 1- and 2-bedroom villas also available. "Drift" lounge has games, tv, and barista. Cotta Restaurant serves Continental and

Indonesian cuisine. Chef can prepare any dish guests desire with prior notice. Coast Café & Bar offers seafood and grill ocean-side. Spa, yoga, gym, spa products refill shop, Internet. Starts from $565/night.

Waka Gangga, Jl. Pantai Yeh Gangga, Sudimara village, tel: 416-256, 416-257, fax: 416-353, www.wakaexperience.com. 10 thatched hillside bungalows and 2 villas on different levels of a slope. A dining pavilion serving excellent food sits on the property's highest ground, affording a 180 degree view over the vast Indian Ocean. Facilities also include swimming pool, library, and spa. $200/bungalows; $450/villa with private pool. Discounted Internet rates available.

DINING

The resorts and bungalows are almost the only dining options; however, large, clean **Warung Putih**, near Sudirmara village and 2 minutes from Bali Wisata Bungalows has a good menu, reasonable prices, and a choice of indoor or outdoor seating.

ACTIVITIES

Alila Villas Soori can arrange **Balinese dance lessons** in Abiantuwung village, 5 km (3.2 miles) east of the resort.

Horse riding. Alila Villas Soori can also arrange horse riding at **The Royal Stable** near Kelating Beach, owned by a noble family. 6 domestic and Australian horses.

Bali Island Horse, Yeh Gangga village, tel: 731-407, 871-8060, www.baliislandhorse.com. Stables are located in a seaside village where rice farming, fishing, and sea salt harvesting are the main activities. Ride through gently sloping rice terraces, pause at a waterfall, visit a temple and a bat cave. 2-hr morning or sunset rides $56/adult and $53/child; 1-hr sunset ride $35/adult or child.

BALIAN BEACH (LALANG LINGGHA BEACH)

(TELEPHONE CODE: 0361)

Ten kilometers (6.2 miles) or so west of Antosari, turning south via Lalang Linggha village, is Balian Beach, a relatively new beach resort. Between Antosari and Balian is Soka, where there are restaurants, a convenience store, and buses going east and west. From Balian, it's another 30 minute drive to Medewi Beach.

There is a new development of villas owned by a Russian national up on the hill behind the lodgings on the beach. Starkly white, they look very much out of place in the otherwise beautiful surroundings.

ACCOMMODATIONS
Budget (Under $25)

Made's Homestay, on Balian beach, mobile: 081-2396-3335. One of the few budget *losmen* on the beach with simple rooms and a *warung*.

Pondok Pitaya Surfer Hotel & Restaurant, on Balian Beach, mobile: 0819-9984-9054, www.baliansurf.com. With classic wooden bungalows and rooms, this is a large complex that's more upscale than the usual surfer dude digs. Toki's Place restaurant & bar can get rowdy at the end of the day when the surf is up. Rooms from $10/night.

Warung Ayu, across the road from Balian Beach, mobile: 081-2399-3353. Locally owned budget backpacker place with 8 simple rooms and a *warung*. From $15.

Intermediate ($25–50)

Istana Balian Beach Villa, Banjar Pengasahan, Lalang Linggha, www.istanabalian.com. At the top of the road within walking distance of the beach, a small, very nice compound of quiet, new rooms owned by a friendly Australian who has worked in this area over 10 years and his Balinese wife, who live on-site. Rooms have AC and flat-screen tv. Swimming pool. Many of the local expats gather here in the evenings during the football (soccer) season to watch the games. From $50.

Pondok Pisces Bungalows & Balian Riverside Sanctuary, Balian Beach, Banjar Pengasahan, Lalang Linggah, tel: 780-1735, mobile: 0813-3879-7722, www.pondokpiscesbali.com. Traditional thatched roof bungalows built with natural materials, beach house and ocean view rooms in lush gardens across the street from the beach. Simple, relaxed, friendly. Attached **Tom's Garden Café** has an interesting Western and Indonesian menu, serving wine, beer, and cocktails. Open breakfast, lunch, dinner. Highly recommended. Rooms from $38.

Luxury ($100–up)

Gajah Mina Beach Resort, Suraberata, Lalang Linggah, mobile: +62 (0) 81-2381-1630, fax: 731-174, www.gajahminaresort.com. A 10-year old resort with private beach. Sprawling property with standard rooms, bungalows, and honeymoon suites with cheerful interiors, mini-fridge, terraces, and sea views. Highly recommended for a relaxing getaway. Offers a wide range of activities: cycling, headland trekking, massage, car tours. **Naga Restaurant**, spa. Villas from $100.

MEDEWI BEACH
(TELEPHONE CODE: 0365)

Take the main highway west of Denpasar via Tabanan for about 75 km (2.5 hrs; or about 1 hr from Tabanan town) to the beginning of Medewi at Pekutan, ending just before **Pura Rambut Siwi** temple. At Pekutan there are surf shops, board rentals, WiFi, Internet cafes, and other services. There is no road that connects one segment of beach to the next; instead, the small roads heading south to the sea from the highway are all lined with accommodations and eateries.

As they are everywhere on Bali, the local people are extremely friendly both in and out of the surf, and Medewi's spectacular sunsets and cool tropical evenings add a touch of glamour. The beach is rocky and not for sunbathing. The best surf is early in the mornings when the most people are out.

ACCOMMODATIONS
Budget (Under $25)
Warung & Homestay Gede II, Pekutatan, mobile: 081-2397-6668. Ideal for surfers, just a short walk along the rocky beach to the north. Funky and clean, the breezy *lumbung*-style, raised thatched bungalows with shared baths, cold water, no fans, are charming. Ibu Ketut—the lady with the big smile—serves up delicious food in her open-air café looking out to sea. Bungalows cost an irresistible $9/double with fan.

Intermediate ($50–75)
Medewi Bay Retreat, Jl. Ciwa, Medewi, Banjar Pekutatan, mobile: +62 812-384-2252, www.medewibayretreat.com. 9 villas with rustic charm in tropical gardens set back from the beach. From $67.
Mediwi Beach Cottages, Medewi Beach, Pekutatan, tel: 852-8521, www.medewibeachcottages.com.

With spacious garden and ocean view rooms (but small terraces), satellite tv, refrigerator, hot water, manicured gardens with stately palms, big pool. Peaceful with just the sound of the surf. Bar and restaurant, swimming pool. From $65.
West Bali Surf Retreat (also called **Mai Malu**), Jl. Pantai Medewi, Medewi beach, tel: 470-0068, www.medewibeach.com. Sits high on a hill with spectacular 360 degree views of mountainous west Bali and the sea. Single, twin, double, and 4-share standard rooms, with fans and private terraces. Surf guides; surfboard, motorbike, and car hire. Restaurant with full bar a popular hangout for surfers and other travelers. See website for Medewi surf spots. Packages from $95 include 4 days/3 nights, airport transfer, and 3 meals/day. Online booking discounts available.

First class ($75–100)
Puri Dajuma Cottages, Beach Eco-Resort & Spa, Pekutatan, tel: 43955, 470-0118, fax: 43966, www.dajuma.com. Swiss-owned but locally managed with concern for the environment, 21 ocean and garden view rooms and 1 new suite in a family-friendly setting. Outside showers, ACs, and fans. Hammocks on the terraces made by Kuta fishermen. Spa, swimming pool, 2 restaurants, one serving teppanyaki and Mongolian barbecue. On the resort's beach is a monument commemorating Balinese freedom fighters on the site where ammunition from Java was brought by sea and unloaded to support the struggle against the Dutch. Every August 17 (Indonesia's Independence Day) west Bali soldiers hold a ceremony here. Margarana Tabanan soldiers' cemetery is nearby. Offers some interesting tours in open-top vehicles for better viewing, 4-wheel drive excursions, village visits. Beginner **surfing lessons** on their safe, private beach and transport to more extreme break sites. From $85.

NEGARA TO GILIMANUK

Bali's Wild West Coast

Bali's west coast has historically been the area least visited by tourists. But that is changing now. The rugged western countryside is now considered a viable nature destination with cultural attributes not seen elsewhere on the island. Thanks to new resorts, villas, and homestays being built by both local and foreign investors, improved infrastructure, and the ingenuity of those involved in tourism development, the wild West Coast is now attracting travelers who love nature.

Western Bali is comprised of two regencies: all of Jembrana, whose main population centers are all found along the 71 km (44 miles) of road that hug the coast, and western Buleleng on the north coast. It is reachable from Denpasar by way of the vast rice fields and brilliant coastline of Tabanan Regency or from Singaraja via the wild, dry forests of the north. The ferry from Java berths at Gilimanuk on the island's western tip.

Temple of the sacred hair

Traveling west along the southern Java-Bali highway 18 km west of Medewi beach is **Pura Rambut Siwi**, near Yeh Embang village. Its entrance is marked by a small shrine at the edge of the road where Balinese travelers stop briefly to pray for safety on their journeys. Two hundred meters (210 yds) from the main road is the main temple complex, perched on a cliff at the edge of the ocean.

Pura Rambut Siwi is one of several important monuments to the priest Danghyang Nirartha, who came to Bali from Java during the decline of the Majapahit Kingdom in the hopes of fortifying Balinese Hinduism against the spread of Islam occurring elsewhere in the archipelago. Between 1546 and 1550 he traveled through the island, teaching and unifying the Hindu populace. According to legend, he stopped to pray at a village temple at Yeh Embang and made a gift of his hair to the temple. Since that time it has been known as Rambut Siwi, which means "worship of the hair".

The complex consists of three temple enclosures in a setting of great natural beauty. The first one when entering from the main road is the largest and most important, the Pura Luhur where Danghyang Nirartha's

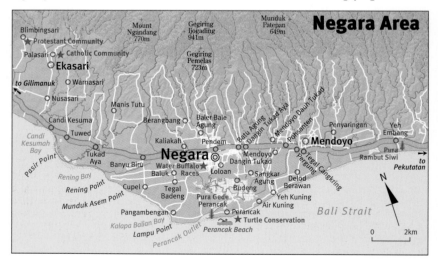

hair is kept. A majestic *candi bentar*, or split gate, on the southern wall of the inner courtyard opens on to the cliff, offering dramatic views of the surf below. Gnarled frangipani trees litter the ground with fragrant blossoms, and incense burns at the feet of moss-covered stone statues swathed in white cloth.

From Pura Luhur it's a short walk east along the cliff to a winding stone stairway that descends to Pura Penataran, the original temple where Danghyang Nirartha is believed to have prayed. When the Balinese worship at Rambut Siwi they first enter this temple.

Walking back westward along the beach there is a small shrine at the entrance to a cave in the cliff wall. This cave is said to be the lair of mystical animals, the *duwe*, or holy beast, of the temple. A well at the mouth of the cave is a source of holy water that is salt free despite its proximity to the ocean. Just beyond the cave, another stairway leads back up to the temple. Atop the edge of the cliff is the tiny Pura Melanting, where merchants stop to pray for prosperity.

A large open-air performance pavilion and two gazebos set amidst lily ponds to the west of Pura Luhur are excellent places to rest and enjoy a panorama of rice fields and white wave crests curling against the black sand coastline as far as the eye can see.

Continuing west along the main road, another important temple is situated along the coast southwest of Mendoyo, **Pura Gede Perancak**, where Danghyang Nirartha is believed to have first landed. A peaceful shrine of white stone sits on the banks of the placid Perancak River, which empties into the sea about 100 m (110 yds) south of the temple. To reach it, turn left off the main road in Tegal Cangkring, 8 km (5 miles) west of Rambut Siwi and follow a narrow back road 1.5 km (1 mile) to an intersection marked by a monument. Turn right and continue west about 9 km (5.6 miles). The temple is on the right where the road turns south along the Perancak River.

At the time of Danghyang Nirartha's arrival, this area was controlled by the debauched ruler, Gusti Ngurah Rangsasa, who obliged the newcomer to pray in his temple. When the holy priest complied, the temple structures collapsed. Gusti Ngurah Rangsasa then fled, and the community rebuilt the temple in honor of Danghyang Nirartha and his teachings.

Off to the races

The Negara **water buffalo races**, known locally as *mekepung*, are the most dramatic of Jembrana Regency's home-grown events. Throughout the westernmost districts, it is still common to see a team of brawny, grey, or pink buffalo pulling wooden carts filled with cacao, coffee or bananas. *Mekepung* began when farmers playfully raced their neighbors in plowing a field or in bringing the harvest home. The races soon became an event in themselves, and the cumbersome *cikar* carts were replaced by light, two-wheeled chariots.

Today, the races are organized by the Jembrana regional government. All participants are members of a racing club (*sekehe mekepung*) and are divided into two divisions: a Western and an Eastern Group, with the Ijo Gading River that bisects Jembrana as the dividing line. These teams compete biannually, in the Regent's Cup Championship on the Sunday before Indonesian Independence Day in August and the Governor's Cup Championship each October. Hundreds of buffalo decorated in colorful ribbons and flowers compete in these events to the delight of onlookers. There are *jegog*, music, and dance performances and traditional foods are sold by vendors.

The buffaloes in each team are ranked prior to the races, and are pitted against their counterparts on the other team. Two pairs run at a time along a circuitous 4 km route. The team with the most winners takes the cup. Apart from this, the only immediate reward for winning is prestige, but owning a prize buffalo does eventually translate into money. A good race animal can fetch almost double the normal price, if its owner is willing to part with it.

If visiting the area in July, inquire at your accommodation about rehearsals that take place every Sunday morning, beginning at 7 am, at an arena on Delod Berawan beach near **Perancak**. Area accommodations often offer tours that generally begin with breakfast at the hotel and also include a stop at the traditional market in Negara.

On the coastline near Perancak are colorful fishing boats originating from eastern Java. The best times to see them lining the beach is early mornings and late afternoons as they prepare to go out to sea. After sunset their twinkling lights, as they go further out to fish, are mesmerizing.

Turtle conservation

Perancak is also the home of a small **turtle conservation** program originated by an NGO many years ago but which is now self-run by a community group called Kurma Asih. In 1997 the first turtle in 37 years nested on this beach, and by 2005 there were 100 turtle nests here. The 10,000 eggs that were recorded in that season were taken to the hatchery and were eventually released back into the sea. Funding received through their "Adopt a Nest" program helps keep the program afloat.

Unity in diversity

Negara is the administrative center of Jembrana Regency and has little to offer tourists. However, there are a few interesting sites in the area. Indonesia's motto "Unity in Diversity" certainly applies here. About 1 km (0.65 miles) south of the city at **Loloan Timur** is a settlement of Buginese from South Sulewesi, bringing their unique architectural style of houses built on stilts with crossed "swords" adorning the roofs. Primarily Muslims, together with the Javanese who immigrated here, they account for the many mosques found in western Bali.

There's a large Protestant community at **Belimbingsari**. To get there, go west from Negara to Melaya and turn northeast. One of the largest of its kind on Bali, the community has an interesting church with Balinese elements. South of Belimbingsari at **Palasari** is a most unusual Catholic church, standing regally among landscaped gardens and agricultural fields, seemingly in the middle of nowhere. Its roof sports features similar to the *meru* pagoda-style seen on Balinese Hindu temples, and a *kul-kul* (warning drum) instead of church bells calls the faithful to services. Both settlements were established in the 1930s by converts of Christian missionaries who were unwelcome in primarily Hindu areas of Bali.

Bamboo tones

Jembrana Regency is home to a number of art forms found nowhere else. By far the most popular and thriving of these is the fabulous *gamelan jegog*, an orchestra comprised of instruments made of various sizes of bamboo which are stricken with mallets—like a xylophone or a metal *gamelan*—to achieve different tones. Travelers may have seen men seated on the floor in hotel lobbies playing melodic, small *jegog* instruments to welcome guests. There are no regularly scheduled performances. Check with your accommodation to determine if there are any local festivals with *jegog* players.

Jegog was created in 1912 by Kiang Geliduh, who was born in Jembrana Regency. Today, I Ketut Suwentra and his family in **Sangkar Agung** village, southeast of Negara, continue the art form and are happy to receive visitors in their home to see the instruments and learn more about them. Upon reaching the village, ask for directions (everyone knows this family). Feel free to drop in without an appointment; whoever is there will act as host.

"To understand *jegog* you must understand Balinese music," says Ketut Suwentra. "It's ethnic; it comes from nature." By understanding bamboo, the characteristics of the many different varieties, and its power, music can be created. The youngest of nine children, all of whom love music, Pak (father) Ketut feels *jegog* is his legacy from his father. His father is undoubtedly proud, as this group performs at ceremonies, wedding parties, hotels, and competitions, and has played in Japan and the United States.

One variation of *gamelan jegog* is an ensemble of 14 instruments, the largest of which are made from giant bamboo, the low-pitched tones of which are so resonant that their vibrations are felt by the body as much as the ears. With the bamboo tubes mounted on tall wooden frames, the musicians sit on elevated platforms, giving them enough leverage to strike the keys with heavy mallets. Medium sized instruments are played with the musician standing, and the smaller ones—with the players seated on the ground—spin out intricately syncopated rhythms with dazzling precision and speed. The result is a dense, multi-layered fabric of sound, above which a single bamboo flute may be added to trill sweet, sinuous melodies.

The awesome *jegog mebarung* is a competition between two or more orchestras, each playing in turn, pitting their skills against one another in a fierce musical battle; it is an unforgettable event to witness. The instruments sway back and forth, the musicians bob up and down, and the onlookers cheer enthusiastically, occasionally helping the musicians to replace a broken key. The winner is the ensemble that can make itself heard above the frenzy and produce the most resonance.

Jegog are also evaluated for their visual appearance. The wooden components of the instruments are all finely carved, and some are brightly painted, with tall ceremonial umbrellas and handsome statues affixed to the big instruments, which stand at the back of the group. A new trend is to leave the wood natural and unpainted.

Other arts

Other interesting art forms of the area include the **Jegog Dance**, as unique as the *gamelan* itself. **Pencak Silat** is a mixture of choral singing, theater, martial arts, and acrobatics, supervised by a sharp-tongued jester named Dag; and there is a daredevil knife dance called **Cabang**. All of these have roots in the performing arts of Java, Madura, and the Malay culture. In recent times, I Ketut Suwentra has been instrumental in creating new music for the younger generation to help keep them connected to their culture, and traditional Balinese dances and dramas from the *gamelan gong* repertoire have been set to *jegog* music.

Kendang Mebarung, a contest of cow hide-covered drums of various sizes and shapes to create different sounds, shares the competitive spirit of *jegog mebarung*. The largest of the drums are 2–3 m (6–9 ft) in length and 1 m (3.2 ft) in diameter, and are sometimes accompanied by an abbreviated *gamelan angklung* ensemble. When they compete at cremation ceremonies, national holidays, or simply for public entertainment, the drummers play interlocking rhythms that challenge each other's resonance, volume, and rhythmic dexterity.

Another type of ensemble indigenous to Jembrana is the **Bumbung Gebyog**. Eight to 12 lengths of bamboo of varying pitches are struck on the ground in rhythmically intricate, interlocking patterns. Probably the only music in Bali that originated and has remained the preserve of women, *bumbung gebyog* derives from the pounding of newly harvested rice in hollowed trees or stone mortars (*lesung*) to remove the husks. Nowadays, it is performed on national holidays and at ceremonies related to rice agriculture, usually accompanied by narrative dances or the playful **Ngibing Dance**, where spectators may take turns joining the performer.

Gilimanuk area

At **Gilimanuk**, on the western tip of Bali, the territory becomes Buleleng Regency, which stretches across Bali's north coastline. The

The passenger ferry leaving Gilimanuk, headed for eastern Java.

ferry from Java berths here. At **Secret Bay**, about 30 minutes from Gilimanuk, there is a mangrove swamp with black sand up to 9 m (30 ft) deep. Its forte is the relatively recent thrill of "muck" diving, where enthusiasts revel in exploring sand and rubbish in shallow waters for tiny creatures: seahorses, frogfish, shrimps, and other tiny, strange creatures. The best time to go is at high tide, when visibility is good.

At **Terima Bay** (**Teluk Terima**), east of the peninsula, visit **Makam Jayaprana**, the gravesite of Jayaprana who, according to Balinese legend, was an orphan raised by the ruler of Kalianget. As an adult he married the lovely Nyoman Layonsari from neighboring Banjar village. However, the ruler himself became enamored of Jayaprana's bride and schemed to kill Jayaprana to have her for himself. To this end, he dispatched Jayaprana with an army to contain a band of pirates who he said had arrived in northwestern Bali. On arrival at Teluk Terima the ruler's minister killed and buried Jayaprana. When the ruler asked Layonsari to marry him, however, she chose to remain faithful to her husband and committed suicide.

The temple marking Jayaprana's grave is a long, steep climb, but the views to Mt. Semeru on Java, Menjangan Island, and Gilimanuk from about halfway up make the effort all worthwhile. The temple, which contains a glass case displaying statues of Jayaprana and Layonsari, is pure kitsch.

South of Gilimanuk at **Cecik** is the West Bali National Park headquarters, where information about the park is available. It was near Cecik that burial mounds were found and evidence of Bali's oldest inhabitants was unearthed, dating back to 1000 B.C.

—*Kate Beddall & others*

WEST BALI NATIONAL PARK AND MENJANGAN ISLAND

First-hand Views of Bali's Native Wildlife

Much of Bali's natural landscape has been altered by the hand of man. Dense tropical forests that once covered the island have mostly now been cleared and the land molded into spectacular rice terraces and sprawling village settlements. But on the westernmost tip of the island, extensive forests, coastal swamps, and marine waters have to be divided into villages and farmland. Today these areas comprise the **West Bali National Park (Taman Nasional Bali Barat)**. Set aside as a nature reserve in 1941 and elevated to national park status in 1984, it consists of 19,012.89 ha: 15,587.89 ha of land and 3,425 ha of water.

Several distinct environments are within the park's protected boundaries. Forested mountains ranging up to 1,414 m (4,639 ft) and arid savannas stand in the central and eastern sectors. The southern slopes are covered with tropical vegetation that is green year round; and the north—which is much drier than the south—hosts deciduous monsoon forests. Palm savannahs and mangrove swamps are found in the coastal areas. Four nearby islands surrounded by coral reefs are rich in sea and bird life.

The park is home to one of the world's rarest birds. The Bali Starling, also known as the Rothschild Myna (*Leucopsar rothschildi*), is indigenous to Bali, but the vast majority of the population is in the hands of bird collectors abroad. It is a small, white bird with black wingtips and a brilliant aqua-blue streak around its eyes. Only 30 or so still live in the wild, mainly on Mt. Prapat Agung on the westernmost peninsula. The park has

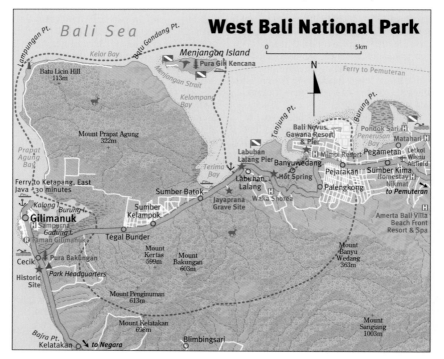

Local boats take passengers back and forth from the mainland to Menjangan Island.

another 100 birds in its breeding center ready for release to their natural habitat; however, this program has not been a resounding success due to competition from other birds for food, predators, and poachers. Fortunately, a Bali Starling captive breeding and release program on Nusa Penida has had a higher success rate by involving local villages that still adhere to *adat* (traditional) law, requiring them to protect nature. (For more information, see www.fnpf.org.)

While the park's best known species is the Bali Starling, it also protects other rare animals: the Javan Pangolin (*Manis javanicus*), Banteng ox (*Bos javanicus*), the tiny Lesser Mousedeer (*Trangulus javanicus*), Marbled Cat (*Felis marmorata*), and Olive Ridley Turtle (*Lepidochelys olivcea*).

As with all protected government lands in Indonesia, one of the park's biggest challenges is to balance conservation with human needs on a limited budget. Additionally, patrolling its expansive boundaries to protect against illegal logging and poaching is a huge undertaking, and large areas are prone to fires during the dry season. This is where eco-tourism can help: three resorts with permits to operate within the park have their own guards, who assist park rangers in patrolling and keeping a watchful eye out for intruders and other irregularities.

Diving and snorkeling off Menjangan Island

If challenges to the West Bali National Park are the bad news, the good news is that Bali's best diving and some good snorkeling is within the park boundaries. Off the coast of **Pulau Menjangan** ("Deer Island") to the northeast of the peninsula are Bali's most beautiful reefs and best diving destinations. Less than 1 km (0.65 miles) from the mainland, Menjangan is surrounded by deep waters with steep walls comprising hundreds of species of coral, gorgonian fans, and sponges, with reefs extending 100–150 m (328–492 ft) from the shore, which then drop 40–60 m (130–195 ft) down to the ocean floor. There are eight dive sites around the island, with drop-offs and slopes with names like Underwater Cave, Anchor Wreck, and Blue Corner. Pos 1 is on the western tip of the island's southern coast and has both hard and colorful soft corals as well as small marine life on a sandy slope. Pos 2 is on the southeast corner, where there is a wall favored by divers; but its shallow reef is also good for snorkeling. Off the northeast coast is Coral Gardens, sloping 8–40 m (26–130 ft) down, with schools of fish in the shallows. Eel Garden, at the west end, is varied enough to satisfy all interests: a wall, gorgonian fans, sponges, angelfish, lionfish, eels, and a current that attracts schools of fish.

Schools of fish swim in the reefs around Menjangan Island.

A 45-minute nature hike on Pulau Menjangan, which is uninhabited except for native deer and a few other animals, affords beautiful panoramic views of the volcanoes on the nearby mainland and the mountains of East Java in the distance. There is a temple on the island, **Pura Gili Kencana**, believed to be Bali's oldest. Annually at Guninghan, villagers flock here to pray.

To reach Pulau Menjangan, boats are available for hire at two piers: **Labuhan Lalang**, just opposite Menjangan Island on the north coast and at **Banyumandi** near Mimpi Resort. Surrounded by mangrove forest, Banyumandi has showers, changing rooms, and a *warung* (small eatery) that also sells bottled water and snacks. When leaving the Banyumandi pier, turn right to visit the **Banyuwedang hot spring**.

There are two park visitor information offices: one at Cekik, south of Gilimanuk near the intersection of the main roads from Singaraja and Denpasar; and the other at Labuan Lalang. At Cekik there is a small library with exhibits and a knowledgeable staff. Either office can organize night dives off Menjangan and can also arrange overnight stays on the island.

Trekking in West Bali National Park

There are many interesting trails within the park. Park officials stress that their guides are part of a community empowerment program, and all are from surrounding villages and have been trained and certified by the park.

The treks are designed to satisfy all types of interests and physical capabilities, and on all expeditions: short, 1–2 hrs; medium, 3 hrs; and long, 6–7 hrs. Visitors may choose between mangrove, savannah, and mountainous terrains. If a savannah hike is chosen, a boat is required, which will be an additional charge. If birdwatching is a special interest, the mangroves and savannah are better choices than the mountains, as they are the habitats of the park's more than 100 species of birds. Short and medium trekkers may choose between the mangrove and mountain forests at Labuan Lalang or south of there, the savannahs on the east side of the peninsula, or the mountains east of Gilimanuk. Long trips can consist of rainforest hiking near Mt. Kelatakan (698 m/2,290 ft) southeast of Gilimanuk, which begins at 6:30 am. Customized hikes to meet special interests can also be arranged. All treks must be booked in advance.

There are three expensive resorts within the national park boundaries and a few more nearby, but many visitors base themselves in cheaper accommodations at Pemuteran, 15 minutes east on the north coast road, to take advantage of the diving and snorkeling there, and making day trips to the park.

—Original text by Kate Beddall; extensively rewritten by Linda Hoffman

VISITING THE FAR WEST COAST

There's actually not an abundance of things to do and see in this area (unless it's buffalo racing season) so most travelers do their sightseeing on a day trip and continue on either to West Bali National Park to the west or to the beaches in the east.

GETTING THERE & GETTING AROUND

Ferries to Java leave Gilimanuk every half hour, 24 hours a day, and arrive at Ketapang terminal in Banyuwangi, East Java, in about 45 minutes. Be aware that loading and unloading cars, buses, and trucks takes awhile, so it's a good idea to get something to eat or drink at a *warung* within view of the dock and get comfortable while waiting. There is always someone to talk to while passing the time, and when it's boarding time, just follow the crowds.

At **Ketapang**, on Java, there are numerous buses, *bemos*, cars, and *ojeks* (motorcycle "taxis") waiting around the clock to take travelers on to their next destination.

Note that security can be tight at both ends of the ferry run. Be sure to have passport available in case of a checkpoint.

ACCOMMODATIONS

Although this region isn't a normal tourist destination, there is an interesting luxury "jungle resort" past the unique Catholic church at Palasari that is so isolated and remote that it feels very far away from Bali. **Taman Wana Villas**, Jl. Taman Wana, Palasari, tel: (0365) 470-2208, fax: 470-2209, www.bali-tamanwa-na-villas.com. Set on 8 ha on the edge of Palasari lake, 90 km (60 miles) from Ngurah Rai airport, surrounded by forest. Reachable over a very bad road, the thatched roof villas were designed with large windows to take in the views. Each villa has 1 bedroom, AC, shower, and balcony. Completely self-contained with activities, tours, treks, spa, and restaurant. From $250–1,000.

ACTIVITIES

Water buffalo races. Every Sunday morning between July and October there are buffalo race practices at Delod Berawan beach near Perancak, south of Negara, which are lots of fun for tourists and local citizens alike. On the Sunday before Indonesian Independence Day (August 17) is the Regent's Cup Championship buffalo races, and in October, the Governor's Cup Championship. Both are hugely important to the racing teams and are accompanied by vendors selling traditional foods and snacks and exuberant onlookers.

JED (Jaringan Ekowisata Desa) Village Ecotourism Network, Jl. Kayu Jati 9Y, Seminyak, tel: (0361) 737-447, www.jed.or.id, organizes tours to the Kurma Asih turtle conservation project at Perancak that (hopefully) includes a chance to encourage a baby turtle to go back to the sea as well as hearing about the project from community supporters. See the Madurese-style fishing boats at Perancak Bay, try musical talents on a giant bamboo *jegog* instrument, and have lunch on the beach. All proceeds go to the turtle conservation project.

WEST BALI NATIONAL PARK

(TELEPHONE CODE: 0362)

Coming from the south, the national park office at Labuhan Lalang (where the boats to Menjangan Island depart) is about 15 minutes from Gilimanuk.

Pemuteran is 12 km (8 miles) from the park office, and it takes about 1.5 hours from the park to Lovina to the east. Many travelers base themselves in either town to take advantage of diving, other activities, and a wider range of accommodations and food choices. Day trips to West Bali National Park are easily arranged from Pemuteran or Lovina.

ACCOMMODATIONS

There are three resorts located inside the park boundaries, having been given permits to establish themselves there in exchange for assistance in patrolling its vast borders. The Mimpi Resort Menjangan is nearby.

Luxury ($100–up)

Menjangan Resort West Bali National Park, Jl. Raya Gilimanuk-Singaraja Km 17, Desa Pejarakan, tel: 94700, fax: 94708, mobile: 0852-3729-4914, www.menjanganresort.com. A true "jungle resort" with an environmental heart. Name card says, "We love trees. Help us protect them. Say no to brochures and visit us online." Choice of rooms on the water, in the forest, or on a cliff overlooking the sea on a property so large that it's a trekking experience to reach the main lodge, housing restaurant and overlook tower, and the adjoining pool. (Or call reception and they will send a golf cart to pick you up.) Inside national park boundaries, the resort's security guards protect the forest there, has a tree planting program with donations helping reforestation and nest boxes for Bali Starlings. Interesting activities include kayaking through a mangrove maze and horse riding through the forest, as well as snorkeling and diving.

Mimpi Resort Menjangan, Banyuwedang, tel: 94497, fax: 94498, www.mimpi.com. A sister to Mimpi Tulamben, East Bali. A boutique resort, dive center, and spa. Complex simulates a Balinese village with 30 terraced patio rooms and 24 walled courtyard villas. Each villa features its own hot spring water tub, and 6 of them have a private natural stone dip pools. Dive tours, PADI courses, equipment rental. From $100–350.

Novus Gawana Resort & Spa, West Bali National Park, Desa Pejarakan, tel: 94598, fax: 94597, www.novushotels.com. Located at the edge of the national park in monsoon forest. 12 Lumbung Suites overlook Menjangan Bay built using indigenous materials, decorated with native fabrics and colors. Lush tropical gardens, sun decks, living rooms, AC bedroom and bathroom, with natural hot spring water. 2 Mangrove Suites with sundecks overlooking mangroves, living rooms, AC bedroom, bathroom with natural hot spring water and private whirlpool. Spa, restaurant and bar, game room with WiFi, games, satellite tv. Dive center.

Waka Shorea, www.wakaexperience.com. Located inside Bali Barat National Park and accessible only by sea, the Waka Shorea follows a "green" philosophy based on a love for the natural environment. 14 lanais and 2 villas were designed to exist in harmony with the landscape; restaurant is on the water's edge. Fresh water swimming pool and spa. Activities include diving, snorkeling, nature treks, and sailing. $185–285. Discounted Internet rates available. Diving packages to Menjangan Island with over-night stays at Waka Shorea begin at $350 for 3 days/2 nights.

ACTIVITIES

Bali Barat National Park Vistor's Centre, Labuhan Lalang. All activities within the national park require paying an entrance fee of $2. Tickets are available at the park headquarters at Cekik or at Labuan Lalang. Both offices are open 7:30 am–3:30 pm Monday–Thursday; 7:30 am–1:00 pm Friday; closed Saturday, Sunday, and public holidays. Ticket offices are open every day.

TREKKING IN THE NATIONAL PARK

All trekking with the park requires a guide, all of whom are selected from local villages and are trained and certified as part of a community empowerment program. The park guides are very knowledgeable and will help select the best location and itinerary to suit individual interests and capabilities. All treks must be booked in advance, and prices include park entrance and guide fee.

Birdwatching treks: $49/1–2 people; 100 species of birds recorded in the park, including the highly endangered Bali Starling. Mangroves and savannah are recommended for birdwatching.

Short trek: 1–2 hrs, $24/1–2 people; $40/3–5 people
Medium trek: 3 hrs, $32/1–2 people; $50/3–5 people
Long trek: 6–7 hrs, $75/1–2 people; $85/3–5 people

Short and medium treks have a choice between the mangroves and mountain forests at Labuan Lalang or south of there, the savannahs on the east side of the peninsula, or the mountains east of Gilimanuk. Note that for savannahs, a boat must be hired for an additional charge.

Long treks can consist of rainforest trekking near Mt. Kelatakan (698 m/2,290 ft)) southeast of Gilimanuk and begin at 6:30 am. Bring your own water and snacks.

Customized treks can also be arranged.

SNORKELING AND DIVING OFF MENJANGAN ISLAND

Hire boats to Menjangan Island at either Labuan Lalang (where the park office is) or Banyumandi near Mimpi Resort.

Banyumandi has showers, changing rooms, and a *warung* that also sells bottled water and snacks. Boats—which can be shared among several passengers—rent for around $33 for foreigners, $7.50 for Indonesians for 2 hours, plus a $2 entrance fee to the park for foreigners, $2.50 for locals. Showers are less than $1. Insider's tip: Look for other travelers hanging around the parking lot who want to charter a boat together and share expenses.

Both park offices can organize night dives off Menjangan, and for packages of 2 night dives can also arrange overnight stays on the island. Bring your own tent and sleeping bag; guides can arrange food for an additional charge.

If booking through one of the park offices for snorkeling at Menjangan, fees are: boat $33/3 hrs on the island (4 hrs total, including 30 minutes each way); park entrance ticket $2/per person; guide $7.50/per person; snorkel, mask, and fin rental $4/set.

DINING

There are many small restaurants in the town and *warungs* near the boat piers. Alternatively, drive 15 minutes east to Pemuteran, where there's a wider range of choices, or splurge at one of the resorts.

Endangered Sea Turtles, Reef Gardeners, and Commerical Pearl Farmers

A 15-minute drive east of West Bali National Park, north coast **Pemuteran** village is 45 minutes west of Lovina, and about three to four hours from the Denpasar airport. It has some of Bali's best beaches, and although there are rocky stretches, it has perfect sandy ones, too. Snorkeling and diving here are nothing short of divine thanks to reef regeneration and protection projects that have been ongoing for nearly two decades, since the arrival of an Australian dive operator and a Balinese resort owner in 1991.

Pemuteran can best be described not as a tourist destination but as a friendly fishing village with a few accommodations and dive shops. It is relatively small and cozy, and definitely laid-back; an ideal spot for honing diving and snorkeling skills or just dropping out for a little while and enjoying life. And it's a bonus is that some of the best snorkeling and diving in Bali is a short hop away on Menjangan Island in the national park.

In addition to these benefits, there are some exciting environmental and community projects here that tourism contributes to; travelers' revenues help support these efforts as well as contribute to local villages, which were previously among Bali's poorest. Acutely aware that healthy reefs benefit their own livelihoods, many of them are now involved in protecting the marine environment.

Saving endangered sea turtles

Pemuteran's **Reef Seen Aquatics Dive Center** has a **Turtle Hatchery Project** (**Proyek Penyu**) established to protect endangered sea turtles. Both the meat and eggs are local delicacies among the Balinese, and although it is illegal to capture and sell them the practice is still rampant and black market prices are so high that they are difficult for impoverished fishermen to pass up.

Reef Seen's turtle project began almost accidently in 1992 when its founder bought a turtle that had been caught by a fisherman,

and later eggs, which he hatched and released back to the sea. The eggs at the hatchery are buried in the sand at optimum temperatures, and after emerging from their shells young turtles are kept in monitored salt water pools until they are old enough to be released, after two to three months. Older turtles accidentally caught in nets are also brought here and are released in a day or two when donors are found to sponsor them. The fishermen who bring them to the center receive half the donation in compensation for lost catch and repair of nets—a controversial exchange that seems to work—with the remainder going either to the hatchery project or to the fishermen's association to encourage participation.

Sea turtles are among the world's oldest living species and can live up to 200 years. Species found in Indonesian waters are Green (*Chelonia mydas*), Hawksbill (*Eretmochelys imbricate*), Olive Ridley (*Lepidochelys olivacea*), Leatherback (*Dermochhelys coriacea*), and Loggerhead (*Caretta caretta*).

Travelers are welcome to visit Proyek Penyu, and money collected from a small entry fee is used to continue their efforts as well as for marine ecology education in local villages. For an additional small donation, guests may release a turtle and become a part of the process of saving these wonderful creatures from extinction.

Local protectors of coral reefs

Reef Seen Aquatics along with The Pemuteran Foundation—supported by Atlas North Bali Pearls, Bali Diving Academy, Easy Divers, Sea Rovers Dive Centre, and Warner Lau Diving Centers—sponsor another community project, called **Reef Gardeners**. It is common throughout Indonesia for local fishermen to collect aquarium fish using cyanide and to use dynamite or "tiger nets" that strip the reefs of practically everything. In addition, between 1996 and 1998 a plague of coral-devastating Crown of Thorns starfish

(*Acanthaster planci*) and Drupella shells (*Drupella cornus*) threatened to decimate reefs throughout the country. Since they were first established, diving centers nationwide have done their best to keep reefs clear of damaging elements and to stop illegal fishing practices, but they have had patchy results due to resistance by local fishermen, who resented their intrusion.

In 2005, AusAID sponsored the Bali Rehabilitation Fund to help create jobs for the local people following the Bali bombings. The Reef Gardeners project applied for a grant and was accepted, and it has continued—employing many villagers and spreading marine environmental awareness through innovative projects—long after the initial funds were used up, thanks to The Pemuteran Foundation.

Under the Reef Gardeners project, young village fishermen were trained as PADI-certified rescue divers. After being taught methods for protecting and repairing coral reefs damaged by careless divers, boat anchoring, nets, and natural causes, they set up patrols of the shoreline to assess and fix damage. The Reef Gardeners now work closely with villagers to protect the reefs and to educate others.

With the assistance of a Balinese resort owner, a *pecalang laut* was also established. This traditional guard comprised of locals now patrols the waters with the authority to arrest fishermen who use explosives or cyanide or who otherwise damage the reefs.

Prime dive sites

The AusAID funding also provided the means for The Pemuteran Foundation to purchase locally-built wooden boats, which were sunk on an offshore reef, employing villagers to provide manpower and creating two excellent dive sites. At **Canyon Wreck**, a massive 30 m (98 ft) Bugis vessel (*pinisi*) rests at 28 m (92 ft) alongside some of Bali's best and most

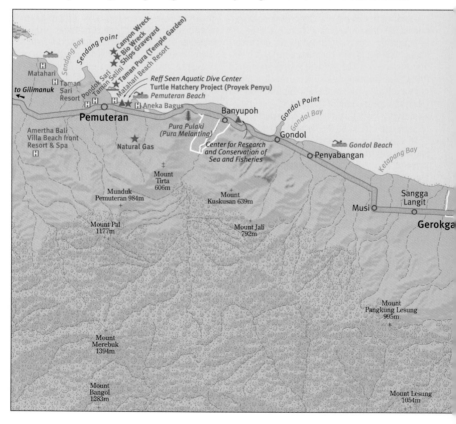

extensive hard coral cover at Tangked Penyu. At **Ships' Graveyard**, another 24 m (78 ft) Bugis timber vessel and nine *prahu* (fishing boats) lie at depths of 14–25 m (45–82 ft). This site also includes a 9 m (30 ft) Madurese *prahu* whose prow is only 5 m (16 ft) from the surface at low tide.

"Biorock" is a technology developed by an architect and a marine biologist to regenerate damaged reefs by charging manmade structures with low-wattage electricity to create limestone formations that quickly promote coral growth. Initially more of a gleam in the developers' eyes than a proven theory, Pemuteran's **Taman Sari Bali Resort** was one of the pioneers in constructing artificial reefs using Biorock techniques, and it worked. Today, the resort remains actively involved in marine ecology and in planning environmentally and culturally friendly tourism development in the area. Using Biorock techniques, The Pemuteran Foundation's next adventure

was to create a **"BioWreck"** structure to add to its sunken ship collection. Measuring 12x3 m (40x10 ft) and made from steel shaped like a boat, it sits on the sand at depths between 7–10 m (23–32 ft). Initially electrified by a generator, solar panels have now been installed on a raft to provide a more environmentally friendly source of power. This site has the largest single species of coral (*Povaris* sp.) found in Bali.

A third manmade site, aptly called **Taman Pura (Temple Garden)**, is an undersea marvel. A recreation of a watery Balinese Hindu temple, 10 large stone statues and a 4 m (13 ft) high Balinese *candi bentar* (split gateway) rest at a depth of 29 m (95 ft). Incorporating a cleaning station with schooling batfish, it is now covered in gorgonian fans. In 2006 a second stage to the garden was constructed at 15 m (49 ft), which is ideal for less experienced divers. Taman Pura was an engineering feat; local divers carried parts of the heavy split

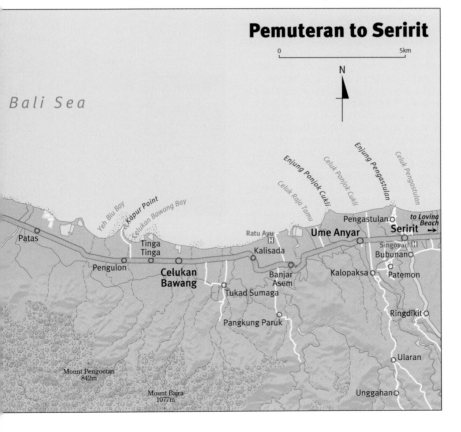

Pemuteran to Seririt

0   5km

N

Bali Sea

Yeh Blu Bay

Kapur Point

Celukan Bawang Bay

Enjung Ponjok Cukli

Celuk Roja Tamu

Celuk Ponjok Cukli

Enjung Pengastulan

Celuk Pengastulan

Patas

Tinga Tinga

Pengulon

Celukan Bawang

Ratu Ayu

Kalisada

Tukad Sumaga

Banjar Asem

Pangkung Paruk

Pengastulan

Ume Anyar

Kalopaksa

Seririt

to Lovina Beach

Singosari

Bubunan

Patemon

Ringdikit

Ularan

Mount Pengootan 842m

Mount Bajra 1077m

Unggahan

gate one-by-one, along with 25 carved sandstone statues of mythical creatures, and anchored them to the seabed. Possibly the only undersea complex of its type in the world, it is quickly becoming a major dive attraction. In 2009, another 5x4 m (16x13 ft) steel structure called **Bio-Boomer**—named in honor of Boomer, a long-term resident turtle of Proyek Penyu—was put into place.

Stay tuned to see what other exciting new adventures the relaxed little village has to offer marine life lovers in the future.

Eastward from Pemuteran

East of Pemuteran is a cluster of temples, the most important and easily accessible of which is **Pura Pulaki**, located in unusual terrain. A rock face rises perpendicularly to the south of the road while the glimmering ocean laps the shore to the north. Pulaki, the home of many monkeys who have a reputation for snatching bags and cameras, was restored and extended about a decade ago. The temple is linked to the legendary personage of Nirartha, the Javanese priest who migrated to Bali in the 16th century and established several of Bali's impressive holy monuments. It is said that prior to his arrival, a village of 8,000 people existed here. When Nirartha visited, the village leader requested a favor that Nirartha granted: the entire village was to be given supernatural knowledge that would enable it to attain an immaterial state. The invisible occupants of this village became known as *gamang* or *wong samar* and form the entourage of the goddess Melanting, whose abode is the nearby **Pura Melanting**.

The Balinese in these parts fervently believe in the existence of the *gamangs* and as a result routinely make offerings to them. For example, it is believed that the entry of *gamangs* into one's garden is heralded by the howling of dogs. Occasionally, sightings of *gamangs* are reported who have momentarily materialized. They are said to have no upper lip and carry a plaited bag over one shoulder.

Turtles, mangrove restoration & pearls

Continuing east, there are further conservation efforts funded by Japan on Turtle Island at **Banyupoh**. Along with turtle conservation, there is also reef restoration and mangrove replanting here. After that, there is a sprawling building complex. This is the Indonesian **Center for Research and Conservation of Sea and Fisheries**.

The next long beach heading east is void of resorts, which seems nothing short of amazing given that all the other beaches in Western Bali are experiencing rapid development. The reason for this dearth of tourism is that the area, called **Gondol**, is a pearl farm established by an Australian-based company that cultivates pearls here and makes them into jewelry. Operating farms across Indonesia since 1992 and on Bali since 2003, Atlas South Sea Pearls uses strict environmental and husbandry guidelines.

Pearls have been cultivated since the 12th century by the Chinese. Cleopatra is said to

Bali's northwest coast offers unspoilt beaches and excellent diving and snorkeling opportunities.

have adored them, and Christopher Columbus introduced them to the New World. In the 20th century, Japanese noodle vendor Mikimoto made round pearls available to the universe, instigating the search for an oyster that could produce even bigger versions of the gem.

At Atlas' hatchery and oyster farm at **Penyabangan**, just a few kilometers east of Pemuteran, visitors can see their sea-farm from the pier that stretches into the ocean, the larva rearing room, the preparation area, and the harvest of pearls. A thoughtfully prepared brochure explains the process and the different varieties of pearls. In the showroom jewelry is for sale in a wide range of prices, the most affordable being mother-of-pearl. There's a coffee shop that serves sandwiches, too, if hunger strikes. This stop is definitely recommended for anyone who has the remotest interest in how pearls are formed or who loves fine jewelry.

The sheltered harbor at **Celukan Bawang** is the main port for Buleleng Regency's import and export trade to other Indonesian islands. Just past the harbor going east, northern Bali begins.

—*Linda Hoffman*

VISITING PEMUTERAN
(TELEPHONE CODE: 0362)

In the far northwest corner of Bali, this cluster of accommodations and restaurants form an out-of-the-way resort area offering expansive corals and marine life, reef regeneration programs and marine conservation projects that don't get the attention they deserve. Nearby Pulau Menjangan (Deer Island)—15 minutes west—has 90 m (290 ft) drop-offs and undersea caves, and its shallow water tempts even beginner snorkelers to come exploring, making it Bali's top diving destinations.

GETTING THERE & GETTING AROUND

It takes 3–4 hrs to reach Pemuteran from Denpasar either traversing the scenic roads going north or looping around via the Denpansar–Gilimanuk south coast road, passing through Gilimanuk. From Lovina in the east, it's about a 45-minute drive. Regular buses and *bemos* service the north coast road to Gilimanuk, stopping in Pemuteran, and **car hires** are easily arranged from Lovina.

Day trips to **West Bali National Park** are available through hotels and dive shops.

Pemuteran is a small village and can easily be navigated on foot or by bicycle. **Motorcycles** are also available for rent. Check with your accommodation for details.

ACCOMMODATIONS

Pemuteran is popular with domestic travelers during public and school holidays and is beginning to be discovered by international tourists as well. Reservations during high seasons are recommended. Expect discounts during low seasons.

Budget (Under $25)

K&K Dive Resort & Rare Angon Homestay, Pemuteran, mobile: +62 812-467-9462, fax: 94747, www.pemuterandive.com/rare-angon.php. Near the beach. Traditional style Balinese bungalows with AC and hot water. From $10.

Kubuku Bed & Breakfast, Pemuteran, tel: 700-5225, mobile: +62 813-3857-5384, www.kubukubali.com. Away from the main road but near a white sand beach and coral project, AC, fan, and deluxe garden view rooms. Can arrange snorkeling and transport. Internet access. $10–30.

Moderate ($25–50)

Adi Assri Hotel Mountain View & Beach Front Cottages, Desa Pemuteran, tel:/fax: 94838, www. adiassri.com. Individual beachfront bungalows near the best diving areas on Bali. Can snorkel from the beach here. Also offers many national park based activities. Dive center, spa, restaurant, swimming pool. $30–60.

Jubawa Homestay, Pemuteran, tel: 94745. Standard AC and fan rooms with hot water shower. Beautiful gardens, swimming pool, massage pavilion. Restaurant serves good Balinese food. $30–35.

Pondok Sari Beach Resort & Spa, on the main road next to Taman Sari Bali Resort & Spa, tel: 94738, tel:/fax: 92337, mobile: 0813-3794-4333, www.pondoksari.com. A wide range of rooms from standard with fan to bungalows with outdoor showers, plus Villa Wayang, a 150-year old Javanese teak wood joglo house with 3 bedrooms, 2 bathrooms, living/dining room, mountain view day bed. Beautiful gardens winding from road to sea, where the restaurant serves excellent food with many choices. Pool. Snorkeling and diving are good from its beach. Werner Lau Diving Center on site. Reservations recommended during school holidays. $30–145.

Intermediate ($50–75)

Aneka Bagus Resort & Spa, Pemuteran, tel: 97498, fax: 94799, www.anekahotels.com/aneka-bagus. Beachside location with standard rooms, suites, and villas. $60–300. Discounted Internet rates available.

Man's Homestay, Pemuteran, mobile: +62 813-3828-7335, www.manshomestay.com. Named after Herman (nicknamed Man), modern minimalist styled rooms with AC, outdoor shower, hot water, and a family touch. $50, including breakfast.

Taman Sari Bali Resort & Spa, on the main road next to Pondok Sari Beach Resort & Spa, tel:/fax: 93264, tel: 94755, www.balitamansari.com. Together with adjacent Pondok Sari this is one of the two best moderately-priced hotels of the area. Stylish, roomy, comfortable AC standard rooms, suites, and bungalows on spacious tropical grounds facing an almost empty black-sand beach. Good restaurant serves a wide variety of cuisines. Very popular and always fully booked during school holidays; reservations recommended. $50–345.

First class ($75–100)

Amertha Bali Villas, Pemuteran, tel: 94831, fax: 94755, www.amerthabalivillas.com. Ocean-front and ocean, mountain, and garden view rooms and suites on the beach with nine mountains as a backdrop. Transfers available with English-speaking drivers from Ngurah Rai airport, with mini-tour available. $76–150.

Villa Semadhi, Pemuteran, tel: 94831, www.villa-semadibali.com. A luxury private villa on the beach with 4 suites, large garden, friendly staff, pool, and Jacuzzi. "Semadhi" means meditation, reflecting the tranquility of the setting. Suites from $75/night (low season); entire villa $185. Reduced rates for weekly stays.

Luxury ($100–up)

Matahari Beach Resort & Spa, Jl. Raya Seririt-Gilimanuk, tel: 92312, fax. 92313, www.mataharibeach-resort.com. A totally surprising find in tiny Pemuteran, the Matahari was named the first prestigious Relais & Chateaux member in Southeast Asia in 2001 and won its Tranquility Trophy in 2007. Also 2008/2009 ASEAN Green Hotel Standard award and Emerald Medal of the Tri Hita Karana award for respecting traditional Balinese values. All this, plus a 5-star villa resort with friendly and courteous staff, full luxury spa, first class restaurant, Balinese dances performed twice a week, all-day dive tours to Menjangan. Highly recommended. $117–484.

Puri Ganesha Villas, Pantai Pemuteran, tel: 94766, fax: 93433, www.puriganesha.com. Another big surprise: ranked one of the World's Best Beach Hideaways by *Travel+Leisure* magazine and in the Top 20 Favorite Hip Hotels Worldwide by Herbert Ypma, author of *Hip Hotels*, this resort is not at all what you'd expect to find in a small fishing village. 4 beautifully decorated, 2-story thatched roof villas with inspiring names such as Senyum (smile), Sepi (quiet), Santai (relaxed) and Senang (happy). Each has AC bedrooms, garden baths, private pool, staff, and masseur on request. Little seaside restaurant serves organic food whenever possible, no red meat, and a menu that changes every night. So important is food here that they offer a "Clean Break-Healing through Food" package. Highly recommended. From $550.

Taman Selini, Pemuteran, tel:/fax: 94746, mobile: +62 813-3878-3434, www.tamanselini.com. 11 simply designed bungalows to encourage rest and relaxation in harmony with local surroundings. Gardens, pool, beach bar. Restaurant on the sandy beach serves Greek and Indonesian food. $120–250.

DINING

There are many simple *warungs* along the road serving Balinese food. Alternatively, try one of the resort restaurants.

DIVING

There are several dive operators in Pemuteran. Expect to pay from $25/dive for local shore dives to $90 for those further afield in West Bali National Park. Equipment rental runs from about $10/dive for a full set of diving gear or a full day of snorkel set use.

Easy Divers Bali, Pemuteran, tel: 753-673, www.easy-divers.eu. PADI dive center emphasizing personal attention, safety, experience, friendliness, and professionalism. 10 years in the business. Supporter of Reef Gardeners.

Reef Seen Aquatics, Pemuteran, mobile: +62 (0)812-389-4051; www.reefseenbali.com. A PADI accredited dive center with heavy emphasis on marine conservation for 20 years. Hatchery at Proyek Penyu (Turtle Project) releases young ones and rescues older turtles to return them to the sea; community marine environment education; supports Reef Gardeners—young village fishermen trained to clean and conserve reefs. Magnificent manmade and natural reefs close by. Dive packages, equipment rental, bungalows, pony rides, sunrise and sunset boat rides. For information on donating to Reef Gardeners, see www.pemuteranfoundation.com.

Sea Rovers, at Hotel Adi Assri, Pemuteran, mobile: +62 812-385-9167, www.searovers.net. Caters to small groups of less than 6, with over 10 years experience. Supporter of Reef Gardeners.

Werner Lau Diving Center, at Pondok Sari Beach Resort & Spa, Pemuteran, www.wernerlau.com. SSI and PADI certifications, shore dives from hotel beach, local dives, night dives, Menjangan Island dives, Secret Bay macro diving, Nitrox course. Equipment rental $15/day; dives from $15/day. Supporter of Reef Gardeners.

Yos Marine Adventures, Pemuteran, tel: 92337, mobile: +62 813-3877-9941, www.yosdive.com. Headquartered in Tanjung Benoa in south Bali with a branch here, an active member of PADI International Resort Association with 20 years experience. Offers tailor-made and daily dive trips and packages, dive safari, and PADI dive courses.

OTHER ACTIVITIES

There are some good **trekking** opportunities in the hills around Pemuteran. Ask at your accommodation for a guide or directions. Local boats can be chartered on the beach for **fishing**.

Shopping

Atlas South Sea Pearls, Jl. Nelayan, Penyabangan village, mobile: 081-2387-77012, farm, www.atlas-southseapearl.com.au. Australian owned, with headquarters in Sanur, this is the pearl oyster hatchery and pearl harvesting center of the organization, just a few kilometers east of Pemuteran. Included in the tour are: larva rearing room, preparation area, and harvest. Call first to find out tour times, as the workers leave early afternoons. The showroom sells fabulous jewelry from reasonable up to extravagant prices, depending on the quality of the pearl(s). There's also a coffee shop that serves sandwiches.

INDONESIA AT A GLANCE

The Republic of Indonesia is the world's fourth most populous nation, with 237 million people (2010 census estimate). The vast majority (87%) are Muslims, making Indonesia home to the largest Islamic population in the world. More than 300 languages are spoken, but Bahasa Indonesia, a variant of Malay, is the national language.

The nation is a republic, headed by a president, with an 560-member legislature making up the elected part of a 695-member People's Consultative Assembly (DPR). There are 33 provinces and special territories. The capital is Jakarta, with a population of 9.6 million. The archipelago comprises nearly 2 million square km (772,000 square miles) of land and sea. Of over 17,000 islands, about 6,000 are named, and 1,000 permanently inhabited.

Indonesia's US$900 billion (2011) gross national product comes from oil, textiles, lumber, fishing, mining, agriculture, and manufacturing; the country's largest trading partner is Japan, followed by neighboring Singapore, the United States, and China. Per capita income is US$3,750 (2011). Much of the population still makes a living through agriculture, chiefly rice-growing. The unit of currency is the rupiah, upon which the government places a value of around Rp 9,000 to $1 (2012).

HISTORICAL OVERVIEW

The Buddhist Sriwijaya empire, based in southeastern Sumatra, controlled parts of western Indonesia from the 7th to the 13th centuries. The Hindu Majapahit kingdom, centered in eastern Java, controlled an even greater area from the 13th to the 16th centuries. However, after contact with Arab traders, beginning in the mid-13th century, local rulers began converting to Islam.

In the 17th century the Dutch East India Company (Vereenigde Oost-Indische Compagnie, or VOC) founded settlements and wrested control of the Indies spice trade from the English. The VOC was declared bankrupt in 1799, and a Dutch colonial government was established.

Anti-colonial uprisings began in the early 20th century, when several nationalist movements were founded by various Muslim, communist, and student groups. Sukarno, who soon emerged as the most charismatic revolutionary leader, was jailed by the Dutch repeatedly during the 1930s. Early in 1942, the Dutch East Indies were overrun by the Japanese army and navy. Treatment by the occupiers was harsh. When Japan saw her fortunes waning toward the end of the war, Indonesian nationalists were encouraged to organize. On August 17, 1945, Sukarno proclaimed Indonesia's independence.

However, the returning Dutch sought to re-establish colonial rule after the war. Four years of fighting ensued between nationalists and the Dutch; full independence was declared by the Indonesians in 1945 but was not recognized by Holland until 1949.

During the 1950s and early 1960s, President Sukarno's government moved steadily to the left, alienating many Western governments. On September 30, 1965, the army put down an attempted coup allegedly attributed to the PKI, or Indonesian Communist Party. Several hundred thousand people were killed as suspected communists and communist sympathizers.

Implicated in the coup, President Sukarno's power was eventually eroded and General Suharto became president in 1968. His administration was friendly to foreign investment and the nation enjoyed three decades of economic growth, but democracy was refused to its people. The Asian financial crisis of 1997 and subsequent political turmoil led to the country's first democratically elected administration in 1999. In 2004, the first direct elections took place, with Susilo Bambang Yudhoyono, known popularly as SBY, assuming the presidency. In 2009 Yuhoyono was re-elected by an overwhelming popular vote. Today, Indonesia has the fourth largest economy in Asia, after Japan, China, and India.

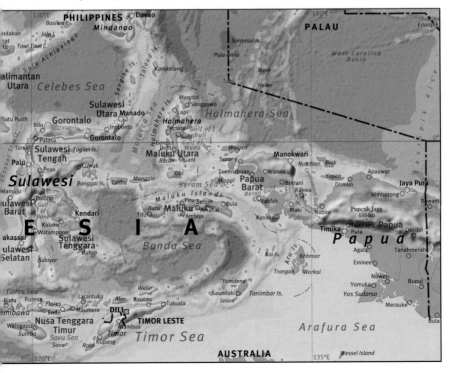

Basic Travel Information

The **Bali Tourism Board**—comprised of a group of private businessmen in the tourism industry—has a good website that might be useful: www.balitourismboard.org. It includes topics such as: how to get to Bali, geography, topography, people and lifestyle, history, flora and fauna, local transportation, economy, and climate.

POLICE

Tourism Police is a specialized force that can lend a hand when trouble arises, for whatever reason, and can be seen patrolling in all tourist areas. Or call the Bali **Police Headquarters** (Jl. Sangian) on tel: 424-346. For emergencies, call 110.

VISAS

Check your passport before leaving for Indonesia, as the following matters are taken very seriously by the Immigration Department. Your passport must be valid for at least six months after the date of arrival, and some immigration officials require at least six empty pages, one of which will be stamped upon arrival.

Upon landing, you will be given a white embarkation/disembarkation card to fill out. Keep this card carefully with your passport as you must present it when leaving the country and will be fined if it is lost.

Tourist Visas on Arrival (VOA)—$25 for a 30-day, $10 for a 3-day stay—are free for citizens of ASEAN countries. Although the list of paying VOA countries is constantly changing, they are currently issued to passport holders of 63 countries:

Algeria,	Czech Republic	Iran
Argentina	Denmark	Ireland
Australia	Egypt	Italy
Austria	Estonia	Japan
Bahrain	Fiji	Kuwait
Belgium	France	Laos
Bulgaria	Finland	Latvia
Brazil	Germany	Libya
Cambodia	Greece	Liechtenstein
Canada	Hungary	Lithuania
China	Iceland	Luxembourg
Cyprus	India	Maldives
Malta	Romania	Switzerland
Monaco	Russia	Taiwan
Mexico	Saudi Arabia	The Netherlands
New Zealand	Slovakia	Tunisia
Norway	Slovenia	United Arab
Oman	South Africa	Emirates
Panama	South Korea	UK
Poland	Spain	USA
Portugal	Suriname	
Qatar	Sweden	

Sixty-day tourist visas are also available but must be applied for in advance of arrival at an Indonesian embassy or consulate in your home country.

Beware: Visitors who overstay their visas will be fined $20 per day. Be aware that Day 1 is the day you arrive. Also know that doing anything other than simply being a tourist—even volunteer work or attending a business-related seminar—can be grounds for immediate deportation.

CUSTOMS

Firearms, weapons, explosives, and ammunition are strictly prohibited.

The standard duty-free allowance is: 1 liter of alcoholic beverages, 200 cigarettes, 50 cigars or 100 gm of tobacco.

Pornography is forbidden, as is "cinematographic films, pre-recorded video tapes, video laser discs, and records". Pornography in particular is a serious issue and possession can get you on the next plane out.

All narcotics, drugs and psychotropic substances are illegal in Indonesia. The use, sale, or purchase of narcotics results in long prison terms, huge fines and death, in some cases. Once caught, you are immediately placed in detention until trial, and the sentences are stiff, as demonstrated by Westerners currently serving sentences in the Kerobokan jail for as long as 10 years for possession of marijuana.

There is no restriction on import and export of foreign currencies in cash or travelers checks, but there is an import limit of 5 million Indonesian rupiah. The customs form also asks if you have bank notes in rupiah or other currency equal to 100 million rupiah or more and goods obtained overseas exceeding $250 per person or $1,000 per family.

The import of animals, fish, and plants, including their products, is also prohibited.

WHEN TO TRAVEL

The best time to visit Bali is during the dry season, April–September, when humidity is down and nights can be cool. Australians, Eastern Europeans, and Asians visit in droves at Christmas and during May–August school holidays. Western Europeans arrive in July and August. Indonesians come during the Ramadan holidays, at Christmas/New Year, during the June–July school break, and any time there is a long weekend public holiday. Book well in advance for cheap flights and accommodations during these periods.

FOREIGN CONSULATES IN BALI

All the consulates and honorary consuls below, except Spain, are located in southern Bali (area code 0361).

Australia, Jl. Tantular 32, Renon, 235-002/3 241-118, fax: 231990/241-120, www.dfat.gov. au (also represents citizens of **Canada, New Zealand, Ireland,** and **Papua New Guinea**).

Brazil (Hon. Consulate), By the Sea Store, Jl. Legian 186, 2nd fl. Kuta, tel: 757-775, fax: 751-006, brazilconsul@bytheseatropical.com.

Czech Republic (Hon. Consul), Jl. Pengembak 17, Sanur, tel: 286-465, fax: 286-408, bali@honorary.mzv.cz.

Chile (Hon. Consulate), Jl. Pengembak Gg. 1/3, tel: 756-781, fax: 756-783, chilehonconsulate@bali-villa.com

Denmark and Norway (Hon. Consulate), Mimpi Resort, Kawasan Bukit Permai, Jimbaran, tel: 701-070, ext. 32, fax: 701-073, mimpi@mimpi.com.

France (Consular Agency), Jl. Mertasari, Gang II No. 8, Sanur, tel: 285-485, fax: 286-406, consul@dps.centrin.net.id.

Germany, Jl. Pantai Karang 17, Sanur, tel: 288-535, fax: 288-826, germanconsul @bali-ntb.com.

Hungary (Hon. Consulate), Marintur, Jl. Bypass Ngurah Rai 219, Sanur, tel: 287-701, fax: 287-456, cristofoli@denpasar.wasantara. net.id.

Italy (Vice Consulato), Lotus Enterprise Building, Jl. Bypass Ngurah Rai, Jimbaran, tel:/fax: 701-005, italconsbali@italconsbali. com.

Japan, Jl. Raya Puputan 170, Renon, tel: 227-628, fax: 265-066, konjpdps@indo.net.id.

Mexico (Hon. Consulate), Puri Astina Bldg,

Jl. Prof. Moh. Yamin 1A, Renon, tel: 223-266, fax: 244-568, astina@denpasar.wasantara.net.id.

Spain (Hon. Consulate), Jl. Raya Sanggingan, Br. Lungsiakan, Kedewatan, Ubud, tel: 975-736, fax: 975-726, rabik@indo.net.id

Sweden & Finland (Hon. Consulate), Jl. Segara Ayu, Sanur, tel: 288-407, fax: 287-242, segara1@denpasar.wasantara.net.id.

Switzerland & Austria (Consulate), Jl. Patih Jelantik, Komplek Istana Kuta Galeri, Blok Valet 2 No. 12, Kuta, tel: 751-735, fax: 754-457, swisscon@telkom.net.

The Netherlands (Hon. Consulate), Jl. Raya Kuta 127, Kuta, tel: 761-506, fax: 752-777, purwa@denpasar.wasantara.net.id.

United Kingdom (Hon. Consulate), Jl. Tirta Nadi #20, Sanur, tel: 270-601, fax: 287-804, bcbali@dps.centrin.net.id.

United States of America (Consular Agency), Jl. Hayam Wuruk 188, Tanjung Bungkak, Denpasar, tel: 233-605, fax: 222-426, amcobali@indo.net.id..

Passport loss

If you lose your passport, it will be difficult to get new documents to leave the country unless you have the proper official forms from the police. Always keep a photocopy of your passport, visa, and international driver's license separate from the originals. You can then prove your identity to your consulate on Bali in case of theft or loss.

When theft occurs, report to the police to get a police report for your consulate. Verification of your identity and citizenship takes two to three weeks and involves going to the immigration office in Renon.

WHAT TO BRING ALONG

When packing, keep in mind that you will be in the tropics, but that it can get cold in the mountains, particularly at night. Generally, you will want to dress light and wear natural fibers that absorb perspiration. Most tourists find a locally-bought cotton batik shirt more comfortable than what they brought along. A medium-weight sweater or wind breaker is a must, as is a sturdy pair of shoes. Suits and ties are almost never worn. Don't bring too much, as you will be tempted by the great variety of inexpensive and stylish clothes available. If you visit a government office, men should wear long trousers, shoes, and a shirt with collar. Women should dress neatly, covering knees and shoulder, with shoes. Never wear flip-flops to a government office.

For those wanting to travel light, a sarong purchased upon arrival in Indonesia ($5–10) is one of the most versatile items you could hope for. It serves as a wrap to get to the bath, a beach towel, required dress for Balinese temples, pajamas, bed sheet, and a fast-drying towel, to name a few of its uses.

Indonesians are renowned for their ability to sleep anytime, anywhere, so they are not likely to understand your desire for peace and quiet at night. Sponge rubber earplugs are available from pharmacies, hardware departments, or travel stores in the West. Many consider them the most important 4 grams they carry.

Tiny padlocks for use on luggage zippers are a handy deterrent to pilfering hands. Some come with combination locks. Flashlights are essential for finding your way along Indonesia's poorly lit roadways and sidewalks; these can be easily purchased locally.

Bring along some pre-packaged alcohol towelettes or better yet, antiseptic hand cleaner (no litter to dispose of). Both are handy for disinfecting hands before eating or after trips to the *kamar kecil* (toilet). Also available at local supermarkets.

The majority of Indonesian department stores and supermarkets in major towns stock Western toiletries. Contact lens supplies for hard and soft lenses are available in well-stocked supermarkets or pharmacies.

Dental floss, tampons, and sanitary napkins are available in large supermarkets and pharmacies. *Kondom* (condoms) are available at all *apotiks* (pharmacies) and large supermarkets. Sunscreen and insect repellent are also available locally. Passport photos may come in handy for applications/permits (for parks) and can be made—or printed from your USB disc—cheaply locally.

On your travels you will meet people who are kind and helpful, yet you may feel too embarrassed to give money. In this kind of situation a small gift is appropriate. Chocolates, biscuits, family photos, pens and pencils, notebooks, and other stationery and T-shirts with foreign designs are all appreciated. A word to the wise: gifts should only be given to adults as a sign of gratitude, and never to children, as it promotes begging. The Indonesian government officially opposes giving money to beggars.

PLANNING A TRIP TO BALI

These days an increasing number of visitors are avoiding the crowded tourist enclaves of southern Bali and Ubud and are heading to other areas directly from the airport: Kintamani, Klungkung, Candidasa, and Amed in the east; Singaraja and Lovina in the north; while surfing, trekking and Bali's best snorkeling and diving in the west all await. Benoa, Kusamba, and Padangbai are launching points for boat journeys to the islands east of Bali, and car and passenger ferries operate between Gilimanuk (west Bali) and Ketapang in east Java. The options are virtually endless.

When planning your trip, avoid impossibly tight schedules. Things happen slowly here, and adjusting to the local pace will make your visit more pleasant. Better to spend more time in a few places and see them in a leisurely way than to end up hot and hassled.

Also keep in mind that the tropical heat takes its toll, and the midday sun should be avoided. Get an early start before the rays become punishing (the tropical light is beautiful at dawn), retreat to a cool place after lunch, and go out again in the afternoon and early evening when it's much more pleasant.

CLIMATE

Indonesia straddles the equator and the climate is tropical. Recent reports indicate that the average temperature on Bali has risen from 28–30°C to 33°C. There are variations, of course. The coasts are drier and hotter, but in the mountains it can drop as low as 5°C at night. Humidity varies but is always high: between 75–100%.

In general, Indonesia has two seasons: the southeast monsoon, bringing dry weather (*musim panas*), and the northwest monsoon, bringing rain (*musim hujan*). In the transition periods between the two seasons, waves can be high (*ombak putih*) and seas rough, which is good if you're a surfer but not great if you're passing between islands by boat.

The rainy season is normally October–April, peaking around January/February, when it rains for several hours each day, after which the sun comes out again. Before it rains, the air gets very sticky; afterwards it is refreshingly cool. The dry season, May–September, is a better time to visit Bali; June–August, the Balinese "winter" is particularly nice. This is perhaps the best time to go climbing or on hikes or bicycle treks; however the island is more crowded then.

TIME ZONES

Bali is on Central Indonesian Standard Time (Waktu Indonesia Tengah, WIT), or Greenwich mean time +8 hours, and lies in the middle of Indonesia's three time zones. It is on the same time as Singapore but is one hour ahead of Jakarata.

MONEY

The Indonesian monetary unit is the rupiah. Notes come in denominations of 100,000, 50,000, 20,000, 10,000, 5,000, 2,000, and 1,000. Coins come in denominations of 1,000, 500, 100, and 50 rupiah. Both old and new issues are circulating. The new coins are very similar in size, so look carefully. Rp 50 are rarely available. In stores small change is often replaced by candies because of a shortage of coins and their relatively low value.

Prices quoted in this book are in US dollars and are intended as a general indication. The exchange rate of the rupiah is relatively stable, fluctuating against the dollar and other major currencies in a range of usually only 10-20% throughout the year. The rate used in this edition is Rp 9,400/US$1.

Banking

Money changers and banks accepting foreign currency are found in most tourist areas. Exchange counters at banks are generally open from 8 am-3 pm Monday-Friday; a few open Saturdays until 11am. Bank lines can be long and slow and are less crowded at opening time. The Bank of Central Asia (BCA), one of Indonesia's oldest and largest banks, has a reliable service with branches and ATMs found virtually everywhere.

The money changers at Bali's international airport offer rates only 5 or 10 points below elsewhere, and are honest. Generally, money changers give better rates than banks, are much more numerous, and keep more convenient hours. Use only licensed money changers, never those who charge a commission. It is also wise to get a receipt and always personally count your money in front of the clerk.

Get a supply of smaller notes when you change money; taxi drivers and vendors often do not have change for big bills, and it's especially hard to break a large note in the countryside.

Carrying cash (US$) can be a handy safety precaution as it is still exchangeable in cities should you lose your passport, but

Indonesian banks and money changers only accept foreign currency that is crisp and clean. New, uncreased, unstained $100 bills command the highest rate of exchange.

Major **credit cards** are accepted in a wide variety of shops, restaurants and hotels in tourist areas. However, a surcharge of 2-3% is often added. All sales are transacted in rupiah, so your monthly statement will indicate interbank exchange rates. Visa and MasterCard are the most frequently accepted.

Automated Teller Machines (ATMs)—where you can get cash advances (in rupiah) on credit cards—are linked to the Cirrus, Plus, and other networks and are most often found in front of banks and in shopping districts in the tourist centers.

There are no exchange controls, and excess rupiah (bills only) can be freely reconverted at the airport upon departure.

Tax, service & tipping

Most larger hotels and higher-priced restaurants add 21% tax and service to your bill, which will be itemized. Actually, tipping is not a custom here, but it is appreciated for outstanding services. In *warungs*, tipping is not expected, but in small cafes that don't charge tax and service, a few rupiah would be nice if the service was good. For room boys and porters, Rp 5,000 per regular-sized bag is the going rate. For huge or heavy bags, give them a little bit more. For taxi drivers, round the metered fare up to the nearest Rp 1,000.

When tipping guides, drivers, or housekeepers in a house in which you've been a guest, put the money in an envelope and present it with the right hand only. Ten percent is appropriate.

OFFICE HOURS

Government offices (except those in Jakarta which operate a five-day work week) are officially open Monday-Thursday, 7 or 8 am until 3 or 4 pm, Fridays until 1 pm, and are usually closed on Saturday. If you want to get anything done, however, be there by at least 10 am. Always dress neatly when visiting government offices and be on your best behavior. Also note that most government offices are open at the regular time on Fridays but there may not be anyone at their desks until around 9 am because of mandatory exercises held on Fridays.

In large cities most private businesses are open 9 am-5 pm; shops often from 9 am-9 pm.

In smaller towns shops close for a siesta at 1 pm and reopen at 5 pm or 6 pm.

MAIL
Indonesia's regular postal service is reliable, albeit not terribly fast. *Kilat* express service is only slightly more expensive but much faster. *Kilat khusus* (domestic special delivery) can deliver overnight to some areas. International express mail gets postcards and letters to North America or Europe in about 7–10 days from most cities.

Kantor Pos (post offices) are found in every town on Bali, open 8 am–2 pm every day except Sunday and 8 am–1 pm on Saturday. The main post office in Denpasar (Jl. Raya Puputan, Renon) remains open until 8 pm. Many smaller post offices close for lunch from noon to 1 pm.

Post offices are often busy and it can be a tedious process to line up at one window for weighing, another window for stamps, etc. Hotels normally sell stamps and will post letters for you, or you can use private postal agents to avoid hassles. Look for the orange *Agen Kantor Pos* (postal agency) signs.

TELEPHONE & FAX
Directory Information: for Bali dial 108, for the rest of Indonesia dial 106.

Long distance phone calls, both within Indonesia and international, are handled by satellite. Domestic long distance calls can be dialed from most landlines. For public telephones, various amounts of phone *pulsa* ("pulses") or units on a magnetic debit (*kartu telpon*) phone card can be purchased at hotels and post offices, eliminating the need for small change.

Public payphones are gradually disappearing, however, as most travelers and many Indonesians have mobile phones. SIM cards can be purchased at any number of kiosks around Bali for both local and international calls.

To dial your own **international calls**, dial 007 or 008 to connect with an international (IDD, International Direct Dial) line, then country code, city code, and telephone number. For operator-assisted calls within Indonesia dial 100, for international calls dial 101. (The international dialing code for Indonesia is 62. Area codes for various regions on Bali are listed in Practicalities.)

If your hotel has no IDD landline link, go to the main telephone office (*kantor telpon*), a *wartel* (*warung telekommunikasi*) or *warpostel*

(*warung* post). These small kiosks are all over Indonesia and are often run by well-trained, efficient staff and offer fast IDD services at the standard rates. Open daily 8 am–10 or 11 pm; some open 24 hours. Night rates are slightly lower than day rates.

An even better option is to purchase a "Telkom Save" card at almost any supermarket or shopping center, in values of Rp 100,000 or Rp 200,000 (plus 10% tax), which enables you to make international calls for as little as Rp 1,000 per minute.

Faxes can be sent and received at *wartel* offices and most main post offices.

E-MAIL
E-mail and Internet services are available in the business centers of many hotels, at any *warnet* (*warung* Internet, kiosks with computers for Internet use paid by the hour), cyber cafés or in the back of the main post office in Renon. If you have your own laptop, WiFi or "hot spots" are found throughout major Indonesian towns in cafés, hotels, and many other places. Note that Internet connections can be maddeningly slow, so be prepared to be patient. In remote locations, there may not be connections at all.

COURIER SERVICES
Most of the big international couriers operate in Indonesia, along with some domestic ones. Bali offices include:
DHL Express, Cargo Area Ngurah Rai Airport, Jl. I Gusti Ngurah Rai, Tuban, tel: 768-282, fax: 768-277; Jl. Legian No. 451, Kuta, tel: 762-138; Jl. Bypass Ngurah Rai No. 155, Sanur.
FedEx, Jl. Raya Nusa Dua 100 X, Denpasar, tel: 701-727, fax: 701-725.
TNT Global Express, Komplek Citra Bali 5-6, Jl. Bypass Ngurah Rai, Jimbaran, Tuban, tel: 703-520, fax: 703-521.
UPS, Cardig Citra Primajasa, Jl. Bypass Ngurah Rai 2005, tel: 766-676, fax: 761-144.

NEWSPAPERS & MAGAZINES
There are several English-language publications to help keep abreast of the news or to find tourist information.
Bali & Beyond (www.baliandbeyond.co.id), **Hello Bali** (www.hellobalimagazine.co.id), and **NowBali** (www.nowbali.co.id), are all aimed at tourists.
Bali Advertiser (www.baliadvertiser.biz) is free and is found in cafés. Primarily pub-

lished for expats, it consists mostly of classified ads but also has performance schedules.
Bali Plus (www.baliplus.com) is a "pocket
guide" for tourists, also free, and lists perti-
nent information, such where to stay, eat, and
shop and what to do while on Bali.
The Jakarta Post (www.thejakartapost.com)
is the largest English-language newspaper
in Indonesia and has amazingly good international coverage.
The Yak (www.theyakmag.com) is an upmarket expat magazine published quarterly. An
interesting read for those who care what the
"locals" are up to.

ELECTRICITY

220 volts at 50 cycles alternating current.
Power failures are common. Voltage can
fluctuate considerably so use a stabilizer for
computers and similar equipment. Plugs are
of the European two-pronged variety.

HEALTH

Check with your physician before leaving home
for the latest news on the need for malaria
prophylaxis and recommended vaccinations.
Frequently considered vaccines are: Diphtheria,
Tetanus (DPT), and Typhoid; Measles, Mumps,
and Rubella (MMR); and the oral Polio
vaccine.

Most doctors recommend being vaccinated
for Hepatitis A and B before traveling to
certain countries and some suggest a cholera
vaccination, which is only partially effective.
Consult your physician. Vaccinations for yellow
fever, smallpox, and cholera are not required,
except for visitors coming from infected areas.

Find out the generic names for whatever
prescription medications you are likely to
need as most are available in Indonesia but
not under the same brand names as they
are known at home. Get copies of doctors'
prescriptions for the medications you bring
into Indonesia so you can renew prescriptions
and avoid questions at the customs desk.
Those who wear spectacles should bring
along prescriptions.

Hygiene

Hygiene cannot be taken for granted in
Indonesia. Very few remote villages have
running water or sewerage. Most water comes
from wells or rivers, and raw sewerage goes
into the ground or the rivers. Tap water is
generally not drinkable and must be boiled.

Most cases of stomach complaints are

attributable to travelers' systems not being
used to the strange foods, overeating tropical
fruits and chilies, and stray bacteria found in
water. To make sure you do not get something
more serious, take the following precautions:
* Never drink unboiled water from a well, tap,
or *bak mandi* (bath tub). Brush your teeth only
with boiled or bottled water. Bottled water, in
various sizes of plastic bottles, is available
everywhere and is usually called "Aqua",
which is the most popular and reliable brand
name.
* Ice on Bali is made in government regu-
lated factories and is deemed safe for local
immunities. If eating in a *warung*, confirm
that the ice is made from boiled water before
relaxing with an iced drink.
* Plates, glasses, and silverware washed in
unboiled water need to be completely dry
before use.
* Fruits and vegetables without skins pose
a higher risk of contamination. To avoid
contamination by food handlers, buy fruits in
the market and peel them yourself.
* To *mandi* (bathe) two or three times a day is
a great way to stay cool and fresh. But be sure
to dry yourself well and perhaps apply a medi-
cated body powder, such as Purol or Herocyn,
to avoid the unpleasantness of skin fungi and
rashes caused by heat, especially during the
October–April rainy season.

Exposure

Many visitors insist on instant suntans, so
overexposure to the heat and sun is a
frequent problem. Be especially careful on
long walks and overcast days. Wear a hat,
loose-fitting, light-colored, long sleeved cotton
clothes and pants, drink plenty of water, and
use a good-quality sunscreen (available in
mini-markets). Do not wear clothing made of
synthetic fibers that don't allow air to
circulate. Tan slowly; don't spoil your trip.

Dehydration

Visitors to Indonesia are usually careful to
eat clean foods and drink safe water, but they
often overlook the need to keep hydrated
in the equatorial climate. Arguably, more
illnesses among tourists are caused by
dehydration than anything else. Don't forget
to drink, drink, drink.

Diarrhea

Diarrhea is a likely traveling companion and
is called **"Bali Belly"** locally. In addition to

strange foods and unfamiliar micro-fauna, diarrhea is often the result of attempting to accomplish too much in one day. Taking it easy can be an effective prevention as can keeping the intake of spices, chilies, and tropical fruits in reasonable amounts; and making sure the food you eat and the water you drink is hygienic. Ask around before leaving home about what the latest of the many remedies are, and bring some along. Imodium is locally available, as are activated carbon tablets (*Norit*) that will absorb the toxins giving you grief.

Symptoms of "Bali Belly" can include watery bowl movements, nausea, vomiting, abdominal cramping, bloating, and fever. When it hits, it usually lasts two to three days. Relax, take it easy, and drink lots of fluids, including rehydration salts such as Servidrat (the local brands are Oralit and Parolit). Especially helpful is water from young coconuts (*air kelapa muda*) or strong, unsweetened tea. The former is an especially pure anti-toxin. Get it straight from the coconut without sugar, ice, or food coloring added. When you are ready to eat again, start with bananas, plain rice, crackers, *tempe* (fermented soybean cakes), and *bubur* (rice porridge). Avoid fried, spicy, greasy, or heavy foods and dairy products for a while. If there's no relief after three days, see a doctor.

Intestinal parasites

It is estimated that 80–90% of all people in Indonesia have intestinal parasites and these are easily passed on by food handlers. Prevention is difficult, short of fasting, when away from luxury hotel restaurants, and while safer than *warungs*, even those places don't carry a guarantee. Before leaving home, ask your physician if it is a good idea to take anti-parasite medicine. If so, brands such as Combantrin are available at all pharmacies.

If you have problems when you get home, even if only sporadic, have stool and blood tests. Left untreated, parasites can cause serious damage.

Cuts & scrapes

Your skin will come into contact with more dirt and bacteria than it did back home, so wash your face and hands more often. Cuts should be taken seriously and cleaned with an antiseptic like Betadine, available from any pharmacy (*apotik*), before applying an anti-bacterial ointment. Cover the cut during the day to keep it clean, but leave it uncovered at night so that it can dry. Constant covering will retain moisture in the wound and only encourage an infection. Repeat this ritual after every bath. Sensitivity and areas of redness around the cut indicate infection, in which case a doctor should be consulted. At the first sign of swelling ask a doctor if you should take broad spectrum antibiotics to prevent a really nasty infection.

Mosquito-borne diseases

Malaria, caused by night-biting mosquitoes, does occur on Bali. Consult a doctor familiar with tropical diseases in Indonesia for the appropriate prophylaxis before leaving, as many must be begun one week before departure. Malaria symptoms are fever, chills, and sweating, headaches and muscle aches.

The other mosquito concern is **dengue fever**, spread by the morning-biting *Aedes aegypti*, which is especially active during the rainy season. The most effective prevention is not getting bitten (there is no prophylaxis for dengue). Symptoms are: severe headache, pain behind the eyes, high fever, back ache, muscle and joint pains, nausea and vomiting, and a rash appearing between the third and fifth days of illness. Within days, the fever subsides and recovery is seldom hampered with complications. The more serious variant, **dengue hemorrhagic fever** (DHF), which can be fatal, may be the reaction of a secondary infection with remaining immunities following a primary attack.

Cases of **Japanese encephalitis**, a viral infection affecting the brain, have been known to occur and are an added reason to take protective measures against mosquito bites.

Preventing getting bitten is the goal. Apply mosquito repellant to your skin (the local brand, Autan, is very effective), and consider wearing long sleeves and pants, especially at sunrise and dusk when mosquitoes are particularly active. Any chemical repellent containing DEET (*diethyl toluamide*) should be applied with caution and never to the face. Application to clothing can also be effective. A local non-chemical solution is citronella oil (*minyak gosok, cap tawon*).

Many *losmen* and bungalows provide mosquito nets, but if they don't, portable mosquito nets (*kelambu*) provide protection at night when sleeping; they are for sale in most general stores for around $5.

Upon request, your room will be sprayed for mosquitoes before sundown. For health reasons, be prepared to leave the room for at least one hour after spraying. Just before going out for dinner is a good time to have your room sprayed.

Slow-burning mosquito coils (*obat nyamuk bakar*) are also widely available. They last 6–8 hours and need to be placed in a safe container to prevent fire hazards (most *losmen* have covered terracotta vases with decorative holes in them expressly for this purpose). Light the coil and leave it in a tightly-enclosed room before going to dinner. When ready to sleep move it outside or to another room away from the bed to avoid the noxious smell and fumes, which can cause headaches. There are many brands, but those that do not contain *pyrethum* are ineffective. Baygon is a good local brand and is sold most places.

Far better than coils are compact electric (smokeless) anti-mosquito devices ($2–$3, available in major towns) that simply plug into a wall outlet. Most varieties have refill pads that must be changed periodically. Check the instructions on the label.

AIDS & Hepatitis B

Surprise! Safe sex is also a good idea. Foreign experts project the HIV/AIDS problem to be of monumental (though relatively unacknowledged) proportions in Indonesia.

Documentation, awareness, and education have only just begun. Another area of concern is the Hepatitis B virus, which affects liver function, is only sometimes curable and can be fatal. The prevalence of Hepatitis B, which is also transmitted by bodily fluids during unprotected sex, is also of concern. In Indonesia, condoms are sold in pharmacies, supermarkets, and mini-markets. Select a reputable brand.

Pharmacies

The Indonesian name for pharmacy is *apotik*. Shopping malls in major cities throughout the country always have at least one pharmacy in them. The most commonly found international chains are **Guardian** and **Century**. Outside of malls the large Indonesian chain, **Apotik Kimia Farma**, is well respected. Most large *apotiks* have a book cross-referencing Latin and generic prescription names, which can be helpful in emergencies. They also carry first aid supplies and sundries.

Medical treatment & insurance

In Indonesian, doctor is *dokter* and hospital is *rumah sakit*. Smaller villages only have small government clinics, *puskesmas*, which are not equipped to deal with anything serious but can be handy in an emergency.

Fancier hotels often have house doctors, physicians on call, or can recommend a nearby clinic. Misuse of antibiotics is a concern in Indonesia. They should only be used for bacterial diseases and then until all the doses are taken to prevent developing antibiotic-resistant strains of your affliction. When consulting with a doctor, Indonesians don't feel they've gotten their money's worth without getting an injection of antibiotics (which is extra). If one is prescribed, be sure it's necessary.

Ensure syringes have never been used. In outlying areas, consider buying your own disposable syringe from an *apotik* and taking it to the clinic.

Some foreigners living on Bali swear by their favorite local clinics and doctors; however there are two internationally-owned clinics in Kuta that have a wide range of specialists and provide the consistently good care and services that most foreigners are accustomed to. No need to call first, just drop in, but be prepared to wait if the clinics are busy.

BIMC, Jl. Bypass Ngurah Rai 100 X, Kuta, tel: 761-263, www.bimcbali.com, is New Zealand owned and operated. It offers first class medical and emergency assistance, primarily for tourists and expats. Centrally located on the big roundabout opposite the Kuta Bali Galeria shopping center.

International SOS Bali, Jl. Bypass Ngurah Rai 505X, Kuta, tel: 710-544, www.internationalsos.com. American owned, located down the street from BIMC. Another excellent clinic with a laboratory, X-ray, and pharmacy. Includes a 24-hr alarm center, dedicated air ambulance fleet, dental, and psychological services, in addition to clinical appointments.

For dentistry, many foreigners living in southern Bali go to **Bali 911 Dental Clinic**, Jl. Patimura No. 9, Denpasar, tel: 249-749, fax: 226-834.

Emergency medical assistance

Outside of the big cities, general health care leaves much to be desired. Often the best course of action in the event of a life-threatening emergency or accident is to get on the first plane to Singapore. Be sure to buy travel insurance before leaving home with emergency evacuation coverage, as Medivac airlifts can cost as much as $30,000. The insurance policy will list emergency telephone numbers to call and describe the procedures to follow.

Both **BIMC** and **SOS** (see above) offer 24-hr emergency services and medical evacuation.

Local emergency telephone numbers:
Police 110
Fire 113
Ambulance 118
Search & Rescue 51111
Red Cross 26465.

WARNINGS

In Indonesia, **possession of drugs** is a serious crime and offences can be punishable by protracted imprisonment or death. Be forewarned.

On Bali, you may be offered **"magic mushrooms"**, which may or may not actually be "entrancing". The legal—and health—position on possession of magic mushrooms is unclear. The best bet is to just say no.

Home-brewed alcohol, *arak*, is 60–100% proof and is distilled from palm or rice wine. Be very wary of any drink called *arak api* (fire *arak*), as it is mixed with additional ingredients—perhaps even gasoline—to give it an extra "kick". In the last few years several partakers have died from drinking it, including foreign tourists.

Rabies has become a problem on Bali in the last few years, with the first case reported in November 2008. If bitten by an infected animal, the incubation period can last from a few weeks to beyond a year. The symptoms are flu-like: headache, fatigue, and fever, later followed by agitation, respiratory problems, fear of water, paralysis, and coma. Injections given immediately after contact with saliva from a rabid animal are effective if the condition is diagnosed in time and the vaccine is available. Massive vaccination, sterilization, and culling of Bali's enormous population of street dogs and public educational campaigns have helped, but it is still best to not invite trouble from dogs, monkeys, or any other animal on Bali.

FOOD AND DRINK

Most Indonesians do not feel they have eaten until they have eaten rice. This is accompanied by side dishes, often just a little piece of meat and some vegetables with a spicy sauce. Other common items include *tahu* (tofu), *tempe* (soybean cake), fried peanuts, and salted fish. Crispy fried tapioca crackers flavored with prawns and spices (*krupuk*) usually accompany a meal.

No meal is complete without *sambal*—a fiery paste of ground chili peppers with garlic, shallots, sugar, and sometimes soy sauce or fish paste. Fruit, especially pineapple and papaya, or cucumbers, provide quick relief for a chili-burned mouth; drinking water will not douse the fire.

In most **Indonesian restaurants** there is a standard menu of *sate* (satay; skewered grilled meat)—often *ayam* (chicken) and *kambing* (goat)—*gado-gado* or *pecel* (boiled vegetables with spicy peanut sauce), and *soto* (vegetable soup with or without meat). Also common are Chinese dishes like *bakmie goreng* (fried noodles), *bakmie kuah* (noodle soup), and *cap cay* (stir-fried vegetables).

In most larger towns there are a number of **Chinese restaurants**, often on the main street. Some have menus in Chinese, but usually the cuisine is very much assimilated to local tastes. Standard dishes, in addition to *bakmie* and *cap cay*, are sweet and sour whole fish (*gurame asam manis*), beef with Chinese greens (*kalian/caisim cay sapi*), and prawns sautéed in butter (*udang goreng mentega*).

Indonesian fried chicken (*ayam goreng*) is common and usually very tasty, although the locally-reared chicken (*ayam kampung*) can be a bit stringy. Note that *ayam goreng* is fried in butter with no batter; for crispy fried skin, order *ayam goreng tepung* (with flour).

Mie goreng (fried noodles) and *nasi goreng* (fried rice) are ubiquitous; *nasi goreng istimewa* (special) comes with an egg on top and a piece of *ayam goreng* or a few sticks of *sate*.

Cooking styles vary greatly from one region to another, and almost all of them are available on Bali. The Sundanese of West Java are fond of raw vegetables, eaten with chili and fermented prawn paste (*lalab/sambal trasi*). Minahasan food from north Sulawesi is very spicy, and includes some interesting specialties: fruit bat wings in coconut milk, sambal rat, and dog.

There are restaurants everywhere in Bali that specialize in food from Padang, West Sumatra. This spicy and very tasty cuisine has a distinctive way of being served. As many as 15–20 different cooked dishes are displayed in a glass case in front of the restaurant. Tell the waiter which dishes are of interest and he will bring them to the table. At the end, you are charged only for what you have eaten, and any untouched plates are put back in the case.

As tempting as fresh vegetables may be, avoid eating garnishes or raw salads unless the vegetables are served in restaurants that cater to tourists, where hygienic preparation conditions are generally observed.

The **beers** available in Indonesia are Bintang and Anker, both brewed under Dutch supervision and rather light (perhaps appropriately for the tropics). In large cities, many imported beers are also available. With electricity such a precious commodity, however, in out-of-the-way places the only way to quaff it cold is to pour it over ice.

Balinese specialties

Balinese specialties include roast pork (*babi guling*) in which pork is rubbed with turmeric, stuffed with spices and roasted over a spit, and roast duck (*bebek betutu*), where duck is stuffed with vegetables and spices, wrapped in banana leaf, and either smoked or steamed in an earth oven. Be aware that on Bali, many Hindus do not eat beef, and local eateries may not serve it.

Balinese brews include *tuak* (palm beer), *arak* (60–100 proof liquor distilled from palm or rice wine) and *brem* (sweet rice wine).

Fruits

Tropical fruits are plentiful and delicious. Bali is known for its sweet *salak*, which has a brown "snakeskin" covering three segments, two of which contain a large brown seed. It tastes like a cross between an apple and a walnut. *Manggis* (mangosteen) is pure heaven hidden within a thick purple-brown cover. The juicy white segments almost melt away. In season November–March. Another favorite is rambutan, about the size of a walnut that ranges in color from pink to cherry red. Peel away the "hairy" outer skin to find delicious, sweet white flesh inside surrounding a large seed.

Warungs (street stalls)

Local restaurant kitchens do not necessarily have healthier food preparation procedures than roadside *warungs*. The important thing at a *warung* is to watch and judge whether or not the cooks maintain cleanliness and

inspire confidence. *Warungs* rarely have a supply of running water, so beware. However, cafes and restaurants that cater to foreigners in tourist areas have a reputation for hygienic food handling and preparation, perhaps out of fear of losing customers.

In *warungs*, the first portion may not fill you up, so a second portion can be ordered by saying "*tambah separuh*" (add half portion), but only the price is halved. The amount of food is more like three-quarters. Finish off with a banana and say "*sudah*" (I've had plenty). The seller will total up the cost of what was served and ask you how many *krupuk, tempe*, or other snacks you helped yourself to, so keep track. The total will come to between Rp 8,000 and Rp 12,000, without a drink.

Vegetarianism

To indicate that you are a vegetarian, say: "*saya tidak makan daging*" (I don't eat meat), "*tidak pakai ayam*" (without chicken), or "*tidak pakai daging*" (without meat). Dietary restrictions are very acceptable and common due to the various religions in Indonesia and spiritual practices involving food. If you want vegetable dishes cooked in tasty and nutritious ways, your best bet are Chinese restaurants.

However, finding food that truly has no animal products is a problem. Often, meals which appear to be made exclusively of vegetables will have a chunk of beef or chicken in them to give flavor. *Tempe* (soybean cakes) and *tahu* (tofu, soybean curd) are excellent sources of protein.

SECURITY

Indonesia is a relatively safe place to travel, and violent crime is rare. However, petty crime is prevalent. Pay close attention to your belongings, especially in big cities and in crowded places, such as markets and bus terminals. Use a small backpack or money belt for valuables. Bags can be snatched by thieves on motorbikes, so be vigilant and always hold your bag facing the sidewalk, away from the street. Be especially wary on crowded *bemos*, buses, and trains where pickpockets lurk. They work in groups and are very clever at distracting you while a confederate slits your bag and extracts valuables unnoticed.

Be sure that the door and windows of your hotel room are locked at night. Big and often mid-size hotels have safes for valuables. If your hotel does not have this facility, it is better to carry all your documents with you. Make sure you have photocopies of your passport, return plane ticket, and travelers' check numbers, and keep them separate from the originals.

Don't take valuables to the beach. Period. Bring your camera only if you're not going to swim or if you are in pairs and one can swim while the other watches. You can ask other tourists to mind your gear while you swim, but they may decide to leave while you're in the water.

ADDRESSES

The Indonesian spelling of geographical features and villages varies considerably as there is no form of standardization that meets with both popular and official approval. Village names can be spelled three different ways, all on signboards in front of various government offices. In this guide, we have tried to use the most common spellings, i.e. Batujimbar instead of Batu Jimbar and Candikuning instead of Candi Kuning.

Every town has streets named after the same national heroes, so you will find Jl. (*jalan* or street) General Sudirman and Ahmad Yani in every city throughout the archipelago. When tracking down addresses you will also find that the numbers are not consecutive. For example, number 38 may be next to number 119. Annoying, but true. As with all things in the tropics, slow down, take a deep breath and try to enjoy being some-where than home.

Another mystery in reading addresses comes of this type: Jl Panti Silayukti 18, Br. Kecil, Padangbai, Amlapura, Bali, Indonesia. You might be asking, "So, where is this place?" Insiders tip: Jl. Pantai Silayukti 18 is the street address; Br. Kecil (found only on Bali) is the *banjar* (neighborhood within the town); Padangbai is the *desa adat* (the town, or on other islands, the *kampung* or village); and Amlapura (which is also the name of a town) is the *kecamatan* (district). Confusing to foreigners, this system helps the post office—and the local people—find addresses more efficiently.

FINDING YOUR WAY

Westerners are used to finding things using telephone directories, addresses, and maps. But in Indonesia, phone books are incomplete (primarily because most people don't have landlines), addresses can be confusing, and maps little understood. The best way to find something is to ask.

To **ask for directions**, it's better to have the name of a person and the name of the neighborhood or village. Thus "Ibu (Mrs.) Murni, Banjar Kalah" is a better address for asking directions even though "Jl. Hanoman 14" is the mailing address. Knowing the language helps, but is not essential.

Clear answers are not common, so be patient. You are likely to get a general indica-tion of direction without the distance given or specific instructions. The assumption is that you will be asking lots of people along the way. Begin by asking three people. Usually two point toward the same general vicinity. Proceed, then ask again. Note: In the country-side or while hiking, it's more useful to ask how long it takes to get someplace than it is to ask how far it is to someplace. Also ask men instead of women, as men travel more.

Maps can be useful, but introducing them into discussions with Indonesians may cause more confusion than clarity.

THE NATIONAL CALENDAR

The Indonesian government sets national holidays every year, both fixed and moveable dates. The fixed **national holidays** on the Gregorian calendar are the international New Year, January 1; Independence Day, August 17; and Christmas, December 25.

The Christian Good Friday, Easter Day, and Ascension Day, the Balinese New Year (Nyepi) and the Buddhist Waisak are also national holidays. These and all the Muslim holy days are based on the lunar cycle. Except for Nyepi, many restaurants, shops, and businesses remain open during public holidays.

The official **Muslim holidays** in Indonesia for 2013 are:

Maulud Nabi Muhammad SAW, January 24—Muhammad's birthday.

Isra Mi'raj Nabi Muhammad SAW, June 5—When Muhammad ascended to heaven.

Idul Fitri, August 8—Also called Lebaran, the end of the Muslim fasting month, Ramadan. Note that it is very difficult to travel just before and just after Idul Fitri everywhere except Bali, as almost everyone returns to their home villages to celebrate and then return to their places of work in the cities.

Idul Adha, October 15—The day of Abraham's sacrifice and when the hajj pilgrims circle the Kaaba in Mecca.

Hijryah, November 5—Islamic New Year, when Muhammad traveled from Mecca to Medina.

THE BALINESE CALENDAR

Bali runs simultaneously on several different calendrical systems, including the Western calendar, a Saka lunar calendar, and a 210-day *pawukon* calendar. The important Balinese holidays include:

Nyepi. Balinese New Year, Nyepi, is a day of silence and meditation. It falls on the day after the new moon, about the time of the vernal equinox. On Nyepi no physical activity occurs. This means no fire (cooking or electricity), no work, no travel, and no entertainment. Even Bali's airport is closed on this day. No touring is allowed, and visitors must stay in their hotels where special permits grant minimal use of the grounds and lights at night. Those staying outside hotels or in *losmens* will also be required to observe the day of silence. This "silence" is taken seriously and should be respected by visitors. The day after Nyepi is Ngembak Nyepi and the roads are crowded with people visiting family, friends, temples, and dance and drama performances.

On the eve of the Nyepi day, hundreds of *ogoh-ogoh* papier maché monsters are carried along the streets in all towns and villages, so be prepared to be caught in big crowds. This extraordinary cavalcade is reminiscent of a small scale South American carnival.

Galungan begins on the Wednesday of Dunggulan, the 11th week of a 30-week *pawukon* cycle. Pre-Galungan rituals involve offerings of animal sacrifices. On Galungan morning, everyone visits temples carrying colorful offerings.

Kuningan. Ten days after Galungan on the Saturday of Kuningan, the 12th week, marks the end of the celebration. It is a time for family gatherings, prayers, and still more offerings as deified ancestors return to heaven.

Saraswati Day, the last day of the *pawukon* calendar (the Saturday of Watugunung week) is when Saraswati, the Goddess of Knowledge, the Arts and Literature, is honored. All books and musical instruments are blessed and no music, reading or writing is allowed on this day. The next day is known as Sinta. This is the first day of the first *pawukon* week, when everyone goes to the beach for cleansing ceremonies.

TEMPLE CEREMONIES

In addition to holy days, Balinese Hindus hold ceremonies and perform rituals on other important days.

Odalan. Bali's temple festivals (*odalan*), based on the 210-day *pawukon* calendar, last alternatively one day or three days. Some of the major ones are listed by the number and name of the Balinese week, then day of the week.

Temple festivals. The temple festivals based on the lunar calendar (Saka) begin on the full moon of the relevant month and last for several days.

Purnama Sasih Kasa. Full moon. Ceremonies are held in Hindu temples all across Bali and believers take offerings of food, fruit, and flowers to the temple to be blessed by a priest. The essence of these offerings will be enjoyed by the deities. The Balinese themselves are then blessed by performing various rituals using holy water, incense smoke, petals, and rice grains.

Tilem Sasih Sada. Dark moon. Celebrated by Balinese Hindus, rituals are held in major temples and family shrines. Offerings to the gods are placed on the ground at the entrance of each housing compound to beg the gods to illuminate dark thoughts.

ART FESTIVALS

As with all Indonesians, the Balinese like a good excuse to have some fun. There are a number of annual festivals held throughout Bali that guarantee educational and entertaining for foreigners and local people alike.

March/April

Bali Spirit Festival, Ubud. Celebrated the end of March-beginning of April to coincide with Nyepi, a four-day festival bringing together music, yoga and dance. www.balispiritfestival.com

May/June

Bali Art Festival, Singaraja, North Bali. Every May or June, one week of performances showcasing dancers and musicians from the region's best village troupes.

June/July

Bali Arts Festival is held from mid-June to mid-July at the Taman Werdi Budaya (Art Center) on Jl. Nusa Indah in Denpasar. A full month of dance, drama, and art and handi-crafts exhibitions. Events include morning and evening performances by the winners of regency competitions from across the island, including the Denpasar arts schools and from other Indonesian islands. The opening ceremony is a parade beginning in downtown Denpasar worthy of international attention. www.baliartsfestival.com

Coca Cola Indonesian Surfing Championship, Seminyak. June events include Pro, Junior, Women's, Master, and Longboard competitions. Local and international surfers participate in a one-week championship competition and surfing film festival. www.isctour.com

MRA Group Bali Triathlon. Held at Four Seasons Resort Jimbaran every June, Olympic and sprint distance events include: 1.5 km (0.9 mile) swim, 40 km (25 mile) bike, 10 km (6.2 mile) run, team relay for teams of three athletes (Olympic distance); 500 m (0.3 mile) swim, 20 km (12.4 mile) bike ride, 5 km (3 mile) run (sprint distance). Pre-race bike tour and Balinese bike blessing ceremony, live music, and beach party. www.balitriathlon.com

Omedomedan Kissing Ceremony. A June event in Banjar Sesetan Kaja, Denpasar Regency held the day after Nyepi. Participants are all single adults 17–30 years old and must be unmarried members of Banjar Kaja. (Outsiders are not allowed to participate.) After prayers, the girls and boys line up facing each other, meet and hug and kiss in this sacred ritual. As expected, things get silly and the ceremony usually ends with everyone being doused with water.

July/August

International Kite Festival, Sanur. Part of the Sanur Village Festival held annually. Teams from Indonesia and abroad fly enormous kites up to 10 m long, taking as many as five men to launch compete in various divisions, including traditional Balinese and contemporary kite designs.

Sanur Village Festival. An annual celebration held July–August, drawing hundreds of locals and tourists to its many events. A four-day feast of contests (water sports and kite flying, to name two), music, dance and food, food, food; a great opportunity to mingle with the local people, hear some great music and to eat some really good food. www.gotosanur.com

August 17

Indonesia's Independence Day. In the week or two leading up to August 17,

Independence Day, games and contests are held throughout Indonesia reminiscent of the U.S. July 4th or French Bastille Day. Culminating on August 17, all celebrations include lots of food, fun, and laughter. Visitors are more than welcome to join.

Negara Buffalo Race Championships, Regent's Cup, Negara, West Bali. In celebration of Independence Day, the Regent's Cup buffalo race—with animals decorated in bright colors and jockeys bouncing and bobbing in attached carts—takes place on the Sunday before August 17 with teams hopeful of being selected to participate in the Governor's Cup Championship in October.

September / October

Nusa Dua Fiesta, Nusa Dua. A three-day festival of music and dance featuring the best of local and national performers held every September or October since 1997. Changing theme every year showcasing Bali's vibrant local culture: art and handicraft exhibitions; dance, drama, music performances, and sporting events.

October

Negara Buffalo Race Championships, Governor's Cup, Negara, West Bali. *Jegog* music, dance performances, and traditional foods accompany an exciting event to the delight of onlookers.

Ubud Writers' and Readers' Festival, Ubud. Brings together authors and readers in a four-day extravaganza of workshops, readings, book launches and performances. Ranked one of the top five literary events in Asia. www.ubudwritersfestival.com

BALINESE CASTES & NAMES

There are four major caste groups among the Balinese: **brahmana** (Brahman), **satria**, **wesya** and **jaba**. The *brahmana* are the priest caste; the *satria*, the nobility; and the *wesya*, the former vassals of the court. Everyone else is *jaba*. Even though castes make no difference in peoples' abilities to hold certain jobs, every Balinese keep track of them for various reasons, for example to decide what level of language to use when speaking Balinese.

Balinese names are coded to reveal caste and birth order within the family. Nothing, of course, is simple, especially when considering inter-caste marriages, and there are always exceptions. The following are clues to interpreting names and their owner's social status:

Ida Bagus (male) and Ida Ayu (female) indicate the brahmanic caste. Gusti is normally used by members of the *wesya* caste, whereas Gusti Agung, Anak Agung, and Cokorda are reserved for the high-ranking members of the *satria* caste. Desak (female) and Dewa (male) are lower-ranking *satria*. I (normally male) and Ni (female) are usually used by the *jaba*.

Wayan, Made, Nyoman, and Ketut mean first-born, second-born, third-born, and fourth-born, respectively. Beginning with the fifth child in the family, the naming cycle is repeated. Also used similarly to indicate birth order are Putu, Kadek, Komang and Ketut. Nengah may be used by either the second- or third-born child. The birth order names are normally used only by the *jaba* caste, so don't call a member of the *satria* caste "Wayan" even if you happen to know that he/she is the oldest in the family!

ETIQUETTE

In the areas of Indonesia most frequented by foreigners, many are familiar with the strange ways and customs practiced outside Indonesia. But it is best to be aware of how certain aspects of your behavior will be viewed. You will not be able to count on an Indonesian to set you straight when you commit a *faux pas*. They are much too polite. They will probably stay silent or even reply "*tidak apa apa*" (no problem) if you ask if you did something wrong. Here are some points to keep in mind:
* The left hand is considered dirty as it is used for cleaning oneself after using the toilet. It is inappropriate to use the left hand to eat or to give or receive anything with it. However, in the event that you do accidentally use your left hand, then say "*ma'af, tangan kiri*" (please excuse my left hand) or a simple "*ma'af*" will do.
* The head is considered the most sacred part of the body, and the feet the least sacred. Avoid touching people on the head. Go for the elbow instead. Never step over food or expose the sole of your foot toward anyone.
* As it is impolite to keep one's head higher than others, it is appropriate to acknowledge the presence of others by stooping (extending the right arm and drooping the right shoulder while leaning forward) when passing closely by someone who is sitting or standing and engaged in a conversation.
* Pointing with the index finger is impolite. Indonesians use their thumbs (palm turned upward, fingers curled in) or open palms instead.
* Summoning people by crooking the forefinger is impolite. Rather, wave with a flat palm facing down.
* Alcohol is frowned upon in Islam, so take a look around you and consider taking it easy.
* Hands on hips is a sign of superiority or anger.
* Take off your shoes when you enter someone's house. Often the host will stop you, but you should at least go through the motions until he/she does.
* Wait for a verbal offer before tucking into food and drinks that have been placed in front of you. Sip your drink and don't finish it in one gulp. Never take the last morsel from a common plate.
* You will often hear the words "*makan, makan*" ("eat, eat") if you pass somebody who is eating. This is not really an invitation, but simply means "Excuse me while I eat."
* If someone prepares a meal or drink for you it is most impolite to refuse. Even if you don't want to partake, it's polite to at least pretend taking a sip of an offered drink and a nibble of the food.
* Some things from the West filter through to Indonesia more pervasively than others, and stories of *free sek* (free sex) made a deep and lasting impression in Indonesia. Expect this topic to appear in lists of questions you will be asked in your cultural exchanges. It is best to explain how things have changed since the free-wheeling 1960s and how we are now stuck with *saf sek*.

Bali may seem to have been placed here just for your personal enjoyment, but it is not a zoo. Be aware of Balinese sensibilities. Remember the Balinese are offended if the casual visitor does not **dress appropriately** when entering a temple. A sash over shorts and very brief tops are not sufficient. Have a *sarung* and sash handy for temple visits and ceremonies, and wear long pants or a skirt and a decent shirt with a collar. Menstruating women are not allowed to enter temples. Never sit higher than the priest, and don't walk in front of people who are praying. Because some ceremonies last for several hours it is permissible to leave after a while, but do so inconspicuously.

Bathing suits and brief shorts and tops are acceptable on the beaches, but nowhere else. When leaving the beach areas it is more polite to wear longer shorts and shirts that cover the midriff.

Keeping your cool

Wherever you are in Indonesia, if problems occur, talking loudly and forcefully doesn't make things easier and in fact can make matters worse. Patience and politeness are the order of the day and will open many doors. Good manners, proper dress, and a pleasant countenance will also work to your advantage.

TRAVELING WITH CHILDREN

Luckily for those with children, all Indonesians love kids. Be sure to bring essentials: sunhats, creams, medicines, special foods, and a separate water container for babies to be sure of always having sterile water. Disposable diapers are available in big supermarkets. Nights can be cool sometimes, so bring some warm clothing for your child. Milk, eggs, fruit which you can peel, and porridges are readily available in the supermarkets. If given advanced notice, babysitters are available for a moderate charge at any hotel.

It's especially important that you have health/medical insurance for children because they can get sick quickly, run high temperatures, get dehydrated, and it can be puzzling what's wrong with them. See "Medical treatment & insurance" (pages 329–30) for recommended medical care.

ACCOMMODATIONS

Indonesia has an extraordinary range of accommodations, much of it good value. All cities and most towns have hotels offering air-conditioned rooms with tv, mini-bar, hot water and swimming pool for $100/night and up. At the other end of the scale, you can stay in a $6/night *losmen* with communal squat toilet (bring your own toilet paper), a tub of cold water with ladle for bathing, and a bunk with no towel or clean linen (provide your own). And there's just about everything in between: from colonial hill stations to luxurious new thatched-roof huts in the middle of rice fields.

A hierarchy of lodgings and official terminology has been set by the government. A "hotel" is a better class establishment catering to businessmen, middle- to upper-class travelers and tourists. A **star-rating** (1–5 stars) is applied according to the range of facilities. Smaller places with no stars and basic facilities are not referred to as hotels but as *losmen*, *wisma* (guesthouse), or *penginapan* (inn) and cater to the traveling masses and budget tourists. In between are "melati-rated" accommodations. The more amenities, the higher the melati rating.

Prices and quality vary enormously. In the major cities that cater to business travelers instead of tourists, such as Jakarta, Surabaya, and Medan, there is little choice in the middle ranges and the choices are to either pay a lot or settle for a room in a *losmen*.

In areas where there are a lot of tourists, such as Bali and Yogyakarta (Jogja), you can get clean and very comfortable rooms with fan or air-conditioning for less than $25 a night. In small towns and remote areas, there's not much choice and all accommodations tend to be very basic. It's common to ask to see the room before checking in. Shop around before deciding, particularly if the hotel offers different rooms at different rates. Avoid carpeted rooms, especially without air-conditioning, as usually they are damp and this makes the room smell.

Advance bookings are necessary during peak tourist seasons (July–August, Christmas and New Year, the Muslim Ramadan holidays, and local public holidays). Popular resorts are always packed on weekends, and prices often double, so travel instead during the week when it's cheaper and quieter.

In this book we have used published rates where available. In many hotels, discounts of up to 40–50% off published rates are to be had for the asking during off-peak seasons. Booking in advance through the Internet, travel agencies, or hotel association counters at airports can also result in a lower rate. Reservations are advisable throughout the year, especially July–August and December–January. Surcharges of 10–20% are added during the peak season.

Larger hotels invariably add 21% tax and service to the bill.

See www.balispirit.com for recommended eco resorts and retreat centers.

BATHROOM ETIQUETTE

When staying in *losmen*, particularly when using communal facilities, don't climb in, do your laundry or drop your soap into the tub of water (*bak mandi*). This is used for storing clean water. Scoop and pour the water over your body standing away from the *bak mandi* with the ladle/dipper (*gayung*) provided.

If you wish to use the native paper-free cleaning method after using the toilet, scoop water or pour with your right hand and clean with the left. This is the reason one only eats with the right hand; the left is regarded as unclean. Use soap and a fingernail brush (villagers use a pumice stone, *batu apung*) for cleaning hands. Pre-packaged alcohol towelettes or antiseptic hand cleaner may make you feel happier about opting for this method. But don't throw the towelettes — or anything else — down the toilet.

Bring along your own towel and soap (although some places provide these). If you ask, *losmen* staff will even provide hot water in a bucket for you which you can dilute with cold water for bathing, but be prepared to wait for it, as it takes awhile to boil large amounts of water.

Staying in villages
Officially, the Indonesian government requires that foreign visitors spending the night in *desa* (villages) report to the local police. This is routinely handled by *losmen* and hotels, which send in a copy of the registration form you fill out when you check in.

Where there are no commercial lodgings, you can often rely on local hospitality. But when staying in a private home, keep in mind the need to inform the local authorities. One popular solution is to stay in the home of the local authority, the village head (*kepala desa*).

Carry photocopies of your passport and embarkation card to give to officials when venturing beyond the usual tourist areas. This saves time and potential hassles for you and your host.

Villagers in rural Bali do not routinely maintain guest rooms. If a cash arrangement has not been prearranged, you should leave a gift appropriate to local needs: rice, fruit, notebooks, pens, clothing, cigarettes or a thick towel. Note down the address of your host and send prints of the photos you took of them.

SHOPPING
Bali is a shopper's paradise. Streets in the resort areas of the south are lined with stores, shops, and stalls selling arts, wood-carvings, handicrafts, hand-woven textiles, gifts, and souvenirs of all types. Lists of local specialties are found in the relevant Practicalities sections. Also among Bali's best buys are ready-made clothes, stylish fashions, and gold and silver designer jewelry. Below are some shopping tips and a general picture of what to look for.

Bargaining
Outside of fixed price shops, the first price is not the last price on Bali. Try to learn the art of bargaining while you're here; it is expected that you will join in this traditional form of socialization. Items in supermarkets, department stores, well-to-do shops, and fees for services are generally fixed, but nearly everything else is fair game. At small hotels try asking for a discount; you'll be surprised at how often at least 10% is granted, particularly in the off-peak seasons.

First ask the price that the vendor expects and then make a counter offer. Keep on asking for the "best price" and keep on smiling. Your initial offer should be much lower than the price you really want to pay. It is advisable not to seem too eager to buy.

Keep a sense of humor about the whole thing. There's no such thing as a "right price". You usually pay more than the locals, but that's the way it is.

Souvenirs
For a wide selection of souvenirs, go to the hundreds of shops along Jl. Legian in Kuta, Legian, and Seminyak; the Ubud Art Market; the Sanur Art Market; and Denpasar's Kumbasari Market. The mother of all souvenir markets (*pasar seni*) is in Sukawati on the way from Denpasar up to Ubud, about 5 km (3.2 miles) south of Ubud.

Carvings
Mas and Kemenuh are the main spots for polished woodcarvings; Batuan is the place for wooden panels. Pujung, Sebatu, and Tegallalang, north of Ubud, specialize in painted carvings and giant statues. For masks, go to Mas, Singapadu, and Batuan.

Traditional Balinese stone carvings made from volcanic pumice (*paras*) are made in Batubulan. See Practicalities for these areas for specific recommendations.

Textiles
Bali is a dreamland for lovers of hand-woven textiles. Big Bali-style *ikat* workshops are concentrated in Gianyar Town, but Klungkung in eastern Bali, and Singaraja in the north also have large well-known producers. For the fancier *songket* with gold and silver threads woven into the weft, go to Sideman, Blayu (between Mengwi and Marga), and Singaraja. There are beautiful woven *selendangs* (temple sashes) in Batuan, Ubud, and Mengwi, but

the exquisite *geringsing* double *ikat* cloths are made only in Tenganan, eastern Bali. Woven textiles from Sumbawa, Sumba, Tanah Toraja (Sulawesi), and Sumatra can be found in Kuta, Legian, and Denpasar.

Some of the batik worn by Balinese and found everywhere is made on Java. However, Bali has its own unique batik styles, often in brighter colors. If you want "genuine" batik be sure that you're getting hand-drawn (*tulis*) or stamped (*cap*) batik, and not the manufactured printed or silk screen batik with traditional designs on machine-processed fabric. The difference is often reflected in the price; hand-drawn batik is always more expensive.

Paintings

Ubud is the place for Balinese paintings, and the surrounding villages Pengosekan, Penestanan, Sanggingan, Peliatan, Mas, and Batuan are all lively breeding grounds for the arts. While the large galleries in Ubud display some of the best work ever produced on the island—past and present—smaller galleries and art shops in Ubud and surrounding hamlets may be your best bet for reasonably priced (but lower quality) local work. You can also visit artists in their homes and strike some good deals. Traditional Balinese calendars and *wayang*-style paintings are produced in Kamasan village near Klungkung, eastern Bali.

Antiques

Kuta, Denpasar, and all along Jl. Bypass Ngurah Rai are hunting grounds for antique dealers from abroad on the lookout for furniture, ornately carved wedding beds, palm-leaf books, fabrics, masks, Chinese ceramics, sculpture, and primitive statues from throughout Indonesia. However, be aware that the antique reproduction market is very active and very lucrative. If you like the look of old furniture but aren't fussy about authenticity, look for reproduction "antiques" in those same areas.

The best idea is to shop around until you have a good sense of quality and prices. To export anything older than 25 years old you must have a letter from the Museum Section of the Education and Culture Department.

Jewelry

Celuk, Kamasan (south of Klungkung), and Bratan in Buleleng (northern Bali) are the traditional centers for gold and silverwork. The silver is 80–90% pure; gold is 22–24 K. If you don't find anything you like ready-made, then custom order. For modern designs, go to Ubud, Kuta, and Legian. Sukawati is a traditional gold working village, or try the gold shops in Denpasar on Jl. Hasanuddin and Jl. Sulawesi. Be sure to bargain.

Beach vendors

Vendors on the beach, especially Kuta, can be rather pushy. They sell everything from chilled pineapple slices to their sisters. They can be annoying, with boxes of fake name-brand watches, perfumes, statuary, and offers for massage, nail decorating, or hair-braiding. There are some good deals on *sarung* and bikinis, but you have to bargain hard. Start out at 50% of their asking price and settle at 25%–30%. To avoid being hassled by them, never make eye contact.

Shipping & freight

Shipping goods home is relatively safe and painless on Bali, though it can be a bit expensive. Items under 1 m (3 ft) long and 10 kg (22 lbs) in weight can be sent by surface mail via most postal agents. All the packing will be done for you at reasonable cost, although it's always advisable to keep an eye on how it's done. Larger purchases are best sent by airfreight or sea cargo. On Bali, freight forwarders are almost as abundant as watch peddlers. Freight forwarders will handle the whole process for a price, from packing to customs. Many retailers are also prepared to send goods if purchased in quantity.

Air cargo is charged by the kilogram (minimum 10 kg/22 lbs), and can be costly. Sea cargo is around $150 per cubic meter to the USA or Europe and takes about 60 days. Don't forget to buy insurance. When shipping cargo, you are responsible for clearing customs back home and for transporting the goods from the port of entry to your destination. This can cost $500 and up, making cargo only economical for large purchases.

PHOTOGRAPHY

Most Indonesians generally enjoy being photographed. But, it's polite to ask—or motion to the camera with a nod and a smile —before taking pictures of the elderly. If you are in doubt or the situation seems awkward, it is always polite to ask. Some religious activities, cockfighting (which is officially banned), eating, praying, and bathing are inappropriate subjects.

Beware of the strong shadows from the equatorial sun. Late afternoon and early morning provide the most pleasing light and the richest colors. The only way to deal with the heavy shadows and glare at midday is to use a fill flash.

The heat and humidity of the tropics is hard on camera equipment. Be particularly careful when moving your camera from an air-conditioned room to the muggy outdoors. Moisture will condense on the inside and outside of the lens. Wait until it evaporates; don't be tempted to wipe it off. Also, always be aware of the location of your camera bag. Temperatures inside cars or on boats can be searing.

In general, stick with reliable equipment you are familiar with and bring extra batteries, memory cards, and a battery charger.

PROTECTED SPECIES

Indonesia is a signatory party to the Convention on International Trade in Endangered Species (CITES) treaty that lists protected species of plants and animals. There are more than 200 endangered species of Indonesian mammals, birds, reptiles, insects, fish, and mollusks, including orangutans, parrots, cockatoos, crocodiles, tortoises, turtles, butterflies, and corals.

There are strict laws and severe penalties for trade in endangered species, so be aware that even though you may see handicrafts for sale made of animal parts—or even the animals or birds themselves—you will not be allowed to take them out of the country. Some of the items you may see for sale that must be avoided are anything made of tortoiseshell (e.g. jewelry, combs, boxes), some clams species, Triton's trumpet shells, and pearly or chambered nautilus shells, just to name a few.

Visitors should also be aware of the fragility of Indonesia's natural environment and not contribute to any further degradation of it. Indonesia is home to more than 500 animal species, more than anywhere else in the world. It also has the greatest number of endangered species in the world. Establishing an effective environmental conservation program is a formidable project.

The Indonesian government, with the help of private conservation agencies, such as the World Wide Fund for Nature, the Nature Conservancy, BirdLife International, and many other international organizations is working to create a viable network of national parks and nature reserves, where fragile ecosystems and threatened species can be protected. Two of these national parks, Ujung Kulon in western Java (home to the world's most endangered large mammal, the Javan rhino), and Komodo in the Lesser Sundas (home to the Komodo dragon), have been declared World Heritage Sites by the World Conservation Union.

Balinese species

Marine turtle meat is considered a delicacy by the Balinese and one of the traditional dishes of ritual feasts. Many organizations are working in the coastal areas throughout Indonesia to educate citizens about the need to protect endangered sea turtles.

The Bali tiger is confirmed to be extinct. Efforts are on-going through the West Bali National Park and on Nusa Penida to preserve the highly endangered Bali Starling, which is indigenous to Bali. See the West Bali National Park and Nusa Penida chapters for more information about this critically endangered bird.

INVESTING IN BALI REAL ESTATE

An investment boom led by foreigners is occurring in Indonesia and is particularly noticeable on Bali with its almost unbelievable number of private villas for rent. As tempting as it might seem to own a home in this exotic land, be aware that the legalities involved—currently, foreigners cannot hold title to property in Indonesia—are incredibly complicated and are changing rapidly. Additionally, land or villas advertised as "freehold" aren't really, at least not to foreigners. If a deal seems too good to be true, then it probably is.

The experts advise that if you're thinking of investing in property anywhere in Indonesia, rent here first for at least one year to see if it's really the right move for you. Next, get the advice of a reputable lawyer who not only knows the changing real estate laws but can explain them in terms you can understand. Do the due diligence, including environmental, zoning, and local *adat* (traditional) restrictions, permits, tax records, and title. After you've done all that, and still think you want to invest, consider it some more before giving anyone any money.

WEDDINGS

Many people from throughout the world dream of a romantic wedding on Bali, and the 5-star resorts have certainly risen to the occasion providing beautiful chapels by the sea, fabulous gardens, and other innovative settings for memorable events. There are also many wedding services that offer complete packages, including "legalities". Do your own research at home first to make sure a marriage officiated overseas is recognizable in your own country.

ACTIVITIES

There are so many choices of activity on Bali that the hardest decision could be how many of them can be squeezed into a holiday. Check Practicalities for each region for specifics, but here is a general overview of options.

Boating & water sports

Cruises. There are a number of vessels that sail from Benoa Harbor, southern Bali, offering day trips for snorkeling and diving at the Nusa islands, dinner cruises, fishing, and charters.
Diving & snorkeling. Bali has several options for snorkeling and diving around Sanur and Nusa Dua, but the most exciting locations are in the island's more remote areas: Pulau Menjangan in West Bali National Park is considered the best, followed by nearby Pemuteran, also in western Bali. Snorkeling and diving are also good at Lovina, in northern Bali; Candidasa, Padangbai, Tulamben, and Amed in the east; and Nusa Penida, Nusa Lembongan, and Nusa Ceningan Island in southern Bali.

It's advisable to use only reputable professional marine sports agencies who provide good quality equipment, current information, and adequate insurance coverage.
Fishing. Good fishing areas are Candidasa and Amed in eastern Bali, where you can go with a local fisherman early morning or late afternoon. Mackerel is the favored catch. There is one boat offering fishing charters to Nusa Penida in southern Bali.
Sailing. The many local outriggers (*jukung*) that line the beaches at Sanur in the south, Padangbai, Candidasa, and Amed in the east, Lovina in the north, and other local boats in the West Bali National Park can be hired for fishing, diving, snorkeling, or sailing trips. Ask about current prices at accommodations.
Surfing. Kuta, Legian, Uluwatu, Canggu, Nusa Dua, some areas of Sanur and the northwest coast of Nusa Lembongan in the south; Medewi and Balian (Lalang Linggih) in western Bali; and Ketewi, Lebih, and

Padangbai on the island's east coast have for many years been surfing areas. Breaks are good throughout the year at various points along the coastlines. Speak to the experts at any of the surf shops, where all the owners are avid surfers. They can provide up-to-the-minute surfing reports and tide charts that are essential for negotiating the currents.

Rip Curl posts important surf news weekly at: www.swellforcast@ripcurl.com.

Magic Wave, a bi-monthly surf community newspaper available free at surf shops in Kuta/Legian, publishes articles, information, and interviews on the Bali surf scene. For almost daily updates on Bali's waves, check out: www.baliwaves.com.

On Kuta, the undertows can be treacherous so always surf between the flags. For protection from the harsh tropical sun be sure to wear sunscreen and a T-shirt. Tend to coral cuts immediately and constantly: they take forever to heal.
Swimming. For the safest and most family-friendly ocean swimming, go to Sanur or Nusa Dua in the south or Lovina on the north coast. The currents along the southern, western, and eastern coasts and at the Nusa islands are extremely strong and the undertow can be very treacherous. Swimming is at your own risk. At Kuta, there are markers to indicate no-swim areas, but no sea markers to indicate safe distance from the beach. Drownings are not uncommon.

Alternatively, the pools at most of the major hotels are open to non-guests for a small fee. There's a water park in Tuban—Waterbom—with pools and slides, rides, a food court, and massage.
White water rafting. Rafting has become a popular way to discover some of the undiscovered parts of Bali around Ubud and in Payangan, northwest of Ubud, both in central Bali. Expect the rivers to be more challenging in the rainy season.

Other water sports

There are several beachside booths at popular water sports locations (Nusa Dua, Benoa, and Sanur in the south, and Lake Bratan's Recreational Park in northern Bali) offering **banana boats**, **jet skis**, **kite surfing** (also called kiteboarding), **sea kayaking**, **parasailing**, **waterskiing**, **wakeboarding**, and **windsurfing**, with many hotels in Sanur and Benoa renting boards and giving lessons for the latter. Prices vary according to the time of year and location.

Biking & hiking

These are the best ways to get to know the hinterlands of Bali intimately. Beware of sunstroke: start off early in the morning, avoid the heat of the day, and drink plenty of bottled water, which is easily obtainable throughout the island. Sunglasses, a hat, comfortable shoes, a sarong, and sash (for entering temples) are useful, as is a map or a clear geographic notion of your destination.

Biking/cycling. The best and most conveniently accessible areas for **biking** are around Ubud and northwest of Ubud in central Bali; Kintamani and Candidasa in eastern Bali; and the Jatuluwih area and the back-country of Lovina in northern Bali. Always check the bike before paying; brake failure half way down a volcano is no fun.

One highly professional bicycling tour organizer is **Bali Cycling Operator**, Jl. Curug Tiga No. 6B, Tuban, www.balicycling.com. While most bicycle tours offered through travel agents and booked at hotels simply take riders from point A to point B, founder I Wayan Kertayasa and his team customize tours for small groups according to their fitness and experience levels, wherever on the island they want to go.

Hiking. Trekking is good almost everywhere away from the traffic of major towns and can be tailored to physical capabilities and interests. Strike out on your own or in some areas getting a good local guide is advisable. Check out the following areas: Kintamani, Toya Bungkah (in the Mt. Batur caldera), Tirta Gangga, and Candidasa in eastern Bali; in and around Ubud and the Pupuan region northwest of Ubud in central Bali; the Bangli and Bedugul areas of northern Bali; and the West Bali National Park in western Bali.

Birdwatching tours of the Ubud area in central Bali, in West Bali National Park in western Bali, and at Nusa Penida (organized by the Friends of the National Parks Foundation) in southern Bali are available.

Climbing. Bali's many volcanoes, mountains, and hills attract climbers from amateurs to extreme. See Practicalities of the various regions for more details.

Other outdoor activities

All-terrain vehicles. Two companies have ATV tours through the countryside northwest

of Ubud, one of which can be combined with a white water rafting outing. The other can include cycling or outbound adventures.

Outbound adventure fun and learning programs. Two organizers offer outbound adventures, one in the Penebel district northwest of Ubud, central Bali, and the other at Bali Botanical Gardens near Bedugul, northern Bali.

Golf

There are five golf courses on Bali: at Nusa Dua, near Tanah Lot, in Sanur, and a new course in Kuta in southern Bali; and near Bedugal in northern Bali. Inquire about packages that often include accommodations or spa treatments, as these can be good bargains.

GETTING TO BALI

You can fly direct to Indonesia from just about anywhere. The country's main international entry points are Sukarno-Hatta airport in Jakarta and Ngurah Rai airport on Bali. Major cities on all the larger islands now also have a few international arrivals from other points in Southeast Asia.

Direct flights connect Bali with many major cities in Asia and Australia. All other international flights transit in Jakarta. At the last count, Bali is served by 17 international air carriers flying non-stop into Bali via major Asian air hubs such as Jakarta, Kuala Lumpur, Bangkok, Singapore, Hong Kong, Taipei, and Seoul, and from Darwin, Melbourne, Sydney, and Perth in Australia.

Several Indonesian domestic carriers offering cheap airfares connect Bali with the rest of Indonesia.

Air fares vary depending on the carrier, the season, and the type of ticket purchased. Check websites for special rates and packages. Also check for round trip excursion fares from Singapore, some of which are valid for one month and include stops in Jakarta and Yogyakarta with multiple overnight stays.

If limited time is not a problem, also check flights from Batam and Bintan, Indonesian islands just south of Singapore, which can be reached via short ferry hops from Singapore's World Trade Center (about $25 one way), then compare with direct Singapore-Bali air discount rates.

Arriving by air

Bali's Ngurah Rai airport is a sophisticated facility with all the amenities of an international airport, yet it still has the feel of a small, user-friendly facility.

Money changers are located inside and outside both terminals. Rates are compatible with reputable money changers in town and are better than hotel or bank rates.

The **domestic** and **international terminals** are only five minutes walk from each other. In the luggage pick-up areas of both terminals are well-staffed hotel reservations counters where English-speaking clerks can arrange free transport to a hotel of your choice. Usually only hotels $30 and up are represented, but this is the place to bargain for a better rate. If you've booked ahead the driver will usually be there to greet you, holding up a sign with your name on it.

Airport area hotels

Most visitors to Bali go straight to their next destination upon arrival, but if arriving late at night with no hotel reservations, unsure of the next day's plans, there are no hotels at the airport. Tuban followed by Kuta are the nearest towns to the airport and any of the accommodations in the Practicalities sections of those two areas will suffice for a last-minute overnight stay.

Airport departure tax

Airport tax for departing passengers is Rp 150,000 (note that it must be paid in rupiah) for international routes and Rp 30,000 for domestic flights.

Domestic airlines

Telephone code: 0361

Airport information, domestic terminal tel: 751-011

Air Asia, **Garuda**, **Lion Air**, and **Mandala** all connect Bali with other cities inside and outside of Indonesia and have extensive online booking facilities.

There are also several strictly domestic carriers. Some of them don't have online booking, but you can make reservations through any local travel agency. All have ticket offices in the domestic terminal at Ngurah Rai airport, and some also have other locations.
Batavia Air, www.batavia-air.co.id. Jakarta

based, established in 2001. Links Jakarta to Bali, Sumatra, Kalimantan, Java, Lombok, Batam, Timor, Sulawesi, and Maluku. Also flies to Guangzhou, Singapore, Riyadh, and Jeddah.
City Link, www.citilink.co.id, contact center: 0804-108-0808, 505-3763 (5 am–9 pm). Garuda's commuter subsidiary, it links Jakarta with Surabaya, Batam, Balikpapan, Banjarmasin, and Ujung Pandang (Makassar).
Merpati Nusantara Airlines, www.merpati. co.id, tel: 235-358. Indonesia's biggest domestic airline connecting towns and cities across the archipelago.
Riau Airlines, www.riau-airlines.com, call center: 0804-133-6699. Links Sumatra and the Riau islands to Jakarta. Also flies to points in Malaysia.
SriWijaya Air, Jl. Teuku Umar No. 97B, tel: 228-461, www.sriwijaya-air-online.com, call center: (021) 6405-566 (24 hours). Jakarta-based, links several points on Java with Sumatra, Sulawesi, Java, Bali, Timor, and Kalimantan.
TransNusa, www.transnusa.co.id, call center: (021) 640-5566 (24 hours). Specializes in the smaller eastern Indonesian islands.

Arriving overland

Traveling overland from Java to Bali requires taking a ferry. It's a pleasant 1-hour trip from Ketapang (east Java) to Gilimanuk (west Bali), with many private and state-owned services that run continuously at 15–25 minute intervals. Getting on can be a hassle during the Indonesian holidays, when there are large crowds, so expect a long wait, or better yet, avoid the journey during those times.

By ferry to Lombok

You may also want to venture over to Lombok. Most ferries leave from Padangbai in east Bali. See Padangbai Practicalities for more information.

By bus

Denpasar's main bus terminal, Ubung, is also a *bemo* terminal, and most buses from and to Java arrive and depart from here. It is a 7–10 hour trip from Denpasar to Surabaya in east Java.

The major advantages of rattling local buses is that they are extremely cheap, run every few minutes between major towns, and can be picked up either at terminals or any point along their routes. This is also their biggest disadvantage: they stop constantly to pick up and drop off passengers, which can make progress agonizingly slow.

Try to find a seat near a window that opens, but be considerate of neighbors. Generally, Indonesians have a strong aversion to wind for fear of *masuk angin* (the wind which enters the body and causes colds).

The seats are very small, both in terms of leg room and width. You and your bag may take up (and be charged for) two seats. This is fair. But be sure you're not being overcharged. Ask someone what the proper fare is to your destination before getting on. People are generally very eager to help you.

Buses depart throughout the day from Ubung terminal in Denpasar for Surabaya (12 hrs), Yogyakarta (15 hrs), Jakarta (24 hrs), and many other destinations, such as Lombok.

Bus company agents are ubiquitous in Denpasar, especially along Jl. Hasanuddin. Someone at your accommodation can point out the nearest agency.

Perama, Jl. Legian 39, tel: 751-551, www. peramatour.com is a reputable private company with offices in Kuta, Sanur, and Ubud. Its buses shuttle back and forth between those areas and Kintamani, Lovina, Padangbai, and Candidasa. Perama also sells long-distance bus tickets to Lombok and beyond and east to Java. Check at their office for schedules. Also ask about pick-up and drop-off, which they provide for a small extra charge. Trips from Kuta to Lovina cost about $10.

Express minibus

Express service comes in two varieties: old, hot *mikrolets* or *bemos* (sit by a window and keep it open) and the newer, much-revered versions with air conditioning that make the Denpasar-Gilimanuk run, called "executive service"— since businessmen often use them—on Java.

These 8-11 passenger vans connect major cities and deliver passengers to their destinations rather than to a terminal. They may also do pick-ups at various offices before leaving the city, but once they're on the highway, there are no stops. They usually travel during the day, though on longer routes they travel at night like the *bis malam*. Express minibuses are slightly more expensive than *bis malam* but more convenient. Buy tickets at the *bemo* office or through bus agencies.

GETTING AROUND
Taxis

Most travelers arrive on Bali through the Ngurah Rai International Airport. Although the airport code is DPS—for Denpasar—the airport is actually in Tuban.

A reliable **taxi cooperative** operates from the airport. Tariffs to various parts of the island are fixed (drivers don't use their meters) and are posted. There are taxi counters at both the domestic and international terminals outside on the left after exiting the baggage claim areas. Prices depend on the destination and range from about $5 to Kuta, Legian, Seminyak, or Denpasar to $15 to Ubud or $25 to Candidasa. Traffic can be heavy during rush hours, but at other times it takes 20-30 minutes to reach Kuta, Legian, Seminyak, or Sanur. Ubud is about 1.5-2 hours north.

If you don't have much luggage and if you want a cheaper taxi, walk through the airport gates and flag one down. Taxis are metered with set government prices and are generally safe, reliable, and can be flagged down anywhere. Highly recommended is **Bali Taxi** (tel: 701-111, 701-621, www.bluebirdgroup.com), part of the well-respected Blue Bird group from Jakarta and the most likely company to have English-speaking drivers. **Praja Taxi** (tel: 289-090) is also good.

Insist that the meter be turned on unless you know where you're going and how much it should cost. Fares are reasonable; a trip within Kuta/Legian, for example, should cost $3-5, depending on traffic.

Car rentals

Both internationally recognized and local self-drive rental car agencies are readily available in major cities. In smaller towns, cars with drivers are available instead. Most accommodations can arrange them.

There are many rental car agencies on Bali offering self-drive or with driver, and all travel agencies have cars with English-speaking drivers for hire. Examine the car and read all contracts carefully before signing. More important than the agency you rent from is to test-drive the car before renting. At the airport, freelance drivers circulate among arriving passengers but they tend to overcharge.

Self-driving

Driving on Bali is not for the faint-hearted. Vehicles, people, and creatures of every size, shape, and description charge onto the road out of nowhere. The traffic is horrendous on the main highways and in southern Bali during peak hours. Drive slowly and carefully and beware of the trucks at night and over-zealous buses at all times. Road construction sites are not marked, few cyclists have reflectors, and motorcycles may have no lights.

The condition and network of major roads has improved considerably in recent years and they are beginning to number some highways. However, driving off the beaten track is one of the best ways to discover Bali and village roads can be unpaved and full of potholes.

Gas stations are found everywhere in towns and cities. Deep in the hinterlands, or if you run out of gas, small roadside fuel stands, indicated by a "Premium" sign, sell gasoline at a bit more per liter than the government-owned Pertamina stations.

A valid **international driving license** is required for driving cars and motorbikes. If you do not have one, you can get a provisional license at the local Polres (police headquarters) on the road between Denpasar and Kerobokan.

Insurance is not compulsory, but strongly recommended. You can get a policy from most of the rental companies and travel agents by paying about $5 extra per day on top of your rental price.

Renting vehicles is very cheap. Small Suzuki Jimny jeeps and larger Toyota Kijangs are available for a daily rate of between $30−40. Discounts are available during the off-season and for longer periods. Beware: vehicles are usually rented with a bone dry gas tank and do not expect you to return them with a full tank.

Chartering a car or minivan with a driver

Hiring a vehicle with a driver is the best way to handle a land tour: someone else worries about the traffic, hills, and dales while you watch the scenery, and you have the freedom to stop whenever things look interesting as well as the flexibility to try out some less traveled routes. This can also be an economical alternative if you can fill up a van. A minibus can take up to seven people, but you need extra space if you are to be in it for a few days, so five passengers is generally maximum.

The quality of both the driver and the vehicle will determine the pleasure of your trip so don't be shy about hiring one for just a day and checking them both out before striking a deal. Your driver should be responsible and have a personality that won't grate on you over the long haul. If he knows the area you will be driving through and can speak some English, so much the better. The air-conditioning should work well enough to overcome the midday heat, and the vehicle should be clean and comfortable.

It's best just to arrange these charters on your own. For traveling around Bali count on paying about $40 a day for an AC van, including fuel but not including parking fees or entrance charges. It is understood that you will pay for the driver's meals and accommo-dation both while he is with you and on his journey back home. If the driver is good, a tip of about $5 per day is gratefully accepted.

For an excellent, professional driver who knows every city street and country road throughout the island, knows which sites are worth stopping for and which ones aren't, and will network with other drivers and guides about new things to see and do while you relax over lunch, contact **Dewa Ny Suweta**, mobile: +62-(0)852-3860-8989.

Privately owned minibuses are widely available on the street. You'll be offered "transport" everywhere you go and prices are negotiated on the spot. To avoid the negotiation process, ask for assistance at your hotel or any one of the abundant travel agent desks. Inspect the vehicle before handing over payment and don't accept substitute vehicles that show up at the last minute.

Rental car agencies at the airport are open 9 am−10 pm. Also recommended are:

Autobagus Rent a Car, Jl. Tukad Balian Renon, Denpasar, tel: 722-222, fax: 722-109, www.autobagus.com. Sedans, jeeps, and limousines, long or short term rental, replacement vehicles, 24-hour call service, experienced driver service or self-drive, comprehensive insurance, and various car makes and models in excellent condition, at reasonable prices.

Golden Bird Limousine & Car Rental, 24-hr reservations tel: 701-111, customer ser-vice tel: 701-621, www.bluebirdgroup.com. A member of the popular Blue Bird Group from Jakarta, in business for nearly 40 years. Excellent service with fully-trained drivers. Bali rentals include sedans, vans, limousines and full-size buses.

Hertz, Inna Grand Bali Beach Hotel, tel: 768-375 or 288-511, ext. 1341, fax: 286-967; and Hotel Putri Bali, Nusa Dua, tel: 771-020, ext. 7186. Offers the usual standard of service found with Hertz throughout the world.

Motorbike rentals

Motorcycling used to be the best way to travel on Bali, but with the exponential increase in traffic it has lost many of its charms and has become increasingly dangerous. Be careful and stick to the back roads.

Motorbikes are available for rent almost everywhere, and prices usually start from $6/day for standard 125cc motorcycles. Check the bike before agreeing to any arrangement and make note of any existing damage so you don't get stuck with repair charges. Helmets and an international driver's license are required.

Make sure you have the registration papers, in case you are stopped by the police. Also ensure you have adequate accident insurance covering emergency air evacuation home or to Singapore in case of a serious accident. Several tourist casualties occur each month. Insurance sold at time of rental normally covers damages or loss of the bike, with a minimal deductible.

Bicycle rentals

Cycling is an enjoyable way to get around and bicycles (and sometimes mountain bikes) are readily available. Note, though, that city traffic can be a nightmare and in some regions the hills require good physical fitness. See individual Practicalities sections for bicycle tours.

Horse and cart

Dokar (**horse carts**) operate in Denpasar. However the best way to navigate that area is on foot. The city center is relatively small, consisting of just a few main (usually one-way) shopping streets crisscrossing the downtown, and you'll want to look in the shops anyway.

HELICOPTER SERVICES

Air Bali, Jl. Bypass Ngurah Rai No. 100X, Dewa Ruci Building, Kuta, tel: 767-466, fax: 766-581, www.airbali.com. Experience Bali by air with the region's only western-managed helicopter and light aircraft company. In addition to flying celebrities and VIPS from place to place Air Bali offers sky tours, picnic flights, excursions to Komodo and Borobudur. Also hotel and villa transfers, golf transfers, private charters, aerial photography. Note that rates are per flight, not per person.

The Indonesian Language

Personal Pronouns
I *saya*
we *kita* (inclusive), *kami* (exclusive)
you *anda* (formal), *saudara* (brother, sister), *kamu* (for friends and children only)
he/she *dia*
they *mereka*

Forms of address
Father/Mr *Bapak* (*"Pak"*)
Mother/Mrs *Ibu* (*"Bu"*)
Elder brother *Abang* (*"Bang"* or *"Bung"*) *Mas* (in Java only)
Elder sister *Mbak* (in Java only)
Elder Brother/sister *Kakak* (*"Kak"*)
Younger brother/sister *Adik* (*"Dik"*)

Note: These terms are used not just within the family, but generally in polite speech.

Basic questions
How? *Bagaimana?*
How much/many? *Berapa?*
What? *Apa?*
What's this? *Apa ini?*
Who? *Siapa?*
Who's that? *Siapa itu?*
What is your name? *Siapa namanya anda/kamu?* (Literally: Who is your name?)
When? *Kapan?*
Where? *Di mana?*
Which? *Yang mana?*
Why? *Kenapa? Mengapa?*

The Basics
Welcome *Selamat datang*
Good morning (7–11 am) *Selamat pagi*
Good midday (11 am–3 pm) *Selamat siang*
Good afternoon (3–7 pm) *Selamat sore*
Goodnight (after dark) *Selamat malam*
Goodbye (to one leaving) *Selamat jalan*

Goodbye (to one staying) *Selamat tinggal*
(Note: *Selamat* is a word from Arabic mean-
ing "May your time (or action) be blessed.")
How are you? *Apa kabar?*
I am fine. *Kabar baik.*
Thank you. *Terima kasih.*
You're welcome. *Kembali.*
Same to you. *Sama sama.*
Pardon me. *Ma'af.*
Excuse me. *Permisi* (when leaving a conver-
sation, etc).

Numbers

1 *satu*	100 *seratus*
2 *dua*	600 *enam ratus*
3 *tiga*	1,000 *seribu*
4 *empat*	3,000 *tiga ribu*
5 *lima*	10,000 *sepuluh ribu*
6 *enam*	1,000,000 *satu juta*
7 *tujuh*	2,000,000 *dua juta*
8 *delapan*	half *setengah*
9 *sembilan*	first *pertama; kesatu*
10 *sepuluh*	second *kedua*
11 *sebelas*	third *ketiga*
12 *dua belas*	fourth *ke'empat*
13 *tiga belas*	
20 *dua puluh*	
50 *lima puluh*	
73 *tujuh puluh tiga*	

Time

minute *menit*
hour *jam* (also clock/watch)
day *hari*
week *minggu*
month *bulan*
year *tahun*
today *hari ini*
yesterday *kemarin*
tomorrow *besok*
later *nanti*
Sunday *Hari Minggu*
Monday *Hari Senin*
Tuesday *Hari Selasa*
Wednesday *Hari Rabu*
Thursday *Hari Kamis*
Friday *Hari Jumat*
Saturday *Hari Sabtu*
What time is it? *Jam berapa?*
(It is) eight thirty. *Jam setengah sembilan*
(Literally: "half nine")
How many hours? *Berapa jam?*
When did you arrive? *Kapan datang?*
Four days ago. *Empat hari yang lalu.*
When are you leaving? *Kapan berangkat?*
In a short while. *Sebentar lagi.*

Useful words

yes *ya*   no, not *tidak, bukan*
(Note: *Tidak* is used with verbs or adverbs;
bukan with nouns.)

and *dan*	better *lebih baik*
with *dengan*	worse *kurang baik*
for *untuk*	this/these *ini*
good *bagus*	that/those *itu*
fine *baik*	same *sama*
more *lebih*	different *lain*
less *kurang*	here *di sini*
from *dari*	there *di sana*
to be *ada*	to be able, can *bisa*
to buy *beli*	correct *betul*
to know *tahu*	wrong *salah*
to get *dapat*	big *besar*
to need *perlu*	small *kecil*
to want *ingin*	pretty *cantik*
to go *pergi*	slow *pelan*
to wait *tunggu*	fast *cepat*
at *di*	stop *berhenti*
to *ke*	old *tua, lama*
if *kalau*	new *baru*
near *dekat*	then *lalu, kemudian*
far *jauh*	only *hanya, saja*
empty *kosong*	crowded *ramai*
	noisy *bising; berisik*

Making small talk

Where are you from? *Dari mana?*
I'm from the U.S. *Saya dari Amerika.*
How old are you? *Umurnya anda/kamu
berapa?*
I'm 31 years old. *Umur saya tiga puluh satu
tahun.*
Are you married? *Sudah nikah belum.*
Yes, I am. *Ya, sudah.* Not yet. *Belum.*
Do you have children? *Sudah punya anak?*
What is your religion? *Agama apa?*
Where are you going? *Mau ke mana?*
I'm just taking a walk. *Jalan-jalan saja.*
Please come in. *Silakan masuk.*
This food is delicious. *Makanan ini enak
sekali.*
You are very hospitable. *Anda sangat
ramah.*

At the hotel

Where's a *losmen*? *Di mana ada losmen?*
cheap losmen *losmen yang murah*
average losmen *losmen biasa*
very good hotel *hotel cukup baik*
hot water *air panas*
Please take me to… *Tolong antar saya ke…*
Are there any empty rooms? *Ada kamar
kosong?*

Sorry there aren't any. *Ma'af, tidak ada.*
How much for one night? *Berapa untuk satu malam?*
One room for two people. *Dua orang, satu kamar.*
I'd like to stay for 3 days. *Saya mau tinggal tiga hari.*
Here's the key to your room. *Ini kunci kamar.*
Please call a taxi. *Tolong panggil taksi.*
Please wash these clothes. *Tolong cucikan pakaian ini.*

Food and eating
to eat *makan*
to drink *minum*
drinking water *air putih, air minum*
Where's a good restaurant? *Di mana ada rumah makan yang baik?*
Let's have lunch. *Mari kita makan siang.*
I want Indonesian food. *Saya mau makanan Indonesia.*
I want coffee, not tea. *Saya mau kopi, bukan teh.*
May I see the menu? *Boleh saya lihat daftar makanan?*
I want to wash my hands. *Saya mau cuci tangan.*
Where is the toilet? *Di mana kamar kecil?*
fish, squid, goat, beef, chicken *ikan, cumi, kambing, sapi, ayam*
salty, sour, sweet, spicy *asin, asam, manis, pedas*

Shopping
I don't understand. *Saya tidak mengerti.*
I can't speak Indonesian. *Saya tidak bisa bicara Bahasa Indonesia.*
Please, speak slowly. *Tolong, berbicara lebih lambat.*
(In this context, *lambat* means "slow"; it would be understood to mean soft, as in a soft voice.)
I want to buy…? *Saya mau beli…*
Where can I buy…? *Di mana saya bisa beli…?*
How much does this cost? *Berapa harga ini?*
2,500 Rupiah. *Dua ribu, lima ratus rupiah.*
That cannot be true! *Masa!*
That's still a bit expensive. *Masih agak mahal.*

Directions
north *utara*
west *barat*
south *selatan*
east *timur*
right *kanan*
left *kiri*
near *dekat*
far *jauh*
inside *di dalam*
outside *di luar*
I am looking for this address. *Saya cari alamat ini.*
How far is it? *Berapa jauh dari sini?*

Pronunciation
Vowels
a As in *father*
e Three forms:
  1) Schwa, like *e* in *the*
  2) Like *é* in *touché*
  3) Short *e*; as in *bet*
i Usually like long *e* (as in *Bali*); when bounded by consonants, like short *i* (*hit*).
o Long *o*, like *go*
u Long *u*, like *you*
ai Long *i*, like *crime*
au Like *ow* in *owl*

Consonants
c Always like *ch* in *church*
g Always hard, like *guard*
h Usually soft, almost unpronounced. It is hard between similar vowels, e.g., *mahal* (expensive).
k Like *k* in *kind*; at the end of word, it is an unvoiced stop.
kh Like *kind*, but harder
r Rolled, like a Spanish *r*
ng Soft, like *fling*
ngg Hard, like *tingle*
ny Like *ny* in *Sonya*

Grammar
Grammatically, Indonesian is in many ways far simpler than English. There are no articles (a, an, the). The verb form "to be" is usually not used. There is no ending for plurals; sometimes the word is doubled, but often the number is understood from the context. And Indonesian verbs are not conjugated. Tense is communicated by context or with specific words for time.

INDEX

Photo Credits

Agung Rai Gallery, Peliatan: page 50

Amir Sidharta: page 65

Bung Karno Foundations: page 51

Canstock: pages 168, 204

Bigstock: page 163

depositphotos.com: pages 87, 96, 264, 307

Dreamstime: pages 2, 3, 4-5, 11 (right), 23, 37, 46, 49, 58, 110, 124, 129, 154, 158, 167, 169, 174, 194, 198, 200, 241, 244, 270, 281, 283, 291, 309, 316-17

Eric Oey: title page, pages 7, 8, 213, 218, 223, 263, 272

iStockphoto: pages 6, 9, 10, 11 (left), 22, 44, 45, 57, 68, 72, 73, 84, 130, 132, 139, 145, 153, 156, 212, 217, 228, 242, 246, 256, 261, 297, 310

Jonathan Copeland: page 238

Leiden University Library: page 16

Linda Hoffman: page 279

National Parks Foundation (FNPF): page 143

Shutterstock: pages 11 (center), 74, 86, 97, 103, 107, 152, 173, 195, 201, 290

Tom Ballinger: page 61

Walter Spies Foundation: page 65

www.bali-travel-life.com: page 112